Leon Trotsky on China

Leon Trotsky on
China

Introduction by Peng Shu-tse

Edited by Les Evans and Russell Block

MONAD PRESS, NEW YORK

DISTRIBUTED BY
PATHFINDER PRESS, INC., NEW YORK

Library of Congress Catalog Card Number 76-25692
ISBN: 0-913460-45-1 (cloth); 0-913460-46-X (paper)
Manufactured in the United States of America

First Edition, 1976

Published by Monad Press for the Anchor Foundation

Distributed by:
Pathfinder Press
410 West Street
New York, N.Y. 10014

CONTENTS

LEON TROTSKY was born Lev Davidovich Bronstein in 1879 in the Ukraine. His first arrest for revolutionary activity was in 1898. He was exiled to Siberia, but escaped to collaborate with Lenin on *Iskra* in London in 1902. He broke with Lenin the following year at the time of the split between Bolsheviks and Mensheviks, was briefly aligned with the Mensheviks, but in 1904 broke with them and began a decade-long effort to reunite the Russian Social Democratic Labor Party. During the 1905 revolution he was the leader of the St. Petersburg Soviet and developed his theory of permanent revolution. He was again exiled to Siberia and again escaped. He was part of the tiny minority in the socialist movement who refused to support their governments in World War I. When the February revolution broke out in 1917 he was in New York, but he arrived back in Russia in May, joined the Bolshevik Party, was elected to its Central Committee, and in October was the leader of the Petrograd Soviet and the chief organizer of the Bolshevik insurrection. As the first commissar of foreign affairs, he headed the Soviet delegation to negotiate a peace with Germany at Brest-Litovsk. As commissar of war (1918-25) he created the Red Army and led it to victory through three years of civil war and imperialist intervention. He was a member of the Politburo of the Russian Communist Party from its formation until 1926, and of the Executive Committee of the Communist International from 1920 to 1927. He formed the Left Opposition in 1923 to fight for the preservation of Leninist internationalism and proletarian democracy. Defeated by the Stalin faction, he was expelled from the party in 1927, exiled first to Siberia in 1928 and then to Turkey in 1929. In 1933 he abandoned his efforts to reform the Communist International and called for the creation of a new International. He viewed his work on behalf of the Fourth International, founded in 1938, as the most important work of his life. In his final exile he was hounded from country to country by both the Stalinists and the fascists. He lived in Turkey until 1933, France until 1935, Norway until 1936, and Mexico until his death in August 1940 at the hands of a Stalinist assassin.

EDITORS' PREFACE

Leon Trotsky's views on the Chinese revolution of 1925-27, a central issue in the struggle between the Left Opposition (Bolshevik-Leninists) and the Stalin faction in the Soviet Communist Party and the Communist International, are known primarily through the collection of documents edited by Max Shachtman for English publication under the title *Problems of the Chinese Revolution* (New York: Pioneer Publishers, 1932). Trotsky's China writings occupy a pivotal place in the history of the Chinese communist movement, whose policies were decided in Moscow during the revolution of the 1920s; in the evolution of Trotsky's theoretical conceptions, particularly on the revolutionary capacities of bourgeois and peasant parties in the colonial world; and in the formation of the policies characteristic of Stalinism.

Until now the majority of Trotsky's work on this subject has remained inaccessible to the ordinary reader—either unpublished, in the author's archives, or scattered in many volumes in or out of print. Even the 1932 collection was difficult to obtain for several decades, until 1967, when the University of Michigan's Ann Arbor Paperbacks placed on the market a photo-offset copy— garnished with a new anticommunist foreword by the editor, Max Shachtman, who had since broken with Trotskyism and departed revolutionary politics for the right wing of the American Socialist Party.

The present collection includes all of the thirteen Trotsky documents in the Shachtman book, and fifty-three more. The material from the 1932 *Problems* makes up only 40 percent of *Leon Trotsky on China*. The reader will now be able to follow the trend of Trotsky's thinking on China after June 1931, the date of the last item in the 1932 book. It is possible, of course, to treat the

Chinese revolution of 1925-27 as a solitary event whose history stands as a test of the policies propounded by the contending forces and factions. But it also set the stage for the overthrow of Chiang Kai-shek in 1949 and the establishment of the People's Republic of China under Mao Tse-tung. Many of the component elements that led to the eventual victory of the Chinese Communist Party (CCP) were assembled in the aftermath of the defeat of 1927 and were discussed by Trotsky at some length in the years before his assassination in 1940. *Leon Trotsky on China* draws together from Trotsky's other published writings, some of which appear here in English for the first time, more than 100 pages of materials written between 1930 and 1940 that did not appear in *Problems of the Chinese Revolution.*

It is in these later writings that the founder of the Soviet Red Army turned his attention to the tactic of rural guerrilla warfare adopted by the CCP after 1927, and outlined his views of the peasant armies that were to bring Mao Tse-tung to power in 1949.

While Trotsky did not live to see the victory of the Chinese Stalinists and was able to observe from afar only the early stage of the so-called soviet areas, after 1930 he did not in general deny the possibility of such a victory on military grounds. What he did point to was the lack of contact with the Chinese working class, the authoritarian and privileged command structure of the peasant armies, the class-collaborationist outlook and program that underlay the military opposition to Chiang's government. Trotsky's conclusion was that a central danger for the socialist revolution in China lurked behind the militancy of the CCP's armed struggle: the likelihood that the peasant armies, if militarily victorious over Chiang Kai-shek, would come into hostile conflict with the city proletariat. These articles and letters provide important elements for the theoretical understanding of the Maoist regime that took shape in China after 1949.

There are two other omissions from the Shachtman collection that have led to occasional misunderstandings or even misrepresentations of the record of the Trotskyist Opposition. These are the absence of any document earlier than May 7, 1927 ("The Chinese Revolution and the Theses of Comrade Stalin"), or of any of the internal discussion inside the United Opposition, the bloc between Trotsky's Left Opposition and the so-called Leningrad Opposition led by Zinoviev and Kamenev. The difficulty arises because the United Opposition, which was formed in April 1926 and lasted until the expulsion of Trotsky and Zinoviev from the party in November 1927, did not accept Trotsky's full position on China. Zinoviev, as president of the Communist International from 1919 until 1926, shared responsibility with Stalin and Bukharin for the class-collaborationist policies imposed on the Chinese Communist Party. He continued after his break with Stalin to defend his role in ordering the CCP to cease its independent activity in 1923 and enter the bourgeois Kuomintang (KMT—Nationalist Party). While Zinoviev came to agree with Trotsky in the spring of 1927 that a call should be issued in China for the formation of independent worker and peasant soviets, one of the key planks in Trotsky's program, the United Opposition never agreed to Trotsky's demand, raised from 1923 onward, that the CCP reject merger with the KMT. In September 1927, after all factions of the KMT had turned on the CCP with savage military repression, the *Platform of the Opposition* in its section on China presented a revolutionary criticism of Stalin's policy of subordination of the Chinese communists to the national bourgeoisie and reiterated the stand that the formation of soviets would have been a correct policy. But this document, coauthored by Zinoviev, makes no mention of the merger between the CCP and Chiang's Kuomintang and does not condemn that policy.

In order to preserve the bloc with Zinoviev and Kamenev, which Trotsky hoped could defeat Stalin on the central issues of Soviet domestic policy and of international communist strategy, he submitted to the majority of the United Opposition and argued publicly only the parts of his program for China that could be accepted by his political collaborators. These amount to a clear counter political line to the positions of Stalin and Bukharin, but do not say everything that Trotsky would have said had he not felt bound by the necessity of striving to retain the unity of the Opposition against the rising Stalin dictatorship.

Trotsky explained these political circumstances in a letter to Max Shachtman of December 10, 1930, which Shachtman quoted in his introduction to *Problems of the Chinese Revolution* and which is reprinted in this collection. In addition to the disagreements with Zinoviev, Trotsky pointed out that several leading members of his own faction—particularly Karl Radek—held positions conciliatory to Zinoviev. Looking back on this experience after several years, Trotsky told Shachtman, "Now I can say with certainty that I made a mistake by submitting formally in this question. In any case, this mistake became quite clear only by the further evolution of the Zinovievists." Trotsky had hoped to convince Zinoviev, but this proved impossible.

There is one further category of documents missing from the 1932 collection that has been added to *Leon Trotsky on China*: the documents of the organizational fight for a hearing inside the Soviet Communist Party. These reveal the conspiracy of silence of the Stalin-controlled apparatus and help to explain why the Opposition's accurate predictions of the outcome of Stalin's policy in China had so little effect on the communist ranks.

To fill these gaps required a collection of a different order than the one already in print. With the help of Louis Sinclair's exhaustive *Leon Trotsky: A Bibliography* (Hoover Institution Press, 1972) and the kind permission of Harvard College Library to examine and use materials from the open section of the Trotsky archive, the full record of this historic struggle is compiled here for the first time.

The collection has been extended back in time some two years, to Trotsky's article on the May Thirtieth Incident, which touched off the revolution of 1925-27. Once top-secret documents of the Soviet Politburo such as the report "Problems of Our Policy with Respect to China and Japan" of March 25, 1926, letters and resolutions directed to the leading bodies of the party and the Communist International, and Trotsky's correspondence within the United Opposition are published here for the first time in any language. Twenty-two of these selections have never before appeared in English.

These documents are indispensable in tracing the development of Trotsky's theory of permanent revolution, which he had first enunciated in 1905 as a theory of the coming Russian revolution. Trotsky had shared Lenin's belief that in Russia, despite its relative backwardness, the proletariat and not the liberal bourgeoisie would have to play the leading role in accomplishing the bourgeois-democratic revolution against tsarist autocracy, especially in promoting a thoroughgoing land reform, the pressing need of the Russian peasantry. He differed with Lenin in adding that the proletariat could hold power only by combining bourgeois-democratic tasks with socialist ones that would strike at capitalist property relations in industry. It was not until the eruption of revolution in China, with its vast peasant population, however, that Trotsky began to apply his theory to countries still more economically backward than tsarist Russia.

Six of the newly translated documents are of special importance in making it possible for the first time to distinguish clearly, as the events unfolded, between Trotsky's views—which underwent an evolution in the course of the revolution—and those of the United Opposition, which he presented in the public debate. These are the three letters to Radek and Alsky, "A Brief Note" (March 22, 1927), and the two articles entitled "The Chinese Communist Party and the Kuomintang" of September 1926 and June 1927. These are written to Trotsky's own faction or to the Zinovievists. They should be read in conjunction with his "Class Relations in the Chinese Revolution" (April 3, 1927), which has had only limited circulation in English and was not included in *Problems of the Chinese Revolution*. These documents show Trotsky's initial thinking on four central strategic questions for the communists of China: (1) the policy of communist membership in the Kuomintang; (2) the role of the "national" bourgeoisie and of the petty bourgeoisie in the anti-imperialist revolution; (3) the applicability of a call for soviets in China; and (4) the class character of the unfolding revolution, i.e., whether it would be held within the bounds of capitalist property relations or would go over to a socialist revolution under the leadership of the Communist Party at the head of the Chinese working class.

The documents listed above show that Trotsky did not at first envisage the Chinese revolution following the same course he had outlined in 1905 for Russia. In 1926 and early 1927 he took up where the first four congresses of the Comintern had left off in the attempt to draw lessons for the colonial world from the Russian October revolution. The early Comintern had concluded that the prospects for the communist movement in the colonies should not be judged solely by the severely limited material prerequisites in the colonies themselves—the lack of industry and the tiny working class. As part of a world capitalist economy and a component part of a world revolution, the working class could play a role far out of proportion to its actual numbers even in very backward lands. Communist policy was to support the independence struggles of oppressed nations against their colonial masters, regardless of whoever momentarily held the leadership of such movements. At the same time the organizational and political independence of the Communist Party was needed to struggle within the national liberation movement for the allegiance of the oppressed worker and peasant masses.

In the early 1920s Lenin and Trotsky still had hopes of a short-term revolutionary victory in Western Europe, where mass

Communist parties existed. The colonial East in comparison was relatively quiescent. The Comintern tended as a consequence to view the possibility of socialist revolution in the colonies as an outgrowth of successful overturns in the imperialist heartland. Victories in Europe could inspire the colonial masses, remove the threat of foreign intervention, and promise massive aid. In December 1922, in his report on the Fourth World Congress of the Comintern to the Russian Communist Party delegates to the Tenth Congress of Soviets, Trotsky summarized the outlook for the colonies as follows:

"It is self-understood that the colonies—Asia and Africa (I speak of them as a unity) . . . if taken independently and isolatedly, are absolutely not ready for the proletarian revolution. . . . But the colonies belong to the metropolitan centers and their fate is intimately bound up with the fate of these European metropolitan centers. . . . The growth of the influence of Socialist and Communist ideas, the emancipation of the toiling masses of the colonies, the weakening of the influence of the nationalist parties can be assured not only by and not so much by the role of the native Communist nuclei as by the revolutionary struggle of the proletariat of the metropolitan centers for the emancipation of the colonies" (*The First Five Years of the Communist International* [New York: Monad Press, 1972], vol. 2, pp. 316-17).

When the Chinese revolution broke out ahead of revolution in the advanced countries, Trotsky at first retained the official Comintern position. He felt that the Chinese proletariat was too small and weak to cement an alliance with the peasantry directly through the Communist Party, as had been done in Russia. Instead, while the CCP should extend its independent influence as far as possible among the workers and peasants, it should seek alliances with revolutionary peasant organizations to establish a "workers' and peasants' democratic dictatorship." Such a government would leave open the question of whether socialist measures such as nationalization of industry could be taken. This would depend on the strength of the Communist Party in the alliance. (The "workers' and peasants' democratic dictatorship" was a slogan first advanced by Lenin for Russia in the epoch of the 1905 revolution. It was rejected by Trotsky for Russia on the grounds that the hostility of the liberal bourgeoisie to mobilizations of the worker and peasant masses, even for limited bourgeois-democratic aims, would leave the working class and its party no alternative but to combine the fight against tsarism with the fight for socialism. Lenin accepted Trotsky's view in April 1917, paving the way for the October revolution.)

Trotsky's initial attack on Stalin's class-collaborationist policy in China centered, then, not on the class character of the unfolding revolution (the "two-stage" theory) but on the need for an independent Communist Party, outside of the Kuomintang. This would allow the communists to consolidate as far as circumstances permitted the power of the Chinese proletariat and its peasant allies.

Trotsky, as the newly translated documents show, in 1926 and early 1927 considered the Kuomintang to be a loose coalition of the radical petty bourgeoisie and the big bourgeoisie, rapidly evolving toward consolidation as a bourgeois party. So long as the KMT participated in the national liberation struggle and retained authority over the masses, Trotsky favored an alliance with it. But this alliance should be between two independent parties, not within a single organization. Trotsky warned, however, of the treachery of the bourgeois wing of the KMT. At the same time, he evidently expected a split in the KMT, through which the communists could possibly cement a closer political alliance with the radical petty-bourgeois forces in the KMT that vacillated between the working class and the bourgeoisie. These sections of the KMT he even considered at one point—see "A Brief Note" (March 22, 1927)—as possible candidates for the role of the peasant component of the workers' and peasants' democratic dictatorship.

Trotsky's views developed in a series of successive approximations. His final judgments were codified in 1928 as the theory of permanent revolution as we know it today—as a general theory of the necessity of socialist revolution in the colonial world. Of the four strategic questions mentioned earlier, Trotsky began with the categorical need for an independent Communist Party and rejection of the subordination to the Kuomintang. He held this position from 1923 and it is a constant thread in even his earliest writings on the Chinese revolution.

The most difficult theoretical problem and the last to be resolved was the class character of the unfolding revolution. Trotsky's ultimate conclusion was that despite the absence of material prerequisites for socialism, and the risks and dangers this imposed on the attempt to create a government based on workers' power and industrial planning in a backward country, no other road was possible. This generalization, which had to be made to ensure against mistaken concessions to the national bourgeoisie in future colonial revolutions, was first made by Trotsky in the late summer of 1927, even before the breakup of the bloc with Zinoviev. In "New Opportunities for the Chinese Revolution, New Tasks, and New Mistakes" (September 1927) he wrote for the first time: "The Chinese revolution at its new stage will win as a dictatorship of the proletariat, or it will not win at all." (This document has never before appeared in English.) Trotsky elaborated these conclusions in the summer of 1928 in his "Summary and Perspectives of the Chinese Revolution."

There remain two strategic points—the role of the national bourgeoisie and the function of soviets—which were key to ensuring a revolutionary policy in the actual course of the Chinese revolution in the decisive spring and summer of 1927. Trotsky was never in doubt as to the reactionary character of the Chinese "national" bourgeoisie. Nor did he have any illusions as to the independent revolutionary qualities of the petty-bourgeois wing of the KMT as long as it remained in the same party with the bourgeoisie (see "The Chinese Communist Party and the Kuomintang" of September 27, 1926). The stumbling block was the organizational form to be taken by the alliance between the workers and the peasantry that would make possible the "workers' and peasants' democratic dictatorship." Until Trotsky definitively rejected this slogan in September 1927 it contained the pitfall of posing the question of the alliance as an alliance between *parties,* and in China the only other party participating in the anti-imperialist struggle was the Kuomintang. For Stalin the independent mobilization of the workers and their alliance with the peasantry was not a question at all—the whole of his policy was designed to strengthen the bourgeoisie. But even for Trotsky the way the problem had been formulated tended to make him look for some means of splitting the Kuomintang as the road to success for the national struggle.

In the decisive last week of March 1927, as major industrial cities fell to the KMT and its true character was revealed, Trotsky made a great theoretical advance and rejected the possibility of any progressive role for any wing of the KMT. In his letter to Alsky (March 29, 1927) he called the KMT as a whole "an organization of the past" as far as the revolution was concerned and issued the call for peasant soviets. These were to be organized directly by the communists as the only practicable form of the worker-peasant alliance. This was the decisive step in his conclusion that the Chinese working class could follow the example of its Russian counterpart and take power directly, supported by worker and peasant soviets.

Readers will note that even after this Trotsky retained the slogan of a "democratic dictatorship of the workers and the peasantry." Like Lenin, he gave to this slogan a revolutionary content: the creation of a workers' and peasants' government in struggle against imperialism and its local bourgeois agents. He left open the question of the material possibilities of such a government: whether it could proceed to socialist tasks or if these would have to await an extension of the world revolution in the imperialist metropolis. Stalin filled the slogan with an opposite content: using the workers and peasants to promote the fortunes of the Kuomintang.

In 1928, looking back on the actual experience of the struggle for an independent workers' and peasants' government, Trotsky rejected the slogan of the "workers' and peasants' democratic dictatorship" as outlived. If the bourgeoisie was incapable of carrying through the democratic revolution, the workers were compelled to take the power; having done so, there was no artificial "democratic" stage at which the revolution could be safely halted without risking a bourgeois counterrevolution.

In addition to its significance for Marxist theory and Soviet and Chinese history, the previously unpublished documentation presented here serves to correct a number of important factual errors in some of the standard accounts by historians such as Isaac Deutscher, E. H. Carr, and others.

An important disputed point concerns Trotsky's alleged belatedness in raising the Chinese question in the Russian party. The facts, accepted by all serious students of the period, are fairly straightforward. The revolution broke out in Central and South China in May 1925, while the fight over strategy and tactics for China became a central issue in the Russian party only in March 1927, almost two years later, and raged on in the USSR through the summer and fall of 1927, when it was carried into the Comintern and continued until the Sixth World Congress in the summer of 1928.

The secondary importance of China in the Soviet disputes before the spring of 1927 is not at all surprising. This period saw the breakup of the Stalin-Zinoviev alliance during the summer and fall of 1925, and the opening in the summer of 1926 of the decisive struggle for the leadership of the Soviet party and Comintern between Stalin-Bukharin on one side and the new United Opposition of Trotsky-Zinoviev-Kamenev on the other. In this fight the principal issues were party democracy, the pace of Soviet industrialization, and the Opposition's call for a repudiation of the Soviet government's alliance with the conservative leaders of the British Trades Union Congress, who used the prestige of the Russian revolution to help strangle the near-revolutionary British general strike of 1926.

The critical point for the revolution in China did not come in the first year of ferment, when the weak Kuomintang government in Canton was trying to consolidate a regional base for use against the more powerful Northern warlord regimes that dominated most of the territory of China. It came only after the launching of the Northern Expedition in July 1926, when major industrial cities began to fall to the KMT, for the first time posing the question of the class character of the new government that would be established. The most decisive turning point was the capture of Shanghai by a workers' insurrection against the local warlord rulers in March 1927. And it was precisely then, before the occupation of proletarian Shanghai by Chiang Kai-shek's Northern Expedition troops, that China became for the Opposition a dominant question in its fight with the Stalinists.

But if China was not the central issue in Trotsky's battle before March 1927, can it be argued that he was silent or that his position was not known to his opponents? Isaac Deutscher in *The Prophet Unarmed* (London: Oxford University Press, 1959), the second volume of his outstanding biography of Trotsky, writes of the period between the spring of 1926 and the Shanghai insurrection:

"During all these events the Chinese issue remained as if outside the Russian inner party controversy. The fact deserves to be underlined: it disposes of one of the legends of vulgar Trotskyism which maintains that the Opposition had from the beginning unremittingly resisted Stalin's and Bukharin's 'betrayal of the Chinese Revolution'" (p. 321). And further: "Then, for a whole year, from April 1926 till the end of March 1927, neither Trotsky nor the other leaders of the Opposition took up the issue" (p. 324).

Deutscher is in error here. He accepts Trotsky's testimony (in his letter to Shachtman in 1930, which is confirmed by Stalin himself in vol. 9 of his Russian *Works*), that in April 1926 he

demanded in the Soviet Politburo the CCP's immediate withdrawal from the Kuomintang and its independent struggle for the
leadership of the Chinese workers and peasants. There is no
evidence, however, that the question did not come up again. The
minutes of the Soviet Politburo have not been published, and
without corroborating documentation it is a matter of speculation
what took place there.

But there is one important piece of evidence that challenges
Deutscher's contention. In addition to Trotsky's correspondence
inside the United Opposition (the letters to Radek), the Trotsky
archive contains a formal resolution by Trotsky ("The Chinese
Communist Party and the Kuomintang") dated September 27,
1926, squarely in the middle of Trotsky's supposed year of silence.
This was an eloquent demand for a complete change in the CCP's
course in China, centering on the call for its immediate
withdrawal from the Kuomintang.

From the internal evidence this document was written for
presentation in the Politburo. The arguments it raised are
directed to the Stalin faction, not to the Zinovievists. This
document shows that Trotsky saw the importance of the Chinese
events and fought for his position well in advance of the
revolutionary crisis the following spring. Trotsky did not succeed
in convincing Zinoviev and Radek of the need for withdrawal
from the KMT, and it is not known whether he submitted this
resolution to the Politburo or if it was vetoed by the steering
committee of the United Opposition. But to say that Trotsky did
not win this battle is very different from saying that he did not
fight.

Whereas Deutscher seems to have overlooked the September
1926 resolution, British historian E. H. Carr, who also studied the
Trotsky archive, makes use of the document in support of a
surprisingly crude variation of the charge that the Opposition
joined the battle over China only after the defeat of the
revolution. In his *History of Soviet Russia* Carr writes:

"It was not till after Chiang Kai-shek's 'betrayal' of the
communists in the summer of 1927 that the opposition, and
especially Trotsky, became anxious to claim credit for having
consistently opposed the Kuomintang alliance. Some members of
the party initially disliked the entry of members of the CCP into
Kuomintang . . . and either Trotsky or Zinoviev may have been
among them; but the policy was not formally opposed, and any
objections to it were forgotten during the next three years.

Trotsky himself was inconsistent in his recollections. In an unpublished memorandum of September 27, 1926, in the Trotsky archives ["The Chinese Communist Party and the Kuomintang"—Eds.], he described the participation of CCP in Kuomintang as 'perfectly correct' for the period before 1925, when it was 'still only preparing itself for *independent* political activity'; in a letter of December 10, 1930 [to Max Shachtman—Eds.], he declared that 'from the very beginning, that is, from 1923', he had been resolutely opposed to participation." (*A History of Soviet Russia: Socialism in One Country, [1924-1926]* [New York: Macmillan, 1964], vol. 3, part 2, p. 784.)

Carr makes a string of assertions here for which he offers not the slightest proof: (1) That the decision of the Soviet Politburo in 1923 to approve the CCP's entry into the KMT was "not formally opposed" by Trotsky; (2) that the Trotskyist Opposition did not "consistently" oppose the alliance with the KMT until after Chiang Kai-shek's April 12, 1927, anticommunist bloodbath in Shanghai (at least that seems to be the sense of Carr's ambiguous formulation); and (3) that Trotsky "was inconsistent in his recollections" of having opposed the CCP-KMT merger.

1. We have Trotsky's testimony in the letter to Shachtman that he opposed the CCP entry into the Kuomintang in 1923, and that "Up to 1926, I always voted independently in the Political Bureau on this question against all the others." Carr provides no evidence from any other source for reducing Trotsky's opposition to a private "dislike." What Trotsky described is his vote cast in the highest decision-making body of the Russian CP.

2. Carr seeks to postpone Trotsky's "consistent" opposition to the entry into the KMT until the summer of 1927. It is less than honest of him, then, to cite a document written in September 1926, which is unavailable to his readers, and mention only that it grants that the collaboration may have been correct until 1925—without mentioning that *this same document is a strongly worded demand for withdrawal.* Even if he discounts Trotsky's later testimony that he formally submitted such a motion to the Politburo in April 1926—substantiated by Stalin's somewhat garbled recollections of the event cited earlier—there remains the fact, not only of the September 27, 1926, resolution, but of two documents submitted formally to the party leadership in advance of Chiang's coup: "To the Politburo of the AUCP(B) Central Committee" (March 31, 1927), and "Class Relations in the Chinese Revolution" (April 3, 1927).

3. This leaves Trotsky's "inconsistent recollections," not a particularly telling point once the record of open opposition to Stalin's policy has been established from April or at the minimum September 1926, in ample time for a change in line to have saved the revolution from disaster. But what shows Trotsky's alleged inconsistency? Carr is not able to produce a single document in which Trotsky advocated CCP membership in the Kuomintang. What he does cite is a resolution demanding immediate withdrawal, the same policy Trotsky later "recollected" that he held, in which Trotsky grants for the sake of argument that the tactic of communists joining the KMT may have been defensible some years in the past. This does not contradict Trotsky's later insistence that he voted against the tactic in 1923. It certainly does not suggest any wavering on this question during the period of the revolution. All that remains is the fact that in the hope of convincing a hostile party leadership of the necessity of an immediate change of course, Trotsky avoided allowing the dispute to hinge on past policy and conceded that the entry could have been justified when the CCP was only a tiny propaganda group and not yet a party. The main point of the document, as readers can see for themselves, is, "To think that the petty bourgeoisie can be won over by clever maneuvers or good advice within the Kuomintang is hopeless utopianism."

There are other more or less serious factual errors in many of the existing treatments of Trotsky's role in the struggle over the strategy and tactics of the Chinese revolution of 1925-27. Benjamin I. Schwartz, in his useful 1951 study *Chinese Communism and the Rise of Mao* (New York: Harper Torchbooks), states that "After Chiang Kai-shek's April [1927] *coup d'etat* . . . Trotsky issued a call for soviets of workers, peasants, and soldiers" (p. 81). This is true, but, as the newly published documentation shows, can be misleading. Trotsky's call for the formation of soviets was first issued not in April 1927, as a means of salvaging a revolution already on the defensive, but in March (see "To the Politburo of the AUCP(B) Central Committee"), as a means of consolidating a proletarian and peasant power still on the rise.

Another factual misrepresentation of Trotsky's views appears in the recently published *The Communist Movement: From Comintern to Cominform* (New York: Monthly Review Press, 1975) by Spanish former Stalinist Fernando Claudin. A member of the Spanish CP from 1933 and of its Politburo from 1947 to 1965, Claudin has awakened late in life to the antirevolutionary character of Stalin and Russian Stalinism. He fails, however, to perceive the continuity of Stalinist policy in the CCP and remains, inconsistently, a devotee of Mao. His idea of Trotsky's positions seems to be derived from a single article, the June 1928 chapter in Trotsky's book *The Third International After Lenin,* entitled "Summary and Perspectives of the Chinese Revolution" (reprinted here). On the basis of this Claudin writes:

"Trotsky's strategic conception of the revolution, which was even more 'European' than that held by Lenin towards the end of his life, was to lead him to another conclusion that history has not validated, namely that the revolution could not triumph in Asia unless it had already triumphed in Europe. Undoubtedly it was his under-estimation of the revolutionary potentialities of the peasant masses in the colonies that induced him to make this assumption" (vol. 1, p. 287).

There is no need to refer to previously unknown materials to refute this latest and lamest "proof" of Trotsky's "underestimation" of the peasantry, a charge leveled against him by the Stalinists since 1924. But it should emphasize the value of bringing together in a single place Trotsky's writings on the subject as an aid in tracing his actual positions. Had Claudin turned, for example, to one of Trotsky's very next articles, "The Chinese Question After the Sixth Congress" (October 4, 1928), which was contained in *Problems of the Chinese Revolution,* he would have found a discussion of the interrelationship between socialist revolution in Europe and Asia:

"In certain countries, the eventuality of the transformation of the potential revolution into an active revolution is closer; in others it is further off. It is all the more difficult to divine in advance what will be the rotation followed, since it is determined not only by the acuteness of the international contradictions, but also by the intersection of world factors. One may very reasonably assume that the revolution will be accomplished in Europe before taking place in North America. But the predictions which announce that the revolution will break out in Asia first and then in Europe already have a more conditional character. It is possible, even probable, but it is not at all inevitable."

Trotsky rejected the schematism of the Stalinist ideologues who claimed the ability to deduce from general historical conditions where and when revolutions would break out. But he directly contradicted Claudin's assertion that Trotsky believed socialist revolution was possible in the colonial countries only after successful revolutions in the imperialist heartland. Trotsky's whole theory of permanent revolution, in fact, is an explanation of why socialist revolution is the only way for oppressed nations to extricate themselves from economic backwardness, despite the lack of the material prerequisites for an industrial planned economy.

In assessing a social revolution as it unfolds, as Trotsky stated here, Marxism does not claim infallible powers of foresight. The present collection does present insights into the workshop, so to speak, in which the leader of one great revolution sought to grasp the dynamic of another in the making. It allows us to see how Trotsky's positions were formed, how they were argued out within his own faction, and how they were presented to the party leadership and ranks. The story is not so simple as earlier collections might have suggested, but for revolutionists and serious students of revolutionary history, it is more instructive.

In addition to Trotsky's work collected here, this volume contains two important documents that stand in their own right as testimony to the events of the second Chinese revolution. These are the accounts by two of the central leaders of the Chinese Communist Party of the time: Peng Shu-tse* and Ch'en Tu-hsiu.

Peng Shu-tse was among the tiny handful of founders of the Chinese Communist Party. In fact he belonged to the Socialist Youth Corps organized in Shanghai by Comintern representative Grigori Voitinsky and Ch'en Tu-hsiu in August 1920, a year before the CCP was created. Peng studied in Moscow in the early 1920s. While there he recruited to the Communist Party Liu Shao-ch'i, later head of state of the People's Republic and the central target of Mao's Cultural Revolution of the 1960s. Peng returned to China in 1924 and was elected to the Central Committee and to the Politburo at the CCP's Fourth Congress in January 1925. In the central leadership he was a close political associate and supporter of the party's first general secretary, Ch'en Tu-hsiu. In the CCP's leading bodies Peng argued for withdrawal from the

---

* Peng's name is also transliterated as P'eng Shu-chih, based on the pronunciation of the Chinese characters in the Peking dialect, which is the standard for foreign translation. He is a native of Hunan and his given name is correctly pronounced Shu-tse.

Kuomintang, and convinced Ch'en of his views. Because of Stalin's censorship none of the Chinese leaders knew of Trotsky's positions, but on the basis of his first-hand experience in China Peng evolved views substantially similar to Trotsky's. Both Ch'en and Peng were compelled under Comintern discipline to carry out Stalin's line, but at a number of key junctures they sought to change the policy that was leading their party to disaster.

In the revolution of 1925-27 Peng headed the party's propaganda department and served as chief editor of its weekly newspaper, *Hsiang-tao* (The Guide), and of its theoretical journal, *Hsin Ch'ing-nien* (New Youth). In this capacity he clashed with Mao Tse-tung, then in the right wing of the CCP and head of the Kuomintang's propaganda department. He worked with all the leading figures in the inner councils where policy was discussed and implemented, including Comintern representatives Mikhail Borodin, M. N. Roy, and Ho Chi Minh, later the Stalinist head of North Vietnam.

After the defeat of the revolution, Stalin made scapegoats of Ch'en Tu-hsiu and Peng for carrying out the policy he had imposed on them. They in turn resisted the bureaucratization of their party. When they finally received copies of some of Trotsky's documents they organized a Left Opposition within the CCP and were expelled in November 1929. Together they founded the Chinese Trotskyist movement. For their organized resistance to Chiang Kai-shek among the workers of Shanghai they were arrested and imprisoned for five years in the jails of the Kuomintang, between 1932 and 1937. Since the Maoist victory and the suppression of all communist opposition by the Stalinist regime, Peng has lived in exile in Europe where he has contributed to the leadership of the Fourth International, the world party of socialist revolution founded by Trotsky in 1938.

In his introduction to Trotsky's writings Peng gives not only a description of the events and of the contending political lines but the fullest account he has yet written of the inner workings of the CCP leadership during those crucial years. This is invaluable primary source material for students of the Chinese revolution.

The second document, published here as an appendix, is Ch'en Tu-hsiu's famous "Appeal to All the Comrades of the Chinese Communist Party," his December 10, 1929, open letter protesting his expulsion from the party he founded, refuting the charges against him, and giving his account of the years of the great revolution. This letter was published in the American *Militant* at the end of 1930 and the beginning of 1931 but has been out of print and unobtainable outside of libraries since that time. The translation has been checked against the original Chinese to rectify errors and omissions in the first English rendering.

Trotsky's text has been annotated and all Chinese names have been corrected to the current Wade-Giles system of transliteration. A biographical glossary has been supplied, with brief data on most of the figures mentioned in the text as well as identification of organizations and periodicals. Where Trotsky quotes Lenin's writings, the editors have used the official Soviet government translation from the fourth English-language edition of Lenin's *Collected Works* (Moscow: Progress Publishers).

A source note follows each item, providing bibliographical information. All translations are from the original Russian unless otherwise specified. Max Shachtman's translation is used for all items credited to *Problems of the Chinese Revolution*. The full Trotsky text from the 1932 book is included here. Omitted are the appendices by Zinoviev, Vujovic, and others. The item in *Problems* entitled "The Canton Insurrection" was an excerpt from Trotsky's essay "Summary and Perspectives of the Chinese Revolution" (June 1928), which appears here in full.

The editors would like to thank the translators, and in particular Marilyn Vogt, who took overall responsibility for the translations from the Russian. Special appreciation is due to Peng Shu-tse, who in addition to contributing the introduction provided valuable aid in compiling the notes.

Les Evans
Russell Block
March 1976

INTRODUCTION

When Monad Press decided to publish a new collection of Trotsky's writings on China, Les Evans, one of the editors, wrote to me and explained that this book would contain a great many more articles than the 1932 *Problems of the Chinese Revolution.* He asked if I would write an introduction for *Leon Trotsky on China*, and he sent me some copies of articles that would be included, along with a complete list of the projected contents. I was happy to take on this task, for it would give me an opportunity to take up some of the historical facts surrounding the second Chinese revolution (1925-27) which have not been discussed before, especially regarding the ideological development of the Chinese Communist Party. It is hoped that this will help readers gain a more concrete understanding of Leon Trotsky's great contribution.

It is difficult for one to overestimate the contribution Trotsky made to understanding the problems of revolution in China. This can be compared with that of Lenin and Trotsky to the successful development of the Russian revolution. Even though the second Chinese revolution was defeated as a result of Stalin's opportunistic leadership, Trotsky's views regarding the theory, strategy, and tactics of revolution were proven completely correct by the historical record. In this way, Trotsky expanded upon, and added to, the lessons of the October revolution in Russia. Just as in the period from February to October 1917 in Russia, there were also two irreconcilable political lines in existence during the second Chinese revolution. Trotsky represented the Bolshevik line, and Stalin represented the Menshevik line. While in the Russian context the Bolshevik line triumphed, bringing about the victory of October 1917, in China, the Menshevik line of the Stalinist bureaucracy caused the Chinese revolution to suffer a tragic defeat. This defeat, however, no less than the success of the Russian revolution, served as a great lesson for China, the colonial and semicolonial countries, and also the advanced capitalist countries. As Trotsky wrote:

> A study of the Chinese revolution is a most important and urgent matter for every communist and for every advanced worker. It is not possible to talk seriously in any country about the struggle of the proletariat for power without a study by the proletarian vanguard of the fundamental events, motive forces, and strategic methods of the Chinese revolution. It is not possible to understand what day is without knowing what night is; it is not possible to understand what summer is without having experienced winter. *In the same way, it is not possible to understand the meaning of the methods of the October uprising without a study of the methods of the Chinese catastrophe.* ["A History of the Second Chinese Revolution Is Needed" (published September 1930), emphasis added.]

I agree completely that the "study of the Chinese revolution is a most important and urgent matter." I would add one more sentence, however: "It is not possible to understand the meaning of the methods of the Chinese catastrophe without a serious study of *Leon Trotsky on China*."

I. The Bolshevism of the Early CCP

Trotsky's systematic presentation of his views regarding the problems of the Chinese revolution did not really begin until August 30, 1926, in a letter to Karl Radek. Even though he stated that in 1923 he was "resolutely opposed to the Communist Party joining the Kuomintang," and in the spring of 1926 he "once more presented the formal proposal that the Communist Party leave the Kuomintang instantly" (see Trotsky's letter to Max Shachtman dated December 10, 1930), we do not have a copy of Trotsky's "formal proposal." Thus, it is difficult to discuss Trotsky's views about revolution in China prior to August 1926, especially as regards the CCP's response to Comintern policies. It is necessary to look deeper into the historical background of the Chinese communist movement in order to gain a more concrete understanding of Trotsky's contribution.

The first Communist group in China was established in Shanghai in May of 1920, with the help of Grigori Voitinsky, the first representative sent to China by the Communist International under the leadership of Lenin and Trotsky. After this communist organization was established, it had to face three urgent tasks: how to recruit and train communist cadres, how to begin to organize the trade unions, and how to spread communist ideas. The Communist parties in the West were in the main established by those who left the Social Democratic parties or labor parties of the Second International under the impact of the victorious October revolution in Russia. China's situation was totally different, however. China had to start from scratch, having no Marxist tradition; even modern industrial unions did not exist. Two months after the establishment of the Shanghai Communist Group, a Socialist Youth Corps (SYC) was founded. The SYC recruited groups of young communists to be sent to study in Moscow. Beginning in August 1920, the Communist Group published a weekly organ, *The Laborer*. It also was responsible for spreading communist ideas among the workers and developing modern trade unions. By September, the famous *New Youth* monthly, edited by Ch'en Tu-hsiu, became the organ of the Shanghai Communist Group and publicly advocated Marxism, while reporting on the true situation in Soviet Russia. Then, in November, the CG published a clandestine monthly, *The Communist*, in which Bolshevik ideas and revolutionary experience were introduced, along with writings about communist movements in other countries. This journal also printed the "Manifesto of the Communist International to the Workers of the World," written by Trotsky, and Lenin's report to the Second Congress of the Communist International. In addition, both *New Youth* and *The Communist* published many articles criticizing anarchist thought (at that time anarchist ideas were quite widespread among radical youth) and the opportunist class collaboration of the Second International, while at the same time advocating the concept of the proletarian dictatorship. In this way, some basic principles were established for the Chinese communist movement. Due to this type of persistent activity by the Shanghai Communist Group, from about October 1920 other communist groups were set up in places like Peking, Wuhan, Changsha, Canton, and Tsinan. This, then, was the foundation upon which the Chinese Communist Party was established in July 1921.

Since Ch'en Tu-hsiu was not able to attend this inaugural congress of the CCP, only a resolution setting up a Bolshevik-style party was passed. There were no other definite decisions made on political matters. However, since the general direction of this new party was to be the proletarian orientation of Bolshevism, a secretariat for organizing the labor movement was established within the CCP. Plans were made to further the workers' movement in the large industrial centers, mines, and railroads, by organizing unions and leading workers' struggles. In 1921-22, the CCP led a series of strikes and won some victories. In light of this, the labor secretariat called the First National Labor Congress to be held in May 1922 in Canton. Those who attended this congress represented 230,000 organized workers. Thus, it is evident that in the space of one short year the CCP had already become the center of the working class movement.

At the same time, the CCP leadership, headed by Ch'en Tu-hsiu, received help from Voitinsky, the Comintern representative. (Voitinsky was then in the process of carefully introducing the CCP to the fundamentals of Russian Bolshevism and Lenin's views on national democratic revolutions.) Thus, in the spring of 1922, the CCP determined its strategic line toward China's national democratic revolution. This line was formally expressed in the "Manifesto of the Second National Congress" in July 1922, and its most important points were:

> The proletariat's support of the democratic revolution is not (equivalent to) its surrender to the capitalists. Not to prolong the life of the feudal system is absolutely necessary in order to raise the power of the proletariat. This is the proletariat's own class interest. . . .
>
> The CCP is the party of the proletariat. Its aims are to organize the proletariat and to struggle for (the establishment of) the dictatorship of the workers and peasants, the abolition of private property, and the gradual attainment of a Communist society. *At present the CCP must, in the interest of the workers and poor peasants, lead the workers to support the democratic revolution and forge a democratic united front of workers, poor peasants, and petty bourgeoisie.* In the interest of the workers, the CCP struggles to secure, within this united front, the following objectives: [Text from *A Documentary History of Chinese Communism* by Conrad Brandt, Benjamin Schwartz, and John K. Fairbank (Cambridge, Massachusetts: Harvard University Press, 1952), pp. 63-64, emphasis added.]

These "objectives" were seven, but here I will mention only a few: "the overthrow of military cliques, and the establishment of internal peace. . . . the removal of oppression by international imperialism and the complete independence of the Chinese nation. . . . a free federation [of China proper with Tibet,

Mongolia, and Sinkiang, i.e., self-determination for national minorities, and]. . . . legislation for workers, peasants, and women. . . ."

The manifesto further pointed out:

> The above seven items are all in the interests of the workers, peasants, and petty bourgeoisie and are prerequisites for their liberation from their present oppression. If we ourselves put up a concerted struggle for liberation, the workers and poor peasants will flock to the banner of (our) Party and the petty bourgeoisie will also link up with us. However, *the workers must not become the appendage of the petty bourgeoisie within this democratic united front, but must fight for their own class interests. Therefore it is imperative that the workers be organized in the Party as well as in labor unions. Ever mindful of their class independence, the workers must develop the strength of their fighting organization (in order to) prepare for the establishment of soviets in conjunction with the poor peasantry and in order to achieve (the goal of) complete liberation.* The CCP is a section of the CI. The Party *calls the Chinese workers and peasants to rush to its banner* for the (coming) struggle: *it asks the oppressed masses of all China to fight in common with the workers and poor peasants under the Party banner;* and it hopes that the revolutionary masses of the whole world will march forward shoulder-to-shoulder. Only an alliance of the world proletariat and the oppressed peoples can lead to the liberation of the world. [Ibid., p. 65, emphasis added.]

I quoted from this particular manifesto because it was the first programmatic document regarding the Chinese revolution to come out of the CCP. It very clearly points out that the workers must be "ever mindful of their class independence" and "prepare for the establishment of soviets in conjunction with the poor peasantry . . . in order to achieve (the goal of) complete liberation." This is the same fundamental line found in Lenin's "Draft Theses on the National and Colonial Questions" which he presented to the Second Comintern Congress in July 1920. The "Theses" say:

> the Communist International should support bourgeois-democratic national movements in colonial and backward countries only on condition that, in these countries, the elements of future proletarian parties, which will be communist not only in name, are brought together and trained to understand *their special tasks, i.e., those of the struggle against the bourgeois-democratic movements within*

their own nations. The Communist International must enter into a temporary alliance with bourgeois democracy in the colonial and backward countries, but *should not merge with it,* and *should under all circumstances uphold the independence of the proletarian movement even if it is in its most embryonic form.* . . . [*Collected Works* (Moscow: Progress Publishers, 1966), vol. 31, pp. 149-50, emphasis added.]

At the close of the Second Congress of the CCP, the Central Committee issued the "First Manifesto of the CCP on the Current Situation." This manifesto, besides reporting on the national political situation and the united front against militarism and imperialism, also stated:

The CP takes the initiative in calling a conference, to be participated in by the revolutionary elements of the KMT [Kuomintang] and revolutionary socialists, to discuss the question of creating a united front for struggle against warlords of the feudal type and against all relics of feudalism. This struggle along a broad united front is a war to liberate the Chinese people from a dual yoke—the yoke of foreigners and the yoke of powerful militarists in our country—a war which is just as urgently needed as it is inevitable. [*A Documentary History,* Brandt et al., p. 63.]

This call for "a united front" to be formed by "the revolutionary elements of the KMT and revolutionary socialists" did not deviate from Lenin's "Draft Theses on the National and Colonial Questions," wherein he advised "a temporary alliance with bourgeois democracy." This way, through practical use of this strategy, the CCP could maintain its working class "independence" and "develop the strength of their fighting organization (in order to) prepare for the establishment of soviets in conjunction with the poor peasantry and in order to achieve (the goal of) complete liberation." This, then, was the fundamental policy of the early CCP toward the national democratic revolution.

II. Repression of the CCP and the Turn Toward Menshevism

Just as the CCP was determining its policy toward the Chinese revolution at its Second Congress, the Communist International made a one-hundred-eighty-degree turn in its policy toward the Chinese revolutionary movement. This was reflected in the instructions brought by the Comintern representative Maring (his original name was Sneevliet).

In early August 1922, Maring arrived at Shanghai and, after meeting with Sun Yat-sen, asked the CCP Central Committee to call a special meeting at which instructions from the Comintern would be discussed. These instructions were: CCP members were to join the KMT as individuals, and use this method to seek KMT-CCP collaboration in advancing the national revolutionary movement. All those in attendance at this meeting opposed this proposal, the main reasons being: the KMT represents the interests of the bourgeoisie, and, since the CCP represented the interests of the proletariat, a merger was out of the question; this type of multiclass organization could only serve to obstruct the CCP's policy of independence.* Maring, however, brought up the question of CCP submission to Comintern discipline. Under this threat of "discipline," the Central Committee reluctantly agreed to the International's proposal, with one condition: the issue was

---

* Harold R. Isaacs, in his *The Tragedy of the Chinese Revolution,* had this to say about the question: "He [Ch'en Tu-hsiu] says that all the Central Committee members opposed Maring, claiming that even at that time the Chinese Communist leaders believed such a step 'would confuse class organizations and curb our independent policy.' This was written, however, after the event" (second edition [New York: Atheneum, 1968], p. 59). As we saw above, the policy of "independence" had been decided at the Second National CCP Congress. Maring's policy was in direct opposition to this, so the Central Committee members fought it.

According to Isaacs: "In 1922, Ch'en had written: 'Co-operation with the revolutionary bourgeoisie is the necessary road for the Chinese proletariat'" (ibid., p. 59). That line quoted by Isaacs was not written in 1922, however; it appeared in an article entitled, "The Bourgeois Revolution and the Revolutionary Bourgeoisie," in the *Hsiang-tao* (Guide Weekly) of April 23, 1923. At that time, Ch'en had already accepted the directive of the Comintern, giving up his original view and moving to the right.

At this point, it is worthwhile to point out that Isaacs' book is a valuable record of the general direction of China's second revolution. However, Isaacs does not allude to CCP internal affairs, conflicting thoughts of its leadership, and especially, its response to Comintern policies. It is as if the CCP mechanically carried out the directives of the Comintern, without any dissent whatsoever. This is the major shortcoming of Isaacs' book, and the main reason I have presented in such detail the record of Comintern leadership and its relation to the development of the CCP.

to be discussed within the whole party and a final decision was to be made at the CCP's Third National Congress.

In the midst of the discussion over whether or not to join the KMT, every branch had experienced sharp debate, the strongest opposition coming from the cadres in the workers' movement. According to Ch'en Tu-hsiu, before he went to Moscow in 1922 to participate in the Fourth Comintern Congress, he still had doubts about the policy requiring CCP members to join the KMT. Because of this, the leaders of the Comintern watched him carefully, considering him a representative of a type of "infantile disorder of 'leftists.'" Radek even went to the point of making a public criticism, saying the task of the CCP was to "bring the workers into a rational relationship with the objectively revolutionary elements of the bourgeoisie" (*A Documentary History*, Brandt et al., p. 53).

Since there was such opposition by the CCP lower-echelon and cadres toward joining the KMT, and, especially since Ch'en Tu-hsiu expressed this opposition when he attended the Fourth Comintern Congress, the chairman of the Comintern, Zinoviev, formally raised the question for discussion in the RCP Politburo in early January 1923. Except for Trotsky, all the others, such as Stalin, Zinoviev, and Bukharin, approved having CCP members join the KMT. As a result of this meeting, Zinoviev wrote a formal resolution on CCP-KMT collaboration, dated January 12, 1923, and adopted by the Executive Committee of the Comintern (ECCI):

1. The only serious national-revolutionary group in China is the Kuomintang, which is based partly on the liberal-democratic bourgeoisie and petty bourgeoisie, partly on the intelligentsia and workers.

2. Since the independent workers' movement in the country is still weak, and since the central task for China is the national revolution against the imperialists and their feudal agents within the country, and since, moreover, the working class is directly interested in the solution of this national-revolutionary problem, while still being insufficiently differentiated as a wholly independent social force, the ECCI considers it necessary that action between the Kuomintang and the young CCP should be co-ordinated.

3. Consequently in present conditions it is expedient for members of the CCP to remain in the Kuomintang.

[*The Communist International, 1919-1943, Documents*, edited by Jane Degras (London: Frank Cass & ·Co., 1971), vol. 2, pp. 5-6.]

The Comintern recognized the KMT as "the only serious national-revolutionary group in China," and, because of this, ordered "members of the CCP to remain in the Kuomintang" with its base in "the liberal-democratic bourgeoisie." The party of the proletariat was thus placed under the control of the party of the bourgeoisie in order to fool the masses. This was in direct opposition to the traditional stand of the Bolsheviks toward the "liberal-democratic bourgeoisie" and Lenin's fundamental views as expressed in the "Draft Theses on the National and Colonial Questions." This Menshevik line, then, was the source of the tragedy of the second Chinese revolution.

Following this Politburo approval of CCP members joining the KMT, Stalin sent the Soviet government representative Adolf Joffe to Shanghai to negotiate directly with Sun Yat-sen regarding cooperation between the two parties and the methods by which the Soviet Union could aid the KMT. On January 26, 1923, a "Joint Manifesto of Sun Yat-sen and A. A. Joffe" was issued; the first part of this manifesto stated:

> Dr. Sun is of the opinion that, because of the non-existence of conditions favourable to their successful application in China, it is not possible to carry out either Communism or even the Soviet system in China. M. Joffe agrees entirely with this view; he is further of the opinion that China's most important and most pressing problems are the completion of national unification and the attainment of full national independence. With regard to these great tasks, M. Joffe has assured Dr. Sun of the Russian people's warmest sympathy for China, and of (their) willingness to lend support. [*A Documentary History*, Brandt et al., p. 70.]

Sun's feelings that "it is not possible to carry out either Communism or even the Soviet system in China" are a candid expression of his bourgeois views. Joffe, the Soviet representative, openly "agrees entirely with this view," and, moreover, promises Soviet "support" for Sun to complete "national unification" and full "national independence." In this way, the CCP was left with only one task: that of following the lead of Soviet policy in support of the KMT efforts to attain this "national unification" and "national independence." This was the concrete manifestation of the January 12, 1923, Comintern resolution, and, it goes without saying, it was carried out in accordance with Stalin's directions.

Following the formal Comintern resolution of January 12, 1923, and the "Joint Manifesto of Sun Yat-sen and A. A. Joffe" of January 26, 1923, the CCP leadership called the Third National Congress for June 1923. The Comintern representative at this congress was, again, Maring. Even though there was sharp debate during this congress, the authority of the Soviet government and the Comintern caused the majority of the delegates to approve the resolution calling for CCP members to join the KMT. The important points of the manifesto which came out of this congress were:

> *The KMT should be the central force of the national revolution and should assume its leadership.* Unfortunately, however, the KMT often suffers from two erroneous notions. Firstly, it relies on foreign powers for help in the Chinese national revolution. . . . Secondly, (the KMT) concentrates all its efforts on military action, neglecting propaganda work among the people. . . .
>
> *We still hope that all the revolutionary elements in our society will rally to the KMT, speeding the completion of the national revolutionary movement.* At the same time, (we also) hope that the KMT will resolutely discard its two old notions of reliance on foreign powers and concentration on military action, and that it *will pay attention to political propaganda among the people—never missing an opportunity for (such) propaganda in order to create a true central force for the national welfare and a true leadership for the national revolution.* [Ibid., pp. 71-72, emphasis added.]

If this manifesto is placed next to that which came out of the Second National Congress, one can clearly see that their contents are in complete contradiction. The CCP had turned from its original Bolshevism and moved into the mire of Menshevism. As a matter of fact, the CCP was even worse off than the Russian Mensheviks; at least they were able to maintain their organizational independence, and did not have to join the party of the Russian bourgeoisie, the Constitutional Democrats, whereas the CCP had to join the party of the Chinese bourgeoisie, the KMT, and expressed the "hope that all the revolutionary elements in our society will rally to the KMT." What was the source for such a surprising change? It was merely this: the change and degeneration of the Soviet Communist Party and Comintern leadership. Here, I must point out one fact, which will clarify things: Following the onset of Lenin's illness in May 1922, Stalin, together with Zinoviev and Kamenev, formed a small group within the Politburo of the Central Committee of the RCP (the so-called triumvirate). Their main objective was to get rid of Trotsky (they feared his assuming a leadership position following Lenin's death). Their foreign policy in China was based on maintaining cooperation with the "democratic faction" of the bourgeoisie. It is because of this that the Comintern ordered the CCP to join the KMT in August 1922 (not yet three months after Lenin became ill).

Following the approval of this policy at the CCP Third National Congress, great changes took place in both the thought and activity of the CCP.

As far as "thought" is concerned, some leaders of the CCP, in order to find some "theoretical" justification for CCP members joining the KMT, exaggerated the revolutionary character of the bourgeoisie and its function in the leadership of the national revolution. The initial advocate and promoter of this type of work was Mao Tse-tung.

Mao was newly elected to the Central Committee at the Third National Congress. Immediately following the close of that congress, he submitted an article to the party organ *Hsiang-tao* (Guide Weekly). The title of this article was, "The Peking Coup d'Etat and the Merchants," and some of its important points are as follows:

> The present political problem in China is none other than the problem of the national revolution. To use the strength of the people to overthrow the militarists and foreign imperialism, with which the former are in collusion to accomplish their treasonable acts, is the historic mission of the Chinese people. This revolution is the task of the people as a whole. The merchants, workers, peasants, students, and teachers should all come forward to take on the responsibility for a portion of the revolutionary work; but *because of historical necessity and current tendencies, the work for which the merchants* [i.e., bourgeoisie—Peng] *should be responsible in the national revolution is both more urgent and more important than the work that the rest of the people should take upon themselves.* We know that the politics of semi-colonial China is characterized by the fact that the militarists and the foreign powers have banded together to impose a twofold oppression on the people of the whole country. The people of the whole country naturally suffer profoundly under this kind of twofold oppression. *Nevertheless the merchants are the ones who feel these sufferings most acutely and most urgently.* [An English translation of this text can be found in *The Political Thought of Mao Tse-tung* by Stuart R. Schram (New York: Praeger, 1969), pp. 206-07, emphasis added.]

"The merchants are the ones who feel these sufferings most acutely and most urgently." Therefore, "the work for which the merchants should be responsible in the national revolution is both more urgent and more important than the work that the rest of the people should take upon themselves." In accordance with this type of analysis, Mao comes to these conclusions:

> The Shanghai merchants have risen and begun to act. We hope that the merchants outside of Shanghai will all rise up and act together. . . . The broader the organization of merchants, the greater will be their influence, *the greater will be their ability to lead the people of the whole country, and the more rapid the success of the revolution!* [Schram, op. cit., p. 208, emphasis added.]

Mao's conclusion that the "hope" for a "success of the revolution" lies in the merchants' (bourgeoisie's) "ability to lead the people of the whole country" (workers, peasants, petty bourgeoisie) is, very clearly, the basest form of Menshevism.

After Ch'en Tu-hsiu received notice of the resolution approved by the Comintern on January 12, 1923, calling for CCP members to join the KMT, and, at the same time, due to the "February Seventh Incident," where Northern railroad workers were seriously attacked on February 7, 1923, he started to retrench on his original opposition to unification with the bourgeoisie. This was first expressed in the article which he wrote for *Hsiang-tao* titled, "The Bourgeois Revolution and the Revolutionary Bourgeoisie." In this article, Ch'en argued that "co-operation with the revolutionary bourgeoisie is the necessary road for the Chinese proletariat" (see Isaacs, p. 59; *Hsiang-tao*, April 23, 1923). Following this, Ch'en wrote an article for the December 1, 1923, *Ch'ien Feng* (Vanguard), titled "The National Revolution and Social Classes." In this article, Ch'en systematically analyzed all Chinese social classes, their situation and function, in the fields of economics, politics, and culture. He felt that the bourgeoisie had the greatest influence in all three sectors and that the working class had very little power in terms of numbers and was poor and ignorant. For these reasons, it was impossible to expect the workers to lead the national revolution. After all, the nature of this revolution was bourgeois, so it was necessary that the working class cooperate with the bourgeoisie in order to successfully complete the national revolution against the imperialists and militarists.

Ch'en Tu-hsiu, stressing the lack of numerical strength of the working class, along with its poverty and ignorance, explained that "the working class cannot lead the revolution, but must cooperate with the bourgeoisie. Only then can they complete . . . the national revolution." When Ch'en's views are placed next to Mao's views that the "merchants" are best able to "feel these sufferings most acutely and most urgently," and, thus have the "ability to lead the people of the whole country" to a quicker "success of the revolution," it is quite clear that we are presented with two manifestations of the same Menshevik thinking.

Another newly elected Central Committee member, Ch'ü Ch'iu-pai, wrote an article just before the reorganization of the KMT. The article was titled "Reform of the Kuomintang and the National Revolutionary Movement," and it appeared in the December 19, 1923, issue of *Hsiang-tao*. In this article Ch'ü expressed the following assessment and hopes about the KMT and its reorganization:

> The author of the 1911 revolution which established the Republic of China was the Kuomintang, and it has been working hard for many years despite hardships and criticisms. Furthermore, it was only the Kuomintang which fought for the rights of the common people in opposition to the Peiyang militarists. . . . (1) since then, the political movement of the common people and military revolutionary activity have both advanced; (2) a mass, democratic party has been organized and corrupt elements have been purged; (3) strict discipline has been established, along with an organized, systematic national movement which always represents the common people against the militarists and the various powers.

Following these highly respectful and hopeful remarks about the KMT's "revolutionary achievements" and the "promising future" to be found in its imminent reorganization, Ch'ü proclaimed:

> People of the whole country! . . . unite and organize the Kuomintang to concentrate our political power. . . . *At present the Kuomintang is the center of power. The only way we can throw off oppression by the great powers and the militarists and establish our own true, common people's republic, a truly independent nation, is to develop the common people's own party. . . . This is our Kuomintang. We must participate, merchants* [bourgeoisie—Peng], *peasants, workers, students, and teachers, all who belong to the common people should join the Kuomintang.*

Besides adding concretization and practice to both Mao's and Ch'en's illusions regarding the bourgeoisie, Ch'ü Ch'iu-pai's remarkable illusions toward the KMT also expressed his own special petty-bourgeois mentality and speculativeness. These views, however, were not merely those of one individual; they were shared by all CCP leaders. The fact that Ch'ü's article was published in a public party organ is proof of this.

Since the KMT "is the common people's own party," and "at present the Kuomintang is the center of power," through this "center" it is possible to "throw off oppression by the great powers [imperialism—Peng] and the militarists and establish our own true common people's republic." Ch'ü's conclusion was that "all work should go toward building the Kuomintang." The facts certainly reflected this!

From the Third National Congress on, the CCP Central Committee ordered all party and SYC members to join the KMT, to mobilize all cadres to assist in the reorganization of the KMT, and to participate in every kind of KMT work. For example, Mao Tse-tung, a standing member of the Central Committee and organizational secretary, put all of his time into propaganda work for the Shanghai executive headquarters of the KMT and completely abandoned organizational work for his own party. Another Central Committe member, T'an P'ing-shan, specialized in working for the KMT's organizational department in its Central Committee. In other provinces and cities, such as Hunan, Hupeh, Szechwan, Peking, and Tientsin, all CCP cadres worked hard to reorganize the KMT and directly took over that party's work. Most prominent among these were: Li Li-san, Hsiang Ying, Teng Chung-hsia, and others, who were originally responsible cadres within the workers' movement, left to do "reorganization" work for the KMT, thus putting a stop to the organizational work of the CCP. The workers' movement was forgotten, even to the point of disbanding the CCP's labor secretariat!

On the other side, the Russian Communist Party sent Mikhail Borodin to Canton in the fall of 1923 to act as Sun Yat-sen's adviser and assist in the reorganization of the KMT. It was Borodin who introduced the KMT to RCP-style party organization in an attempt to turn it into "the center of power," a party in which "strict discipline has been established." Furthermore, he developed a program for the KMT, utilizing such reformist and abstract phrases as "equalization of land rights," "restriction of private capital," etc., to prettify the true reactionary nature of this representative of the bourgeoisie. Thus, in January 1924, the KMT held its First Reorganization Congress, during which it adopted Borodin's platform and party system. This congress also elected some CCP leaders to the KMT's Central Committee (Li Ta-chao, T'an P'ing-shan, Lin Po-ch'ü) and some as alternates (Ch'ü Ch'iu-pai, Mao Tse-tung, Chang Kuo-t'ao, and others). In this way, the KMT, which was originally completely corrupt and disorganized, put on a new mask and became what Ch'ü Ch'iu-pai hoped for, "our common people's party," under the influence of Soviet aid through Borodin and using the skills of CCP members!

In the spring of 1924, the Soviet Union sent another representative, General Galen (his real name was Vassily Blücher), to Canton to act as military adviser for the KMT. He brought with him many military experts and weapons to help reorganize KMT military units. He also introduced the Soviet Red Army's political commissar system to KMT units. First of all, he helped Chiang Kai-shek establish the Whampoa Military Academy, trained military cadres, and made preparations for the establishment of a new army. This was the foundation for all later developments, and, because of it the KMT was not only "armed" politically, but militarily as well.

The old cadres in the KMT, however, felt that the policy to "unite with Soviet Russia, take in the Communist Party" was dangerous to the KMT. They asserted: "Since the Communist Party joined the Kuomintang . . . all its propaganda against British, American, French, and Japanese imperialism has served to undermine the Kuomintang's international image . . . and that against militarism has served to destroy any chance for cooperation between the Kuomintang and powerful internal forces, their plan is to destroy the Kuomintang" (see Chang Chi et al., "Bill of Impeachment," in *Ko-ming wen-hsien* IX, 72-80). Sun Yat-sen gave the following explanation to these old cadres:

> If Russia wants to co-operate with China, she must co-operate with our Party and not with Ch'en Tu-hsiu. If Ch'en disobeys our Party, he will be ousted.
> The Chinese revolution has never been welcomed by the foreign powers, which have often helped our opponents [militarists—Peng] in attempts to destroy our Party. . . . Sympathy can only be expected from Russia. . . . It was not Ch'en Tu-hsiu's but Russia's idea to befriend us. [*A Documentary History,* Brandt et al., p. 73.]

Sun's explanation is very clear: all he needed was Russia's "sympathy," that is, Soviet military and financial aid. This, even to the point of ousting Ch'en Tu-hsiu's CCP at any time. This, then, foreshadowed the later moves by Chiang Kai-shek and Wang Ching-wei to purge the KMT of CCP members.

In order to soothe the opposition within his own party, Sun initiated further controls over CCP members. In August 1924 he called a plenum of the KMT Central Committee, during which he not only reiterated the policy of taking in CCP members, but also presented a motion calling for KMT Central Committee review of all Comintern resolutions and orders to the CCP. Ch'ü Ch'iu-pai, who attended this meeting, expressed his agreement with Sun's motion but stated that he must ask the opinion of the CCP Central Committee on this question.

III. The CCP Turns to the Left—Toward the Working Class

When I returned to Shanghai from Moscow in August 1924, Ts'ai Ho-sen (standing member of CCP Central Committee and editor of *Hsiang-tao*) told me about Sun's motion regarding KMT review of all Comintern resolutions and orders to the CCP and asked what I thought about it. "Has the Central Committee accepted this demand?" I asked. Ts'ai replied, "They are thinking it over now." "The Central Committee must refuse Sun's demand," I said strongly, "otherwise, our party will become a mere appendage to the Kuomintang." Ts'ai talked this over with Ch'en Tu-hsiu (Ch'en and Ts'ai were the only standing members of the Central Committee left in Shanghai), and they sent a telegram to Ch'ü Ch'iu-pai ordering him to refuse Sun's demand. This was the turning point in the CCP attitude toward the KMT.

After this, I presented three formal resolutions to the Central Committee: (1) we should assume a critical attitude toward the policies and activities of the KMT; (2) we must renew our local party organizations everywhere; we should call on those comrades who have returned from the University of the Toilers of the East in Moscow to take responsibility for this renewal of party organizations and the workers' movement; (3) we should establish a Labor Movement Committee in order to plan for and lead the national workers' movement. The Central Committee adopted these three resolutions and directed Li Li-san, Hsiang Ying, Li Ch'i-han, and myself to form the Labor Movement Committee. This committee established workers' evening schools and workers' clubs in the West Shanghai area. This, then, was the foundation on which the great strike in Shanghai's Japanese cotton mills was built in February 1925.

On the occasion of the seventh anniversary of the October revolution, I wrote an article titled, "The October Revolution and Leninism," which appeared in the November 7, 1924, issue of *Hsiang-tao*. After I discussed the great accomplishments of the October revolution, I pointed out, "The October revolution is the model for the world revolution; China's revolution must follow this path." In other words, China's national revolution, under the leadership of the proletariat, would move directly into a socialist revolution. At about this same time, Ch'en Tu-hsiu and I carried on a serious discussion about which class should lead the national revolution. Even though, throughout this discussion, Ch'en still maintained his view that the bourgeoisie should lead the national revolution, he had modified this view somewhat. Just at that time, the Central Committee appointed me editor of *New Youth* (the party theoretical journal). I planned to make the December 1924 issue of this journal a special one on "The National Revolution." Besides translation of those resolutions from the Second Comintern Congress on national and colonial questions and Lenin's remarks, this issue also contained an article I wrote, "Who Is the Leader of the National Revolution?" Before the issue was published, I gave the original draft of my article to Ch'en Tu-hsiu and asked him to write something on the question. The idea was to further public discussion on the issue if he disagreed with my views and wished to criticize me.

As a matter of fact, my article was written in answer to Ch'en's article on "The National Revolution and Social Classes." After analyzing the material advantages and mutual relations of each class in Chinese society, I pointed out that the bourgeoisie, due to its close ties with the warlords and imperialists, could never lead the national revolution against these evils. Moreover, because of its fear of the proletariat, the bourgeoisie would inevitably become reactionary. From this, I concluded:

> After analyzing all the classes . . . we may now affirm that from the standpoint of their material basis, revolutionary consciousness, and the conditions of the international revolution . . . *only the working class can become the leader of the national revolution.* [Emphasis in original.]

Ch'en Tu-hsiu's article for the special issue of *New Youth* was titled, "The Lessons of the National Movement over the Past

Twenty-seven Years." His conclusion was that only with proletarian leadership could the national revolution be victorious; he had already given up on the idea of bourgeois leadership. As a result, Ch'en and I reached agreement on the basic principle of which class was to lead the national revolution.

In January 1925, the CCP held its Fourth National Congress. A resolution was written calling for proletarian leadership of the revolution, and plans were made to rebuild and develop the workers' movement of the entire nation. First of all, the Second Congress of the National General Union of Railway Workers was called, in order to rebuild the Northern railway workers' movement. Further, plans were made to hold the Second National Labor Congress to unify the workers' movement. If we compare this Fourth Congress with the Third Congress, we find that, whereas the Third Congress determined the "leader of the national revolution" to be the representative of the bourgeoisie, the KMT, this Fourth Congress formally resolved that the proletariat was the leader of the national revolution and that all work should be concentrated on developing the workers' movement. This congress marked the return of the CCP to Bolshevism and the setting of conditions for the second Chinese revolution.

The Second Congress of the National General Union of Railway Workers opened on February 7, 1925 (the second anniversary of the "February Seventh Incident"), in Chengchow, Honan (the place where the union's First Congress had been closed down). There were forty-five delegates representing twelve branches of the union, and they passed resolutions concerning workers' economic interests and political rights. This lent great impetus to the future struggles of the railway workers.

At about the same time, the strike in Shanghai's Japanese cotton mills was going on. About seventy thousand people were involved in this strike, developed and advanced under the leadership of the "workers' clubs" in West Shanghai. This strike was a great victory. Not only were wages increased and working conditions improved, but the legal right to organize unions was established. This was the first great accomplishment in the history of the Shanghai workers' movement.

The Second National Labor Congress convened on May Day 1925, in Canton. There were 281 delegates representing 166 unions with a membership of over 570,000. Besides passage of resolutions regarding the economic interests and political rights of workers, this congress took pains to point out that the working class should participate in the national democratic liberation struggles and must be the leading force in these struggles. As a result, the National Congress was imbued with the conviction that the working class should lead the national revolution and in turn carried this idea to the working masses.

Immediately following the Second National Labor Congress, the workers in Shanghai's Japanese cotton mills again went on strike. This was a direct result of a counterattack by the Japanese capitalists. First of all, they forbade any union activity, then followed this up with bloody repression. On May 15, Ku Cheng-hung, a leader of the workers, was killed. This caused an immediate protest by the students and working masses in anti-imperialist demonstrations and street meetings. This anti-imperialist movement reached its peak on May 30, when thousands of students and workers gathered in front of the Laocha Police Station on Nanking Road and demanded the release of arrested demonstrators. The British police raised their guns and fired, killing seven and wounding dozens of demonstrators. This was the "May Thirtieth Incident," which shook the whole of China and started the second Chinese revolution. It was these events that Trotsky was responding to in the first article in this book, "The 'Moscow Spirit,'" which was published in the press of the Comintern a few days later.

IV. The Revolution Begins—The Conflict Between the Policies of the Comintern and Those of the CCP

Following the May Thirtieth Incident, all of Shanghai's students, workers, and merchants went on strike. This became a great wave of anti-imperialism by the "whole people." In the midst of this wave, the CCP mobilized all of its members and the members of the SYC to lead the students in organizing the Shanghai Student Federation. At the same time, with the cotton mill unions as a foundation, the Shanghai General Labor Union was established in less than a week. This General Labor Union became the general headquarters in leading the later struggles of the Shanghai workers' movement.

Under the strong influence of the anti-imperialist movement in Shanghai, every major city, such as Nanking, Wuhan, and Peking, saw students, workers, and the general public rise up together in strikes and demonstrations; it was a veritable flood of anti-imperialist sentiment in the national liberation movement.

Finally, in Canton, the masses of students and workers held a demonstration on June 23 to protest the butchery carried out by British imperialism in Shanghai. The demonstration followed along Shakee Road, and, as it approached Shameen, the imperialist concession area, the British and French military police strafed the crowd with machine guns. Fifty-seven people were killed, and one hundred and seventeen were injured in the famous "Shakee Incident."

Immediately upon hearing of the butchery by the British imperialists in Canton, the workers in Hong Kong called a general strike, and many traveled to Canton. It was at this time that the Canton–Hong Kong Strike Committee was established; this became the bastion for the anti-imperialist movement in South China, initiating the blockade of Hong Kong. This was a very grave attack against British imperialism.

When the bourgeoisie saw the unparalleled heroism, spirit of sacrifice, and strong leadership expressed by the workers of Shanghai, Hong Kong, and Canton in the anti-imperialist national revolution, especially with CCP members in the leadership, they were terrified. They moved quickly to come to terms with the imperialists in order to stop the movement. The first move was made by the Shanghai General Merchants Association (representative of the big bourgeoisie) when it publicly changed the anti-imperialist positions of the Workers, Merchants [small and medium], and Students Association, and then ordered the merchants to open their stores. Eventually they used all kinds of plots and methods to break the strikes. The bourgeoisie had discovered that its fundamental conflict with the working class overrode its conflict with imperialism. Thus, the struggle between the bourgeoisie and working class was raised another level. This situation was reflected in the party of the bourgeoisie, the KMT, and became a struggle against the working class and the Communist Party. In July 1925, Tai Chi-t'ao, a leading theoretician for the KMT, published "The Fundamentals of Sun Yatsenism" with emphasis on "national interest and unification" and attacking the concept of class struggle, especially the workers' struggles under the leadership of the CCP. This article expressed the views and hopes of the bourgeoisie, and soon after it appeared, Chiang Kai-shek organized the Society for the Study of Sun Yat-senism at the Whampoa Military Academy and the units under his direct command. This organization spread out immediately and specialized in opposing the communists.

The Shanghai bourgeoisie, after seeing this public expression by the KMT's leading theoretician, Tai Chi-t'ao, moved quickly to ally itself with the local warlords and initiate a policy of repression. Thus, on September 20, 1925, they closed down the Shanghai General Labor Union, hoping to defuse the workers' struggle. The fact of being "closed down" did not keep the Shanghai General Labor Union from leading the workers' movement, however. It merely went underground to help in the workers' struggle.

I wrote an article titled, "The Closing of the Shanghai General Labor Union and the Present Responsibilities of the Workers," which appeared in the October 5, 1925, issue of *Hsiang-tao*. In light of the leadership function of the working class in the May Thirtieth Movement, I pointed out:

> The success of the Chinese national revolution is possible only on the condition that the Chinese workers arise and fight. Shanghai . . . is the equivalent of Russia's Petrograd—the February revolution and the October revolution in Russia were under the leadership of the workers in Petrograd.

Then, I concluded:

> The hundreds of thousands of workers in Shanghai have gained much experience in the May Thirtieth Movement under the leadership of the General Labor Union, and have become familiar with a number of the elementary methods of carrying out a revolution. *In the future they will advance further along the road of armed insurrection . . . following the example set by the workers of Petrograd from the February revolution to the October revolution.* [Emphasis in original.]

At this juncture, I must point out one thing: when I stressed the decisive function of the workers in the May Thirtieth Movement and foresaw the need for an armed insurrection to take power, I was in direct contradiction with the official policy of the Comintern.

Ch'en Tu-hsiu had personally seen the working class demonstrate its leadership function during the May Thirtieth Movement. He felt very strongly that the CCP should base itself on the working class, and, because of this, he made a public statement in *Hsiang-tao* calling on workers to join the CCP. This was a fundamental change from the propaganda of Ch'ü Ch'iu-pai, who called on workers, merchants, and students to join "our common people's Kuomintang."

When Ch'en Tu-hsiu criticized Tai Chi-t'ao's "Fundamentals of Sun Yat-senism" (Ch'en's article appeared in an August 1925 issue of *Hsiang-tao*), even though he had quite effectively refuted the latter's argument against the class struggle, he could not publicly criticize the reactionary anti-class-struggle views of Sun Yat-sen because of the policy of "KMT-CCP collaboration." At the same time, Ch'en witnessed those members of the Society for the Study of Sun Yat-senism moving closer to the right wing of the KMT, while carrying out anticommunist activities. This all caused Ch'en to believe that this policy which required the CCP to remain within the KMT only served to restrain the CCP's own independence in leading the masses. Because of this, Ch'en formally proposed that the CCP quit the KMT and only cooperate with it outside of the party. This proposal was made at a plenum of the CCP Central Committee which met in October 1925. The Comintern representative, however, felt that the most immediate task for the CCP was to try to use the upcoming Second Congress of the KMT to push the whole party into the hands of the left wing, and thus take over leadership of the national revolutionary movement. In this way, Ch'en's proposal to leave the KMT was defeated. This was the first instance of conflict between the CCP and the Comintern over the "KMT-CCP collaboration" policy.

The Second Congress of the KMT was held in Canton in January 1926. This congress issued a shallow statement which expressed its determination to carry out the revolution to the end. "Leftist leader" Wang Ching-wei, in his remarks, was very pretentious in expressing his sincerity toward the work of revolution and collaboration with the CCP. In the Central Executive Committee elections, a great many KMT left-wingers and CCP members were added, while some rightists were kicked out. Chiang Kai-shek, acting as a "leftist leader," was elected to the CEC for the first time. The newly elected heads of the KMT Central Headquarters, Organizational Section, and Peasant Section, were all CCP members. Others, such as the Propaganda Section, Workers' Section, Youth Section, Women's Section, etc., all had secretaries who were from the CCP. Mao Tse-tung was a secretary in the Propaganda Section under Wang Ching-wei. In this way, "the whole Kuomintang" became the "left wing." CCP members held "leadership positions" in the Central Committee of the KMT; however, in less than two months this "left wing

Kuomintang" failed in the face of a minor attack, Chiang Kai-shek's coup of March 20, 1926.

This anticommunist coup was plotted and carried out by members of the Society for the Study of Sun Yat-senism under the direction of Chiang Kai-shek. More than fifty CCP members who were doing political work in military units under Chiang's direct control were immediately arrested on the day of the coup. At the same time, weapons were taken from Strike Committee pickets and Soviet Russian guard units, and Chiang established his own personal military dictatorship after chasing out Wang Ching-wei, the chairman of the national government.

The CCP Central Committee hoped for some guidance from Moscow as to the policy to be followed in dealing with this attack by the forces of Chiang Kai-shek. After three weeks, however, there was no word (because Stalin, frightened and confused, just sat on the sidelines watching the situation develop). Because of this, it became necessary that we determine our own policy toward Chiang. The important points of this policy were: unite with the left wing of the KMT and their military forces in order to oppose Chiang Kai-shek; expand the military units under the leadership of Yeh T'ing, a CCP member (close to 3,000 men); furnish arms to the workers and peasants so that they might function as the basic force of the revolution. Moreover, it was decided to send me to Canton to organize a special committee (this consisted of CC members T'an P'ing-shan and Chang Kuo-t'ao and Kwangtung Provincial Committee members Ch'en Yen-nien, Chou En-lai, and Chang T'ai-lei) to discuss with the Comintern representative Borodin concrete measures for dealing with Chiang Kai-shek.

I arrived in Canton toward the end of April 1926. At the same time Borodin had just returned from the Soviet Union with directives from Stalin. Immediately, I called a meeting of the special committee and invited Borodin to attend. After I had reported on the resolutions of the CCP Central Committee regarding Chiang Kai-shek, Borodin emphasized the "extreme danger inherent in the present situation" and used this as a reason for opposing any discussion of the CC resolutions. When I proposed that CCP members leave the KMT and only cooperate outside of party ranks, Borodin seized the pretext that "the question of leaving the Kuomintang must be agreed upon by the left wing of the Kuomintang." In summary, Borodin expressed Stalin's orders that no matter how serious the results of Chiang's

March coup might be, the policy of "KMT-CCP collaboration" must be maintained. He openly proposed that the CCP should accept the situation which resulted from the March coup, recognize Chiang's military dictatorship, and accept his "Resolution Adjusting Party Affairs,"* while assisting him in the leadership of the Northern Expedition. Borodin soothed the other comrades, saying, "The advancement of the Northern Expedition will have advantages for us in the future." Except for myself, all other members of the special committee gave their approval to Borodin's views. In this way, the policy of opposition to Chiang Kai-shek, which had been put forth by the Central Committee of the CCP, was turned into a policy of surrender to Chiang Kai-shek. This, then, smoothed the way for his next coup. This was the turning point which led the second Chinese revolution to defeat.

Both Ch'en Tu-hsiu and I felt the great danger which was inherent in this shameless policy of surrender followed by the Comintern, but there was, once again, no way to publicly oppose it. All we could do was call a plenum of the CC to discuss the situation and attempt to recover from this danger. This plenum was held in mid-July 1926, just one week after Chiang Kai-shek took command of the general headquarters of the Northern Expedition and announced its mobilization. Thus, the situation had become more intense and severe. Ch'en Tu-hsiu and I put forth a resolution: All CCP members should leave the KMT, should only cooperate with it outside party ranks, and should establish a united front with the left wing of the KMT. We explained that only by throwing off the control of the CCP by the KMT could we carry out a truly independent policy of leadership of the movement of workers and peasants. Under pressure from the Comintern representative, a majority of the CC, led by Ch'ü Ch'iu-pai, refused to accept our resolution, but agreed to forward it to the Comintern for consideration. The Comintern not only refused to consider our resolution, but Bukharin also published

---

* The basic points of Chiang's "Resolution Adjusting Party Affairs" were: CCP members could not criticize the "Three People's Principles" of Sun Yat-sen; they could no longer assume positions as heads of departments in the KMT Central Committee; CCP members could not make up more than one-third of any local party committee; the CCP must turn over the names of its members in the KMT and of Communist Youth Corps (CYC) members who had joined the KMT.

an article in *Pravda* wherein he charged that those who advocated CCP withdrawal from the KMT were just as wrong as those in the Soviet Opposition who advocated Soviet withdrawal from the Anglo-Russian Committee. Trotsky, however, said later:

> It is necessary to approve as unconditionally correct the resolution of the June plenum of the CC of the Chinese CP, which demands that the party withdraw from the Kuomintang and conclude a bloc with that organization through its left wing. ["Class Relations in the Chinese Revolution" (April 3, 1927).*]

V. Comintern Policy of Collaboration with the KMT Leads the CCP into a Blind Alley

The resolution which was put forth by Ch'en Tu-hsiu and Peng Shu-tse and called for "CCP members [to] leave the KMT, only to cooperate with the KMT outside party ranks, and to establish a united front with the left wing of the KMT"—this "unconditionally correct" resolution was finally rejected by the Comintern. After this, the CCP could only remain active within the restraints of the policy of "KMT-CCP collaboration." This, then, describes the difficult and contradictory situation with which the CCP had to deal during the great tide of revolution from July 1926 to March 1927.

Under this kind of situation, the CCP was restrained from criticizing the infantile Three People's Principles of Sun Yat-sen and the reactionary behavior of Chiang Kai-shek. An even more serious restriction was the prohibition on advocating agrarian revolution, calling on the peasantry to struggle for the land, and organizing workers', peasants', and soldiers' soviets, pulling soldiers into revolutionary units. All of this would have been in direct opposition to the Comintern policy of "KMT-CCP collaboration." The CCP's mission, according to the Comintern, was to "bend all efforts toward mobilizing the workers and peasants into support for the Northern Expedition."

In fact, the Chinese Communist Party did mobilize the workers and peasants in support of the Northern Expedition against the Peiyang warlords. They mobilized all party members and Youth

---

* The "resolution of the June plenum of the CC of the Chinese CP" which Trotsky mentions is that resolution of Ch'en Tu-hsiu and Peng Shu-tse which the July plenum of the CC of the CCP agreed to turn over to the Comintern for consideration.

Corps members on every front to propagandize in opposition to the Northern militarists and to encourage the forces of the Northern Expedition in their fighting. They also organized workers and peasants into all types of commando units to handle reconnaissance, spying, and scouting. These units were also responsible for sabotage of communications behind enemy lines (railroads, electrical lines, ships, etc.), and for collection of abandoned weapons when the enemy retreated. Among the official positions in the National Revolutionary Army, there were dozens of CCP members acting as company commanders, battalion commanders, and regimental commanders. They were all indifferent to their personal safety, fought bravely, and some of them were sacrificed in battle. Thus, in less than four months (July to October 1926), and with few serious battles, the Western Route Northern Expeditionary Forces (by way of Hunan) reached the banks of the Yangtze River and secured the mercantile and industrial center of Central China—Wuhan. The Central Route Forces, under the direct command of Chiang Kai-shek, occupied the city of Nanchang, Kiangsi, in November 1926. The Eastern Route Forces, passing through Fukien, occupied Hangchow, Chekiang, in February 1927. All of these quick and surprising victories were the direct result of the active aid rendered by the worker and peasant masses which had been mobilized by members of the Chinese Communist Party.

At the time the workers and peasants had been mobilized to assist the Northern Expeditionary Forces, especially when victories had been attained, they were quickly organizing their own unions and peasant associations. For example, Hunan in the short period of five months had organized peasant associations with a total membership of more than four million. The Hunan General Union had a membership of about 500,000. In October 1926, after the Northern Expeditionary Forces had occupied Wuhan, 300,000 workers, with the assistance of CCP members, organized the Hupeh General Union. The peasant movement in Hupeh also developed rapidly. At about the same time, the working class in Shanghai, under the influence of victories of the Northern Expedition, had turned from economic strikes to political strikes and demonstrations, while preparing for armed insurrection. On another side, the masses in Hankow and Chiuchiang moved spontaneously in early January 1927 and took over the concession areas under the control of English imperialism. In summary, from the time these forces entered the Yangtze

River valley, the worker-peasant movement in Hunan and Hupeh billowed like an angry tide, overturning all social relations. The workers, from strikes for a better life and better working conditions, had come to the verge of attacking the system of private ownership itself. They even went to the point of directly taking over the concessions previously controlled by imperialism. The peasants, especially those of Hunan, had gone from struggles aimed at lowering rents and interest rates directly to revolutionary activity to get rid of the landlords and gentry and take over the land. In fact, the peasant associations became the governing organizations in most villages. Thus, one can see the new high point which the tide of revolution had reached.

However, the representative of counterrevolution, Chiang Kai-shek, was also moving at the same speed in carrying out counterrevolutionary activities. First of all, he turned around and repressed those workers and peasants who had already helped the Northern Expedition in its battles, and through whom so many victories were won. He closed down the unions, abolished the peasant associations, and assassinated the leaders of the workers and peasants. He even went to the point of disbanding provincial branches of the left wing of the KMT if they were sympathetic to the worker-peasant movement (this happened to the Kiangsi branch, for instance), and then organizing his own KMT branches. Secondly, he began talks with those militarists in league with Japanese imperialism in an attempt to establish an "anti-Red united front." In Shanghai, his party henchmen got together with some reactionary politicians (Huang Fu, Kuo T'ai-ch'i, etc.) and gangster leaders (such as Huang Chin-jung, Tu Yueh-sheng, etc.), and approved their collaboration with the imperialist concessions in developing schemes to oppose the working masses and the Communist Party. This situation became very clear by early March, 1927, so I wrote an article titled, "The Present Revolutionary Crisis of the Rightward Tendency" (published in *Hsiang-tao* on March 6, 1927), which described the dangerous situation as follows:

> *The whole situation of the Chinese revolution is already clearly apparent. . . . On the one hand, the power of the revolution, especially the power of the National Revolutionary Army, the workers, and the peasants, is developing with exceptional rapidity. The tide of revolution is still swelling and deepening. . . . On the other hand. . . . A compromising and reactionary tendency among*

the leaders of the National Revolutionary Army has become apparent. . . . They have attempted, publicly or secretly, to make a compromise with the enemy against the masses they confront. This is the most dangerous phenomenon in the revolution at present, and it may well destroy the whole revolution. [Emphasis in original.]

Besides pointing out these grave dangers in the general situation, I also revealed the bourgeois counterrevolutionary tendency represented by Chiang Kai-shek in the KMT (at that time, both the Northern warlords and the imperialists called Chiang's faction the "moderate group"):

The so-called moderate group in the Kuomintang has fully disclosed its bourgeois tendency; *they . . . have seen the workers and peasants rising to fight not only for general revolutionary interests but in the interests of the workers and peasants themselves. They have also noted the concessions granted by the imperialists and the warlords. Hence this group aims at stopping the revolutionary process . . . in order to unify all the compradors, bureaucrats, and landlords, the rotten gentry and those enemies of the revolution, the imperialists and the warlords, for the purpose of striking back at the worker and peasant masses.* [Emphasis in original.]

Chiang Kai-shek's group then unified all counterrevolutionary forces, and plotted the attack on the worker-peasant masses and the Communist Party. As a matter of fact, they had already begun the work of repression in many places in Kiangsi and Anhwei provinces. When faced with this kind of danger, what kind of policy should have been adopted by the Chinese Communist Party? There was no other route but to carry out an armed uprising for power and establish a revolutionary dictatorship. At that time the CCP was already preparing for the armed uprising in Shanghai. As far as this was concerned, since it was a matter of tactics I could not initiate a public discussion of the problem. However, in the same article I did set down the following opinions as to what the regime following the victory of the armed uprising should be like:

The Chinese revolution should create a regime of revolutionary democracy, and, above all, should not create a personal military dictatorship (Chiang Kai-shek). . . . The present revolution is urgently in need of a revolutionary regime of democratic dictatorship. That means a regime for the masses in their majority, composed of workers, peasants, and petty bourgeois, in which they participate directly, thus controlling the government in order to carry out their interest in *striking down all the elements of the counterrevolution and in enforcing a revolutionary dictatorship over them.* [Emphasis in original.]

In the above analysis of the dangers to the revolution, I concentrated on exposing the counterrevolutionary tendencies and plans of the bourgeoisie represented by Chiang Kai-shek's group in the KMT. On March 18, 1927, I published "After Reading Chiang Kai-shek's Speech of February 21" (in *Hsiang-tao*). In this article I more concretely exposed the facts of Chiang's counterrevolutionary activities, including his "March 20 coup," his personal military dictatorship, his unification of all reactionary forces and alignment with imperialism, and the repression of the worker-peasant mass movement and persecution of the CCP, etc. Finally, I expressed the following warning: *"The coming struggle in China is a life and death struggle between the forces of the revolution and the antirevolutionary forces represented by Chiang Kai-shek"* (emphasis in original). In the main, the idea of a revolutionary democratic dictatorship was put forth in opposition to the bourgeois dictatorship which Chiang represented, thus placing the bourgeoisie outside of any new regime.

But, what was the Comintern's view of the situation at that time? What was its estimate of Chiang Kai-shek's Northern Expedition, or his national government in Canton? For the answer, one needs only to look at remarks made by Stalin at the Seventh Plenum of the Executive Committee of the Comintern, which met in Moscow in November–December 1926. In these remarks, titled "Prospects of the Revolution in China," there are two sections which should help clarify the problem.

When Stalin mentioned the Northern Expedition led by Chiang Kai-shek, he declared:

> The advance of the Canton troops meant a blow aimed at imperialism, a blow aimed at its agents in China. It meant the freedom of assembly, freedom to strike, freedom of the press, freedom of coalition for all the revolutionary elements in China and for the workers in particular. . . . [Isaacs, p. 119, emphasis added.]

As a matter of fact, as soon as the Northern Expedition began, under Chiang's leadership, it imposed severe limitations on the freedom of assembly, press, and especially the freedom to strike.

The "advance" of the "Canton troops" under his leadership was certainly not "a blow aimed at imperialism," rather, it was a method by which he could attain an advantageous position for coming to an agreement with imperialism.

When Stalin spoke of Chiang's national government, he emphasized:

> What is important is not the bourgeois-democratic character of the Canton government, which *forms the nucleus of the future all-Chinese revolutionary power. The most important thing is that this power is an anti-militarist power, and can be nothing else, that every advance of this power is a blow aimed at world imperialism and is therefore a stroke in favor of the world revolutionary movement.* [Loc. cit., emphasis added.]

Stalin's words were the exact opposite of the facts. "The Canton government . . . forms the nucleus of the future all-Chinese *counterrevolutionary* power." "Every advance of this power is *a blow aimed at* the world revolutionary movement."

The policies of the Comintern's Seventh Plenum regarding the Chinese revolution were decided by the expressed attitude of Stalin toward Chiang Kai-shek's Northern Expedition and the national government. So, the plenum invited Chiang's personal representative, Shao Li-tzu, to attend, recognized Chiang's KMT as a "sympathizing party," determined that the Chinese communists should participate in his national government, and assigned to the Chiang-led Northern Expedition the role of expelling imperialism and defeating its Chinese representative, the warlords, and gaining national independence and national unification. Naturally, under this kind of thinking, the CCP could not launch any effective opposition to Chiang Kai-shek's counterrevolutionary activities and plots, let alone prepare its own forces to overthrow him. *In this way, the CCP gradually was forced into a blind alley from which it could not escape.*

Thus, even though the CCP led the Shanghai workers in an armed insurrection on March 21, 1927, which succeeded in destroying the control of the Northern warlords and occupying Shanghai (except for the foreign concessions), with armed workers organized to maintain peace and order, they could not establish a revolutionary regime based on the working class. Such a regime would have initiated a dictatorship against the counterrevolutionary bourgeoisie and, in particular, would have opposed and defeated the coup plotted by Chiang Kai-shek's bandit gang. They could not do this because it would destroy "KMT-CCP collaboration," obstruct the line of a "bloc of four classes," and would especially disrupt the business of Chiang Kai-shek's Northern Expedition. Even though the CCP had taken Shanghai and gained the support of the entire working class and a majority of the lower petty-bourgeoisie, along with the sympathy of a section of the soldiers, in order to adhere to the Comintern's policy of a "coalition government of four classes," the CCP could do nothing but establish a Shanghai provisional government in collaboration with the bourgeoisie. Those representatives of the bourgeoisie "elected" to serve in the provisional government used sabotage and opposition, under Chiang Kai-shek's direction, to paralyze the government and prepare the way for Chiang's next coup.

Under these circumstances, the CCP slipped into a period of exceptional distress and dilemma. At that time the only members of the Central Committee left in Shanghai were Ch'en Tu-hsiu and myself, since Ch'ü Ch'iu-pai (a Central Committee member) had gone to Wuhan a few days after the Shanghai workers' victory, without first obtaining the permission of the Central Committee.* Ch'en and I had discussed many times how to get out of the critical situation the party had fallen into. We felt that without extensively arming the workers and building an alliance with those units of the National Revolutionary Army who were sympathetic to the workers' movement, there was no other way to defend ourselves against the coup then being planned by Chiang

---

* Ch'ü Ch'iu-pai went to Wuhan to personally organize the takeover of the party leadership and get rid of Ch'en and me, because he always defended Comintern policies. He especially defended Stalin's theory of revolution by stages as against Trotsky's theory of permanent revolution. At that time he wrote a small pamphlet titled *The Problem of the Chinese Revolution* especially to attack me and my position on "permanent revolution." This was in answer to an article I wrote to commemorate the third anniversary of Lenin's death. The article was titled "Is Leninism Applicable to the National Peculiarities of China?" and appeared in *Hsiang-tao* of January 21, 1927. In this article I analyzed the similarities between China's social and economic conditions and class relationships and the situation in Russia before the October revolution. I concluded that Leninism was entirely applicable to China. Thus, I suggested the slogan of "permanent revolution" and pointed out: "China's revolution will move directly from a national revolution to a proletarian revolution." Ch'ü retorted that this was "copying Trotskyism," thus maintaining his good relations with Stalin.

Kai-shek (at that time nearly everyone was aware of Chiang's plans; only Moscow still denied such plans existed). Our plans for armed struggle against Chiang ran up against a fundamental problem in the relationship between the CCP and the Comintern, however; that of discipline. To go ahead with our plans would have been in direct opposition to the Comintern Seventh Plenum policy toward Chiang and his KMT; it would have meant a complete break with the Comintern. Regarding this problem, both Ch'en Tu-hsiu and I were undecided as to how to deal with it. So, we asked the Shanghai regional secretary, Lo I-nung, and Chou En-lai, then directing the Shanghai insurrection, to discuss this difficult question. They completely agreed with our position: there was no other way except armed struggle against Chiang. However, they also agreed with Ch'en that it was not possible to go against Comintern policy. In the midst of this immensely contradictory situation, Ch'en Tu-hsiu asked me to travel to Wuhan and discuss the problem of armed struggle against Chiang with the Comintern representatives and the rest of the Central Committee. Then we would make a final decision.

At the end of March 1927, I left Shanghai and went to Nanking, because the Second and Sixth armies of the National Revolutionary Army were based there. These two units were still part of the Kuomintang left wing and opposed to Chiang Kai-shek. The political commissars in these units were Communist Party members; there were also a great number of CP members in these units who were responsible for other political and military work. So, after I arrived in Nanking an emergency meeting was called by the secretary of the Nanking branch of the CCP with the cadres in the Second and Sixth armies, along with the Russian advisers. At this meeting I reported that the CCP Central Committee advocated the use of armed struggle against the anticommunist coup being prepared by Chiang Kai-shek. The discussion resulted in total approval of the CC plan, especially by the Russian advisers. According to the analysis of units based in Shanghai, Nanking, and Wu-hsi, etc., victory over Chiang Kai-shek could be gained through the use of military force. Because of this, they requested the CC representative to give the order to initiate military action against Chiang. I told them that, since armed struggle against Chiang would be in opposition to Moscow's official policy, the Central Committee was sending me to Wuhan to discuss the problem with Comintern representatives and other CC members. Upon hearing this, the cadres of the Second and Sixth armies and the Russian advisers urged me to hurry on to Wuhan; they would wait to find out the results of the discussion before initiating any action.

Since I had spent a few days in Nanking, I didn't arrive in Wuhan until April 10, 1927. But on April 12 Chiang Kai-shek began his coup in Shanghai. Thousands of fighting workers and Communist Party members were massacred. Workers' organizations (unions) were destroyed. Communist Party members were hunted by the reactionaries. All of the industries in Shanghai and the southeast were taken over by Chiang's forces. This, then, was Stalin's final reward for his policy of KMT-CCP collaboration, his unconditional support of the Chiang-led Northern Expedition, his concealment and defense of all of Chiang's counterrevolutionary activity, and his hopes for Chiang's success in destroying imperialism and the warlords and completing the struggle for national independence.

VI. The Turn from Chiang Kai-shek to Wang Ching-wei

Two weeks after Chiang Kai-shek's coup, the Fifth Congress of the CCP was held (April 27, 1927, to the beginning of May). It would certainly have been reasonable to place the coup first on the agenda and submit the question to a thorough discussion, so lessons could be learned from the experience and a new political line could be developed for the party. However, when the Comintern representative M. N. Roy made the first report to the congress, he didn't even mention Chiang's coup; he merely emphasized the abstract:

> The differentiation of the classes within the Kuomintang has strengthened the bonds between its Left Wing and the Communist Party. The departure of the big bourgeoisie has permitted the transformation of the Kuomintang into a revolutionary bloc composed of the industrial proletariat, the peasants, and the petty bourgeoisie (in addition to several strata of the bourgeoisie). . . . The Chinese revolution continues to develop on the basis of a class coalition and cannot yet be submitted to the exclusive leadership of the proletariat. . . . The leading members of the Kuomintang participated in the opening meeting of the Congress and declared that *they were ready to fortify the bloc with the Communist Party.* [Isaacs, p. 218, emphasis added.]

If Roy's abstract terms were translated into concrete language, we would end up with: Chiang Kai-shek's anticommunist coup "has strengthened the bonds between the KMT's left wing and the Communist Party." Thus, the "bloc of four classes" remained; it merely became necessary to get rid of that part of the big bourgeoisie represented by Chiang Kai-shek. The policy of "KMT-CCP collaboration" remained; it was only necessary to get rid of the "KMT right wing" which Chiang represented, and replace it with the "KMT left wing" led by Wang Ching-wei. This, then, was the direction given to the Fifth Congress of the CCP by the Comintern representative.

In my own speech at the Fifth Congress, I concentrated on an analysis of the connection between Chiang's first coup (March 20, 1926) and his second coup (April 12, 1927). I pointed out: the latest coup was a logical development from the earlier one. Since our party adopted a policy of extreme compromise following Chiang's first coup, and not only did not carry out any opposition activity, but recognized his personal military dictatorship, accepted his "Resolution Adjusting Party Affairs," and, moreover, expended the greatest effort to aid his leadership of the Northern Expedition and overlooked all of his counterrevolutionary activities in the progress of the Northern Expedition, we thus failed to adopt any effective method to stop this latest coup. Finally, I called upon this congress to carry out a thorough discussion of this experience. Following my remarks, during a break in congress activities, M. N. Roy said informally to me: "Your analysis of events is Marxist." He did not say anything about my proposal to discuss the coup, however. He had received orders from the Comintern and a draft of Stalin's article on "Questions of the Chinese Revolution," which appeared in *Pravda* on April 21, 1927. When this article discussed the past line, it declared: "The line adopted was the only correct line." Since "the line adopted was the only correct line," naturally, it was impermissible to discuss the mistakes of the past line; it was especially so as regards the coup of Chiang Kai-shek, which was a product of this past incorrect line.

According to that "only correct line," Stalin made the following elucidation:

> Chiang Kai-shek's coup means that from now on there will be in South China two camps, two governments, two armies, two centres, *the centre of revolution in Wuhan* and the centre of counter-revolution in Nanking. . . .
> *This means that the revolutionary Kuomintang in Wuhan, by a determined fight against militarism and imperialism, will in fact be converted into an organ of the revolutionary-democratic dictatorship*

of the proletariat and the peasantry. . . . [We must adopt] the *policy of concentrating the whole power in the country in the hands of the revolutionary Kuomintang. . . .* It further follows that *the policy of close co-operation between the Lefts and the Communists within the Kuomintang in this stage acquires special force and special significance . . . and that without such co-operation the victory of the revolution is impossible.* ["The Questions of the Chinese Revolution: Theses of Comrade Stalin for Propagandists, Approved by the C.C. of the C.P.S.U.," *International Press Correspondence,* April 28, 1927, emphasis added.]

Roy's report, and especially Stalin's article, placed the Fifth Congress of the CCP in a straitjacket. Because of this, all questions discussed by the congress were limited to the following: how to "strengthen the bonds between the Kuomintang's left wing and the Communist Party"; how to push forward the day when "the revolutionary Kuomintang in Wuhan . . . will in fact be converted into an organ of the revolutionary-democratic dictatorship of the proletariat and the peasantry"; and, how to strengthen "the centre of revolution in Wuhan." In order to complete these tasks, the CCP naturally could not have its own independent stance. Everything must accommodate the intentions of the KMT left wing. For example, regarding the urgent and grave problem of land at that time, the Fifth Congress resolution completely surrendered to Wang Ching-wei's views: "no confiscation of the land of small landlords and Revolutionary Army officers." This was equivalent to giving up on land reform in actuality, since the "Revolutionary Army officers" were either landlords or closely related to landlords.

To "strengthen the center of revolution in Wuhan," the Fifth Congress formally approved sending two CCP members (T'an P'ing-shan and Su Chao-cheng) to join the KMT government in Wuhan as heads of the Agriculture and Labor ministries, respectively. Officially, they were to protect the interests of the workers and peasants, but in fact, they were sent to contain any revolutionary activity by the workers and peasants. That is, to stop what the KMT left wing propagandized as "worker-peasant excesses." In this way, they paved the way for the later counterrevolutionary attack.

During the first week of the Fifth Congress and two weeks following its close, the revolutionary movement in Hunan and Hupeh among the workers and peasants reached its height. At the same time, the counterrevolutionary forces were making frantic plans to suppress the revolutionary mass movement. In Wuhan and Changsha, because of currency devaluation and rising prices, life was already unbearably difficult for the working masses. Added to this, the closing of many factories and stores resulted in a great number of unemployed. The workers and clerks could not accept this, so they demanded that those factories and stores be turned over to them to run. The peasants, especially those in Hunan, chased out many of the landlords and took over the land; they established "peasant associations" (a miniature form of peasant soviets) to handle rural administration; they organized armed units to carry out direct battle against the armed landlords and gentry. This indicated the critical juncture reached by the worker-peasant revolutionary movement, and the urgent need which existed for the unification of workers and peasants in an organized form if the movement was to advance. This type of "organized form" could only be the soviet. On another side, those masses of soldiers who, while in the process of carrying out military operations during the Northern Expedition, were aided and influenced by the worker and peasant masses, had no way to develop an organized connection with them since these soldiers were under the control of reactionary officers. *The only way to attain this kind of connection is, again, through the organization of soviets.*

At this time the unions in Hunan and Hupeh had a membership of over one million. The Hunan Peasant Association had close to ten million members, while that in Hupeh had close to three million. This was a great organized mass force. *If the CCP had followed Trotsky's advice* at that time and relied upon this great mass of organized force, while calling for the organization of worker-peasant-soldier soviets to become the central revolutionary organization, and, through these armed soviets carried out the agrarian revolution, giving land to the peasants and revolutionary soldiers, they not only could have assembled all the poor masses of Hunan and Hupeh into soviets, but they could have destroyed the foundation of the reactionary officers immediately, and indirectly destabilized Chiang's army. In this way, the revolution could have developed from the destruction of the roots of counterrevolutionary power and advanced along the road of proletarian dictatorship.*

Quite unfortunately, however, under Stalin's "policy of close

---

* See in particular the "Letter to Alsky" (March 29, 1927) and "Class Relations in the Chinese Revolution" (April 3, 1927).

cooperation between the Lefts and the Communists within the Kuomintang," the CCP not only failed to organize soviets (because this was absolutely forbidden by Stalin) and initiate the agrarian revolution, but also failed to warn the worker-peasant masses and help them plan self-defense measures, such as the expansion of the workers' deputies and the peasants' armed self-defense units in order to prepare against a sneak attack by counterrevolutionary forces. At that time, the CCP leadership still put all its hope in the leader of the KMT left wing, Wang Ching-wei. They sought "close cooperation" with him, asked him to improve the conditions of the workers and initiate land reform, while they would make every effort to contain the "worker-peasant excesses." For example, the CCP would forbid the takeover of factories and stores by the workers and clerks, along with the takeover of the land by the peasants, in order to avoid undermining the policy of cooperation with the KMT left wing, which might push the "revolutionary officers" on the road to reaction. *In this way, on the one hand, the revolutionary activity of the workers and peasants was paralyzed, while on the other hand, those officers had sufficient time to prepare their counterrevolutionary attack. The result was a counterrevolutionary rebellion by Hsia Tou-yin in Hupeh on May 17, 1927. Four days later, Hsü K'e-hsiang* (T'ang Sheng-chih's subordinate) *carried out a counterrevolutionary coup in the city of Changsha, in Hunan province* (these were developments from Chiang Kai-shek's April coup). While Hsia Tou-yin's rebellion was destroyed by military units under the command of Yeh T'ing, a CCP member, the coup by Hsü K'e-hsiang met with no resistance whatsoever, and he took control of Changsha. From this point on, the organizations of the workers and peasants (unions and peasant associations) were attacked one by one.

What policy did the CCP leadership adopt toward Hsü K'e-hsiang's counterrevolutionary coup, then? Its policy was the same as that following Chiang's Shanghai coup; the KMT government in Wuhan was requested to send units to punish Hsü. Wuhan, however, asked Hsü's superior, T'ang Sheng-chih, to go to Changsha to investigate and handle the situation. T'ang's report to Wuhan following his "investigation" in Changsha stated:

I have found that the workers' and peasants' movement, under the misguidance of their leaders, has broken loose from control and precipitated a reign of terror against the people. . . . the soldiers who were stationed in Hunan rose for their self-defense. . . . Although Hsü K'e-hsiang's actions were animated by a passion for justice, he has overstepped the limits of law and discipline. He should receive a light punishment in the form of a demerit but should be retained in the army service. [Isaacs, p. 250.]

Hsü K'e-hsiang "should be retained in the army service," that is, allow him to finish the counterrevolutionary coup to the point of destroying all workers' and peasants' organizations—unions and peasant associations, and get rid of all communists. In the following few months, Hsü was to complete this mission. Then, Hunan, which had originally been the center of revolutionary power, became the strongest counterrevolutionary bastion.

Two days after Hsü K'e-hsiang's coup in Changsha (May 23, 1927), the Eighth Plenum of the Executive Committee of the Communist International began in Moscow. Actually, this plenary session should have discussed the situation of the Chinese revolution following the Changsha coup, and come up with the necessary conclusion. However, this session reacted to Hsü's coup in the same way as to Chiang's Shanghai coup; they made every effort to cover it up. So, in Stalin's speech to the session on May 24 not one word was said about Hsü's counterrevolutionary coup. All he emphasized was an attack on the Trotskyist Opposition and their advocacy of the establishment of soviets:

> Does the Opposition understand that the creation of Soviets of workers' and peasants' deputies now is tantamount to the creation of a dual government, shared by the Soviets and the Hankow government, and necessarily and inevitably leads to the slogan calling for the overthrow of the Hankow Government? . . . It would be quite another matter were there no popular, revolutionary democratic organization such as the Left Kuomintang in China. But since there is such a specific revolutionary organization, adapted to the peculiarities of Chinese conditions and demonstrating its value for the further development of the bourgeois democratic revolution in China—*it would be stupid and unwise to destroy this organization,* which it has taken so many years to build, at a moment when the bourgeois democratic revolution has just begun, has not yet conquered, and cannot be victorious for some time. [Isaacs, p. 241, emphasis added.]

The above quote, besides exposing Stalin's "stupid" illusions regarding the already reactionary KMT left wing, further makes clear his own reactionary thinking about the establishment of soviets. He was afraid that "Soviets . . . leads to the slogan calling for the overthrow of the Hankow Government." What was Stalin's appraisal of the "Hankow Government," then? It was as follows:

> Since *China is experiencing an agrarian revolution, . . . since Hankow is the center of the revolutionary movement in China, it is necessary to support the Kuomintang in Wuhan*. . . . Is the present Hankow government an organ of the revolutionary dictatorship of the proletariat and the peasantry? No. So far it is not, nor will it be so very soon, *but it has all the chances of developing into such an organ in the further development of the revolution*. . . . [Isaacs, p. 241, emphasis added.]

Stalin certified that the "Hankow Government. . . . has all the chances of developing into ["an organ of the revolutionary dictatorship of the proletariat and the peasantry"] in the further development of the revolution." For this reason, it could take the place of soviets in completing the "agrarian revolution." There is no need to look at past incidents to prove that Stalin's viewpoint was based on exaggerated illusions. One only needs to look at the reactionary situation which resulted from Hsü K'e-hsiang's coup to realize that Stalin had already closed his eyes and was speaking nonsense. In this way he manufactured the final disaster for the revolution. Thus, during that plenary session, Trotsky delivered a strategic attack on Stalin's disastrous policy, and, furthermore, appealed directly to the Chinese peasants and workers:

> Stalin has again declared himself here against workers' and peasants' soviets with the argument that the Kuomintang and the Wuhan government are sufficient means and instruments for the agrarian revolution. Thereby Stalin assumes, and wants the International to assume, the responsibility for the policy of the Kuomintang and the Wuhan government, as he repeatedly assumed the responsibility for the policy of the former "national government" of Chiang Kai-shek (particularly in his speech of April 5, the stenogram of which has, of course, been kept hidden from the International).
>
> We have nothing in common with this policy. We do not want to assume even a shadow of responsibility for the policy of the Wuhan government and the leadership of the Kuomintang, and we urgently advise the Comintern to reject this responsibility. We say directly to

the Chinese peasants: The leaders of the left Kuomintang of the type of Wang Ching-wei and Company will inevitably betray you if you follow the Wuhan heads instead of forming your own independent soviets. The agrarian revolution is a serious thing. Politicians of the Wang Ching-wei type, under difficult conditions, will unite ten times with Chiang Kai-shek against the workers and peasants. Under such conditions, two communists in a bourgeois government become impotent hostages, if not a direct mask for the preparation of a new blow against the working masses. We say to the workers of China: The peasants will not carry out the agrarian revolution to the end if they let themselves be led by petty-bourgeois radicals instead of by you, the revolutionary proletarians. Therefore, build up your workers' soviets, ally them with the peasant soviets, arm yourselves through the soviets, draw soldiers' representatives into the soviets, shoot the generals who do not recognize the soviets, shoot the bureaucrats and bourgeois liberals who will organize uprisings against the soviets. Only through peasants' and soldiers' soviets will you win over the majority of Chiang Kai-shek's soldiers to your side. You, the advanced Chinese proletarians, would be traitors to your class and to your historic mission, were you to believe that an organization of leaders, petty bourgeois and compromising in spirit, which has no more than 250,000 members (see the report of T'an P'ing-shan) is capable of substituting for workers', peasants', and soldiers' soviets embracing millions upon millions. *The Chinese bourgeois democratic revolution will go forward and be victorious either in the soviet form or not at all.* ["Second Speech on the Chinese Question" (May 24, 1927), emphasis in original.]

If the Comintern had adopted Trotsky's proposals and sent them on to China, the revolution might have been saved. However, because of Stalin's control of the Comintern and his suppression of Opposition documents, Trotsky's urgent call to the workers and peasants not only never reached China, but it was never published in the Comintern's internal bulletins. Because of this, Trotsky's final proposal to save the Chinese revolution in this critical period only served to prophesy the tragedy of the second Chinese revolution.

Thus, the Eighth Plenum of the Comintern was completely under Stalin's control, and so, the resolution which came out of this session regarding the China question was Stalin's resolution. For example:

No matter what the political situation may be, the Communist Party must never become merged with any other political organization. It must represent an independent force. . . . For that reason the Communist Party must never allow restrictions to be imposed on it in advocating its views and mobilising the masses under its own banner. . . .

The independence of the Communist Party of China must not, however, be interpreted to mean that it must become exclusive and isolated from the non-proletarian toiling strata and particularly from the peasantry. On these grounds, the E.C.C.I. resolutely rejects all demands for the Communist Party to leave the Kuomintang, or that it should take up a position which would actually lead to its leaving the Kuomintang. . . . It is impossible to claim the role of leader for the proletariat *unless* the Communist Party, as the Party of the working class, claims the role of leader *within* the Kuomintang. [Emphasis in original.]

And further:

The E.C.C.I. regards as incorrect the view which underestimates the Hankow Government and which in fact denies its great revolutionary role. The Hankow Government and the leaders of the Left Kuomintang by their class composition represent not only the peasants, workers and artisans, but also a section of the middle bourgeoisie. Therefore, the Hankow Government, being the government of the Left Kuomintang, is not yet the dictatorship of the proletariat and the peasantry, but is on the road to it and will inevitably, in the course of the victorious class struggle of the proletariat and in discarding its radical bourgeois camp followers, develop in the direction of such dictatorship. ["Resolution on the Chinese Question," adopted by the Eighth Plenum of the Executive Committee of the Communist International, May 30, 1927, published in *International Press Correspondence,* June 16, 1927.]

If one wished to give a fair evaluation of the above, it could only be that the resolution was a mixture of illusion and contradiction, and could only bring about disastrous results.

It seems that Stalin had already discovered that the "revolutionary left Kuomintang" did not correspond very well with his ideals; he especially felt that those generals controlling the "Hankow government" were "unreliable." For this reason, at the closing of the Comintern plenary session, on June 1, 1927, he sent a telegram to the CCP. This directive contained five important points, of which the most outstanding were:

A large number of new peasant and working class leaders from the ranks must be drawn into the Central [Executive] Committee of the Kuomintang. Their bold voice will stiffen the backs of the old leaders or throw them into the discard. . . .

It is necessary to liquidate the unreliable generals. Mobilize about

20,000 Communists and about 50,000 revolutionary workers and peasants from Hunan and Hupeh, form several new army corps . . . and organize your own reliable army. . . . [*M. N. Roy's Mission to China* by Robert C. North and Xenia J. Eudin (Berkeley: University of California Press, 1963), p. 107.]

But how were the "new peasant and working class leaders" to be placed on the KMT Central Executive Committee? How were we to "liquidate the unreliable generals"? And where were we to obtain the weapons necessary to "organize our own reliable army"? Stalin did not deal with these problems at all in his directive. It was as if Wuhan were under his direct control and he could use dictatorial bureaucratic directives to obtain whatever he wanted. Thus, when the Politburo of the CCP received Stalin's directive, they were frightened and didn't know how to deal with it. All they could do was to set up a meeting with Comintern representatives to discuss the matter. As a result of this meeting, everyone felt there was no way to carry out Stalin's directive. But the naive M. N. Roy decided to turn the directive over to Wang Ching-wei, hoping that after some thought he would agree to its contents. By that time, however, Wang had already decided to drive out the Communist Party. After he saw Stalin's telegram, it not only added to his determination to oppose the communists, but it also speeded up his plans to clear them out of the KMT.

On June 12, 1927, Wang Ching-wei and other anticommunist officials went to Chengchow, Honan, to hold a secret meeting with General Feng Yü-hsiang. The major problems discussed were how to oppose the Communist Party and Chiang Kai-shek. Feng advocated the immediate expulsion of the Communist Party and the suppression of the workers' and peasants' movement in Hunan and Hupeh; afterwards, he favored negotiations with Chiang Kai-shek. A week after his meeting with Wang in Chengchow, however, Feng met with Chiang Kai-shek in Soochow, Kiangsu. Following this meeting, Feng publicly declared to newspaper reporters his "sincere desire to cooperate with the Nationalists and to extirpate militarism and Communism." This was the final expression of the man whom Moscow had already recognized and proclaimed as the "son of a laborer" and a "most reliable ally."

Following the Chengchow meeting between Wang and Feng, the atmosphere in Wuhan—"the center of the revolution"— suddenly became very tense; everywhere one could smell the breath of anticommunist terror. The leadership of the CCP and the Comintern representatives all felt as if a frightening shadow were resting on their heads. It was as if a great calamity were very near. On June 20, 1927, the CCP called an enlarged meeting of the Central Committee in order to try and avoid the calamity. This meeting issued a statement which expressed the CCP attitude toward the left wing Kuomintang. The statement was issued following a discussion between Ch'ü Ch'iu-pai and the Comintern representatives, and its important points were:

> The Kuomintang, since it is the bloc of the workers, peasants, and petty bourgeoisie opposed to imperialism, is naturally in the leading position of the national revolution. . . .
> The workers' and peasants' mass organizations should accept the leadership and control of the Kuomintang. . . .
> According to Kuomintang principles, the masses must be armed. But the armed groups of the workers and peasants should submit to the regulation and training of the government. In order to avoid political troubles, the present armed pickets at Wuhan can be reduced or incorporated into the army. [Isaacs, pp. 262-63.]

It is unnecessary to elaborate; this statement was the final document of surrender by the CCP to the KMT. One week following the issuance of the statement, the General Trades Union of Hupeh, on June 28, voluntarily disbanded their pickets and turned their weapons and ammunition over to the military guard in Wuhan. Two days later (June 30), the CCP ordered T'an P'ing-shan and Su Chao-cheng to resign their positions in the Wuhan government. This all shows that the CCP voluntarily quit the field of battle and turned the workers and peasants over to the Kuomintang left wing to do with as it would.

In the middle of June, Ch'en Tu-hsiu felt that the collaboration between the CCP and the KMT left wing had reached a dead end. Because of this, he proposed that the CCP should quit the KMT, appraise the situation once again, and determine its own independent policy. However, the Comintern absolutely rejected Ch'en's proposal, feeling that to quit the KMT would be tantamount to giving up the KMT's revolutionary banner to the reactionary right wing. Because of this, Ch'en resigned as CCP general secretary early in July 1927. Ch'ü Ch'iu-pai became the acting general secretary. Ch'ü's only task was to wait to see how the CCP would be treated by the left KMT.

On July 15, 1927, the Central Executive Committee of the left Kuomintang issued an order requiring all CCP members in the

KMT and the Revolutionary Army to withdraw from the CCP or be severely punished. Stalin's policy of "KMT-CCP collaboration" was thus brought to a shameful conclusion, and the second Chinese revolution was mortally wounded. Let us recall Trotsky's words:

> Politicians of the Wang Ching-wei type, under difficult conditions will unite ten times with Chiang Kai-shek against the workers and peasants. . . . *The Chinese bourgeois-democratic revolution will go forward and be victorious either in the soviet form or not at all.*

In less than seven weeks, the prediction which Trotsky made during the Eighth Plenum of the ECCI was completely verified.

VII. The Leap from Ultraright Opportunism to Ultraleft Adventurism

Stalin reacted in the same manner to Wang Ching-wei's "July 15 expulsion of Communists" as he had to Chiang Kai-shek's "April 12 coup." He not only refused to consider the situation and learn the lessons, but he also analyzed the revolution's defeat as a "development of the revolution to a higher stage." Then, from his previous opportunism, which led the revolution to defeat, he jumped into adventurism. This, then, produced a chain of blind adventurist armed insurrections through the next few months:

1. *The Nanchang uprising.* After Wang Ching-wei announced the expulsion of the communists, Stalin hurriedly sent his cousin, Lominadze, to Wuhan. This frivolous scoundrel, without so much as investigating the grave situation of the revolution's defeat, or assembling those leading CCP cadres who still remained in Wuhan to discuss the situation and determine a new political direction, merely gave Stalin's new directive calling for armed struggle to the CCP's acting general secretary, Ch'ü Ch'iu-pai, to have carried out. This was the background of the Nanchang uprising of August 1, 1927.

Those military forces participating in this insurrection included Ho Lung's independent Fifteenth Division, Yeh T'ing's Twenty-fourth Division in the Eleventh Army, and Chu Te's model unit (formerly belonging to Chu P'ei-teh's Third Army), a total of about 30,000 men. After these units took over the city of Nanchang, Kiangsi, they announced the establishment of a "Revolutionary Committee." Included among those on this committee were KMT Central Executive Committee member

Soong Ch'ing-ling (Sun Yat-sen's widow), and the head of the National Revolutionary Army's Fourth Army, Chang Fa-k'uei. The committee had no program and carried out no revolutionary measures. Furthermore, the insurrection was carried out quite clearly under the banner of the KMT, so, in the eyes of the general public, this was merely a coup of the left Kuomintang against the right.

Less than three days after the insurrectionists had taken Nanchang, the forces led by Ho Lung and Yeh T'ing were forced to retreat from the city because they were attacked by the forces of Chang Fa-k'uei. They fled to the south and, after a tortuous journey of more than a month, took the towns of Chaochow and Swatow in Kwangtung on September 13. In less than a week, the Ho-Yeh forces were again dispersed by an encircling attack on the part of the reactionary units in the KMT army. Ho and Yeh escaped; and Chu Te brought a small unit composed of remnants out of Kwangtung and on to Chingkangshan, where they converged with Mao Tse-tung's forces, later to become the basic cadre for the "Red Army." Thus, those basic CCP military forces left over after the defeat of the revolution were destroyed by the blind adventurism of the Nanchang uprising.

Two days after the defeat of the Nanchang uprising, on August 7, Ch'ü Ch'iu-pai, under Lominadze's direction, called an emergency conference of the Central Committee (actually, only a few CC members attended), the so-called "August 7 Emergency Conference." This conference approved the "Circular Letter of the CC to All Party Members," in which the responsibility for the revolution's defeat was placed upon Ch'en Tu-hsiu and T'an P'ing-shan. This relieved Stalin and Bukharin of all responsibility and guilt for their leadership over the defeat of the Chinese revolution. The "August 7 Emergency Conference" not only failed to discuss the lessons of the defeat of the Nanchang uprising, it even decided to initiate Autumn Harvest uprisings in Hunan and Hupeh.

2. *The Hunan-Hupeh Autumn Harvest uprisings.* Since Hsü K'e-hsiang's revolt in Changsha, Hunan had become a frightening world of "white terror." Almost all of the unions and peasant associations had been destroyed. All that were left were some worker and peasant cadres hiding in mines, factories, and smaller villages, who maintained some amount of secret contact with the workers and peasants. The situation in Hupeh was even worse. In these kinds of circumstances, to carry out armed

insurrections to take power would be, if not insane, at least infantile. Actually, few people participated in the insurrection.

Approximately 3,000 people took part in the armed insurrection in Hunan. Cadres from among the miners and peasants in P'inghsiang and Anyuan organized with CCP members, and, between September 8 and 12, 1927, started moving in such counties as P'inghsiang and Liling. They quickly took over the major cities in these counties, but were defeated by the KMT army in a few days. Most of the insurrectionists were dispersed, and only a small number followed Mao Tse-tung to Chingkangshan. As for the uprising in Hupeh, only a minority of peasants from a few southern counties, such as Tungshan, Tungcheng, P'uch'e, actually participated. Moreover, these were quickly suppressed by reactionary military units. The so-called Hunan-Hupeh Autumn Harvest uprising not only brought unfavorable results, but many heroic cadres were killed or wounded. The worst of it was that many cadres who had been concealed in the mines and villages were now exposed. As a result, the CCP lost its contacts with the workers and peasants, which in effect meant that it lost its base for activity among the workers and peasants.

3. *The Hailufeng soviet movement.* The origin of China's peasant associations was in the counties of Haifeng and Lufeng, in Kwangtung province. These were built up from 1922 on through the tireless efforts of the hero of the peasant movement, P'eng P'ai. The peasant association in these two counties contained about 200,000 members, had passed through a long period of struggle, developed a very strong organization, and trained a great number of cadres. Thus, they became the model and the bastion for the peasant movement in Kwangtung. Even after Li Chi-shen, following Chiang Kai-shek's lead, had carried out the "April 15 coup," the Hailufeng peasant association was able to maintain its power. Following the defeat of both the Nanchang uprising and the Autumn Harvest uprising, the adventurists in the CCP chose Hailufeng to be the experimental ground for the soviet movement. This was in line with Stalin's report of September 30, 1927, where he said: "The propaganda slogan of soviets must now become a slogan of action!"

The Hailufeng insurrection began toward the end of October, and by November 1 the major towns of Haifeng were taken. Following this, the major towns of Lufeng, along with those of neighboring counties such as Chiehshih and Chiehcheng, were also taken. During the insurrection, soviets were established, a peasant army was organized, and it was announced that land would be taken from the landlords and distributed to the peasants. About two or three hundred thousand peasants and handicraft workers took part in this movement. It could be said this was a true agrarian revolution on the part of the peasants. This movement, however, received no leadership or support whatsoever from the working class in Canton, Hong Kong, or other large cities (as a matter of fact, the working class in both Canton and Hong Kong was itself in the midst of a period of extreme oppression and exploitation due to the grave defeat it suffered as a result of opportunist policies); thus, it became totally isolated. Finally, due to encirclement and constant attacks by counterrevolutionary KMT troops, the movement was destroyed.

The number of peasant fighters who were killed or wounded was never recorded after the defeat of the insurrection. However, there is one fact which cannot be denied. That is: following the abortion of this soviet movement, the strong peasant associations of Hailufeng were destroyed, and thousands of peasant cadres and fighters, if not killed, were driven away. As a result, the peasant masses were once again in the condition of arbitrary exploitation and enslavement under the landlords and gentry.

4. *The Canton insurrection.* After Stalin saw the Nanchang uprising and the Autumn Harvest uprising defeated he ordered Lominadze to prepare a new insurrection immediately, and he also sent Heinz Neumann to China to assist in planning this undertaking. From a report delivered by Ch'ü Ch'iu-pai, the leader of the Central Committee, Lominadze learned that there was part of a military force (a model unit under Chang Fa-k'uei) in Canton, which took orders from CCP members. Furthermore, even though the Canton–Hong Kong Strike Committee had been dispersed, there were a great many cadres left, which included former pickets. For this reason, Lominadze chose Canton to be the base of the final insurrection. Just around that time (mid-November, 1927), a civil war broke out between KMT militarists Chang Fa-k'uei (representing the Kwangtung clique) and Li Chi-shen (representing the Kwangsi clique) over control of the Kwangtung region. Lominadze took advantage of this situation, and immediately ordered the Kwangtung CCP organization to carry out an insurrection in Canton. He also sent Neumann to Canton to directly control the insurrection.

The Canton insurrection began on December 11, 1927. The major force of the insurrection came from model units and Red

Guards (organized by those workers' cadres and pickets who were formerly in the Canton–Hong Kong Strike Committee). In addition, there were thousands of party members and workers actively participating in the insurrection. On the very first day, an announcement was made reporting the establishment of a "Soviet Government" (delegates were appointed by the party), along with some decrees of a socialist nature, such as: nationalization of the large industries and banks; confiscation of land from the landlords for the use of the peasants; confiscation of the houses of the bourgeoisie for the use of the common people, etc. This insurrection only lasted three days, however, before being destroyed by the combined forces of Chang Fa-k'uei and Li Chi-shen (they got together solely to wipe out the Communist Party). According to official KMT reports, more than 5,700 people were killed in this insurrection. They were just one small part of the most daring and most heroic revolutionary fighters left over from the second Chinese revolution. Now they had paid with their lives for Stalin's adventurist policies. Henceforth, Canton's working class became disappointed in the revolution and disgusted with the Communist Party, thus falling into a long period of pain and discouragement.

VIII. Trotsky's Contribution to the Study of the Problems of the Chinese Revolution

In order to help younger readers understand more concretely, more deeply, the great contribution made by Trotsky, I have presented above a description of the changes in thought and policy inside the Chinese Communist Party from the period of preparation for revolution through the progress of the second Chinese revolution, along with a description of the CCP's relationship with the Communist International. The content of this book is exceptionally rich, and the discussion of all of the problems touched on is very comprehensive. Thus, it is not easy for younger readers to grasp the center of each problem and the interconnection between each type of problem. Because of this, I feel it is necessary to present a simple explanation of the most important (and most meaningful for today) problems that Trotsky wrote about, especially those he debated with Stalin.

1. *The attitude of each class toward the anti-imperialist revolution.* Stalin felt that, under imperialist oppression, each class, from the bourgeoisie, petty bourgeoisie, and peasantry, to

the proletariat, would all feel equally the need for a united anti-imperialist struggle. In this way, the internal struggles between each class would become less significant. So he advocated the "bloc of four classes" as the foundation upon which to fight against imperialism.

Trotsky's views were exactly opposite to those of Stalin. Imperialist aggression not only would not weaken the class struggle, especially between the bourgeoisie and the proletariat, but would necessarily sharpen this struggle. He pointed out:

> It is a gross mistake to think that imperialism mechanically welds together all the classes of China from without. . . . The revolutionary struggle against imperialism does not weaken, but rather strengthens the political differentiation of the classes. Imperialism is a highly powerful force in the internal relationships of China. The main source of this force is not the warships in the waters of the Yangtze Kiang . . . but the economic and political bond between foreign capital and the native bourgeoisie. . . . everything that brings the oppressed and exploited masses of the toilers to their feet, inevitably pushes the national bourgeoisie into an open bloc with the imperialists. The class struggle between the bourgeoisie and the masses of workers and peasants is not weakened, but on the contrary, it is sharpened by imperialist oppression, to the point of bloody civil war at every serious conflict. ["The Chinese Revolution and the Theses of Comrade Stalin" (May 7, 1927).]

In accordance with the precise analysis given above, Trotsky charged Stalin's policy of a "bloc of four classes" with being the most effective way to destroy the national revolution. The only hope for the anti-imperialist revolution was for the proletariat, along with the peasants and the poor from urban and rural areas, to crush the bourgeoisie's attempts to compromise with imperialism.

2. *The problem of independence for the Communist Party.* Stalin thought the KMT was a party of all classes, the best organized form of the "bloc of four classes." Because of this, he ordered the CCP to enter the KMT and carry out "inner-party collaboration." Through this kind of collaboration, Stalin believed they could lead the national revolution and complete its bourgeois-democratic tasks.

Trotsky's attitude toward the KMT was completely different. It did not matter how many petty bourgeoisie, or workers, or peasants were in the KMT, it was still fundamentally a party of the bourgeoisie, led by representatives of the bourgeoisie. For the

CCP to join the KMT meant that it would become a tool in the bourgeoisie's plot to cheat the workers and the peasants. For this reason, Trotsky expressed absolute opposition to the policy in a discussion within the Politburo of the Russian Communist Party early in 1923. In 1926, when the revolution began, he "advocated that the Communist Party immediately withdraw from the Kuomintang." On March 4, 1927, in a letter to Radek, Trotsky again stressed the absolute necessity for the CCP to quit the KMT. Moreover, he predicted: "For the Communist Party to remain in the Kuomintang any longer threatens to have dire consequences for the proletariat and for the revolution." This prediction was quickly verified by Chiang Kai-shek's April 12 coup.

In another article, on May 10, 1927, "The Communist Party and the Kuomintang," Trotsky presented a detailed refutation of the fundamental arguments used to oppose withdrawal from the Kuomintang. He further warned: "By remaining in the same organization with the Wang Ching-weis, we are sharing the responsibility for their waverings and betrayals." As a result, after "sharing the responsibility for their waverings and betrayals," we were then purged by Wang Ching-wei.

According to Marxist theory, especially as developed by Lenin and the practical experience of the Bolsheviks, the complete political and organizational independence of the party of the proletariat is absolutely indispensable. This is because the historical mission of the party of the proletariat is to unite the vanguard of that class, become the leader of the revolution, expose all types of frauds by bourgeois and petty-bourgeois politicians, organize all the exploited and oppressed masses, and prepare for armed struggle to destroy the bourgeois state and establish its own regime in order to follow the road to socialism. Stalin, however, completely renounced Marxist theory and Bolshevik experience by turning over all hopes for leadership of the revolution and social change to the top leadership of the bourgeoisie and petty bourgeoisie (Chiang Kai-shek and Wang Ching-wei). This, then, was the reason behind the defeat of the second Chinese revolution.

From the beginning, Trotsky opposed the Communist Party's entrance into the Kuomintang. Afterwards, he unceasingly called for the CCP's withdrawal from the KMT and the carrying out of an independent proletarian policy. In this way, Trotsky was merely remaining true to, and developing, the Bolshevik tradition. If the CCP had been under the leadership of Trotsky's thought at that time, the possibilities for victory would have been very great, because by the time the revolution had reached its greatest height (March-April 1927) the CCP had in fact become a mass party. Even though the party, including the members of the Communist Youth Corps, numbered only about 100,000, it nevertheless led three million organized workers (unions) and fifteen million organized peasants (peasant associations). This was an overwhelming revolutionary force. Its defeat was totally due to the opportunist policies of Stalin. The lesson we gain from this is: if a mass proletarian party lacks correct political leadership it cannot avoid defeat.

3. *The problem of soviets.* If the Communist Party is the proletariat's revolutionary staff, leading the working masses to revolution and the taking of power, then the soviets are the instrument through which the workers, peasants, and soldiers are united. They become the organizational center of the revolution. They are the command posts through which the masses are armed, carry out the insurrection, and, finally, take power. After taking power, they become the basic organ of the state. This is the experience and lesson gained from three revolutions in Russia. Lenin, in the founding documents of the Communist International, emphasized soviets as a fundamental part of the political program. Stalin, however, completely forgot about this program, and placed all hopes for the organization of the masses and the taking of power in the Kuomintang. From the beginning, he looked upon the KMT as a "revolutionary parliament," and, because of this, opposed the establishment of soviets. After Chiang Kai-shek's April 12 coup took away this "revolutionary parliament," Stalin still thought the left-wing Kuomintang, the "revolutionary Kuomintang," could take the place of soviets. Since he asserted that "the revolutionary Kuomintang in Wuhan . . . will in fact be converted into an organ of the revolutionary-democratic dictatorship of the proletariat and peasantry," it would decide the democratic tasks, such as national independence and the land problem. As a result, however, "the revolutionary Kuomintang" quickly "converted" into an executioner of the Communist Party and the workers and peasants.

According to his personal experience in twice leading the soviet movement (1905 and 1917), Trotsky felt that through no other organizational form except workers', peasants', and soldiers' soviets could preparations be made for armed insurrection and the taking of power. So, from the start of the second Chinese revolution, Trotsky advocated the establishment of soviets. On March 29, 1927, in a letter to Alsky, Trotsky wrote:

> It is precisely through soviets that the crystallization of the class forces can keep pace with the new stage of the revolution instead of conforming to the organizational-political traditions of a bygone day, of the kind being offered by the present-day Kuomintang. . . . The indispensable condition is an independent proletarian party. The form for its closest collaboration with the rural and urban petty bourgeoisie is the soviets *as organs of the struggle for power or as organs of power.*
>
> *Large sections of the Chinese National Revolutionary Army are still green, and bourgeois landowners' sons wield great influence within the ranks of the commanding staff. Because of this the future of the revolution is in danger. Once more, I do not see any other way to oppose this danger than soldiers' deputies joining workers' deputies, and so on.* [Emphasis added.]

The above quotation had spoken quite clearly about the basic functions and capabilities of the soviets, especially where he pointed out the great danger of the National Revolutionary Army and the fact that he did "not see any other way to oppose this danger than soldiers' deputies joining workers' deputies" in united soviets. This conclusion was of decisive and urgent significance. If the CCP had had the benefit of Trotsky's guidance at that time, and had immediately established workers' and soldiers' soviets in Shanghai, the situation would have been altered. At that time, most of the soldiers stationed in Shanghai were sympathetic to the working masses.* Even a division commander, Hsueh Yüeh, was sympathetic to the Communist Party and requested cooperation to oppose Chiang Kai-shek. Other than this, troops stationed in Wu-hsi and Soochow, under division commander Yian Chung, were also against Chiang. In

---

* On March 21, the fifth day after the victory of the Shanghai workers' insurrection, both the workers and the soldiers elected representatives—about 1,000—and held a meeting at the Shanghai Commercial Press Guild. First to speak at this meeting was the commander in chief of the advance forces, Pai Ch'ung-hsi. Following his speech, there was very little applause. Next, I spoke as a representative of the Chinese Communist Party and received a very warm welcome from all the deputies. This instance is real evidence as to the coldness felt toward the KMT generals by workers and soldiers, and their closeness to the CCP.

this kind of situation, if the CCP had called for the organization of workers' and soldiers' soviets, Chiang's troops could have been immediately dispersed, and his April coup would have been completely overturned. From this, we can see that at a critical point in revolution the correct policy, such as the organization of soviets, can be most important, and moreover, have decisive significance.

Following Chiang Kai-shek's April coup, Trotsky even more urgently called for the establishment of workers', peasants', and soldiers' soviets. He carefully explained the decisive significance and power of the soviets in a revolutionary situation (see "The Chinese Revolution and the Theses of Comrade Stalin"). He repeatedly pointed out that only the soviets can bring life into a dormant situation and extend the horizons of the revolution. At that time, the "critical point" was about to be reached in Hunan and Hupeh. On the one hand, the workers and peasants had already been organized by the Communist Party. The workers were demanding better living conditions, and the peasants were demanding a redistribution of the land. On the other hand, the soldiers remained under the control of those officers who were related to the landlords and the bourgeoisie. This, then, became a barrier of mutual opposition between the workers and soldiers. In order to break up this extremely dangerous situation, it would be necessary to establish workers', peasants', and soldiers' soviets. This way closer cooperation could be obtained between the workers' and peasants' deputies and those of the soldiers, throwing off the control of the bourgeois officers. However, Stalin absolutely opposed these soviets. His reason was that if soviets were established it would push the officers into the reactionary camp. The facts, however, were exactly the opposite. Only the soviets could have stopped the reactionary officers; for, if soldiers' soviets were already established, the reactionary officers would have already lost their base for counterrevolution. The October revolution in Russia is the greatest proof of this.

The freshest lesson on this point is the recent tragedy in Chile. Chile between 1971 and 1973 was very similar to the situation in Wuhan in April–May 1927: on the one hand, the revolutionary movement of the worker and peasant masses was growing. On the other hand, the soldiers were completely in the hands of reactionary officers. This situation was bordering on a show-down, but Allende had no thought whatsoever of setting up workers', peasants', and soldiers' soviets to deprive these reactionary officers of their base. He only brought a few generals into his appointed cabinet, thinking that this would moderate their counterrevolutionary activities. Actually, this only gave the generals more time and more advantage to organize their counterrevolutionary military coup. As a result, thousands of worker and peasant fighters lost their lives. Allende himself became a sacrificial victim of his own policy. This lesson should be written in the program of every revolutionary party.

4. *The problem of strategy following the defeat of the revolution.* After the second Chinese revolution was completely defeated, Stalin turned from opportunism to adventurism and initiated a series of armed insurrections which destroyed the remaining revolutionary forces and only deepened the degree of defeat. After he had helped Chiang Kai-shek to stabilize his counterrevolutionary military dictatorship, Stalin suddenly discovered the philosophy of the "Third Period." According to this philosophy, the world revolution was growing each day, and it had become an immediate and urgent task for the proletariat to prepare insurrections for the taking of power. So, the "Theses on the Revolutionary Movement in the Colonies and Semicolonies" passed by the Sixth Comintern Congress set up the following line for the Chinese Communist Party:

> Already at the present time, the Party must everywhere propagate among the masses the idea of Soviets, the idea of the dictatorship of the proletariat and peasantry, and the inevitability of the coming revolutionary mass armed uprising. It must already now emphasise in its agitation the necessity of overthrow of the ruling bloc and the mobilisation of the masses for revolutionary demonstrations . . . it must consistently and undeviatingly follow the line of seizure of State power, organisation of Soviets as organs of the insurrection, expropriation of the landlords and big property-owners, expulsion of the foreign imperialists and the confiscation of their property. . . . In China, the future growth of the revolution will place before the Party as an immediate practical task the preparation for and carrying through of armed insurrection as the sole path to the completion of the bourgeois-democratic revolution and to the overthrow . . . of the Kuomintang. [*International Press Correspondence,* December 12, 1928.]

The later protracted guerrilla war, the organization of the "Red Army," and the establishment of "soviets" by the CCP, were all in accordance with the line set down at the Sixth Comintern Congress.

Following Wang Ching-wei's "July Communist expulsion," Trotsky pointed out that since the second Chinese revolution had been defeated the CCP should adopt a defensive policy. He argued that Stalin's policy of armed insurrection could only serve to destroy the remaining revolutionary forces. However, Stalin called Trotsky's defensive policy "liquidationism" because it would "liquidate" Stalinist adventurism.

When Trotsky saw the adventurist strategic line set down for the CCP at the Sixth Comintern Congress, he wrote:

> Bolshevik policy is characterized not only by its revolutionary scope, but also by its political realism. These two aspects of Bolshevism are inseparable. The greatest task is to know how to recognize in time a revolutionary situation and to exploit it to the end. But it is no less important to understand when this situation is exhausted and is converted, from the political point of view, into its antithesis. Nothing is more fruitless and worthless than to show one's fist after the battle. . . . It must be distinctly understood that there is not, at the present time, a revolutionary situation in China. It is rather a counterrevolutionary situation that has been substituted there, transforming itself into an interrevolutionary period of indefinite duration. ["The Chinese Question After the Sixth Congress" (October 4, 1928).]

In accordance with the fact that "a counterrevolutionary situation . . . has been substituted there, transforming itself into an interrevolutionary period of indefinite duration," Trotsky proposed a transitional program of democratic demands for the Chinese Communist Party, in place of Stalin's adventurist line. This program contained the most fundamental democratic demands: an eight-hour work day; freedom of speech, press, assembly, and association; and the right to strike. These demands were all contained in one general political slogan: convene a constituent assembly with full powers, elected by universal, equal, and direct suffrage. While propagandizing for the convening of a constituent assembly, the party should also propagandize for the expropriation of the landlords and national independence. The task of this program of transitional demands was to renew the spirit and confidence of the masses through the political struggle for everyday demands, while at the same time helping them to unite in opposition to the KMT military dictatorship. In other words, the party should gradually develop from a defensive to an offensive struggle against the ruling class. When the revolutionary tide returned, soviets should be established, and the proletariat should prepare to lead the peasants in a struggle for power. The Left Opposition in the CCP, which was formed in 1929, based all its propaganda and activity on this transitional program.

Naturally, the CCP did not get to see Trotsky's proposals, since the party was under Stalin's very strict control at that time. It could only honor the resolution of the Sixth Comintern Congress in "the preparation for and carrying through of armed insurrection as the sole path to the completion of the bourgeois-democratic revolution and to the overthrow . . . of the Kuomintang." So, from the fall of 1928, in Kiangsi, Fukien, Hupeh, and Anhwei provinces, the CCP initiated many small-scale guerrilla wars and organized the "Red Army" and "soviets." They even announced the establishment of the "Chinese Soviet Republic." In one period (1930-34), the CCP's guerrilla movement experienced widespread development. This forced Chiang Kai-shek to concentrate his full force in an encircling attack, thus precipitating a fierce civil war. However, by the fall of 1934, under pressure of Chiang's fierce attacks, the CCP finally gave up the "soviet" in southern Kiangsi and began the "Long March," escaping to the Northwest. Finally, in the fall of 1935, they reached Yenan, in the northern part of Shensi. As a result, not only were millions of peasants in Kiangsi, Fukien, Anhwei, and Hupeh left to the cruel oppression levied by Chiang Kai-shek, with hundreds of thousands killed, but 90 percent of the Long March troops were also lost. The Long March began with three hundred thousand people, and when the march reached Yenan, only 30,000 were left.

After these remnants of the CCP escaped to Yenan, Chiang Kai-shek immediately transferred Chang Hsueh-liang's Manchurian army (troops that escaped from Manchuria when the Japanese imperialists invaded) to surround Yenan, and prepared the final armed force to destroy the CCP. Meanwhile in Moscow the Seventh World Congress of the Comintern in the summer of 1935 adopted Stalin's Popular Front line of offering support to friendly bourgeois governments. Carrying out Stalin's line and trying to extricate itself from the military trap in which it found itself, the CCP reversed its previous policy. They turned from a policy designed to "overthrow . . . the Kuomintang" to asking the KMT to establish a "national united front" to resist the Japanese invasion. However, in Chiang Kai-shek's view, before they could resist the Japanese, the armed force of the CCP had to be destroyed. So, in December 1936, he personally went to Sian to inspect Chang Hsueh-liang's troops and prepare the attack on Yenan.

After Chiang arrived at Sian, a small group of officers in Chang's unit carried out a little coup, capturing Chiang Kai-shek and threatening to kill him because his "nondefensism" during the Japanese attack on Manchuria had rendered them homeless. This was the famous "Sian incident."

When Stalin heard about the incident in Sian, he thought this to be a great opportunity to renew collaboration between the CCP and Chiang Kai-shek in order to resist Japan. He immediately telegraphed orders to the CCP to find a way to "save Chiang Kai-shek" and hold talks with him regarding collaboration to fight the Japanese. The CCP, already in great danger, sent Chou En-lai to Sian to talk directly with Chiang. The results were: (1) the CCP guaranteed Chiang's safety if he would consent to lead the struggle against Japan, and (2) the CCP agreed to abolish the "Red Army" and the "soviets" and give up the agrarian revolution. The CCP's armed forces would participate in the war against Japan under the command of Chiang Kai-shek. This, then, was the outcome of the CCP having followed the resolution of the Sixth Comintern Congress in the "carrying through of armed insurrection . . . to overthrow . . . the Kuomintang," and passing through ten years (1925-36) of bloody struggle, sacrificing hundreds of thousands of lives. Trotsky drew a lesson from this outcome and wrote in the Fourth International's Transitional Program:

> Following the inevitable collapse of the Canton uprising, the Comintern took the road of guerrilla warfare and peasant soviets with complete passivity on the part of the industrial proletariat. Landing thus in a blind alley, the Comintern took advantage of the Sino-Japanese War to liquidate "Soviet China" with a stroke of the pen, subordinating not only the peasant "Red Army" but also the so-called "Communist" Party to the identical Kuomintang, i.e., the bourgeoisie. ["The Death Agony of Capitalism and the Tasks of the Fourth International" (1938) in *The Transitional Program for Socialist Revolution* (New York: Pathfinder Press, 1974), p. 98.]

5. *The problem of the nature of the Chinese revolution.* While the second Chinese revolution was unfolding, even though Trotsky did not explicitly advocate permanent revolution as a strategic line for the Chinese revolution, in many of the articles

he wrote about China, especially those criticizing Stalin, his analysis of events and his proposals were all in accordance with and developed the theory of permanent revolution.

The line which Stalin adopted for the Chinese revolution was quite clearly in accordance with the Menshevik theory of revolution by stages. He consistently argued for the completion of the democratic tasks of the bourgeois revolution first (national independence and land reform), and then the carrying through of the proletariat's socialist revolution (when the proletariat takes state power and confiscates the property of the bourgeoisie).

In order to first complete the democratic tasks of the bourgeois revolution, Stalin argued that the proletariat must "collaborate" with the bourgeoisie and establish the "bloc of four classes." The concrete manifestation of this "bloc" was the entrance of the CCP into the KMT, carrying out "KMT-CCP collaboration." In order to maintain the policy of "collaboration," Stalin forced the CCP to honor Sun Yat-sen's *San-min chu-i* (Three People's Principles), and carry out the policies of the KMT and its government. Stalin absolutely supported Chiang Kai-shek. Even after Chiang had carried out his "March coup" (1926) and established his military dictatorship, Stalin still totally supported Chiang's Northern Expedition. He had hoped (obviously an illusion) that Chiang would defeat imperialism and the warlords, and complete the tasks of national independence and national unification. It wasn't until after Chiang's "April coup" (1927), the large-scale massacre of CCP members, workers, and peasants, and the surrender to imperialism, that Stalin gave up his hopes for Chiang. However, once again, he placed his hopes for completion of the democratic revolution in the KMT, the left KMT of Wang Ching-wei, and the Wuhan government. Only after Wang Ching-wei copied Chiang's "April coup" and initiated the "July Communist expulsion," did Stalin finally resign his illusions about the KMT completing the tasks of the bourgeois-democratic revolution.

Stalin's strong opposition to the CCP quitting the KMT to carry out an independent revolutionary policy and organize workers', peasants', and soldiers' soviets was in keeping with his basic attitude of revolution by stages. In Stalin's view, these actions would go beyond his "stage of the democratic revolution." Thus, the second Chinese revolution was strangled with the rope of Stalin's theory of revolution by stages.

Trotsky's stand was the exact opposite. He had determined that the bourgeoisie not only could *not* complete the tasks of the democratic revolution, moreover, they could not avoid coming to terms with imperialism in opposition to the democratic demands of the worker and peasant masses. So, he consistently opposed Stalin's "bloc of four classes" and the policy of "KMT-CCP collaboration" based on this "bloc." He felt that this would "have dire consequences for the proletariat and for the revolution." Because of this, he opposed the CCP joining the KMT from the beginning, and later always advocated its withdrawal to carry out an independent revolutionary policy. During the rising tide of revolution, he unceasingly promoted the organization of soviets to oppose the KMT of Chiang Kai-shek and Wang Ching-wei, and to prepare to take power when the opportunity presented itself, establish the dictatorship of the proletariat, complete the democratic tasks, and follow the road to socialism.

Why didn't Trotsky publicly promote the line of permanent revolution during the second Chinese revolution? The main reason was: not only did the Stalinists hysterically oppose the theory of permanent revolution, but some of the important leaders in the Left Opposition, such as Radek, Preobrazhensky, and Smilga, also disagreed with the theory. In order to obtain their cooperation, Trotsky found it necessary to refrain from using the term "permanent revolution"; but actually, the outlook of permanent revolution permeated all of Trotsky's analyses of events and concrete proposals for solving problems. As I pointed out earlier, his analysis of the reactionary nature of the Chinese bourgeoisie, his criticism of the bloc of four classes and the KMT-CCP coalition government, and his promotion of complete independence for the CCP and the establishment of soviets—all were practical manifestations of a concrete program grounded in the theory of permanent revolution.

The first time Trotsky openly pointed out the permanent nature of the Chinese revolution was after the defeat of the Canton insurrection. After presenting a precise analysis of the soviet regime which resulted from this insurrection, along with its socialist policies, Trotsky concluded that in the coming third Chinese revolution, the dictatorship of the proletariat would settle the democratic tasks and follow the road to socialism, because

the class dialectics of the revolution, having spent all its other resources, clearly and conclusively put on the order of the day the *dictatorship of the proletariat*, leading the countless millions of oppressed and disinherited in city and village. . . . the Canton insurrection which, with all its prematurity, with all the adventurism of its leadership, raised the curtain of a new stage, or, more correctly, of the coming *third* Chinese revolution. . . .

The workers of Canton outlawed the Kuomintang, *declaring all of its tendencies illegal.* This means that for the solution of the basic national tasks, not only the big bourgeoisie but also the petty bourgeoisie was incapable of producing a political force, a party, or a faction, in conjunction with which the party of the proletariat might be able to solve the tasks of the bourgeois-democratic revolution. The key to the situation lies precisely in the fact that *the task of winning the movement of the poor peasants already fell entirely upon the shoulders of the proletariat,* and directly upon the Communist Party; and that the approach to a genuine solution of the bourgeois-democratic tasks of the revolution necessitated the concentration of all power in the hands of the proletariat. . . .

These fundamental and, at the same time, incontrovertible social and political prerequisites of the third Chinese revolution demonstrate not only that the formula of the democratic dictatorship has *hopelessly outlived its usefulness,* but also that the third Chinese revolution . . . will not have a "democratic" period . . . but it will be compelled from the very outset to effect the most decisive shake-up and abolition of bourgeois property in city and village. ["Summary and Perspectives of the Chinese Revolution" (June 1928), emphasis in original.]

The third Chinese revolution (1949), led by the CCP, took power under the exceptionally advantageous conditions created by the Sino-Japanese War and World War II. However, the CCP still upheld the theory of revolution by stages, established an alliance with the bourgeoisie and petty bourgeoisie (called the "Consultative Conference"), and organized a "coalition government of four classes." Not only did they protect the property of the bourgeoisie and the imperialists, but they postponed land reform, in an attempt to realize the stage of Mao Tse-tung's "New Democracy." Still, under the pressure of the dialectical logic of the class struggle and the grave threats from hostile classes both inside and outside of China (especially the threat from American imperialism after the outbreak of the Korean War in 1950, and the counterattack on the part of the internal bourgeoisie against the revolution), the CCP, in order to maintain its existence, could not but adopt some socialist measures, such as a planned economy and monopolization of foreign trade, in order to limit the activities of the bourgeoisie. They also used the method of "state and private joint ownership" (1955) to gradually take away bourgeois property rights. Finally, in 1956, at the CCP's Eighth National Congress, Liu Shao-ch'i announced that the "dictatorship of the proletariat" now existed, to show that the "coalition government of four classes" had come to an end. All of this makes it very clear that under the irresistible pressure of objective conditions the CCP, in order to protect itself, was forced to yield to the laws of permanent revolution and nationalize the property of the bourgeoisie, thereby making China a workers' state. This, then, proves that Trotsky's prediction regarding the permanent development of the Chinese revolution was basically correct.

However, the CCP was forced to yield to the permanent revolution; it was unconscious and empirical, thus greatly distorting the natural development of the permanent revolution. The manifestation of this kind of distortion can be seen in the CCP's substitution of an all-inclusive "People's Congress" for workers' and peasants' soviets, and then its substitution of a *bureaucratic dictatorship* for the dictatorship of the proletariat. This became an irreconcilable contradiction between the society's economic foundation and its political superstructure. The only way to get rid of this kind of contradiction, allow the revolution to develop, destroy all internal exploitative relations, and push forward the world revolution, is for China (as well as the Soviet Union, Eastern Europe, North Korea, and North Vietnam) to go through a political revolution, which would get rid of the bureaucratic dictatorship and establish a proletarian democratic system.

6. *The problem of policy toward the Sino-Japanese War.* The Sino-Japanese War, which began in July 1937, was the most important incident in modern Chinese history. It not only had decisive significance for Chinese national independence, but it was also one of the most explosive factors in the world situation of that time. Hitler, who initiated the Second World War, utilized the Sino-Japanese War to obtain a military alliance with Japan. Regarding the nature of the Sino-Japanese War, on the Japanese side it was clearly a war of aggression, and thus reactionary. Because of this, the Chinese war of resistance was just and progressive, but its leader, Chiang Kai-shek, was extremely reactionary. He was not only the butcher of the second Chinese revolution, but, for a very long period (from September 1931,

when Japan invaded Manchuria) he consistently followed a
policy of "nondefensism," which allowed Japanese imperialism
to unscrupulously initiate this war of aggression in an attempt to
take over all of China. Under this extremely contradictory
situation, many tendencies developed regarding attitudes and
policies toward the war of resistance, two of which were
completely opposed: ultrarightist opportunism and ultraleftist
sectarianism.

The Chinese Communist Party represented the first tendency.
Based on the progressiveness of the war of resistance, it not only
abolished the "Red Army" and the "soviets," but it also gave up
on all demands for democratic reforms and unconditionally
supported Chiang Kai-shek, voluntarily placing itself under his
direction in the war. This was a repetition of the opportunist
policy carried out by Stalin in the second Chinese revolution. The
other kind of tendency felt that, since Chiang Kai-shek was a
counterrevolutionary, the war of resistance under his leadership
could not be progressive. This tendency thought that "the Sino-
Japanese War was a war between the Japanese emperor and
Chiang Kai-shek," and both sides were reactionary. Because of
this, they advocated the adoption of a defeatist policy toward the
war of resistance. Unfortunately, one of the representatives of
this defeatist tendency was a Trotskyist, Cheng Ch'ao-lin. In the
early period of the war of resistance this tendency did not have
much influence. But about the time of American involvement in
the war, another Trotskyist, Wang Fan-hsi, felt that if war broke
out between Japan and the United States, the Chinese war of
resistance would become subsumed in an imperialist war, thus
losing its progressive nature and becoming reactionary. He then
used this "theory of the changing nature of the war of resistance"
to support defeatism. From this, there developed within the
Chinese Trotskyist organization extreme confusion and fierce
debate. This lasted until the organization split.

The advocates of the defeatist policy toward the war of
resistance were by no means limited to a few Chinese Trotskyists;
this was an international tendency. For instance, in America
Oehler and Eiffel publicly challenged Trotsky's stand on the
Sino-Japanese War. In order to answer this challenge, Trotsky
wrote a letter to Diego Rivera (September 23, 1937) which
carefully and correctly exposed the absurd proposals of Oehler
and Eiffel, while expressing his own basic views on the Sino-
Japanese War. It could be said that this letter contained the

strategic line which Trotsky offered regarding the Chinese war of resistance, while, at the same time, being his final major contribution to the study of the problems of the Chinese revolution. It is worth quoting from quite extensively:

> In my declaration to the bourgeois press, I said that the duty of all the workers' organizations of China was to participate actively and in the front lines of the present war against Japan, without abandoning, for a single moment, their own program and independent activity. But that is "social patriotism" the Eiffelites cry! It is capitulation to Chiang Kai-shek! It is the abandonment of the principle of class struggle! Bolshevism preached revolutionary defeatism in the imperialist war. Now, the war in Spain and the Sino-Japanese war are both imperialist wars. " . . . The only salvation of the workers and peasants of China is to struggle independently against the two armies, against the Chinese army in the same manner as against the Japanese army." These four lines, taken from an Eiffelite document of September 10, 1937, suffice entirely for us to say: we are concerned here with either real traitors or complete imbeciles. But imbecility, raised to this degree, is equal to treason.
>
> We do not and never have put all wars on the same plane. Marx and Engels supported the revolutionary struggle of the Irish against Great Britain, of the Poles against the tsar, even though in these two nationalist wars the leaders were, for the most part, members of the bourgeoisie and even at times of the feudal aristocracy . . . at all events, Catholic reactionaries. . . . Lenin wrote hundreds of pages demonstrating the primary necessity of distinguishing between imperialist nations and the colonial and semicolonial nations which comprised the great majority of humanity. To speak of "revolutionary defeatism" in general, without distinguishing between exploiter and exploited countries, is to make a miserable caricature of Bolshevism and to put that caricature at the service of the imperialists.
>
> In the Far East we have a classic example. China is a semicolonial country which Japan is transforming, under our very eyes, into a colonial country. Japan's struggle is imperialist and reactionary. China's struggle is emancipatory and progressive.
>
> But Chiang Kai-shek? We need have no illusions about Chiang Kai-shek, his party, or the whole ruling class of China, just as Marx and Engels had no illusions about the ruling classes of Ireland and Poland. Chiang Kai-shek is the executioner of the Chinese workers and peasants. But today he is forced, despite himself, to struggle against Japan for the remainder of the independence of China. Tomorrow he may again betray. It is possible. It is probable. It is even inevitable. But today he is struggling. Only cowards, scoundrels, or complete imbeciles can refuse to participate in that struggle. . . .
>
> But can Chiang Kai-shek assure the victory? I do not believe so. It

is he, however, who began the war and who today directs it. *To be able to replace him it is necessary to gain decisive influence among the proletariat and in the army, and to do this it is necessary, not to remain suspended in the air, but to place oneself in the midst of the struggle. We must win influence and prestige in the military struggle against the foreign invasion and in the political struggle against the weaknesses, the deficiencies, and the internal betrayal. At a certain point, which we cannot fix in advance, this political opposition can and must be transformed into armed conflict, since the civil war, like war generally, is nothing more than the continuation of the political struggle. It is necessary, however, to know when and how to transform political opposition into armed insurrection.* . . .

The Eiffelite imbeciles try to jest about this "reservation." "The Trotskyists," they say, "want to serve Chiang Kai-shek in action and the proletariat in words." *To participate actively and consciously in the war does not mean "to serve Chiang Kai-shek" but to serve the independence of a colonial country in spite of Chiang Kai-shek. And the words directed against the Kuomintang are the means of educating the masses for the overthrow of Chiang Kai-shek. In participating in the military struggle under the orders of Chiang Kai-shek, since unfortunately it is he who has the command in the war for independence—to prepare politically the overthrow of Chiang Kai-shek . . . that is the only revolutionary policy.* The Eiffelites counterpose the policy of "class struggle" to this "nationalist and social patriotic" policy. Lenin fought this abstract and sterile opposition all his life. To him, the interests of the world proletariat dictated the duty of aiding oppressed peoples in their national and patriotic struggle against imperialism. Those who have not yet understood that, almost a quarter of a century after the World War and twenty years after the October revolution, must be pitilessly rejected as the worst enemies on the inside by the revolutionary vanguard. This is exactly the case with Eiffel and his kind! ["On the Sino-Japanese War" (September 23, 1937), emphasis added.]

From the quotes above, we can see that, through Marxist principles and historical experience, Trotsky not only presented a precise analysis and judgment of the nature of the Sino-Japanese War, but he also pointed out the strategic direction for the Chinese in the war of resistance: "In participation in the military struggle under the orders of Chiang Kai-shek . . . to prepare politically the overthrow of Chiang Kai-shek." This strategic line was not just "the only revolutionary policy" for that period of the war of resistance, but moreover, in a very fundamental way it could be utilized by any oppressed nation in their revolutionary struggle against aggression (the oppressed nation's struggles against aggression are frequently forced upon the ruling class for its own protection). This strategic direction can also be used in the workers' states controlled by Stalinist parties, when these states are confronted with armed aggression from the imperialists, "In participation in the military struggle under the orders of the bureaucracy . . . to prepare politically the overthrow of the bureaucracy."

With regard to Trotsky's correct criticism of the "imbecility" or "treason" of the Eiffelites, it not only destroyed the Eiffelites, but it also indirectly levied a serious attack against those few "defeatists" in China. This, then, helped the Chinese Trotskyist organization to lessen the damages of splitting. Thus, Trotsky wrote about both the Sino-Japanese War and the Spanish civil war in the Transitional Program of the Fourth International, to serve as models, and to alert against sectarian imbeciles.

IX. Conclusion

In order to clearly understand the evolution of the political lines carried out by the CCP and Trotsky's contribution to the analysis of the problems of the Chinese revolution, we can utilize the above explanation to divide the history of the CCP (up to the assassination of Trotsky by Stalin) into seven periods:

1. Under the influence of the ideas of Lenin and Trotsky, the CCP follows the Bolshevik line (1920 to July 1922).

2. Through Stalin's orders for the CCP to join the KMT, the CCP turns from the Bolshevik line to Menshevik opportunism (August 1922 to August 1924).

3. One part of the CCP leadership, in accordance with some basic principles of Bolshevism, participates in the leadership of the working class movement (August 1924 to December 1925).

4. Because of the problem of "KMT-CCP collaboration," the CCP and the Comintern develop a sharp disagreement (December 1925 to July 1926).

5. The CCP, forced to follow Stalin's Menshevik line, is defeated in the revolution. This is also the period during which the debate over China between Trotsky and Stalin reached its fiercest level (1926 to July 1927).

6. Under the control of Stalin, the CCP jumps from ultrarightist opportunism to ultraleftist adventurism; at the same time, Trotsky turns from opposition to Stalin's opportunism to

opposition to his adventurism (July 1927 to July 1937).*

7. Following the defeats of the adventurist armed insurrections initiated by the CCP, under Stalin's direction, the party again returns to an opportunist line and carries out, for the second time, a policy of "KMT-CCP collaboration"; once again, Trotsky turns from opposition to Stalin's adventurist policy to opposition to his opportunist policy (1937 to 1940).

It is especially worthwhile to point out: from the sixth period on (after the defeat of the revolution), the Chinese Communist Party became Stalinist, both politically and organizationally. Its leadership by then had become a tool for the blind carrying out of Stalin's policies. On the other hand, a part of the CCP leadership and some cadres, learning the lesson from the defeat of the revolution, accepted Trotsky's ideas and organized a Left Opposition inside the party. From this point on, there developed in China an irreconcilable struggle between Trotskyists and Stalinists.

Finally, the methods used by Trotsky in his writings on China are worth pointing out. I have already quoted Trotsky's words: "It is not possible to understand the meaning of the methods of the October uprising without a study of the methods of the Chinese catastrophe." But what are "the methods of the Chinese catastrophe"? They are Stalin's methods of empiricism, as well as formalistic logic. For example, when Stalin observed "imperialist oppression," he thought that this type of oppression was the same toward all classes. Thus, class contradictions could be liquidated, or at least weakened. From this, he arrived at the conclusion of class collaboration, upon which the policies of the "bloc of four classes" and "KMT-CCP collaboration" were based.

---

* In the West, Stalin turned from adventurism to opportunist popular frontism at the time of the Seventh Congress of the Comintern in 1935. Many of the Communist parties in Europe immediately followed the new policy. In China the turn was delayed by the fact that the period of adventurism had resulted in an armed struggle between the two sides. Mao announced his readiness to change the policy after his army arrived in the Northwest in 1936. The CCP from this point on advocated the policy of the national front, but Chiang Kai-shek refused to accept collaboration. It was not until after the Sian incident that the CCP was able to carry out in practice the turn to popular frontism, two years behind the CPs in the West.

Trotsky, in accordance with the dialectical method, believed that imperialist oppression "inevitably pushes the national bourgeoisie into an open bloc with imperialism. The class struggle between the bourgeoisie and the masses of workers and peasants is not weakened, but on the contrary, it is sharpened by imperialist oppression to the point of bloody civil war at every serious conflict." The complete history of the second Chinese revolution vividly verifies Trotsky's analysis and predictions, while, at the same time, proving the complete bankruptcy of Stalin's analysis and predictions. It demonstrates the decisive significance of the use of Marxist methods—dialectics—in a revolution.

Peng Shu-tse
April 26, 1974

Translated from the Chinese by Joseph T. Miller and Hui-fang Miller.

THE "MOSCOW SPIRIT"[1]

To the Memory of the Murdered Workers and Students of Shanghai

June 6, 1925

The *Times,* the leading newspaper of the English bourgeoisie, writes that the movement of the Chinese masses reveals a "Moscow spirit." Well, for once in a way we are prepared to agree with the conservative denunciators. The English press in China and in the British Isles brands the striking workers and students as Bolshevists. Well, we are prepared to a certain extent to support even this terrible revelation. The fact is the Chinese workers object to being shot down by the Japanese police, so they have declared a protest strike and are proclaiming their indignation in the streets. Is it not evident that here the "Moscow spirit" prevails? The Chinese students, filled with sympathy for the workers in their struggle, have joined in the strike against the exercise of violence by foreigners. It is evident, as far as the students are concerned, that we have to deal with Bolshevists.

We of Moscow are prepared to accept all these accusations and revelations. We should like however to add that the best agents for spreading the "Moscow spirit" in the East are the capitalist politicians and journalists. To the question of the ignorant coolie: "What is a Bolshevist?" the English bourgeois press replies: "A Bolshevist is a Chinese worker who does not wish to be shot by Japanese and English police; a Bolshevist is a Chinese student who stretches out a brotherly hand to the Chinese worker who is streaming with blood; a Bolshevist is a Chinese peasant who resents the fact that foreigners, whose arguments are deeds of violence, behave on his land as though they were lord and master." The reactionary press of both hemispheres gives this excellent description of Bolshevism.

Is it possible to carry on in the East a better, more convincing, more stirring propaganda? And to what purpose, may we ask, do we need in the East or, for that matter, in the West either, secret agents with Moscow gold in one pocket and with poison and dynamite in the other? Would any trained agents be capable of doing a thousandth part of the educational work which the *Times* and its companions carry on gratuitously—this must be acknowledged—throughout the world? If a so-called Moscow agent were to tell the oppressed Chinese that the policy of Moscow is a policy of the liberation of the oppressed classes and subjugated nations, the Chinese would very likely not believe him—has he not often been deceived by foreigners! But when Moscow's worst enemy, in the form of the English Conservative newspapers, tells him the same about Moscow, he will believe it implicitly.

When the half-naked and half-starved Chinese worker who is oppressed and degraded begins to become conscious of his dignity as a human being, he is told: Moscow agents have egged you on! If he allies himself with other workers to defend his elementary human rights, he is told: this is the "Moscow spirit." If in the streets of his own town, he tries to defend his right to existence and development, he hears cries of: This is Bolshevism!

Thus the course of revolutionary education advances step by step under the direction of the foreign police and of the journalists, whose attitude of mind is similar to that of the police. And in order to imprint the political lessons deeply on his memory, the English police, after having shot down dozens and hundreds of Chinese workers and students, drags him into the cellars of the English prisons in Shanghai. Thus a shortcut to political knowledge is accomplished. From now onwards every Chinese will know that the "Moscow spirit" is the spirit of revolutionary solidarity which unites the oppressed in the fight against the oppressors; and that on the other hand the atmosphere which pervades the cellars of the English prisons of Shanghai incorporates the spirit of "British freedom."

We would have concluded at this point, for, is there much to add to this eloquent and convincing propaganda of the capitalist press on behalf of Moscow? But it occurs to us that liberal Labour politicians of the MacDonald type are eagerly listening to our conversation with the Conservatives. "You see," they say, pointing didactically at the chief editor of the *Times*, "we have always said that our Conservatives work for Bolshevism." And this also is true. The Conservatives, or rather the reactionaries— all capitalist parties are now reactionary—represent an enormous historical force which is supported by capital and gives expression to its chief interests. MacDonald is right in that there would be no Bolshevism, either in the East or in the West, if the forces of capital did not exist. As long, however, as the force and the yoke of capital does exist, the "Moscow spirit" will make its way throughout the world.

For the "adjustment" of events in Shanghai, and in order to counteract the influence of "Moscow," the liberals and Mensheviks suggest the idea of an international conference on the Chinese question, but they are shutting their eyes to the fact that at this conference the decision would lie in the hands of the same gentlemen at whose command workers and students are shot down in Shanghai.

Possibly MacDonald has a program ready for this conference. If not, we can submit our own to him. It is very simple. The Chinese house belongs to the Chinese. No one has a right to enter this house without knocking at the door. The owner has the right to admit none but friends and to refuse entrance to those whom he considers his enemies. This is the beginning of our program. You will certainly reject it, because to your nostrils it seems to be thoroughly saturated with the explosive "Moscow spirit." But just for this reason it will penetrate into the consciousness of the oppressed Chinese and of every honest English worker. This program contains in itself the most powerful innate force. This is the banner under which the workers and students of Shanghai are dying. The blood which has been shed in the streets of Shanghai will infect the masses with the "Moscow spirit." This spirit penetrates everywhere and is invincible. It will overcome the whole world by liberating it.

From *International Press Correspondence,* vol. 5, no. 51, June 15, 1925.

PROBLEMS OF OUR POLICY WITH RESPECT TO CHINA AND JAPAN[2]

March 25, 1926

1. In the case of China we must take into consideration factors which fall into three categories: (a) China's internal forces; (b) the militarist organizations which, while expressing China's internal forces in one or another form, are to a great extent dependent upon foreign governments; (c) foreign imperialist forces on the one hand, and the forces of the USSR and the proletarian revolutionary movement on the other.

All of the difficulty in finding an orientation flows from the interrelation of factors in these three categories from which everything derives its internal logic and tempo of development.

Of course, in the development of a newly awakened country with a population of 400 million, domestic factors are, in the last analysis, decisive. We must base our fundamental orientation on the development of these internal forces, i.e., chiefly on drawing the peasantry into the revolution and ensuring that proletarian organizations are in the leadership. Our decisive advantage is that we have the opportunity to conduct in China a policy of great historic scope.

While doing this it goes without saying that we cannot ignore the struggle of the militarist groups with all its episodic ups and downs, but we must not allow these episodes to draw us away from our fundamental political line.

I. The International Orientation of the Chinese Revolution and the USSR

1. There is no information which would make us think that there will be a pause, however temporary, in the development of the internal forces of the Chinese revolution. On the contrary, we

have every reason to believe that in the period ahead the movement of the broad popular masses—of workers and peasants—will be developed and consolidated. We, for our part, must do everything possible to give this movement its maximum scope. But the international situation has become far more difficult in light of Europe's well-recognized stabilization, the Locarno Pact,[3] and particularly given the way *the imperialists have posed the China problem in its full scope.* Under these circumstances China's leading revolutionary forces, and even more, the Soviet government must do everything possible to impede the formation of a united imperialist front against China. At the present moment Japan could become extremely dangerous to the Chinese revolution in view of both its geographic position and its vital economic and military interests in Manchuria. *The Chinese revolutionary movement has approached that stage when the question of its relations with Japan takes on the greatest importance.* It is necessary to try to gain a respite, and this means in fact to "postpone" the question of the political fate of Manchuria, i.e., to actually be reconciled to the fact that southern Manchuria will remain in Japanese hands *in the period ahead.*[4]

2. This political orientation, which in no case means, of course, a cessation of the general political struggle against Japanese imperialism, must be submitted in its entirety for the approval of the Chinese Communist Party and the Kuomintang. It is necessary however to consider in advance how difficult it will be for the revolutionary elements and broad public opinion in China to accept this orientation in view of the intense hostility toward Japan. Nevertheless, this orientation is dictated by the internal needs of the Chinese revolution which, until there is a new revolutionary wave in Europe and Asia, will not be able to withstand a combined onslaught from the imperialists.

The interests of the Chinese revolution fully coincide in this case, as in others, with the interests of the Soviet Union, which needs an extended respite just as much as the Chinese revolutionary movement needs to gain time.

3. From what has been said it is clear that the orientation toward intensifying the contradictions between the imperialist powers in the Far East and above all the orientation toward coming to a certain understanding with Japan must be carefully prepared with respect to the general attitude of China's revolutionary forces so that this policy will not be incorrectly

interpreted by ill-informed elements as a sacrifice of China's interests, for purposes of a settlement in Soviet-Japanese political relations.

4. To properly orient Chinese public opinion it is particularly important to recognize the need to strengthen revolutionary and anti-imperialist influence on the Chinese press, not only by creating new organs but by influencing those already in existence.

5. In the event that Manchurian autonomy is established, which is what Japan is trying to bring about, we should get Chang Tso-lin to give up his campaign into the South and generally to stop meddling in the internal affairs of the rest of China. Under no circumstances, of course, can we take the initiative or even indirect responsibility in this matter, but a clear understanding of the implication of Manchurian autonomy under the present conditions in itself dictates the necessary line of conduct for the leading circles of the Chinese revolutionary movement on the one hand, and for us on the other.

6. In view of the general political plan outlined above, it is now more important for us than ever before to eliminate all unnecessary, incidental, and secondary issues that disturb Chinese public opinion. There is absolutely no doubt that in the actions of the various departmental representatives there were inadmissible great-power mannerisms compromising the Soviet administration and creating an impression of Soviet imperialism.

It is necessary to impress upon the corresponding agencies and persons the vital importance for us of such a policy and of even such an *external form* of the policy in relation to China so that any trace of suspicion of great-power intentions will be eliminated. This line—based on the closest attention to China's rights, emphasizing its sovereignty, etc.—must be carried out on every level. In every individual instance of a violation of this policy, no matter how slight, the culprits should be punished and this fact brought to the attention of Chinese public opinion.

7. We must in various ways openly declare: Our policy is based fully on sympathy with the struggle of the Chinese popular masses for a single independent government and for democracy. We reject, however, the idea of any kind of military intervention whatever on our part. The Chinese problem can and must be solved by the Chinese people themselves. Until the realization of a unified China, the Soviet government endeavors to establish and maintain loyal relations with all of the governments existing in China, central as well as provincial.

8. In Manchuria our diplomatic work must be wholly and completely transferred from Harbin to Mukden.[5]

9. We should negotiate with Chang Tso-lin on the following basis: It is clear to us that under the existing circumstances the Manchurian government must maintain good, stable relations with Japan. We will not encroach upon these relations. But at the same time it is to the Manchurian government's advantage to maintain stable and peaceful relations with us, thereby guaranteeing itself a certain independence in relation to Tokyo.

During the negotiations we must point out to Chang Tso-lin that certain Japanese circles are ready to have him replaced with another buffer general, but that we see no reason for him to be replaced with another person while normal relations exist.

10. Working out a strictly businesslike administrative structure for the CER [Chinese Eastern Railroad] is the basic element in negotiations with *Manchuria,* i.e., an explicit procedure for settling (on an equal footing) all contested or disputed questions; in the event of any complications turning the question over to Mukden.

Simultaneously our railway administrator, the consul in Harbin, and the consul general in Mukden will be instructed that any attempt by the railway authorities to solve problems unilaterally, over the head of the Chinese authorities or—even worse—by means of ultimatums to the latter must be punished without mercy.

11. Following an agreement with Chang Tso-lin and the corresponding recognition of this agreement in Peking, an effort should be made to have a Chinese-Japanese-Soviet railway conference called with the aim of all three powers working out a joint economic and construction plan for the railroad in Manchuria, and an economic agreement concerning Manchuria based on full respect for mutual interests and rights.

12. While strictly keeping the actual apparatus of the CER in the hands of the Soviet government—which in the next period is the only way to protect the railroad from imperialist seizure—it is necessary to immediately adopt broad measures of a cultural-political nature aimed at the *Sinification* of the railroad. (a) The administration should be bilingual; station signs and instructions posted in the stations and in the cars, etc., should be bilingual. (b) Chinese schools for railroad workers should be established combining technical and political training. (c) At appropriate points along the railroad, cultural-educational institutions should be established for the Chinese workers and

the Chinese settlements adjacent to the railroad.

13. It is necessary (for Comrade Serebryakov) to check whether turning the railroad directly over to the People's Commissariat of Communications could be interpreted by the Chinese as a step toward our unilateral seizure of the railroad.

All details of changing the railroad's administrative structure must be carefully thought through and worked out with the appropriate Chinese authorities.

14. We must take advantage of the present moment, while our activity on the railroad is totally unencumbered, to conduct a purge of the CER over a month-long period in accordance with the Politburo's decision . . . transferring the elements of the administration and the workers who are of little use or who have compromised themselves to the railroads of the Soviet Union and replacing them in Manchuria with workers from the central railroads who are thoroughly reliable and politically educated.

15. On the other hand, it is necessary right now to carefully compile (and subsequently examine) all cases of tyranny and violence on the part of Chinese militarists, police, and Russian White Guard elements against Russian workers and employees of the CER, and also all cases of conflict between Russians and Chinese on national-social grounds. It is also necessary to devise the course and means for defending the personal and national dignity of Russian workers so that conflicts on this basis, rather than kindling chauvinist sentiments on both sides, on the contrary, will have a political and educational significance. It is necessary to set up special conciliation commissions or courts of honor attached to the trade unions, with both sides participating on an equal basis, under the actual guidance of serious communists who understand the full importance and acuteness of the national question.

The means for protecting the railroad employees from the tyranny of local Chinese authorities must be worked out in an appropriate agreement (with Mukden and Peking) and furnished with all of the necessary organizational guarantees.

In this regard it is necessary to issue instructions and proclamations in Russian and Chinese and distribute them along the railroad line, posting them in the stations and similar premises as well as in the cars.

16. The staff of the consulate general in Harbin should be reorganized to conform with the policies described above.

17. One of the points of the agreement with Chang Tso-lin (and

later on with Japan) should protect People's Revolutionary Mongolia from Chang Tso-lin's encroachments.

18. Instead of immediately starting joint negotiations with Japan, we should concentrate on actually improving relations by carrying out all of the measures outlined above, and by influencing *Japanese public opinion* accordingly; and the People's Commissariat of Foreign Affairs shall be instructed to work out systematic measures in keeping with this approach. Without deciding beforehand the form of a possible tripartite agreement (USSR, Japan, China) the ground should be prepared politically and diplomatically in such a way that it will be impossible for the Chinese to interpret any concessions China may find itself temporarily forced to make to Japan as a division of spheres of influence with our participation. Chinese public opinion, especially in left-wing circles, should be made well aware that the only Chinese concessions to Japanese imperialism that we are prepared to tolerate are those necessary for the popular revolutionary movement in China itself in order to defend itself against a united imperialist offensive. With this perspective the possible joint negotiations should have as their aim, at the cost of some concessions, driving a wedge between Japan and Britain

19. In case it turns out that the people's armies have to surrender ground to Wu P'ei-fu for a long period, it may prove expedient to try to reach an agreement with the latter in order to weaken his dependence on Britain while at the same time carrying out an ongoing struggle against Britain, the main and implacable foe of Chinese independence.[6]

20. With regard to the people's armies it is necessary to conduct comprehensive political, educational, and organizational work (in the Kuomintang and Communist Party) in order to convert them into an effective stronghold of the popular revolutionary movement, independent of personal influence.

21. Canton: During a period of slow development of the revolutionary movement in China, Canton has to be considered as not just a temporary revolutionary beachhead, but also an enormous country with a population of 37 million. It needs a correct and stable economic and political administration. The Canton government should concentrate all its efforts on strengthening the republic internally by means of agrarian, financial, administrative, and political reforms; by drawing the broad popular masses into the political life of the South Chinese Republic, and by strengthening the latter's internal defensive capacity.

The Canton government should in the present period emphatically reject any idea of an aggressive military campaign and, in general, any activity that would push the imperialists onto the path of military intervention.*

Note: Inquire of Comrade Rakovsky whether there is some chance for the Canton government to arrange either officially or unofficially some kind of modus vivendi with France, and if it would not be expedient to send a representative of the Canton government to Paris with the aim of sounding out the French government along this line.[7]

22. In view of the fact that in a whole number of resolutions that have been adopted there are components that urge the leadership of the Kuomintang to assume a cautious and yielding stance on questions raised and meticulously outlined here, in order to avoid any kind of political deviation whatever from the general line, it is necessary to thoroughly explain that such concessions as are made necessary by circumstances must in no way reduce the revolutionary scope of the movement or curtail the broadest agitation either in China or beyond its borders for purposes of assisting the revolutionary movements of the neighboring oppressed colonial countries, etc., etc.

23. In view of the fact that the Chinese reactionaries, at the instigation of the imperialists, have demanded that Comrade Karakhan be recalled, we must recognize the necessity for organizing a very energetic political campaign in China (and as much as possible in other countries, above all in Britain and Japan) against this outrageous demand, explaining the meaning and content of the liberation policy Comrade Karakhan has been pursuing as a representative of the Soviet Union.

II. Railroad Problems in Manchuria

1. It would be advisable to postpone the Manchurian railroad conference until attitudes toward the CER have improved.

2. On railroad construction the CER should make preliminary arrangements with Mukden, keeping in mind that the USSR cannot proceed independently with railroad construction in Manchuria.

3. For the purpose of expanding CER railroad construction,

---

* Stalin's amendment—L.T., March 25, 1926. [Marginal notation by Trotsky next to the sentence in italics. Chiang Kai-shek launched the Northern Expedition against the warlords on July 26, 1926.—Eds.]

expenditures on CER improvements should be cut back so that all available resources can be diverted toward construction.

4. The plan advanced by the People's Commissariat of Communications for CER construction should be adopted.

5. For the construction of the individual spur tracks it would be advisable to form joint-stock companies that can attract local Chinese capital, with the Chinese taking the initiative wherever possible.

6. The CER should not restrict its tasks to laying spur tracks, but should also project the construction of paved roads for automobile transport and the development of shipping.

7. The CER should try with every means available to prevent the Japanese from constructing railroad lines to its north and also toward Hailun and to prevent linking up railroad lines such as the Kirin line with the CER.

8. In order to exert pressure on Japan we should spread information that we are constructing railroads from China across eastern Mongolia.

9. Our aim should be to begin work as soon as possible on a railroad running from Verkhneudinsk to Urga and Kalgan, and from Khabarovsk to Sovetskaya Gavan.

10. The People's Commissariat of Communications should be instructed to ascertain what kind of disagreements between the CER and the Southern Manchurian Railroads on the questions of tariffs, rebates, or cost reductions on poor-quality goods, and freight distribution should be brought up at the conference of the governments.

11. We should reply in the following manner to Dobuchi in connection with Comrade Serebryakov's trip: that the problems facing us will be ascertained on the spot since Serebryakov will personally visit Tokyo.[8] After that our side will make concrete proposals aimed at settling disputed questions and eliminating friction on the basis of principles of mutual respect for the interests of all three parties concerned.

III. On Japanese Immigration

When resolving the question of Japanese immigration to the Soviet Far East we must take into account the intense interest the Japanese public is showing in this matter. However, in view of the danger of Japanese colonization in the Far East, every step we take will have to be cautious and gradual. It is premature at this time to fix the number of Japanese immigrants who are to be allowed into the USSR, but, in any case, Japanese immigration should not be large. It should be strictly regulated and should result in the breaking up of Japanese-controlled resources by means of a special agency set up for that purpose. The Japanese colonists should be settled in a checkerboard fashion, being alternated with a reinforcement of colonization from central Russia. The land that is parceled out should be acceptable to the Japanese peasants and should be suited to the peculiarities of Japanese agriculture. There are areas of land suitable for the Japanese colonists in the vicinity of Khabarovsk and further south, but not in the Siberian interior. We must not allow Korean immigration into these regions under the pretense that it is Japanese. The question of Korean immigration must be examined separately. The Koreans can be granted land that is considerably farther into the depths of Siberia.

Published for the first time in any language. By permission of Harvard College Library. Translated for this volume by Ivan Licho.

FIRST LETTER TO RADEK

August 30, 1926

Dear Karl Berngardovich:

1. I'm writing to you on the question of the Chinese Communist Party in the Kuomintang. This question deserves attention and elaboration. I agree entirely with what you wrote in this regard. But it must be made concrete for the uninitiated readers, and that is essentially everyone. It is extremely important to organize the basic factual data on the development of the Kuomintang and the Communist Party (the areas where they have spread; the growth of the strike movement, the Kuomintang, the Communist Party, and the trade unions; the conflicts within the Kuomintang; etc.).

It is very important, in my opinion, to compare the situation in China with the situation in India. Why is it that the Indian Communist Party is not joining a national-revolutionary organization? How are things going in this regard in the Dutch Indies? The fact of the matter is that the existence of national and even colonial oppression does not at all necessitate the entry of the Communist Party into a national-revolutionary party. The question depends above all on the differentiation of class forces and how this is bound up with foreign oppression. Politically the question presents itself thus: is the Communist Party destined for an extended period of time to play the role of a propaganda circle recruiting isolated co-thinkers (inside a revolutionary democratic party), or can the Communist Party in the coming period assume the leadership of the workers' movement? In China there is no doubt that the conditions are of the second order. But this must be demonstrated, perhaps if only in a very general way, but with an accompanying selection of the essential factual material. Do not forget that at the party conference Bukharin will give a report on questions of international policy, and the question of the Kuomintang will also undoubtedly come up there.

2. How are "questions and answers" going?[9]

3. Did you write the letter?

4. On the agenda of the party conference is the question of trade unions. As far as I know, you have been following *Trud* and the trade union press. It is very important to expand this work and systematize it in view of the exceptional importance of the question.

I am writing a little, receiving guests, being photographed with comrades at the spa, and shooting quail, which I hope you are doing too.

Published for the first time in any language. By permission of Harvard College Library. Translated for this volume by Carol Lisker.

THE CHINESE COMMUNIST PARTY
AND THE KUOMINTANG

September 27, 1926

Facts and documents from the political life of China in the recent period provide an absolutely indisputable answer to the problem of further relations between the Communist Party and the Kuomintang. The revolutionary struggle in China has, since 1925, entered a new phase, which is characterized above all by the active intervention of broad layers of the proletariat, by strikes and the formation of trade unions. The peasants are unquestionably being drawn into motion to an increasing degree. At the same time, the commercial bourgeoisie, and the elements of the intelligentsia linked with it, are breaking off to the right, assuming a hostile attitude toward strikes, communists, and the USSR.

It is quite clear that in the light of these fundamental facts the question of revising relations between the Communist Party and the Kuomintang must necessarily be raised. The attempt to avoid such a revision by claiming that national-colonial oppression in China requires the permanent entry of the Communist Party in the Kuomintang cannot stand up under criticism. At one time, the Western European opportunists used to demand that we Russian Social Democrats should work in the same organization not only with the Social Revolutionaries but also with the "Liberationists" on the grounds that we were all engaged in the struggle against tsarism. On the other hand, with regard to British India or the Dutch Indies, the very question of the Communist Party entering the national-revolutionary organizations does not arise. As far as China is concerned, the solution to the problem of relations between the Communist Party and the Kuomintang differs at different periods of the revolutionary movement. The main criterion for us is not the constant fact of national oppression but the changing course of the class struggle, both within Chinese society and along the line of encounter between the classes and parties of China and imperialism.

The leftward movement of the masses of Chinese workers is as certain a fact as the rightward movement of the Chinese bourgeoisie. Insofar as the Kuomintang has been based on the political and organizational union of the workers and the bourgeoisie, it must now be torn apart by the centrifugal tendencies of the class struggle. There are no magic political formulas or clever tactical devices to counter these trends, nor can there be.

The participation of the CCP in the Kuomintang was perfectly correct in the period when the CCP was a propaganda society which was only preparing itself for future *independent* political activity but which, at the same time, sought to take part in the ongoing national liberation struggle. The last two years have seen the rise of a mighty strike wave among the Chinese workers. The CCP report estimates that the trade unions during this period have drawn in some 1.2 million workers. Exaggeration in such matters is of course inevitable. Moreover, we know how unstable new union organizations are in situations of constant ebb and flow. But the fact of the Chinese proletariat's mighty awakening, its desire for struggle and for independent class organization, is absolutely undeniable.

This very fact confronts the CCP with the task of graduating from the preparatory class it now finds itself in to a higher grade. Its immediate political task must now be to fight for direct independent leadership of the awakened working class—not of course in order to remove the working class from the framework of the national-revolutionary struggle, but to assure it the role of not only the most resolute fighter, but also of political leader with hegemony in the struggle of the Chinese masses.

Those who favor the CCP's remaining in the Kuomintang argue that "the predominant role of the petty bourgeoisie in the composition of the Kuomintang makes it possible for us to work within the party for a prolonged period on the basis of our own politics." This argument is fundamentally unsound. The petty bourgeoisie, by itself, however numerous it may be, cannot decide the main line of revolutionary policy. The differentiation of the political struggle along class lines, the sharp divergence between the proletariat and the bourgeoisie, implies a struggle between them for influence over the petty bourgeoisie, and it implies the vacillation of the petty bourgeoisie between the merchants, on the one hand, and the workers and communists, on the other. To think that the petty bourgeoisie can be won over by clever maneuvers or good advice within the Kuomintang is hopeless utopianism. The Communist Party will be more able to exert direct and indirect influence upon the petty bourgeoisie of town and country the stronger the party is itself, that is, the more it has won over the Chinese working class. But that is possible only on the basis of an independent class party and class policy.

We have taken the above-quoted argument in favor of the CCP's remaining in the Kuomintang from the July 14, 1926, resolution of the CCP Central Committee plenum. This resolution, along with other documents of the plenum, testifies to the extremely contradictory policies of the CCP and to the dangers flowing from that. The documents of the July plenum of the CCP Central Committee testify at every step to the "intensified process, during the past year, by which each of the two poles—bourgeoisie and proletariat—has defined its own separate position" (quoted from the same resolution).

The resolutions, documents, and reports record, first, the growth of the Kuomintang right wing, then the rightward movement of the Kuomintang center, and after that, the vacillations and splits in the Kuomintang left. And all of this has followed the pattern of stepped-up attacks on the communists. For their part, the communists have been retreating steadily, from one position to the next, within the Kuomintang. Their concessions, as we shall see, are both of an organizational nature and of the kind involving matters of principle. They have agreed to limit the number of communists on leading bodies of the Kuomintang to no more than one-third. They have even agreed to accept a resolution declaring the teachings of Sun Yat-sen inviolable. But, as ever, each new concession only brings renewed pressure against the communists on the part of the Kuomintang forces. All of these processes, as we have said, are absolutely inevitable, given the class differentiation.

Nevertheless the Central Committee plenum rejected the views of those Chinese communists who proposed withdrawal from the Kuomintang. The resolution states:

A completely incorrect point of view, which distorts the prospects for development of the liberation struggle in China, is held by those comrades who think that the Communist Party—if it were to break organizationally with the Kuomintang, that is, if it were to dissolve the alliance with the urban commercial and professional bourgeoisie, the revolutionary intelligentsia, and partly, the government—could now, by itself, lead the proletariat and behind it the other oppressed masses to carry out the bourgeois-democratic revolution.

This line of argument seems to us, however, completely untenable. Whether the CCP will prove capable *in the future,* as an independent and decisive force, of leading the proletariat and peasantry to liberate and unify the country, no one can now predict. The further course of the revolutionary struggle in China depends on the play of far too many internal and international forces. Of course, the Communist Party's struggle for influence over the proletariat and for the hegemony of that class in the national-revolutionary movement may not lead to victory in the next years. But that is no argument at all against an independent class policy, which is inconceivable without an independent class organization. It is fundamentally wrong to suggest that withdrawal from the Kuomintang means the breakup of the alliance with the petty bourgeoisie. The essential point is that the vague and formless alliance of the proletariat with the petty-bourgeois, merchant, and other elements, which is reflected in the Kuomintang, is now no longer even possible. The class differentiation has passed over into the realm of politics. From now on the alliance between the proletariat and the petty bourgeoisie can be based only on strictly defined and clearly stated agreements.

The drawing of organizational lines, which inevitably flows from the class differentiation, does not rule out but, on the contrary, presupposes—under existing conditions—a political bloc with the Kuomintang as a whole or with particular elements of it, throughout the republic or in particular provinces, depending on the circumstances. But first of all, the CCP must ensure its own complete organizational independence and clarity of political program and tactics in the struggle for influence over the awakened proletarian masses. Only with this kind of approach can one speak seriously of drawing the broad masses of the Chinese peasantry into the struggle.

The direction of the CCP's thinking can best be made clear by quoting the most striking passages from the CCP declaration issued by the July Central Committee plenum (July 12, 1926):

The urgent demand of the Chinese people is for the alleviation of all these sufferings. This is not Bolshevism. Perhaps one could say that it is Bolshevism for the sake of saving our people, but it is not Bolshevism for the sake of communism.

Further on, this manifesto states:

They [the bourgeoisie] do not understand that the minimal expression of the class struggle that has occurred in the organization of the workers and in the strikes does not at all reduce the fighting capacity of the anti-imperialist and antimilitarist forces. Moreover, they do not understand that the welfare of the Chinese bourgeoisie depends on the success of the war waged in conjunction with the proletariat against the imperialists and militarists, and not at all upon the continuation of the class struggle by the proletariat.

The path of struggle is to "call for a nationwide conference." This should be done by the Kuomintang "as the party whose mission it is to carry out the national revolution." To the objection that the militarists would make it impossible to convene a national assembly truly representative of the people, the manifesto replies with generalities about control being exercised by the parties and unity of all classes. In Point 23 of the platform a demand is inserted, and only in twelfth place, for freedom to form coalitions, freedom of assembly, etc.

The concluding section of the declaration states:

They [the militarists] say that our platform is revolutionary. That may be. However, it corresponds to the most urgent and vital demands and needs of all layers of the people. And a united fighting front of all classes of the population should be based on a common platform. Those who take part in this struggle should firmly defend these demands. They should fight for the common interests, not egoistically defend the interests of their own class. . . .

The entire declaration is permeated from beginning to end with the desire to convince the bourgeoisie and not to win the proletariat. This kind of position establishes the premises for inevitable retreats before the right, center, and pseudoleft leaders of the Kuomintang. The politics expressed in this declaration in fact have nothing to do with Marxism. This is Sun Yat-senism, slightly touched up with Marxist terminology.

Under these conditions it can no longer come as a surprise that the communists found it possible to accept the following policy statement of the Kuomintang Central Committee, adopted on Chiang Kai-shek's motion:

> The Kuomintang must see to it that every member of another party entering the Kuomintang [i.e., the Communist Party—L.T.] understands that Sun Yat-senism, founded by Sun Yat-sen, is the basic principle of the Kuomintang and that there must not be any doubts or criticism expressed in regard to Sun Yat-sen or Sun Yat-senism.

It is quite obvious that when matters are presented this way, the whole reason for the CCP's existence disappears.

Sun Yat-senism as an idealist, petty-bourgeois doctrine of national solidarity was able to play a relatively progressive role in the period when the communists could get along in the same organization with the students and progressive merchants on the basis of a vague and informal alliance. The present class differentiation within Chinese society and within the Kuomintang is not only an irreversible but also a profoundly progressive fact.

Moreover, it means that Sun Yat-senism has become altogether a thing of the past. It would be suicidal for the CCP to refrain from criticizing this doctrine which, as events unfold, is sure to bind the Chinese revolution hand and foot and ever more tightly. The imposition of this kind of obligation results from enforced organizational cohabitation within the bounds of a single political organization in which the communists voluntarily accept the position of a systematically discriminated-against minority.

The way out of this profoundly contradictory and absolutely unacceptable situation cannot be found along the lines pursued by the last plenum of the CCP. The way out does not lie in trying to "take the place of" the left wing in the Kuomintang, or in gently and unobtrusively trying to educate and nudge them along, nor in trying to "help create a left-Kuomintang periphery out of the organizations of the petty bourgeoisie." All these recipes and even the way they are formulated are cruelly reminiscent of the old Menshevik cuisine. The way out is to draw the line organizationally as the necessary prerequisite for an independent policy, keeping one's eyes, not on the left Kuomintang, but above all, on the awakened workers. Only under this condition can a bloc with the Kuomintang or with any of its elements be anything more than a castle of sand. The sooner the policy of the CCP is turned around the better for the Chinese revolution.

Two Conclusions

1. In the foregoing we have criticized the recent decisions of the CCP Central Committee. On the basis of past experience we can expect attempts to depict our criticism as an expression of hostility toward the fraternal Chinese party.

One or another sentence may be torn out of context with the aim of showing that to us, the CCP is a "brake" on the revolutionary movement. There is no need to comment on the harm done by such lowgrade "criticism." But facts are stronger than fabrications and insinuations. Properly evaluated and foreseen in time, the facts can still prove convincing even if the insinuations are disseminated in huge editions. Our criticism of the central leadership of the CCP is dictated by the desire to help the proletarian revolutionists of China to avoid mistakes that have long since been tested out in the experience of other countries. The responsibility for the CCP Central Committee's mistakes lies first of all with the leading group of our own party. The policy of remaining in the Kuomintang in spite of the whole trend of developments was dictated from Moscow, as the highest precept of Leninism. The Chinese communists had no alternative but to accept the political conclusions flowing from this organizational precept.

2. Politics is expressed through organization. That is why opportunism in organizational matters is entirely possible, as Lenin taught us. Such opportunism can be expressed in various ways, depending on the circumstances. One form of organizational opportunism is tailendism, i.e., the desire to hold on to organizational forms and relations that have become outdated and therefore turn into their opposites. We have seen organizational tailendism in the recent period in two cases: (a) on the question of the Anglo-Russian Committee;[10] and (b) on the question of the relations between the CCP and the Kuomintang. In both cases, the tailendism consisted in clinging to an organizational form that had already been stood on its head by the course of the class struggle. In both cases the outdated organizational form has helped right-wing elements and bound the left hand and foot. We must learn from these two examples.

[Postscript dated September 30, 1926.]

From Comintern leaders in China we have heard a voice of warning—though phrased, to be sure, in a very cautious way—on the question of relations between the CCP and Kuomintang. Thus, the report on CCP tactics toward the Kuomintang which was received after the May plenum of the Kuomintang Central Committee states:

> In carrying out these decisions [i.e., the decisions defining our organizational ties with the Kuomintang], we should stretch them somewhat, that is, remain formally within the Kuomintang, but in practice, make a division of labor that would, as much as possible, give them the form of collaboration between two parties, i.e., make a gradual transition from the form of collaboration based on inner unity to that of contacts and consultations between allies.

Thus, from China the proposal has come that we, without formally negating the directives, should violate them in fact and turn the relations between the CCP and Kuomintang in the direction of an alliance between two independent parties. This proposal, which was called for by the whole course of events, met with no sympathy, however, and as a result we have had the decisions of the July plenum of the CCP Central Committee, decisions that are obviously mistaken, profoundly contradictory, and tending in a dangerous direction.

Published for the first time in any language. By permission of Harvard College Library. Translated for this volume by George Saunders.

SECOND LETTER TO RADEK

March 4, 1927

Dear Friend:

It seems to me that your way of formulating the problems with respect to the Chinese Communist Party is inadequate, and owing to what it leaves out, must inevitably lead, upon its subsequent application, to mistaken conclusions, i.e., for all intents and purposes to support for the status quo with some left-wing criticism.

You write that the treacherous bourgeois politics of the Kuomintang have "not yet created a mass movement against the Kuomintang and have not fostered an understanding of the need for a special class party of the proletariat and the poorest peasantry." Undoubtedly, the supporters of the present situation will try to latch onto these words. This was precisely the reason Stalin revived the "theory of stages," explaining that "it is impossible to skip over a stage," etc. Since the masses have not become conscious of the need, therefore . . . and so on. Our reasoning is just the opposite: in order to make it easier for the masses to understand how treacherous Kuomintang policy is, what is needed is an absolutely independent party, even if small, criticizing, explaining, exposing, and so forth; and by so doing, paving the way for the new "stage."

It is as if the present situation in China had been specifically created so that the masses would not understand the need for an independent party. Indeed, with the full authority of the International and the Russian revolution we are telling China's working class vanguard that they already have an independent party—the Communist Party; that by force of the peculiar conditions in China this Communist Party must become a part of the Kuomintang at the present stage of the revolution; that Lenin's precepts demand this, and so on. Then the Kuomintang tells the communists: "Since Lenin's precepts demand that you join the Kuomintang, I, the Kuomintang, demand that you renounce Lenin's precepts and recognize the precepts of Sun Yat-sen."

To pose in the abstract the question of a painless transition from Sun Yat-sen to Lenin by presenting Leninism as the logical extension of Sun Yat-senism (although this method can in certain instances be used pedagogically with respect to the young revolutionary dilettantes of China) has, of course, proven to be untenable on the great historical scale. The class struggle has torn up the little artificial bridge we had constructed between Sun Yat-sen and Lenin. The Chinese proletariat must go through the process of directly and openly overcoming Sun Yat-sen, through an open struggle against Sun Yat-senism. If Marx demanded this even with respect to Lassalle, can it really be that we must not pose such a task with respect to Sun Yat-sen? Any moves to obscure, delay, or camouflage on this fundamental question will be not only dangerous but utterly disastrous for the Chinese proletariat.

When should the communists have withdrawn from the Kuomintang? My memory of the history of the Chinese revolution in recent years is not concrete enough, and I do not have the materials at hand; therefore, I will not venture to say whether it was necessary to pose this question point-blank as early as 1923, 1924, or 1925. In that period the preparatory arrangement expressed in your letter, evidently counting on a transitional state of a year or two, would have, perhaps, been admissible. But we are dreadfully late. We have turned the Chinese Communist Party into a variety of Menshevism, and worse yet, not into the best variety; i.e., not into the Menshevism of 1905, when it temporarily united with Bolshevism, but into the Menshevism of 1917, when it joined hands with the right SR movement and supported the Cadets. In giving our blessing to or merely tolerating this situation, we hamper the development of the class consciousness of the Chinese workers, only to afterward cite the insufficient development of their consciousness as the reason for dragging out still further the present state of things. With such a policy we are caught in a vicious circle.

If it were to turn out that the Chinese communists *do not want* to withdraw from the Kuomintang even in the present conditions of an unfolding class struggle, this would mean not that withdrawal is unnecessary, but that what we have there is a Martynovist party. I am afraid that to a large degree this is precisely how things stand.

Our task would then be reduced to extracting the genuinely revolutionary elements from the Martynovist party and beginning the work of building a Bolshevik party, outside not only the Kuomintang, but also outside the present "Communist" Party of China. I say this hypothetically because I do not know the actual relationship of forces inside the Communist Party; in fact, I doubt that it could have developed much at all yet in view of the absence of a clear and precise formulation of the problem by any side whatever. If we want to try to save the Chinese Communist Party from ultimately degenerating into Menshevism, we do not have the right to put aside one day longer the demand for withdrawal from the Kuomintang.

You propose that we restrict ourselves to the call for the Communist Party to emerge *from underground*. But this misses the point. To emerge from underground work means to breach Kuomintang legality. How would it be done? On the spur of the moment? Without warning? Without an attempt to come to an understanding with the Kuomintang on new terms? Without making an agreement with the left wing? But this would be the worst kind of breach; one that would be depicted as treachery. We are not starting out in China with a blank slate. All aspects of the problem of the relationship between the communists and the Kuomintang have been discussed in China. The problem brought about conflicts, was resolved, and resulted in a specific structuring. To ignore what has gone on before is impermissible. The problem must be posed in terms of revising the party constitution. The communists should directly and openly propose that the organizational structure be revised, by mutual agreement, to provide for the full independence of both parties. In the absence of such a clear and precise formulation, the tactic of "emerging from underground" will be incomprehensible to the communists themselves; but the fact of the matter is that they must understand what the tactic will lead to and have a perspective for the future. Of course, withdrawal from the Kuomintang is a painful process. A neglected illness always requires more drastic treatment. It is wrong to be afraid that we will "alienate the petty bourgeoisie." There will be an endless number of zigzags and waverings on the part of the petty bourgeoisie. It is very likely that our withdrawal from the Kuomintang will at first give rise to just such a zigzag. But the petty bourgeoisie can be won over only by a concrete policy, not by maintaining disguises, making diplomatic maneuvers, etc. In order to develop a policy that has the potential for winning over the petty bourgeoisie, it is necessary to have the instrument for this policy, i.e., an independent party.

That is why I have come to the following conclusions:

1. We must recognize that for the Communist Party to remain in the Kuomintang any longer threatens to have dire consequences for the proletariat and for the revolution; and above all, it threatens the Chinese Communist Party itself with a total degeneration into Menshevism.

2. We must recognize that if there is to be a leadership for the Chinese proletariat, a systematic struggle to gain influence in the trade unions, and finally, a leadership in the struggle of the proletariat to influence the peasant masses, there must be a totally independent, i.e., truly Communist (Bolshevik) Party.

3. The question of the forms and methods of coordination of the activities of the Communist Party and the Kuomintang must be fully and completely subordinated to the demand for the independence of the party.

4. All the genuinely revolutionary elements of the Chinese Communist Party must advance the program for action indicated above, demanding that its Central Committee raise before the Kuomintang and the working masses—in its full scope and unequivocally—the question of revising organizational relationships. Simultaneously, communists must everywhere "emerge from underground," i.e., actually begin to work as an independent party.

5. A congress of the Chinese Communist Party must be prepared under the call for the organizational independence of the Chinese Communist Party and the complete independence of its class politics and on the basis of a merciless struggle of its Bolshevik elements against the Menshevik elements within the party itself.

L. Trotsky

Published in English for the first time. By permission of Harvard College Library. Translated for this volume by Marilyn Vogt.

A BRIEF NOTE[11]

March 22, 1927

I confess that at the present time the situation in China arouses in me far greater concern than does any other problem. I have just received a telegram to the effect that Shanghai has been occupied by Nationalist troops. The wider the territory under Nationalist rule and the more the Kuomintang takes on the character of a governing party, the more it becomes bourgeois. In this regard, the inclusion of Shanghai in the territory of the Nationalist government has an out-and-out decisive character.

At the same time we read Kalinin's and Rudzutak's speeches, in which they expound and repeat the idea that the Nationalist government is the government of all the classes of the Chinese people (those are their words!). Thus, it seems that in China a government can exist that transcends class lines. Marxism has been completely forgotten. Forgotten too have been Lenin's theses on democracy (the First Congress of the Comintern). When you read such things in *Pravda*, at first you do not believe your eyes, you reread it and reread it again. . . . But then, on this question Kalinin and Rudzutak are expressing in full the policy of the Chinese Communist Party, i.e., to put it more accurately, the Comintern's present policy on the Chinese question. The greater the successes of the national revolution in China, the greater are the dangers that await us with the present policy. (There will be some wise soul who will conclude from these words that I am against reaping the Chinese "harvest"—in other words, against the victory of the national revolution in China.)

The present policy is incorrect, even if we approach the matter from a "purely national" point of view, "abstracted" from the international revolution. There can be no doubt that the

Nationalist government in China, upon seizing huge territories and finding itself face to face with gigantic and extremely difficult problems, upon experiencing the need for foreign capital and clashing daily with the workers, will make a sharp turn to the right, toward America to a certain extent and Britain. At this moment the working class finds itself without leadership, for it is quite impossible to consider as an independent leadership of the working class the "communist" appendage of the Kuomintang, which puts into the workers' heads the idea that the Nationalist government is a government of all classes. We find ourselves in the position of a hen who has hatched a duckling. . . .

Evidently those who are in charge of this policy conceive of the following course of development: first we will carry things to a complete victory for the Nationalist troops, i.e., the unification of China; then we will begin to remove the Communist Party from the Kuomintang. The concept is Menshevik through and through. First we complete the bourgeois revolution, and then, . . . etc. With this concept, we are turning ourselves into not a class force of history, but some sort of classless inspectorate above the historical process as a whole. And, of course, we will fall flat on our faces at the very first turn. This turn will in all likelihood be the occupation of Shanghai.[12]

The communists cannot, of course, relinquish support for the Nationalist army and the Nationalist government, nor, it appears, can they refuse to become part of the Nationalist government. But the question of the complete organizational independence of the Communist Party, i.e., of its withdrawal from the Kuomintang, must not be put off one day longer. We have lost far too much time as it is. The communists can form a united government with the Kuomintang on the condition of the total separation of the parties forming the political bloc. So it was with us and the left SRs.[13] Vladimir Ilyich demanded that the Hungarian communists follow the same course and reproached them for having entered into an amalgamation of parties—that act having been, incidentally, one of the reasons the Hungarian revolution was crushed so quickly.[14]

Is it permissible to continue any longer the flirtation with Sun Yat-senism, which is turning into the ideological shackles of the Chinese proletariat and tomorrow will become (is already becoming today) the main instrument of the Chinese bourgeois reaction! I believe that this sort of flirtation is criminal. But in order to cut the umbilical cord of Sun Yat-senism, there must be someone to cut it. An independent Communist Party is needed. Revolutionary selection within the Communist Party itself, i.e., its Bolshevization not in word but in deed, will undoubtedly occur around this question.

References to national oppression as a justification for a Menshevik policy are absolutely untenable. First of all one must remember that the whole Second International (Jaurès, Vandervelde, and the others) in demanding the unity of the Bolsheviks not only with the Mensheviks but also with the SRs was taking as its starting point the oppression of tsarism. As if a struggle against tsarism or against national oppression is not the class struggle! In Georgia, Finland, Latvia, etc., the yoke of tsarism took the form of the most savage national oppression, more complete than Britain's or even Japan's oppression of China. However, from this it did not follow that the Georgians, Finns, or Latvians should not build an independent party.

It seems to me that we must again, in one way or another, present this question to the Politburo. Of course, there is the danger that instead of a serious discussion of this problem in the Central Committee, there will be factional slander. But can we be silent when nothing less than the head of the Chinese proletariat is at stake?

L.T.

Published in English for the first time. By permission of Harvard College Library. Translated for this volume by Carol Lisker.

LETTER TO ALSKY

March 29, 1927

Dear Comrade Alsky:

Thank you for sending me the book. I read it today, all to my interest and benefit. I think you are absolutely right when you object to naming the Southern Nationalist government "workers' and peasants'." Defining it in such a way is, of course, a serious mistake as should be especially obvious now after the occupation of Shanghai with the powerful class contradictions this entails.

But this is precisely why I believe that you have made an error, expressed with particular clarity on page 141, where you say that in China, "two camps that are bitterly hostile to one another" have come into being: in one are the imperialists and militarists and certain layers of the Chinese bourgeoisie; and in the other are "the workers, artisans, petty bourgeoisie, students, intelligentsia, and certain groups from the middle bourgeoisie with a nationalist orientation. . . ." In fact, there are three camps in China—the reactionaries, the liberal bourgeoisie, and the proletariat—fighting for hegemony over the lower strata of the petty bourgeoisie and peasantry. It is true that before 1926 this division was less obvious than it is now, but even then it was a fact. But your book was published in 1927, and it was of the utmost importance to specifically describe this situation. If not, your review of Mif's book, and your evaluation in a number of places, and especially on page 141, would—in my opinion—provide the basis for grossly incorrect and dangerous conclusions. The Kuomintang in its present form creates the *illusion* that two camps exist, furthering the national-revolutionary disguise of the bourgeoisie, and consequently, making its betrayal easier. The Communist Party's entry into the Kuomintang, on the other hand, makes an independent proletarian policy impossible. It would be the purest charlatanism and betrayal of Marxism—you, of course, would agree—to point to the revolutionary heroism of the proletariat and the successes of the Canton forces as proof that in the sphere of proletarian politics everything is going favorably. That the workers and the revolutionary soldiers won back Shanghai is magnificent. But the question still remains: Who did they win it back for? If one thinks that "two bitterly hostile camps" exist in China, it is clear that Shanghai has passed from the hands of one camp into the hands of the other. But if one bears in mind that there are *three* camps in China, then the question posed above takes on its full meaning.

The problem of a struggle for a workers' and peasants' government should in no case be identified with the problem of "noncapitalist roads" of development for China. The latter can only be posed provisionally and only within the perspective of the development of world revolution. Only an ignoramus of the socialist-reactionary variety could think that *present-day* China, with its *current* technological and economic foundations, can through its *own* efforts jump over the capitalist phase. A conception of this type would be the worst caricature of the theory of socialism in one country, and carrying this conception to the absurd would render the Comintern a service, clearing its activity of such rubbish once and for all thereafter.[15] If, thus, the problem of the Chinese revolution growing over into a socialist revolution is right now merely a long-term option wholly dependent upon the development of the world proletarian revolution, the problem of the *struggle for a workers' and peasants' government* has the most immediate importance for the course of the Chinese revolution as well as for the education in revolution of the proletariat and its party.

We know how complex and contradictory the course of the revolution is, especially in such a huge and—to an overwhelming extent—backward country like China. The revolution can still pass through a series of ebbs and flows. What we must safeguard in the course of the revolution is above all the independent party of the proletariat that is constantly evaluating the revolution from the point of view of three camps, and is capable of fighting for hegemony in the third camp and, by so doing, in the entire revolution.

I must say, I totally fail to comprehend *why the call for soviets is not being raised in China*. It is precisely through soviets that the crystallization of the class forces can keep pace with the new stage of the revolution instead of conforming to the organizational-political traditions of a bygone day, of the kind being offered by the present-day Kuomintang. How the Kuomintang will reorganize itself after the Communist Party withdraws from it—this particular question is of secondary importance to us. The indispensable condition is an independent proletarian party. The form for its closest collaboration with the rural and urban petty bourgeoisie is the soviets as organs of the struggle for power or as organs of power.

Large sections of the Chinese National Revolutionary Army are still green, and bourgeois landowners' sons wield great influence within the ranks of the commanding staff. Because of this, the future of the revolution is in danger. Once more, I do not see any other way to oppose this danger than soldiers' deputies joining workers' deputies, and so on.

It goes without saying, the means for selecting the deputies would have to be very carefully adapted to suit the conditions and particular features of a city, a village of a given area, the army, etc., so as not to give an accidental advantage to the reactionary elements or bring disorganization to the revolutionary forces, and so on. But I repeat: I see no other means for testing and organizing the revolutionary movement and the revolutionary power that grows out of it than a system of soviets. Why is nothing said about it? Explain it to me, please! This is what I can in no way understand.

Instead of clearly and concisely posing the question of the struggle for a workers' and peasants' (and artisans' and soldiers') soviet of deputies they are devoting themselves to the artificial and, therefore, reactionary perpetuation of an organization of the past—the Kuomintang—forcing the Communist Party to submit to the discipline of a bourgeois organization, at the same time consoling the party with talk about "noncapitalist roads" of development.

In his speech, Comrade Rafes stated that the present-day Kuomintang must be preserved "as a transmission belt." When people move away from Marxism, they invariably substitute all sorts of meaningless images for a class understanding. A transmission belt is an excellent device. One only needs to know what it is transmitting from and what it is transmitting toward. While driving the Communist Party away from a strictly defined organizational position and subjecting it to the ideological discipline of Sun Yat-senism, the Kuomintang will necessarily and inevitably transfer power to the most influential, weighty, and organized elements of the "united" national camp, i.e., bluntly speaking, to the liberal bourgeoisie. Thus, the Kuomintang under the present conditions is a "transmission belt" for delivering the revolutionary popular masses into the hands of the bourgeoisie, for politically subjugating them to it. Any other interpretation is stupidity or charlatanism.

Members of the Kuomintang (those with brains) not only demand that communists unconditionally observe "revolutionary discipline" but when doing this they refer to the experience of the October revolution with its dictatorship of *one* party. We, for our part, are supporting such a way of formulating the question insofar as we are compelling the Chinese Communist Party—against its will—to be part of a united Kuomintang and to submit to its discipline. In so doing we are leaving out of our reckoning the "petty detail" that what is taking place in China is not a socialist overturn but a bourgeois-national revolution, the "completion" of which means not the dictatorship of one party but a guarantee of the maximum democracy; so, from our point of view it means above all total freedom for the party of the proletariat. Now, when the wave is rising, there is nothing easier than to warm up our singing voices on "noncapitalist roads of development." But with the first big revolutionary lull, or especially a full-fledged ebb, it can become immediately obvious that China lacks the fundamental instrument for revolutionary struggle and revolutionary successes—an independent Communist Party acquiring experience and understanding the situation.

[Postscript, March 29, 1927]

PS: In your book it says that the Hong Kong–Canton Strike Committee represented the "Chinese version of the soviet of workers' deputies."[16] This is absolutely true if "Chinese version" is understood not in the sense of some sort of decisive national peculiarity, but in the sense of the character of a stage of development of the soviet system: it was a soviet of deputies of the type that existed in the summer of 1905 in Ivanovo Voznesensk. Why can't this system be developed further? What is standing in its way? I maintain that it is the fact that the Communist Party has been bound hand and foot. If it is called upon to openly struggle for influence over the workers and—

through the workers—over the peasantry under the banner of Marxism, and not Sun Yat-senism, and in direct struggle against the reactionary application of Sun Yat-senism, simultaneously collaborating with all revolutionary elements, groups, and layers of the petty bourgeoisie in the city and in the countryside; then it is impossible to devise a better form for such a struggle and for such collaboration than soviets.

PPS: I would not attach such great importance to your words about "two camps" if in the beginning of your book there were not a dedication to the Kuomintang and the Communist Party. I believe such a dedication is a serious mistake. The Kuomintang and the Communist Party are parties representing two opposing classes. It is not possible for one and the same book to be simultaneously dedicated to both. It is permissible to be in an alliance with the Kuomintang, but such an ally must be as carefully watched as an enemy. However, to be sentimental about such an ally is impermissible.

L. Trotsky

Published in English for the first time. By permission of Harvard College Library. Translated for this volume by Marilyn Vogt.

TO THE POLITBURO OF THE
AUCP(B) CENTRAL COMMITTEE

March 31, 1927

Dear Comrades:

It is only through the papers that I am able at present to follow the events in China. What instructions you have given I do not know. But one cannot help noticing that nowhere in our press, in dealing with the development of the Chinese revolution (primarily its military aspect), has the question of *soviets* been raised. But it seems to me that at the present stage this question takes on absolutely decisive significance.

1. The Chinese revolution has taken over such major proletarian centers as Shanghai and Hankow, not to mention other less important places. Everything seems to point to the fact that the *first thing* that should be done in these proletarian centers is to organize soviets of workers' deputies.

2. Revolutionary collaboration between the proletariat and the urban and rural poor is a matter of life and death for the further progress of the Chinese revolution. Regardless of how one views the question of the further relations between the CCP and the Kuomintang, one thing is clear: day-to-day political, administrative and practical collaboration between the hundreds of thousands of workers and the millions of semiproletarian and petty-bourgeois elements in town and countryside cannot be achieved solely through the essentially elitist organization of the Kuomintang, with its roughly 300,000 party members. This kind of actual, genuine, day-to-day collaboration among the masses of the people awakened by the revolution can only be brought about in reality through the creation of soviets of workers', artisans', and peasants' deputies.

3. The national army, whose political education has only

begun, will inevitably become swollen out of proportion as it is joined by new, provincial forces, completely green and raw as far as politics is concerned. The officer cadre, as far as one can tell from the available materials, is characterized by bourgeois and landlord origins and by sympathies tending to favor those same classes. Apprehensions regarding a Chinese variant of Bonapartism are apparently rather strong among revolutionary circles in China, nor can one say by any means that these fears are unfounded. Under existing conditions it would seem there is no more effective measure for countering such dangers than the establishment of soldiers' sections of soviets, beginning with *the garrisons in the major proletarian centers.*

4. It goes without saying that the formation of soviets must be done very carefully, in accordance with all the class relations, local conditions, and other special features and factors, so as not to give any accidental advantage to reactionary elements in one place or another, not to cause disturbances among the troops, etc. Nevertheless, everything points to the fact that this task of truly consolidating the conquered territories by forming soviets of the working and exploited masses of the Chinese population cannot be postponed any longer.

5. Only in this way can there, and will there, be a radical agrarian transformation—by "reformist" means where circumstances permit, and by "revolutionary" means where there are landlords with military detachments supporting them.

6. Today, many are being persuaded to desert or betray, especially if they are generals. The creation of rank-and-file soviets would help to radically alter this pattern. Without ruthless reprisals against the militarists, the heads of outlaw bands, the innumerable "generals" and bandits, it will be impossible, in a China that has suffered years of civil war, to establish a stable democratic system. But stern measures of reprisal are unthinkable without the creation of a firm base of support for them among the lower ranks of society. Such a base can only be found in soviets of workers', soldiers', and poor people's deputies.

7. Needless to say, such soviets should and will become agencies in the struggle for power or actual organs of power on the local level.

8. All social layers and groups which in fact cooperate with and support the revolution in particular situations, at particular times, in particular localities, would elect their deputies to the soviets. This cooperation and support would be shown, on the one

hand, by the attitude of such layers toward the workers, their strikes, etc., and on the other, by their attitude toward the national army. The lines of political cooperation as well as of political demarcation would follow the course of the class struggle, and not the artificial organizational schemes of the Kuomintang (such as the formula of one-third for the communists and two-thirds for merchants and intellectuals, etc.).

9. I will not raise the question of the relations between the CCP and the Kuomintang here. But I do think that a system of soviets would also help to place this question in its proper framework in a very short time. A system of soviets in China would not be, at least not in the coming period, an instrument of proletarian dictatorship, but one of revolutionary national liberation and democratic unification of the country. The soviets in this period would not be under the dictatorship of one party but under the direction of a bloc of parties with inevitable internal struggle between them, inevitable shifts, etc. The Kuomintang's attempt, using the model of the Russian experience, to set up a one-party dictatorship, i.e., of the Kuomintang, with the Communist Party totally subordinated to it, is in essence *counterrevolutionary* and will inevitably produce fascist tendencies. The dictatorship of the proletariat in the Soviet Union, under conditions of capitalist encirclement, was possible only in the form of the dictatorship of the Communist Party. But in China, what is occurring is a national-democratic revolution, not a socialist one. A national democratic revolution is supposed to assure the proletariat *full freedom for the class struggle* and, consequently, full independence for the Communist Party as the leader of that struggle. The revolution cannot succeed without prolonged, close, and even more deepgoing collaboration between the proletariat and the plebeian masses of the towns and villages. This can be realized through the soviets in the form of blocs between parties, through the influence of worker delegates on nonparty deputies, etc.

L. Trotsky
Gagry

Published for the first time in any language. By permission of Harvard College Library. Translated for this volume by George Saunders.

CLASS RELATIONS
IN THE CHINESE REVOLUTION[17]

April 3, 1927

Issue 11 of the *Communist International* (March 18, 1927) printed as an editorial an article on the Fifth Congress of the Chinese CP and the Kuomintang which is in every way an exceptional mockery of the basic elements of Marxist theory and Bolshevik politics. This article cannot be characterized otherwise than as the worst expression of right Menshevism on questions of revolution.

As its starting point the article takes the proposition that "the problem of problems of the Chinese revolution at the present moment is the position of the Kuomintang, the further development of the Kuomintang as a party at the head of the South China state" (p. 4). Thus the problem of problems is not the awakening and the unification of millions of workers under the leadership of trade unions and the Communist Party, nor the drawing of poor peasants and artisans into the mainstream of the movement, nor the deepening of the struggle of the CP to win over the proletariat, nor the struggle of the proletariat for influence over the many-millioned masses of the disinherited—no, "the problem of problems"(!) is the position of the Kuomintang, i.e., a party organization which embraces, according to official figures, some 300,000 members—students, intellectuals, liberal merchants in general, and in part peasants and workers.

"For a political party," declares the article, "300,000 members is quite a considerable number." A paltry parliamentary appraisal! If these 300,000 had emanated from the experience of past class struggles, and the experience of leading proletarian strikes and peasant movements, then, naturally, even a smaller number of members could successfully assume the leadership of the revolution on its new and broader mass stage. But these 300,000 represent in their majority the result of individual recruitment among the tops. We have here the unification of national-liberals or Cadets with right SRs, with an admixture of young communists who are compelled in the period of their political training to submit to the discipline and even the ideology of a bourgeois-nationalist organization.

"The development of the Kuomintang," continues the article, "reveals alarming [!] symptoms from the standpoint of the interests of the Chinese revolution" (p. 4). And what is the nature of these "alarming" symptoms? Apparently it is this, that the power is in the hands of the Kuomintang center, and "the center has in the recent period gravitated in most instances definitely to the right." It should be noted that all political definitions in this article are of a formal, parliamentary, and ceremonial character, emptied of all class content. What is the meaning of this gravitation—to the right? What kind of Kuomintang "center" is this? It consists of the tops of the petty-bourgeois intelligentsia, middle-ranking functionaries, and so on. Like all petty bourgeois, this center is incapable of carrying out an independent policy, especially in the period when millions of workers and peasants have entered the arena. This petty-bourgeois center can produce an ally for the proletariat only on the condition that the proletariat carries out an independent policy. But there cannot even be talk of such a policy in China in the absence of an independent class party there.

Communists do not simply "join" the Kuomintang but they submit to its discipline and even obligate themselves not to criticize Sun Yat-senism. Under these conditions, the petty-bourgeois intellectual center can only trail behind the nationalist-liberal bourgeoisie, which is bound up by imperceptible gradations with the compradorian, i.e., overtly imperialist bourgeoisie; and, in proportion as the struggle of the masses sharpens, go over openly to its side. Thus the Kuomintang is a party apparatus adapted for the political subjection of the mass movement through the medium of a top intellectual center to an out-and-out right, i.e., manifestly bourgeois leadership, which under these conditions unfailingly subjects the Nationalist government to itself, and will continue to do so. The article cites the fact that "lefts" predominate in conferences, congresses, and the Executive Committee of the Kuomintang, but that this solacing circumstance is "not reflected in the composition and politics of the

Nationalist government." How astonishing! But, after all, the left petty bourgeoisie exists only to display its radicalism in articles, and at conferences and banquets, while handing the power over to the middle and big bourgeoisie.

Thus the "alarming" symptoms in the Kuomintang consist in this, that the Kuomintang does not personify the pure idea of a national liberation revolution, which the author of the article sucked out of his thumb, but rather reflects the class mechanics of the Chinese revolution. The author finds "alarming" the fact that the history of the Chinese people is unfolding in the form of a class struggle, proving thereby no exception to the history of all mankind. The article further informs us that the "Kuomintang and the Nationalist government are seriously concerned [a remarkable expression!] about the growth of the labor movement." What does this mean? It only means that the intellectual petty bourgeoisie has become scared by fear of the bourgeoisie before the awakening of the working masses. In proportion as the revolution extends and deepens its base, radicalizes its methods, sharpens its slogans, groups and layers of proprietors and intellectual burghers bound up with them will inevitably split from it at the top.

One part of the national government is joined with blood-ties to the bourgeoisie, and another part, fearful of breaking with it, becomes "concerned" about the growth of the labor movement, and seeks to harness the latter. By this delicate expression, "concerned," as previously by the words "alarming symptoms," the article refers to the sharpening of class relations, and to the attempts of the nationalist-liberal bourgeoisie, by using the Kuomintang as a tool and by issuing orders through it to the Nationalist government, to place a halter on the proletariat. When and where have we ever appraised class relations as is done by the lead article in the *Communist International?* Whence come these ideas? What is their source?

What methods are proposed in the article to overcome these "alarming symptoms"? On these questions the article polemicizes against the June (1926) plenum of the Central Committee of the Chinese CP, which adopted the position that it was necessary for the CP as an independent organization to conclude a bloc with the Kuomintang. The article rejects this idea. It also rejects the proposal to organize a left faction in the Kuomintang as an ally of the CP. No, the task—it teaches—consists in "assuring a firm left orientation to the whole Kuomintang." The question is solved easily. What is needed at the new stage of development, at a time when the workers are engaging in strikes against the capitalists, when the peasants are seeking, against the opposition of the Nationalist government, to drive out the landlords—what is needed at this new stage is to assure "a firm left orientation" to the Kuomintang, which represents the unification of a section of the bourgeoisie suffering from the strikes, a section of the landed intelligentsia suffering from the agrarian movement, the urban petty-bourgeois intellectuals who are fearful of "repelling" the bourgeoisie to the side of reaction, and finally the Communist Party which is bound hand and foot. It is this Kuomintang which must acquire "a firm left orientation."

Nobody knows what *class* line this "firm left orientation" must express. And how is it to be attained? Very simply: It is necessary "to saturate it [the Kuomintang] with revolutionary worker and peasant elements" (p. 6). Saturate the Kuomintang with workers and peasants? But the whole trouble is that workers and peasants, unacquainted with the pure idea of national revolution, are trying to utilize the revolution in order to "saturate" themselves a little before they saturate the Kuomintang with themselves. To this end they are engaging in strikes and agrarian uprisings. But these unpleasant manifestations of class mechanics hinder the Kuomintang from acquiring "a firm left orientation." To call a striking worker to join the Kuomintang is to run up against his objection: Why should I join a party that crushes strikes through the government appointed by it? The resourceful author of the article would probably reply to him: By joining a common party with the bourgeoisie, you will be able to push it to the left, you will eliminate "alarming symptoms" and dispel the clouds of its "concern." In answer to this, the Shanghai striker will say that workers can exert pressure on their government and even achieve a change in government not through individual pressure on the bourgeoisie within the framework of a common party, but through an independent class party. Incidentally, it may well be that the Shanghai striker, who has already given evidence of advanced maturity, would not even continue to discuss any further, but shrug his shoulders, and give up his interlocutor as hopeless.

The article goes on to quote one of the leading communists who stated at the December 1926 party conference that the Kuomintang was dead and decomposing and that the communists have no reason for hanging on to a stinking corpse. In this connection the article says: "This comrade obviously [!!] had in mind the fact that recently the Nationalist government and especially government organs in the provinces have come out on a number of occasions against the development of the revolutionary struggle of the working class and peasantry" (p. 7).

The penetration of the author of this article is truly astounding. When a Chinese communist says that the bourgeois-nationalist tops are dead so far as the revolution is concerned, he "obviously" has in mind the fact that the Nationalist government has been shooting strikers on a small scale. "Obviously"! Of course, "alarming symptoms" are in evidence, but "this danger may be averted, if we do not look upon the Kuomintang as a stinking corpse" (p. 7). The whole thing depends, it seems, on how one looks upon the Kuomintang. Classes and their parties depend on how we view them. The Kuomintang is not a corpse, it is only ailing. What of? Of a lack of blood of revolutionary workers and peasants. It is necessary for the Communist Party to "assist in the influx of this blood," etc. In short, what is needed is to perform the very-popular-of-late operation of blood transfusion, not on an individual but on a class scale. But, after all, the gist of the matter is that the bourgeoisie has begun to transfuse blood in its own way, by shooting, or helping to shoot, or winking its eyes at shootings of strikers and revolutionary peasants. In short, while fulfilling this splendid prescription we run up against one and the same difficulty, to wit, the class struggle.

The gist of the entire article is in its desire to have the Chinese revolution make a detour around the class struggle, by taking an economic, rational, and expedient road. In a word by using the method of the Mensheviks, and at that, in the periods of their greatest backsliding. And this article appears in the theoretical organ of the Communist International which was founded on an irreconcilable break with the Second International!

The article upbraids the Chinese communists for not participating in the Nationalist government and its local organs. They would be able there to push the government to the left from within, guard it against false actions toward the masses, etc., etc. The entire experience of the past, and above all the experience of the Russian revolution, has been scrapped. The authority of the leadership of the revolution is handed completely over to the Kuomintang, the responsibility for violence over the workers must be assumed by the communists. Bound hand and foot within the Kuomintang, the communists are powerless to offer the many-millioned masses an independent line in the field of foreign and domestic politics. But the workers are justified in charging the communists, especially if they participate in the Nationalist government, with complicity in all antiproletarian and antipeople's actions of the nationalist bourgeoisie. The entire experience of our revolution has been scrapped.

If the communists, despite the mass labor movement, despite the powerful growth of the trade unions and the revolutionary agrarian movement in the villages, are obliged as hitherto to constitute a subordinate section of a bourgeois party, and enter as an impotent appendage into a national government formed by this bourgeois party, then it must be flatly stated that the time has not yet come for the formation of the Communist Party of China. For it is far better not to build a Communist Party at all than to compromise it in the epoch of revolution, i.e., precisely at the time when the ties between the party and the working masses are sealed with blood, and when great traditions are created which exert their influence for decades.

Developing a scintillating program in the spirit of right Menshevism in its period of decline, the article refurbishes it in the modest modern spirit by consoling China with the fact that she possesses objective preconditions for "skipping over the capitalist stage of development." Not a word is said in this connection to the effect that the anticapitalist perspective of China's development is unconditionally and directly dependent upon the general course of the world proletarian revolution. Only the proletariat of the most advanced capitalist countries—with the organized assistance of the Chinese proletariat—will be able to take in tow the 400 million atomized, pauperized, backward peasant economy, and through a series of intermediate stages lead it to socialism, on the basis of a worldwide exchange of commodities, and direct technical and organizational assistance from the outside. To believe that without the victory of the proletariat in the most advanced capitalist countries, and prior to this victory, China is capable with her own forces of "skipping over the capitalist stage of development" is to trample underfoot the ABCs of Marxism. This does not concern our author. He simply promises China a noncapitalist path—obviously in recompense for injuries she has borne, and also for the dependent character of the proletarian movement, and especially the degraded, disfranchised position of the Chinese CP.

How can and must the question of the capitalist and socialist paths of China's development be posed in reality?

Above all it must be made clear to the vanguard of the Chinese proletariat that China has no prerequisites whatever economically for an *independent* transition to socialism; that the revolution now unfolding under the leadership of the Kuomintang is a bourgeois-national revolution, that it can have as its consequence, even in the event of complete victory, only the further development of productive forces on the basis of capitalism. But it is necessary to develop no less forcefully before the Chinese proletariat the converse side of the question as well: The belated bourgeois-national revolution is unfolding in China in conditions of the imperialist decay of capitalism. As Russian experience has already shown—in contrast, say, to the English—politics does not at all develop in parity with economics. China's further development must be taken in an international perspective. Despite the backwardness of the Chinese economy, and in part precisely due to this backwardness, the Chinese revolution is wholly capable of bringing to political power an alliance of workers and peasants, under the leadership of the proletariat. This regime will be China's political link with the world revolution.

In the course of the transitional period, the Chinese revolution will have a genuinely democratic, worker-and-peasant character. In its economic life, commodity-capitalist relations will inevitably predominate. The political regime will be primarily directed to secure the masses as great a share as possible in the fruits of the development of the productive forces and, at the same time, in the political and cultural utilization of the resources of the state. The further development of this perspective—the possibility of the democratic revolution growing over into the socialist revolution— depends completely and exclusively on the course of the world revolution, and on the economic and political successes of the Soviet Union, as an integral part of this world revolution. If the Chinese revolution were to triumph under its present bourgeois-nationalist leadership, it would very quickly go to the right, demonstrate its good intentions to the capitalist countries, soon gain recognition on their part, offer them concessions on new bases, obtain loans, in a word, enter into the system of capitalist states as a less degraded, less colonial, but still profoundly dependent entity. Furthermore, the Chinese republic would hold in relation to the Soviet Union *in the best variant* the same position as the present Turkish republic.

A *different* path of development can be opened up only if the proletariat plays the leading role in the national democratic revolution. But the first and most elementary precondition for this is the complete independence of the Communist Party, and an open struggle waged by it, with banners unfurled, for the leadership of the working class and the hegemony in the revolution. Failing this, all talk of noncapitalist paths of development serves only to cover up right Menshevist politics by left SR phraseology of the [Russian] prerevolutionary period—the most revolting of all conceivable combinations. A program of assisting in the "influx of workers' and peasants' blood into the Kuomintang" (what an infamous phraseology!) gives nothing and means nothing. There also happen to be different kinds of workers' and peasants' blood. The blood which is being shed by workers of China is not blood shed for class-conscious tasks. Workers who enter the Kuomintang will become followers of the Kuomintang, i.e., the proletarian raw material will be recast in the petty-bourgeois Sun Yat-senist mold. To prevent this from taking place, the workers must receive their education in a Communist Party. And for this, the Communist Party must be completely free from *any outward* restrictions to leading the workers in their struggle and opposing Leninism to Sun Yat-senism.

However, it may be the author of the article envisions, in the ancient and truly Martynovist style, the following perspective: First, the national bourgeoisie completes the national-bourgeois revolution through the medium of the Kuomintang which is, with the assistance of Chinese Mensheviks, infused with workers' and peasants' blood. And following this so-to-speak Menshevik stage of the national revolution will come the turn of the Bolshevik stage: The Communist Party withdraws from the Kuomintang, the proletariat breaks with the bourgeoisie, wins the peasantry away from it and leads the country to a "democratic dictatorship of workers and peasants." It is very likely that the author is guided by a conception which is a result of his failure to digest the two stratifications in the 1905 period—the Menshevik and the Bolshevik. But such a perspective must be declared pedantic nonsense.

It is impossible to achieve the national democratic revolution twice: first in the bourgeois and then in the proletarian spirit. To be sure, if we were to hinder the proletarian vanguard from breaking with the bourgeoisie in time and utilizing the revolutionary situation to prove to the masses in the nonrecurring events of the supreme struggle its energetic and unwavering loyalty to the cause of the toilers; if we were to accomplish this end by further enslaving the CP to the Kuomintang, then the time would sooner or later come when the proletarian vanguard would break belatedly with the bourgeoisie, in all likelihood not under the banner of communism, and would perhaps renounce politics altogether. The past of the European labor movement would provide the revolutionary proletarians of China with a corresponding ideology in the shape of syndicalism, anarchism, etc. Under these conditions, the Chinese nationalist-democratic state would very easily arrive at methods of fascism or semifascism.

We have observed this in the case of Poland. Was it so very long ago that Pilsudski was one of the leaders of the petty-bourgeois revolutionary organization, the Polish Socialist Party? Was it so very long ago that he sat in the Peter and Paul Fortress? His entire past gave him influence and authority among petty-bourgeois circles and in the army; and he used this authority for a fascist coup directed wholly against the proletariat. Will anyone wish to deny that in the staff of the Kuomintang its own Pilsudskis will be found? They will. Candidates can already be designated. If the Polish Pilsudski required three decades to complete his evolution, then the Chinese Pilsudski will require an interval far more brief to accomplish his transition from the national revolution to national fascism. We are living in the imperialist epoch when the tempo of development is extremely accelerated, when convulsions follow upon convulsions, and each country learns from the experience of another. To pursue the policy of a dependent Communist Party supplying workers to the Kuomintang is to prepare the conditions for the most successful and triumphant establishment of a fascist dictatorship in China at that not very distant moment when the proletariat, despite everything, will be forced to recoil from the Kuomintang.

Menshevism, even in the period of its revolutionary "flowering," sought to be not the class party of the proletariat which rises to all-national and then world tasks (Bolshevism) but a supervisor of national development, in which capacity the party of the proletariat was assigned in advance a subordinate place (to collaborate, to push, to effect blood transfusion, and so on). But aspiring to such pseudo-Marxist supervision of history has always proved in action to be pedantic idiocy. The Mensheviks completely revealed this as far back as 1905; Kautsky did likewise somewhat later but no less decisively.

A national revolution in the sense of a struggle against national dependency is achieved through the mechanics of classes. Chinese militarists represent a class organization. The compradorian bourgeoisie represents the most "mature" detachment of the Chinese bourgeoisie which does not want a Chinese February lest it arrive at a Chinese October or even a semi-October. The section of the Chinese bourgeoisie which still participates in the Kuomintang, constituting there an internal brake and an auxiliary detachment of the compradorian bourgeoisie and of the foreign imperialists, will on the morrow seek to lean upon the bombardment of Nanking in order to exert pressure on the revolutionary rank and file and above all to put a harness on the proletariat.[18] They will succeed in doing so unless the proletariat is able to counteract them from day to day by a well-directed class resistance. This is impossible so long as the Communist Party remains subordinate to the Kuomintang, which is headed by the auxiliary detachment of the compradorian bourgeoisie and foreign imperialists. It is indeed embarrassing to have to explain this in the year 1927 and doubly embarrassing to have to direct these ideas against the lead article in the organ of the Comintern!

As the Chinese revolution extends geographically it at the same time deepens socially. Shanghai and Hankow—the two most important industrial centers which together embrace about three-quarters of a million workers—are in the hands of the Nationalist government.[19] Nanking was subjected to a bombardment by the imperialists. The struggle immediately passed into a higher stage. Having captured Hankow and Shanghai, the revolution has thereby drawn into itself the most developed class contradictions in China. It will no longer be possible to orient the policies on the handicraft–petty-trade peasant of the South. It is necessary to orient either on the proletariat or the bourgeoisie.

The proletariat must orient itself on the many-millioned rank and file in the struggle against the bourgeoisie. We have this on the one hand. And on the other—the imperialists show by their Nanking butchery that they are in no jesting mood. Are they hoping in this way to terrorize Chinese workers or to bring the agrarian movement to a halt? Hardly. In any case, this is not their immediate aim. They desire above all to compel the bourgeois tops of the nationalist movement to understand that the time has come for them to break with the rank and file if they do not wish to have the guns of world imperialism trained upon them. The bombardment of Nanking is propaganda for the ideas of compradorism, i.e., the salutary nature of ties with world capitalism which is mighty, united, and armed, which can provide not only profits but also armed aid against one's own workers and peasants.

It is frivolous to assert that the bombardment of Nanking will fuse the whole Chinese nation as one man, etc. Such declamation suits middle-class democrats. The revolution has risen to a new level and a more profound differentiation within the nationalist camp. Its splitting into a revolutionary and a reformist-compradorian wing flows with iron necessity from the situation as a whole. The British guns, after the initial wave of "universal" indignation, will only speed this process. Hereafter, to drive workers and peasants into the political camp of the bourgeoisie and to keep the Communist Party as a hostage within the ranks of the Kuomintang is objectively tantamount to conducting a policy of betrayal.

Should the representatives of the CP participate in the Nationalist government? Into a government that would correspond to the new phase of the revolution, into a revolutionary workers' and peasants' government, they must unquestionably enter. Into the present Nationalist government, under no conditions. But before raising the question of communist representation in a revolutionary power, it is necessary to consider the question of the Communist Party itself. After the capture of Shanghai by the revolution, former political relations have already become absolutely intolerable. It is necessary to approve as unconditionally correct the resolution of the June plenum of the CC of the Chinese CP, which demands that the party withdraw from the Kuomintang and conclude a bloc with that organization through its left wing.

To deny the need of organizing a left faction within the Kuomintang and to recommend instead that the Kuomintang as a whole be made to acquire a left orientation, as is done by the leading article in the *Communist International,* is merely to occupy oneself with babbling. How can a political organization be given a left orientation if not by gathering within it the partisans of this orientation and setting them up against their opponents? The Kuomintang will, of course, object to this. It is quite possible that they will begin citing the resolution of our

Tenth Party Congress against factions. We have already witnessed a masquerade of this kind on the question of the dictatorship of a single party. The arch-right-wingers in the Kuomintang insist upon its unconditional necessity, citing the AUCP as an example in point. Similarly they will insist that a single party effecting the revolutionary dictatorship cannot tolerate factions in its midst. But this only signifies that the right wing of the nationalist camp, which assumed power through the Kuomintang, seeks in this way to prohibit the independent party of the working class and to deprive the radical elements of the petty bourgeoisie of any possibility of obtaining within the party a real influence on its leadership. The author of the article which we analyzed above goes all the way in all these questions to meet the bourgeois wing of the Kuomintang.

We must clearly understand that the Chinese bourgeoisie is still trying to cover itself with the authority of the Russian revolution and that, in particular, it is plagiarizing from the forms of the future dictatorship of the Chinese proletariat in order to strengthen its own dictatorship against the proletariat. That is why it is of utmost importance today not to permit any muddling in the determination of the stage through which the Chinese revolution is passing. It is a question not of the socialist but of a bourgeois-democratic revolution. And within the latter, it is a question of the struggle between two methods: bourgeois-conciliationist as against worker-peasant. It is possible today only to speculate as to the manner and conditions in which the national democratic revolution can rise to the socialist revolution, whether it will occur with or without an interruption and whether this interruption will be long or brief. The further march of events will bring the necessary clarification. But to smear over the question of the bourgeois character of the present revolution with general considerations of a noncapitalist development is to befuddle the Communist Party and to disarm the proletariat. Let us hope we shall not live to see the International Central Control Commission calling the Chinese communists to account for an attempt to build a left faction in the Kuomintang.

From the standpoint of the class interests of the proletariat—and we take them as our criterion—the task of the bourgeois revolution is to secure the maximum of freedom for the workers in their struggle against the bourgeoisie. From this standpoint the philosophy of the leaders of the Kuomintang in regard to a single centralized party that permits neither any other parties nor any factions within itself is a philosophy hostile to the proletariat, a counterrevolutionary philosophy which lays down the ideological foundations for Chinese fascism in the future. It is absurd to say that the withdrawal of the Chinese CP from the Kuomintang signifies a break of collaboration. It is the termination not of collaboration but of servitude. Political collaboration presupposes equality between the sides and an agreement between them. Such is not the case in China. The proletariat does not enter into an agreement with the petty bourgeoisie but rather submits to its leadership under a veiled form, with an organizational seal set upon this submission. In its present form the Kuomintang is the embodiment of an "unequal treaty" between the bourgeoisie and the proletariat. If the Chinese revolution as a whole demands the abrogation of unequal treaties with the imperialist powers, then the Chinese proletariat must liquidate the unequal treaty with its own bourgeoisie.

It is necessary to summon the Chinese workers to the creation of soviets. The proletariat of Hong Kong during the general strike created an organization very close in structure and functions to the elementary type of workers' soviets. With this experience as a basis, it is necessary to go further. The Shanghai proletariat already possesses the priceless experience of struggle and is fully capable of creating soviets of workers' deputies which will set an example for all China and thereby become the center of attraction for all genuinely revolutionary organizations.

From *New International* (New York), March and April 1938.

ON THE SLOGAN OF SOVIETS IN CHINA

April 16, 1927

Dear Comrades,

Yesterday, during the discussion on the Chinese question, one of Comrade Stalin's main retorts to Comrade Zinoviev's criticisms and mine of the basic errors in our policy on the problems of the Chinese revolution was to repeat the words: "Why didn't Zinoviev say . . . ?" "Why didn't Trotsky write . . . ?" I will not undertake here to go back to what we have said and written on this question. Undoubtedly, if our suggestions and advice had been treated with less prejudice and hostility and given more serious consideration at the time we could have avoided the most important errors.

I will not dwell on the fact that of late fundamental questions are being resolved in closed sessions of the Politburo to which members of the Central Committee are not admitted. The object of this letter is not to recall what has happened in the past, but to pose the basic problem of the present and future: *the question of soviets in China.* Comrade Stalin has now opposed the call for the Chinese workers and oppressed masses in general to set up soviets. However, this question has *decisive importance* for the further development of the Chinese revolution. Without soviets the entire Chinese revolution is going to serve the upper stratum of the Chinese bourgeoisie and through it the imperialists.

The plenum did not address itself to this fundamental question. However, the question is becoming extremely acute. It cannot be postponed any longer because the entire fate of the Chinese revolution is bound up with the question of the formation of soviets. That is why I am raising this question here.

This is Comrade Stalin's reasoning: "Soviets are the essential

149

organs of the struggle for power; to call for soviets means in fact to usher in the proletarian dictatorship, the Chinese October." But why did we have soviets in 1905? "We were struggling against tsarism," answers Stalin. "There is no struggle against tsarism in China. Since we are not heading directly for an October, we should not call for the formation of soviets."

This entire logic represents such a flagrant distortion of the meaning of our entire revolutionary experience, illuminated theoretically by Lenin, that I could never have believed a serious and responsible revolutionary would say such things if I had not heard them with my own ears.

Let us try to briefly analyze the problem.

1. Against the tsar it was permissible to form soviets while not yet conducting a struggle for the proletarian dictatorship. Why, then, is it impermissible, by means of soviets, to wage a struggle against the bloc of Chinese militarists, compradors, landlords, and foreign imperialists without posing as the immediate task the establishment of a proletarian dictatorship? Why?

If one thinks, as Stalin did (and still does?), that the unification of China must be achieved by the bourgeois Kuomintang leadership which, through the Kuomintang, has made the Communist Party subordinate to itself, deprived the CP of its elementary independence (even its press!), and ruled captured territories by means of a reactionary bureaucracy—if this represents the national revolution, then, of course, there can be no place for soviets. If one recognizes, however, that the bourgeois Kuomintang leadership, not just the right wing but the left centrists, too, are incapable of carrying the democratic nationalist revolution to its conclusion or even halfway, and that it will without fail reach an agreement with the imperialists—if this is understood, then it was necessary in good time and now it is even more necessary to prepare *to replace* that leadership. A *replacement* does not mean the pure and simple replacement of Chiang Kai-shek with Wang Ching-wei: that would turn out to be the same old brew, with some more slops added. The problem will not be solved by changing the faces. A change means preparing a revolutionary government that relies not on the verbal, but on the real and practical support of the workers, petty bourgeoisie, peasants, and the masses of soldiers in the army. This can be achieved only by providing the masses with the kind of organization that meets the needs of the revolutionary conditions and of the awakening masses with their yearning for independence, a change in their living conditions, etc. This organization is the soviet.

2. Stalin imagines that first the bourgeoisie, with the support of the masses who are not organized for revolution (organized, they would not have begun to support it), must carry to completion the struggle against imperialism, and then we will begin preparations for soviets. This idea is false to the core! The whole question is *how* the struggle against imperialism and Chinese reaction will be waged and *who* will play the leading role in this struggle. It is possible to proceed toward the democratic worker-peasant dictatorship *only* on the basis of the unfolding struggle against imperialism which will be long and drawn out; *only* on the basis of a struggle against the national-liberal bourgeoisie for influence over the workers and peasants; *only* on the basis of a mass organization of workers and peasants not just against imperialism but also against the Chinese bourgeoisie. The only form this organization can take is soviets.

3. "Soviets must not be organized in the army's rear," says Stalin. This is the generals' point of view but not ours. The generals also think that trade unions should not be organized in the army's rear. We know, however, that both soviets and trade unions in the rear are an excellent aid to the revolutionary army. "But, don't you see, soviets are organs for insurrection," replies Stalin. "That means you intend to organize an insurrection at the army's rear and seize power." This is a false and caricatured formulation of the problem! It is true that soviets are organs of the struggle for power. But they are not at all born as such; they *develop* in this direction. But only through the experience of struggle can they mature for the role of organs for the dictatorship (in this case, the democratic dictatorship). If we seriously intend to strive for a democratic workers' and peasants' dictatorship, the soviets will have to have the necessary time to develop and intervene in the unfolding events—those involving the military included—so that they, the soviets, can become firmly established, gain experience, and subsequently make a bid for power.

"But, you see, the [KMT] center will not permit soviets." We have nothing in common with this point of view. What the center permits or does not permit will depend on the relationship of forces. This relationship must be shifted to the advantage of the proletariat. While the awakened but unorganized masses follow the lead of the political organization of the Kuomintang upper echelon, they necessarily give the big bourgeoisie and the generals a powerful advantage over the proletariat. To argue that China has not yet reached its October and for *this* reason to keep the masses in a state of disarray actually means to weaken the proletariat by our own efforts while strengthening the bourgeoisie and its center, and then to plead that this center will not permit soviets at the army's rear.

4. But why can't the workers simply join the Kuomintang? Really, isn't it an adequate organization? To pose the question thus, one has to forget completely everything we have done and learned. The Kuomintang is a party organization tightly controlled by the topmost layer, despite the popularity of its banner. Is it really conceivable that hundreds of thousands, even millions of workers and peasants will join a party organization during the revolution? Where and when has this happened? In fact, the importance of a soviet is that there, on the spot, it draws in those sections of the masses who have in no way become mature enough for the party and will not be for a number of years. To declare that the Kuomintang is a *substitute* for soviets is to engage in intolerable sophistry. The Kuomintang has 300,000 members. At present these 300,000 (if the number is not exaggerated) are dispersed. Only now is there talk about the need for Kuomintang elections, i.e., elections to fill the leadership organs by polling party members; but it goes without saying that there is no talk of the election of Kuomintang members by the millions of the masses. The fact is that to have to resort to such sophisms as equating the Kuomintang with soviets shows that soviets are knocking at the door and that they cannot be driven off by doctrinaire schemas about whether it is October or not October.

5. But wouldn't the formation of soviets lead to "a premature insurrection"? Premature insurrections erupt more easily and frequently in cases where the masses lack an authoritative organization that embodies their revolutionary will. That is to say, the absence of soviets in the major revolutionary centers will lead to chaotic, premature, and pointless outbreaks as a result of the unorganized state of the class struggle and the absence of correct political leadership. This has always been the case. Every revolutionary experience testifies to it.

6. What will soviets do? The first and most urgent thing they will do is provide an organization for the workers and help them in organizing their fraternization with the soldiers. The first order of business for the soviet of workers' deputies of a given

industrial city or region should be to draw into its ranks soldiers' deputies, representatives from the garrisons. This is the surest way—or, to be precise, the only way—to effect a serious guarantee against Bonapartist[20] and fascist attempts by the Kuomintang higher-ups and any other riffraff. Failure to organize soviets of workers' and soldiers' deputies will mean turning the soldier into cannon fodder for Chiang Kai-shek and setting the stage for a bloody massacre of the workers like the one that occurred in Shanghai.

7. In the cities, this must obviously not be restricted to workers only. It is necessary that the petty artisans, small shopkeepers, and the city's oppressed lower strata in general be drawn into the soviets. This will facilitate the workers' revolutionary envelopment of the army. If this is not done, however, the fate of Shanghai, and with it the revolution, will depend on some vile Bonapartist.

8. This should by no means be limited to the cities. The network of soviets should be extended as soon as possible from the major industrial centers to the countryside, relying on the existing peasant unions, broadening their framework, expanding their program, and linking them up with the workers and soldiers.

9. What will the soviets do? They will struggle against the local reactionary bureaucracies, learning and teaching the masses to understand the connection between the local authorities and those who rule the country. They will struggle against those same bureaucracies, against the militarist gangs, against the landlords, etc., in the rural areas. They thus become organs of the agrarian revolution that cannot be postponed until China is unified ("until there is a constituent assembly").

10. Commissars are powerless figures under the reactionary generals, often outright lackeys who are appointed by these very generals. The only way a commissar can have any weight in the present epoch is by relying on strong local mass organs, and not simply on a political party—especially one like the Kuomintang, which has no serious organizational structure or one like the Communist Party, which is bound hand and foot and deprived of even an independent newspaper. The formation of workers', peasants', and soldiers' soviets prepares the ground for a really revolutionary democratization of the National Revolutionary Army which otherwise will inevitably become the tool of a homegrown Chinese Bonapartism.

11. Through the soviets a real and genuine—not doctrinaire

and artificial—regroupment of forces will take place. All of the classes, layers, and strata that are involved in or that will become involved in the real, present struggle against native and foreign reactionaries will enter the soviets. The goading by the various Kuomintang "leaders," the conniving, the counterposing of one person to another, and combinations of these things—all of this backstage chicanery, inadequacy, and impotence, now fully exposed, will be replaced by the other, far more serious, real *revolutionary class selection*. The alignment of forces will proceed as follows: for or against the soviets, i.e., for preparing the transition of the revolution to a higher stage, or for a deal between the Chinese bourgeoisie and imperialism. If the question is not posed this way, all prospects for a democratic worker-peasant dictatorship, etc.—not to mention *noncapitalist* paths of development—will remain merely talk to console us while the masses of Chinese people remain the cannon fodder of a revolution led by corrupt nationalist liberals.

12. Whoever opposes the formation of soviets must say: All power to the Kuomintang. But the Kuomintang tells the communists, "place yourself under my command," prohibits them from criticizing Sun Yat-senism, and does not even let them have a newspaper, pointing out that in Russia, too, there is a one-party dictatorship. But, in Russia the one-party dictatorship is the expression of the proletarian dictatorship and the socialist revolution, whereas the Kuomintang is a bourgeois party in a bourgeois revolution. Without soviets a dictatorship in the existing concrete situation means disarming the workers, gagging the communists, a state of disorganization among the masses, and Chiang Kai-shek-type coups.

13. Does this mean war with the Kuomintang? Nonsense! Nonsense! Nonsense! The problem here is organizing collaboration with the Kuomintang on a far broader and deeper basis—on the basis of millions of workers, soldiers, peasants, and other deputies' soviets. Of course, this collaboration presupposes the full and unconditional freedom for the Communist Party to criticize the Kuomintang, and this freedom to criticize presupposes the freedom of the communist press and communist organization.

14. Unless there is a total political split in the Kuomintang, unless it is purged of all Chiang Kai-shekist elements in general, there can be no joint revolutionary work with it. The differentiation, cleansing, and tempering within the Kuomintang will

proceed more easily and most assuredly on the question of soviets than on any other. We will work hand in hand with the section of the old Kuomintang that will support the soviets and participate in them, i.e., that will get into *real* contact with the *real* masses. Of course, while working hand in hand with a *revolutionary* Kuomintang, we will keep a very vigilant eye on this ally and openly criticize its indecisiveness, retreats, and errors, not to mention possible treachery. In this way, on the basis of the closest collaboration with the Kuomintang, we will strive to further broaden the Communist Party's influence on the soviets and through the soviets.

15. But wouldn't soviets mean *dual power* for an indefinite period?[21] On one side would be the national-revolutionary government (if, when thoroughly reorganized, it holds its own and experiences an upturn), and on the other side, the soviets. Yes, this means dual power or elements of dual power. "But we were against dual power." We were against a dual-power regime insofar as we were striving to seize power ourselves as the proletarian party. We were for dual power, i.e., a system of soviets, while there was a Provisional Government insofar as soviets restricted any bourgeois pretensions to dictatorship. Dual power during the February revolution was progressive insofar as it contained new revolutionary possibilities. But this progressiveness was only temporary. The way out of the contradiction was the proletarian dictatorship. Dual power lasted only eight months in our case. In China this transitional regime under certain conditions could last considerably longer, and vary in different parts of the country. To call for and begin organizing soviets means in fact to begin introducing in China elements of dual power. This is both necessary and healthy. This alone will open up further prospects of a revolutionary democratic dictatorship of the proletariat and peasantry. Without this, all talk about this dictatorship is simply chatter which the Chinese popular masses know nothing about.

16. I will not examine here the very important question of future possibilities and paths for the development of the future worker-peasant dictatorship into the proletarian dictatorship and an immediate socialist revolution since it is *not now* on the agenda. That there is such a perspective and that it has every chance of becoming a reality—given a favorable tempo of development of the proletarian revolution in the West—is, for every Marxist, indisputable. This can and should be discussed.

But this perspective need not turn into a philosophic compensation for the present situation when the armed bourgeois traitors have the upper hand. The basic and vital task now is to prepare for the *next stage,* the only one from which subsequent prospects and possibilities can emerge.

17. That the Chinese revolution at this stage is national-democratic, i.e., bourgeois, is elementary to us all. Our politics, however, do not flow simply from the revolution having a bourgeois label but from the actual development of class relations within this revolution. Comrade Martynov proceeds very clearly and explicitly from the old Menshevik conception that since the revolution is bourgeois but anti-imperialist, the section of the Chinese bourgeoisie whose interest is to overthrow imperialism cannot step aside from this revolution. Chiang Kai-shek answered Martynov on this score by making a deal with the imperialists and crushing the Shanghai proletariat. This is precisely where Comrade Stalin goes astray, since his general definition of the revolution as nonproletarian and bourgeois leads to the conclusion that, therefore, soviets are not necessary. He wants to replace the actual course of the class struggle with a timetable for the classes. But this timetable is derived from formalistically defining the revolution as bourgeois. This totally incorrect position contradicts everything Lenin taught.

L. Trotsky

Published in English for the first time. By permission of Harvard College Library. Translated for this volume by Ivan Licho.

THE FRIENDLY EXCHANGE OF PORTRAITS BETWEEN STALIN AND CHIANG KAI-SHEK[22]

April 18, 1927

To the Eastern Secretariat of the ECCI:

Returned from leave of absence, I found the photograph of Chiang Kai-shek sent me through the Eastern Department of the ECCI and the request promptly to send him my autographed picture. Had I received such a request through the Foreign Office, then, regardless of my attitude toward this request, I would find the fact itself explainable. But it is absolutely incomprehensible to me why the Eastern Department of the ECCI—the international organization of the communist vanguard of the proletariat—occupies itself with such a thoroughly compromising matter as the spreading of portraits of Chiang Kai-shek. And this, moreover, as a result of a malicious irony of fate, on the eve of the coup d'etat carried out by him. I do not doubt that this job, unseemly for the ECCI, was done by some employee of the Eastern Department not empowered to do it, without the knowledge of the leading persons and especially of the Presidium of the ECCI, as a consequence of which I deem it necessary to bring this distasteful affair to your attention. The picture of Chiang Kai-shek I am herewith returning.

With communist greetings,
L. Trotsky

Copy: To the Presidium of the ECCI and the Political Bureau of the Central Committee

From the *Militant* (New York), September 17, 1932.

THE CHINESE REVOLUTION AND
THE THESES OF COMRADE STALIN[23]

May 7, 1927

The theses of Comrade Stalin, entitled "Questions of the Chinese Revolution," were published in *Pravda* on April 21, 1927, a few days after the close of the plenary session of the Central Committee* to which these theses were never presented and at which they were never discussed (although all the members of the plenum were still in Moscow).

Moreover, the theses of Comrade Stalin are erroneous to such a point, they turn the matter upside down to such a degree, they are so permeated with the spirit of tailendism, they are so inclined to perpetuate the mistakes already made, that to remain silent about them would be a positive crime.

The Lessons of the Chinese Events Must Be Drawn

1. The prohibition of an open discussion of the theoretical and tactical problems of the Chinese revolution has been motivated of late by the fact that such a discussion would delight the enemies of the USSR. Naturally it would be quite impermissible to make public facts that could be seized upon by enemies, who,

---

* The theses of Comrade Stalin are published in the name of the Central Committee. This does not change the fact that the theses were not examined by the plenum of the Central Committee. The Political Bureau charged three of its members, Comrades Stalin, Bukharin, and Molotov, to look over the theses of Comrade Stalin and in case of agreement, to publish them in the name of the Central Committee. Naturally, it is not a question of the formal side of the matter, which nobody raises. But it is quite clear that such a "simplified" method of deciding questions of world importance, after the mistakes made and the heavy defeats, in no way serves the interests of the party and of the Chinese revolution.

incidentally, do not shrink from the direct invention of "facts" and "documents." But there is no need at all for such a discussion. It is only a question of determining the driving forces of the Chinese revolution and of estimating the basic line of its political direction. In other words, it is a question of discussing *the same questions to which the theses of Comrade Stalin are devoted.* If these theses can be published, then why cannot a criticism of them be published?

It is an unheard-of mistake to contend that a discussion of the problems of the Chinese revolution can injure our state interests. If this were so, then not only the Communist Party of the Soviet Union but every other party of the Communist International, including the Chinese, would have to abstain from any discussion. But the interests of the Chinese revolution, as well as the interests of the education of all the Communist parties in the world, demand an open, energetic, exhaustive discussion of all the problems of the Chinese revolution, especially those in dispute. It is not true that the interests of the Communist International conflict with the state interests of the USSR. The renunciation of discussion of the mistakes is not dictated by the interests of a workers' state, but by a false "apparatuslike," bureaucratic attitude toward the Chinese revolution as well as toward the interests of the USSR.

2. The April defeat of the Chinese revolution is not only a defeat for the opportunist line but also a defeat for the bureaucratic methods of the leadership, through which the party is confronted with every decision as an accomplished fact: the decision, it is explained, does not justify criticism until facts demonstrate its annulment, whereupon it is just as automatically, that is, behind the back of the party, replaced by a decision which is frequently more erroneous, like the present theses of Stalin. Such a method, which, in and by itself, is incompatible with the development of a revolutionary party, becomes an especially heavy obstacle to young parties that can and should learn independently from the experiences of defeats and mistakes.

The theses of Comrade Stalin are published. At least within the limits of these theses, the questions of the Chinese revolution can and must be discussed openly and from every angle.

The Yoke of Imperialism and the Class Struggle

3. The peculiarity of the Chinese revolution—in comparison, for example, with our revolution of 1905—lies above all in the

semicolonial position of China. A policy that disregarded the powerful pressure of imperialism on the internal life of China would be radically false. But a policy that proceeded from an abstract conception of national oppression without its class refraction and reflection would be no less false. The main source of the mistakes in the theses of Comrade Stalin, as in the whole leading line in general, is the false conception of the role of imperialism and its influence on the class relationships of China.

The imperialist yoke is supposed to serve as a justification for the policy of the "bloc of four classes." The yoke of imperialism leads allegedly to the fact that "all" (!) the classes of China look upon the Canton government as the "national government of the whole of China in the same way" (!) (speech of Comrade Kalinin, *Izvestia,* March 6, 1927). This is essentially the position of the right Kuomintang man Tai Chi-t'ao, who pretends that the laws of the class struggle do not exist for China—because of imperialist pressure.

China is an oppressed semicolonial country. The development of the productive forces of China, which is proceeding in capitalist forms, demands the shaking off of the imperialist yoke. The war of China for its national independence is a progressive war, because it flows from the necessities of the economic and cultural development of China itself, as well as because it facilitates the development of the revolution of the British proletariat and that of the whole world proletariat.

But this by no means signifies that the imperialist yoke is a mechanical one, subjugating "all" the classes of China in the "same" way. The powerful role of foreign capital in the life of China has caused very strong sections of the Chinese bourgeoisie, the bureaucracy, and the military to join their destiny with that of imperialism. Without this tie, the enormous role of the so-called militarists in the life of modern China would be inconceivable.

It would further be profound naiveté to believe that an abyss lies between the so-called comprador bourgeoisie, that is, the economic and political agency of foreign capital in China, and the so-called national bourgeoisie. No, these two sections stand incomparably closer to each other than the bourgeoisie and the masses of workers and peasants. The bourgeoisie participated in the national war as an internal brake, looking upon the worker and peasant masses with growing hostility and becoming ever readier to conclude a compromise with imperialism.

Installed within the Kuomintang and its leadership, the

national bourgeoisie has been essentially an instrument of the compradors and imperialism. It can remain in the camp of the national war only because of the weakness of the worker and peasant masses, the lack of development of the class struggle, the lack of independence of the Chinese Communist Party, and the docility of the Kuomintang in the hands of the bourgeoisie.

It is a gross mistake to think that imperialism mechanically welds together all the classes of China from without. That is the position of the Chinese Cadet, Tai Chi-t'ao, but in no wise ours. The revolutionary struggle against imperialism does not weaken, but rather strengthens the political differentiation of the classes. Imperialism is a highly powerful force in the internal relationships of China. The main source of this force is not the warships in the waters of the Yangtze Kiang—they are only auxiliaries—but the economic and political bond between foreign capital and the native bourgeoisie. The struggle against imperialism, precisely because of its economic and military power, demands a powerful exertion of forces from the very depths of the Chinese people. Really to arouse the workers and peasants against imperialism is possible only by connecting their basic and most profound life interests with the cause of the country's liberation.

A workers' strike—small or large—an agrarian rebellion, an uprising of the oppressed sections in city and country against the usurer, against the bureaucracy, against the local military satraps, all that arouses the multitudes, that welds them together, that educates, steels, is a real step forward on the road to the revolutionary and social liberation of the Chinese people. Without that, the military successes and failures of the right, semiright or semileft generals will remain foam on the surface of the ocean. But everything that brings the oppressed and exploited masses of the toilers to their feet inevitably pushes the national bourgeoisie into an open bloc with the imperialists. The class struggle between the bourgeoisie and the masses of workers and peasants is not weakened, but, on the contrary, it is sharpened by imperialist oppression, to the point of bloody civil war at every serious conflict. The Chinese bourgeoisie always has a solid rearguard behind it in imperialism, which will always help it with money, goods, and shells against the workers and peasants.

Only woeful philistines and sycophants, who hope in their hearts to obtain freedom for China as an imperialist bounty for the good behavior of the masses, can believe that the national liberation of China can be achieved by moderating the class struggle, by curbing strikes and agrarian uprisings, by abandoning the arming of the masses, etc. When Comrade Martynov proposes that strikes and the struggle in the countryside be replaced by a solution of the questions through the medium of governmental arbitration, then he differs in no way from Tai Chi-t'ao, the philosophical inspirer of Chiang Kai-shek's policy.

Democratic or Socialist Revolution?

4. The senseless contention is attributed to the Opposition that China now stands on the eve of a socialist dictatorship of the proletariat. There is nothing original in this "criticism." On the eve of 1905 and later on, the Mensheviks frequently declared that Lenin's tactic would be correct if Russia were directly on the eve of the socialist revolution. Lenin, however, explained to them that his tactic was the only road to the radical victory of the democratic revolution which, under favorable conditions, would begin to grow over into a socialist revolution.

The question of the "noncapitalist" path of development of China was posed in a conditioned form by Lenin, for whom, as for us, it was and is ABC wisdom that the Chinese revolution, left to its own forces, that is, *without the direct support of the victorious proletariat of the USSR and the working class of all advanced countries,* could end only with the conquest of the broadest possibilities for the capitalist development of the country, with more favorable conditions for the labor movement.

5. No less basically false is the contention that the question as to whether the Chinese proletariat needs an independent party; whether this party needs a bloc with the Kuomintang or must subordinate itself to it; whether soviets are necessary, etc., must be solved in accordance with how we conceive the course and the tempo of the *further* stages of the Chinese revolution. It is quite possible that China will have to pass through a relatively prolonged stage of parliamentarism, beginning with a constituent assembly. This demand is inscribed on the banner of the Communist Party. If the bourgeois-democratic revolution does not grow into a socialist revolution in the near future, then in all probability the workers' and peasants' soviets will pass from the scene for a definite stage and give way to a bourgeois regime, which, depending on the progress of the world revolution, will in turn give way, at a new historical stage, to the dictatorship of the proletariat.

6. But first of all, the inevitability of the capitalist path has by no means been proved; and secondly—this argument is now incomparably more timely for us—the bourgeois tasks can be solved in various ways. The slogan of the constituent assembly becomes an empty abstraction, often simple charlatanry, if one does not add who will convoke it and with what program. Chiang Kai-shek can raise the slogan of a constituent assembly against us even tomorrow, just as he has now raised his "workers' and peasants' program" against us. We want a constituent assembly convoked not by Chiang Kai-shek but by the executive committee of the workers' and peasants' soviets. That is the only serious and sure road.

7. Basically untenable is the endeavor of Comrade Bukharin to justify the opportunist and compromising line by referring to the allegedly predominant role of the "remnants of feudalism" in Chinese economy. Even if Comrade Bukharin's estimation of Chinese economy rested on an economic analysis and not on scholastic definitions, the "remnants of feudalism" would still be unable to justify the policy which so manifestly facilitated the April coup.

The Chinese revolution has a national-bourgeois character principally because the development of the productive forces of Chinese capitalism collides with its governmental customs, dependence upon the countries of imperialism. The obstruction of the development of Chinese industry and the throttling of the internal market involve the conservation and rebirth of the most backward forms of production in agriculture, of the most parasitic forms of exploitation, of the most barbaric forms of oppression and violence, the growth of surplus population, as well as the persistence and aggravation of pauperism and all sorts of slavery.

No matter how great the specific weight of the typically "feudal" elements in Chinese economy may be, they can be swept away only in a revolutionary way, and consequently not in alliance with the bourgeoisie but in direct struggle against it.

The more complicated and tortuous is the interlacing of feudal and capitalist relations, the less the agrarian question can be solved by legislation from above, the more indispensable is the revolutionary initiative of the peasant masses in close union with the workers and the poor population of the cities, the falser is the policy that clings convulsively to the alliance with the bourgeoisie and the large landowner and subordinates its work among the masses to this alliance. The policy of the "bloc of four classes" not only prepared the bloc of the bourgeoisie with imperialism, but also meant the preservation of all the survivals of barbarism in administration and in economy.

To invoke the bourgeois character of the Chinese revolution, in particular against the soviets, is simply to renounce the experiences of our bourgeois revolutions of 1905 and February 1917. In these revolutions, the immediate and essential objective was the abolition of the autocratic and feudal regime. This aim did not exclude, but demanded the arming of the workers and the formation of soviets. Here is how Lenin treated the subject after the February revolution:

> No, if there is to be a real struggle against the tsarist monarchy, if freedom is to be guaranteed in fact and not merely in words, in the glib promises of Milyukov and Kerensky, the workers must *not* support the new government; the government must "support" the workers! For the only *guarantee* of freedom and of the complete destruction of tsarism lies in *arming the proletariat,* in strengthening, extending and developing the role, significance and power of the Soviet of Workers' Deputies.
>
> All the rest is mere phrase-mongering and lies, self-deception on the part of the politicians of the liberal and radical camp, fraudulent trickery.
>
> Help, or at least do not hinder, the arming of the workers, and freedom in Russia will be invincible, the monarchy irrestorable, the republic secure.
>
> Otherwise the Guchkovs and Milyukovs will restore the monarchy and grant *none,* absolutely none of the "liberties" they promised. All bourgeois politicians in *all* bourgeois revolutions "fed" the people and fooled the workers with promises.
>
> Ours is a bourgeois revolution, *therefore,* the workers must support the bourgeoisie, say the Potresovs, Gvozdyovs and Chkheidzes, as Plekhanov said yesterday.[24]
>
> Ours is a bourgeois revolution, we Marxists say, *therefore* the workers must open the eyes of the people to the deception practised by the bourgeois politicians, teach them to put no faith in words, to depend entirely on their *own* strength, their *own* organization, their *own* unity, and their own *weapons.* [*Collected Works,* vol. 27, pp. 305-06; from *Pravda* (March 21, 1917).]

The Chinese revolutionist who clears his mind of the over-cunning resolutions and comments on the bloc of four classes will firmly grasp the sense of these simple words of Lenin, will be sure not to go astray, and will attain the goal.

The School of Martynov
on the Chinese Question

8. The official leadership of the Chinese revolution has been oriented all this time on a "general national united front" or on the "bloc of four classes" (cf., the report of Bukharin; the lead article in the *Communist International,* no. 11; the unpublished speech of Stalin to the Moscow functionaries on April 5, 1927; the article of Martynov in *Pravda* on April 10; the lead article in *Pravda* of March 16; the speech of Comrade Kalinin in *Izvestia* of March 6, 1927; the speech of Comrade Rudzutak in *Pravda* of March 9, 1927; etc., etc.). Matters had gone so far on this track that on the eve of Chiang Kai-shek's coup, *Pravda,* in order to expose the Opposition, proclaimed that revolutionary China was not being ruled by a bourgeois government but by a "government of the bloc of four classes."

The philosophy of Martynov, which has the sorry courage to carry all the mistakes of Stalin and Bukharin in the questions of Chinese policy to their logical conclusion, does not meet a trace of objection. Yet it is tantamount to trampling underfoot the fundamental principles of Marxism. It reproduces the crudest features of Russian and international Menshevism, applied to the conditions of the Chinese revolution. Not for nothing does the present leader of the Mensheviks, Dan, write in the last number of *Sotsialistichesky Vestnik:*

> "In principle" the Bolsheviks were also for retaining the "united front" in the Chinese revolution up to the completion of the task of national liberation. On April 10, Martynov, in *Pravda,* most effectively and, despite the obligatory abuse of the Social Democracy, in a quite "Menshevik manner" showed the "left" Oppositionist Radek the correctness of the *official* position, which insists on the necessity of retaining the "bloc of four classes," on not hastening to overthrow the coalition government in which the workers sit side by side with the big bourgeoisie, not to impose "socialist tasks" upon it prematurely. [No. 8 (April 23, 1927), p. 4.]

Everyone who knows the history of the struggle of Bolshevism against Menshevism, particularly in the question of relations to the liberal bourgeoisie, must acknowledge that Dan's approval of the "rational principles" of the Martynov school is not accidental, but follows with perfect legitimacy. It is only unnatural that this school should raise its voice with impunity in the ranks of the Comintern.

The old Menshevik tactic of 1905 to 1917, which was crushed underfoot by the march of events, is now transferred to China by the Martynov school, much the same as capitalist trade dumps its most inferior merchandise, which finds no market in the mother country, into the colonies. The merchandise has not even been renovated. The arguments are the same, letter for letter, as they were twenty years ago. Only where formerly the word *autocracy* stood, the word *imperialism* has been substituted for it in the text. Naturally, British imperialism is different from autocracy. But the Menshevik reference to it does not differ in the slightest from its reference to autocracy. The struggle against foreign imperialism is as much a class struggle as the struggle against autocracy. That it cannot be exorcised by the idea of the national united front is far too eloquently proved by the bloody April events, a direct consequence of the policy of the bloc of four classes.

What the "Line" Looked Like in Practice

9. On the past period, which terminated with the April coup, the theses of Comrade Stalin announce: "The line adopted was the only correct line."

What did it look like in practice? An eloquent reply is supplied by T'an P'ing-shan, the communist minister of agriculture, in his report at the Seventh Plenum of the ECCI in December 1926.

> Since the establishment of the national government in Canton last July, which is nominally a government of the left wing, *the power has actually been in the hands of the right wing.* . . . The movement of the workers and peasants cannot develop to its full breadth as a result of various obstacles. After the March putsch a *military dictatorship of the center* [that is, Chiang Kai-shek] was established, while the political power remained as before in the hands of the right wing. The whole political power, which should properly [!] have belonged to the left wing, is finally lost.

So: the left "should have" had the power, but finally lost it; the state power belonged to the right, the military authority, which is incomparably more powerful, and was entirely in the hands of the "center" of Chiang Kai-shek, which became the center of the conspiracy. Under such conditions, it is not difficult to understand why "the movement of the workers and peasants" could not develop as it should have.

T'an P'ing-shan gives an even more precise characterization of what the "only correct line" looked like in reality:

> . . . *We sacrificed the interests of the workers and peasants in practice.* . . . After lengthy negotiations with us, the government did not as much as promulgate a trade union law. . . . The government did not accept the demands of the peasantry, which we presented to it in the name of various social organizations. When conflicts arose between the large landowners and the poor peasants, the government always took the side of the former.

How could all this happen? T'an P'ing-shan cautiously gives two reasons:

(a) "The left leaders are not capable of consolidating and extending their influence by means of political power";

(b) The right wing "won the possibility to act partly *as a result of our wrong tactic.*"

10. Such are the political relations that received the pompous title of the "bloc of four classes." Such "blocs" abound in the revolutionary as well as the parliamentary history of bourgeois countries: the big bourgeoisie leads the petty-bourgeois democrats, the phrasemongers of the national united front, behind it, and the latter, in turn, confuse the workers and drag them along behind the bourgeoisie. When the proletarian "tail," despite the efforts of the petty-bourgeois phrasemongers, begins to stir too violently, the bourgeoisie orders its generals to stamp on it. Then the opportunists observe with an air of profundity that the bourgeoisie has "betrayed" the national cause.

11. But did not the Chinese bourgeoisie "nevertheless" fight against imperialism? This argument too is an empty commonplace. The compromisers of every country, in similar cases, have always assured the workers that the liberal bourgeoisie is fighting against the reaction. The Chinese bourgeoisie utilized the petty-bourgeois democracy only in order to conclude an alliance with imperialism against the workers. The Northern Expedition only served to strengthen the bourgeoisie and weaken the workers. A tactic that prepared such a result is a false tactic. "We sacrificed the interests of the workers and peasants in practice," says T'an P'ing-shan. What for? To support the bloc of four classes. And the results? A colossal success of the bourgeois counterrevolution, the consolidation of shattered imperialism, the weakening of the USSR. Such a policy is criminal. Unless it is mercilessly condemned, we cannot take a step forward.

The Theses Justify a Line
for Which There Is No Justification

12. The theses endeavor even now to justify the policy which united the party of the proletariat with the big bourgeoisie within the framework of one organization, the Kuomintang, where the whole leadership was in the hands of the bourgeoisie. The theses declare: "This was the line . . . for the utilization of the rightists, their connections and experiences, insofar as they submitted [!] to the discipline of the Kuomintang." Now we know very well how the bourgeoisie submitted to "discipline" and how the proletariat utilized the rights, that is, the big and middle bourgeoisie, their "connections" (with the imperialists) and their "experiences" (in strangling and shooting the workers). The story of this "utilization" is written in the book of the Chinese revolution with letters of blood. But this does not prevent the theses from saying: "The subsequent events fully confirmed the correctness of this line." Further than this no one can go!

From an enormous counterrevolutionary coup, the theses of Stalin draw the positively miserable conclusion that the policy of "isolating the right" within the united Kuomintang must be "replaced" by a policy of "determined struggle" against the right. All this after the right-wing "comrades" have begun to speak in the language of machine guns.

13. The theses refer, to be sure, to a "previous prediction" on the inevitability of the bourgeoisie's withdrawal from the revolution. But are such prophecies by themselves sufficient for a Bolshevik policy? The prediction that the bourgeoisie will quit is an empty commonplace unless definite political conclusions are drawn from it. In the already quoted article, which approves the semiofficial line of Martynov, Dan writes: "In a movement that embraces such antagonistic classes, *the united front cannot of course last forever"* (*Sotsialistichesky Vestnik,* April 23, 1927, p. 3).

So Dan also acknowledges the "inevitability of the bourgeoisie's withdrawal." In practice, however, the policy of Menshevism in the revolution consists of retaining the united front at any cost, as long as possible, at the price of adapting its own policy to the policy of the bourgeoisie, at the price of cutting down the slogans and the activity of the masses, and even, as in China, at the price of the organizational subordination of the workers' party to the political apparatus of the bourgeoisie. The Bolshevik way, however, consists of an unconditional political and organizational demarcation from the bourgeoisie, of a relentless exposure of the bourgeoisie from the very first steps of the revolution, of a destruction of all petty-bourgeois illusions about the united front with the bourgeoisie, of tireless struggle with the bourgeoisie for the leadership of the masses, of the merciless expulsion from the Communist Party of all those elements who sow vain hopes in the bourgeoisie or idealize them.

Two Paths and the Mistakes of the Past

14. The theses of Comrade Stalin, to be sure, seek to oppose to each other the two paths of development of the Chinese revolution: one under the leadership of the bourgeoisie, with its suppression of the proletariat and an inevitable alliance with foreign imperialism; the other under the leadership of the proletariat against the bourgeoisie.

But in order that this second perspective of the bourgeois-democratic revolution should not remain an empty phrase, it must be said openly and plainly that the whole leadership of the Chinese revolution up to now has been in irreconcilable contradiction to it. The Opposition has been and is subjected to a rabid criticism precisely because, from the very beginning, it brought to the fore the Leninist manner of putting the question, that is, the path of the struggle of the proletariat against the bourgeoisie for the leadership of the oppressed masses of city and country within the framework and on the foundation of the national democratic revolution.

15. From the theses of Stalin it follows that the proletariat can separate itself from the bourgeoisie only after the latter has tossed it aside, disarmed it, beheaded it, and crushed it underfoot. But this is precisely the way the abortive revolution of 1848 developed, where the proletariat had no banner of its own, but followed at the heels of the petty-bourgeois democracy, which in turn trotted behind the liberal bourgeoisie and led the workers under the saber of Cavaignac. Great though the real peculiarities of the Chinese situation may be, the fundamentals that characterize the development of the 1848 revolution have been repeated in the Chinese revolution with such deadly precision as though neither the lessons of 1848, 1871,[25] 1905, and 1917, nor those of the Communist Party of the Soviet Union and the Comintern had ever existed.

That Chiang Kai-shek played the role of a republican-liberal

Cavaignac has already become a commonplace. The theses of Stalin, following the Opposition, recognize this analogy. But the analogy must be supplemented. Cavaignac would have been impossible without the Ledru-Rollins, the Louis Blancs, and the other phrasemongers of the all-inclusive national front.[26] And who played these roles in China? Not only Wang Ching-wei, but also the leaders of the Chinese Communist Party, above all their inspirers of the ECCI. Unless this is stated openly, explained, and deeply impressed, the philosophy of the two paths of development will only serve to screen opportunism à la Louis Blanc and Martynov, that is, to prepare a repetition of the April tragedy at a new stage of the Chinese revolution.

The Position of the Chinese Communist Party

16. In order to have the right to speak about the struggle for the Bolshevik path of the democratic revolution, one must possess the principal instrument of proletarian policy: *an independent proletarian party* which fights under its own banner and never permits its policy and organization to be dissolved in the policy and organization of other classes. Without assuring the complete theoretical, political, and organizational independence of the Communist Party, all talk about "two paths" is a mockery of Bolshevism. The Chinese Communist Party, in this whole period, has not been *in alliance* with the revolutionary petty-bourgeois section of the Kuomintang, but *in subordination* to the whole Kuomintang, led in reality by the bourgeoisie, which had the army and the power in its hands. The Communist Party submitted to the political discipline of Chiang Kai-shek. The Communist Party signed the obligation not to criticize Sun Yat-senism, a petty-bourgeois theory which is directed not only against imperialism, but also against the class struggle. The Communist Party did not have its own press, that is, it lacked the principal weapon of an independent party. Under such conditions, to speak of the struggle of the proletariat for hegemony means to deceive oneself and others.

17. By what is the submissive, indistinct, and politically unworthy position of the Communist Party in Chiang Kai-shek's Kuomintang to be explained? By the insistence upon the unity of the national front under the actual leadership of the bourgeoisie which allegedly "could not" withdraw from the revolution (the school of Martynov); that is, the rejection in practice of the

second, Bolshevik path of which the theses of Stalin speak as an afterthought, solely for camouflage purposes.

To justify such a policy by the necessity for an alliance of the workers and peasants is to reduce this alliance itself to a phrase, to a screen for the commanding role of the bourgeoisie. The dependence of the Communist Party, an inevitable result of the "bloc of four classes," was the main obstacle in the path of the workers' and peasants' movement, and therefore also of the real alliance between the proletariat and the peasantry, without which the victory of the Chinese revolution cannot even be thought of.

18. What should the Communist Party do in the future?

In the theses, there is only a single sentence on this, but one capable of sowing the greatest confusion and causing irreparable harm. ". . . While fighting in the ranks of the revolutionary Kuomintang," say Stalin's theses, "the Communist Party must *preserve its independence* more than ever before." Preserve? But to this day the Communist Party has had no such independence. Precisely its lack of independence is the source of all the evils and all the mistakes. In this fundamental question, the theses, instead of making an end once and for all to the practice of yesterday, proposes to retain it "more than ever before." But this means that they want to retain the ideological, political, and organizational dependence of the proletarian party upon a petty-bourgeois party, which is inevitably converted into an instrument of the big bourgeoisie.

In order to justify a false policy, one is forced to call dependence independence, and to demand the preservation of what ought to be buried for all time.

19. Chinese Bolshevism can rise only under a merciless self-criticism by the best elements of the Communist Party. To support them in this is our direct duty. The attempt to cover up the mistakes of the past by artificially curbing a discussion of them will cause enormous harm, primarily to the Chinese Communist Party. If we do not help it to purge itself, in the shortest period, from Menshevism and the Mensheviks, it will enter a prolonged crisis, with splits, desertions, and an embittered struggle of various groups. What is more, the heavy defeats of opportunism may clear a road to anarcho-syndicalist influences.

If, in spite of a workers' mass movement, in spite of the powerful rise of the trade unions, in spite of the revolutionary agrarian movement on the land, the Communist Party should remain as before an integral appendage to a bourgeois party, and what is more, should it enter the national government created by this bourgeois party, it would be better to say frankly: the time has not yet come for a Communist Party in China. It is better not to constitute any Communist Party at all than to discredit it so cruelly at the time of a revolution, that is, just at the time when the party is being joined to the working masses with bonds of blood and when great traditions are being created that are destined to live for decades.

Who Was Mistaken on the Tempo?

20. In Stalin's theses there is of course a whole section devoted to the "mistakes of the Opposition." Instead of hitting out at the right, that is, at the mistakes of Stalin himself, the theses are intent upon striking at the left, thereby deepening the mistakes, piling up confusion, making the way out more difficult, and driving the line of the leadership down into the swamp of compromise.

21. The main accusation: the Opposition "does not understand that the revolution in China cannot develop at a rapid tempo." For some reason or other, the theses drag in here the tempo of the October revolution. If the question of tempo is raised, it must not be measured with the external yardstick of the October revolution, but with the internal class relationships of the Chinese revolution itself. The Chinese bourgeoisie, as is known, paid no attention to the precepts about a slow tempo. In April 1927, it considered it quite opportune to throw off the mask of the united front, which had served it so well, in order to open an attack upon the revolution with all its strength. The Communist Party, the proletariat, as well as the left Kuomintang people, showed themselves completely unprepared for this blow. Why? Because the leadership counted upon a slower tempo, because it remained hopelessly behindhand, because it was infected with tailendism.

On April 23, that is, after the coup by Chiang Kai-shek, the Central Committee of the Kuomintang[27] together with the "left" Wuhan government published a manifesto, which said:

"It only remains for us to regret [!] *that we did not act when there was still time.* For that we apologize [!] sincerely" (*Pravda*, April 23, 1927).

In these doleful and whining avowals there is revealed, against the will of their authors, a pitiless refutation of the Stalinist philosophy on the "tempo" of the Chinese revolution.

22. We continued to maintain the bloc with the bourgeoisie at a time when the working masses were driving toward independent struggle. We attempted to utilize the experiences of the "rights" and became playthings in their hands. We carried on an ostrich policy in the press by suppressing and concealing from our own party the first coup by Chiang Kai-shek in March 1926, the shootings of workers and peasants, and in general all the facts that marked the counterrevolutionary character of the Kuomintang leadership. We neglected to look after the independence of our own party. We founded no newspaper for it. "We sacrificed the interests of the workers and peasants in practice" (T'an P'ing-shan). We did not take a single serious step to win over the soldiers. We allowed the Chiang Kai-shek band to establish a "military dictatorship of the center," that is, a dictatorship of the bourgeois counterrevolution. On the very eve of the coup we blew the trumpets for Chiang Kai-shek. We declared that he had "submitted to discipline," and that we had succeeded "by a skillful tactical maneuver in forestalling an abrupt turn to the right that threatened the Chinese revolution" (Raskolnikov's foreword to the pamphlet by T'an P'ing-shan).

We remained behind the events all along the line. At every step we lost in tempo to the benefit of the bourgeoisie. In this way we prepared the most favorable conditions for the bourgeois counterrevolution. The left Kuomintang at least offers us its "sincere apology." The theses of Stalin, on the contrary, draw from this whole chain of truly unparalleled tailendist mistakes the remarkable conclusion that the Opposition demands . . . a too rapid tempo.

23. Ever more frequently one hears accusations at our party meetings against the "ultraleft" Shanghaiers and in general against the Chinese workers for having provoked Chiang Kai-shek by their "excesses." No one cites any examples; and what would they prove, anyway? Not a single real people's revolution, drawing millions into its vortex, proceeds without so-called excesses. A policy that seeks to prescribe for the masses just awakening a line of march that will not disturb the bourgeois "order" is a policy of incurable philistines. It will always break its head against the logic of civil war when, while pronouncing belated curses upon the Cavaignacs and Kornilovs, it denounces at the same time the alleged "excesses" of the left.

The "mistake" of the Chinese workers lies in the fact that the critical moment of the revolution found them unprepared, unorganized, and unarmed. But that is not their mistake, it is their misfortune. The responsibility for it falls entirely upon a bad leadership, which let every interval pass.

Does a New Revolutionary Center Already Exist or Must One First Be Created?

24. On the present state of the Chinese revolution, the theses proclaim:

> Chiang Kai-shek's coup means that there will now be two camps, two governments, two armies, two centers in the South: a revolutionary center in Wuhan and a counterrevolutionary center in Nanking.

What an inexact, superficial, vulgar characterization. It is not simply a question of two halves of the Kuomintang but of a new grouping of class forces. To believe that the Wuhan government is already a finished center, which will simply continue the revolution from the point where it was brought to a stop and beaten to the ground by Chiang Kai-shek is to regard the counterrevolutionary coup in April as a personal "desertion," an "episode"; in a word, it is to understand nothing.

The workers were not simply crushed. They were crushed by those who led them. Can one believe that the masses will now follow the left Kuomintang with the same confidence that they accorded the whole Kuomintang yesterday? From now on the struggle must be conducted not only against the former militarists allied with imperialism, but also against the "national" bourgeoisie which, as a result of our radically incorrect policy, has captured the military apparatus and considerable sections of the army.

For the struggle on a new, higher stage of the revolution, the deceived masses must above all be inspired with confidence in themselves, and the not yet awakened masses must be aroused. For this, it must first of all be demonstrated that not a trace has been left of that disgraceful policy that "sacrificed the interests of the workers and peasants" (cf. T'an P'ing-shan) in order to support the bloc of four classes. Anyone who will lean in the direction of this policy must be mercilessly driven out of the Chinese Communist Party.

The miserably superficial and bureaucratic idea must be thrown aside that now, after the sanguinary experiences, millions of workers and peasants can be set in motion and led if only the "banner" of the Kuomintang is waved around in the air a little. ("We will surrender the blue banner of the Kuomintang to nobody!" cries Bukharin.)

No, the masses need a revolutionary program and a fighting organization that grows out of their own ranks and contains within itself the guarantee of contact with the masses and of loyalty to them. The Wuhan authorities are not enough for this: workers', peasants', and soldiers' soviets are needed for this, soviets of the toilers.

Soviets and the Arming of the Workers and Peasants

25. After rejecting the vital and indispensable slogan of soviets, the theses of Comrade Stalin declare somewhat unexpectedly that the principal "antidote [?] to the counterrevolution is the arming of the workers and peasants." The arming of the workers is undoubtedly a necessary thing. We will have no differences at all on this point. But how are we to explain why it was considered correct up to now to arm the workers to a "minimum" extent for the welfare of the revolution? that the representatives of the Comintern actually *opposed* the arming of the workers? (cf. the letter of the three comrades to the delegation of the AUCP in the Comintern[28]); that in spite of the full possibility of arming themselves the workers found themselves unarmed at the moment of the coup? All this is to be explained by the desire not to break with Chiang Kai-shek, not to offend Chiang Kai-shek, not to push him to the right. The marvelous "antidote" was lacking precisely on the day it was most needed. Today the workers are not arming themselves in Wuhan either—so as "not to drive away" Wang Ching-wei.

26. The arming of the workers and peasants is an excellent thing. But one must be logical. In South China there are already armed peasants; they are the so-called national armies. Yet, far from being an "antidote to the counterrevolution," they have been its tool. Why? Because the political leadership, instead of embracing the masses of the army through soldiers' soviets has contented itself with a purely external copy of our political departments and commissars, which, without an independent revolutionary party and without soldiers' soviets, have been transformed into an empty camouflage for bourgeois militarism.

27. The theses of Stalin reject the slogan of soviets with the

argument that it would be a "slogan of struggle against the government of the revolutionary Kuomintang." But in that case, what is the meaning of the words: "The principal antidote to the counterrevolution is the arming of the workers and peasants"? Against whom will the workers and peasants arm themselves? Will it not be against the governmental authority of the revolutionary Kuomintang?

The slogan of arming the workers and peasants, if it is not a phrase, a subterfuge, a masquerade, but a call to action, is not less sharp in character than the slogan of workers' and peasants' soviets. Is it likely that the armed masses will tolerate at their side or over them the governmental authority of a bureaucracy alien and hostile to them? The real arming of the workers and peasants under present circumstances inevitably involves the formation of soviets.

28. Further: Who will arm the masses? Who will direct the armed men?

So long as the nationalist armies marched forward and the Northern armies yielded ground, the arming of the workers could proceed with relative ease. The timely organization of workers', peasants', and soldiers' soviets would have meant a real "antidote" to the counterrevolution. Unfortunately, the mistakes of the past are irreparable. The whole situation has now taken a sharp turn for the worse. The few weapons seized spontaneously by the workers (are not these the "excesses" that are spoken of?) have been torn from them. The advance to the North has been suspended. Under these conditions the arming of the workers and peasants is a laborious and difficult task. To declare that the time for the soviets has not yet arrived and at the same time to launch the slogan for arming the workers and peasants is to sow confusion. Only the soviets, at a further development of the revolution, can become the organs capable of really conducting the arming of the workers and of directing these armed masses.

Why Is It Impossible to Form Soviets?

29. To this, the theses reply: "In the first place soviets cannot be created at every convenient moment, they are created only in the period of a special rise of the revolutionary wave." If these words have any sense at all, it is this: We let pass the favorable moment when we did not call upon the masses to create soviets at the beginning of the last period of powerful revolutionary rise.

Once again: the mistakes of the past are irreparable. If we are of the opinion that the Chinese revolution has been crushed for a long time, then the slogan of soviets will naturally find no echo in the masses. But all the more unfounded then is the slogan of the arming of the workers and peasants. We do not believe, however, that the consequences of the false policy pursued are so heavy and profound. There are many facts that speak for the possibility and the likelihood of a new revolutionary rise in the near future. Among other things, it is indicated by the fact that Chiang Kai-shek is forced to flirt with the masses, to promise the workers the eight-hour day, and all sorts of relief to the peasants, etc.

In the event of a further extension of the agrarian movement and a turning of the petty-bourgeois masses of the city against Chiang Kai-shek as an open agent of imperialism, more favorable conditions can arise in the near future under which the now battered proletarian vanguard will reassemble the ranks of the toilers for a new offensive. Whether this will take place a month sooner or later is of no concern; in any case we must prepare for it now with our own program and our own organizations. In other words: *the slogan of soviets will henceforth accompany the whole further course of the Chinese revolution and reflect its destinies.*

30. "In the second place," say the theses, "soviets are not formed for chattering; they are created primarily as organs of struggle against the existing state power, and for the conquest of power." That soviets are not created for chattering is perhaps the only correct point in the theses. But a revolutionist does not propose the arming of the workers and peasants for chattering either. Whoever says here: at the present stage only chatter can be the result of soviets, but on the contrary, something serious will come out of the arming of the workers and peasants, is either making fun of himself or of others.

31. A third argument: since there is now a series of left Kuomintang organizations in Wuhan, which in their solemn manifesto of April 23 apologized for having overslept Chiang Kai-shek's coup, the theses draw the conclusion: the creation of soviets would mean an insurrection against the left Kuomintang, "for there is no other governmental authority in this region at present than that of the revolutionary Kuomintang."

These words fairly reek with the apparatuslike bureaucratic conception of revolutionary authority. The government is not regarded as the expression and consolidation of the developing struggle of the classes, but as the self-sufficient expression of the will of the Kuomintang. The classes come and go but the continuity of the Kuomintang goes on forever. But it is not enough to call Wuhan the center of the revolution for it really to be that. The provincial Kuomintang of Chiang Kai-shek had an old, reactionary, mercenary bureaucracy at its disposal. What has the left Kuomintang? For the time being, nothing or almost nothing. The slogan of soviets is a call for the creation of real organs of the new state power right through the transitional regime of a dual government.

32. And what will be the attitude of the soviets to the "government of the revolutionary Kuomintang," allegedly the "only" governmental authority "in this region"? A truly classic question! The attitude of the soviets to the revolutionary Kuomintang will correspond to the attitude of the revolutionary Kuomintang to the soviets. In other words: to the extent that the soviets arise, arm themselves, consolidate themselves, they will tolerate over them only such a government as bases itself upon the armed workers and peasants. What makes the soviet system valuable is the fact that, especially in directly revolutionary epochs, it furnishes the best means of guaranteeing agreement between the central and local government authorities.

33. Comrade Stalin, as far back as 1925, called the Kuomintang a "workers' and peasants' party" (!?) (*Problems of Leninism*, p. 264). This definition has nothing in common with Marxism. But it is clear that with this incorrect formulation Comrade Stalin wanted to express the idea that the basis of the Kuomintang is an antibourgeois alliance of the workers and peasants. This was absolutely false for the period in which it was said: the workers and peasants, it is true, did follow the Kuomintang, but they were led by the bourgeoisie and we know where it led them. Such a party is called bourgeois, but not workers' and peasants'. After the "withdrawal" of the bourgeoisie (that is, after it massacred the unarmed and unprepared proletariat), the revolution, according to Stalin, passes over to a new stage, in which it is to be led by the left Kuomintang, that is, by one, at least so we are to assume, that will finally realize the Stalinist idea of the "workers' and peasants' party." The question arises: why then will the creation of workers' and peasants' soviets mean a war against the authority of the workers' and peasants' Kuomintang?

34. Another argument: To call for the creation of soviets "means to hand the enemies of the Chinese people a new weapon

to combat the revolution, to manufacture new legends, and to pretend that there is no national revolution in China, but an artificial transplanting of Moscow sovietization."

This stupefying argument means that if we develop, extend, and deepen the revolutionary movement of the masses, the enemies of the Chinese people will redouble their efforts to calumniate it. This argument has no other sense. Therefore it has no sense at all.

Perhaps the theses have not in mind the enemies of the Chinese people, but the fear of the popular masses themselves of a Moscow sovietization? But on what is such a consideration based? It is well known that all the varieties of the "national" bourgeoisie, right, center, and left, zealously smear themselves with a protective Muscovite coloration in all their political work: they create commissars, political army posts, political departments, plenums of the central committee, control commissions, etc. The Chinese bourgeoisie is not at all afraid of transplanting Muscovite forms, which it carefully debases to serve its own class aims. But why do they apply them? Not out of love for Moscow, but rather because they are popular with the masses of the people.

The Chinese peasant knows that the soviets gave the land to the Russian peasant, and whoever does not know this ought to learn it. The Chinese workers know that the soviets guaranteed the liberty of the Russian proletariat. The experience of the counterrevolution of Chiang Kai-shek must have made the advanced workers understand that without an independent organization embracing the whole proletariat and assuring its collaboration with the oppressed masses in the city and on the land, the revolution cannot triumph. The creation of soviets follows for the Chinese masses from their own experience, and is far from being an "artificially transplanted sovietization" for them. A policy that is afraid to call things by their right name is a false policy. One must be guided by the revolutionary masses and by the objective needs of the revolution, but not by what the enemy will say.

35. It is said: The Hankow government is nevertheless a fact. Feng Yü-hsiang is a fact, T'ang Sheng-chih is a fact, and they have armed forces at their disposal; neither the Wuhan government, nor Feng Yü-hsiang, nor T'ang Sheng-chih wants soviets. To create soviets would mean to break with these allies. Although this argument is not openly formulated in the theses, it is

nevertheless decisive for many comrades. We have already heard from Stalin on the Hankow government; the "revolutionary center," the "only governmental authority." At the same time an advertising campaign is launched for Feng Yü-hsiang in our party meetings: "a former worker," "a faithful revolutionist," "a reliable man," etc. All this is a repetition of the past mistakes under circumstances in which these mistakes can become even more disastrous. The Hankow government and the army command can be against the soviets only because they will have nothing to do with a radical agrarian program, with a real break with the large landowners and the bourgeoisie, because they secretly cherish the thought of a compromise with the right. But then it becomes all the more important to form soviets. This is the only way to push the revolutionary elements of Hankow to the left and force the counterrevolutionists to retire.

36. But even if the soviets do not carry on a war with the "only" government of Hankow, will they not still bring with them the elements of dual power? Without a doubt. Whoever is really for the course toward a workers' and peasants' government, not only in words but in deeds, must understand that this course leads through a certain period of dual power. How long this period will last, what concrete forms it will assume, will depend upon how the "only" government in Hankow conducts itself, upon the independence and initiative of the Communist Party, upon how rapidly the soviets develop, etc. It will be our task, in any case, to strengthen the element of the workers and peasants in the dual power and by that provide the genuine workers' and peasants' soviet government with a fully developed democratic program.

37. But dozens of foreign warships are anchored in the Yangtze river which can sweep away Shanghai, Hankow, etc. Is it not insanity to form soviets under such conditions? This argument too is of course not formulated in Stalin's theses, but it is paraded around everywhere in party meetings (Martynov, Yaroslavsky, and others). The school of Martynov would like to kill the idea of the soviets with fear of the British naval artillery. This artifice is not a new one. In 1917, the Social Revolutionaries and the Mensheviks sought to frighten us by declaring that the seizure of power by the soviets would mean the occupation of Kronstadt and Petrograd by the Allies. We answered: only the deepening of the revolution can save it. Foreign imperialism will only reconcile itself to such a "revolution" as strengthens its own positions in

China at the price of a few concessions to the Chinese bourgeoisie. Every real people's revolution that undermines the colonial foundation of imperialism will inevitably meet with the latter's furious resistance.

We did try to stop halfway, but this "only correct line" protected Nanking from the cannons of imperialism as little as it did the Chinese workers from the machine guns of Chiang Kai-shek. Only the transition of the Chinese revolution to the phase of real mass action, only the formation of workers', peasants', and soldiers' soviets, only the deepening of the social program of the revolution, are capable, as our own experiences prove, of bringing confusion into the ranks of the foreign army forces by arousing their sympathy for the soviets and thus really protecting the revolution from blows from without.

What Do the Theses of Stalin Propose in Place of Soviets?

38. The creation of "revolutionary peasant committees, workers' trade unions, and other mass organizations as preparatory elements for the soviets of the future." What should be the course of these organizations? We do not find a single word on this in the theses. The phrase that these are "preparatory elements for the soviets of the future" is only a phrase and nothing more. What will these organizations do now? They will have to conduct strikes, boycotts, break the backbone of the bureaucratic apparatus, annihilate the counterrevolutionary military bands, drive out the large landowners, disarm the detachments of the usurers and the rich peasants, arm the workers and peasants, in a word, solve all the problems of the democratic and agrarian revolution that are on the order of the day, and in this way raise themselves to the position of local organs of power. But then they will be soviets, only of a kind that are badly suited to their tasks. The theses therefore propose, if these proposals are to be taken seriously at all, to create substitutes for soviets, instead of soviets themselves.

39. During all the preceding mass movements, the trade unions were compelled to fulfill functions closely approaching the functions of soviets (Hong Kong, Shanghai, and elsewhere). But these were precisely the functions for which the trade unions were entirely insufficient. They embrace a too small number of workers. They do not at all embrace the petty-bourgeois masses in

the city that incline toward the proletariat. But such tasks as the carrying through of strikes with the least possible losses to the poorer population of the city, the distribution of provisions, participation in tax policy, participation in the formation of armed forces, to say nothing of carrying through the agrarian revolution in the provinces, can be accomplished with the necessary sweep only when the directing organization embraces not only all the sections of the proletariat, but connects them intimately in the course of its activities with the poor population in the city and country.

One would at least think that Chiang Kai-shek's military coup had finally hammered into the mind of every revolutionist the fact that trade unions separated from the army are one thing, and united workers' and soldiers' soviets, on the other hand, are quite another thing. Revolutionary trade unions and peasants' committees can arouse the hatred of the enemy no less than soviets. But they are far less capable than soviets of warding off its blows.

If we are to speak seriously of the alliance of the proletariat with the oppressed masses in the city and country—not of an "alliance" between the leaders, a semiadulterated alliance through dubious representatives, but of a real fighting alliance built and steeled in the struggles of the masses against the enemy—then such an alliance can have no other organizational form than that of soviets. This can be denied only by those who rely more upon compromising leaders than upon the revolutionary masses below.

Should We Break with the Left Kuomintang?

From the foregoing remarks may be seen how ill-founded are the whispers about a break of the Communist Party with the Kuomintang. "This is tantamount," say the theses, "to deserting the field of struggle and leaving our allies in the Kuomintang in the lurch to the delight of the enemies of the revolution." These pathetic lines are quite out of place. It is not a question of a break but of preparing a bloc, not on the basis of subordination but on the basis of a genuine equality of rights. A revolutionary Kuomintang has yet to be formed. We are in favor of the communists working inside the Kuomintang and patiently drawing the workers and peasants over to their side. The Communist Party can gain a petty-bourgeois ally, not by prostrating itself before the Kuomintang at every one of its vacillations, but only if it appeals to the workers openly and directly, in its own name, under its own banner, organizes them around it, and shows the Kuomintang by example and by deed what a party of the masses is, by supporting every forward step of the Kuomintang, by relentlessly unmasking every vacillation, every step backward, and by creating a real revolutionary foundation for a bloc with the Kuomintang in the form of workers', peasants', and soldiers' soviets.

40. It is absurd to assert that the Opposition stands for the "political isolation" of the Communist Party. This assertion contains just as much truth as the one that the Opposition stood for withdrawing from the British trade unions. Both accusations have only served to mask the bloc with the right Kuomintang and with the traitorous General Council.[29] The Opposition is energetically in favor of strengthening and developing the bloc with the revolutionary elements of the Kuomintang, for a compact fighting alliance of the workers with the poor population of the city and country, for the course toward the revolutionary dictatorship of the workers, peasants, and the urban petty bourgeoisie.

For this it is necessary:

(a) to establish as disastrous such forms of the bloc in which the Communist Party sacrifices the interests of the workers and peasants to the utopian aim of holding the bourgeoisie in the camp of the national revolution;

(b) to reject categorically such forms of the bloc which directly or indirectly hinder the independence of our own party and subordinate it to the control of other classes;

(c) to reject categorically such forms of the bloc in which the Communist Party hauls down its banner and sacrifices the growth of its own influence and its own authority in the interest of its allies;

(d) to establish the bloc with clearly formulated common tasks, but not to base it upon misunderstanding, diplomatic maneuvers, sycophancy, and hypocrisy;

(e) to establish the conditions and limits of the bloc with thorough precision and let them be known to all;

(f) for the Communist Party to retain full freedom of criticism, and to watch over its allies with no less vigilance than over an enemy, without forgetting for a moment that an ally who bases himself upon other classes or depends upon other classes is only a temporary confederate who can be transformed by the force of circumstances into an opponent and an enemy;

(g) to set the connection with the petty-bourgeois masses higher than a connection with their party leaders;

(h) finally, to rely only upon ourselves, upon our own organization, arms, and power.

Only by observing these conditions will a really revolutionary bloc of the Communist Party with the Kuomintang become possible, not a bloc of the leaders, which vacillates and is subject to contingencies, but a bloc based upon all the oppressed masses of the city and country under the political hegemony of the proletarian vanguard.

The Problems of the Chinese Revolution and the Anglo-Russian Committee

41. In the direction of the Chinese revolution we are confronted not by tactical errors, but by a radically false line. This follows clearly from everything that has been presented above. It becomes still clearer when the policy in China is compared with our policy toward the Anglo-Russian Committee. In the latter case the inconsistency of the opportunist line did not express itself so tragically as in China, but no less completely and convincingly.

42. In Britain, as in China, the line was directed toward a rapprochement with the "solid" leaders, based on personal relations, on diplomatic combinations, while renouncing in practice the deepening of the abyss between the revolutionary or leftward developing masses and the traitorous leaders. We ran after Chiang Kai-shek and thereby drove the Chinese communists to accept the dictatorial conditions put by Chiang Kai-shek to the Communist Party. Insofar as the representatives of the All-Union Central Council of Trade Unions ran after Purcell, Hicks, Citrine, and Company and adopted in principle the position of neutrality in the trade union movement, they recognized the General Council as the only representative of the British proletariat and obligated themselves not to interfere in the affairs of the British labor movement.[30]

43. The decisions of the Berlin conference of the Anglo-Russian Committee mean our renunciation of support in the future to the strikers against the will of averred strikebreakers. They are tantamount to a condemnation and a flat betrayal of the trade

union minority, all of whose activity is directed against the traitors whom we have recognized as the sole representatives of the British working class. Finally, the solemn proclamation of "noninterference" signifies our capitulation in principle to the national narrowness of the labor movement in its most backward and most conservative form.

44. Chiang Kai-shek accuses us of interfering in the internal affairs of China just as Citrine accuses us of interfering in the internal affairs of the trade unions. Both accusations are only transcriptions of the accusation of world imperialism against a workers' state that dares to interest itself in the fate of the oppressed masses of the whole world. In this case as in others, Chiang Kai-shek, like Citrine, under different conditions and at different posts, remains the agent of imperialism despite temporary conflicts with it. If we chase after collaboration with such "leaders," we are forced ever more to restrict, to limit, and to emasculate our methods of revolutionary mobilization.

45. Through our false policy we not only helped the General Council to maintain its tottering positions after the strike betrayal, but, what is more, we furnished it with all the necessary weapons for putting impudent demands to us which we meekly accepted. Under the tinkling of phrases about "hegemony," we acted in the Chinese revolution and the British labor movement as if we were morally vanquished, and by that we prepared our material defeat. An opportunist deviation is always accompanied by a loss of faith in its own line.

46. The businessmen of the General Council, having received a guarantee of noninterference from the All-Union Central Council of Trade Unions, are undoubtedly persuading Chamberlain that their method of struggle against Bolshevik propaganda is far more effective than ultimatums and threats. Chamberlain, however, prefers the combined method and combines the diplomacy of the General Council with the violence of British imperialism.

47. If it is alleged against the Opposition that Baldwin or Chamberlain "also" wants the dissolution of the Anglo-Russian Committee, then one understands nothing at all of the political mechanics of the bourgeoisie. Baldwin justly feared and still fears the harmful influence of the Soviet trade unions upon the leftward developing labor movement of Britain. The British bourgeoisie set its pressure upon the General Council against the pressure of the All-Union Central Council of Trade Unions upon

the traitorous leaders of the trade unions, and on this field the bourgeoisie triumphed all along the line. The General Council refused to accept money from the Soviet trade unions and to confer with them on the question of aid for the mine workers. In exercising its pressure upon the General Council, the British bourgeoisie, through its medium, exerted pressure upon the All-Union Central Council of Trade Unions and at the Berlin conference obtained from the latter's representatives an unprecedented capitulation in the fundamental questions of the class struggle. An Anglo-Russian Committee *of this kind* only serves the British bourgeoisie (cf. the declaration of the *Times*). This will not hinder it from continuing its pressure in the future upon the General Council, and demanding of it a break with the All-Union Central Council of Trade Unions, for by such a policy of pressure and blackmail the British bourgeoisie wins everything we lose by our senseless and unprincipled conduct.

48. The insinuations that Chiang Kai-shek is "in solidarity" with the Opposition, because he wants to drive the communists out of the Kuomintang, have the same value. A remark by Chiang Kai-shek is being circulated in which he is supposed to have said to another general that he agrees with the Opposition in the CPSU on this point. In the text of the document from which this "quotation" was picked out, the words of Chiang Kai-shek are not adduced as an expression of his views, but as a manifestation of his readiness and aptitude to deceit, to falsehood, and even to disguise himself for a few days as a "left communist" in order to be better able to stab us in the back. Still more, the document in question is one long indictment against the line and the work of the Comintern's representatives in China. Instead of picking quotations out of the document and giving them a sense contrary to that contained in the text, it would be better to make the document itself known to the Comintern.[31]

Leave aside, however, the misuse of alleged "quotations" and there remains the "coincidence" that Chiang Kai-shek has always been against a bloc with the communists, while we are against a bloc with Chiang Kai-shek. The school of Martynov draws from this the conclusion that the policy of the Opposition "generally" serves the reaction. This accusation is not new either. The whole development of Bolshevism in Russia proceeded under the accompaniment of Menshevik accusations that the Bolsheviks are playing the game of the reaction, that they are aiding the monarchy against the Cadets, the Cadets against the SRs and Mensheviks, and so on without end. Renaudel accuses the French communists of rendering aid to Poincaré when they attack the bloc of the Radicals and the Socialists. The German Social Democracy has more than once pretended that our refusal to enter the League of Nations plays the game of the extreme imperialists, etc., etc.

The fact that the big bourgeoisie, represented by Chiang Kai-shek, needs to break with the proletariat, and the revolutionary proletariat on the other hand needs to break with the bourgeoisie, is not an evidence of their solidarity, but of the irreconcilable class antagonism between them. The hopeless compromisers stand between the bourgeoisie and the proletariat and accuse both the "extreme" wings of disrupting the national front and rendering assistance to the reaction. To accuse the Opposition of playing the game of Chamberlain, Thomas, or Chiang Kai-shek is to show a narrow-minded opportunism, and at the same time to recognize involuntarily the proletarian and revolutionary character of our political line.

49. The Berlin conference of the Anglo-Russian Committee which coincided with the beginning of British intervention in China did not even dare to allude to the question of effective measures to take against the hangman's work of British imperialism in the Far East. Could a more striking proof be found that the Anglo-Russian Committee is incapable of moving as much as a finger toward really preventing war? But it is not simply useless. It has brought immeasurable harm to the revolutionary movement, like every illusion and hypocrisy. By referring to its collaboration with the All-Union Central Council of Trade Unions in the "struggle for peace," the General Council is able to soothe and lull the consciousness of the British proletariat, stirred by the danger of war. The All-Union Central Council of Trade Unions now appears before the British working class and the working class of the whole world as a sort of guarantor for the international policy of the traitors of the General Council. The criticism directed by the revolutionary elements in Britain against the General Council thereby becomes weakened and blunted.

Thanks to Purcell, Hicks, and Company, the MacDonalds and Thomases get the possibility of keeping the working masses in a stupor up to the threshold of war itself, in order to call upon them then for the defense of the democratic fatherland. When Comrade

Tomsky, in his last interview (*Pravda,* May 8), criticized the Thomases, Havelock Wilsons and the other hirelings of the stock exchange, he did not mention by a single word the subversive, disintegrating, lulling, and therefore much more pernicious work of Purcell, Hicks, and Company. These "allies" are not mentioned by name in the interview as though they do not even exist. Then why a bloc with them? But they do exist. Without them Thomas does not exist politically. Without Thomas there exists no Baldwin, that is, the capitalist regime in England. Contrary to our best intentions, our support of the bloc with Purcell is actually support of the whole British regime and the facilitation of its work in China. After all that has happened, this is clear to every revolutionist who has gone through the school of Lenin. In a like manner, our collaboration with Chiang Kai-shek blunted the class vigilance of the Chinese proletariat, and thereby facilitated the April coup.

The Theory of Stages and the Theory of Socialism in One Country

50. The tailendist theory of "stages" or "steps" repeatedly proclaimed by Stalin in recent times has served as the motivation in principle for the opportunist tactic. If the complete organizational and political independence of the Chinese Communist Party is demanded, it means that steps are being skipped over. If soviet organizations are demanded for drawing the worker and peasant masses into the civil war, it means that "stages" are being skipped over. If the dissolution of the political bloc with the traitors of the General Council, who are now carrying on the basest work, is demanded, it means that stages are being skipped over. The conservative bourgeois-national Kuomintang government, the military command of Chiang Kai-shek, the General Council—in a word, any one of the institutions created by the pressure of the possessing and ruling classes, and constituting a barrier for the revolutionary class movement, becomes, according to this theory, a great historical stage, to which one's policy must be adapted until "the masses themselves" pass through it. Once we set out on this road, our policy must be inevitably transformed from a revolutionary factor into a conservative one. The course of the Chinese revolution and the fate of the Anglo-Russian Committee are an imminent warning in this regard.

51. Such facts as the defeat of the great strikes of the British

proletariat last year, as the Chinese revolution this year, cannot go by without consequences for the international labor movement, just as the defeat of the German proletariat in the autumn of 1923 did not pass without leaving its traces.[32] An unavoidable temporary weakening of the revolutionary positions is in itself a great evil. It can become irreparable for a long time if the orientation is wrong, if the strategic line is false. Precisely now, in the period of a temporary revolutionary ebb, the struggle against all manifestations of opportunism and national limitedness and for the line of revolutionary internationalism is more necessary than ever.

By recognizing the principle of noninterference, our delegation, regardless of its intentions, promotes the most conservative, most defeatist tendencies in the working class. There is nothing perplexing in the fact that the most backward and weariest sections of the workers of the USSR consider interference in the British strike struggle or the Chinese revolution a mistake. Ever more frequently they argue: "Are we not taught that we can build up socialism in our country, even without the victory of the revolution in other countries, if only there will be no intervention? Then we must carry on such a policy as does net provoke intervention. Our interference in British and Chinese affairs is a mistake because without yielding positive results it drives the world bourgeoisie to the road of military intervention and thus threatens the construction of socialism in our country."

There is no doubt and there can be none that now, after the new defeats of the international revolutionary movement, the theory of socialism in one country will serve, independent of the will of its creators, to justify, to motivate, and to sanctify all the tendencies directed toward restricting the revolutionary objectives, toward quenching the ardor of the struggle, toward a national and conservative narrowness.

The slightest digression toward the side of "noninterference," whether covered or not with the theory of socialism in one country, only increases the imperialist danger instead of diminishing it.

It is perfectly clear and incontestable with regard to the Chinese revolution that only a deeper mass impulsion, a more radical social program, the slogan of the workers' and peasants' soviets, can seriously shield the revolution against a military attack from without. Only a revolution on whose banner the toilers and oppressed write plainly their own demands is capable of gripping the feelings not only of the international proletariat but also of the soldiers of capital. We know this well enough from our own experiences. We saw and proved it in the years of the civil war at Archangel, Odessa, and elsewhere. The compromising and traitorous leadership did not protect Nanking from destruction. It facilitated the penetration of the enemy ships into the Yangtze. A revolutionary leadership, with a powerful social movement, can make the waters of the Yangtze too hot for the ships of Lloyd George, Chamberlain, and MacDonald. In any case, this is the only way and the only hope of defense.

The extension of the Soviet front is simultaneously the best defense of the USSR. Under the present circumstances, the talk that our international position has become worse or can in any way become worse as a result of some kind of "left" mistake sounds absurd. If our position has grown worse, it is a result of the defeat of the Chinese revolution, a historical and international event, regardless of whether or not we interfere in it. Were we not to interfere in the intervention of imperialism, we would only facilitate its work—against China, and against ourselves as well. But there are different kinds of "interference." The falsest and most dangerous interference consists of the endeavor to halt the development of the revolution halfway. The struggle for peace occupies the center of our international policy. But even the most extreme representative of the Martynov school would never dare to contend that our policy of peace can be in contradiction to the development of the Chinese revolution, or conversely, that its development can be in contradiction to our policy of peace. The one supplements the other. The best way to defend the USSR is to vanquish the Chiang Kai-shek counterrevolution and to raise the movement to a higher stage. Whoever rejects soviets for China under such conditions, disarms the Chinese revolution. Whoever proclaims the principle of noninterference in the relations of the European proletariat, weakens its revolutionary vanguard. Both weaken the position of the USSR, the principal fortress of the international proletariat.

Thus we see how one mistake is heaped upon the others and together produce a line that digresses ever more from the line of Bolshevism. Critical voices and warnings are regarded as obstructions. The shifting of the official line toward the right is supplemented by blows at the left. To continue on this path would involve the greatest dangers for the Soviet state as well as for the Comintern. Were we to conceal these dangers from the international proletarian vanguard, we would be betraying the banner of communism.

*   *   *

We do not doubt for a moment that the mistakes can be repaired, the deviations overcome, and the line rectified without violent crises and convulsions. The language of facts is all too eloquent, the lessons of experience all too plain. It is only necessary that our party, of the Soviet Union as well as of the International, obtain the full possibility to weigh the facts and draw the proper conclusions from them. We firmly believe that they will draw these conclusions in the spirit of revolutionary unity.

Comrade Ch'en Tu-hsiu's Speech on the Tasks of the Chinese Communist Party

[Postscript, May 17, 1927]

52. What purpose does Marxism serve in politics? To understand that which is and to foresee that which will be. Foresight must be the foundation of action. We already know what has happened to the predictions of Comrade Stalin: one week before the coup d'etat of Chiang Kai-shek, he defended him and blew the trumpet for him by calling for the utilization of the right wing, its experiences, its connections (speech to the Moscow functionaries on April 5). In the theses analyzed by us, Stalin gives another example of foresight that has also been tested by life. The central question of our criticism of Stalin's theses was formulated by us above as follows: "Does there already exist a new center of the revolution or must one first be created?" Stalin contended that after Chiang Kai-shek's coup there were *"two governments, two armies, two centers: the revolutionary center in Wuhan and the counterrevolutionary center in Nanking."* Stalin contended that no soviets can be built because that would signify an uprising against the Wuhan center, against the *"only government"* in South China. We called this characterization of the situation "false, superficial, vulgar." We called this so-called Wuhan government the *"leaders of Wuhan"* and showed that in South China, after the abrupt veering of the civil war to another class

line, there is no government as yet, that one must first be created.

In *Pravda* of May 15 the speech of Comrade Ch'en Tu-hsiu at the convention of the Chinese Communist Party (April 29) is reprinted.[33]

Neither Stalin nor we had this speech when Stalin wrote his theses and we wrote a criticism of them. Ch'en Tu-hsiu characterizes the situation not on the basis of a general analysis of the circumstances but on the basis of his direct observations. Now, what does Ch'en Tu-hsiu say of the new revolutionary movement? He declares plainly that "it would be a mistake" to consider the Wuhan government an organ of the revolutionary democratic dictatorship: "It is *not yet a government of the worker and peasant masses but solely a bloc of leaders.*" But is this not word for word what we said against Stalin?

Stalin wrote: "There is now no other governmental power than the government of the revolutionary Kuomintang." We answered him on that: "These words fairly reek with the apparatuslike and bureaucratic conception of revolutionary authority . . . the classes come and go but the continuity of the Kuomintang government goes on forever [allegedly]. But it is not enough to call Wuhan the center of the revolution for it really to be that" (cf. above). Instead of making it clear to the Chinese revolutionists, to the communists primarily, that the Wuhan government will break its head against a wall if it imagines that it is itself already the only government in China; instead of turning relentlessly against the decorative hypocrisy of the petty-bourgeois revolutionists who have already destroyed so many revolutions; instead of shouting right into the ear of the uncertain, faltering, vacillating center of Wuhan: "Do not be misled by outward appearances, do not be dazzled by the glitter of your own titles and manifestos, begin to perform the hard daily work, set masses in motion, build up workers', soldiers', and peasants' soviets, build up a revolutionary governmental power"—instead of all this, Stalin hurls himself against the slogan of the soviets and supports the worst, the most provincial and bureaucratic prejudices and superstitious views of those ill-fated revolutionists who fear people's soviets, but for that, have faith in the sacred inkblots on the notepaper of the Kuomintang.

53. Comrade Ch'en Tu-hsiu characterizes the situation on the basis of his own observations with exactly the same words with which we characterized the situation on the basis of theoretical consideration. No revolutionary government but only a bloc of

leaders. But this does not at all mean that Comrade Ch'en Tu-hsiu himself draws correct conclusions from the circumstances correctly characterized by him. Since he is bound hand and foot by false directives, Ch'en Tu-hsiu draws conclusions that radically contradict his own analysis. He says: "We have before us the task of beginning to build up a genuinely revolutionary and democratic government *as soon as the situation in the sphere of the national government has changed and the threat of foreign intervention and the offensive of the militarists has disappeared.*"

Here we must say directly and openly: pose the question this way and you adopt the surest and shortest road to ruin. The creation of a genuinely revolutionary government basing itself on the popular mass is relegated to the moment when the dangers have disappeared. But the central danger consists precisely of the fact that instead of a revolutionary government in South China, there is for the time being only a bloc of leaders. Through this principal evil, all the other dangers are increased tenfold, including also the military danger. If we are to be guarded to the highest possible degree against the foreign and our "own" militarist bands, we must become strong, consolidate ourselves, organize, and arm ourselves. There are no other roads. We should not stick our heads in the sand. No artifice will help us here. The enthusiasm of the masses must be aroused, their readiness to fight and to die for their own cause. But for this the masses must be gripped as deeply as possible, politically and organizationally. Without losing even an hour, they must be given a revolutionary program of action and the organizational form of the soviets. There are no other roads. Postpone the creation of a revolutionary government until somebody has eliminated the danger of war in some way or other, and you take the surest and shortest road to ruin.

54. With regard to the agrarian movement, Comrade Ch'en Tu-hsiu admits honestly that the agrarian program of the party (reduction of rent payments) is completely insufficient. The peasant movement, he says, "is being transformed into the struggle for land. The peasantry arises spontaneously and wants to settle the land question itself." Further on, Comrade Ch'en Tu-hsiu declares openly: "*We followed a too pacific policy.* Now it is necessary to confiscate the large estates. . . ." If the content of these words is developed in a Marxist manner, it constitutes the harshest condemnation of the whole past line of the Communist

Party of China, and the Comintern as well, in the agrarian question of the Chinese revolution. Instead of anticipating the course of the agrarian movement, of establishing the slogans in time and throwing them among the peasant masses through the workers, the revolutionary soldiers, and the advanced peasants, the Chinese Communist Party remained a vast distance behind the spontaneous agrarian movement. Can there be a more monstrous form of tailendism? *"We followed a too pacific policy."* But what does a pacific policy of a revolutionary party mean in the period of a spontaneous agrarian revolution? It signifies the most grievous historical mistake that a party of the proletariat can possibly commit. A pacific policy (the reduction of rent payments), while the peasant is already fighting spontaneously for land, is not a policy of Menshevik compromise but of liberal compromise. Only a philistine corrupted by an alleged statecraft can fail to understand this, but never a revolutionist.

55. But from his correct, and therefore deadly, characterization of the relations of the party to the agrarian movement, Comrade Ch'en Tu-hsiu draws not only false, but positively disastrous conclusions. "It is now necessary," he says, "to confiscate the large estates, but at the same time to make concessions to the small landowners who must be reckoned with." In principle, such a way of posing the question cannot be assailed. It must be clearly determined who, and in what part of China, is to be considered a small landowner, how and to what limits he must be reckoned with. But Ch'en Tu-hsiu says further:

"Nevertheless, it is necessary to await *the further development of the military actions* even for the confiscation of the large estates. The only correct decision at the present moment is the principle of deepening the revolution *only after its extension."*

This road is the surest, the most positive, the shortest road to ruin. The peasant has already risen to seize the property of the large landowners. Our party, in monstrous contradiction to its program, to its name, pursues a pacific-liberal agrarian policy. Ch'en Tu-hsiu himself declares that it is "now [?] necessary to confiscate the large estates," but he immediately recalls that we "must not fall into left extremism" (Ch'en Tu-hsiu's own words) and he adds that we must "await the further development of the military actions" for the confiscation of the property of the large landowners, that the revolution must first be extended and only later deepened.

But this is simply a blind repetition of the old, well-known, and outworn formula of national-liberal deception of the masses: First the victory, then the reform. First we will "extend" the country—for whom: for the large landowner?—and then, after the victory, we will concern ourselves very tranquilly with the "deepening." To this, every intelligent and halfway sensible peasant will answer Comrade Ch'en Tu-hsiu: "If the Wuhan government today, when it finds itself encircled by foes and needs our peasant support for life and death—if this government does not dare now to give us the land of the large landowners or does not want to do it, then after it has extricated itself from its encirclement, after it has vanquished the enemy with our help, it will give us just as much land as Chiang Kai-shek gave the workers of Shanghai." It must be said quite clearly: The agrarian formula of Comrade Ch'en Tu-hsiu, who is bound hand and foot by the false leadership of the representatives of the Comintern, is objectively nothing else than the formula of the severance of the Chinese Communist Party from the real agrarian movement which is now proceeding in China and which is producing a new wave of the Chinese revolution.

To strengthen this wave and to deepen it, we need peasants' soviets with the unfurled banner of the agrarian revolution, not after the victory but immediately, in order to guarantee the victory.

If we do not want to permit the peasant wave to come to naught and be splattered into froth, the peasants' soviets must be united with workers' soviets in the cities and the industrial centers, and to the workers' soviets must be added the soviets of the poor population from the urban trade and handwork districts.

If we do not want to permit the bourgeoisie to drive a wedge between the revolutionary masses and the army, then soldiers' soviets must be fitted into the revolutionary chain.

As quickly as possible, as boldly as possible, as energetically as possible, the revolution must be deepened, not after the victory but immediately, or else there will be no victory.

The deepening of the agrarian revolution, the immediate seizure of the land by the peasants, will weaken Chiang Kai-shek on the spot, bring confusion into the ranks of his soldiers, and set the peasant hinterland in motion. There is no other road to victory and there can be none.

Have we really carried through three revolutions within two decades only to forget the ABCs of the first of them? Whoever carries on a *pacific* policy during the agrarian revolution is lost.

Whoever postpones matters, vacillates, temporizes, loses time, is lost. The formula of Ch'en Tu-hsiu is the surest road to the destruction of the revolution.

Slanderers will be found who will say that our words are dictated by a hatred of the Chinese Communist Party and its leaders. Was it not once said that our position on the Anglo-Russian Committee signified a hostile attitude toward the British Communist Party? The events confirmed the fact that it was we who acted as loyal revolutionists toward the British communists, and not as bureaucratic sycophants. Events will confirm the fact—they confirm it every day—that our criticism of the Chinese communists was dictated by a more serious, more Marxist, revolutionary attitude toward the Chinese revolution than was the attitude of the bureaucratic sycophants who approve of everything after the fact, provided that they do not have to foresee for the future.

The fact that the speech of comrade Ch'en Tu-hsiu is reprinted in *Pravda* without a single word of commentary, that no article revealing the ruinous course of this speech is devoted to it—this fact by itself must fill every revolutionist with the greatest misgivings, for it is the central organ of Lenin's party that is involved!

Let not the pacifiers and flatterers tell us about "the unavoidable mistakes of a young Communist party." It is not a question of isolated mistakes. It is a question of the mistake of mistakes. It is a question of the false basic line, the consummate expression of which are the theses of Comrade Stalin.

The Necessary Final Accord

In the May 9 number of *Sotsialistichesky Vestnik,* it says in the article devoted to the theses of Comrade Stalin:

> If we strip the envelope of words that is obligatory for the theses of a communist leader, then very little can be said against the essence of the "line" traced there. As much as possible to remain in the Kuomintang, and to cling to its left wing and to the Wuhan government to the last possible moment: "to avoid a decisive struggle under unfavorable conditions"; not to issue the slogan "all power to the soviets" so as not "to give new weapons into the hands of the enemies of the Chinese people for the struggle against the revolution, for creating new legends that it is not a national revolution that is taking place in China, but an artificial transplanting of Moscow

sovietization"—what can actually be more sensible for the Bolsheviks now, after the "united front" has obviously been irremediably destroyed, and so much porcelain has been smashed under the "most unfavorable conditions"? [*Sotsialistichesky Vestnik,* no. 9 (151), p. 1.]

Thus, after the *Sotsialistichesky Vestnik,* in its April 23 number, acknowledged that Martynov analyzed the tasks of the Chinese revolution in *Pravda* "very impressively" and "entirely in the Menshevik manner," the leading article in the central organ of the Mensheviks declares in its latest number that "very little can be said against the essence of the 'line' traced" in the theses of Comrade Stalin. This harmony of political lines hardly requires special elucidation.

But still more: The same article in *Sotsialistichesky Vestnik* speaks further on in a mocking tone—we quote literally!—of "*the line of Radek which, covered with extreme 'left' slogans (withdrawal from the Kuomintang, 'propaganda of the soviet system,' etc.), simply desires in reality to give up the game and to step aside . . .*" (ibid., p. 2). The line of Radek is characterized here with the words of the leading articles and the feuilletons of *Pravda.* After all, it cannot be otherwise: Radek cannot say anything openly in the press about his line, for otherwise the party would learn that Radek's line is being confirmed by the whole course of events. The editors of *Sotsialistichesky Vestnik* not only describe "the line of Radek" with the words of *Pravda* but also evaluate them in full accord with the articles of *Pravda:* The line of the Opposition, according to Dan, gives the possibility, "covered with extreme 'left' slogans," in reality "to give up the game and to step aside."

We have already read in the articles of *Pravda* that "a mass for the dead must be read" for the Chinese revolution, that the Chinese communists must "retire within themselves," that they must renounce "great deeds and great plans," and that all this is the "sermon of the liquidation of the Chinese revolution"—if the line of the Opposition is adopted. This was said literally, for example, in the leading article in *Pravda* of May 16, 1927. As we see, it is word for word the same thing that Dan says, or more correctly, Dan says of the Opposition word for word what *Pravda* has said in a series of its articles. Dan approves the theses of Stalin and derides the "liquidator" Radek, who covers his liquidation with extremely left phrases. Everything is clear now: The liquidationism of Radek is the same liquidationism that is evaluated as such by the renowned revolutionist Dan. That is the lesson that the leading article in *Sotsialistichesky Vestnik* presents to those who are still capable of learning anything.

It is surely portentous that the quoted number of *Sotsialistichesky Vestnik* should arrive in Moscow on the eve of the opening of the session of the Executive Committee of the Communist International, which must consider the problem of the Chinese revolution in its full scope.

From *Problems of the Chinese Revolution.*

THE COMMUNIST PARTY
AND THE KUOMINTANG[34]

May 10, 1927

I think the new situation calls for a review of the relationship between the Communist Party and the Kuomintang. Why should we remain in the left Kuomintang?

1. On this point the following argument is often repeated: "Since the workers and peasants support the left Kuomintang, we should remain in it in order to win them over to the Communist Party." This argument scarcely holds up. Far more workers support the Social Democracy and Amsterdam[35] than the Kuomintang. The same argument could also fully apply to the Anglo-Russian Committee.

As a general rule, when we want to break workers away from some organization and win them over, we do not join the organization; we leave it.

2. Another argument is: "Now, while they are smashing both us and the left Kuomintang, withdrawal is out of the question." I think it is much more dangerous for the organization to be combined when they are dealing us blows than it is when we are the ones dealing the blows. Bela Kun's experience in Hungary is eloquent testimony to this. Under such difficult conditions, the meaning of revolutionary firmness is clearer than ever. By remaining in the same organization with the Wang Ching-weis, we are sharing the responsibility for their waverings and betrayals. There must be unity in striking the enemy—but a separation of political responsibility.

3. From the first argument it follows that we should remain in the left Kuomintang until we have drawn all of the workers and peasants away from it. But if this is the case, we will never leave the Kuomintang. First, because China's national democracy will

have behind it not only peasants but workers as well for a good while yet. And second, by remaining in the Kuomintang we do not confront the workers with the necessity of choosing between it and the Communist Party.

As for the peasants, they could continue to look to the Kuomintang as our peasants looked to the Social Revolutionaries, right up to the proletarian dictatorship. From precisely this flows the necessity of a bloc.

The second argument states that we should remain in the Kuomintang until our retreat is over (i.e., until our destruction). But if our retreat were to shift to an attack, then they would say: it is impermissible to disrupt the offensive by withdrawing from the Kuomintang.

4. The analogy of the British Communist Party's entry into the Labour Party falls apart under its own weight. The British Labour Party is proletarian in composition and political differentiation is proceeding slowly by comparison. The Kuomintang is a "party" of different classes, and political differentiation among them is proceeding with extreme rapidity because of the revolution. The Chinese Communist Party has lagged behind this differentiation the whole time.

5. After the Chiang Kai-shek coup the question becomes even more crucial. As it turns out, the most vile proposals against the Communist Party and the working class at the Kuomintang's last plenum were made by Wang Ching-wei. That was on the eve of the coup.[36] All available information indicates that the Hankow government at this moment continues to pursue the same line, yet the Communist Party remains the left opposition in the Kuomintang. Moscow can talk about "remaining in the Kuomintang with full [?] political and organizational [?!] independence." But what does this mean in practice? In Hankow, surely, all of these questions are being posed at the point of a sword. The Central Committee of the Chinese Communist Party will be totally unable to comprehend what we are in fact proposing. And in moments as critical as this nothing is worse than confusion.

6. This kind of argument was also advanced: *It is necessary to leave the Kuomintang, but the Communist Party must be allowed a certain time to prepare.* It is easier to accept this kind of formulation. But then the Chinese Communist Party must be told openly about it. Obviously, the preparation must include the perspective that withdrawal from the Kuomintang will give way

to a bloc with it and collaboration on all policy—however, with a separation of political responsibility. Unfortunately this purely practical way of posing the question has been withdrawn and replaced with the arguments of a general nature, examined briefly above.

7. Meanwhile, there can be no doubt that the Communist Party's remaining in the left Kuomintang will in the future mean the subordination of its policy to its organizational dependence, and—considering how young and inexperienced it is—this will inevitably lead it to repeat all the mistakes of the past period.

*   *   *

In Comrade Radek's letter of March 3, the need to remain for a time within the Kuomintang was argued as follows: "All the activity of the Kuomintang, or more precisely, its right wing and military units—directed as they are against the interests of the masses and in defense of the interests of the landlords and capitalists, as well as the Blanquist policies of the Kuomintang Central Committee—*have still not produced among the masses any opposition to the Kuomintang nor led to an understanding of the need for a separate class party of the proletariat and the poorest peasantry.*"

At the time, I objected to this argument on the basis of which the organization of an independent workers' party is put off until the masses understand the need for such a party. But right now I will leave aside the question of principle on this matter. The meaning of the words we have quoted from Comrade Radek is clear: It is necessary to wait for actions on the part of the right wing and units of the army so that the masses understand the need for their own party. Were the "April actions" not sufficient for this? It would seem that they were.

However, new difficulties now crop up: The "April actions" which, according to the March 3 letter, should have served as the signal for an independent Communist Party, are now being proclaimed the main obstacle to this independence. We are creating an organizational trap for ourselves—one we will not be able to escape from by continually finding new political arguments.

I understand very well that on *this* aspect of the question *our* differences are not differences in principle, but how the question is interpreted organizationally under the present conditions in

China has enormous significance. The very same Chinese communists who were the left appendage under Chiang Kai-shek will in a year or two become in turn the left appendage under Wang Ching-wei.

[Postscript, June 9, 1927]

The above lines were written about a month ago. Everything that has transpired since then confirms the need for clarity on the fundamental question of independence for the Chinese Communist Party. To depict the Kuomintang as a formless organization committed to no one is to distort the very meaning of the question. No matter how formless the Kuomintang is at its periphery, its central apparatus has the revolutionary dictatorship firmly in hand. The Canton Kuomintang has imitated the AUCP in this respect. The Hankow Kuomintang imitates the one in Canton (or Nanking). For the Central Committee of the Communist Party in Hankow the proposal that it enter the Kuomintang while retaining full political and organizational independence is no more than an unsolvable riddle. We know that even the present Central Committee of the present Chinese Communist Party declared itself last year in favor of a bloc *from without* rather than a bloc *from within,* that is, *in favor of withdrawing from the Kuomintang.* But now the Chinese Central Committee is no doubt repeatedly being told: "Look, even the Opposition in the AUCP is against withdrawing from the Kuomintang." In China this argument is undoubtedly being used, and will continue to be used, just as widely as we use the argument that the Opposition is for withdrawing from the Kuomintang.

T'an P'ing-shan's speech at the time he became minister[37] shows all too clearly that for this Communist Party to remain in the Kuomintang—not "in general" but under the given concrete conditions of time and place—permits its leaders to declare they will implement the program of the Kuomintang and not that of their own party, and what is even worse, permits the party to put up with such leaders, thereby blurring the lines defining the party. This has to be stopped at all costs. A real differentiation of Bolsheviks from Mensheviks within the Communist Party itself is bound to occur over this question.

What is necessary at the present time? It is necessary to formulate the reasons we have remained in the Kuomintang up to the present. At the same time—and this is most important of all—

it is necessary to formulate with just as much clarity and accuracy the reasons we must now leave the Kuomintang. The reasons for leaving it multiply by the day—one need only look at the dispatches "not for publication."

To postpone dealing with this question can only worsen the situation.

L. Trotsky

Enclosed:
1. Comrade Radek's letter of March 3, 1927.
2. Comrade Trotsky's reply of March 4, 1927.
3. Comrade Trotsky's memorandum of March 22, 1927.
4. Comrade Trotsky's letter of March 29, 1927.

Published for the first time in any language. By permission of Harvard College Library. Translated for this volume by Ivan Licho.

THE SURE ROAD

May 12, 1927

The Shanghai correspondent of the *Daily Express* reports:

The peasants of Honan province are occupying the land and executing the big landlords who resist most stubbornly. Everywhere, control is in the hands of the communists. Workers' soviets are formed locally which take over administrative authority. [*Pravda,* May 11, 1927.]

We do not know to what extent the dispatch is correct in depicting the situation with such bold strokes. We have no other reports save the dispatch. What is the real extent of the movement? Is it not deliberately exaggerated in order to influence the power of imagination of Messrs. MacDonald, Thomas, Purcell, and Hicks with the intention of making them more pliant to the policy of Chamberlain? We do not know. But in this case, it has no decisive significance.

The peasants are seizing the land and exterminating the most counterrevolutionary big landlords. Workers' soviets are formed locally which take over administrative authority. That is what a correspondent of a reactionary paper communicates. The editorial board of *Pravda* considers this report sufficiently important to incorporate it in the contents table of the most important daily events in the world. We too are of the opinion that this is correct. But it would naturally be premature to contend that the Chinese revolution, after the April coup d'etat of the bourgeois counterrevolution, has already entered a new and higher stage. After a great defeat, it frequently happens that a part of the attacking masses, which was never submitted to any direct blows, passes over to the next stage of the movement and for a while outstrips the leading detachments which suffered with especial severity in the defeat. Were we to have before us such a phenomenon, the soviets of Honan would soon disappear, temporarily washed away by the general revolutionary ebb tide.

But there is not the slightest reason to contend that we have before us only sharp rearguard encounters of a revolution that is ebbing for a long period. In spite of the fact that the April defeat was no separate "episode," but a very significant stage in the development of the counterrevolution; in spite of the agonizing blood drawn from the vanguard detachments of the working class, there is not the least reason to contend that the Chinese revolution has been beaten back for years.

The agrarian movement, since it is more scattered, is less subject to the direct operations of the hangmen of the counterrevolution. There is the possibility that the further growth of the agrarian movement will give the proletariat the opportunity to rise again in the relatively near future and to pass over once more to the attack. Naturally, exact predictions on this point are impossible, especially from afar. The Chinese Communist Party will have to follow attentively the actual course of events and the class groupings in order to catch the moment of a new wave of attack.

The possibility of a new attack, however, will depend not only on the evolution of the agrarian movement but also upon the side toward which the broad petty-bourgeois masses of the city develop in the next period. Chiang Kai-shek's coup does not signify only the consolidation of the power of the Chinese bourgeoisie (perhaps less so), but also the reestablishment and the consolidation of the positions of foreign capital in China with all the consequences that flow from this. From this follows the probability, perhaps even the inevitability—and this in the fairly near future—of a turn of the petty-bourgeois masses against Chiang Kai-shek. The petty bourgeoisie, which is submitted to great suffering not only by foreign capital but also by the alliance of the national Chinese bourgeoisie with foreign capital, must, after some vacillations, turn against the bourgeois counterrevolution. It is precisely in this that lies one of the most important manifestations of the class mechanics of the national democratic revolution.

Finally, the young Chinese proletariat, by all the conditions of its existence, is so accustomed to privation and sacrifice, has so well "learned," together with the whole of the oppressed Chinese people, to look death in the eye, that we may expect from the Chinese workers, once they are properly aroused by the revolution, a highly exceptional self-abnegation in struggle.

All this gives us the full right to count upon the new wave of the Chinese revolution being separated from the wave that ended with the April defeat of the proletariat, not by long years but by short months. Naturally, nobody can establish the intervals for this either. But we would be incompetent revolutionists if we were not to steer our course upon a new rise, if we were not to work out any program of action for it, any political road, and any organizational forms.

The April defeat was no "episode," it was a heavy class defeat; we will not take up here an analysis of the reasons for it. We want to speak in this article of tomorrow and not of yesterday. The heaviness of the April defeat lies not only in the fact that the proletarian centers were struck a sanguinary blow. The heaviness of the defeat lies in the fact that the workers were crushed by those who until then had stood at their head. Such a violent turn must produce not only a physical disorganization but also political confusion in the ranks of the proletariat. This confusion, which is more dangerous to the revolution than the defeat itself, can be overcome only by a clear, precise, revolutionary line for the morrow.

In this sense, the dispatch of the Shanghai correspondent of the reactionary British newspaper has a special significance. In it is shown what road the revolution in China can tread should it succeed in the next period in reaching a higher level.

We have said above that the peasants' liquidation of the big landlords of Honan, like the creation of workers' soviets, may be the sharp conclusion of the last wave or the commencement of a new one, since the matter is considered from afar. This contrast of two waves can lose its significance if the interval between them is long, namely, a few weeks or even a few months. However the matter may be (and here only advice can be given, especially from a distance), the symptomatic significance of the Honan events is thoroughly clear and incontestable, regardless of their extent and sweep. The peasants and the workers of Honan are showing the road that their movement can tread, now that the heavy chains of their bloc with the bourgeoisie and the big landlords have been smashed. It would be contemptible and philistine to believe that the agrarian problem and the workers' problem in this revolution, gigantic in its tasks and in the masses it has drawn in its train, can be solved by decree from above and by arbitration committees. The worker himself wants to break the backbone of the reactionary bourgeoisie and to teach the manufacturers to respect the proletarian, his person and his rights. The peasant himself wants to sever the ties of his dependence upon the big landlords who exhaust him with their usurious practices and enslave him. Imperialism, which violently hampers the economic development of China by its customs, its financial and its military policy, condemns the worker to beggary and the peasant to the cruelest enslavement.

The struggle against the big landlords, the struggle against the usurer, the struggle against the capitalists for better working conditions, is thus raised by itself to the struggles for the national independence of China, for the liberation of its productive forces from the bonds and chains of foreign imperialism. There is the principal and the mightiest foe. It is mighty not only because of its warships, but also directly by its inseparable connections with the heads of the banks, the usurers, the bureaucrats, and the militarists, with the Chinese bourgeoisie, and by the more indirect but no less intimate ties with the big commercial and industrial bourgeoisie.

All these facts demonstrate that the pressure of imperialism is in no sense an external, mechanical pressure that welds all the classes together. No, it is a very deep-seated factor of internal action that accentuates the class struggle. The Chinese commercial and industrial bourgeoisie carries behind it the supplementary force of foreign capital and foreign bayonets in every one of its serious collisions with the proletariat. The masters of this capital and these bayonets play the role of more experienced and more adroit agitators, who include the blood of the Chinese workers in their accounts just as they do with raw rubber and opium. If one wants to drive out foreign imperialism, if one wants to conquer the enemy, then his "peaceful," "normal" hangman's and robber's work in China must be rendered impossible. This cannot be attained, naturally, on the road of compromise of the bourgeoisie with foreign imperialism. Such a compromise may increase the share of the Chinese bourgeoisie in the labor products of the Chinese workers and peasants by a few percent. But it will signify the deeper penetration of foreign imperialism in the economic and political life of China, the deeper enslavement of the Chinese worker and peasant.

The victory over foreign imperialism can only be won by means of the toilers of town and country driving it out of China. For this, the masses must really rise millions strong. They cannot rise under the bare slogan of national liberation, but only in direct struggle against the big landlords, the military satraps, the usurers, the capitalist brigands. In this struggle, the masses are already rising, steeling themselves, arming themselves. There is no other road of revolutionary training. The big-bourgeois leadership of the Kuomintang (the gang of Chiang Kai-shek) has opposed this road with all means. At first, only from within, by means of decrees and prohibitions, but when the "discipline" of the Kuomintang did not suffice, with the aid of machine guns. The petty-bourgeois leadership of the Kuomintang hesitates out of fear of a too stormy development of the mass movement. By its whole past, the petty-bourgeois radicals are more accustomed to looking to the top, to seek combinations of all sorts of "national" groups, than down below, to the real struggle of millions of workers. But if vacillations and irresolution are dangerous in all things, then in the revolution they are disastrous. The workers and peasants of Honan are showing the way out of the vacillations, and by that, the road to save the revolution.

It is not necessary to explain that only this road, that is, the deeper mass sweep, the greater social radicalism of the program, the unfurled banner of workers' and peasants' soviets, can seriously preserve the revolution from military defeats from without. We know this from our own experience. Only a revolution on whose banner the toilers and the exploited plainly inscribe their own demands, is capable of winning the living sentiments of the soldiers of capitalism. We experienced and tested this out in the waters of Archangel, Odessa, and other places. The leadership of compromise and treason did not preserve Nanking from destruction, and gave the enemy ships access to the Yangtze. A revolutionary leadership, given a mighty social sweep of the movement, can succeed in making the waters of the Yangtze too hot for the ships of Lloyd George, Chamberlain, and MacDonald. In any case, it is only along this road that the revolution can seek and find its defense.

We have repeatedly said above that the agrarian movement and the formation of soviets can signify the conclusion of the yesterday and the beginning of the tomorrow. But this does not depend upon objective conditions alone. Under present conditions, the subjective factor has an enormous, perhaps a decisive significance: a correct formulation of the tasks, a firm and clear leadership. If a movement like the one that has begun in Honan is left to its own resources, it will inevitably be crushed. The confidence of the insurrectionary masses will be increased tenfold as soon as it feels a firm leadership and greater cohesion with it. A clear-headed leadership, generalizing matters in the political field and connecting them up organizationally, is alone capable of preserving the movement to a greater or lesser degree from incautious or premature side leaps and from so-called excesses, without which, however, as the experience of history teaches, no really revolutionary movement of the millions can reach its goal.

The task consists of giving the agrarian movement and the workers' soviets a clear program of practical action, and internal cohesion, and a broad political goal. Only on this basis can a really revolutionary collaboration of the proletariat and the petty bourgeoisie be constituted and developed, a genuine alliance of struggle of the Communist Party with the left Kuomintang. The cadres of the latter can in general only constitute and steel themselves if they do it in most intimate contact with the revolutionary struggles of the peasants and the poor population of the city. The agrarian movement, led by peasants' and workers' soviets, will confront the left Kuomintang people with the necessity of finally choosing between the Chiang Kai-shek camp of the bourgeoisie and the camp of the workers and peasants. To put the fundamental class questions openly, that is the only way under present conditions to put an end to the vacillation of the petty-bourgeois radicals and to compel them to tread the only road that leads to victory. This can be done by our Chinese party with the support of the whole Communist International.

From *Problems of the Chinese Revolution.*

A PROTEST TO THE CENTRAL CONTROL COMMISSION

May 17, 1927

Politburo, Presidium of the Central Control Commission:

1. The Politburo decided on May 12 not to publish my articles. It seems this concerns two articles, one, "The Chinese Revolution and the Theses of Comrade Stalin," which I sent to *Bolshevik,* and the other, "The Sure Road," which I sent to *Pravda.* I was not summoned to be present for the Politburo discussion of this question, although such would be required for even a pretense of fairness.

2. The reason given for not carrying the articles was that they criticize the Central Committee and are in the nature of a discussion. In other words, a rule is being established whereby all party members and the entire party press can only echo the Central Committee, whatever it says, whatever it does, no matter what the circumstances.

3. I consider the line of the Central Committee on the Chinese question to be fundamentally wrong. It was precisely this erroneous line that ensured the success of the April coup of the Chinese counterrevolution. Confuting the widely circulated lies and slander that the Opposition "is trying to profit from the difficulties," Zinoviev et al. offered to discuss the question of the future line for China and all of the most important questions of our policy *in a closed plenum.* This in itself indicated our intention to study and decide these questions on their merits, in a formal manner, without stenographic records—consequently without seeking to "exploit" anything. The Politburo, together with the Presidium of the Central Control Commission, refuses to convene such a plenum. Thus the attempt to correct a line that is false to the core and disastrous in its effects, by means of a

serious discussion in the Central Committee, has failed through the fault of the Politburo, automatically backed up as always by the Presidium of the Central Control Commission.

4. Then, Comrade Stalin's theses suddenly appear, representing a reinforcement and deepening of the most erroneous aspects of a thoroughly erroneous policy. And finally, to top it all off, the Politburo, having refused to discuss the Chinese question with us at a closed plenum (of course, it was discussed—without us—at "private" meetings) sanctioned Stalin's theses, and afterward refuses to allow anybody to pose in the press the question of why Chiang Kai-shek triumphed so easily, why the Chinese proletariat proved to be so unprepared, why our party has gotten so horribly entangled in the web of Martynovism, why Stalin's theses are pushing the Chinese Communist Party and the entire International into the swamp of opportunism, and why the *Sotsialisticheşky Vestnik* so emphatically approved Martynov's article earlier, and Stalin's theses now (May 9, 1927).

5. Are the Chinese revolution and the Comintern's entire political line really such small items that they can be swept under the rug? Can this really further the process of education in the Chinese Communist Party? Is this really the way for foreign sections of the Comintern to be developed? Can our party really survive following this course? Is such a bureaucratic utopia really conceivable?

6. The resolution of the Politburo states that we want to force the party into a discussion. If by discussion what is meant is the roar of the apparatus, the shouts and whistling of the claques that have been organized in advance, the packing of cells with goons trained to use violence against the Opposition, the overwhelming of workers' cells with threats and cries about a split—then, of course, we do not want such "discussion." But it is this very type of discussion our party life is brimming with. We want the party to discuss the question of the Chinese revolution, beginning as a minimum with the party's theoretical and central organs.

7. Yes, we want a discussion on the question of the fate of the Chinese revolution and consequently of our own fate. Why was such a discussion considered normal under Lenin throughout our party's entire history? Can anyone really believe that the theses Stalin, Molotov, and Bukharin pronounce at any given moment are the last word in historical development for the party? Yes, we want a discussion of these questions in order to demonstrate and

make clear to the party that these theses are false to the core, and that *carrying them out threatens to break the neck of the Chinese revolution.*

8. The Central Committee does not want a discussion. Yet what this discussion would entail is criticism of the Central Committee itself. It can be said as a general rule that the more erroneous any Central Committee line proves to be, and the more strikingly and harshly it is refuted by events, the less taste there will be for a discussion. I don't think there were ever any mistakes in the history of our party that compare with those made by Stalin and Bukharin on the Chinese question or on the question of the Anglo-Russian Committee. But the point is not what happened yesterday. Every one of us has been ready, and is ready now, to give it all up as a bad job. But these mistakes, promulgated by decree, are being extended into the future with their magnitude increased tenfold. This is what I am talking about. It is understandable that the Politburo "does not want" a discussion. But does the Politburo really have the right to *forbid* a discussion of the issue, when involved are fundamental errors of the Politburo itself on questions of world-historic importance?

9. The Politburo does not want a discussion. Why? Ostensibly so as "not to upset" the party. However, the Politburo opened up an artificial discussion, contrived by the leadership, about the allegedly antiparty statement of Comrade Zinoviev at an alleged nonparty meeting.[38] The party was not told anything about what Comrade Zinoviev said (as for me, I subscribe to every word he said). Comrade Zinoviev's speech has not been published. The affair is presented as though it was a nonparty meeting, whereas in fact the entire meeting had the character of a party meeting, even though a certain number of people who are not in the party may have been present. The "discussion" against Comrade Zinoviev proceeds at full tilt. The Central Control Commission is quiet. It is not stepping in. But when the "discussion" has made its way along the line, the Central Control Commission will also pronounce a "verdict."

10. Now, during the discussion of the Chinese question, *open meetings of the party cells* have been specially set up all over the country so as not to allow anyone to speak out on the mistakes of the revolutionary leadership and in order to have a chance to hold anyone who makes criticisms accountable for speaking against the party at a nonparty meeting. This is the system. It is a system organized by the leadership, a system organized for the

purpose of stifling thought within the party. Actually, one could get the idea that there is no real need for members of the Bolshevik party to exchange opinions on the question of the Chinese revolution, especially now that it has become clear that the Politburo, instead of learning from its errors, is imposing these errors on the party by decree. Compelled to make a choice in a situation like this, every honest party member should say: "It will be immeasurably more dangerous if I conceal my criticism of the party than if, against my will, a few people who aren't in the party hear my criticism."

11. We want a party discussion of the conditions and causes of the Chinese catastrophe. Irt order to hinder this, the Central Committee converts Comrade Zinoviev's supremely calm and supremely moderate statement into a party "catastrophe." Despite the critical situation, the difficulties, the dangers, etc., the leadership whips up the party, shakes it up, terrorizes it, and deliberately shouts in the party's ear the lie that Comrade Zinoviev is mobilizing nonparty elements against it. By means of a one-sided, fierce, envenomed discussion on grounds that have been artificially blown up, they want to prevent the party from calmly discussing the basic issues of the Chinese revolution. Amidst the noise, fuss, and clamor of a one-sided apparatus discussion, our articles are forbidden publication. Why are they forbidden? *Because Stalin cannot answer them.* Because the pathetic, empty, hurriedly stuck-together sentences of his theses that so satisfied Dan fly to pieces at a puff of criticism.

12. Discussion of the most basic issues is forbidden by referring to the difficulties of the situation, the dangers from without, and the approaching threat of war. As for these undeniable dangers, the Opposition stands out if only because it foresaw them earlier and assessed them in greater depth. The dangers are present, and moreover gigantic. But the fact is that *every one of these dangers will become a hundred times more dangerous as a result of the mistakes of the leadership.* The main source of the dangers lies in the defeat of the Chinese revolution, so swiftly brought about through the absence of the necessary class base. We prevented this base from being created at the proper time by our false policy. At the present stage this is a blow to the revolution and our international position. If we go further along the path of Stalin's theses, the position of the Chinese revolution—and that means ours as well—will further deteriorate (see Ch'en Tu-hsiu's speech[39]). Then they can point to a position that has deteriorated

doubly and they can doubly forbid all criticism. The more in error the leadership is, the less possible will it be—given the present course—to criticize it.

13. They will turn the whole question inside out. In favorable conditions it is still possible to make headway even with an incorrect line. But a serious situation demands a correct line, all the more imperatively the more serious it is. If the line is incorrect and if a leadership's persistence in following the incorrect line threatens the workers' state and the international revolution with new defeats and jolts, only a pathetic bureaucrat who has lost any feeling of personal responsibility or a base careerist—of whom, by the way, there are more than a few around—can keep silent about the mistakes, once having seen them and recognized them. Stifling a principled political discussion of the disputed issues with the noise, clamor, and hooting of the artificially contrived "discussion" directed against Comrade Zinoviev means terrorizing the rank-and-file party members, depriving them of any feeling of personal responsibility, raising the apparatchik even higher above them, and allowing the careerist to thrive like a fish in water.

14. I am calling things by their proper names because innuendo can help nothing in a situation like this. It is possible to mechanistically suppress anything for a short period of time: doubts, questions, and outraged protests. But Lenin called such methods rude and disloyal. They are rude and disloyal, not because they have an unpleasant form, but because *they are inherently incompatible with the nature of the party*. The Chinese revolution cannot be stuck in a bottle and sealed up. Nobody will succeed in doing this. The move to crush the Opposition that is being secretly prepared can be successful only superficially and mechanistically. The line we defend has been tested in the fire of the greatest events in world history, confirmed by the entire experience of Bolshevism, and reaffirmed, even though negatively, by the tragic experience of the Chinese revolution and the Anglo-Russian Committee. This line cannot be suppressed. However, it is entirely possible to do irreparable damage to the party and the Comintern.

This is what I want to state clearly and unequivocally to the Central Committee and the Central Control Commission.

Published for the first time in any language. By permission of Harvard College Library. Translated for this volume by Ivan Licho.

LETTER TO THE SECRETARIAT OF THE CENTRAL COMMITTEE[40]

May 18, 1927

1. My request of May 11 of this year that the Secretariat of the Central Committee indicate where and when I would be able to familiarize myself with the Politburo's decision on the Chinese question after what has transpired over the past two months has remained unanswered.

2. My request of May 11 of this year that Comrade Bukharin's draft theses on the Chinese question be made known in time for the amendments to be introduced has remained unanswered.

3. In view of the fact that Comrade Bukharin's theses basically repeat all the mistakes of Comrade Stalin's theses, I am forwarding to the Executive Committee of the Comintern my theses on the basic questions of the Chinese revolution in connection with criticism of Comrade Stalin's theses.

Published for the first time in any language. By permission of Harvard College Library. Translated for this volume by Carol Lisker.

STATEMENT TO THE PLENUM OF THE ECCI[41]

May 1927

The new resolution against the Opposition represents the high point of a line which is clearly and unequivocally a right deviation from the Marxist-Leninist line.

The objective causes of this deviation are: the defeats of the international proletariat, the temporary stabilization of capitalism, and the slowed tempo of socialist development in the USSR.

As the result of a series of defeats—under incorrect leadership that crawled after the bourgeoisie—the right deviation has increased and gathered strength. This deviation magnifies the consequences of the defeats of the working class and makes the preparations for its victories more difficult.

The defeat of the German proletariat in 1923, the defeats in Bulgaria and Estonia, the defeats in the great strikes in Britain, and, finally, the defeat of the Chinese proletariat have not only strengthened the Social Democracy at the expense of the Communist Party, but they have also strengthened the right wing within the Communist Party at the expense of the left. The right wing, for its part, exploits the huge apparatus, directs its blows exclusively against the left, uses repression, punitive transfers, firings, and expulsions to shift the balance of forces against the left wing to an even greater extent.

These are the general reasons why we, the Left Opposition, appear as a minority, while communists the likes of Martynov, Smeral, Pepper, Thälmann, etc., denounce us in the name of the majority. On the question of the Anglo-Russian Committee, the plenum approved the outrageous capitulation to the strikebreakers and traitors in Berlin. Like it or not, this is the line that leads to Amsterdam. And furthermore! If this line is maintained,

216

unavoidably tendencies will arise within the Comintern demanding that a bridge be built to the Second International. We can see these tendencies forming at this very moment. We issue a warning against them. We declare an implacable struggle against them in due course.

Speculations about help from the reformist British leaders against the war [danger] have revealed themselves to be sad illusions. The behavior of the leaders of the General Council and the Labour Party before and during the severing of diplomatic relations was dictated by cowardliness and baseness. As war really approaches, these two characteristics will only become more pronounced.[42]

On the question of the Chinese revolution, the plenum has accepted a resolution that approves the false line of the past and prepares the way for new defeats in the future. The leading Kuomintang people in Hankow, people the likes of Wang Ching-wei and Company, are beginning to become involved with the bourgeoisie, holding back the agrarian movement and the workers' movement, and if they do not succeed in holding these back, they will unite with Chiang Kai-shek against the workers and peasants. Those who, under these conditions, oppose soviets and are for subordination to the Kuomintang, i.e., to Wang Ching-wei, are preparing the way for a new and perhaps even more serious defeat for the Chinese revolution. We pledge ourselves to an all-out struggle within the Comintern for a change in this grossly opportunistic political line.

You have not allowed Comrade Zinoviev, who for seven years was president of the Comintern, to appear here. Our speeches and articles are not printed. The work of the Executive Committee itself is shrouded in a thick veil of secrecy. Is this the way to prepare the working class for the war danger? But now it is already no longer sufficient to suppress just the speeches and articles of the Opposition. Every day, dispatches from China, England, from all over are hidden from the workers simply because the course of events runs against the leadership's false line.

More and more frequently facts have to be suppressed. In doing this the party is disarmed, the errors compounded, and the ground is laid for new defeats.

The attempt to represent the struggle against the Opposition as a struggle against Trotskyism is a woeful, cowardly way of masking the right deviation, particularly when seen in the light of the Chinese events. You try to artificially breathe life into differences that Trotsky had with Bolshevism but which he settled long before most of you present here joined the ranks of the Bolsheviks. In vain! The most complete expression of the official line on the Chinese question was presented here by Martynov, who has taken an active counterrevolutionary position in three revolutions. He repeats here, applied to China, everything he said in 1905 and 1917. The Menshevik leader Dan acknowledges Martynov's position as correct and truly Menshevik. You call Lenin's fundamental views on revolution "Trotskyism" in order to justify the Martynovist struggle against them. Such a facade is a necessity given the level of ideological degradation. But it will not help. The views we put forward are the views of Bolshevism tried and tested throughout the entire history of our party.

A few days ago, approximately one hundred Old Bolsheviks, the pillars on which our party is built, delivered a declaration of solidarity with the basic positions of the Opposition to the Central Committee.[43] This fact discredits the false appeals to "Trotskyism" once and for all. The percentage of those who signed who come from other parties is far smaller than the percentage of such people in the leadership of the Comintern or the AUCP.[44]

The attempt to expel Comrades Trotsky and Vujovic from the Executive Committee of the Comintern is as flagrant a violation of the statutes of the Communist International as the refusal to allow Comrade Zinoviev to attend the sessions of the executive. Both are the expression of ideological weakness and bureaucratic arbitrariness. Both are the clearest expressions of Stalin's line, the dangers of which Lenin warned against in his Testament.[45] Instead of correcting the obvious errors of the leadership, errors the party has already paid for so dearly, Stalin wants to get rid of those who anticipate these errors and warn against them. The immediate object of barring Zinoviev and attempting to expel Trotsky and Vujovic is to shield the Sixth World Congress against criticism. It will be followed by the expulsion of the Oppositionists from the CC of the AUCP so that not one voice of criticism can ring out at the similarly prepared Fifteenth Party Congress.[46] The application of such shabby methods will only undermine the authority of the Sixth Congress of the Comintern. In the meantime a decision of yesterday's Executive Committee meeting unexpectedly postponed without discussion the convening of the Sixth Congress for a whole year (until four years after the Fifth Congress). The purpose of this postponement is to present the International with faits accomplis, especially with regard to the Opposition, and to demand that the congress merely give its approval after the fact to what has already taken place. This, to use Lenin's expression, is the "rude and disloyal" method which is intended to make it impossible for the party to introduce corrections through normal party channels. It will do no good. The line will be corrected. But the Comintern and international proletariat will have to pay much more dearly for this correction.

In anticipation of our resolution, work is being carried out for the preparation of a new and even more blatant repression. Your resolution is supposed to place the stamp of approval on it. But this will not advance the cause a single step. Truth and justice are on our side. The period of international upheavals which we are now entering will affirm the correctness of our views with each passing day and at the same time discredit every attempt at hypocrisy and double-dealing. We have set down our views in the documents we have introduced. You have condemned us, but the international working class has a right to know why you have condemned us. Suppressing our documents—this is only possible with an open awareness of one's own impotence. Articles can be hidden from view. Facts cannot. You will have to revise your resolutions. We are preparing for tomorrow. We embody the continuity of revolutionary Bolshevism. After this plenum we are more convinced than ever that revolutionary Bolshevism will triumph. For, apart from it, there is only confusion, vacillation, retreats into Menshevism, and defeats.

Long live the Third International! Long live revolutionary Bolshevism!

L. Trotsky
V. Vujovic

Published in English for the first time. From *Der Kampf um die Kommunistische Internationale* (Berlin: Die Fahne des Kommunismus, 1927). Translated from the German for this volume by Russell Block.

FIRST SPEECH ON THE CHINESE QUESTION[47]

May 1927

Comrades! In the question under discussion you have been given the theses of Comrade Zinoviev, which have remained unknown to the Russian party up until now.[48] Zinoviev was not permitted to come here, although he has the full right—politically as well as formally—to do so. I am defending here the theses of Comrade Zinoviev as representing our common views.

The first rule of the political education of a mass party is: It must know not only what is adopted by the Central Committee but also what it rejects, for only in this way does the line of the leadership become clear and comprehensible to the party masses. And that is how it always went with us until now. The refusal to show the party the theses of Comrade Zinoviev and my own reveals the intellectual weakness, the lack of certainty in their own position, the fear that the theses of the Opposition will appear more correct to the public opinion of the party than the theses of the majority. There can be no other motives for the concealment of the theses.

My attempt to publish the criticism of the theses of Stalin in the theoretical organ of the party remained unsuccessful. The Central Committee, against whose line on this question my theses are directed, prohibited its publication, as well as the publication of other articles by Zinoviev and me.

Yesterday a decision of the Editorial Committee, signed by Comrade Kurella, was distributed here. It relates to information on our proceedings. What is meant by this is not quite clear to me. In any case, the Executive Committee is meeting in a strange atmosphere of silence of the press. Only one article in *Pravda* has been devoted to the plenum and this article contains a phrase of unheard-of impudence: "He would be a criminal who would think of shaking the unity of the ranks of the Comintern," etc., etc. Everyone understands what is meant by this. Even before the drafts of the resolutions have been published, *Pravda* brands as a criminal whoever will polemicize against the future resolutions. One can imagine how *Pravda* will inform the party tomorrow about what is taking place here. Meanwhile, here in Moscow every expression of opinion, oral or written, in favor of the Opposition on the basic problems of the Chinese revolution is treated as a crime against the party.

The completely false theses of Comrade Stalin have been declared de facto inviolable. Still more, in the very days of the proceedings of the executive, those comrades who, in the discussions in their cells, protested against the baiting of Comrade Zinoviev, are simply expelled from the party or are at least threatened with expulsion. It is in this atmosphere, comrades, that you are acting and deciding. I propose that the executive shall decide that every party, the Communist Party of the Soviet Union as well, shall publish completely exact and objective reports on our deliberations, supplemented by all the theses and documents distributed here. The problems of the Chinese revolution cannot be stuck into a bottle and sealed up.

Comrades, the greatest of all dangers is the ever-sharpening party regime. Every mistake of the leadership is made "good," so to speak, through measures against the Opposition. The day the dispatch on Chiang Kai-shek's coup was made known in Moscow, we said to each other: The Opposition will have to pay dearly for this—especially when demands for payment on their part have not been lacking recently.

The opportunity is always found to frame up a new "case" against Zinoviev, Kamenev, Trotsky, Pyatakov, Smilga, etc., so as to distract the attention of the party from the most burning question; expulsions of the Opposition, despite the approach of the party congress or rather just because of it—constantly increase. The same methods in every section of the party: in every factory, in every district, in every city. With this, there frequently emerge, of necessity, those elements who are always ready to accept in advance everything from above, because nothing is difficult for them. They lull themselves into the hope that after Trotsky or Zinoviev have been overcome, everything will be in order. On the contrary: the regime has its own inner logic. The list has only been opened, not closed. On this road there are only difficulties and further convulsions.

This regime weighs heavily on the International. One does not trust himself to speak a word of criticism openly, on the false pretense of not wanting to harm the Soviet Union. But that is exactly how the greatest harm is done. Our internal policy needs revolutionary international criticism, for the false tendencies in foreign policies are only the extension of the incorrect tendencies in our internal policy.

I now turn to the draft resolution of Comrade Bukharin. First a question that directly touches the point on the agenda already acted upon. Listen, comrades:

> The Communist International is of the opinion that parties and in general all organizations that call themselves workers' parties and workers' organizations and do not conduct the *most decisive struggle* against intervention in China, who *lull the vigilance of the working class* and propagate a *passive attitude* in this question, objectively (sometimes also subjectively) help the imperialists . . . in the preparation of the war against the Soviet Union and in the preparation of new world wars in general.

These ring like honest words. But they become honest only when they are applied also to the Anglo-Russian Committee. For does it "conduct the most decisive struggle against intervention in China"? No! Does it not lull the vigilance of the working class? It does. Does it not propagate a passive attitude on this question! Without a doubt. Does it not thereby objectively (in its British half also subjectively) help the imperialists of Great Britain in their work of preparing the war? Obviously and without a doubt.

Compare this with what was declaimed here yesterday by Kuusinen on the Anglo-Russian Committee in the language of Kuusinenized Purcellism. Whence this duplicity? The philosophy of customs certificates is far more appropriate in the customs office of a border state than on the tribune of the Comintern. This false and unworthy philosophy must be swept away with a broom.

Let us listen further to the resolution of Bukharin:

> The ECCI declares that the development of events [in the Chinese revolution, the estimate of its driving forces made at the last enlarged plenum of the CI] has confirmed the prognosis. The ECCI declares especially that the course of events has fully confirmed the prognosis of the enlarged plenum on the inevitable departure of the bourgeoisie

from the national-revolutionary united front and its going over to the side of the counterrevolution.

The workers of Shanghai and Hankow will surely be surprised when they read that the April events developed in complete harmony with the historical line of march that Comrade Bukharin had previously outlined for the Chinese revolution. Can one ever imagine a more malicious caricature and more ridiculous pedantry? The vanguard of the Chinese proletariat was smashed by that same "national" bourgeoisie that occupied the leading role in the joint party of the Kuomintang, subordinating the Communist Party on all decisive questions to the organizational discipline of the joint party. After the counterrevolutionary overthrow, which struck the Chinese workers and the huge majority of the working class of the world like a bolt from the blue, the resolution says: It all took place in accordance with the best rules of the Bukharinist prognosis. It really sounds like a misplaced anecdote.

What is to be understood here by a prognosis, what does this so-called prognosis signify under the given conditions? Nothing but an empty phrase on the fact that the bourgeoisie, at a given stage of the bourgeois revolution, must separate itself from the oppressed masses of the people. That this commonplace is pathetically called "prognosis" is a disgrace to Marxism. This banality does not separate Bolshevism from Menshevism for an instant. Ask Kautsky, Otto Bauer, and Dan, and the answer will be: the bloc of the proletariat with the bourgeoisie cannot last forever. Dan scribbled that in his rag only a short time ago.

But the kernel of the question is the following: To say that the bourgeoisie must separate itself from the national revolution is one thing; to say that the bourgeoisie must take hold of the leadership of the revolution and the leadership of the proletariat, deceive the working class and then disarm it, smash it, and bleed it to death, is something quite different. The whole philosophy of Bukharin, in his resolution, is founded on the identity of these two prognoses. But this means that one does not want to make any fundamental contrast between the Bolshevik and Menshevik perspectives.

Let us listen to what Lenin said on this question:

> All bourgeois politicians in *all* bourgeois revolutions "fed" the people and fooled the workers with promises.
> Ours is a bourgeois revolution, *therefore,* the workers must support

the bourgeoisie, say the Potresovs, Gvozdyovs and Chkheidzes, as Plekhanov said yesterday.

Ours is a bourgeois revolution, we Marxists say, *therefore* the workers must open the eyes of the people to the deception practised by the bourgeois politicians, teach them to put no faith in words, to depend entirely on their *own* strength, their *own* organisation, their *own* unity, and their own *weapons*. [*Collected Works,* vol. 23, p. 306.]

Foreseeing the inevitable departure of the bourgeoisie, Bolshevik policy in the bourgeois revolution is directed toward creating an independent organization of the proletariat as soon as possible, to impregnate it as deeply as possible with mistrust of the bourgeoisie, to embrace the masses as soon as possible in the broadest form and to arm them, to aid the revolutionary uprising of the peasant masses with all means. The Menshevik policy in foreseeing the so-called departure of the bourgeoisie is directed toward postponing this moment as long as possible, while the independence of policy and organization of the proletariat is sacrificed to this aim, the workers are instilled with confidence in the progressive role of the bourgeoisie, and the necessity of political self-restraint is preached. In order to maintain the alliance with Purcell, the great strikebreaker, he must be palliated by declaiming about hearty relations and political agreement. In order to maintain the so-called bloc with the Chinese bourgeoisie, they must always be whitewashed anew, thereby facilitating the deluding of the masses by the bourgeois politicians.

Yes, the moment of the departure of the bourgeoisie can thereby be postponed. But this postponement is utilized by the bourgeoisie against the proletariat: It seizes hold of the leadership thanks to its great social advantages, it arms its loyal troops, it prevents the arming of the proletariat, politically as well as militarily, and after it has acquired the upper hand it organizes the counterrevolutionary massacre at the first serious collision.

It is not the same thing, comrades, whether the bourgeoisie is tossed to one side or it tosses the proletarian vanguard to one side. These are the two roads of the revolution. On what road did the revolution travel up to the overthrow? The classic road of all previous bourgeois revolutions, of which Lenin said:

"All bourgeois politicians in *all* bourgeois revolutions 'fed' the people and fooled the workers with promises."

Did the false position of the leadership obstruct or facilitate this road of the Chinese bourgeoisie? It facilitated it to a great extent.

To prevent the departure of the bourgeoisie from becoming the destruction of the proletariat, the miserable theory of the bloc of four classes should have been denounced from the very beginning as genuine theoretical and political treason to the Chinese revolution. Was this done? No, just the contrary.

I have not time enough to present the historical description of the development of the revolution and of the differences, which Bukharin had the full opportunity to do—so extensively and so falsely. I am prepared to undertake this retrospective treatment in the theoretical organ of the party or of the International. Unfortunately, Bukharin touches this question only where we have no opportunity to answer him properly, that is, with facts and quotations.

The following will suffice for today:

1. On March 16, one short month before the overthrow by Chiang Kai-shek, an editorial in *Pravda* indicted the Opposition for believing that the bourgeoisie stands at the head of the Kuomintang and the Nationalist government and is preparing treason. Instead of making this truth clear to the Chinese workers, *Pravda* denied it indignantly. It contended that Chiang Kai-shek submitted to the discipline of the Kuomintang, as if the conflicting classes, especially in the feverish tempo of the revolution, could submit to common political discipline. Incidentally: if the Opposition had never anything to say against the official line, as was said here by Smeral in his mammoth manner, then why are the speeches and articles by Bukharin for the last year filled with accusations against the Opposition on the most burning questions of the Chinese revolution?

If I have time, I will read here a letter by Radek; it is a repetition of his letter of last July. This letter was written last September and takes up the most burning questions of the Chinese revolution.[49]

2. Only on April 5, that is, a week before Chiang Kai-shek's coup, Stalin rejected Radek's opinion in a meeting of Moscow functionaries and declared again that Chiang Kai-shek is submitting to discipline, that the admonitions are baseless, that we will use the Chinese bourgeoisie and then toss it away like a squeezed-out lemon. The whole speech of Stalin meant the pacification, the allaying of the uneasiness, the lulling to sleep of our party and the Chinese party. Thousands of comrades listened to this speech. This was on April 5. Truly, the prognosis is not so remarkable as Bukharin may pretend. The stenogram of this speech by Stalin was never made public, because a few days later

the squeezed-out lemon seized power and the army. As a member of the CC, I had the right to get the stenogram of this speech. But my pains and attempts were in vain. Attempt it now, comrades, perhaps you will have better luck. I doubt it. This concealed stenogram of Stalin alone, without any other document, suffices to reveal the erroneousness of the official line and to demonstrate how out of place it is to maintain that the events in Shanghai and Canton "confirmed" the very line that Stalin defended in Moscow a week before.

3. The CC received a report on March 17 from China from three comrades who were sent there by the CC.[50] This highly important document gives an actual description of what the line of the CI really looked like. Borodin acted, in the words of the document, sometimes as a right, at other times as a left Kuomintang man, but never as a communist. The representatives of the CI also acted in the same spirit, by transforming it a little into the Kuomintern; they hindered the independent policy of the proletariat, its independent organization, and especially its armament; to reduce this to a minimum, they considered their sacred duty. Heaven forbid, with arms in hand the proletariat would frighten the great specter of the national revolution, hovering over all the classes. Demand this document! Read it! Study it, so that you will not have to vote blindly.

I could name dozens of other articles, speeches, and documents of this type for the period of about one and a half to two years. I am prepared to do it in writing at any moment, with complete accuracy and a statement of date and page. But what has been said is already enough to prove how basically false is the assertion that the events confirmed the "prognosis" of that time.

Read further in the resolution: "The ECCI is of the opinion that the tactic of a bloc with the national bourgeoisie in the period of the revolution already passed was fully correct."

Still more. Bukharin contends even today that the renowned formula of Martynov that the national government is the government of the bloc of four classes, suffers from only one trifling defect, that Martynov did not emphasize that the bourgeoisie stands at the head of the bloc. A quite insignificant trifle! Unfortunately, Martynov's masterpiece shows many other defects. For Martynov contends quite openly and clearly in his *Pravda* article that this national Chiang Kai-shek government was no (no!) bourgeois government, but (but!) the four-class-bloc government. Thus is it written for him in the holy scriptures.

What does this mean, anyway—bloc of four classes? Have you ever encountered this expression in Marxist literature before? If the bourgeoisie leads the oppressed masses of the people under the bourgeois banner, and takes hold of the state power through its leadership, then this is no bloc but the political exploitation of the oppressed masses by the bourgeoisie. But the national revolution is progressive, you reply. To be sure, Capitalist development in backward countries is also progressive. But its progressive character is not conditioned by the economic *cooperation* of the classes, but by the economic *exploitation* of the proletariat and the peasantry by the bourgeoisie. Whoever does not speak of the class struggle but of class cooperation in order to characterize capitalist progress, is not a Marxist but a prophet of peace dreams. Whoever speaks of the bloc of four classes so as to emphasize the progressive character of the political exploitation of the proletariat and peasantry by the bourgeoisie, has nothing to do with Marxism, for herein really lies the political function of the opportunists, of the "conciliators," of the heralds of peace dreams.

The question of the Kuomintang has the closest connection with this. What Bukharin makes out of it is real political trickery. The Kuomintang is so "peculiar," something unprecedented, something that can only be characterized by the blue flag and blue smoke—in a word: whoever does not understand this highly complicated "peculiarity"—and it cannot be understood for, according to Bukharin, it is just too "peculiar"—understands nothing about the Chinese revolution. What Bukharin himself understands about it, however, is not to be understood at all from Bukharin's words. The Kuomintang is *a party,* and in the time of revolution, it can be understood only as a party. In the last period, this party has not embodied the "bloc of four classes," but the leading role of the bourgeoisie over the masses of the people, the proletariat and the Communist Party included.

The word "bloc" should not be misused, especially not in this case where it is done only for the good of the bourgeoisie. Taken politically, a bloc is the expression of an alliance of sides "with equal rights," who come to an understanding on a certain joint action. Only this was not the case in China, and still is not to this day. The Communist Party was a subordinated part of a party at whose head stood the national-liberal bourgeoisie. Last May, the Communist Party obligated itself not to criticize even the teachings of Sun Yat-sen, that is, the petty-bourgeois doctrine that is aimed not only against imperialism but also against the proletarian class struggle.

This "peculiar" Kuomintang has assimilated the lesson of the *exclusiveness* of the party which exercises the dictatorship and draws from this the conclusion toward the communists: "Hold your tongue!"—for in Russia—they say—there is also only one party at the head of the revolution.

With us the dictatorship of the party (quite falsely disputed theoretically by Stalin) is the expression of the socialist dictatorship of the proletariat. In China we have the bourgeois revolution, and the dictatorship of the Kuomintang is directed not only against the imperialists and the militarists but also against the proletarian class struggle. In that way, the bourgeoisie, supported by the petty bourgeoisie and the radicals, curbs the class struggle of the proletariat and the uprisings of the peasantry, strengthens itself at the cost of the masses of the people and the revolution. We stood for this, we made it easier for them to go on with it, we want to sanction it now also by talking nonsense about the peculiarity of the Kuomintang without showing the proletariat the vicious class maneuvers that have been and are concealed behind this "peculiarity."

The dictatorship of a party is a part of the socialist revolution. In the bourgeois revolution, the proletariat must absolutely insure the independence of its own party—at any price, cost what it may. The Communist Party of China has been a shackled party in the past period. It did not have so much as its own newspaper. Imagine what this means in general and especially in a revolution! Why has it not had, and has not yet to this day, its own daily paper? Because the Kuomintang does not want it. Can we tolerate something like this? This means to disarm the proletariat politically. Then you must be for withdrawal from the Kuomintang, shouts Bukharin. Why? Will he say, then, that the Communist Party cannot exist as a party within the "revolutionary" Kuomintang? I can accept remaining within the really revolutionary Kuomintang only on the condition of complete political and organizational freedom of action of the Communist Party with a guaranteed, common basis for actions of the Kuomintang together with the Communist Party.[51]

The political conditions therefore have been enumerated in the theses of Zinoviev as well as in my own (no. 40) more precisely in points a, b, c, d, e, f, g, and h.[52] These are the conditions for remaining in the left Kuomintang. If Comrade Bukharin is for remaining unconditionally—under all circumstances and at any price—then we do not go along.

(*Remmele:* Where is that in the resolution?)

The maintenance of a bloc or the organizational form of a bloc at any price leads to the necessity of throwing oneself at the feet of his partner. The Berlin session of the Anglo-Russian Committee teaches us that.

The Communist Party must create its own completely independent daily press at any price. Thereby it will first really begin to live and act as a political party.

Let us read further: "The ECCI considers radically false the liquidatory [look, look!] view that the crisis of the Chinese revolution is a long-lasting defeat."

On this point, we have expressed ourselves in our theses with complete clarity. That the defeat is great I consider self-evident. To seek to minimize it only means to stand in the way of the education of the Chinese Party.

No one is today in a position to prophesy exactly if the defeat will last and for how long. At any rate, in our theses we proceed from the possibility of the speedy overcoming of the defeat by the proletariat. But the preliminary condition for this is a correct policy on our part. The policy represented by Comrade Ch'en Tu-hsiu, the leader of the party, in his speech at the latest convention of the Communist Party of China (published recently in *Pravda*) is basically false in the two most important questions: in that of the revolutionary government, and in that of the agrarian revolution. If we do not correct with the greatest energy the policy of the Chinese and our own party in these two decisive questions, the defeat will become deeper and weigh heavily on the Chinese working people for a long time. What is most essential concerning this has been said in my theses, in the postscript on the speech of Comrade Ch'en Tu-hsiu. I must limit myself greatly and I point to the theses and the other documents. I have promised to read also the letter of Radek to the Central Committee. Unfortunately I cannot here refute the wholly frivolous and absurd assertions about the "surrender" of the Chinese Eastern Railroad, etc. Bukharin, like myself, has no documents on this, because the question was considered quite cursorily in one session of the Politburo.[53]

(*Bukharin:* It is shameless to deny this.)

If I am given three minutes for it, I will immediately refute the shamefaced Bukharin, for what he says is a lie. The only thing I proposed at that time—after the words of Comrade Rudzutak who said this railroad becomes an instrument of imperialism now and then (for which Bukharin attacked Rudzutak)—was a declaration from our side in which we repeat in an open and solemn manner that which we had already said once in the Peking decisions: The moment the Chinese people has created its own democratic unified government, we will freely and gladly deliver the railroad to them under the most favorable conditions. The Politburo said: No, at this time such a declaration will be interpreted as a sign of weakness, we will make this declaration a month from now. Although not in agreement with this, I raised no protest against it. It was a fleeting discussion which was only later, transformed in a wretched manner, in an untruthful way, presented as a definite formula and launched in the party organization, in the cells, with warped insinuations in the press—in a word, just as it has become the custom and practice with us in recent times.

Chairman: Comrade Trotsky, I call your attention to the fact that you have only eight more minutes to speak. The Presidium granted you forty-five minutes and after that I must let the plenum decide.

Remmele: Besides that I must request the plenum to reject certain imputations and expressions; to speak of a shameless Bukharin is the lowest I have yet heard.

Trotsky: If I am reproached for shamelessness and I speak of the shamefaced, protest is made—against me. I speak of the shamefaced Bukharin who accuses me of shamelessness. It is you who speak of shamelessness, I always speak only of shamefacedness.

Chairman: I strongly request you to abstain from such expressions. Do not think that you can behave here just as you please.

Trotsky: I bow before the objectivity of the chairman and withdraw every suspicion of "shamefacedness."

I cannot read Radek's whole letter; perhaps I will do it when I speak a second time. Radek's letter, which was sent to the CC in full agreement with me and Zinoviev, and which raised the most burning questions of the Chinese revolution which we are discussing here today, was not answered by the Politburo of the party. I must therefore now speak only on the general political consequences created by the very heavy defeat of the Chinese revolution.

Comrade Bukharin has already made the attempt to refer to the fact that Chamberlain broke off diplomatic relations. We were—I have already observed—in a very difficult situation, where we were surrounded by enemies and Bukharin and other comrades participated then in a great party discussion to find the correct way out of the difficult situation.[54] A revolutionary party can renounce its right to analyze the situation and draw the necessary conclusions for its policy just as little in a difficult situation as in a favorable one. For I repeat again, if a false policy can be harmless in a favorable situation, it can become fatal in a difficult situation.

Are the differences of opinion great? Very great, very significant, very important! It cannot be denied that they have become deeper in the course of the last year. No one would have believed in the possibility of the Berlin decisions of the Anglo-Russian Committee a year ago, no one in the possibility that the philosophy of the bloc of four classes would be flaunted in *Pravda,* that Stalin would present his squeezed-out lemon on the eve of Chiang Kai-shek's coup, just as Kuusinen yesterday presented his customs certificate. Why did this quick development become possible? Because the incorrect line was checked by the two greatest events of the last year, the great strikes in Britain and the Chinese revolution.

Comrades have come forth—and we will surely hear such voices again—who said: since the contradictions have become sharpened, the road leads necessarily to two parties. I deny this. We live in a period where the contradictions do not ossify because the great events teach us better. There is a great and dangerous push toward the right in the line of the CI. But we have enough confidence in the force of the Bolshevik idea and the power of the great events to reject decisively and determinedly every prophecy of split.

The theses of Comrade Bukharin are false. And withal in the most dangerous manner. They suppress the most important points of the question. They contain the danger that we will not only fail to make up for lost time but that we will lose still more time.

1. Instead of continually sounding alarms about wanting to withdraw from the Kuomintang (which is not proposed at all) the political independence of the Communist Party must be put above

all other considerations, even that of remaining in the Kuomintang. A separate daily press, relentless criticism also against the
left Kuomintang.

2. The postponement of the agrarian revolution until the
territory is secured militarily—the idea of Ch'en Tu-hsiu must be
condemned formally, for this program endangers the life of the
revolution.

3. The postponement of the reorganization of the government
until the military victory—a second idea of Ch'en Tu-hsiu—must
also be characterized as endangering the life of the revolution.
The bloc of Hankow leaders is not yet a revolutionary government. To create and spread any illusions on this score means to
condemn the revolution to death. Only the workers', peasants',
petty-bourgeois', and soldiers' soviets can serve as the basis for
the revolutionary government.

Naturally, the Hankow government will have to adapt itself to
the soviets in some way or other, or else—disappear.

4. The alliance between the Communist Party and the real
revolutionary Kuomintang must not only be maintained but must
be extended and deepened on the basis of mass soviets.

Whoever speaks of arming the workers without permitting the
workers to build soviets is not serious about arming them. If the
revolution develops further—and we are fully confident that it
will—the impulse of the workers to build soviets will grow ever
stronger. We must prepare, strengthen, and extend this movement, but not hamper and apply brakes to it as the resolution
proposes.

The Chinese revolution cannot be advanced if the worst right
deviations are abetted, and smuggled Menshevik goods are
allowed to be circulated under the customs seal of Bolshevism—
Comrade Kuusinen did this for a whole hour yesterday—while on
the other hand the real revolutionary warnings of the left are
mechanically smothered.

Bukharin's resolution is false and dangerous. It directs the
attacks toward the left. The Communist Party of China, which
can and must become a really Bolshevik party in the fire of the
revolution, cannot accept this resolution. Our party and the entire
Comintern cannot declare this resolution their own. The world-
historical problem must be openly and honestly discussed by the
whole International. The discussion, may it be ever so sharp
politically, should not be conducted in the tone of envenomed,
personal baiting and slander. All the documents, the speeches,

the theses, the articles must be made available to the membership of the International.

The Chinese revolution cannot be stuffed into a bottle and sealed from above with a signet.

From *Problems of the Chinese Revolution.*

SECOND SPEECH ON THE
CHINESE QUESTION[55]

May 1927

We are all of the opinion that the Chinese revolution lives and will continue to live. That is why the main question is not whether the Opposition issued a warning, and when, and where (I assert that it did warn and take it upon myself to prove it); the question is not whether Trotsky or Maslow wanted to surrender the Chinese Eastern Railroad; the question is rather what is to be done from now on to pull the revolution out of the morass into which it was led by false policy and to set it on the correct road. I want, in a few words, to go to the heart of the question and show the irreconcilable divergence between our position and Stalin's.

Stalin has again declared himself here against workers' and peasants' soviets with the argument that the Kuomintang and the Wuhan government are sufficient means and instruments for the agrarian revolution. Thereby Stalin assumes, and wants the International to assume, the responsibility for the policy of the Kuomintang and the Wuhan government, as he repeatedly assumed the responsibility for the policy of the former "national government" of Chiang Kai-shek (particularly in his speech of April 5, the stenogram of which has, of course, been kept hidden from the International).

We have nothing in common with this policy. We do not want to assume even a shadow of responsibility for the policy of the Wuhan government and the leadership of the Kuomintang, and we urgently advise the Comintern to reject this responsibility. We say directly to the Chinese peasants: The leaders of the left Kuomintang of the type of Wang Ching-wei and Company will inevitably betray you if you follow the Wuhan heads instead of forming your own independent soviets. The agrarian revolution is

234

a serious thing. Politicians of the Wang Ching-wei type, under difficult conditions, will unite ten times with Chiang Kai-shek against the workers and peasants. Under such conditions, two communists in a bourgeois government become impotent hostages, if not a direct mask for the preparation of a new blow against the working masses. We say to the workers of China: The peasants will not carry out the agrarian revolution to the end if they let themselves be led by petty-bourgeois radicals instead of by you, the revolutionary proletarians. Therefore, build up your workers' soviets, ally them with the peasant soviets, arm yourselves through the soviets, draw soldiers' representatives into the soviets, shoot the generals who do not recognize the soviets, shoot the bureaucrats and bourgeois liberals who will organize uprisings against the soviets. Only through peasants' and soldiers' soviets will you win over the majority of Chiang Kai-shek's soldiers to your side.

You, the advanced Chinese proletarians, would be traitors to your class and to your historic mission, were you to believe that an organization of leaders, petty bourgeois and compromising in spirit, which has no more than 250,000 members (see the report of T'an P'ing-shan) is capable of substituting for workers', peasants', and soldiers' soviets embracing millions upon millions. *The Chinese bourgeois-democratic revolution will go forward and be victorious either in the soviet form or not at all.*

We will say to the Chinese communists: The program of comrade Ch'en Tu-hsiu, namely, to postpone the "reorganization" of the Hankow regime and the confiscation of the large landowners' land until the war danger is eliminated, is the surest and swiftest road to ruin. War danger is class danger. It can only be ended by crushing the great landowners, by annihilating the agents of imperialism and of Chiang Kai-shek, and by the building of soviets. Precisely in that lies the agrarian revolution, the people's revolution, the workers' and peasants' revolution, i.e., the genuine national revolution (in the Leninist, but not in the Martynovist sense of the term).

Now on the internal questions of the Communist Party of the Soviet Union.

In critical moments like the present, the principal rule of revolutionary policy consists of thinking out a question to the very end and expressing one's opinion completely, with entire clarity, without any hypocrisy, without reservations. It is a question of the Opposition in the CPSU and of what is going to happen in connection with the international difficulties and the perspective of war.

It would be manifestly absurd to believe that the Opposition can simply renounce its views. Such questions are decided by the test of events. An examination of the last half year since the Seventh Plenum has, in our opinion, shown and proved that the line of the Opposition stood the test of the greatest events of the Chinese revolution and gave the possibility to foresee and foretell correctly every stage in the question of the Anglo-Russian Committee, that is, in essence, the question of Amsterdam, and consequently also of the Second International.

Is common work possible? I have enumerated to you our diplomats, and I named only the most important ones. I could name hundreds and thousands of Opposition party workers at various posts at home. Will anyone dare to say that such Oppositionists, for example, as the people's commissar for postal and telegraphic communications, Ivan Nikitich Smirnov, or the head of the Workers' and Peasants' Inspection for the Army and Navy, Muralov, or the people's commissar for the interior, Byeloborodov, fulfill their duties worse than others? But the whole trick of the party apparatus consists of removing the Oppositionists from their work, beginning with the skilled workers in the factories. They are persecuted, shifted around, driven out, regardless of the quality of their work, solely and exclusively because of their Opposition viewpoint, which they defend with party methods.

As the party congress approaches, they are trying to send the member of the Central Committee, Comrade Smilga, one of the oldest Bolsheviks, one of the heroes of the October revolution and the civil war, one of our outstanding economists, to the Far East, to Khabarovsk, for planning work, that is, simply to isolate him politically. In the same manner, they are trying to get rid of Comrade Safarov, who has more than twenty years of uninterrupted party work behind him, by proposing to him to leave as soon as possible, be it for Turkey, or Tierra del Fuego, or the planet Mars, or anywhere else, so long as he disappears. They are trying at all costs to ship one of the oldest party members, Kuklin, a proletarian to the core, a former member of the Central Committee (he was removed from it for supporting the Opposition) to Great Britain, where he would be practically like a fish out of water. All of them are stainless revolutionists, fighters of the October revolution and the civil war. The number of examples could be multiplied endlessly. This method is ruinous. It disorganizes the party. A common practical work is entirely possible. This has been demonstrated by all our experience. The guarantee for such a common work in the interest of our workers' state depends entirely upon the Central Committee which is, it is true, pursuing an exactly contrary course.

I repeat: conscientious common work is possible, despite the deepening of the differences during the last year. In international questions this has appeared clearly, because tremendous events have taken place there. But now developments are entering a new phase in internal questions. Not only war, but also the danger of war puts all the questions harshly before us. Every class necessarily examines the fundamental questions of policy before a war. The kulak, the functionary, and Nepman raise their heads and ask: What kind of a war will this be, what will we get out of it, with what methods will it be conducted? On the other hand, the city worker, the agricultural worker, and the poor peasant will also examine more sharply, in face of the war danger, the achievements of the revolution, the advantages and disadvantages of the Soviet regime, and will ask: In which direction will the relationship of forces be changed by the war? Will it increase the role of the men on top or the masses below? Will it straighten out the proletarian class line of the party or will it accelerate the shift toward the leaders under the pretext of a "national war" (in the Stalinist interpretation)?

The bourgeois elements among us have grown very strong; the struggle of the two tendencies has its roots in the classes. Since there is only one party in our country, the struggle goes on through our party.

With the greatest light-mindedness, or more correctly, with the most criminal light-mindedness, they have spoken here of shattering the Opposition, of splitting off the Opposition, and the speakers were those whose whole past gives them the least right to do so. But I shall not dwell on them. Such people are washed ashore by one wave and washed away by another.

Ustryalov, the shrewdest enemy of Bolshevism, has for some time demanded the expulsion of the Opposition and the split with it. Ustryalov is the representative of the new bourgeoisie which grows out of the NEP, and of the most virile section of the old bourgeoisie which wants to support itself upon the new. Ustryalov does not want to "skip over any stages." Ustryalov openly supports the policy of Stalin and only demands of Stalin greater determination in liquidating the Opposition. Ponder over these facts.

On the other hand, when MacDonald appeals against intervention, he demands that the sensible "practical politicians" should not be prevented from putting an end to "the propagandists of the Third International"—these are literally MacDonald's words—that is, that Stalin should not be disturbed in his work of smashing the Opposition. Chamberlain, with his brigand's methods, wants to hasten the same process. The various methods are directed toward one aim: to smash the proletarian line, to destroy the international connections of the Soviet Union, to force the Russian proletariat to renounce its intervention in the affairs of the international proletariat. Can it be doubted that MacDonald will raise no objection to your refusal to permit Comrade Zinoviev to attend the sessions of the Comintern? MacDonald will boast of his own farsightedness if you should carry out the policy of destroying and splitting off the Opposition. MacDonald will say: The practical politicians are breaking with the propagandists of the Third International.

The attempt to depict the Opposition as a group of leaders is a gross deception. The Opposition is an expression of the class struggle. The organizational weakness of the Opposition by no means corresponds to its specific weight in the party and the working class. The strength of the present party regime lies, among other things, in the fact that it changes the relation of forces in the party by artificial means. The present heavy bureaucratic regime in the party reflects the pressure of other classes upon the proletariat. Yesterday, eighty old party members, tested Bolsheviks, sent a declaration to the Central Committee in which they fully support the standpoint which we are developing here. They are all comrades who have behind them, ten, fifteen, twenty, and more years of uninterrupted work in the Bolshevik party. To speak of any kind of "Trotskyism" in the face of all these facts is to falsify the question in a ridiculous and wretched manner. The revisionists label the revolutionary content of Marxism with the word Blanquism, more easily to enable them to fight against Marxism. The comrades who are turning away from the Bolshevik line label the revolutionary content of Leninism "Trotskyism," more easily to enable them to fight against Leninism. We have had a classic example of this in the speech of Comrade Kuusinen, out of whose mouth spoke a provincial German Social Democrat.

During the last period of party development, the blows have been directed only against the left. The basic reason for this is the defeats of the proletariat in the international field and the strengthening of the right course flowing from them. The whole history of the working class movement proves that great defeats result in a temporary triumph of the opportunist line. After the defeat of the great strikes in Britain and of the Chinese revolution, they want to deliver a new blow to the Opposition, that is, to the left, revolutionary line in the Communist Party of the Soviet Union and the Communist International. There is no doubt that the most principled, most consummate speech was delivered here by the new leader of the new course, Martynov, the mountebank of the bloc of four classes. What does this signify? A still greater strengthening of the shift to the right. It means the threat that the tendencies of Ustryalov will triumph. The Ustryalovs do not want to skip over any stages or phases, that is why the Ustryalovs are now openly for Stalin. But they do not, of course, think of remaining with him. For them, he is only a stage. For them, it is a question of destroying the left barrier in the AUCP, of weakening the proletarian line, of transforming the Soviet system into an instrument of the petty bourgeoisie, so as to proceed from there on the direct road toward the restoration of capitalism, most probably in the Bonapartist form.

The war danger puts all questions harshly. Stalin's line is the line of indecision, of vacillation between left and right tendencies with actual support for the right course. The growth of the war danger will force Stalin to choose. He has made an effort here to show that the choice has already been made. After the massacre of the Chinese workers by the bourgeoisie, after the capitulation of the Political Bureau to Purcell, after the speech of Ch'en Tu-hsiu in *Pravda,* Stalin sees the enemy only on the left and directs his fire against them. Dozens of old and tested Bolshevik party comrades, chiefly from Moscow and Leningrad, warn the party in their collective letter of the threatening internal dangers. We do not doubt that thousands of party fighters will join with them, fighters who do not fear threats or provocations, and who, despite all mechanical barriers, will understand how to penetrate to the public opinion of the party, and to redress the revolutionary line of Bolshevism through the party and by party methods.

Fraternization with Purcell and baiting Zinoviev, eulogizing and painting up the bourgeois leaders of the Kuomintang and baiting the Left Opposition in the AUCP and in other parties—

one goes closely together with the other. This is a definite course. Against this course we will fight to the end. Stalin said, the Opposition stands in one front with Chamberlain, with Mussolini, and Chang Tso-lin. To that I answer: Nothing has facilitated the work of Chamberlain so much as the false policy of Stalin, particularly in China. The revolution cannot be made by halves. The London blow is the receipt for the Martynovist course in China. On this path, only defeats can be accumulated.

Stalin obviously wants to make the attempt to present the Opposition as something like a defense corps of Chamberlain. This is wholly in the spirit of his methods. Yesterday Mikhail Romanov,[56] today Chamberlain. But here he will miscalculate even more than he did with his hopes in Chiang Kai-shek and Purcell. Chamberlain must be seriously fought and the working class in the country and throughout the world must be brought to its feet and united. The masses can be brought to their feet, united, and strengthened only through a correct class line. While we fight for a correct revolutionary line against the line of Stalin, we are preparing the best conditions for the struggle against Chamberlain. It is not we who are helping Chamberlain; it is the false policy.

Not a single honest proletarian will believe the insane infamy about the united front between Chamberlain and Trotsky. But the reactionary section of the petty bourgeoisie, the rising kulakdom of the Black Hundreds, can believe this, or pretend to believe this, so as to carry through to the end the suppression of the revolutionary proletarian line and its representatives. If you give the devil of chauvinism a finger, you perish. With his poisoned accusations, Stalin is extending this finger. We say this here and we will say it openly before the international proletariat.

From *Problems of the Chinese Revolution.*

IT IS TIME TO UNDERSTAND,
TIME TO RECONSIDER,
AND TIME TO MAKE A CHANGE[57]

May 27, 1927

Every day and, one might say, every hour brings news from China demonstrating the complete erroneousness of the line adopted by the plenum and the equally complete correctness of our predictions and proposals. This information is being concealed from the press. After the national bourgeoisie, exploiting the Kuomintang and our policy in the Kuomintang, smashed the workers, the so-called left Kuomintang—to whom the Communist Party was now subordinating itself—made an appeal in which it was proclaimed that "the peasants, workers, owners of businesses, and merchants—are all allies in the national revolution. . . . The Kuomintang is placing before itself the task of freeing from oppression not only the workers and peasants, but also the industrialists and merchants." (See the TASS dispatch—concealed from the press—dated May 25 from Hankow: *Bulletin not for publication,* no. 117.)

This is precisely why the left Kuomintang is demanding that the workers observe "revolutionary discipline"—with respect to the industrialists and merchants. The left Kuomintang prohibits trade unions from arresting a counterrevolutionary, just as it prohibits peasants from seizing the landlords' land. By misleading us, the Chinese Communist Party is helping the Kuomintang in these efforts. Step by step, events are demolishing a policy based on illusions, conciliation, disregard for the class struggle, and the bloc of four classes, which was invented by Martynov and approved by Dan. This policy is erroneous, and it is ruinous. In light of the new facts and the recent dispatches, the plenum would do well to bury Bukharin's resolution, replacing it with a resolution of a few lines:

In the first place, peasants and workers should place no faith in the leaders of the left Kuomintang but they should instead build their soviets jointly with the soldiers. In the second place, the soviets should arm the workers and the advanced peasants. In the third place, the Communist Party must assure its complete independence, create a daily press, and assume the leadership in creating the soviets. Fourth, the land must be immediately taken away from the landlords. Fifth, the reactionary bureaucracy must be immediately dismissed. Sixth, perfidious generals and other counterrevolutionists must be summarily dealt with. And finally, the general course must be toward the establishment of a revolutionary dictatorship through the soviets of workers' and peasants' deputies.

Published in English for the first time. By permission of Harvard College Library. Translated for this volume by Carol Lisker.

HANKOW AND MOSCOW

May 28, 1927

What is happening in Hankow now? We can only judge from the fragments of dispatches that TASS does not give to the press.

The left Kuomintang continues to chew the cud of the theory of the solidarity of the workers, peasants, and the bourgeoisie in the "national revolution" and recommends to the workers and peasants to observe discipline—toward the bourgeoisie.

The Central Committee of the Communist Party (or the Executive Committee of the Kuomintang?) calls upon the trade unions to mind "their own affairs" and to leave to the authorities of the Kuomintang the struggle against the counterrevolution.

The leader of the Communist Party, Ch'en Tu-hsiu, adjures the peasants *to wait* for land until the external foe is conquered.

From Moscow comes the warning not to create soviets "prematurely."

In the meantime, imperialism exerts pressure upon Chiang Kai-shek, and Chiang Kai-shek, through the bourgeoisie of Hankow, upon the left Kuomintang.

The left Kuomintang demands discipline and patience from the workers and the peasants.

This is the general picture. Its meaning is completely clear.

What is the Moscow leadership doing these days? We know nothing about it. But we need not doubt that under the influence of the recent extremely disquieting dispatches from Hankow, Moscow is sending advice there with approximately the following content: "As much of the agrarian revolution as possible, as many of the masses as possible in the Kuomintang," and so forth. The communist ministers transmit these counsels to the government and to the Central Executive Committee of the Kuomintang.

In this manner, the work of the Communist Party is divided into two parts: aloud, it implores the workers and peasants *to wait;* but in an undertone it whisperingly adjures the bourgeois government *to make haste.* But the revolution is a revolution precisely because the masses do not want to wait. The bourgeois "radicals" are afraid to make haste precisely because they are bourgeois radicals. And the Communist Party, instead of bringing the masses to their feet, instead of occupying the land, and building soviets, loses time with sterile counsels to both sides, in accordance with the sacrosanct prescription of Martynov on the bloc of four classes and on the replacement of the revolution by an arbitration committee.

The collapse of this policy is absolutely inevitable. Unless we correct it sharply, instantly, and resolutely, the collapse will take place in the immediate future. Then a lot of papers, with the Moscow advice in them, will be brandished before our eyes: "As much of the agrarian revolution as possible, as many of the masses as possible in the Kuomintang." But then we will repeat just what we say today: Such counsels are humbug. The whole revolution cannot be made dependent upon whether or not the pusillanimous bourgeois leadership of the Kuomintang accepts our well-meaning advice. It cannot accept it. The agrarian revolution cannot be accomplished with the consent of Wang Ching-wei, but in spite of Wang Ching-wei and in struggle against him.

That is why the first task is to free our hands, to withdraw the communist ministers from the national government, to call upon the masses to occupy the land immediately, and to build soviets.

But for this we need a really independent Communist Party, which does not implore the leaders, but resolutely leads the masses. There is no other road and there can be none.

From *Problems of the Chinese Revolution.*

IS IT NOT TIME TO UNDERSTAND?

May 28, 1927

Today's *TASS Bulletin,* no. 118, not for the press, contains a few dispatches of exclusively political importance. These dispatches are not kept concealed from public opinion because they may cause harm to the Soviet state or the Chinese revolution, but because they prove the faultiness of the official course and the correctness of the line of the Opposition. We cite only two especially striking telegrams:

> Shanghai, May 24, TASS—The central political council in Nanking has decided to make Feng Yü-hsiang a member of the council.

That Chiang Kai-shek has made Feng Yü-hsiang a member of the council (for the time being, perhaps, without the consent of the "cautious" Feng Yü-hsiang), is now known to the whole world. But it must remain a secret to the Soviet workers. Why? Because Feng Yü-hsiang has until recently been presented to us at home as a genuine "worker" or "peasant," as a reliable revolutionist, and so forth, that is, all the mistakes that were previously made with Chiang Kai-shek were again made with Feng Yü-hsiang. Now, for the last few weeks, all dispatches concerning the more than dubious conduct of Feng Yü-hsiang have been concealed. Why? To what end? Obviously, because some are waiting with the secret hope: perhaps he will not betray us after all! And if he does betray us, they will say: this completely verifies our prediction on the abandonment of the national revolution by the bourgeoisie. But now? Instead of warning the Chinese workers and the party, instead of stirring the masses of workers, peasants, and soldiers to adopt really

245

revolutionary measures against the treason of the general, we keep still, we conceal the dispatches in our pockets. That will not help. The class logic of the revolutionary struggle cannot be concealed in one's pocket.[58]

The second telegram:

> THE SITUATION IN HANKOW. Hankow, May 23, TASS—The Central Committee of the Communist Party has proposed to the Hupeh League for Strengthening the Revolutionary Front to set in order the relations between the workers and the petty bourgeoisie. The Central Committee emphasized the necessity of increasing discipline among the workers and of obedience to the decrees of the national government and declared that the trade unions have not the right to arrest anyone, and must always apply to the authorities when they consider the arrest of this or that person necessary.

This dispatch is even more important than the first. For every serious revolutionist, it illuminates the whole situation and shows the absolute faultiness of the official line, the downright disastrousness of this line, and the absolute correctness of the line of the Opposition.

Just think: the trade unions in the territory of the Hankow government are arresting the enemies of the revolution. This means that the trade unions, by the whole logic of the situation, are forced to assume the tasks of the revolutionary soviets. Now what does the Central Committee of the Communist Party do? It recommends to the trade unions to refrain from nonlegal action, to submit to the "decrees" of the Wuhan authorities, and in case of emergency, when a counterrevolutionist, a traitor, a conspirator has to be arrested or shot, to apply respectfully to the authorities who, in all probability, are related or allied to the conspirator. Is this not a mockery of the revolution, of its needs and of its most elementary tasks? Instead of arousing the masses to settle with the enemy right on the spot, the Wuhan government forbids it. Still more, it forbids it not in its own name, but through the medium of the Communist Party. The Central Committee of the Communist Party, in this case, plays the role of a political clerk to cowardly bourgeois radicals and pseudoradicals, who tremble before the revolutionary masses and believe together with Martynov that the revolution can be carried out through arbitration commissions but not through the liquidation of the enemy by the masses. Isn't this monstrous? Isn't this a mockery of the revolution?

It is noteworthy, besides, that the "Hupeh League for the Strengthening of the Revolutionary Front" is given a special commission, namely, to set in order "the relations between the workers and the petty bourgeoisie." These relations cannot be set in order by a special league nor by special instruction, but only by a correct policy. The soviets of workers and of semiproletarian city poor must be the broad organs of such a daily revolutionary policy. If the trade unions are forced to assume the functions of soviets, they will in certain cases almost inevitably leave out of consideration or injure the legitimate interests of the city petty bourgeois. Thus, the absence of soviets also hits the petty bourgeoisie and undermines its alliance with the proletariat.

Such is the situation in reality. The trade unions, driven forward by the masses, seek to correct the errors of the Chinese and Moscow leadership and are proceeding to the immediate liquidation of the enemy. The Central Committee of the Communist Party, however, which ought to be the inspirer and leader of this summary liquidation, holds back the workers, and calls upon them to increase their "discipline" (toward the bourgeoisie), and to bow mutely before the connivance of the Hankow Kerenskys and Tseretellis with the agents of imperialism, of the bourgeoisie, and of Chiang Kai-shek.

There is the Martynovist policy for you, not in words but in deeds!

A whole series of dispatches, especially from Tokyo, speak of the "crumbling" of the Hankow government, of its impending downfall, and so forth. Of course such dispatches must be taken with the greatest caution. These are the dispatches of an enemy, who awaits the downfall of the revolution, hopes for it, is on the watch for it, and thinks up all kinds of stories and lies. But the two above-mentioned dispatches, like many others of a similar kind that arrive almost every day, compel us to recognize the fact that *the position of the Hankow government can become hopeless.* If it prevents the workers and peasants from putting an end to the counterrevolutionists, it will collapse. By its false policy, the Central Committee of the Communist Party is accelerating its collapse. Should the Hankow government crash under the assault of the workers', peasants', and soldiers' soviets, we will surely not regret it. And it will collapse because it opposes the creation of soviets. If the Hankow government is supported in this ruinous policy, if the Chinese workers and peasants are restrained from immediately eliminating the enemy and from building soviets, then *the Chinese Communist Party is helping the Hankow government to collapse in the shortest time,* and to die an inglorious death, not at the hand of the worker and peasant masses, but at the hand of the bourgeois reaction. What is more, with such a policy the Hankow government, before it "collapses," will most probably unite with Chiang Kai-shek— against the workers and peasants.

Is it not really time to understand this?

From *Problems of the Chinese Revolution.*

WHY HAVE WE NOT CALLED FOR WITHDRAWAL FROM THE KUOMINTANG UNTIL NOW?[59]

June 23, 1927

The reasons we have not called for withdrawal from the Kuomintang until now (a serious blunder) can be correctly formulated in only one way that will account for both past and present. That is approximately as follows:

We have proceeded from the fact that the Communist Party has spent too much time in the Kuomintang, and that our party and the Comintern have been overly occupied with this question, but that openly calling for immediate withdrawal from the Kuomintang would even further sharpen the contradictions within our own party. We formulated the kind of conditions for the Chinese Communist Party's remaining in the Kuomintang, which—in practice, if not on paper—essentially excluded the possibility that the Chinese Communist Party would remain within the Kuomintang organization for a long period. We tried in this way to devise a *transitional* formula that could become a bridge our Central Committee could use to retreat from its erroneous course to a correct one. We posed the question *pedagogically* and not *politically*. As always in such cases, this turned out to be a mistake. While we were busy trying to enlighten a mistaken leadership, we were sacrificing political clarity with respect to the ranks. Because of this, the very way in which the question was raised was distorted. The Central Committee did not use our bridge, crying that the Opposition was in fact *in favor of* withdrawal from the Kuomintang. We were compelled to "justify" ourselves and argue that we were *not* in favor of withdrawal. This clear contradiction between the pedagogical and the political was reflected in the very first lines of the Declaration of the Eighty-three.[60]

Our basic approach on this question was correct, since we all held to the course for withdrawal from the Kuomintang. Our mistake was in pedagogically watering down, softening, and blunting our position on the basic question. It has yielded nothing but minuses for us: vagueness of position, defensive protestation, and lagging behind the events. We are putting an end to this error by openly calling for immediate withdrawal from the Kuomintang!

Published for the first time in any language. By permission of Harvard College Library. Translated for this volume by Ivan Licho.

FOR A SPECIAL SESSION OF THE PRESIDIUM OF THE ECCI[61]

July 1927

To the Presidium of the Executive Committee
of the Communist International:

The recent news from China shows that placing our stakes on the Wuhan government as the "organizing center of the revolution" was a devastating mistake. Within the territory of the Wuhan government the counterrevolution organized with ease at the same time that the workers' movement was suppressed. The situation is extremely serious for both the Chinese revolution and the USSR because a defeat for the Chinese revolution increases the danger of war tenfold.

In view of this, we consider it especially necessary to immediately convene the Presidium of the ECCI along with members and alternates of the EC who are in Moscow to discuss the situation and correct the mistaken line that is being carried out by the Comintern in China and that was approved by the last plenum of the ECCI.

Vujovic
Zinoviev
Trotsky

Published for the first time in any language. By permission of Harvard College Library. Translated for this volume by Carol Lisker.

WHAT ABOUT CHINA?[62]

August 1, 1927

Let us take the entire tactical, or rather strategical line in China as a whole. The Kuomintang is the party of the liberal bourgeoisie in the period of revolution—the liberal bourgeoisie that draws behind it, deceives, and betrays the workers and peasants.

The Communist Party, in accordance with your directives, remains throughout all the betrayals within the Kuomintang and submits to its bourgeois discipline.

The Kuomintang as a whole enters into the Comintern and does not submit to its discipline, but merely utilizes the name and the authority of the Comintern to dupe the Chinese workers and peasants.

The Kuomintang serves as a shield for the landlord-generals who hold in their grip the soldier-peasants.

Moscow—at the end of last October—demands that the agrarian revolution be kept from developing so as not to scare away the landlords in command of the armies. The armies become mutual insurance societies for the landlords, large and small alike.

The landlords do not raise any objection to their military expeditions being called national revolutionary, so long as the power and the land remain in their hands. The proletariat, which composes a young revolutionary force in no way inferior to our own proletariat in 1905, is driven under the command of the Kuomintang.

Moscow offers counsel to the Chinese liberals: "Issue a law for the organization of a *minimum* of workers' detachments." This, in March 1927! Why the counsel to the tops—Arm yourselves to the minimum? And why not a slogan to the rank and file—Arm yourselves to the maximum? Why the minimum and not the maximum? In order not to "scare away" the bourgeoisie, so as not to "provoke" a civil war. But the civil war came inevitably, and proved far more cruel, catching the workers unarmed and drowning them in blood.

Moscow came out against the building of soviets in the "army's rear"—as if the revolution is the rump of an army!—in order not to disorganize the rear of the very same generals who two days later crushed the workers and peasants in their rear.

Did we reinforce the bourgeoisie and the landlords by compelling the communists to submit to the Kuomintang and by covering the Kuomintang with the authority of the Comintern? Yes, we did.

Did we weaken the peasantry by retarding the development of the agrarian revolution and of the soviets? Yes, we did.

Did we weaken the workers with the slogan of "minimum arming"—nay, not the slogan but the polite counsel to the bourgeois tops: "minimum arming," and "no need for soviets"? Yes, we did. Is it to be wondered at that we suffered a defeat, having done everything that could have made victory difficult?

Voroshilov gave the most correct, conscientious, and candid explanation for this entire policy. "The peasant revolution," he said, "might have interfered with the Northern Expedition of the generals." You put a brake on the revolution for the sake of a military expedition. That is exactly how Chiang Kai-shek viewed the matter. The development of the revolution might, you see, make an expedition difficult for a "nationalist" general. But, after all, the revolution itself is indeed an actual and a real expedition of the oppressed against the oppressors. To help the expedition of the generals, you put a brake on the revolution and disorganized it. Thereby the expedition of the generals was turned into a spearhead not only against the workers and the peasants but also—precisely because of that—against the national revolution.

Had we duly secured the complete independence of the Communist Party, assisted it to arm itself with its press and with correct tactics; had we given it the slogans "Maximum arming of the workers!" "Extend the peasant war in the villages!" the Communist Party would have grown, not from day to day, but from hour to hour, and its cadres would have been tempered in the fires of revolutionary struggle. The slogan of soviets should have been raised from the very first days of the mass movement. Everywhere, wherever the slightest possibility existed, steps for the actual realization of soviets should have been taken. Soldiers should have been drawn into the soviets. The agrarian revolution would have disorganized the pseudorevolutionary armies but it would have likewise transmitted the infection to the counterrevolutionary armies of the enemy. Only on this foundation could it have been possible to forge gradually a real revolutionary, i.e., workers' and peasants' army.

Comrades! We have heard here a speech made not by Voroshilov, the people's commissar for the army and navy, but by Voroshilov, a member of the Political Bureau. This speech, I say, is in itself a catastrophe. It is equivalent to a lost battle.

(Shouts from the Opposition benches: "Correct!")

Trotsky: Last May, during the plenum of the ECCI, when after finally assigning Chiang Kai-shek to the camp of reaction, you put your stakes on Wang Ching-wei, and then on T'ang Shengchih, I wrote a letter to the ECCI. It was on May 27. "This policy is erroneous, and it is ruinous." What did I propose? Here is literally what I wrote. On May 27, I wrote:

> The plenum would do well to bury Bukharin's resolution, replacing it with a resolution of a few lines:
> In the first place, peasants and workers should place no faith in the leaders of the left Kuomintang but they should instead build their soviets jointly with the soldiers. In the second place, the soviets should arm the workers and the advanced peasants. In the third place, the Communist Party must assure its complete independence, create a daily press, and assume the leadership in creating the soviets. Fourth, the land must be immediately taken away from the landlords. Fifth, the reactionary bureaucracy must be immediately dismissed. Sixth, perfidious generals and other counterrevolutionists must be summarily dealt with. And finally, the general course must be toward the establishment of a revolutionary dictatorship through the soviets of workers' and peasants' deputies. ["It Is Time to Understand, Time to Reconsider, and Time to Make a Change."]

Now, compare this with: "There is no need for a civil war in the villages"; "Do not alarm the fellow travelers"; "Do not irritate the generals"; "Minimum arming of the workers"; and so on. This is Bolshevism! While our position is called in the Political Bureau . . . Menshevism. Having turned yourselves inside out, you have firmly resolved to call white, black. But your misfortune is that international Menshevism—from Berlin to New York—approves of the Chinese policy of Stalin-Bukharin, and being fully cognizant of the issues, solidarizes with your political line on the Chinese question.

Please try to understand that in question here is not the individual betrayals of the Chinese members of the Kuomintang, or of the right and left Chinese army commanders, or British trade unionists, and Chinese or British communists. When one rides in the train, it is the earth that appears to be in motion. The whole trouble lies in the fact that you placed hopes on those who were not to be relied upon; you underestimated the revolutionary training of the masses, the principal requirement for which is inoculating the masses with mistrust toward reformists, vague "left" centrists, and all vacillators in general. The fullest measure of this mistrust is the supreme virtue of Bolshevism. Young parties have still to acquire and assimilate this quality. Yet you have acted and are acting in a diametrically opposite fashion. You inoculate young parties with the hopes that the liberal bourgeoisie and the liberal labor politicians from the trade unions will move to the left. You hinder the education of the British and Chinese Bolsheviks. That is the source whence come these "betrayals" that each time catch you unaware.

Excerpted from "The War Danger—the Defense Policy and the Opposition," in *The Stalin School of Falsification* (New York: Pathfinder Press, 1971). Translated by John G. Wright.

NEW OPPORTUNITIES FOR THE CHINESE REVOLUTION, NEW TASKS, AND NEW MISTAKES

September 1927

Stalin and Bukharin's main concern at the present time is to claim that on the question of China the Opposition was always in complete solidarity with the Politburo majority until only recently. All the sections of the Comintern have been ordered to sermonize on this theme. This unexpected turn only serves to show how deepgoing the bankruptcy of the Stalin group is—just yesterday they were still arguing that the Opposition, unlike Stalin-Bukharin, had a Social Democratic, semi-Menshevik position on all questions. And now they are boasting that Stalin and Bukharin have acted and spoken exactly as the Opposition has, in every respect. But since all of yesterday's writings have not yet been burned, their pitiful attempt to hide their mistakes can be exposed without difficulty.

The July 1926 plenum adopted the following resolution:

> The plenum of the Central Committee, in approving the action of the Politburo and of the delegation of the All-Union Communist Party on the Chinese question, finds the *proposals of the Opposition (Zinoviev-Trotsky) patently opportunistic and in part openly capitulationist* on the following points: recalling Comrade Karakhan, relinquishing control over the Chinese Eastern Railroad, and withdrawing from the Kuomintang. The Central Committee holds that such a position would make sense only in the event of a total liquidation of the national revolutionary movement in China. . . .

And so forth.

If the "China" policy of the Opposition even before July 1926 was "opportunistic and in part openly capitulationist," how can it now be said that the policy on the Chinese question was carried out with unanimous consent? It is hardly worth pausing on the questions of Karakhan's recall or the alleged relinquishing of the Chinese Eastern Railroad. The crux of the matter is our attitude toward the Kuomintang. The resolution accused the Opposition of favoring withdrawal from the Kuomintang. The Opposition stated that it was prepared to form a bloc with the Kuomintang and establish a workable understanding with its rank and file, *on the condition of full and genuine independence for the Communist Party,* since in general such independence is the first lesson in the ABCs of Bolshevism. A struggle along this line has been going on since 1925. This struggle was recorded in numerous resolutions, reports, and articles written by the majority, where the Opposition's point of view is termed capitulationist precisely on the basis of the fact that the Opposition insisted on the independence of the Communist Party as the prerequisite for all revolutionary politics.

The Opposition exposed the incorrect policy with respect to Chiang Kai-shek. If not everyone knows of the relevant statements in the Politburo or in the Central Committee, Radek's speech at the Hall of Columns on April 5 is widely known. The most complete expression of opportunistic blindness was Stalin's speech at this same meeting, the record of which has been hidden from the party to this day. It would be sufficient to print the verbatim records of these two speeches—Radek's and Stalin's—to eliminate the possibility of any further allegations to the effect that the Opposition never opposed Stalin's pro-Chiang Kai-shek line.

After Chiang Kai-shek's coup, in May 1927, the Opposition introduced the following proposal in the plenum of the Executive Committee of the Comintern:

> The plenum would do well to bury Bukharin's resolution, replacing it with a resolution of a few lines:
> In the first place, peasants and workers should place no faith in the leaders of the left Kuomintang but they should instead build their soviets jointly with the soldiers. In the second place, the soviets should arm the workers and the advanced peasants. In the third place, the Communist Party must assure its complete independence, create a daily press, and assume the leadership in creating the soviets. Fourth, the land must be immediately taken away from the landlords. Fifth, the reactionary bureaucracy must be immediately dismissed. Sixth, perfidious generals and other counterrevolutionists

must be summarily dealt with. And finally, the general course must be toward the establishment of a revolutionary dictatorship through the soviets of workers' and peasants' deputies. ["It Is Time to Understand, Time to Reconsider, and Time to Make a Change."]

This proposal was only a brief summary of a whole series of documents previously submitted to the Politburo by the Opposition. Much time had been lost. However, if the Executive Committee of the Comintern had adopted the proposal of the Opposition in May 1927, so that it could have been put into practice, we would not have had this second, Wuhan chapter, which is even more disgraceful than the first, Chiang Kai-shek chapter. And we would be immeasurably stronger today.

Finally, now—in September 1927—we are introducing our current proposals, which correspond to the new stage in the development of the Chinese events.

1. It is necessary to again pose the problems of the Chinese revolution point-blank. An overall orientation is again needed because the official leadership while attempting to make some outward display of initiative in action (Bukharin's remarks at the last joint session of the Politburo and the Presidium of the Central Control Commission concerning Ho Lung and Yeh T'ing's detachments[63]) is in fact floundering without rudder or sail. With such a policy, new defeats are inevitable. These defeats will compromise the Chinese Communist Party and the Comintern directly—i.e., not through the buffer of the Kuomintang, as has been the case until now.

2. What does the movement of new, and, to all appearances, truly *revolutionary detachments of Ho Lung and Yeh T'ing* signify? Is it the brief epilogue common enough after great historic defeats, with the appearance on the scene of the extreme left wing—which didn't know how or was not able to act when it should have and is therefore doomed to defeat? Or is it the spontaneous beginning of a great new chapter in the Chinese revolution? This question is key in determining our "strategic" orientation and the tactical measures that flow from it.

3. If this question is to be defined more precisely in terms of the relations between the classes, then it must be formulated roughly as follows: After the bourgeoisie and the conciliationist petty-bourgeois higher-ups have gone over completely to the camp of the counterrevolution—having taken advantage of the workers'

and peasants' movement, Moscow's backing, and the authority of Bolshevism and the Comintern, and having reduced all of this to an instrument for the political exploitation and deception of the workers and peasants—can we expect that in the antibourgeois, anticonciliationist camp there will be enough political and organizational forces that will prove capable of inspiring the masses, who have been betrayed and, for the most part, beaten and bled white, with confidence in themselves and their own leadership? For this is the only way that a *new upsurge of the Chinese revolution* can be assured.

4. It is impossible to give an unqualified answer to this question, especially from the sidelines and from afar. However, it is doubtful that anyone, even in China itself—in this immense, far-flung country—can say yet whether China is fated to go through a more or less prolonged period of revolutionary decline before the movement is revived on a new, more advanced class base; or whether we can expect that, given the presence of huge masses of people living in horrifying conditions, given their exceptional readiness for self-sacrifice, given the presence of a young proletariat scattered widely throughout the country, given the people's experiences in civil war, and given the presence of the USSR and possible help from it, a new wave of uprisings can lead directly to a victorious struggle of the proletariat and the peasant masses for power. This last, of course, provided there is the correct leadership. Neither of these possibilities is excluded. Which will prevail depends not only on the so-called objective conditions, which, moreover, do not lend themselves to any kind of complete a priori calculation, but also on our own policies— their correctness, their energetic implementation, and so on.

5. About two months ago *Pravda,* to everyone's surprise (including, apparently, its own), advanced the *slogan of soviets for China.* Until then Stalin had explained that soviets are appropriate only during the transitional period where the bourgeois revolution passes over into the socialist revolution. This explanation stood in glaring contradiction to the entire experience of our three revolutions, all our party's traditions, and Lenin's theroetical teachings on revolutions in the East. Nonetheless, Stalin's new teachings became the official teachings of the party—i.e., of its apparatus. (It should be noted that the new "discoveries" and "teachings," at odds with one another and, above all, with the facts, wash off the party ranks like watersoluble paints. This does not mean that they are harmless:

when watersoluble paints run together, they turn everything to a dingy gray color.)

6. Advancing the slogan for soviets in July—i.e., after the revolution has suffered serious defeats—obviously ought to mean that the Chinese revolution had directly entered the period of transition into a socialist revolution. But the question remains: why was this slogan, advanced in a single editorial only, afterward so thoroughly forgotten?[64] And why does *Pravda* say nothing about it now, when the movement of revolutionary detachments is having notable successes with the assistance of the working class and peasant masses? Or does the slogan for soviets, which served at a certain point as camouflage (for Stalin and Bukharin), prove unsuitable for the new offensive of the revolution?

7. As is apparent from several commentaries in *Pravda,* the official leadership is exercising restraint and caution with respect to the new revolutionary movement that is linked to the detachments of Ho Lung and Yeh T'ing—i.e., in essence it is not running the risk of *openly* assuming the same responsibility for an authentic revolutionary movement of workers and peasants as it did for the armies of Chiang Kai-shek, Feng Yü-hsiang, and Wang Ching-wei.

8. It is not at all a matter of "guaranteeing" success. It is a matter of politically identifying the development of the revolution in the next period with the fate of this movement and of arming this movement with the correct perspective and the correct demands, without which victory is unthinkable. A movement of numerically small and, it goes without saying, poorly armed revolutionary armies can be successful only with the active intervention in events by the workers and the rural poor peasants—in particular only if workers' and peasants' soviets are established as the organs of power. Meanwhile, *Pravda* has again concealed this slogan. Why? Apparently because it fears that the movement will be more or less rapidly crushed. Of course, such a defeat is always possible; but in the absence of the correct slogans it is inevitable. To abstain "for the time being" from advancing fundamental, vitally necessary slogans for fear of defeat means, for fear of defeat, to in fact pave the way for it.

9. To identify the revolution with Chiang Kai-shek's armies was not only supremely "ill-considered," but also the greatest of historical mistakes and the gravest of crimes. To assume responsibility for Wuhan as the center of the agrarian revolution

was the second "ill-considered" act, no less serious than the first, and the second crime, no less grave. Once burned, twice shy. "Wait-and-see" type caution with respect to the independent workers' and peasants' movement, a reluctance for the time being to arm it with the necessary slogans, i.e., to say openly to the Chinese workers and peasants for the whole world to hear: "This movement is yours"—such "caution" threatens to become the third successive error of "ill-consideration" and the worst of them all.

10. What is involved here is not whether or not we are sympathetic toward the military revolutionary movement that has begun, and not even of organizational and material aid to it. There is no need at all to waste words on that score. Bragging about aid to revolutionary armies, or for example, to the British coal miners is what an overblown functionary would do, but not a revolutionary. Every bit of aid that comes from the sidelines is necessary, but it is not decisive. *The relations among the Communist Party, the revolutionary troops, the workers, and the poor peasants is what is decisive.* And these relations are determined to a great extent by politics as a system of slogans and actions. You can give any kind of material aid you want to a rebelling army, but if the question of power is not posed point-blank, if the slogan for soviets is not raised, and if a complete program of economic measures linked to the establishment of soviet power is not put forward, then outside material aid to the armies will not produce the desired results, just as our aid to the British coal miners did not produce the desired results when it was accompanied by our political bloc with the General Council. In the last analysis it is not material aid that is decisive, but the correct political line.

11. Right now, on the road, I'm reading in the Ukrainian organ *Visty* [News] of September 13 a dispatch from Shanghai about the fact that, in the face of the approach of Ho Lung's and Yeh T'ing's revolutionary troops to Swatow, the Kuomintang authorities and garrisons abandoned the city. The editor entitled the dispatch "Kuomintang Flees from Swatow." For many months now we have been living with the charge of "underestimating"— first the Kuomintang as a whole, then the left Kuomintang, which Stalin had authorized as the revolutionary center. Bukharin vowed that he would never give up the blue flag of the Kuomintang, but meanwhile it turns out that the Kuomintang powers "flee" from Swatow with the blue flag in their hands—

since (as the British so aptly say in such cases) one cannot simultaneously "run with the foxes and hunt with the hounds." Combining the red and the blue—a bloc of four classes—did not originate with Martynov. Bukharin vowed to hold onto the blue flag for a bloc of three classes. But now there turns out to be a civil war between the blue and the red flags. And one would have to be a hopeless idiot not to understand that only this civil war— against the landlords, the bourgeoisie, and the conciliators—can produce a genuine bloc of the workers and the poor, rural and urban. Those who up to now have isolated the Communist Party from the workers and the rural poor in China are precisely the ones who, in chasing after the blue flag of the Kuomintang, compromised the red flag of the proletariat.

12. But from the circumstance that a state of civil war has broken out between the revolutionary troops and the Kuomintang flows the fact that *the revolutionary movement can win only under the leadership of the Communist Party* and only in the form of soviets of workers', soldiers', and peasants' deputies. This presupposes a readiness on the part of the Communist Party to take on the leadership of a movement of this kind. And that in turn calls for a complete program in the period of struggle for power and the conquest of power, and after the establishment of the new regime.

13. The previous policy was deadly for the training of the Communist Party. Perhaps the most serious consequence of the wrong line of the previous period was not so much the material defeats and sacrifices as the loss of historical conditions unique for training revolutionary cadre, tempering the proletarian vanguard, and strengthening within it a sense of independence and confidence in its strength and in its leadership. Now, on the threshold of a new stage of the revolution, the Communist Party is immeasurably weaker than it should and could be. But one must accept the facts as they are as the result of a whole combination of factors, including the criminally erroneous line of the leadership. Only the Communist Party can now assume the leadership of the revolutionary movement. The blue flag of the Kuomintang can now be had not by way of new blocs, but through civil war—that is by tearing it like a trophy from the hands of the vanquished enemy. Therefore, we must put an end to shameful, reactionary fictions: We must openly announce a break of the Communist Party with the Kuomintang, openly declare the Kuomintang an instrument of bourgeois reaction, and expel it in

disgrace from the ranks of the Comintern. To fail to do so means to condemn the new movement to vacillations, confusion, and defeat.

14. This does not necessarily mean that the Communist Party will be the only revolutionary political organization in the next period. On the basis of the peasant unions and the Red Spears,[65] in direct struggle against the Kuomintang powers and military forces, a political organization can be formed alongside the Communist Party but more or less independent of it, relying on the support of a section of the rural poor. It is fruitless to try to guess how this will occur—at least from here, where the nature of the movement's organization and cadre are not well enough visible. But one thing is obvious: the Communist Party must clearly realize that the revolution can be victorious only through it and only under its leadership, and that the peasant organizations can fight successfully only side by side with it, only under its slogans, and only under its direct political and organizational influence. But this is possible only with a clear and precise formulation of all the political and economic tasks of the revolution by the Communist Party itself.

15. In order to justify collaboration with the bourgeoisie in the revolution (i.e., the Menshevik policy), Stalin and Bukharin have advanced two factors in turn. First it was *foreign imperialism,* which supposedly brings the classes of China together. It soon became obvious, however, that the bourgeoisie, in alliance with foreign imperialism, was smashing the workers and peasants. Then they advanced the second factor, *Chinese feudalism,* which they say impels the more "left-wing" section of the very same bourgeoisie and the real revolutionary ally, the loyal Wang Ching-wei, to struggle along with the workers and peasants against feudalism. But as it turned out, the bourgeoisie did not put forward a single political group that would agree to participate in revolutionary struggle against Bukharin's feudalism. And it is not accidental. In China there are no noble lords standing in opposition to the bourgeoisie. The landholder as a general rule is the urban bourgeois. The small landholder—the kulak, the gentry—is closely linked with the usurer and the urban bourgeois.

Unless one is playing with words, there is no feudalism in China. In the Chinese village there are serf-owner relations which are crowned, however, not by feudal, but by bourgeois property forms and a bourgeois sociopolitical order. This type of serf-owner relationship, which is a result of agrarian overpopulation, given the overall lag in capitalist development, can be found—of course in much more "mild" forms—in several Balkan countries, which have known neither feudalism nor the noble estate since their emancipation from the Turkish yoke. Of course, in China poverty and bondage take inhumane forms such as were hardly to be encountered even in the age of feudalism. Nonetheless, the attempt to create feudalism in China, still more its prevalence, relies not on facts, but on the naked desire to justify collaboration with the bourgeoisie. The facts have avenged themselves. In China there has been found no such bourgeoisie or section of the bourgeoisie that would agree to carry on a revolutionary struggle against feudalism, i.e., against itself. That is why, upon the approach of revolutionary troops to Swatow, the Kuomintang takes to its heels, carrying the blue flag under its arm and the Comintern membership card in its pocket.

16. *The struggle for an agrarian revolution* is a struggle against the bourgeoisie, which means against the Kuomintang. Not one section of the bourgeoisie has supported or is supporting this struggle. In the countryside, the chief enemy, due to their numerical strength, will be the gentry, the kulak, the small landed proprietor. In China, a refusal to expropriate the small exploiters, the kulaks, would mean renunciation of the agrarian revolution. The agrarian revolution in China—not according to Bukharin but in reality—is an antibourgeois revolution. Because of this—and only because of this—Martynov and Bukharin's schemes failed. But this also means that the proletariat will complete the agrarian revolution, taking behind it the poor masses of the Chinese countryside, i.e., 80, 90, or more percent of the peasantry—in direct and unmitigated struggle against the bourgeois, the landowner, and the kulak, and against their political arm, the Kuomintang.

17. The way the question of revolutionary power is posed is determined in the same way.

The experience with Chiang Kai-shek signified the failure of the idea of a bloc with the entire "bourgeois nation" in a struggle against imperialism and feudalism.

The experience with Wang Ching-wei signified the failure of the bloc of "the revolutionary democracy" in the spirit of Kerensky and Tseretelli.

Right now the business at hand for the proletariat is to win over to "revolutionary democracy" the poor lower classes of the city and countryside and lead them forward for the conquest of power, of the land, of national independence, and better living conditions for the toiling masses. In other words, the business at hand is the *dictatorship of the proletariat.*

18. The call for a democratic dictatorship of the proletariat and peasantry, if it had been advanced, let us say, at the beginning of the Northern Expedition, in connection with the call for soviets and the arming of the workers and peasants, would have played a tremendous role in the development of the Chinese revolution, would have completely assured a different course for it. It would have isolated the bourgeoisie and thereby the conciliationists, and it would have led to the posing of the question of the dictatorship of the proletariat under conditions infinitely more favorable than in the past. But we cannot reverse the course of history. The bourgeoisie retreated from the revolution on its own initiative—under circumstances chosen by it and most favorable to it. Exactly the same is true of the conciliationists. Because we were afraid to isolate them at the right time, they successfully isolated us. It always happens that way—and at that, not only in Shanghai, but also in Edinburgh, as is shown by the last congress of trade unions.[66]

But in any case, the retreat from the revolution by the bourgeoisie—the big bourgeoisie and the middle and upper petty bourgeoisie in the city and the countryside, and the intelligentsia as well—is an accomplished fact. Under these conditions, the call for a democratic dictatorship of the proletariat and peasantry— given a new revolutionary upsurge—will prove to be vague and amorphous. And any vague and amorphous slogan in a revolution becomes dangerous for the revolutionary party and the oppressed masses.

There can be virtually no doubt that Stalin will come forward tomorrow under the banner of the democratic dictatorship of the proletariat and the peasantry after giving it a conciliationist character. It would be incorrect to think that Stalin and Bukharin have understood their mistakes. The course of events in China is pushing them to the left, but they are bracing themselves and pulling to the right. In the future, too, they will strive to blunt the tasks and conceal the "isolation" of the proletariat by means of a bloc with the last two honorable figures in the Kuomintang—the wife and the protégé of Sun Yat-sen.[67] Blocs of this type, organized from the top, already nothing more than a masquer- ade, will, however, call for very real sacrifices on the part of the proletarian party in the sense of a retreat from decisive slogans and methods of struggle. Mme. Sun Yat-sen can manage the Chinese revolution a little more cheaply than Chiang Kai-shek and Wang Ching-wei.

19. If the revolutionary movement expands, the subsequent success of Ho Lung and Yeh T'ing's troops will inevitably push a section of the left conciliationists in the direction of a "bloc" with the revolutionary forces in order to co-opt the movement and neutralize it. The conciliators will be able to move toward this goal under the very slogan of a democratic dictatorship of the proletariat and the peasantry so as to once again even more surely and at a higher level, subordinate the proletariat to themselves, narrow the scope of the movement, and prepare a new disaster, the third one in a row.

The Leninist slogan for a democratic dictatorship of the proletariat and the peasantry that was not applied at the right time cannot be mechanically carried over into the third stage that is taking shape on the basis of a new relationship of forces. We must clearly understand that after the experience with the Kuomintang in general and with the left Kuomintang in particular, *a historically overdue slogan will become a weapon of the forces working against the revolution.* And for us it is no longer a question of the democratic dictatorship of the proletariat and the peasantry, but of the dictatorship of the proletariat supported by the inexhaustible masses of urban and rural poor— a dictatorship that poses for itself the objective of solving *the most* urgent and vital problems of the country and its working masses and in the process inevitably passes over to the path of making socialist inroads on property relations.

20. The task of the Communist Party is first and foremost *the creation of a revolutionary army.* A Red army of regulars must be constructed on the basis of the movement of the workers and peasants that is actually unfolding. The principle of operating with mercenary soldiers must be replaced by the principle of a systematic class levy. The organs for this levy should be trade unions and peasant unions under the leadership of the soviets and the Communist Party. It is necessary to skillfully and persistently include partisan detachments of peasants (the Red Spears, etc.) in the regular ranks. The question of the composition of the command must be correctly resolved on the basis of all the experiences of the Russian as well as the Chinese revolutions. The exploiter and the counterrevolutionary elements should be mercilessly driven out of the army.

21. The task of feeding the armies and the cities poses *the problem of the food policy.* Resolving this problem under conditions of civil war and blockade is inconceivable without measures of iron discipline regarding food, without the seizure of the food supplies of the big landholders, kulaks, the speculators, and without rationing in one form or another.

22. Civil war at the present stage is inconceivable in China without *the dispossession of the kulaks.*

23. The same tasks that the Opposition has formulated more than once, in particular at the May plenum of the Executive Committee of the Comintern, remain the most important part of the practical program for the soviets and revolutionary armies.

The land must be immediately confiscated from the landlords—big and small—as the armies advance and as local uprisings are successful. The reactionary bureaucracy must be immediately rooted out. Traitors, counterrevolutionaries, and agents of Chiang Kai-shek and Wang Ching-wei must be dealt with on the spot.

24. *Problems of industry and transport* will rise point-blank before the revolutionary government. In one of his countless speeches on China, Bukharin whiningly complained about the sabotage of the bourgeoisie, who export capital and are leaving no circulating media and thus create great difficulties that the Opposition does not want to concern itself with. Bukharin has proposed no means for overcoming these difficulties. A general reference to the difficulties as an excuse for one's flabbiness is a common trick of opportunism.

It is patently obvious that under conditions of civil war, the bourgeoisie can be prevented from sabotaging the economy, above all industry and transport, not by admonishment, but by the measures of the dictatorship—through organized proletarian control of industry in those instances where it is feasible and through workers taking enterprises into their own hands in every case where it is otherwise impossible to secure a continuity of production. The same applies with respect to rail and water transportation. In short, the overall plan should be to transfer the most important enterprises, i.e., the industries and transportation facilities ripest for it, into the hands of the soviet state. The necessary steps and preparatory organizational measures to be adopted must be worked out in accordance with the entire situation—depending on the overall course of development of the revolution, the strength of the enemy's resistance, etc.

It goes without saying, all this applies first and foremost to foreign concessions.

25. There will be philistines who will cry out about our utopianism, ultraleftism, etc. They will moan about China's backwardness, the small numerical size of the proletariat, etc.

To this we answer first of all that we do not intend to build *socialism in a single country* in China either. The Chinese revolution is not an independent, isolated phenomenon that must find solutions to all the problems posed by the revolution within the borders of China. The Chinese revolution is one link of that chain of which the following are among the other links: the Soviet Union, the forthcoming imperialist wars, impending proletarian uprisings, etc.—in other words, the chain of wars and revolutions that constitute today's imperialist epoch. It is precisely the epoch of imperialism that has led to such a sharpening of class relations in China and made the solution of the most important tasks of the revolution impossible, not only under the leadership of the bourgeoisie, but also through the democratic dictatorship of the petty bourgeoisie and the proletariat; and by so doing the task of establishing the dictatorship of the proletariat supported by the rural and urban poor has been put on the agenda. The dictatorship of the proletariat means making socialist inroads in property relations and a transition to production under state control, i.e., passing over to the rail of the socialist revolution.

26. But are the forces of the Chinese proletariat sufficient to get the support of the hundreds of millions of Chinese poor, seize power, set up an army and state apparatus, withstand blockade and sabotage, safeguard the country's most important economic operations, etc.? In essence, this question is tantamount to another question: Does the Chinese revolution in fact have a chance for further development and victory, since roads and methods other than those designated above do not exist? Naturally, nobody will say for certain that the Chinese proletariat will succeed in coming to power in the near future. Only the actual struggle will be able to tell whether or not that is true. Only correct leadership can provide a victory. The revolutionary "limit," as they say, i.e., that quantity that restricts all the others, at the present time is not in the least the Chinese proletariat, but the Chinese Communist Party, which incorrect theory, an incorrect line, and incorrect leadership have weakened to the worst degree. By its numbers, its productive role, and the way it is distributed in the country as a whole, the Chinese proletariat represents a tremendous force and can become the leading and

ruling force in the country provided there is a rapid growth and tempering of the Chinese Communist Party. Can it make up for lost and wasted time? It can. If there is a revolutionary upsurge, the party can quickly rise to the level of events. But for this to happen, it must have a clear perspective before it—not halfway measures, reluctance, or playacting with Mme. Sun Yat-sen. *The task of the dictatorship of the proletariat in a country of poor peasants* should be presented clearly and distinctly, and in its full scope.

Without this, support to the troops of Ho Lung and Yeh T'ing would be the purest adventurism, which could have as its only result a new crushing defeat for the movement, a new monstrous bloodletting, and a new strengthening of the forces of reaction.

The Chinese revolution at its new stage will win as a dictatorship of the proletariat, or it will not win at all.

Published in English for the first time. By permission of Harvard College Library. Translated for this volume by Carol Lisker.

SPEECH TO THE PRESIDIUM
OF THE ECCI[68]

September 27, 1927

1. You accuse me of violating discipline. I have no doubt that your verdict is already prepared. Today there is not one organization that discusses and decides; they only *carry out orders*. Even the Presidium of the Communist International is no exception.

2. What do you call *factional work?* Anything that is not authorized by the AUCP Secretariat. But the Secretariat tramples the rules underfoot, shatters the very foundations of party discipline, and imposes a ban on what is the inalienable right and primary duty of every party member.

The Chinese Revolution

3. Here is a vivid and burning example. Today's papers report that the revolutionary army has occupied Swatow. It is already several weeks that the armies of Ho Lung and Yeh T'ing have been advancing. *Pravda* calls these armies revolutionary armies. Here, at any rate, it is much closer to the truth than in regard to the armies of Chiang Kai-shek, Feng Yü-hsiang, or T'ang Sheng-chih.

But I ask you: What prospects does the movement of the revolutionary army that captured Swatow raise before the Chinese revolution? What are the slogans of the movement? What is its program? What should be its organizational forms? What has become of the slogan of Chinese soviets, which *Pravda* suddenly advanced for a single day in July? On this point we hear not one word in the press if we exclude the fundamentally wrong article by Comrade Lozovsky.

Why is the press of the AUCP silent? Why does the Comintern press hold its tongue? After all, the resolution of the last ECCI plenum, approved following the report by Comrade Bukharin, remains in force to this day. That resolution is totally wrong. It helped the Wuhan government complete what Chiang Kai-shek had not yet accomplished.

The opportunist theses and resolutions of Stalin and Bukharin, which have twice led the Chinese revolution to the most severe defeats, are printed without any prohibition. Marxist criticism and Marxist formulations of the problems are placed under a ban. Anyone who circulates our theses is accused of violating discipline and expelled from the party. But we say that every honest party member is duty bound to demand the publication of all the documents on the Chinese question and is duty bound to circulate our criticism of the opportunist line of Stalin-Bukharin, and to do so with all the forces and resources possible. The question of the fate of the Chinese revolution stands immeasurably higher than the bureaucratic orders and bans of the CC Secretariat, which are presented as measures of revolutionary proletarian discipline.

4. I have said that the organs of the Comintern have remained silent in regard to the third stage of the Chinese revolution, which could mark the beginning of a new rise, but which could also—with incorrect policies—prepare the way for a third defeat that would be the most severe and the most devastating, that would enfeeble the revolution for a number of years to come.

While the entire press remains silent and the Comintern says nothing, a new opportunist combination is all the while being quietly prepared, entirely in the spirit of the Chinese policy of Stalin-Bukharin. In Moscow a new and ever-so-modern Kuomintang is in formation, centering around the widow of Sun Yat-sen and a comrade-in-arms of Chiang Kai-shek, Eugene Ch'en. The first stage was Chiang Kai-shek; the second stage, Wang Ching-wei; the third stage is Eugene Ch'en and Company. The first two stages ended with the workers and peasants being crushed and shot down. The third stage will lead to the same thing. Instead of assuring the full independence of the Chinese Communist Party, raising its self-esteem, broadening its outlook, confronting it with the tasks of a dictatorship of the soviets that would unite the proletariat and the many millions of poor peasants in China— instead of that, Stalin-Bukharin are preparing a new inspectorate to be placed over the Chinese Communist Party, a new petty-bourgeois compromiser form of supervision over it, that is, new shackles to bind the proletarian vanguard hand and foot. We say to you: This will end in a third catastrophe. And do you really think we are going to keep quiet?

5. Since 1925 we have been carrying on a struggle for the independence of the Chinese Communist Party, for its emancipation from the discipline of Chiang Kai-shek. This crucial, fundamental slogan of Bolshevism was called Trotskyism. In China, the agents of the Comintern used the term "Trotskyist" for those genuine proletarian revolutionists who upheld the fundamental precondition of Bolshevik politics: the independence of the proletarian party. Against them, the Comintern agents supported Ch'en Tu-hsiu, who translated the politics of Martynov into Chinese.

What is the Opposition guilty of? Only that it paid too much attention to the prohibitions of the Stalinist Secretariat, which have been fatal to the revolution, and that it did not immediately and publicly place before the entire Comintern, with full firmness and determination, the call for the complete independence of the Chinese Communist Party.

6. In May of this year, during the ECCI plenum, we proposed a briefly worded motion in opposition to the thoroughly opportunist resolution of Bukharin. Our motion was as follows:

The plenum would do well to bury Bukharin's resolution, replacing it with a resolution of a few lines:

In the first place, peasants and workers should place no faith in the leaders of the left Kuomintang but they should instead build their soviets jointly with the soldiers. In the second place, the soviets should arm the workers and the advanced peasants. In the third place, the Communist Party must assure its complete independence, create a daily press, and assume the leadership in creating the soviets. Fourth, the land must be immediately taken away from the landlords. Fifth, the reactionary bureaucracy must be immediately dismissed. Sixth, perfidious generals and other counterrevolutionists must be summarily dealt with. And finally, the general course must be toward the establishment of a revolutionary dictatorship through the soviets of workers' and peasants' deputies. ["It Is Time to Understand, Time to Reconsider, and Time to Make a Change."]

These lines are the voice of genuine Bolshevism, temporarily stifled by the bureaucratic apparatus in service to opportunist policies. And do you really think we will fail to make these lines known to the Chinese and world proletariat? Whoever thinks that is no revolutionist.

7. To this day the China resolution of the last ECCI plenum has not been withdrawn. To this day the position of Stalin, who at first called for confidence in Chiang Kai-shek and then proclaimed the Wuhan government the leading center of the agrarian revolution, has not been condemned.

Isn't Comrade Treint correct when he says that the Stalin-Bukharin policy—given the organized silence of the entire Comintern—led the vanguard of the international proletariat astray? Didn't *l'Humanité* send a telegram greeting the butcher Chiang Kai-shek as the hero of the Shanghai Commune? Isn't a policy that loses sight of the deep abyss between the proletarian Communard and the general Galliffet—isn't this a criminal policy that must not only be condemned but branded criminal?

8. Even worse, the Kuomintang, to this day, remains a member of the Comintern. Which Kuomintang? The Kuomintang of Chiang Kai-shek or that of Wang Ching-wei? But now they have united. Thus the united Kuomintang of Chiang Kai-shek and Wang Ching-wei still belongs to the Comintern. You are in a hurry to expel Vujovic and myself. But you have forgotten to expel the comrades-in-arms Chiang Kai-shek and Wang Ching-wei. Perhaps you will agree to place this question on the agenda today as well.

9. The fight for the independence of the Communist Party, the fight of the proletariat for the peasantry and against the bourgeoisie, the fight for soviets of workers', peasants', and soldiers' deputies is called by the opportunists *Trotskyism*. Why? In order the more surely to fight against Leninism. Trotskyism is an epithet the bankrupt hide behind when they have nothing to say. The silence of the Comintern in regard to the new stage of the Chinese revolution, unfolding before our eyes, is evidence of unparalleled confusion. The right road and destination must be pointed out clearly. We cannot be silent. We will not be silent, because we are revolutionists and not bureaucrats.

Published for the first time in any language (excerpts). By permission of Harvard College Library. Translated for this volume by George Saunders.

THE CANTON UPRISING[69]

December 1927

4. Control in the party, and therefore in the country too, is in the hands of the Stalin faction, which has all the features of centrism, a centrism which is, moreover, in the period of decline and not of upsurge. That means short zigzags to the left, longer zigzags to the right. One can have no doubt that the last move to the left (the jubilee manifesto[70]) produces the necessity of placating the right wing and its real supports in the country—not with words, but with deeds.

5. The zigzags to the left are not only expressed in hastily prepared jubilee manifestoes. The Canton rising is unquestionably an *adventurist* zigzag by the Comintern to the left, after the disastrous consequences of the Menshevik policy in China have made themselves fully apparent. The Canton episode is a worse and more pernicious repetition of the Estonian putsch of 1924, after the revolutionary situation in Germany of 1923 had been missed.[71] Menshevism plus bureaucratic adventurism have dealt a double blow to the Chinese revolution; we need not doubt that the revenge for Canton will be a new and longer zigzag to the right in the field of international politics, especially Chinese.

Published in English for the first time. Excerpted from "On the New Stage." Text from *Die Fahne des Kommunismus* (Berlin), December 21 and 28, 1928. Translated from he German by Iain Fraser.

THE CLASSIC MISTAKES OF OPPORTUNISM[72]

January 1928

The outcome and the lessons of the Chinese revolution, a revolution that constitutes one of the greatest events in world history, have been kept in obscurity, barred from discussion, and have not been assimilated by the public opinion of the proletarian vanguard. In reality the Central Committee of the Russian Communist Party has prohibited discussion of the questions related to the Chinese revolution. But without studying the mistakes that were committed—the classic mistakes of opportunism—it is impossible to imagine the future revolutionary preparation of the proletarian parties of Europe and Asia.

Aside from the question of knowing who was directly responsible for the leadership of the December events in Canton, these events furnish a striking example of putschism during the ebb of the revolutionary wave. In a revolutionary period, a deviation towards putschism is often the result of defeats whose direct cause is to be found in an opportunist leadership. The Communist International cannot take a single new step forward without first drawing the lessons of the experience of the Canton uprising, in correlation with the course of the Chinese revolution as a whole. This is one of the main tasks of the Sixth World Congress. The repressive measures taken against the left wing will not only fail to correct the mistakes already made, but even more serious, they will teach nothing to anyone.

Published in English for the first time. Excerpted from "Appeal of the Deportees." Text from *Contre le Courant* (Paris), February 11, 1928. Translated from the French by Jeff White.

THREE LETTERS TO
PREOBRAZHENSKY

March-April 1928[73]

First Letter, March 2, 1928

Pravda prints in several installments an extensive article entitled, "The Significance and Lessons of the Canton Insurrection." This article is truly remarkable for the invaluable, substantiated, and firsthand information it contains as well as for its lucid exposition of contradictions and confusion of a principled nature.

It begins with an evaluation of the social nature of the revolution itself. As we all know, it is a bourgeois-democratic, a workers' and peasants' revolution. Yesterday it was supposed to unfold under the banner of the Kuomintang—today it unfolds against the Kuomintang.

But according to the author's appraisal, the character of the revolution, and even the entire official policy, remains bourgeois democratic. We turn next to the chapter that deals with the policy of the soviet power. Here we find stated that: "in the interests of the workers, the Canton Soviet issued decrees establishing . . . workers' control of production, effecting this control through factory committees [and] . . . nationalization of large-scale industry, transport, and banks."

It goes on to enumerate the following measures: "the confiscation of all the apartments of the big bourgeoisie for the use of the toilers. . . ."

Thus the workers were in power in Canton, through their soviets. Actually the entire power was in the hands of the Communist Party, i.e., the party of the proletariat. The program included not only the confiscation of whatever feudal estates still exist in China, not only the workers' control of production, but also the nationalization of large-scale industry, banks, and transport, as well as the confiscation of bourgeois apartments, and all their property for the use of the toilers. The question arises: If *such* are the methods of a bourgeois revolution, then what would the socialist revolution look like in China? What other class would do the overthrowing and by what sort of different measures? We observe that given a real development of the revolution, the formula of a bourgeois-democratic, a workers' and peasants' revolution applied to China in the present period, in the given stage of its development, proved to be a hollow fiction, a bagatelle. Those who insisted upon this formula prior to the Canton insurrection, and above all those who insist on it now, after this insurrection, are repeating (under different conditions) the principled mistake committed by Zinoviev, Kamenev, Rykov, and the rest in the year 1917.[74]

An objection may be raised that the problem of the agrarian revolution in China has not been solved as yet! True. But neither was it solved in our own country prior to the establishment of the dictatorship of the proletariat. In our country it was not the bourgeois-democratic but the proletarian socialist revolution that achieved the agrarian revolution which, moreover, was far more deepgoing than the one that is possible in China, in view of the historical conditions of the Chinese system of land ownership. It may be said that China has not matured for the socialist revolution as yet. But that would be an abstract and a lifeless manner of posing the question. Was Russia, then, if taken by itself, ripe for socialism? Russia was ripe for the dictatorship of the proletariat as the only method of solving all national problems; but so far as socialist development is concerned, the latter, proceeding from the economic and cultural conditions of a country, is indissolubly bound up with the entire future development of the world revolution. This applies in whole and in part to China as well. If eight or ten months ago this was a forecast (rather belated, at that), then today it is an irrefutable deduction from the experience of the Canton uprising. It would be erroneous to argue that the Canton uprising was an adventure by and large, and that the actual class relations were reflected in it in a distorted form.

In the first place the author of the above-mentioned article does not at all consider the Canton insurrection as an adventure, but as an entirely lawful stage in the development of the Chinese revolution. The general official point of view is to combine the appraisal of the revolution as bourgeois democratic with an approval of the program of action of the Canton government. But even from the standpoint of appraising the Canton insurrection as a putsch, one could not arrive at the conclusion that the formula of the bourgeois-democratic revolution is viable. The insurrection was obviously untimely. It was. But the class forces and the programs that inevitably flow from them were disclosed by the insurrection in all their lawfulness. *The best proof of this is: that it was possible and necessary to foresee in advance the relation of forces that was laid bare by the Canton insurrection. And this was foreseen.*

This question is most closely bound up with the paramount question of the Kuomintang. Incidentally, the author of the article relates, with assumed satisfaction, that one of the fighting slogans of the Canton overturn was the cry: "Down with the Kuomintang!" The banners and insignia of the Kuomintang were torn down and trampled underfoot. But only recently, even after the "betrayal" of Chiang Kai-shek, and after the "betrayal" of Wang Ching-wei, we heard solemn vows that: "We will not surrender the banner of the Kuomintang!" Oh, these sorry revolutionists! . . .

The workers of Canton outlawed the Kuomintang, *proclaiming all its tendencies illegal.* What does this imply? It implies that for the solution of the fundamental national tasks, not only the big but also the petty bourgeoisie could not put forward such a force as would enable the party of the proletariat to solve jointly with it the tasks of the "bourgeois-democratic revolution." But *"we"* are overlooking the many-millioned peasantry and the agrarian revolution. . . . A pitiable objection . . . for the key to the entire situation lies precisely in the fact that the task of conquering the peasant movement falls upon the proletariat, i.e., directly upon the Communist Party; and this task cannot be solved in reality differently than it was solved by the Canton workers, i.e., in the shape of the dictatorship of the proletariat whose methods from the very outset grow over inevitably into socialist methods. Conversely, the general fate of these methods, as well as of the dictatorship as a whole, is decided in the last analysis by the course of world development, which naturally does not exclude but on the contrary presupposes a correct policy on the part of the proletarian dictatorship, that consists of strengthening and developing the alliance between the workers and peasants, and of an all-sided adaptation to national conditions, on the one hand,

and to the course of world development, on the other. To play with the formula of the bourgeois-democratic revolution, after the experience of the Canton insurrection, is to march against the Chinese October, for without a correct general political orientation, revolutionary uprisings cannot be victorious, no matter how heroic and self-sacrificing they may be.

To be sure, the Chinese revolution has "passed into a new and higher phase"—but this is correct not in the sense that it will begin surging upward tomorrow or the next day, but in the sense that it has revealed the hollowness of the slogan of the bourgeois-democratic revolution. Engels said that a party that misses a favorable situation and suffers a defeat as a result, turns into a nonentity. This applies to the Chinese party as well. The defeat of the Chinese revolution is not a bit smaller than the defeat in Germany in 1923. Of course, we must understand the reference to "nonentity" in a sensible way. Many things bespeak the fact that the next period in China will be a period of revolutionary reflux, a slow process of assimilating the lessons of the cruelest defeats, and consequently, the weakening of the direct influence of the Communist Party. Thence flows the necessity for the latter to draw profound conclusions in all questions of principles and tactics. And this is impossible without an open and all-sided discussion of all the fatal mistakes perpetrated hitherto.

Of course this activity must not turn into the activity of self-isolation. It is necessary to keep a firm hand on the pulse of the working class in order not to commit a mistake in estimating the tempo, and not only to identify a new mounting wave, but also to prepare for it in time.

Second Letter [Undated]

Your letter was also twenty-two days in transit. It is difficult to discuss vital questions under such conditions, and in my opinion the Chinese question belongs among the most vital ones, because the struggle is still unfolding in China, the partisan armies are in the field, and an armed insurrection has been placed on the agenda, as you no doubt know from the resolution of the last plenum of the ECCI.[75]

To begin, I want to reply to a minor but aggravating point. You say that I needlessly polemicize against you under the pseudonym of Zinoviev. In this you are entirely mistaken. I believe, incidentally, that the misunderstanding arose as a result of the irregular mail delivery. I wrote about the Canton affair at a time when I was apprised of the famous letter of the two musketeers[76]; in addition to this, reports came from Moscow that they had been supplied with secretaries in order to expose "Trotskyism." I felt certain that Zinoviev would publish several of my letters on the Chinese question in which I set out to prove that in no case would there be such a special epoch in the Chinese revolution as an epoch of the democratic dictatorship of the proletariat and peasantry, because incomparably fewer preconditions exist there than in our own country, and as experience, and not theory, has already shown us, the democratic dictatorship of the proletariat and peasantry as such failed to materialize in our own country. Thus, my entire letter was written with a view to the past and future "exposures" on the part of Zinoviev.

In referring to the charge of *ignoring the peasantry,* I did not for a moment forget certain of our disputes on China—but I had no reason whatever to put in your lips this banal charge against me: for you, I trust, recognize that it is possible, without in the least ignoring the "peasantry," to arrive at a conclusion that the only road for solving the peasant question lies through the dictatorship of the proletariat. So that you, my dear E.A.—please do not take offense at a hunter's simile—assume gratuitously the role of a startled hare who concludes that the rifle is being aimed at him when the pursuit follows a totally different track.

I came to the opinion that there would not be any democratic dictatorship of the proletariat and peasantry in China from the time the Wuhan government was first formed. I based myself precisely upon the analysis of the most fundamental social facts, and not upon the manner in which they were refracted politically, which, as is well known, often assumes peculiar forms, since, in this sphere, factors of a secondary order enter in, including national tradition. I became convinced that the basic social facts have already cleared the road for themselves through all the peculiarities of political superstructures, when the Wuhan shipwreck destroyed utterly the legend of the left Kuomintang, allegedly embracing nine-tenths of the entire Kuomintang. In 1924-25, it was almost an accepted commonplace that the Kuomintang was a workers' and peasants' party. This party "unexpectedly" proved to be bourgeois capitalist. Then another version was created, that the latter was only a "summit," but that the genuine Kuomintang, nine-tenths of the Kuomintang, was a revolutionary peasant party. Once again, it turned out "unexpectedly" that the left Kuomintang, in whole and in part, proceeded to smash the peasant movement which, as is well known, has great traditions in China and its own traditional organizational forms that became widespread during these years. That is why, when you write in the spirit of absolute abstraction that "it is impossible to say today whether the Chinese petty bourgeoisie will be able to create any sort of parties analogous to our SRs, or whether such parties will be created by the right-wing communists who split off, etc.," I reply to this argument from "the theory of improbabilities" as follows:

In the first place, even were the SRs to be created, there would not at all follow from this any dictatorship of the proletariat and peasantry, precisely as none followed in our own country, despite immeasurably more favorable conditions; secondly, instead of *guessing* whether the petty bourgeoisie is capable in the future— i.e., with the further aggravation of class relations—of playing a greater or lesser independent role (suppose a piece of wood suddenly fires a bullet?), one should rather ask why did the petty bourgeoisie prove *incapable* of playing such a role in the recent past, when it had at its disposal the most favorable conditions— the Communist Party was driven into the Kuomintang, the latter was declared a workers' and peasants' party, it was supported by the entire authority of the Communist International and the USSR, the peasant movement was far-flung and sought for leadership, the intelligentsia was widely mobilized since 1919, etc., etc.

You write that China still faces the "colossal problem of the agrarian bourgeois-democratic revolution." To Lenin, this was the root of the question. Lenin pointed out that the peasantry even as *an estate* is capable of playing a revolutionary role in the struggle against the *estate of the landed nobility,* and the bureaucracy indissolubly linked up with the latter, crowned by the tsarist autocracy. In the subsequent stage, says Lenin, the kulaks will break with the workers, and together with them a considerable section of the middle peasants, but this will take place during the transition to the proletarian revolution, as an integral part of the international revolution. But how do matters stand in China? China has no landed nobility; no peasant estate, fused by community of interests against the landlords. The agrarian revolution in China is aimed *against the urban and rural bourgeoisie.* Radek has stressed this often—even Bukharin has half-understood this now. In this lies the gist of the matter!

You write that "the social content of the first stage of the future third Chinese revolution cannot be characterized as a socialist overturn." But we run the risk here of falling into Bukharinistic scholasticism, and of occupying ourselves with splitting hairs over terminology instead of with a living characterization of the dialectic process. What was the content of our revolution from October 1917 to July 1918? We left the mills and factories in the hands of the capitalists, confining ourselves to workers' control; we expropriated the landed estates and put through the petty-bourgeois SR program of the socialization of land; and to crown it all, during this period, we had a coparticipant in power in the form of the Left SRs. One could say with complete justification that "the social content of the first stage of the October revolution cannot be characterized as a socialist overturn." I believe it was Yakovlev and several other Red professors who spilled a great deal of sophistry over this. Lenin said that we completed the bourgeois revolution en route. But the Chinese revolution (the "third") will have to begin the drive against the kulak at its very first stages; it will have to expropriate the concessions of foreign capitalists, for, without this, there cannot be any unification of China in the sense of a genuine state sovereignty in economics and politics. In other words, the very first stage of the third Chinese revolution will be less bourgeois in content than the first stage of the October revolution.

On the other hand, the Canton events (as earlier Chinese events, etc.) demonstrated that the "national" bourgeoisie, too, having behind it Hong Kong,[77] foreign advisers, and foreign cruisers, assumes such a position in relation to the slightest independent movement of workers and peasants as renders workers' control of production even less likely than was the case among us. In all probability we shall have to expropriate mills and factories, of any size, at the very first moments of the "third Chinese revolution."

To be sure, you propose simply to set aside the evidence of the Canton uprising. You say: "since" the Canton insurrection was an adventure—i.e., not an undertaking that grew out of a mass movement—therefore "how can *such* an undertaking create a new situation . . . ?" Now, you yourself know that it is entirely impermissible thus to simplify the question. I would be the last person to argue against the fact that there were elements of adventurism in the Canton uprising. But to picture the Canton events as some sort of hocus-pocus from which no conclusions flow is an oversimplified attempt at *evading* the analysis of the actual content of the Canton experience. Wherein did adventurism lie? In the fact that the leadership, striving to cover up its past sins, monstrously forced the course of events, and caused a miscarriage. The mass movement existed, but it was inadequate and immature. It is wrong to think that presumably a miscarriage can teach us nothing about the maternal organism and the process of gestation. The enormous and theoretically decisive significance of the Canton events for the fundamental questions of the Chinese revolution lies precisely in the fact that we have here—"thanks to" the adventure (yes! of course!)—what happens so rarely in history and politics: *virtually a laboratory experiment on a gigantic scale.* We paid very dearly for it, but that is all the less reason to wave its lessons aside.

The conditions for the experiment were almost "chemically pure." All the previously adopted resolutions had set down, sealed, and canonized, just like two times two equals four, that the revolution is bourgeois-agrarian, that only those "who leap over stages" could babble about the dictatorship of the proletariat based upon an alliance with the peasant poor, who compose 80 percent of the Chinese peasantry, etc., etc. The last convention of the Communist Party of China met under this banner. A special representative of the Comintern, Comrade N., was present.[78] We were told that the new CEC of the Chinese CP was above all suspicion. During this time, the campaign against so-called Trotskyism attained the wildest tempo, in China as well. Yet, on the very threshold of the Canton events, the CEC of the Chinese CP adopted, in the words of *Pravda,* a resolution declaring that the *Chinese revolution had assumed a "permanent" character.* Moreover, the representative of the Comintern, Comrade N., held the same position.

Under the "permanent" character of the revolution we must here understand the following: Face to face with the supremely responsible practical task (though it was posed prematurely) the Chinese communists and even the representative of the Comintern, after taking into account the entire past experience and, as it were, all the political assets, drew the conclusion that only the workers led by the communists could lead the peasants against the landowners (the urban and rural bourgeoisie); and that only the dictatorship of the proletariat based on an alliance with the hundreds of millions of peasant poor could ensue from such a victorious struggle.

Just as during the Paris Commune, which also had in it elements of a laboratory experiment (for the uprising took place there in a single city isolated from the rest of the country), the Proudhonists and Blanquists had to resort to steps directly contrary to their own doctrines, and thus (according to Marx) revealed all the more clearly the actual logic of class relations—so in Canton, too, the leaders, who were stuffed to the ears with prejudices against the bogie of the "permanent revolution," once they set to work, proved guilty of committing this original permanent sin from their very first steps. What happened, then, to the antitoxin of Martynovism that had been injected in bovine and asinine doses? Oh no! If this were *only* an adventure, i.e., a sort of hocus-pocus, showing nothing and proving nothing, then this adventure would have assumed the image and likeness of its creators. But no! This adventure came in contact with the earth, it was fed by the juices of real (though immature) mass movements and relations; and it was on this account that the said "adventure" seized its own creators by the scruff, impolitely picked them up, shook them in the air, and then deposited them on their heads, tapping their skulls, for firmness' sake, against the Chinese pavements. . . . As the latest resolutions and the latest article on this subject testify, these said "creators" are still standing on their heads, "permanently" dancing with their feet in the air.

It is ludicrous and impermissible to say that it is "inopportune" to draw conclusions from living events which every worker-revolutionist must think through to the end. At the time of the Ho Lung-Yeh T'ing uprising I wanted to pose openly the question that, in view of the consummation of the Kuomintang cycle of development, only the vanguard of the proletariat could aspire to power. This would presuppose a new standpoint for it, a new self-appraisal on its part—after a reevaluation of the objective situation—and this very thing would have excluded such an adventuristic approach to the situation as: "We'll bide our time in a little corner, the peasant will come to our assistance by starting things, and somebody will somehow seize power and do something." At that time, certain comrades said to me, "It is inopportune to raise these questions now in connection with Ho Lung who apparently has been crushed already." I did not at all tend to overestimate Ho Lung's uprising; I did consider, nevertheless, that it was the last signal in favor of the necessity to review the orientation in the Chinese revolution. Had these questions been *opportunely* posed at that time, then, perhaps, the ideological authors of the Canton adventure might have been compelled to think things over, and the Chinese party might not have been so ruthlessly destroyed; and if not, then in the light of our prognosis and our warning, the Canton events would have entered as a weighty lesson into the consciousness of hundreds and thousands, as for example, did Radek's warning about Chiang Kai-shek, on the eve of the Shanghai coup d'etat. No, the propitious time has passed. I do not know when the Chinese revolution will revive. But we must utilize whatever time remains at our disposal entirely for preparation and, moreover, on the basis of the fresh course of events.

You write that it is necessary to study the history of China, its economic life, statistical data, etc. Nobody can object to this (unless this is intended as an argument to postpone the question to doomsday). In my own justification, however, I must say that since my arrival in Alma-Ata I have occupied myself only with China (India, Polynesia, etc., for comparative study). Of course more gaps remain than complétely covered places, but I must say nevertheless that in all the new (for myself) books I am reading, I find even today nothing new in principle. But the chief point still remains—*the confirmation of our prognoses by experience*—first in relation to the Kuomintang as a whole, then in relation to the "left" Kuomintang and the Wuhan government, and finally, in relation to the "deposit" on the third revolution, in the shape of the Canton uprising.

That is why I consider that there cannot be any postponement.

Two final questions:

You ask: Was Lenin right when during the war he defended against Bukharin the idea that Russia was still facing a bourgeois revolution? Yes, he was right. The Bukharin formulation was schematic and scholastic, i.e., it represented the self-same caricature of the permanent revolution that Bukharin tries to ascribe to me now. But there is also another side to this same question: Was Lenin right when against Stalin, Rykov, Zinoviev, Kamenev, Frunze, Kalinin, Tomsky, etc., etc. (let alone all the Lyadovs), he advanced his April theses? Was he right when against Zinoviev, Kamenev, Rykov, Milyutin, etc., etc., he defended the seizure of power by the proletariat? You know better than I that had Lenin failed to reach Petrograd in April 1917, there would have been no October revolution. Up to February 1917, the slogan of the dictatorship of the proletariat and peasantry was historically progressive; after the February overturn the same slogan—of Stalin, Kamenev, and the rest— became a reactionary slogan.

From April to May 1927 I supported the slogan of the democratic dictatorship of the proletariat and peasantry for China (more correctly, I concurred with this slogan) inasmuch as the social forces had not as yet passed their political verdict, although the situation in China was immeasurably less propitious for this slogan than in Russia. After this verdict was passed by a colossal historical action (the experience of Wuhan) the slogan of democratic dictatorship became a reactionary force and will lead inevitably either to opportunism or adventurism.

You further argue that for the October leap we had the February running start. That is correct. If, even at the beginning of the Northern Expedition, we had begun to build soviets in the "emancipated" regions (and the masses were striving for that), we would have obtained the necessary running start, would have disintegrated the armies of the enemies, obtained *our own* army, and we would have assumed power—if not in the whole of China at once, then in a very considerable section of it. At present, of course, the revolution is on the decline. The babbling of the light-minded scribblers about the fact that the revolution is on the verge of a new upswing, inasmuch as, in China, if you please, countless executions are taking place and a cruel commercial and industrial crisis is raging—this is criminal idiocy. After three of the greatest defeats, the crisis does not arouse but on the contrary oppresses the proletariat, while the executions are destroying the politically weakened party.

We have entered the period of reflux. What will provide the impulse for a new mounting wave? Or to put it differently: What conditions will provide the necessary running start for the proletarian vanguard at the head of the worker and peasant masses? This I do not know. The future will show whether only internal processes will suffice or an impulse from without will be necessary. I am willing to allow that the first stage of the movement may repeat in an abridged and altered form the stages of the revolution that we have already passed (for example, some new parody of the "all-national front" against Chang Tso-lin); but this first phase will perhaps suffice only in order to enable the Communist Party to advance and proclaim to the popular masses its "April theses," i.e., its program and strategy of the conquest of power by the proletariat. If, however, we enter into the new upswing, which will unfold with an incomparably more rapid tempo than in the past, with a schema of a "democratic dictatorship" that is already outworn today, then one could stake his head beforehand that in China very many Lyadovs will be found, but hardly a Lenin in order to effect (against all the Lyadovs) the tactical rearming of the party on the day after the revolutionary spurt.

Third Letter [Undated]

Dear E.A.:

Received your airmail letter yesterday. Thus, all the letters have arrived. The last letter took sixteen days in transit, i.e., six days less than ordinary mail. Two days ago I sent you a detailed answer to your objections on the Chinese revolution. But on awakening this morning I recalled that I had failed (apparently) to reply to the argument you deem most important, as I understand it. You write:

"Your basic error lies in the fact that you determine the character of a revolution on the basis of who makes it, which class, i.e., by the effective subject, while you seem to assign secondary importance to the objective social content of the process."

Then you go on to adduce as examples the November revolution in Germany, the 1789 revolution in France, and the future Chinese revolution.

This argument is in essence only a "sociological" generalization (to use Johnsonian terminology) of all your other concrete economic and historical views. But I want also to reply to your views in their generalized sociological formulation, for in so doing the "fundamental error" (on your part and not mine) stands out most clearly.

How to characterize a revolution? By the class which achieves it or by the social content lodged in it? There is a theoretical trap lodged in counterposing the former to the latter in such a general form. The Jacobin period of the French revolution was of course the period of petty-bourgeois dictatorship, in addition to which, the petty bourgeoisie—in complete harmony with its "sociological nature"—cleared the way for the big bourgeoisie. The November revolution in Germany was the beginning of the proletarian revolution but it was checked at its very first steps by the petty-bourgeois leadership, and succeeded only in achieving a few things unfulfilled by the bourgeois revolution.[79] What are we to call the November revolution—bourgeois or proletarian? Both the former and the latter would be incorrect. The place of the October revolution will be determined when we both give the *mechanics* of this revolution and determine its results. There will be no contradiction in this case between the mechanics (understanding under it, of course, not only the motive force but also the leadership) and the results—both the former and the latter are "sociologically" indeterminate in character. I take the liberty to put the question to you: What would you call the Hungarian revolution of 1919? You will say: *proletarian*. Why? Didn't the social "content" of the Hungarian revolution prove to be capitalist! You will reply: This is the social content of the counterrevolution. Correct. Apply this now to China. The "social content" under the dictatorship of the proletariat (based on an alliance with the peasantry) can remain during a certain period of time not socialist *as yet,* but the road to bourgeois development from the dictatorship of the proletariat can lead only through counterrevolution. For this reason, so far as the social content is concerned, it is necessary to say: "We shall wait and see."

The gist of the matter lies precisely in the fact that although the political mechanics of the revolution depend in the *last analysis* upon an economic base (not only national but international) they cannot, however, be deduced with abstract logic from this economic base. In the first place, the base itself is very contradictory and its "maturity" does not allow of bald statistical determination; secondly, the economic base as well as the political situation must be approached not in the national but in the international framework, taking into account the dialectic action and reaction between the national and the international; thirdly, the class struggle and its political expression, unfolding on the economic foundations, also have their own imperious logic of development, which cannot be leaped over. When Lenin said in April 1917 that only the dictatorship of the proletariat could save Russia from disintegration and doom, Sukhanov (the most consistent opponent) refuted him with two fundamental arguments: (1) the social content of the bourgeois revolution has not yet been achieved; (2) Russia had not yet matured economically for a socialist revolution. And what was Lenin's answer? Whether or not Russia has matured is something that "we shall wait and see"; this cannot be determined statistically; this will be determined by the trend of events and, moreover, only on an international scale. But, said Lenin, independently of how this social content will be determined in the end, at the present moment, today, there is no other road to the salvation of the country—from famine, war, and enslavement—except through the seizure of power by the proletariat.

That is precisely what we must say now in relation to China. First of all, it is incorrect to allege that the agrarian revolution composes the basic content of the present historical struggle. In what must this agrarian revolution consist? The universal partition of the land? But there have been several such universal partitions in Chinese history. And then the development always returned to "its proper orbit." The agrarian revolution is the destruction of the Chinese landlords and Chinese functionaries. But the national unification of China and its economic sovereignty imply its emancipation from *world imperialism,* for which China remains the most important safety valve against the collapse of European and, tomorrow, of American capitalism. The agrarian overturn in China *without* national unification and tariff autonomy (in essence: monopoly of foreign trade) would not open any way out or any perspectives for China. This is what predetermines the gigantic sweep and the monstrous sharpness of the struggle facing China—today, after the experience already undergone by all the participants.

What then should a Chinese communist say to himself under these conditions? Can he really proceed to reason as follows: The social content of the Chinese revolution can only be bourgeois (as proved by such and such charts). Therefore we must not pose ourselves the task of the dictatorship of the proletariat; the social content prescribes, in the most extreme case, a coalition dictatorship of the proletariat and peasantry. But for a coalition (in question here, of course, is a *political* coalition, and not a "sociological" alliance of classes) a partner is needed. Moscow taught me that the Kuomintang is such a partner. However, no left Kuomintang materialized. What to do? Obviously, there only remains for me, a Chinese communist, to console myself with the idea that "it is impossible to say today whether the Chinese petty bourgeoisie will be able to create any sort of parties" . . . or whether it will not. Suppose it suddenly does?

A Chinese communist who reasons along such a prescription would cut the throat of the Chinese revolution.

Least of all, of course, is it a question here of summoning the Communist Party of China to an immediate insurrection for the seizure of power. The tempo depends entirely upon the circumstances. The task lies in seeing to it that the Communist Party is permeated through and through with the conviction that the third Chinese revolution can come to a triumphant conclusion only with the dictatorship of the proletariat under the leadership of the Communist Party. Moreover, it is necessary to understand this leadership not "in a general" sense, but in the sense of the direct wielding of complete revolutionary power. And so far as the tempo with which we shall have to build socialism in China is concerned, about this—"we shall wait and see."

Leon Trotsky

From *New International* (New York), April 1936.

SUMMARY AND PERSPECTIVES
OF THE CHINESE REVOLUTION[80]

Its Lessons for the Countries of the Orient and for the Whole of the Comintern

June 1928

Bolshevism and Menshevism and the left wing of the German and international Social Democracy took definite shape on the analysis of the experiences, mistakes, and tendencies of the 1905 revolution. An analysis of the experiences of the Chinese revolution is today of no less importance for the international proletariat.

This analysis, however, has not even begun—it is prohibited. The official literature is engaged in hastily selecting facts to suit the resolutions of the ECCI, the hollowness of which has been completely revealed. The draft program dulls the sharpest points of the Chinese problem whenever possible, but it sets the seal of approval upon the essential points of the fatal line followed by the ECCI on the Chinese question. The analysis of the great historical process is replaced by a literary defense of bankrupt schemas.

1. On the Nature of the Colonial Bourgeoisie

The draft program states: "Temporary agreements [with the national bourgeoisie of colonial countries] are admissible only insofar as the bourgeoisie does not obstruct the revolutionary organization of the workers and peasants and wages a genuine struggle against imperialism."

This formula, although it is deliberately tacked on as an incidental proposition, is one of the central postulates of the draft, for the countries of the Orient, at any rate. The main proposition deals, naturally, with the "emancipation [of the workers and peasants] from the influence of the national bourgeoisie." But we judge not from the standpoint of grammar but politically and, moreover, on the basis of experience, and therefore we say: The main proposition is only an incidental one here, while the incidental proposition contains what is most essential. The formula, taken as a whole, is a classic Menshevik noose for the proletariat of the Orient.

What "temporary agreements" are meant here? In politics, as in nature, all things are "temporary." Perhaps we are discussing here purely practical agreements *from one occasion to the next?* It goes without saying that we cannot renounce in advance such rigidly delimited and rigidly practical agreements as serve each time a quite definite aim. For example, such cases as involve agreements with the student youth of the Kuomintang for the organization of an anti-imperialist demonstration, or obtaining assistance from the Chinese merchants for strikers in a foreign concession, etc. Such cases are not at all excluded in the future, even in China. But in that case why are *general* political conditions adduced here, namely, ". . . insofar as the bourgeoisie does not obstruct the revolutionary organization of the workers and peasants and wages a genuine [!] struggle against imperialism"?

The sole "condition" for every agreement with the bourgeoisie, for each separate, practical, and expedient agreement adapted to each given case, consists in not allowing either the organizations or the banners to become mixed directly or indirectly for a single day or a single hour; it consists in distinguishing between the red and the blue, and in not believing for an instant in the capacity or readiness of the bourgeoisie either to lead a *genuine* struggle against imperialism or *not to obstruct* the workers and peasants. For practical and expedient agreements we have absolutely no use for such a condition as the one cited above. On the contrary, it could only cause us harm, running counter to the general line of our struggle against capitalism, which is not suspended even during the brief period of an "agreement." As was said long ago, purely practical agreements, such as do not bind us in the least and do not oblige us to anything politically, can be concluded with the devil himself if that is advantageous at a given moment. But it would be absurd in such a case to demand that the devil should *generally* become converted to Christianity, and that he use his horns not against workers and peasants but exclusively for pious deeds. In presenting such conditions we act in reality as the devil's advocates, and beg him to let us become his godfathers.

By its absurd conditions, which serve to paint the bourgeoisie in bright colors in advance, the draft program states clearly and definitely (despite the diplomatic and incidental character of its thesis) that involved here are precisely long-term political blocs and not agreements for specific occasions concluded for practical reasons and rigidly confined to practical aims. But in such a case, what is meant by demands that the bourgeoisie wage a "genuine" struggle and that it "not obstruct" the workers? Do we present these conditions to the bourgeoisie itself, and demand a public promise from it? It will make you any promises you want! It will even send its delegates to Moscow, enter the Peasants' International, adhere as a "sympathizing" party to the Comintern, peek into the Red International of Labor Unions. In short, it will promise anything that will give it the opportunity (with our assistance) to dupe the workers and peasants, more efficiently, more easily, and more completely to throw sand in their eyes— until the first opportunity, such as was offered in Shanghai.

But perhaps it is not a question here of political obligations exacted from the bourgeoisie which, we repeat, it will immediately agree to in order thus to transform us into its guarantors before the working masses? Perhaps it is a question here of an "objective" and "scientific" evaluation of a given national bourgeoisie, an expert a priori "sociological" prognosis, as it were, of its capacity to wage a struggle and not to obstruct? Sad to say, as the most recent and freshest experience testifies, such an a priori prognosis makes fools out of experts as a rule. And it would not be so bad, if only they alone were involved. . . .

There cannot be the slightest doubt on the matter: the text deals precisely with long-term political blocs. It would be entirely superfluous to include in a program the question of occasional practical agreements. For this purpose, a matter-of-fact tactical resolution "On Our Current Tasks" would suffice. Involved here is a question of justifying and setting a programmatic seal of approval upon yesterday's orientation toward the Kuomintang, which doomed the second Chinese revolution to destruction, and which is capable of destroying revolutions in the future.

According to the idea advanced by Bukharin, the real author of the draft, all stakes are placed precisely upon the general evaluation of the colonial bourgeoisie, whose capacity to struggle and not to obstruct must be proved not by its own oaths but in a rigorous "sociological" manner, that is by a thousand and one scholastic schemas adapted to opportunist purposes.

To bring this out more clearly let us refer back to the Bukharin evaluation of the colonial bourgeoisie. After citing the "anti-imperialist content" of colonial revolutions, and quoting Lenin (without any justification whatever), Bukharin proclaims:

"The liberal bourgeoisie in China played an objectively revolutionary role over a period of a number of years, and not months. Then it exhausted itself. This was not all a political 'twenty-four hour' holiday of the type of the Russian liberal revolution of 1905."

Everything here is wrong from beginning to end.

Lenin really taught us to differentiate rigidly between an oppressed and oppressor bourgeois nation. From this follow conclusions of exceptional importance. For instance, our attitude toward a war between an imperialist and a colonial country. For a pacifist, such a war is a war like any other. For a communist, a war of a colonial nation against an imperialist nation is a bourgeois-revolutionary war. Lenin thus *raised* the national liberation movements, the colonial insurrections, and wars of the oppressed nations, to the level of the bourgeois-democratic revolutions, in particular, to that of the Russian revolution of 1905. But Lenin did not at all place the wars for national liberation *above* bourgeois-democratic revolutions as is now done by Bukharin, after his 180 degree turn. Lenin insisted on a distinction between an oppressed bourgeois nation and a bourgeois oppressor nation. But Lenin nowhere raised and never could raise the question as if the bourgeoisie of a colonial or a semicolonial country in an epoch of struggle for national liberation must be more progressive and more revolutionary than the bourgeoisie of a noncolonial country in the epoch of the democratic revolution. This does not flow from anything in theory; there is no confirmation of it in history. For example, pitiful as Russian liberalism was, and hybrid as was its left half—the petty-bourgeois democrats, the Social Revolutionaries, and Mensheviks—it would nevertheless hardly be possible to say that Chinese liberalism and Chinese bourgeois democracy rose to a higher level or were more revolutionary than their Russian prototypes.

To present matters as if there must inevitably flow from the fact of colonial oppression the revolutionary character of a national bourgeoisie is to reproduce inside out the fundamental error of Menshevism, which held that the revolutionary nature of the Russian bourgeoisie must flow from the oppression of feudalism and the autocracy.

The question of the nature and the policy of the bourgeoisie is settled by the entire internal class structure of a nation waging the revolutionary struggle; by the historical epoch in which that struggle develops; by the degree of economic, political, and military dependence of the national bourgeoisie upon world imperialism as a whole or a particular section of it; finally, and this is most important, by the degree of class activity of the native proletariat, and by the state of its connections with the international revolutionary movement.

A democratic or national liberation movement may offer the bourgeoisie an opportunity to deepen and broaden its possibilities for exploitation. Independent intervention of the proletariat on the revolutionary arena threatens to deprive the bourgeoisie of the possibility to exploit altogether.

Let us observe some facts more closely.

The present inspirers of the Comintern have untiringly repeated that Chiang Kai-shek waged a war "against imperialism" whilst Kerensky marched hand in hand with the imperialists. Ergo: Whereas a ruthless struggle had to be waged against Kerensky, it was necessary to support Chiang Kai-shek.

The ties between Kerenskyism and imperialism were indisputable. One can go even still further back and point out that the Russian bourgeoisie "dethroned" Nicholas II with the blessings of British and French imperialism. Not only did Milyukov-Kerensky support the war waged by Lloyd George-Poincaré, but Lloyd George and Poincaré also supported Milyukov's and Kerensky's revolution first against the tsar, and later against the workers and peasants. This is absolutely beyond dispute.

But how did matters stand in this respect in China? The "February" revolution in China took place in 1911. That revolution was a great and progressive event, although it was accomplished with the direct participation of the imperialists. Sun Yat-sen, in his memoirs, relates how his organization relied in all its work on the "support" of imperialist states—either Japan, France, or America. If Kerensky in 1917 continued to take part in the imperialist war, then the Chinese bourgeoisie, the one that is so "national," so "revolutionary," etc., supported Wilson's intervention in the war with the hope that the Entente would help to emancipate China. In 1918 Sun Yat-sen addressed to the governments of the Entente his plans for the economic development and political emancipation of China.[81] There is no foundation whatever for the assertion that the Chinese bourgeoisie, in its struggle against the Manchu dynasty, displayed any higher revolutionary qualities than the Russian bourgeoisie in the struggle against tsarism; or that there is a principled difference between Chiang Kai-shek's and Kerensky's attitude toward imperialism.

But, says the ECCI, Chiang Kai-shek nevertheless did wage war against imperialism. To present the situation in this manner is to put too crude a face upon reality. Chiang Kai-shek waged war against certain Chinese militarists, the agents of *one* of the imperialist powers. This is not at all the same as to wage a war against imperialism. Even T'an P'ing-shan understood this. In his report to the Seventh Plenum of the ECCI (at the end of 1926) T'an P'ing-shan characterized the policy of the Kuomintang center headed by Chiang Kai-shek as follows:

> In the sphere of international policy it occupies a passive position in the full meaning of that word. . . . It is inclined to fight only against British imperialism; so far as the Japanese imperialists are concerned, however, it is ready under certain conditions to make a compromise with them. [*Minutes of the Seventh Plenum, ECCI,* vol. I, p. 406.]

The attitude of the Kuomintang toward imperialism was from the very outset not revolutionary but entirely opportunist. It endeavored to smash and isolate the agents of certain imperialist powers so as to make a deal with the self-same or other imperialist powers on terms more favorable for the Chinese bourgeoisie. That is all. But the gist of the matter lies in the fact that the entire formulation of the question is erroneous.

One must measure not the attitude of every given national bourgeoisie to imperialism "in general," but its attitude toward the immediate revolutionary historical tasks of its own nation. The Russian bourgeoisie was the bourgeoisie of an imperialist oppressor state; the Chinese bourgeoisie, a bourgeoisie of an oppressed colonial country. The overthrow of feudal tsarism was a progressive task in old Russia. The overthrow of the imperialist yoke is a progressive historical task in China. However, the conduct of the Chinese bourgeoisie in relation to imperialism, the proletariat, and the peasantry, was not more revolutionary than the attitude of the Russian bourgeoisie toward tsarism and the revolutionary classes in Russia, but, if anything, viler and more reactionary. That is the only way to pose the question.

The Chinese bourgeoisie is sufficiently realistic and acquainted intimately enough with the nature of world imperialism to understand that a really serious struggle against the latter requires such an upheaval of the revolutionary masses as would primarily become a menace to the bourgeoisie itself. If the struggle against the Manchu dynasty was a task of smaller historical proportions than the overthrow of tsarism, then the struggle against world imperialism is a task on a much larger scale. And if we taught the workers of Russia from the very beginning not to believe in the readiness of liberalism and the ability of petty-bourgeois democracy to overthrow tsarism and to destroy feudalism, we should no less energetically have imbued the Chinese workers from the outset with the same spirit of distrust. The new and absolutely false theory promulgated by Stalin-Bukharin about the "immanent" revolutionary spirit of the colonial bourgeoisie is, in substance, a translation of Menshevism into the language of Chinese politics. It serves only to convert the oppressed position of China into an internal political premium for the Chinese bourgeoisie, and it throws an additional weight on the scale of the bourgeoisie against the scale of the trebly oppressed Chinese proletariat.

But, we are told by Stalin and Bukharin, the authors of the draft program, Chiang Kai-shek's Northern Expedition roused a powerful movement among the worker and peasant masses. This is incontestable. But did not the fact that Guchkov and Shulgin brought with them to Petrograd the abdication of Nicholas II play a revolutionary role? Did it not arouse the most downtrodden, exhausted, and timid strata of the populace? Did not the fact that Kerensky, who but yesterday was a Trudovik, became the president of the Council of Ministers and the commander in chief rouse the masses of soldiers? Did it not bring them to meetings? Did it not rouse the village to its feet against the landlord?

The question could be posed even more widely. Did not the entire activities of capitalism rouse the masses, did it not rescue them, to use the expression of the *Communist Manifesto,* from the idiocy of rural life? Did it not impel the proletarian battalions to the struggle? But does our historical evaluation of the objective role of capitalism as a whole or of certain actions of the bourgeoisie in particular become a substitute for our active class revolutionary attitude toward capitalism or toward the actions of the bourgeoisie? Opportunist policies have always been based on this kind of nondialectical, conservative, tailendist "objectivism." Marxism on the contrary invariably taught that the revolutionary consequences of one or another act of the bourgeoisie, to which it is compelled by its position, will be fuller, more decisive, less doubtful, and firmer, the more independent the proletarian vanguard will be in relation to the bourgeoisie, the less it will be inclined to place its fingers between the jaws of the bourgeoisie, to see it in bright colors, to overestimate its revolutionary spirit or its readiness for a "united front" and for a struggle against imperialism.

The Stalinist and Bukharinist appraisal of the colonial bourgeoisie cannot stand criticism, either theoretical, historical, or political. Yet this is precisely the appraisal, as we have seen, that the draft program seeks to canonize.

*   *   *

One unexposed and uncondemned error always leads to another, or prepares the ground for it.

If yesterday the Chinese bourgeoisie was enrolled in the united revolutionary front, then today it is proclaimed to have "definitely gone over to the counterrevolutionary camp." It is not difficult to expose how unfounded are these transfers and enrollments which have been effected in a purely administrative manner without any serious Marxist analysis whatever.

It is absolutely self-evident that the bourgeoisie in joining the camp of the revolution does so not accidentally, not because it is light-minded, but under the pressure of its own class interests. For fear of the masses the bourgeoisie subsequently deserts the revolution or openly displays its concealed hatred of the revolution. But the bourgeoisie can go over "*definitely* to the counterrevolutionary camp," that is, free itself from the necessity of "supporting" the revolution again, or at least of flirting with it, only in the event that its fundamental class aspirations are satisfied either by revolutionary means or in another way (for instance, the Bismarckian way). Let us recall the history of the period of 1848-71. Let us recall that the Russian bourgeoisie was able to turn its back so bluntly upon the revolution of 1905 only because the revolution gave it the State Duma, that is, it received the means whereby it could bring direct pressure to bear on the bureaucracy and make deals with it. Nevertheless, when the war of 1914-17 revealed the inability of the "modernized" regime to secure the basic interests of the bourgeoisie, the latter again turned toward the revolution, and made its turn more sharply than in 1905.

Can anyone maintain that the revolution of 1925-27 in China has at least partly satisfied the basic interests of Chinese capitalism? No. China is today just as far removed from real national unity and from tariff autonomy as it was prior to 1925.[82] Yet, the creation of a unified domestic market and its protection from cheaper foreign goods is a life-and-death question for the Chinese bourgeoisie, a question second in importance only to that of maintaining the basis of its class domination over the proletariat and the peasant poor. But, for the Japanese and the British bourgeoisie the maintenance of the colonial status of China is likewise a question of no less importance than economic autonomy is for the Chinese bourgeoisie. That is why there will still be not a few leftward zigzags in the policy of the Chinese bourgeoisie. There will be no lack of temptations in the future for the devotees of the "national united front." To tell the Chinese communists today that their alliance with the bourgeoisie from 1924 to the end of 1927 was correct but that it is worthless now because the bourgeoisie has definitely gone over to the counterrevolutionary camp, is to disarm the Chinese communists once again in face of the coming objective changes in the situation and the inevitable leftward zigzags of the Chinese bourgeoisie. The war now being conducted by Chiang Kai-shek against the North already overthrows completely the mechanical schema of the authors of the draft program.

*   *   *

But the principled error of the official formulation of the question will doubtless appear more glaringly, more convincingly, and more incontrovertibly if we recall the fact which is still fresh in our minds, and which is of no little importance, namely, that tsarist Russia was a combination of oppressor and oppressed nations, that is of Great Russians and "foreigners," many of whom were in a completely colonial or semicolonial status. Lenin not only demanded that the greatest attention be paid to the national problem of the peoples in tsarist Russia but also proclaimed (against Bukharin and others) that it was the elementary duty of the proletariat of the dominant nation to support the struggle of the oppressed nations for their self-determination, up to and including separation. But did the party conclude from this that the bourgeoisie of the nationalities oppressed by tsarism (the Poles, Ukrainians, Tatars, Jews, Armenians, and others) were more progressive, more radical, and more revolutionary than the Russian bourgeoisie?

Historical experience bears out the fact that the Polish bourgeoisie—notwithstanding the fact that it suffered both from the yoke of the autocracy and from national oppression—was more reactionary than the Russian bourgeoisie and, in the State Dumas, always gravitated not toward the Cadets but toward the Octobrists. The same is true of the Tatar bourgeoisie. The fact that the Jews had absolutely no rights whatever did not prevent the Jewish bourgeoisie from being even more cowardly, more reactionary, and more vile than the Russian bourgeoisie. Or perhaps the Estonian bourgeoisie, the Latvian, the Georgian, or the Armenian bourgeoisie were more revolutionary than the Great Russian bourgeoisie? How could anyone forget such historical lessons!

Or should we perhaps recognize today, after the event, that Bolshevism was wrong when—in contradistinction to the Bund, the Dashnaks, the Polish Socialist Party, the Georgian and other Mensheviks—it called upon the workers of *all* the oppressed nationalities, of all the colonial peoples in tsarist Russia, at the very dawn of the bourgeois-democratic revolution, to dissociate themselves and form their own autonomous class organizations, to break ruthlessly all organizational ties not only with the liberal bourgeois, but also with the revolutionary petty-bourgeois parties, to win over the working class in the struggle against these parties, and through the workers, fight against these parties for influence over the peasantry? Did we not commit here a "Trotskyist" mistake? Did we not skip over, in relation to these oppressed, and in many cases very backward nations, the phase of development corresponding to the Kuomintang?

As a matter of fact how easily one could construct a theory that the Polish Socialist Party, Dashnaktsutiun, the Bund, etc., were "peculiar" forms of the necessary collaboration of the various classes in the struggle against the autocracy and against national oppression! How can such historical lessons be forgotten?

For a Marxist it was clear even prior to the Chinese events of the last three years—and today it should be clear even to the blind—that foreign imperialism, as a direct factor in the internal life of China, renders the Chinese Milyukovs and Chinese Kerenskys in the final analysis even more vile than their Russian prototypes. It is not for nothing that the very first manifesto issued by our party proclaimed that the further east we go, the lower and viler becomes the bourgeoisie, the greater are the tasks that fall upon the proletariat. This historical "law" fully applies to China as well.

> Ours is a bourgeois revolution, *therefore,* the workers must support the bourgeoisie, say the Potresovs, Gvozdyovs and Chkheidzes, as Plekhanov said yesterday.
> Ours is a bourgeois revolution, we Marxists say, *therefore* the workers must open the eyes of the people to the deception practised by the bourgeois politicians, teach them to put no faith in words, to depend entirely on their *own* strength, their *own* organization, their *own* unity, and their own *weapons.* [Lenin, *Collected Works,* vol. 27, pp. 305-06.]

This Leninist thesis is compulsory for the Orient as a whole. It must by all means find a place in the program of the Comintern.

2. The Stages of the Chinese Revolution

The first stage of the Kuomintang was the period of domination of the national bourgeoisie under the apologetic label of a "bloc of four classes." The second period, after Chiang Kai-shek's coup d'etat, was an experiment of parallel and "independent" domination of Chinese Kerenskyism, in the shape of the Hankow government of the "left" Wang Ching-wei. While the Russian Narodniks, together with the Mensheviks, lent to their short-lived "dictatorship" the form of an open dual power,[83] the Chinese "revolutionary democracy" did not even reach that stage. And inasmuch as history in general does not work to order, there only remains for us to understand that *there is not* and *will not be* any other "democratic dictatorship" except the dictatorship exercised by the Kuomintang since 1925. This remains equally true regardless of whether the semiunification of China accomplished by the Kuomintang is maintained in the immediate future or the country is again dismembered. But precisely at a time when the class dialectics of the revolution, having spent all its other resources, clearly and conclusively put on the order of the day the *dictatorship of the proletariat,* leading the countless millions of oppressed and disinherited in city and village, the ECCI advanced the slogan of a *democratic* (i.e., bourgeois-democratic) dictatorship of the workers and peasants. The reply to this formula was the Canton insurrection which, with all its prematurity, with all the adventurism of its leadership, raised the curtain of a new stage, or, more correctly, of the coming *third* Chinese revolution. It is necessary to dwell on this point in some detail.

Seeking to insure themselves against their past sins, the leadership monstrously forced the course of events at the end of last year and brought about the Canton miscarriage. However, even a miscarriage can teach us a good deal concerning the organism of the mother and the process of gestation. The tremendous and, from the standpoint of theory, truly decisive significance of the Canton events for the fundamental problems of the Chinese revolution is conditioned precisely upon the fact that we have here a phenomenon rare in history and politics, a virtual *laboratory experiment on a colossal scale.* We have paid for it dearly, but this obliges us all the more to assimilate its lessons.

One of the fighting slogans of the Canton insurrection, according to the account in *Pravda* (no. 31.), was the cry "Down with the Kuomintang!" The Kuomintang banners and insignia were torn down and trampled underfoot. But even after the "betrayal" of Chiang Kai-shek, and the subsequent "betrayal" of Wang Ching-wei (betrayals not of their own class, but of our . . . illusions), the ECCI had issued the solemn vow that: "We will not surrender the banner of the Kuomintang!" The workers of Canton outlawed the Kuomintang, *declaring all of its tendencies illegal.* This means that for the solution of the basic national tasks, not only the big bourgeoisie but also the petty bourgeoisie was incapable of producing a political force, a party, or a faction, in conjunction with which the party of the proletariat might be able to solve the tasks of the bourgeois-democratic revolution. The key to the situation lies precisely in the fact that *the task of winning the movement of the poor peasants already fell entirely upon the shoulders of the proletariat,* and directly upon the Communist Party; and that the approach to a genuine solution of the bourgeois-democratic tasks of the revolution necessitated the concentration of all power in the hands of the proletariat.

Pravda carried the following report about the policies of the short-lived Canton Soviet government:

"In the interests of the workers, the Canton Soviet issued decrees establishing . . . workers' control of industry through the factory committees . . . the nationalization of big industry, transportation, and banks."

Further on such measures are mentioned as: "The confiscation of all dwellings of the big bourgeoisie for the benefit of the toilers. . . ."

Thus it was the Canton workers who were in power and, moreover, the government was actually in the hands of the Communist Party. The program of the new state power consisted not only in the confiscation of whatever feudal estates there may be in Kwangtung in general; not only in the establishment of workers' control of production; but also in the nationalization of big industry, banks, and transportation, and even the confiscation of bourgeois dwellings and all bourgeois property for the benefit of the toilers. The question arises: if these are the methods of a bourgeois revolution then what should the proletarian revolution in China look like?

Notwithstanding the fact that the directives of the ECCI had nothing to say on the subject of the proletarian dictatorship and socialist measures; notwithstanding the fact that Canton is more petty bourgeois in character than Shanghai, Hankow, and other industrial centers of the country, the revolutionary overturn effected *against the Kuomintang* led automatically to the dictatorship of the proletariat which, at its very first steps, found itself compelled by the entire situation to resort to more radical measures than those with which the October revolution began. And this fact, despite its paradoxical appearance, flows quite lawfully from the social relations of China as well as from the entire development of the revolution.

Large and middle-scale landed estates (such as exist in China) are most closely interlinked with city capital, including foreign capital. There is no caste of feudal landlords in China in opposition to the bourgeoisie. The most widespread, common, and hated exploiter in the village is the kulak-usurer, the agent of finance capital in the cities. The agrarian revolution is therefore just as much antibourgeois as it is antifeudal in character. In China, there will be practically no such stage as the first stage of our October revolution in which the kulak marched with the middle and poor peasant, frequently at their head, against the landlord. The agrarian revolution in China signifies from the outset, as it will signify subsequently, an uprising not only against the few genuine feudal landlords and the bureaucracy, but also against the kulaks and usurers. If in our country the poor peasant committees appeared on the scene only during the second stage of the October revolution, in the middle of 1918, in China, on the contrary, they will, in one form or another, appear on the scene as soon as the agrarian movement revives. The drive on the rich peasant will be the first and not the second step of the Chinese October.

The agrarian revolution, however, is not the sole content of the present historical struggle in China. The most extreme agrarian revolution, the general division of land (which will naturally be supported by the Communist Party to the very end), will not by itself provide a way out of the economic blind alley. China requires just as urgently national unity and economic sovereignty, that is, customs autonomy, or more correctly, a monopoly of foreign trade. And this means *emancipation from world imperialism*—imperialism for which China remains the most important prospective source not only of enrichment but also of actual existence, constituting a safety valve against the internal explosions of European capitalism today and American capitalism tomorrow. This is what predetermines the gigantic scope and monstrous sharpness of the struggle that faces the masses of China, all the more so now when the depth of the stream of the struggle has already been plumbed and felt by all of its participants.

The enormous role of foreign capital in Chinese industry and its way of relying directly in defense of its plunder on its own "national" bayonets, render the program of workers' control in China even less realizable than it was in our country.[84] The direct expropriation first of the foreign capitalist and then of the Chinese capitalist enterprises will most likely be made imperative by the course of the struggle, on the day after the victorious insurrection.

Those objective sociohistorical causes that predetermined the "October" outcome of the Russian revolution rise before us in China in a still more accentuated form. The bourgeois and proletarian poles of the Chinese nation stand opposed to each other even more irreconcilably, if this is at all possible, than they did in Russia, since, on the one hand, the Chinese bourgeoisie is directly bound up with foreign imperialism and the latter's military machine, and since, on the other hand, the Chinese proletariat has from the very beginning established a close bond with the Comintern and the Soviet Union. Numerically the Chinese peasantry constitutes an even more overwhelming mass than the Russian peasantry. But being crushed in the vise of world contradictions, upon the solution of which in one way or another its fate depends, the Chinese peasantry is even less capable of playing a *leading* role than the Russian. At present this is no longer a matter of theoretical forecast, but a fact verified completely in all its aspects.

These fundamental and, at the same time, incontrovertible social and political prerequisites of the third Chinese revolution demonstrate not only that the formula of the democratic dictatorship has *hopelessly outlived its usefulness,* but also that the third Chinese revolution, despite the great backwardness of China, or more correctly, because of this great backwardness as compared with Russia, will not have a "democratic" period, not even such a six-month period as the October revolution had (November 1917 to July 1918); but it will be compelled from the very outset to effect the most decisive shake-up and abolition of bourgeois property in city and village.

To be sure, this perspective does not harmonize with the pedantic and schematic conceptions concerning the interrelations between economics and politics. But the responsibility for this disharmony so disturbing to the prejudices which have newly taken root and which were already dealt a not inconsiderable blow by the October revolution must be placed not on "Trotsky-ism" but on the *law of uneven development.* In this particular case this law is especially applicable.

It would be unwise pedantry to maintain that, had a Bolshevik policy been applied in the revolution of 1925-27, the Chinese Communist Party would *unfailingly* have come to power. But it is contemptible philistinism to assert that such a possibility was entirely out of the question. The mass movement of workers and peasants was on a scale entirely adequate for this, as was also the disintegration of the ruling classes. The national bourgeoisie sent its Chiang Kai-sheks and Wang Ching-weis as envoys to Moscow, and through its Hu Han-mins knocked at the door of the Comintern, precisely because it was hopelessly weak in face of the revolutionary masses; it realized its weakness and sought to insure itself. Neither the workers nor the peasants would have followed the national bourgeoisie if we ourselves had not dragged them by a rope. Had the Comintern pursued any sort of correct policy, the outcome of the struggle of the Communist Party for the masses would have been predetermined—the Chinese proletariat would have supported the communists, while the peasant war would have supported the revolutionary proletariat.

If at the beginning of the Northern Expedition we had begun to organize soviets in the "liberated" districts (and the masses were instinctively aspiring for that with all their might and main) we would have secured the necessary basis and a revolutionary running start, we would have rallied around us the agrarian uprisings, we would have built *our own* army, we would have disintegrated the enemy armies; and despite the youthfulness of the Communist Party of China, the latter would have been able, thanks to proper guidance from the Comintern, to mature in these exceptional years and to assume power, if not in the whole of China at once, then at least in a considerable part of China. And above all, we would have had a *party*.

But something absolutely monstrous occurred precisely in the sphere of leadership—a veritable historical catastrophe. The authority of the Soviet Union, of the Bolshevik party, and of the Comintern served entirely, first, to support Chiang Kai-shek against an independent policy of the Communist Party, and then to support Wang Ching-wei as the leader of the agrarian revolution. Having trampled underfoot the very basis of Leninist policy and after breaking the spine of the young Communist Party of China, the ECCI predetermined the victory of Chinese Kerenskyism over Bolshevism, of the Chinese Milyukovs over the Kerenskys, and of British and Japanese imperialism over the Chinese Milyukovs.

In this and in this alone lies the meaning of what took place in China in the course of 1925-27.

3. Democratic Dictatorship or a Dictatorship of the Proletariat?

But how did the last plenum of the ECCI evaluate the experiences of the Chinese revolution, including the experience of the Canton insurrection? What further perspectives did it outline? The resolution of the February (1928) plenum, which is the key to the corresponding sections of the draft program on this subject, says concerning the Chinese revolution:

> It is incorrect to characterize it as a "permanent" revolution [the position of the representative of the ECCI]. The tendency to skip [?] over the bourgeois-democratic stage of the revolution while simultaneously [?] appraising the revolution as a "permanent" revolution is a mistake analogous to that committed by Trotsky in 1905 [?].

The ideological life of the Comintern since Lenin's departure from its leadership, that is, since 1923, consisted primarily in a struggle against so-called Trotskyism and particularly against the "permanent revolution." How is it, then, that in the fundamental question of the Chinese revolution not only the Central Committee of the Communist Party of China, but also the official delegate of the Comintern, i.e., a leader who was sent with special instructions, happen to commit the very same "mistake" for which hundreds of men are now exiled to Siberia and put in prison? The struggle around the Chinese question has been raging for some two and a half years. When the Opposition declared that the old Central Committee of the Communist Party of China (Ch'en Tu-hsiu), under the influence of the false directives from the Comintern, conducted an opportunist policy, this evaluation was declared to be "slander." The leadership of the Communist Party of China was pronounced irreproachable. The celebrated T'an P'ing-shan declared amid the general approval of the Seventh Plenum of the ECCI that "At the very first manifestations of Trotskyism, the Communist Party of China and the Young Communist League immediately adopted a unanimous resolution against Trotskyism" (*Minutes,* p. 205).

But when, not withstanding these "achievements," events unfolded their tragic logic which led to the first and then to the second and even more frightful debacle of the revolution, the leadership of the Communist Party of China, formerly flawless, was rebaptized as Menshevik and deposed in the space of twenty-four hours. At the same time a decree was promulgated that the new leadership fully reflected the line of the Comintern. But no sooner did a new and a serious test arise than it was discovered that the new Central Committee of the Communist Party of China was guilty (as we have already seen, not in words, but in actions) of swerving to the position of the so-called permanent revolution. The delegate of the Comintern took the very same path. This astonishing and truly incomprehensible fact can be explained only by the yawning "scissors" between the instructions of the ECCI and the real dynamics of the revolution.

We shall not dwell here upon the myth of the "permanent

revolution" of 1905 which was placed in circulation in 1924 in order to sow confusion and bewilderment. We shall confine ourselves to an examination of how this myth broke down on the question of the Chinese revolution.

The first paragraph of the February resolution, from which the above-quoted passage was taken, gives the following motives for its negative attitude toward the so-called permanent revolution:

> The current period of the Chinese revolution is a period of a bourgeois-democratic revolution which has not been completed either from the economic standpoint (the agrarian revolution and the abolition of feudal relations), or from the standpoint of the national struggle against imperialism (the unification of China and the establishment of national independence), or from the standpoint of the class nature of the state (the dictatorship of the proletariat and the peasantry). . . .

This presentation of motives is an unbroken chain of mistakes and contradictions.

The ECCI taught that the Chinese revolution must secure for China the opportunity to develop along the road to socialism. This goal could be achieved only if the revolution did not halt merely at the solution of the bourgeois-democratic tasks but continued to unfold, passing from one stage to the next, i.e., continued to develop uninterruptedly (*or permanently*) and thus lead China toward a socialist development. This is precisely what Marx understood by the term "permanent revolution." How then can we, on the one hand, speak of a noncapitalist path of development for China and, on the other, deny the permanent character of the revolution in general?

But—insists the resolution of the ECCI—the revolution has not been completed, either from the standpoint of the agrarian revolution or from the standpoint of the national struggle against imperialism. Hence it draws the conclusion about the bourgeois-democratic character of the "present period of the Chinese revolution." As a matter of fact the "present period" is a period of counterrevolution. The ECCI doubtlessly intends to say that the new resurgence of the Chinese revolution, or *the third Chinese revolution,* will bear a bourgeois-democratic character because the second Chinese revolution of 1925-27 solved neither the agrarian question nor the national question. However even thus amended, this reasoning is based upon a total failure to understand the experiences and lessons of both the Chinese and the Russian revolutions.

The February 1917 revolution in Russia left unsolved all the internal and international problems that had led to the revolution—serfdom in the villages, the old bureaucracy, the war, and economic debacle. Taking this as a starting point, not only the SRs and the Mensheviks, but also a considerable section of the leadership of our own party tried to prove to Lenin that the "present period of the revolution is a period of the bourgeois-democratic revolution." In this, its basic consideration, the resolution of the ECCI merely copies the objections that the opportunists raised against the struggle for the dictatorship of the proletariat waged by Lenin in 1917.

Furthermore, it appears that the bourgeois-democratic revolution remains unaccomplished not only from the economic and national standpoint, but also from the "standpoint of the class nature of the state (the dictatorship of the proletariat and the peasantry)." This can mean only one thing: that the Chinese proletariat is forbidden to struggle for the conquest of power so long as no "genuine" democratic government stands at the helm in China. Unfortunately, no instructions are forthcoming as to where we can get it.

The confusion is further increased by the fact that the slogan of soviets was rejected for China in the course of these two years on the ground that the creation of soviets is permissible presumably only during the transition to the proletarian revolution (Stalin's "theory"). But when the soviet revolution broke out in Canton and when its participants drew the conclusion that this was precisely the transition to the proletarian revolution, they were accused of "Trotskyism." Is the party to be educated by such methods? Is this the way to assist it in the solution of supreme tasks?

To save a hopeless position, the resolution of the ECCI (without any connection whatever with the entire trend of its thought) rushes in posthaste to its last argument—taken from imperialism. It appears that the tendency to skip over the bourgeois-democratic stage ". . . is all the more [!] harmful because such a formulation of the question eliminates [?] the most important national peculiarity of the Chinese revolution, which is a semicolonial revolution."

The only meaning that these senseless words can have is that the imperialist yoke will be overthrown by some sort of nonproletarian dictatorship. But this means that the "most important national peculiarity" has been dragged in at the last moment in order to paint the Chinese national bourgeoisie or the

Chinese petty-bourgeois "democracy" in bright colors. This argument can have no other meaning. But this only "meaning" has been adequately examined by us in our chapter "On the Nature of the Colonial Bourgeoisie." There is no need to return to this subject.

China is still confronted with a vast, bitter, bloody, and prolonged struggle for such elementary things as the liquidation of the most "Asiatic" forms of slavery, national emancipation, and unification of the country. But as the course of events has shown, it is precisely this that makes impossible in the future any petty-bourgeois leadership or even semileadership in the revolution. The unification and emancipation of China today is an international task, no less so than the existence of the USSR. This task can be solved only by means of a desperate struggle on the part of the downtrodden, hungry, and persecuted masses under the direct leadership of the proletarian vanguard—a struggle not only against world imperialism, but also against its economic and political agency in China, against the bourgeoisie, including the "national" bourgeoisie and all its democratic flunkies. And this is nothing else than the road toward the dictatorship of the proletariat.

Beginning with April 1917, Lenin explained to his opponents, who accused him of having adopted the position of the "permanent revolution," that the dictatorship of the proletariat and the peasantry was realized partially in the epoch of dual power. He explained later that this dictatorship met with its further extension during the first period of soviet power from November 1917 until July 1918, when the entire peasantry, together with the workers, effected the agrarian revolution while the working class did not as yet proceed with the confiscation of the mills and factories, but experimented with workers' control. So far as the "class nature of the state" was concerned, the democratic SR-Menshevik "dictatorship" gave all that it could give—the miscarriage of dual power. As to the agrarian overturn, the revolution gave birth to a perfectly healthy and strong baby, but it was the proletarian dictatorship that functioned as the midwife.

In other words, what the theoretical formula of the dictatorship of the proletariat and the peasantry had combined, was dissociated in the course of the actual class struggle. The hollow shell of semipower was provisionally entrusted to Kerensky-Tseretelli, while the real kernel of the agrarian-democratic revolution fell to the share of the victorious working class. This dialectical dissociation of the democratic dictatorship, the leaders of the ECCI failed to understand. They drove themselves into a political blind alley by condemning mechanically any "skipping over the bourgeois-democratic stage" and by endeavoring to guide the historical process in accordance with circular letters. *If we are to understand by the bourgeois-democratic stage the accomplishment of the agrarian revolution by means of a "democratic dictatorship," then it was the October revolution itself that audaciously "skipped" over the bourgeois-democratic stage.* Should it not be condemned for it?

Why is it then that the historically inevitable course of events that was the highest expression of Bolshevism in Russia must prove to be "Trotskyism" in China? No doubt owing to the very same logic that declares to be suitable for China the theory of the Martynovs, a theory fought by Bolshevism for two decades in Russia.

But is it at all permissible to draw here an analogy with Russia? Our answer is that the slogan of a democratic dictatorship of the proletariat and the peasantry was constructed by the leaders of the ECCI exclusively and entirely in accordance with the method of analogy, but a formal and literary analogy and not a materialist and historical analogy. An analogy between China and Russia is entirely admissible if we find the proper approach to it, and Lenin made excellent use of such an analogy. Moreover he did so not *after* but before the events, as if he had foreseen the future blunders of the epigones. Hundreds of times Lenin had to defend the October revolution of the proletariat that had the audacity to conquer power *notwithstanding the fact* that the bourgeois-democratic tasks had not been solved. Precisely *because of that, and precisely in order to do that,* replied Lenin. Addressing himself to the pedants, who in their arguments against the conquest of power referred to the economic immaturity of Russia for socialism, which was "incontrovertible" for him ["Our Revolution," *Collected Works,* vol. 33, p. 478], Lenin wrote on January 16, 1923:

> For instance, it does not even occur to them that because Russia stands on the border-line between the civilised countries and the countries which this war has for the first time definitely brought into the orbit of civilisation—all the Oriental, non-European countries— she could and was, indeed, bound to reveal certain distinguishing features; although these, of course, are in keeping with the general

line of world development, they distinguish her revolution from those which took place in the West-European countries and introduce certain partial innovations as the revolution moves on to the countries of the East. [Ibid., p. 477.]

The "distinguishing feature" that brings Russia *closer* to the countries of the Orient was seen by Lenin precisely in the fact that the young proletariat, at an early stage, had to grasp the broom and sweep feudal barbarism and all sorts of rubbish from its path toward socialism.

If, consequently, we are to take as our starting point the Leninist analogy between China and Russia, then we must say: from the standpoint of the *"political nature of the state,"* all that could have been obtained through the democratic dictatorship in China has been put to the test, first in Sun Yat-sen's Canton, then on the road from Canton to Shanghai, which culminated in the Shanghai coup, and then in Wuhan where the left Kuomintang appeared in its chemically pure form, i.e., according to the directives of the ECCI, as the organizer of the agrarian revolution, but in reality as its hangman. But the social *content* of the bourgeois-democratic revolution will fill the initial period of the coming dictatorship of the Chinese proletariat and the peasant poor. To advance now the slogan of a democratic dictatorship of the proletariat and the peasantry after the role not only of the Chinese bourgeoisie, but also of Chinese "democracy" has been put to a thorough test, after it has become absolutely incontestable that "democracy" will play even a greater hangman's role in the coming battles than in the past—to advance this slogan now is simply to create the means of covering up the new varieties of Kuomintangism and to prepare a noose for the proletariat.

Let us recall for the sake of completeness what Lenin tersely said about those Bolsheviks who insisted upon counterposing to the SR–Menshevik experience the slogan of a "genuine" democratic dictatorship:

> The person who *now* speaks only of a "revolutionary-democratic dictatorship of the proletariat and the peasantry" is behind the times, consequently, he has in effect *gone over* to the petty bourgeoisie against the proletarian class struggle; that person should be consigned to the archive of "Bolshevik" pre-revolutionary antiques (it may be called the archive of "old Bolsheviks"). ["Letters on Tactics," April 1917, *Collected Works*, vol. 24, p. 45.]

These words ring as if they were actually spoken today.

Of course it is not at all a question of calling the Communist Party of China to an immediate insurrection for the seizure of power. The pace depends entirely upon the circumstances. The consequences of defeat cannot be removed merely by revising the tactic. The revolution is now subsiding. The half-concealing resolution of the ECCI, the bombast about imminent revolutionary onslaughts, while countless people are being executed and a terrific commercial and industrial crisis rages in China, are criminal light-mindedness and nothing else. After three major defeats an economic crisis does not rouse, but on the contrary, depresses the proletariat which, as it is, has already been bled white, while the executions only destroy the politically weakened party. We are entering in China into a period of reflux, and consequently into a period in which the party deepens its theoretical roots, educates itself critically, creates and strengthens firm organizational links in all spheres of the working class movement, organizes rural nuclei, leads and unites partial, at first defensive and later offensive, battles of the workers and the peasant poor.

What will turn the tide in the mass movement? What circumstances will give the necessary revolutionary impulsion to the proletarian vanguard at the head of the many-millioned masses? This cannot be predicted. The future will show whether internal processes alone will be sufficient or an added impulsion will have to come from without.

There are sufficient grounds for assuming that the smashing of the Chinese revolution, directly due to the false leadership, will permit the Chinese and foreign bourgeoisie to overcome to a lesser or greater degree the frightful economic crisis now raging in the country. Naturally, this will be done on the backs and bones of the workers and peasants. This phase of "stabilization" will once again group and fuse together the workers, restore their class self-confidence in order subsequently to bring them into still sharper conflict with the enemy, but on a higher historical stage. It will be possible to speak seriously about the perspective of an agrarian revolution only on the condition that there will be a new mounting wave of the proletarian movement on the offensive.

It is not excluded that the first stage of the coming third revolution may reproduce in a very abridged and modified form the stages that have already been passed, presenting, for instance, some new parody of the "national united front." But this first stage will be sufficient only to give the Communist Party a chance to put forward and announce its "April" thesis, that is, its program and tactics of the seizure of power, before the popular masses.

But what does the draft program say on this?

> The transition to the proletarian dictatorship is possible here [in China] only after a series of preparatory stages [?], only as a result of a whole period of the growing over [??] of the bourgeois-democratic revolution into the socialist revolution.

In other words, all the "stages" that have already been gone through are not to be taken into account. The draft program still sees ahead what has already been left behind. This is precisely what is meant by a tailendist formulation. It opens wide the gates for new experiments in the spirit of the Kuomintang course. Thus the concealment of the old mistakes inevitably prepares the road for new errors.

If we enter the new upsurge, which will develop at an incomparably more rapid tempo than the last one, with a blueprint of "democratic dictatorship" that has already outlived its usefulness, there can be no doubt that the third Chinese revolution, like the second, will be led to its doom.

4. Adventurism as the Product of Opportunism

The second paragraph of the same resolution of the February plenum of the ECCI says:

> The first wave of the broad revolutionary movement of workers and peasants which in the main proceeded under the slogans and to a considerable extent *under the leadership of the Communist Party,* is over. It ended in several centers of the revolutionary movement with *heaviest defeats* for the workers and peasants, the physical extermination of the communists and revolutionary cadres of the labor and peasant movement in general. [Our emphasis.]

When the "wave" was surging high, the ECCI said that the whole movement was entirely under the blue banner and leadership of the Kuomintang, which even took the place of soviets. It is precisely on that ground that the Communist Party was subordinated to the Kuomintang. But that is exactly why the revolutionary movement ended with "heaviest defeats." Now when these defeats have been recognized, an attempt is being made to erase the Kuomintang from the past as if it had never existed, as if the ECCI had not declared the blue banner its own.

There have been no defeats either in Shanghai or in Wuhan in the past; there were merely transitions of the revolution "into a higher phase"—that is what we have been taught. Now the sum total of these transitions is suddenly declared to be "heaviest defeats for the workers and peasants." However, in order to mask to some extent this unprecedented political bankruptcy of forecasts and evaluations, the concluding paragraph of the resolution declares:

"The ECCI makes it the duty of all sections of the CI to fight against the Social Democratic and Trotskyist slanders to the effect that the Chinese revolution has been liquidated [?]."

In the first paragraph of the resolution we were told that "Trotskyism" was the idea of the *permanent* Chinese revolution, that is, a revolution that is precisely at this time growing over from the bourgeois to the socialist phase; from the last paragraph we learn that according to the "Trotskyists," "the Chinese revolution has been liquidated." How can a *"liquidated"* revolution be a *permanent* revolution? Here we have Bukharin in all his glory.

Only complete and reckless irresponsibility permits of such contradictions which corrode all revolutionary thought at its roots.

If we are to understand by "liquidation" of the revolution the fact that the labor and peasant offensive has been beaten back and drowned in blood, that the masses are in a state of retreat and decline, that before another onslaught there must be, apart from many other circumstances, a molecular process at work among the masses that requires a certain period of time, the duration of which cannot be determined beforehand; if "liquidation" is to be understood in this way, it does not in any manner differ from the "heaviest defeats" which the ECCI has finally been compelled to recognize. Or are we to understand liquidation literally, as the actual elimination of the Chinese revolution, that is, of the very possibility and inevitability of its rebirth on a new plane? One can speak of such a perspective seriously and so as not to create confusion only in two cases—if China were doomed to dismemberment and complete extirpation, an assumption for which there is no basis whatever, or if the Chinese bourgeoisie would prove capable of solving the basic problems of Chinese life in its own nonrevolutionary way. Is it not this last variant that the theoreticians of the "bloc of four classes," who directly drove the Communist Party under the yoke of the bourgeoisie, seek to ascribe to us now? History repeats itself. The blind men who did not understand the scope of the defeat of 1923, for a year and a half accused us of "liquidationism" toward the German revolution. But even this lesson, which cost the International so dearly, taught them nothing. At present they use their old rubber stamps, only this time substituting China for Germany. To be sure, their need to find "liquidators" is more acute today than it was four years ago, for this time it is much too obviously apparent that if anybody did "liquidate" the second Chinese revolution it was the authors of the "Kuomintang" course.

The strength of Marxism lies in its ability to foretell. In this sense the Opposition can point to an absolute confirmation in experience of its prognosis. At first concerning the Kuomintang as a whole, then concerning the "left" Kuomintang and the Wuhan government, and, finally, concerning the "deposit" on the third revolution, that is the Canton insurrection. What further confirmation could there be of one's theoretical correctness?

The very same opportunist line, which through the policy of capitulation to the bourgeoisie has already brought the heaviest defeats to the revolution during its first two stages, "grew over" in the third stage into a policy of adventurous raids on the bourgeoisie and thus made the defeat final.

Had the leadership not hurried yesterday to leap over the defeats which it had itself brought about, it would first of all have explained to the Communist Party of China that victory is not gained in one sweep, that on the road to the armed insurrection there still remains a period of intense, incessant, and savage struggle for political influence on the workers and peasants.

On September 27, 1927, we said to the Presidium of the ECCI:

> Today's papers report that the revolutionary army has occupied Swatow. It is already several weeks that the armies of Ho Lung and Yeh T'ing have been advancing. *Pravda* calls these armies revolutionary armies. . . . But I ask you: What prospects does the movement of the revolutionary army that captured Swatow raise before the Chinese revolution? What are the slogans of the movement? What is its program? What should be its organizational forms? What has become of the slogan of Chinese soviets, which *Pravda* suddenly advanced for a single day in July?

Without first counterposing the Communist Party to the Kuomintang as a whole, without the party's agitation among the masses for soviets and a soviet government, without an independent mobilization of the masses under the slogans of the agrarian revolution and of national emancipation, without the creation, broadening, and strengthening of the local soviets of workers', soldiers', and peasants' deputies, the insurrection of Ho Lung and Yeh T'ing, even apart from their opportunist policy, could not fail to be only an isolated adventure, a pseudocommunist Makhno feat;[85] it could not fail to crash against its own isolation. And it has crashed.

The Canton insurrection was a broader and deeper repetition of the Ho Lung–Yeh T'ing adventure, only with infinitely more tragic consequences.

The February resolution of the ECCI combats putschistic moods in the Communist Party of China, that is, tendencies toward armed uprisings. It does not say, however, that these tendencies are a reaction to the entire opportunist policy of 1925-27, and an inevitable consequence of the purely military command issued from above to "change the step," without an evaluation of all that had been done, without an open revaluation of the basis of the tactic, and without a clear perspective. Ho Lung's campaign and the Canton insurrection were—and under the circumstances could not fail to be—breeders of putschism.

A real antidote to putschism as well as to opportunism can be only a clear understanding of the truth that the leadership of the armed insurrection of the workers and poor peasants, the seizure of power, and the institution of a revolutionary dictatorship fall henceforth entirely upon the shoulders of the Communist Party of China. If the latter is permeated thoroughly with the understanding of this perspective, it will be as little inclined to improvise military raids on towns or armed insurrections in traps as to chase humbly after the enemy's banner.

The resolution of the ECCI condemns itself to utter impotence by the fact alone that in arguing most abstractly concerning the inadmissibility of leaping over stages and the harmfulness of putschism, it entirely ignores the class content of the Canton insurrection and the short-lived soviet regime that it brought into existence. We Oppositionists hold that this insurrection was an adventure of the leaders in an effort to save their "prestige." But it is clear to us that even an adventure develops according to laws that are determined by the structure of the social milieu. That is why we look to the Canton insurrection for the features of the future phase of the Chinese revolution. These features fully correspond with our theoretical analysis made prior to the

Canton uprising. But how much more imperative it is for the ECCI, which holds that the Canton uprising was a correct and normal link in the chain of struggle, to give a clear class characterization of the Canton insurrection. However, there is not a word about this in the resolution of the ECCI, although the plenum met immediately after the Canton events. Is this not the most convincing proof that the present leadership of the Comintern, because it stubbornly pursues a false policy, is compelled to occupy itself with the fictitious errors of 1905 and other years without daring to approach the Canton insurrection of 1927, the meaning of which completely upsets the blueprint for revolutions in the East that is set down in the draft program?

5. Soviets and Revolution

In the February resolution of the ECCI the representatives of the Comintern, "Comrade N. and others," are made responsible for the "absence of an *elected* soviet in Canton as an organ of insurrection" (emphasis in the original). Behind this charge in reality lies an astounding admission.

In the report of *Pravda* (no. 31), written on the basis of first-hand documents, it was stated that a soviet government had been established in Canton. But not a word was mentioned to indicate that the Canton Soviet was *not* an elected organ, i.e., that it was not a *soviet*—for how can there be a soviet that was not elected? We learn this from the resolution. Let us reflect for a moment on the significance of this fact. The ECCI tells us now that a soviet is necessary to effect an armed insurrection, but by no means prior to that time. But lo and behold! When the date for the insurrection is set, there is no soviet. To create an elected soviet is not an easy matter. It is necessary that the masses know from experience what a soviet is, that they understand its form, that they have learned something in the past to accustom them to an elected soviet organization. There was not even a sign of this in China, for the slogan of soviets was declared to be a Trotskyist slogan precisely in the period when it should have become the nerve center of the entire movement. When, however, helter-skelter, a date was set for an insurrection so as to skip over their own defeats, they simultaneously had to *appoint* a soviet as well. If this error is not laid bare to the core, the slogan of soviets can be transformed into the hangman's noose of the revolution.

Lenin in his time explained to the Mensheviks that the

fundamental historical task of the soviets is to organize, or help organize, the conquest of power so that on the day after the victory they become the organ of that power. The epigones—and not the disciples—draw from this the conclusion that soviets can be organized only when the twelfth hour of the insurrection has struck. Lenin's broad generalization they transform post factum into a little recipe which does not serve the interests of the revolution but imperils it.

Before the Bolshevik soviets in October 1917 captured power, the SR and Menshevik soviets had existed for nine months. Twelve years before, the first revolutionary soviets existed in Petersburg, Moscow, and scores of other cities. Before the soviet of 1905 was extended to embrace the mills and factories of the capital, there was created in Moscow, during the strike, a soviet of printers' deputies. Several months before this, in May 1905, a mass strike in Ivanovo Voznesensk set up a leading body that already contained all the essential features of a soviet of workers' deputies. Between the first experiment of setting up a soviet of workers' deputies and the gigantic experiment of setting up a soviet government, more than twelve years rolled by. Of course, such a period is not at all required for all other countries, including China. But to think that the Chinese workers are capable of building soviets on the basis of the little recipe that has been substituted for Lenin's broad generalization is to substitute impotent and importunate pedantry for the dialectic of revolutionary action.

Soviets must be set up not on the eve of the insurrection, not under the slogan of immediate seizure of power—for if the matter has reached the point of the seizure of power, if the masses are prepared for an armed insurrection *without a soviet,* it means that there have been other organizational forms and methods that made possible the performance of the preparatory work to insure the success of the uprising. Then the question of soviets becomes of secondary importance and is reduced to a question of organizational technique or merely to a question of denomination. The task of the soviets is not merely to issue the call for the insurrection or to carry it out, but *to lead the masses toward the insurrection through the necessary stages.* At first the soviet rallies the masses not to the slogan of armed insurrection, but to partial slogans, so that only later, step by step, the masses are brought toward the slogan of insurrection without scattering them on the road and without allowing the vanguard to become isolated from the class.

The soviet appears most often and primarily in connection with strike struggles that have the perspectives of revolutionary development, but are in the given moment limited merely to economic demands. The masses must sense and understand while in action that the soviet is *their* organization, that it marshals the forces for a struggle, for resistance, for self-defense, and for an offensive. They can sense and understand this not from an action of a single day nor in general from any single act, but from the experience of several weeks, months, and perhaps years, with or without interruptions. That is why only an epigonic and bureaucratic leadership can restrain the awakening and rising masses from creating soviets in conditions when the country is passing through an epoch of revolutionary upheavals and when the working class and the poor peasants have before them the prospect of capturing power, even though this is a perspective of one of the subsequent stages and even if this perspective can be envisaged in the given phase only by a small minority. Such was always our conception of the soviets. We evaluated the soviets as that broad and flexible organizational form that is accessible to the masses who have just awakened at the very first stages of their revolutionary upsurge; and which is capable of uniting the working class in its entirety, independent of the size of that section which, in the given phase, has already matured to the point of understanding the task of the seizure of power.

Is any documentary evidence really necessary? Here, for instance, is what Lenin wrote about the soviets in the epoch of the first revolution:

> The R.S.D.L.P. [Russian Social Democratic Labor Party—the name of the party at that time—L.T.] has never renounced its intention of utilising certain non-party organisations, such as the Soviets of Workers' Deputies, in periods of more or less intense revolutionary upheaval, to extend Social-Democratic influence among the working class and to strengthen the Social Democratic labour movement. ["Non-Party Workers' Organizations and the Anarcho-Syndicalist Trend Among the Proletariat," Draft Resolution for the Fifth Congress of the RSDLP, written February 15-18, 1907, *Collected Works,* vol. 12, p. 143.]

One could cite voluminous literary and historical evidence of this type. But one would imagine that the question is sufficiently clear without them.

In contradistinction to this the epigones have converted the soviets into an organizational parade uniform with which the party simply dresses up the proletariat on the eve of the capture of power. But this is precisely the time when we find that the soviets cannot be improvised in twenty-four hours, by order, for the direct purpose of an armed insurrection. Such experiments must inevitably assume a fictitious character and the absence of the most necessary conditions for the capture of power is masked by the external ritual of a soviet system. That is what happened in Canton where the soviet was simply appointed to observe the ritual. That is where the epigone formulation of the question leads.

*   *   *

During the polemics on the Chinese events the Opposition was accused of the following alleged flagrant contradiction: whereas from 1926 on the Opposition advanced the slogan of soviets for China, its representatives spoke against the slogan of soviets for Germany in the autumn of 1923. On no other point perhaps has scholastic political thought expressed itself so glaringly as in this accusation. Yes, we demanded for China a *timely* start for the creation of soviets as *independent* organizations of workers and peasants, *when the wave of revolutionary upsurge was mounting.*

The chief significance of the soviets was to be that of *opposing the workers and peasants to the Kuomintang bourgeoisie* and its left Kuomintang agency. The slogan of soviets in China meant above all the break with the suicidal and infamous "bloc of four classes" and the withdrawal of the Communist Party from the Kuomintang. The center of gravity consequently lay not in bare organizational forms, but in the class line.

In the autumn of 1923 in Germany it was a question of organizational form only. As a result of the extreme passivity, backwardness, and tardiness of the leadership of the Comintern and the Communist Party of Germany, the moment for a timely call for the organization of soviets was missed. The factory committees, due to pressure from below and of their own accord, had occupied in the labor movement of Germany by the autumn of 1923 the place that would no doubt have been much more successfully occupied by soviets had there been a correct and daring policy on the part of the Communist Party. The acuteness of the situation had in the meantime reached its sharpest point. To lose any more time would have meant definitely to miss the revolutionary situation. The insurrection was finally placed on the order of the day, with very little time left.

To advance the slogan of soviets under such conditions would have been the greatest pedantic stupidity conceivable. The soviet is not a talisman with omnipotent powers of salvation. In a situation such as had then developed, the hurried creation of soviets would only have duplicated the factory committees. It would have become necessary to deprive the latter of their revolutionary functions and to transfer them to the newly created and still utterly unauthoritative soviets. And when was this to be done? Under conditions in which each day counted. This would have meant to substitute for revolutionary action a most pernicious game in organizational gewgaws.

It is incontestable that the organizational form of a soviet can be of enormous importance; but only at a time when it furnishes a timely reflection of the correct political line. And conversely, it can acquire a no less negative meaning if it is converted into a fiction, a fetish, a bagatelle. The German soviets created at the very last moment in the autumn of 1923 would have added nothing politically; they would only have caused organizational confusion. What happened in Canton was even worse yet. The soviet that was created in a hurry to observe the ritual was only a masquerade for the adventurist putsch. That is why we discovered, after it was all over, that the Canton Soviet resembled an ancient Chinese dragon simply drawn on paper. The policy of pulling rotten strings and paper dragons is not our policy. We were against improvising soviets by telegraph in Germany in September 1923. We were for the creation of soviets in China in 1926. We were against the masquerade soviet in Canton in 1927. There are no contradictions here. We have here instead the profound unity of the conception of the dynamics of the revolutionary movement and its organizational forms.

The question of the role and significance of the soviets, which had been distorted and confused and obscured by the theory and practice of recent years, has not been illuminated in the least in the draft program.

6. The Question of the Character of the Coming Chinese Revolution

The slogan of the dictatorship of the proletariat, which leads behind it the peasant poor, is inseparably bound up with the question of the socialist character of the coming third revolution in China. And inasmuch as not only history repeats itself but also the mistakes that people counterpose to its requirements, we can already hear the objection that China has not yet matured for a socialist revolution. But this is an abstract and lifeless formulation of the question. For has Russia, taken by itself, matured for socialism? According to Lenin—*no!* It has matured for the dictatorship of the proletariat as the only method for solving unpostponable national tasks. But the destiny of the dictatorship as a whole is determined in the last analysis by the trend of *world* development, which, of course, does not exclude but rather presupposes a correct policy on the part of the proletarian dictatorship, the consolidation and development of the workers' and peasants' alliance, an all-sided adaptation to national conditions on the one hand, and to the trend of world development on the other. This fully holds true for China as well.

In the same article, entitled "Our Revolution" (January 16, 1923), in which Lenin establishes that the peculiarity of Russia proceeds along the lines of the peculiar development of the Eastern countries, he brands as "infinitely stereotyped" the argument of European Social Democracy to the effect "that we are not yet ripe for socialism, that, as certain 'learned' gentlemen among them put it, the objective economic premises for socialism do not exist in our country" [*Collected Works,* vol. 33, pp. 477-78]. But Lenin ridicules the "learned" gentlemen not because he himself recognized the *existence* of the economic prerequisites for socialism in Russia but because he holds that the rejection of the seizure of power does not at all follow, as pedants and philistines think, from the absence of these prerequisites necessary for an *independent* construction of socialism. In this article of his, Lenin for the hundred and first time, or, rather, for the thousand and first time replies to the sophisms of the heroes of the Second International: "They keep harping on this incontrovertible proposition in a thousand different keys, and think that it is the decisive criterion of our revolution" [ibid., p. 478]. That is what the authors of the draft program refuse and are unable to understand. In itself the thesis of the economic and cultural immaturity of China as well as Russia—China, of course, more so than Russia—is incontrovertible. But hence it does not at all follow that the proletariat has to renounce the conquest of power when this conquest is dictated by the entire historical context and the revolutionary situation in the country.

The concrete, historical, political, and actual question is reducible not to whether China has economically matured for "its own" socialism, but whether China has ripened politically for the proletarian dictatorship. These two questions are not at all identical. They might be regarded as identical were it not for the law of uneven development. This is where this law is in place and fully applies to the interrelationship between economics and politics. Then China has matured for the dictatorship of the proletariat? Only the experience of the struggle can provide a categorical answer to this question. By the same token, only the struggle can settle the question as to when and under what conditions the real unification, emancipation, and regeneration of China will take place. Anyone who says that China has not matured for the dictatorship of the proletariat declares thereby that the third Chinese revolution is postponed for many years to come.

Of course, matters would be quite hopeless if feudal survivals did really *dominate* in Chinese economic life, as the resolutions of the ECCI asserted. But fortunately, *survivals* in general cannot dominate. The draft program on this point, too, does not rectify the errors committed, but reaffirms them in a roundabout and nebulous fashion. The draft speaks of the "predominance of medieval feudal relations both in the economics of the country and in the political superstructure. . . ." This is false to the core. What does *predominance* mean? Is it a question of the number of people involved? Or the dominant and leading role in the economics of the country? The extraordinarily rapid growth of home industry on the basis of the all-embracing role of mercantile and bank capital; the complete dependence of the most important agrarian districts on the market; the enormous and ever-growing role of foreign trade; the all-sided subordination of the Chinese village to the city—all these bespeak the unconditional predominance, the direct domination of capitalist relations in China. The social relations of serfdom and semiserfdom are undeniably very strong. They stem in part from the days of feudalism; and in part they constitute a new formation, that is, the regeneration of the past on the basis of the retarded development of the productive forces, the surplus agrarian population, the activities of merchants' and usurers' capital, etc. However, it is capitalist relations that *dominate* and not "feudal" (more correctly, serf and, generally, precapitalist) relations. Only thanks to this dominant role of capitalist relations can we speak seriously of the prospects of the proletarian hegemony in the national revolution. Otherwise, there is no making the ends meet.

> The strength of the proletariat in any capitalist country is far greater than the proportion it represents of the total population. That is because the proletariat economically dominates the centre and nerve of the entire economic system of capitalism, and also because the proletariat expresses economically and politically the real interests of the overwhelming majority of the working people under capitalism.
>
> Therefore, the proletariat, even when it constitutes a minority of the population (or when the class-conscious and really revolutionary vanguard of the proletariat constitutes a minority of the population), is capable of overthrowing the bourgeoisie and, after that, of winning to its side numerous allies from a mass of semi-proletarians and petty bourgeoisie who never declare in advance in favour of the rule of the proletariat, who do not understand the conditions and aims of that rule, and only by their subsequent experience become convinced that the proletarian dictatorship is inevitable, proper and legitimate. [Lenin, "The Constituent Assembly Elections and the Dictatorship of the Proletariat," December 16, 1919, *Collected Works,* vol. 30, p. 274.]

The role of the Chinese proletariat in production is already very great. In the next few years it will only increase still further. Its political role, as events have shown, could have been gigantic. But the whole line of the leadership was directed entirely against permitting the proletariat to conquer the leading role.

The draft program says that successful socialist construction is possible in China "only on the condition that it is directly supported by countries under the proletarian dictatorship." Thus, here, in relation to China, the same principle is recognized that the party has always recognized in regard to Russia. But if China lacks sufficient inner forces for an *independent* construction of socialist society, then according to the theory of Stalin-Bukharin, the Chinese proletariat should not seize power at any stage of the revolution. Or it may be that the existence of the USSR settles the question in just the opposite sense. Then it follows that our technology is sufficient to build a socialist society not only in the USSR but also in China, i.e., in the two economically most backward countries with a combined population of 600 million. Or perhaps the *inevitable* dictatorship of the proletariat in China, is "inadmissible" because that dictatorship will be included in the chain of the worldwide socialist revolution, thus becoming not only its link, but its driving force? But this is precisely Lenin's basic formulation of the October revolution, the "distinguishing feature" of which follows precisely along the lines of development of the Eastern countries. We see thus how the revisionist theory of socialism in one country, evolved in 1924 in order to wage a struggle against Trotskyism, distorts and confuses matters each time a new major revolutionary problem is approached.

The draft program goes still further along this same road. It counterposes China and India to "Russia before 1917" and Poland ("etc.,"?) as countries with a "certain *minimum* of industry sufficient for the triumphant construction of socialism," or (as is more definitely and therefore more erroneously stated elsewhere) as countries possessing the "necessary and sufficient material prerequisites . . . for the complete construction of socialism." This, as we already know, is a mere play upon Lenin's expression " necessary and sufficient" prerequisites; a fraudulent and impermissible jugglery because Lenin definitely enumerates the *political and organizational prerequisites,* including the *technical, cultural, and international* prerequisites. But the chief point that remains is: how can one determine a priori the "minimum of industry" sufficient for the complete building of socialism once it is a question of an uninterrupted world struggle between two economic systems, two social orders, and a struggle, moreover, in which our *economic* base is infinitely the weaker?

If we take into consideration only the economic lever, it is clear that we in the USSR, and all the more so in China and India, have a far shorter arm of the lever than world capitalism. But the entire question is resolved by the *revolutionary struggle* of the two systems on a world scale. In the political struggle, the long arm of the lever is *on our side,* or, to put it more correctly, it can and must prove so in our hands, if our policy is correct.

Again, in the same article, "Our Revolution," after stating that "a definite level of culture is required for the building of socialism," Lenin adds: "although nobody can say just what that definite 'level of culture' is. . . ." Why can no one say? Because the question is settled by the struggle, by the rivalry between the two social systems and the two cultures, *on an international scale.* Breaking completely with this idea of Lenin's, which flows from the very essence of the question, the draft program asserts that in 1917 Russia had precisely the "minimum technology" and consequently also the culture necessary for the building of socialism in one country. The authors of the draft attempt to say in the program that which "nobody can say" a priori.

It is impermissible, impossible, and absurd to seek a criterion for the "sufficient minimum" within national states ("Russia prior to 1917") when the whole question is settled by international dynamics. In this false, arbitrary, isolated national criterion rests the theoretical basis of national narrowness in politics, the precondition for inevitable national-reformist and social-patriotic blunders in the future.

7. On the Reactionary Idea of "Two-Class Workers' and Peasants' Parties" for the Orient

The lessons of the second Chinese revolution are lessons for the entire Comintern, but primarily for all the countries of the Orient.

All the arguments presented in defense of the Menshevik line in the Chinese revolution must, if we take them seriously, hold trebly good for India. The imperialist yoke assumes in India, the classic colony, infinitely more direct and palpable forms than in China. The survivals of feudal and serf relations in India are immeasurably deeper and greater. Nevertheless, or rather precisely for this reason, the methods that, applied in China, undermined the revolution, must result in India in even more fatal consequences. The overthrow of Hindu feudalism and of the Anglo-Hindu bureaucracy and British militarism can be accomplished only by a gigantic and indomitable movement of the popular masses that precisely because of its powerful sweep and irresistibility, its international aims and ties, cannot tolerate any halfway and compromising opportunist measures on the part of the leadership.

The Comintern leadership has already committed not a few mistakes in India. The conditions have not yet allowed these errors to reveal themselves on such a scale as in China. One can, therefore, hope that the lessons of the Chinese events will permit of a more timely rectification of the line of the leading policy in India and in other countries of the East.

The cardinal question for us here, as everywhere and always, is the question of the Communist Party, its complete independence, its irreconcilable class character. The greatest danger on this path is the organization of so-called workers' and peasants' parties in the countries of the Orient.

Beginning with 1924, a year that will go down as the year of open revision of a number of fundamental theses of Marx and Lenin, Stalin advanced the formula of the "two-class workers' and peasants' parties for the Eastern countries." It was based on the self-same national oppression that served in the Orient to camouflage opportunism, as did "stabilization" in the Occident. Cables from India, as well as from Japan, where there is no national oppression, have of late frequently mentioned the activities of provincial "workers' and peasants' parties," referring to them as organizations that are close and friendly to the Comintern, as if they were almost our "own" organizations, without, however, giving any sort of concrete definition of their political physiognomy; in a word, writing and speaking about them in the same way as was done only a short while ago about the Kuomintang.

Back in 1924, *Pravda* reported that: "There are indications that the movement of national liberation in Korea is gradually taking shape in the form of the creation of a workers' and peasants' party" (March 2, 1924).

And in the meantime Stalin lectures the communists of the Orient that

> They [the communists] will have to transcend the policy of the united nationalist front, and adopt the policy of forming a revolutionary coalition between the workers and the petty bourgeois. This coalition may find expression in the creation of a single party whose membership will be drawn from among the working class and the peasantry, after the model of the Kuomintang. [Stalin, *Problems of Leninism*, p. 264.[86]]

The ensuing tiny "reservations" on the subject of the independence of the Communist parties (obviously, "independence" like that of the prophet Jonah inside the whale's belly) served only for the purpose of camouflage. We are profoundly convinced that the Sixth Congress must state that the slightest equivocation in this sphere is fatal and will be rejected.

It is a question here of an absolutely new, entirely false, and thoroughly anti-Marxist formulation of the fundamental question of the party and of its relation to its own class and other classes.

The necessity for the Communist Party of China to enter the Kuomintang was defended on the ground that in its social composition the Kuomintang is a party of workers and peasants, that nine-tenths of the Kuomintang—this proportion was repeated hundreds of times—belonged to the revolutionary tendency and were ready to march hand in hand with the Communist Party. However, during and since the coups in Shanghai and Wuhan, these revolutionary nine-tenths of the

Kuomintang disappeared as if by magic. No one has found a trace of them. And the theoreticians of class collaboration in China—Stalin, Bukharin, and others—did not even take the trouble to explain what has become of the nine-tenths of the members of the Kuomintang—the nine-tenths workers and peasants, revolutionists, sympathizers, and entirely our "own." Yet, an answer to this question is of decisive importance if we are to understand the destiny of all these "two-class" parties preached by Stalin; and if we are to be clarified upon the very conception itself, which throws us far behind not only of the program of the RCP of 1919, but also of the *Communist Manifesto* of 1847.

The question of where the celebrated nine-tenths vanished can become clear to us only if we understand, first, the impossibility of a bicomposite, that is a two-class party, expressing simultaneously two mutually exclusive historical lines—the proletarian and petty-bourgeois lines; secondly, the impossibility of realizing in capitalist society an independent peasant party, that is, a party expressing the interests of the peasantry, which is at the same time independent of the proletariat and the bourgeoisie.

Marxism has always taught, and Bolshevism, too, accepted, and taught, that the peasantry and proletariat are two different classes, that it is false to identify their interests in capitalist society in any way, and that a peasant can join the Communist Party only if, from the property viewpoint, he adopts the views of the proletariat. The alliance of the workers and peasants under the dictatorship of the proletariat does not invalidate this thesis, but confirms it, in a different way, under different circumstances. If there were no *different* classes with *different* interests, there would be no talk even of an *alliance*. Such an alliance is compatible with the socialist revolution only to the extent that it enters into the iron framework of the dictatorship of the proletariat. In our country the dictatorship is incompatible with the existence of a so-called Peasants' League precisely because every "independent" peasant organization aspiring to solve all national political problems would inevitably turn out to be an instrument in the hands of the bourgeoisie.

Those organizations that in capitalist countries label themselves peasant parties are in reality one of the varieties of bourgeois parties. Every peasant who has not adopted the proletarian position, abandoning his proprietor psychology, will inevitably follow the bourgeoisie when it comes to fundamental political issues. Of course, every bourgeois party that relies or seeks to rely on the peasantry and, if possible, on the workers, is compelled to camouflage itself, that is, to assume two or three appropriate colorations. The celebrated idea of "workers' and peasants' parties" seems to have been specially created to camouflage bourgeois parties that are compelled to seek support from the peasantry but are also ready to absorb workers into their ranks. The Kuomintang has entered the annals of history for all time as a classic type of such a party.

Bourgeois society, as is known, is so constructed that the propertyless, discontented, and deceived masses are at the bottom and the contented fakers remain on top. Every bourgeois party, if it is a real party, that is, if it embraces considerable masses, is built on the self-same principle. The exploiters, fakers, and the despots compose the minority in class society. Every capitalist party is therefore compelled in its internal relations, in one way or another, to reproduce and reflect the relations in bourgeois society as a whole. In every mass bourgeois party the lower ranks are therefore more democratic and further to the "left" than the tops. This holds true of the German Center, the French Radicals, and particularly the Social Democracy. That is why the constant complaints voiced by Stalin, Bukharin, and others that the tops do not reflect the sentiments of the "left" Kuomintang rank and file, the "overwhelming majority," the "nine-tenths," etc., etc., are so naive, so unpardonable. That which they represented in their bizarre complaints to be a temporary, disagreeable misunderstanding which was to be eliminated by means of organizational measures, instructions, and circular letters, is in reality a cardinal and basic feature of a bourgeois party, particularly in a revolutionary epoch.

It is from this angle that the basic arguments of the authors of the draft program in defense of all kinds of opportunist blocs in general—both in England and China—must be judged. According to them, fraternization with the tops is done exclusively in the interests of the rank and file. The Opposition, as is known, insisted on the withdrawal of the party from the Kuomintang:

"The question arises," says Bukharin, "why? Is it because the leaders of the Kuomintang are vacillating? And what about the Kuomintang masses, are they mere 'cattle'? Since when is the attitude to a mass organization determined by what takes place at the 'high' summit!" (*The Present Situation in the Chinese Revolution*).

The very possibility of such an argument seems impossible in a revolutionary party. Bukharin asks, "And what about the Kuomintang masses, are they mere cattle?" Of course they are cattle. The masses of any bourgeois party are always cattle, although in different degrees. But for us, the masses are not cattle, are they? No, that is precisely why we are forbidden to drive them into the arms of the bourgeoisie, *camouflaging the latter under the label of a workers' and peasants' party*. That is precisely why we are forbidden to subordinate the proletarian party to a bourgeois party, but on the contrary, must at every step, oppose the former to the latter. The "high" summit of the Kuomintang of whom Bukharin speaks so ironically, as of something secondary, accidental, and temporary is in reality the soul of the Kuomintang, its social essence. Of course, the bourgeoisie constitutes only the "summit" in the party as well as in society. But this summit is powerful in its capital, knowledge, and connections: it can always fall back on the imperialists for support, and what is most important, it can always resort to the actual political and military power that is intimately fused with the leadership in the Kuomintang itself. It is precisely this summit that wrote laws against strikes, throttled the uprisings of the peasants, shoved the communists into a dark corner, and, at best, allowed them to be only one-third of the party, exacted an oath from them that petty-bourgeois Sun Yat-senism takes precedence over Marxism.

The rank and file were picked and harnessed by this summit, serving it, like Moscow, as a "left" support, just as the generals, compradors, and imperialists served it as a right support. To consider the Kuomintang not as a *bourgeois party, but as a neutral arena of struggle for the masses*, to play with words about nine-tenths of the left rank and file in order to mask the question as to who is the real master, meant to add to the strength and power of the summit, to assist the latter to convert ever broader masses into "cattle," and, under conditions most favorable to it, to prepare the Shanghai coup.

Basing themselves on the reactionary idea of the two-class party, Stalin and Bukharin imagined that the communists, together with the "lefts," would secure a majority in the Kuomintang and thereby power in the country, for, in China, power is in the hands of the Kuomintang. In other words, they imagined that *by means of ordinary elections at Kuomintang congresses power would pass from the hands of the bourgeoisie to the proletariat*. Can one conceive of a more touching and idealistic idolization of "party democracy" . . . in a bourgeois party? For indeed, the army, the bureaucracy, the press, the capital, are all in the hands of the bourgeoisie. Precisely because of this and this alone it stands at the helm of the ruling party.

The bourgeois "summit" tolerates or tolerated "nine-tenths" of the lefts (and lefts of *this sort*), only insofar as they did not venture against the army, the bureaucracy, the press, and against capital. By these powerful means the bourgeois summit kept in subjection not only the so-called nine-tenths of the "left" party members, but also the masses as a whole. In this the theory of the bloc of classes, the theory that the Kuomintang is a workers' and peasants' party, provides the best possible assistance for the bourgeoisie. When the bourgeoisie later comes into hostile conflict with the masses and shoots them down, in this clash between the two real forces, the bourgeoisie and the proletariat, not even the bleating of the celebrated nine-tenths is heard. The pitiful democratic fiction evaporates without a trace in face of the bloody reality of the class struggle.

Such is the genuine and only possible political mechanism of the "two-class workers' and peasants' parties for the Orient." There is no other and there will be none.

*   *   *

Although the idea of the two-class parties is motivated on national oppression, which allegedly abrogates Marx's class doctrine, we have already heard about "workers' and peasants'" mongrels in Japan, where there is no national oppression at all. But that isn't all, the matter is not limited merely to the Orient. The "two-class" idea seeks to attain universality. In this domain, the most grotesque features were assumed by the above-mentioned Communist Party of America in its effort to support the presidential candidacy of the bourgeois, "antitrust" Senator La Follette, so as to yoke the American farmers by this means to the chariot of the social revolution. Pepper, the theoretician of this maneuver, one of those who ruined the Hungarian revolution because he overlooked the Hungarian peasantry, made a great effort (by way of compensation, no doubt) to ruin the Communist Party of America by dissolving it among the farmers.[87] Pepper's theory was that the superprofit of American capitalism converts the American proletariat into a world labor aristocracy, while the agrarian crisis ruins the farmers and drives them onto the path of social revolution. According to Pepper's conception, a party of a few thousand members, consisting chiefly of immigrants, had to fuse with the farmers through the medium of a bourgeois party and by thus founding a "two-class" party, insure the socialist revolution in the face of the passivity or neutrality of the proletariat corrupted by superprofits.

This insane idea found supporters and half-supporters among the upper leadership of the Comintern. For several weeks the issue swayed in the balance until finally a concession was made to the ABCs of Marxism (the comment behind the scenes was: Trotskyist prejudices). It was necessary to lasso the American Communist Party in order to tear it away from the La Follette party which died even before its founder.

Everything invented by modern revisionism for the Orient is carried over later to the West. If Pepper on one side of the Atlantic Ocean tried to spur history by means of a two-class party then the latest dispatches in the press inform us that the Kuomintang experience finds its imitators in Italy where, apparently, an attempt is being made to foist on our party the monstrous slogan of a "republican assembly on the basis [?!] of workers' and peasants' committees." In this slogan the spirit of Chiang Kai-shek embraces the spirit of Hilferding [38] Will we really come to that?

*   *   *

In conclusion there remains for us only to recall that the idea of a workers' and peasants' party sweeps from the history of Bolshevism the entire struggle against the Populists (Narodniks), without which there would have been no Bolshevik party. What was the significance of this historical struggle? In 1909, Lenin wrote the following about the Social Revolutionaries:

> The main *idea* in their programme was not that an "alliance of the forces" of the proletariat and the peasantry was necessary, but that there was *no class gulf* between them, that no class distinction should be drawn between them, and that the Social-Democratic idea concerning the petty-bourgeois character of the peasantry, as distinct from the proletariat, is utterly false. ["How the Socialist-Revolutionaries Sum Up the Revolution and How the Revolution Has Summed Them Up," January 7, 1909, *Collected Works,* vol. 15, p. 331. Emphasis in original.]

In other words, the two-class workers' and peasants' party is the central idea of the Russian Narodniks. Only in the struggle against this idea could the party of the proletarian vanguard in peasant Russia develop.

Lenin persistently and untiringly repeated in the epoch of the 1905 revolution that it was necessary

> to be wary of the peasantry, to organise separately from it, to be ready to combat it, *insofar as* this peasantry acts in a reactionary or anti-proletarian manner. ["The Proletariat and the Peasantry," March 23, 1905, *Collected Works,* vol. 8, p. 234.]

In 1906 Lenin wrote:

> The third and last advice is: proletarians and semi-proletarians of town and country, organise separately. Don't trust any petty proprietors—not even small, or "working", proprietors. . . . We stand by the peasant movement to the end; but we have to remember that it is the movement of another class, *not the one* which can and will bring about the socialist revolution. ["Revision of the Agrarian Programme of the Workers' Party," March 1906, *Collected Works,* vol. 10, p. 191.]

This idea reappears in hundreds of Lenin's major and minor works. In 1908, he explained:

> "The alliance of the proletariat and the peasantry", let us note in passing, should not in any circumstances be understood as meaning the *fusion of various classes, or of the parties* of the proletariat and the peasantry. Not only fusion, but *any prolonged agreement* would be destructive for the socialist party of the working class, and would *enfeeble* the revolutionary-democratic struggle. ["The Assessment of the Russian Revolution," April 1908, *Collected Works,* vol. 15, p. 57. First two emphases added.]

Could one condemn the very idea of a workers' and peasants' party more harshly, more ruthlessly, and more devastatingly? Stalin, on the other hand, teaches that

> The revolutionary anti-imperialist bloc . . . must, though not always necessarily [!], assume the form of a single workers' and peasants' party, bound formally [?] by a single platform. [*Problems of Leninism,* p. 265.]

Lenin taught us that an alliance between workers and peasants must in no case and never lead to merger of the parties. But Stalin makes only one concession to Lenin: although, according to Stalin, the bloc of classes must assume "the form of a single party," a workers' and peasants' party like the Kuomintang—*is not always obligatory.* We should thank him for at least this concession.

Lenin put this question in the same irreconcilable spirit during the epoch of the October revolution. In generalizing the experience of the three Russian revolutions, Lenin, beginning with 1918, did not miss a single opportunity to repeat that there are two decisive forces in a society where capitalist relations predominate—the bourgeoisie and the proletariat.

> Owing to their economic status in bourgeois society the peasants must follow either the workers or the bourgeoisie. *There is no middle way.* ["Deception of the People with Slogans of Freedom and Equality," speech to the First All-Russian Congress on Adult Education, May 19, 1919, *Collected Works,* vol. 29, p. 370. Emphasis in original.]

Yet a "workers' and peasants' party" is precisely an attempt to create a middle way.

Had the vanguard of the Russian proletariat failed to oppose itself to the peasantry, had it failed to wage a ruthless struggle against the all-devouring petty-bourgeois amorphousness of the latter, it would inevitably have dissolved itself among the petty-bourgeois elements through the medium of the Social Revolutionary Party or some other "two-class party" which, in turn, would inevitably have subjected the vanguard to bourgeois leadership. In order to arrive at a revolutionary alliance with the peasantry— this does not come gratuitously—it is first of all necessary to separate the proletarian vanguard, and thereby the working class as a whole, from the petty-bourgeois masses. This can be achieved only by training the proletarian party in the spirit of unshakable class irreconcilability.

The younger the proletariat, the fresher and more direct its "blood ties" with the peasantry, the greater the proportion of the peasantry to the population as a whole, the greater becomes the importance of the struggle against any form of "two-class" political alchemy. In the West the idea of a workers' and peasants' party is simply ridiculous. In the East it is fatal. In China, India, and Japan this idea is mortally hostile not only to the hegemony of the proletariat in the revolution but also to the most elementary independence of the proletarian vanguard. The workers' and peasants' party can only serve as a base, a screen, and a springboard for the bourgeoisie.

It is fatal that in this question, fundamental for the entire East, modern revisionism only repeats the errors of old Social Democratic opportunism of prerevolutionary days. Most of the leaders of European Social Democracy considered the struggle of our party against SRs to be mistaken and insistently advocated the fusion of the two parties, holding that for the Russian "East" a two-class workers' and peasants' party was exactly in order. Had we heeded their counsel, we should never have achieved either the alliance of the workers and the peasants or the dictatorship of the proletariat. The "two-class" workers' and peasants' party of the SRs became, and could not help becoming in our country, the agency of the imperialist bourgeoisie, i.e., it tried unsuccessfully to fulfill the same historic role that was successfully played in China by the Kuomintang in a different and "peculiar" Chinese way, thanks to the revisionists of Bolshevism. Without a relentless condemnation of the very idea of workers' and peasants' parties for the East, there is not and there cannot be a program of the Comintern.

8. The Advantages Secured from the Peasants' International Must Be Probed

One of the principal, if not *the* principal, accusations hurled against the Opposition was its "underestimation" of the peasantry. On this point, too, life has made its tests and rendered its verdict along national and international lines. In every case the official leaders proved guilty of *underestimating the role and significance of the proletariat in relation to the peasantry*. In this the greatest shifts and errors took place, in the economic and political fields and internationally. At the root of the internal errors since 1923 lies an underestimation of the significance, for the whole of national economy and for the alliance with the peasantry, of state industry under the management of the proletariat. In China, the revolution was doomed by the inability to understand the leading and decisive role of the proletariat in the agrarian revolution.

From the same standpoint, it is necessary to examine and evaluate the entire work of the Krestintern,[89] which from the beginning was merely an experiment—an experiment, moreover, that called for the utmost care and rigid adherence to principles. It is not difficult to understand the reason for this.

The peasantry, by virtue of its entire history and the conditions of its existence, is the least international of all classes. What are commonly called national traits have their chief source precisely in the peasantry. From among the peasantry, it is only the semiproletarian masses of the peasant poor who can be guided along the road of internationalism, and only the proletariat can guide them. Any attempt at a shortcut is merely playing with the classes, which always means playing to the detriment of the proletariat. The peasantry can be attracted to internationalist politics only if it is torn away from the influence of the bourgeoisie by the proletariat and if it recognizes in the proletariat not only its ally, but its leader. Conversely, attempts to organize the peasants of the various countries into an independent international organization, over the head of the proletariat and without regard to the national Communist parties, are doomed in advance to failure. In the final analysis such attempts can only harm the struggle of the proletariat in each country for hegemony over the agricultural laborers and poor peasants.

In all bourgeois revolutions as well as counterrevolutions, beginning with the peasant wars of the sixteenth century and even before that time, the various strata of the peasantry played an enormous and at times even decisive role. But it never played an *independent* role. Directly or indirectly, the peasantry always supported one political force against another. By itself it never constituted an independent force capable of solving national political tasks. In the epoch of finance capital the process of the polarization of capitalist society has enormously accelerated in comparison to earlier phases of capitalist development. This means that the specific gravity of the peasantry has diminished and not increased. In any case, the peasant is less capable in the imperialist epoch of *independent* political action on a national, let alone international scale, than he was in the epoch of industrial capitalism. The farmers of the United States today are incomparably less able to play an independent political role than they were forty or fifty years ago when, as the experience of the populist movement shows, they could not and did not organize an independent national political party.

The temporary but sharp blow to agriculture in Europe resulting from the economic decline caused by the war gave rise to illusions concerning the possible role of the "peasant," i.e., of bourgeois pseudopeasant parties demagogically counterposing themselves to the bourgeois parties. If in the period of stormy peasant unrest during the postwar years one could still risk the experiment of organizing a Peasants' International, in order to test the new relations between the proletariat and the peasantry and between the peasantry and the bourgeoisie, then it is high time now to draw the theoretical and political balance of the five years' experience with the Peasants' International, to lay bare its vicious shortcomings and make an effort to indicate its positive aspects.

One conclusion, at any rate, is indisputable. The experience of the "peasant" parties of Bulgaria, Poland, Romania, and Yugoslavia (i.e., of all the backward countries); the old experience of our Social Revolutionaries, and the fresh experience (the blood is still warm) of the Kuomintang; the episodic experiments in advanced capitalist countries, particularly the La Follette-Pepper experiment in the United States—have all shown beyond question that in the epoch of capitalist decline there is even less reason than in the epoch of rising capitalism to look for *independent,* revolutionary, antibourgeois peasant parties.

> The town cannot be equal to the country. The country cannot be equal to the town under the historical conditions of this epoch. The town inevitably *leads* the country. The country inevitably *follows the town.* The only question is *which class,* of the "urban" classes, will succeed in leading the country, will cope with this task, and what forms will *leadership by the town* assume? ["The Constituent Assembly Elections and the Dictatorship of the Proletariat," December 16, 1919, *Collected Works,* vol. 30, p. 257.]

In the revolutions of the East the peasantry will still play a decisive role, but once again, this role will be neither leading nor independent. The poor peasants of Hupeh, Kwangtung, or Bengal can play a role not only on a national but on an international scale, but only if they support the workers of Shanghai, Canton, Hankow, and Calcutta. This is the only way out for the revolutionary peasant on an *international* road. It is hopeless to attempt to forge a direct link between the peasant of Hupeh and the peasant of Galicia or Dobruja, the Egyptian fellah and the American farmer.

It is in the nature of politics that anything which does not serve a direct aim inevitably becomes the instrument of other aims, frequently the opposite of the one sought. Have we not had examples of a bourgeois party, relying on the peasantry or seeking to rely upon it, deeming it necessary to seek insurance for itself in the Peasants' International, for a longer or shorter period, if it could not do so in the Comintern, in order to secure protection from the blows of the Communist Party in its own country? Like Purcell, in the trade-union field, protected himself through the Anglo-Russian Committee? If La Follette did not try to register in the Peasants' International, that was only because the American Communist Party was so extremely weak. He did not have to. Pepper, uninvited and unsolicited, embraced La Follette without that. But Radic, the banker-leader of the Croatian rich peasants, found it necessary to leave his visiting card with the Peasants' International on his way to the cabinet. The Kuomintang went infinitely further and secured a place for itself not only in the Peasants' International and the League Against Imperialism, but even knocked at the doors of the Comintern and was welcomed there with the blessing of the Politburo of the AUCP, marred by only one dissenting vote.[90]

It is highly characteristic of the leading political currents of recent years that at a time when tendencies in favor of liquidating the Profintern[91] were very strong (its very name was deleted from the statutes of the Soviet trade unions), nowhere, so far as we recall, has the question ever been raised in the official press as to the precise conquests of the Krestintern.

The Sixth Congress must seriously review the work of the Peasants' "International" from the standpoint of proletarian internationalism. It is high time to draw a Marxist balance to this long drawn-out experiment. In one form or another the balance must be included in the program of the Comintern. The present draft does not breathe a single syllable either about the "millions" in the Peasants' International, or for that matter, about its very existence.

Conclusion

We have presented a criticism of certain fundamental theses in the draft program; extreme pressure of time prevented us from dealing with all of them. There were only two weeks at our disposal for this work. We were therefore compelled to limit ourselves to the most pressing questions, those most closely bound up with the revolutionary and internal party struggles during the recent period.

Thanks to our previous experience with so-called discussions, we are aware beforehand that phrases torn out of their context and slips of the pen can be turned into a seething source of new theories annihilating "Trotskyism." An entire period has been filled with triumphant crowing of this type. But we view with utmost calm the prospect of the cheap theoretical scorpions that this time, too, may descend upon us.

Incidentally, it is quite likely that the authors of the draft program, instead of putting into circulation new critical and expository articles, will prefer to resort to further elaboration of the old Article 58.[92] Needless to say, this kind of argument is even less valid for us.

The Sixth World Congress is faced with the task of adopting a program. We have sought to prove throughout this entire work that there is not the slightest possibility of taking the draft elaborated by Bukharin and Stalin as the basis of the program.

The present moment is the turning point in the life of the AUCP and the entire Comintern. This is evidenced by all the recent decisions and measures of the CEC of our party and the February plenum of the ECCI. These measures are entirely inadequate, the resolutions are contradictory, and certain among them, like the February resolution of the ECCI on the Chinese revolution, are false to the core. Nevertheless throughout all these resolutions there is a tendency to take a turn to the left. We have no ground whatever for overestimating it, all the more so since it proceeds hand in hand with a campaign of extermination against the revolutionary wing, while the right wing is being protected. Notwithstanding all this, we do not for a moment entertain the notion of ignoring this leftward tendency, forced by the impasse created by the old course. Every genuine revolutionist at his post will do everything in his power to facilitate the development of these symptoms of a left zigzag into a revolutionary Leninist course, with the least difficulties and convulsions in the party. But we are still far removed from this today. At present the Comintern is perhaps passing through its most acute period of development, a period in which the old course is far from having been liquidated, while the new course brings in eruptions of alien elements. The draft program reflects in whole and in part this transitional condition. Yet, such periods, by their very nature, are least favorable for the elaboration of documents that must determine the activity of our international party for a number of years ahead. Difficult as it may be, we must bide our time—after so much time has been lost already. We must permit the muddled waters to settle. The confusion must pass, the contradictions must be eliminated, and the new course take definite shape.

The congress has not convened for four years. For nine years the Comintern has existed without a definitive program. The only way out at the present moment is this: that the Seventh World Congress be convened a year from today, putting an end once and for all to the attempts at usurping the supreme powers of the Comintern as a whole, a normal regime be reestablished, such a regime as would allow of a genuine discussion of the draft program and permit us to oppose to the eclectic draft, another, a Marxist-Leninist draft. There must be no forbidden questions for the Comintern, for the meetings and conferences of its sections, and for its press. During this year the entire soil must be deeply plowed by the plow of Marxism. Only as a result of such labor can the international party of the proletariat secure a program, a beacon that will illuminate with its penetrating rays, and throw reliable beams far into the future.

From *The Third International After Lenin* (New York: Pathfinder Press, 1970). Translated by John G. Wright.

DEMOCRATIC SLOGANS IN CHINA[93]

October 1928

The history of this work ("The Chinese Question After the Sixth Congress") is the following: When I wrote the criticism of the draft program, I wanted to include the call for a constituent assembly as one to be raised in China in the present period. Then I decided that it was better in a programmatic document for me to confine myself for the time being to a general description of the counterrevolutionary and nonrevolutionary epoch that has come about in China, i.e., the epoch of a certain political and economic stabilization of the bourgeoisie (a "year of '49" as Lenin put it[94]). I thought that the only dispute over principles that could arise would be over whether the "year of '49" has begun or not. If it has, the call for soviets as a practical slogan falls by the wayside as a matter of course. This is precisely why, in addition to demonstrating the reactionary nature of the call for a "democratic dictatorship," I also argued that a revolutionary situation did not exist in China and that there was a need for a policy that coincided with the inevitable intensification of the tendencies toward stabilization.

I admit that I was still apprehensive that if in passing I raised the call for a constituent assembly—especially important, in my opinion, for showing the character of the political change that had occurred—then Bukharin and Manuilsky would hasten to forbid a constituent assembly. So I decided to wait. But the discussion at the congress on the question of China showed that there could be no waiting. The fundamental features of my work had been written when I received the resolution of the ECCI, declaring the call for a national assembly to be opportunistic. At that point I very much regretted that I had not included the call for a constituent assembly in my programmatic work. In the meantime I wrote a number of comrades very briefly about the need to advance in China the democratic demand for popular representation. It could be that excessive brevity gave rise to a misunderstanding. I have already received several telegrams raising objections to this demand. Some comrades inform me by telegram that they have sent detailed letters on this question. I am forwarding my work without waiting for these letters, which, very likely, will have to be answered individually. I must say, some of the objections in the telegrams did seem quite incredible to me. For example, two comrades say that the call for a constituent assembly is "not a class demand," and that, therefore, they reject it. Such an understanding of the class character of demands has an anarcho-syndicalist and not a Marxist character. To the extent that Chinese politics have switched from a revolutionary track to the track of bourgeois stabilization, with the question of a national assembly already having become the central question (tomorrow this will be conclusively revealed), to that extent the class interests of the proletariat, correctly understood, require that "democratic slogans be carried out to the fullest extent." Don't forget that in 1912 the Bolsheviks in the legal press called themselves "consistent democrats." This pseudonym to pass the censors expressed all the same a very important political tendency of the party's work at that time. Several telegrams advance the call for soviets instead of the call for a constituent assembly. This is not in the least a serious alternative. If it were, it would serve us well to reexamine either the entire question of the role of soviets or the question of the character of the period China is passing through. Otherwise we are only confusing the Chinese party and ourselves. But as I already said, I will have to speak about this a little more after receiving the letters, if the present work does not dispel some of the misunderstandings provoked, in part, by the brevity of my letter.

I believe that it is necessary to devote separate documents, like the one I was trying to do on China, to the most important countries ("The French Question After the Sixth Congress," "The English Question . . . ," etc.). It would only be possible to carry out this work well by doing it collectively, for example, if Comrade Radek took responsibility for Germany, Holland, and Scandinavia, possibly England as well; Comrade Dingelstedt— India; Comrade Rakovsky—France and possibly England, etc.

Other comrades could send me their observations on different questions or countries. It is necessary right now to pose all the questions raised in the Comintern fully in the concrete, but by separate countries—and in good time. From Comrades Smilga, Palatnikov, Livshits, and our economists in general we expect concrete theses on the internal working of the "present period" domestically. Of course it goes without saying, I am naming comrades here only by way of example. But time is precious.

Warm greetings.

Yours,
L. Trotsky

Published for the first time in any language. By permission of Harvard College Library. Translated for this volume by Ivan Licho.

THE CHINESE QUESTION AFTER THE SIXTH CONGRESS

October 4, 1928

The lessons and the problems in the strategy and tactics of the Chinese revolution constitute at the present time the greatest teaching for the international proletariat. The experience gained in 1917 has been altered, disfigured, and falsified to the point of unrecognizability by the epigones led to power on the waves of defeats of the world's working class. Henceforth, one is compelled to extract the 1917 revolution from beneath mountains of impurities under which it has been buried. The revolution has verified the policy of Bolshevism by resorting to the method of the absurd. The strategy of the Communist International in China was a gigantic game of "losers take all." The young generation of revolutionists must be taught the alphabet of Bolshevism by using the Chinese antithesis contrasted to the experience gained in October.

China itself has a world importance. But what happens in this country decides not only its own fate, but the destiny of the Communist International in the full sense of the word. Not only has the Sixth Congress not drawn up the correct balance or introduced clarity, but on the contrary, it has consecrated the errors committed and has supplemented them by a new confusion which can create for the Chinese Communist Party a hopeless situation for a whole number of years. The bureaucratic thunderbolts of excommunication will manifestly fail to reduce us to silence when the fate of the international revolution is at stake. It is just those who excommunicate us who are the ones directly responsible for the defeats suffered; that is why they dread the shedding of light.

In the past five years, no party has suffered so cruelly from the opportunist leadership of the Communist International as the Chinese CP. We have had in China a perfect example (and that is just the reason why it led to a catastrophe) of the application of the Menshevik policy to a revolutionary epoch. What is more, Menshevism had a monopoly at its disposal, for it was protected against Bolshevik criticism by the authority of the Communist International and by the material apparatus of the Soviet power. This combination of circumstances is unique in its kind. As a result, one of the greatest revolutions, in terms of its possibilities, was completely confiscated by the Chinese bourgeoisie; it served to strengthen the latter, something which, from all the data in our possession, the bourgeoisie had no reason to count on.

The mistakes of opportunism have not yet been repaired. The whole course of the congress discussion, the reports of Bukharin and Kuusinen, the speeches of the Chinese communists—all these indicate that the line of conduct followed by the leadership in Chinese politics not only was false but remains false to this day. Passing over from the opportunism openly practiced in the form of collaboration (1924-27), it made an abrupt zigzag at the end of 1927 by resorting to adventures. After the Canton insurrection, it rejected putschism· and passed into the third phase, the most sterile one, seeking to combine the old opportunistic premises with a purely formal, ineffectual radicalism, which at a certain period bore the name of "ultimatism" in Russia, and "Otzovism," and which constitutes the worst variety of ultraleftism.[95]

No Chinese communist can any longer take a single step forward now without first having estimated at its right value the opportunist leadership that led to destruction in the three stages (Shanghai, Wuhan, Canton) and without having completely understood the immense break produced by these defeats in the social and political, the internal and international position of China.

The congress discussion showed what gross and perilous illusions still subsist in the conceptions of Chinese communist leaders. While defending the Canton insurrection, one of the Chinese delegates referred triumphantly to the fact that after the defeat suffered in this city, the membership of the party did not decrease but grew. Even here, thousands of miles from the theater of the revolutionary events, .it seems incredible that such monstrous information could have been presented to a world congress without immediately encountering an indignant refutation. However, thanks to observations made on another point by a speaker, we learn that while the CCP has gained (for how long?) tens of thousands of new members among the peasants, it has on the other hand lost the majority of its workers. It is this menacing process, characterizing without the possibility of error a certain phase of *decline* of the party, that the Chinese communists describe at the congress as a sign of growth and progress. While the revolution is beaten in the cities and in the most important centers of the workers' and the peasants' movement, there will always be, especially in a country as vast as China, fresh regions, fresh just because they are backward, containing not yet exhausted revolutionary forces. On the distant periphery, the beginnings of the revolutionary wave will yet swell for a long time.

Without having direct data on the situation in the Chinese Muslim regions of the Southwest, it is difficult to speak with precision of the probability of a revolutionary ferment being produced there in the approaching period. But the whole past of China renders such an eventuality possible. It is quite evident that this movement would only be a belated echo of the battles of Shanghai, Hankow, and Canton. After the decisive defeat suffered by the revolution in the cities, the party, for a certain time, can still draw tens of thousands of new members from the awakening peasantry. This fact is important as a precursory sign of the great possibilities in the future. But in the period under consideration it is only one form of the dissolution and the liquidation of the CCP, for, by losing its proletarian nucleus, it ceases to be in conformity with its historical destination.

An epoch of revolutionary decline is by its very essence pregnant with dangers for a revolutionary party. In 1852, Engels said that such a party, having let a revolutionary situation escape it, or having suffered a decisive defeat in it, inevitably disappears from the scene for a certain period of history. The counterrevolutionary epoch strikes a revolutionary party all the more cruelly if the crushing of the revolution is caused, not by an unfavorable relationship of forces, but by the patent and indisputable blunders of the leadership, as was exactly the case in China. Add to all this the brief existence of the Chinese party, the absence in it of firmly tempered cadres and solid traditions; add to it, finally, the alterations made so lightheartedly in the leadership which, there as everywhere else, was converted into the responsible manager expiating the mistakes of the Communist International. Taken together, all this creates veritably fatal conditions for the CCP—during the counterrevolutionary epoch, whose duration cannot be determined in advance.

It is only by clearly and courageously posing the fundamental questions of today and yesterday that one can avert for the CCP the fate that Engels spoke of, in other words, liquidation, from the political point of view, for a certain period.

We have examined the class dynamics of the Chinese revolution in a special chapter of the criticism to which we submitted the fundamental theses of the draft program of the Communist International. Today, we see no need of adding anything to this chapter, or, for that matter, of introducing any modifications into it. We arrived there at the conclusion that the subsequent development of the Chinese revolution can only take place in the form of the struggle of the Chinese proletariat, drawing hundreds of millions of poor peasants to the conquest of power. The solution of fundamental bourgeois and democratic problems in China ends entirely in the dictatorship of the proletariat. To oppose to it the democratic dictatorship of the proletariat and peasantry is to devote oneself to a reactionary attempt that seeks to drag the revolution back to stages already traversed by the coalition of the Kuomintang. This general political diagnosis, containing the strategical line of conduct for the coming period of the Chinese revolution, or more exactly, of the third Chinese revolution of the future, in no case annuls the question of the tactical problems of today and tomorrow.

1. The Permanent Revolution and the Canton Insurrection

In November 1927, the plenum of the Central Committee of the Chinese party decided that

> The objective circumstances existing at the present time in China are such that the duration of a directly revolutionary situation will be measured not by weeks or by months, but by long years. The Chinese revolution has a lasting character, but on the other hand, it has no stops. By its character, it constitutes what Marx called a permanent revolution.

Is this right? Intelligently understood, it is right. But it must be understood according to Marx and not according to Lominadze.

Bukharin, who showed up the latter precisely for having employed this formula, was no closer to Marx than the author of it. In capitalist society, every real revolution, above all if it takes place in a large country, and more particularly now, in the imperialist epoch, tends to transform itself into a permanent revolution, in other words, not to come to a halt at any of the stages it reaches, not to confine itself up to the complete transformation of society, up to the final abolition of class distinctions, consequently, up to the complete and final suppression of the very possibility of new revolutions. That is just what the Marxist conception of the proletarian revolution consists of, being distinguished by that from the bourgeois revolution, limited by its national scope as much as by its specific objectives.

The Chinese revolution contains within itself tendencies to become permanent insofar as it contains the possibility of the conquest of power by the proletariat. To speak of the permanent revolution without this and outside of it, is like trying to fill the cask of the Danaides.[96] Only the proletariat, after having seized the state power and having transformed it into an instrument of struggle against all the forms of oppression and exploitation, in the interior of the country as well as beyond its frontiers, gains therewith the possibility of assuring a continuous character to the revolution, in other words, of leading it to the construction of a complete socialist society. A necessary condition for this is to carry out consistently a policy that prepares the proletariat in good time for the conquest of power. Now, Lominadze has made of the possibility of a permanent development of the revolution (on the condition that the communist policy be correct) a scholastic formula guaranteeing at one blow and for all time a revolutionary situation "for many years." The permanent character of the revolution thus becomes a law placing itself above history, independent of the policy of the leadership and of the material development of revolutionary events. As always in such cases, Lominadze and Company resolved to announce their metaphysical formula relative to the permanent character only after the political leadership of Stalin, Bukharin, Ch'en Tu-hsiu, and T'an P'ing-shan had thoroughly sabotaged the revolutionary situation.

After having assured the continuity of the revolution for many years, the plenum of the Central Committee of the Chinese Communist Party, freed from any further doubts, deduces from this formula conditions favorable to the insurrection.

Not only is the strength of the revolutionary movement of the toiling masses of China not yet exhausted, but it is precisely only now that it is beginning to manifest itself in a new advance of the revolutionary struggle. All this obliges the plenum of the Central Committee of the Chinese Communist Party to recognize that a directly revolutionary situation exists today (November 1927) throughout China.

The Canton insurrection was deduced from a similar evaluation of the situation with a perfect inevitability. Had a revolutionary situation really existed, the mere fact of the defeat of Canton would have been a special episode, and in any case, would not have transformed the uprising of this city into an adventure. Even in face of unfavorable conditions for the insurrection of Canton itself or its environs, the leadership had as its duty to do all that was necessary to realize the revolt most rapidly in order thus to disperse and weaken the forces of the enemy and to facilitate the triumph of the uprising in the other parts of the country.

However, not after "many years" but after a few months, it had to be acknowledged that the political situation had declined abruptly, and that before the Canton insurrection. The campaign of Ho Lung and Yeh T'ing was already developing in an atmosphere of revolutionary decline, the workers were separating themselves from the revolution, the centrifugal tendencies were gaining in strength. This is in no way contradictory to the existence of peasant movements in various provinces. That is how it always is.

Let the Chinese communists ask themselves now: Would they have dared to decide upon fixing the Canton insurrection for December had they understood that for the given period the fundamental forces of the revolution were exhausted and that the great decline had commenced? It is clear that if they had understood at the time this radical break in the situation, they would in no case have put on the order of the day the appeal for the armed uprising in Canton. The only way of explaining the policy of the leadership, in fixing and carrying out this revolt, is that it *did not understand the meaning* and the consequences of the defeats of Shanghai and Hupeh. There can be no other interpretation of it. But the lack of understanding can all the less excuse the leadership of the Communist International since the Opposition had warned in good time against the new situation and the new dangers. It found itself accused for this by idiots and calumniators of having the spirit of liquidators.

The resolution of the Sixth Congress confirms the fact that an inadequate resistance to "putschistic moods" produced the fruitless uprisings of Hunan, of Hupeh, etc.[97] What is to be understood by "putschistic moods"? The Chinese communists, in conformity with the directions of Stalin and Bukharin, judged that the situation in China was directly revolutionary and that the partial revolts had every chance of being extended successfully to the point of becoming a general insurrection. In this way, the launching of these surprise attacks resulted from an erroneous estimation of the circumstances in which China found itself toward the second half of 1927, as a result of the defeats suffered.

In Moscow, they could prattle about the "directly revolutionary situation," accuse the Oppositionists of being liquidators, while providing for themselves beforehand against the future (especially after Canton) by making reservations on the subject of "putschism." But in the theater of events, in China itself, every honest revolutionist was duty bound to do everything he could in his corner to hasten the uprising, since the Communist International had declared that the general situation was propitious for an insurrection on a national scale. It is in this question that the regime of duplicity divulges its deliberately criminal character.

At the same time the resolution of the congress says:

> The congress deems it entirely inexact to attempt to consider the Canton insurrection as a putsch. It was a heroic rearguard [?] battle of the Chinese proletariat, fought in the course of the period which has just passed in the Chinese revolution; in spite of the crude mistakes committed by the leadership, this rising will remain the standard of the new soviet phase of the revolution.

Here confusion reaches its zenith. The heroism of the Cantonese proletariat is placed in evidence as a screen to cover up the faulty leadership, not of Canton (which the resolution casts off completely) but of Moscow, which only yesterday spoke not of a "rearguard battle" but of the overthrow of the government of the Kuomintang.

Why is the appeal to insurrection denounced as putschism *after* the experience of Canton? Because thanks to this experience, the inopportuneness of the uprising was confirmed. The leadership of the Communist International had need of a new lesson by example in order to discover what already appeared quite clear without it. But are not these practical supplementary lessons for the retarded too costly for the proletariat?

Lominadze, one of the infant prodigies of revolutionary strategy, swore at the Fifteenth Congress of the Communist Party of the Soviet Union that the Canton insurrection was necessary, right, and salutary, precisely because it inaugurated an era of the direct struggle of the workers and peasants for the conquest of power. He met with agreement. At the Sixth Congress, Lominadze recognized that the insurrection did not inaugurate an era of triumph but concluded one of defeat. Nevertheless, just as before, the uprising is considered necessary, right, and salutary. Its name has simply been changed: from a clash between the vanguard of the forces at hand, they made a "rearguard battle." Everything else remains as in the past. The attempt to escape the criticism of the Opposition by hiding behind the heroism of the Cantonese workers has as much weight as, let us say for example, the attempt of General Rennenkampf to take shelter behind the heroism of the Russian soldiers whom he drowned by his strategy in the Masurian swamps. The proletarians of Canton are guilty, without having committed mistakes, simply of an excess of confidence in the leadership. Their leadership was guilty of having had a blind confidence in the leadership of the Communist International which combined political blindness with the spirit of adventurism.

It is radically false to compare the Canton insurrection of 1927 with that of Moscow in 1905. During the whole of 1905, the Russian proletariat rose from one plane to the other, wresting concessions from the enemy, sowing disintegration in its ranks, concentrating around its vanguard ever greater popular masses. The October 1905 strike was an immense victory, having a world-historical importance. The Russian proletariat had its own party, which was not subordinated to any bourgeois or petty-bourgeois discipline. The self-esteem, the intransigence, the spirit of offensive of the party, rose from stage to stage. The Russian proletariat had created soviets in dozens of cities, not on the eve of the revolt but during the process of a strike struggle of the masses. Through these soviets, the party established contact with vast masses; it registered their revolutionary spirit; it mobilized them. The tsarist government, seeing that each day brought a change in the relationship of forces favorable to the revolution, passed over to the counteroffensive and thus prevented the revolutionary leadership from being able to gain the time needed for continuing to mobilize its forces. Under these conditions, the leadership could and should have staked everything so as to be able to test by deeds the state of mind of the last decisive factor—the army. This was the meaning of the insurrection of December 1905.

In China, the events developed in a directly opposite way. The Stalinist policy of the Chinese Communist Party consisted of a series of capitulations before the bourgeoisie, accustoming the workers to support patiently the yoke of the Kuomintang. In March 1926, the party capitulated before Chiang Kai-shek; it consolidated his position while weakening its own; it discredited the banner of Marxism; it converted itself into an auxiliary instrument of the bourgeois leadership. The party extinguished the agrarian movement and the workers' strikes by putting into practice the directions of the Executive Committee of the Communist International on the bloc of four classes. It renounced the organization of soviets so as not to disturb the situation at the rear of the Chinese generals. It thus delivered to Chiang Kai-shek the workers of Shanghai, bound hand and foot.

After the crushing of Shanghai, the party, in conformity with the directions of the Executive Committee of the Communist International, placed all its hopes in the left Kuomintang, the so-called "center of the agrarian revolution." The communists entered the Wuhan government, which repressed the strike struggle and the peasants' uprisings. They thus prepared a new and still crueler devastation of the revolutionary masses. After all this, an instruction entirely penetrated with the spirit of adventurism was issued, ordering an immediate orientation toward the insurrection. It is from this that was first born the adventure of Ho Lung and Yeh T'ing, and the even more painful one of the Canton coup.

No, all this does not resemble the insurrection of December 1905 at all.

If an opportunist calls the events of Canton an adventure, it is because it was an *insurrection*. If a Bolshevik employs the same designation for these facts, it is because it was an *inopportune insurrection*. It is not for nothing that a German proverb says that when two men say the same thing it does not mean the same thing. The officials à la Thälmann can continue, on the subject of the Chinese revolt, to recount to the German communists the "apostasy" of the Opposition. We will know how to teach the German communists to turn their backs on the Thälmanns. In actuality, the question of evaluating the Canton insurrection is the question of the teachings drawn from the Third Congress, in other words, of a lesson where the life of the German proletariat was at stake.

In March 1921, the Communist Party of Germany sought to engage in an insurrection by basing itself upon an active minority of the proletariat in the face of the passive spirit of the majority, which was tired, distrustful, expectative, as a result of all the preceding defeats. Those who directed this attempt at the time also sought to take shelter behind the heroism of which the workers gave proof in the March battles. However, the Third Congress did not congratulate them for this attempt when it condemned the spirit of adventurism of the leadership. What was our judgment in those days of the March events?

> Their gist [we wrote] comes down to this, that the young Communist Party, taking fright at the obvious revolutionary ebb of the labor movement, made a desperate bid to exploit the action of one of the dynamically inclined detachments of the proletariat for the purpose of "electrifying" the working class and of doing everything possible to bring matters to a head, to precipitate the decisive battle. [*Pravda,* December 25, 1921. In *The First Five Years of the Communist International* (New York: Monad Press, 1972), vol. 2, pp. 77-78.]

From July 1923 on, we demanded, to the great astonishment of Clara Zetkin, Warski, and other old, very venerable, but incorrigible Social Democrats, that the date of the insurrection in Germany be fixed. Then, at the beginning of 1924, when Zetkin declared that at that moment she envisaged the eventuality of an uprising with much "more optimism" than during the preceding year, we could only shrug our shoulders.

> It is the *ABC* of Marxism that the tactics of the socialist proletariat cannot be the same both when there is a revolutionary situation and when there is no revolutionary situation. [Lenin, "The Proletarian Revolution and the Renegade Kautsky," October-November 1918, *Collected Works,* vol. 28, p. 289. Emphasis in original.]

Today, everybody acknowledges this ABC verbally, but how far they still are from applying it in reality!

It is not a question of knowing what the communists must do when the masses are rebelling *of their own accord.* That is a special question. When the masses arise, the communists must be with them, organizing and instructing them. But the question is posed differently: What did the leadership do and what should it have done during the weeks and months that immediately preceded the Canton insurrection? The leadership was duty bound to explain to the revolutionary workers that as a consequence of defeats, due to an erroneous policy, the relationship of forces had veered entirely in favor of the bourgeoisie. The great masses of workers who had fought tremendous battles, dispersed by the encounters, abandoned the field of battle.

It is absurd to believe that one can march toward a peasant insurrection when the proletarian masses are departing. They must be grouped together again, fight defensive battles, avoiding a general battle, which obviously does not hold out any hope. If *in spite of* such a work of clarification and education, *contrary* to it, the masses of Canton had rebelled (which is very unlikely) the communists would have had to put themselves at their head. But it is just the reverse that happened. The uprising had been commanded in advance, deliberately and with premeditation, based upon a false appreciation of the whole atmosphere. One of the detachments of the proletariat was drawn into a struggle that obviously held out no hope, and made easier for the enemy the annihilation of the vanguard of the working class. Not to say this openly is to deceive the Chinese workers and to prepare new defeats. The Sixth Congress did not say it.

Does all this signify that the Canton insurrection *was only an adventure,* allowing of but one conclusion, that is, that the leadership was entirely incompetent? No, that is not the sense of our criticism. The Canton insurrection showed that even after enormous defeats, with the manifest decline of the revolution, even in nonindustrialized Canton, with its petty-bourgeois traditions of Sun Yat-senism, the proletariat was able to rise in revolt, to fight valiantly, and to conquer power. We have here a fact of enormous importance. It shows anew how considerable is the weight of the proletariat in its own right, how great is the political role that it can eventually play, even if the working class is relatively weak in numbers, in a historically backward country, where the majority of the population is composed of peasants and scattered petty bourgeois. This fact, once more after 1905 and 1917, completely demolishes the philistines à la Kuusinen, Martynov, and consorts, who teach us that one cannot dream of speaking of the dictatorship of the proletariat in "agrarian"

China. Yet the Martynovs and the Kuusinens are at the present time the daily inspirers of the Communist International.

The Canton insurrection showed at the same time that at the decisive moment, the proletariat was unable to find even in the petty-bourgeois capital of Sun Yat-senism a single *political ally* having a distinct form, not even among the debris of the Kuomintang, of the left or the ultraleft. This means that the vital task of establishing the alliance between the workers and the poor peasants in China devolves exclusively and directly upon the Communist Party. The accomplishment of this task is one of the conditions for the triumph of the coming third Chinese revolution. And the victory of the latter will restore the power to the vanguard of the proletariat, supported by the union of the workers and the poor peasants.

*   *   *

If "apostasy" must be spoken of, the traitors to the heroes and the victims of the Canton insurrection are those who seek to rid themselves of the teachings of this uprising in order to conceal the crimes of the leadership. The lesson to draw is the following:

1. The Canton insurrection showed that only the proletarian vanguard in China is capable of carrying out the uprising and of capturing power. The revolt showed, after the experience of collaboration between the Communist Party and the Kuomintang, the complete lack of vitality and the reactionary character of the slogan of the democratic dictatorship of the proletariat and the peasantry, opposed to the slogan of the dictatorship of the proletariat drawing the poor peasants behind it.

2. The Canton insurrection, conceived and executed contrary to the course of development of the revolution, accelerates and deepens the decline of the latter, facilitating the annihilation of the proletarian forces by the bourgeois counterrevolution. This stamps the interrevolutionary period with a painful, chronic, and lasting character. The greatest problem now is the renascence of the Communist Party as the organization of the vanguard of the proletariat.

These two conclusions are equally important. It is only by considering them simultaneously that the situation can be judged and the perspectives fixed. The Sixth Congress did neither the one nor the other. By taking as its point of departure the resolutions of the Ninth Plenum of the Executive Committee of the Communist International (February 1928) which assured us that the Chinese revolution "is continuing," the congress slipped up in its flight to the point of declaring that this revolution has now entered into a preparatory phase. But this flight will not help anything. We must speak clearly and sincerely, recognize firmly, openly, brutally the breach that has taken place, adapt the tactics to it and at the same time follow a line of conduct that leads the vanguard of the proletariat through the insurrection to its preponderant role in the soviet China of the future.

2. The Interrevolutionary Period and the Tasks That Present Themselves in the Course of It

Bolshevik policy is characterized not only by its revolutionary scope, but also by its political realism. These two aspects of Bolshevism are inseparable. The greatest task is to know how to recognize in time a revolutionary situation and to exploit it to the end. But it is no less important to understand when this situation is exhausted and is converted, from the political point of view, into its antithesis. Nothing is more fruitless and worthless than to show one's fist after the battle. That, however, is just where Bukharin's specialty lies. First, he proved that the Kuomintang and the soviets are the same thing, and that the communists can conquer power through the Kuomintang, avoiding the fray. And when this same Kuomintang, with the aid of Bukharin, crushed the workers, he begins to hold out the fist. Insofar as he did nothing but amend or "complete" Lenin, his caricatured aspect did not exceed certain modest limits. Insofar as he pretends to give leadership himself, profiting by the total lack of knowledge in international questions on the part of Stalin, Rykov, and Molotov, the little Bukharin swells up until he becomes a gigantic caricature of Bolshevism. His strategy reduces itself to finishing off and mutilating, in the epoch of decline, that which escaped alive in the abortive and besmirched revolutionary period.

It must be distinctly understood that there is not, at the present time, a revolutionary situation in China. It is rather a counterrevolutionary situation that has been substituted there, transforming itself into an interrevolutionary period of indefinite duration. Turn with contempt from those who would tell you that this is pessimism and lack of faith. To shut one's eyes to facts is the most infamous form of lack of faith.

There remains in China a revolutionary situation in all its profundity, insofar as all the internal and international contradictions of the country can find their solution only on the road of the revolution. But from this point of view, there is not a single country in the world where there does not exist a revolutionary situation which must inevitably manifest itself openly, with the exception of the USSR where, in spite of five years of opportunist backsliding, the soviet form of the proletarian dictatorship still opens up the possibility of a renascence of the October revolution by means of reformist methods.

In certain countries, the eventuality of the transformation of the potential revolution into an active revolution is closer; in others it is further off. It is all the more difficult to divine in advance what will be the rotation followed, since it is determined not only by the acuteness of the international contradictions, but also by the intersection of world factors. One may very reasonably assume that the revolution will be accomplished in Europe before taking place in North America. But the predictions which announce that the revolution will break out in Asia first and then in Europe already have a more conditional character. It is possible, even probable, but it is not at all inevitable. New difficulties and complications, like the occupation of the Ruhr in 1923, or else the accentuation of the commercial and industrial crisis, under the pressure of the United States, can in the nearest future put the European states before a directly revolutionary situation, as was the case in Germany in 1923, in England in 1926, and in Austria in 1927.[98]

The fact that only yesterday China was passing through a stirring revolutionary phase does not bring closer the revolution for today and tomorrow, but on the contrary, makes it more distant. In the course of the period that followed the revolution of 1905, it produced great revolutionary disturbances and coups d'etat in the countries of the East (Persia, Turkey, China). But in Russia itself, the revolution revived only twelve years later, in connection with the imperialist war. Naturally, these intervals are not obligatory for China. The general speed of the evolution of world contradictions has now been accelerated. That is all that can be said. But one must take into account and bear in mind that in China itself the revolution is at the present time laid over into an indefinite future. And moreover: the consequences of the defeat of the revolution have not yet been completely exhausted. With us, the wave of fall and decline went through the years 1907-

08, 1909, and partly 1910, when, thanks in large measure to the revival of industry, the working class began to come to life. A no less abrupt descent confronts the Chinese Communist Party. The latter must know how to cling to every ledge, to hold tenaciously to every point of support so as not to tumble down and be smashed.

The Chinese proletariat, beginning with its vanguard, must assimilate the enormous experiences of the defeats and, by acting with new methods, recognize the new environment; it must redress its shattered ranks; it must renew its mass organizations; it must establish with greater clarity and distinctness than before what its attitude must be toward the problems that are arising before the country: national unity and liberation, revolutionary agrarian transformation.

On the other hand, the Chinese bourgeoisie must squander the capital accumulated by its victories. The contradictions which exist within itself, as well as between it and the outside world, must once more lay themselves bare and become sharpened. A new regrouping of forces must have its repercussions in the peasantry, reviving its activity. It is precisely all this that will signify that there is a renascence of the revolutionary situation on a higher historical basis.

> . . . those who have had to live [said Lenin on February 23, 1918] through the long years of revolutionary battles in the period of the upswing of the revolution and the period when the revolution fell into decline, when revolutionary calls to the masses obtained no response from them, know that all the same the revolution always arose afresh. ["Report at the Meeting of the All-Russian CEC," *Collected Works,* vol. 27, p. 46.]

The pace that the Chinese revolution will follow in "rising anew" will depend not only upon objective conditions but also upon the policy of the Communist International.

The resolution of the congress wheels diplomatically around these essential questions, planting reservations to the right and the left that will permit it to save itself, that is, like the lawyers, it creates motives in advance that will permit it to quash the case or appeal it.

It is true that this resolution recognizes that "the slogan of mass uprising becomes a propaganda slogan and it is only to the extent . . . that a new rise of the revolution matures that it will again become immediately applicable in practice." Let us point out in passing that as late as February of this year such an attitude was called Trotskyism. No doubt it must be understood that this term signifies the ability to take into account facts and their consequences more rapidly than is done by the leadership of the Communist International.

But the resolution of the congress does not go beyond this transformation of the armed insurrection into a propaganda slogan. The reports say nothing more on this point. What is to be expected in the very next period? What must be prepared for? What line must be followed in the work to be effected? No perspective is established. To understand how much needs to be learned over again from the very bottom in this question, let us again cast a glance upon the yesterday, upon the very same resolution of the Chinese Central Committee, which furnishes the most striking manifestation of "revolutionary" light-mindedness doubled by opportunism.*

The plenum of the Central Committee of the Chinese Communist Party, directed by the infant prodigies of left centrism, decided in November 1927, on the eve of the insurrection at Canton:

> In evaluating the general political situation created in China after the counterrevolutionary coup of Hunan, the Central Committee of the Chinese Communist Party, already in its theses of August, formulated the affirmation that the stabilization of the bourgeois military reaction in China was *entirely impossible* on the basis of the present social, economic, and political relationships.

In this remarkable thesis, dealing with the *stabilization,* the same operation was carried through as was done with the *revolutionary situation.* These two conceptions have been transformed into certain substances, irremediably opposed to each other. If the revolutionary situation is assured for "many years" in the face of no matter what circumstances, it is clear

---

* It goes without saying that *Pravda* has not published this resolution to which we have already referred above. It can only be found in the "Material on the Chinese Question" (no. 10, 1928, issued by the Chinese Sun Yat-sen University), and is very hard to procure. It is this same resolution that is officially charged with "Trotskyism," although it is, in reality, nothing but Stalino-Bukharinist opportunism upside down.

that the stabilization, no matter what happens, is "absolutely impossible." The one supplements the other in a system of metaphysical principles. Bukharin and his friendly adversary, Lominadze, do not understand in such a case that the *revolutionary situation,* as well as its opposite, the *stabilization,* are not only the premises of the class struggle but also constitute its living content. Outside of this struggle, neither the one nor the other exists.

We once wrote that the stabilization is an "object" of the class struggle and not an arena established for it in advance. The proletariat wants to develop and utilize a situation of crisis, the bourgeoisie wants to put an end to it and to overcome it by its stabilization. The stabilization is the "object" of the struggle of these fundamental class forces. Bukharin first sneered at this definition; then he introduced it textually, as contraband, into his printed report to one of the plenums of the Executive Committee of the Communist International. But in acknowledging our formula, directed especially against his scholasticism, Bukharin failed absolutely to understand the meaning of our definition. As to the capricious leaps that Lominadze executes toward the left, their radius is very restricted, for the valiant infant prodigy does not dare break Bukharin's thread. Naturally, absolute stabilization is absolutely opposed to an absolute revolutionary situation. The conversion of these absolutes into each other is "absolutely impossible." But if one descends from these ridiculous theoretical summits, it turns out that before the complete and final triumph of socialism, the relatively revolutionary situation will very likely be converted more than once into relative stabilization (and vice. versa). All other conditions remaining equal, the danger of the conversion of a revolutionary situation into bourgeois stabilization is all the greater the less capable the proletarian leadership is of exploiting the situation.

The leadership of the Chiang Kai-shek clique was superior to that of Ch'en Tu-hsiu and of T'an P'ing-shan. But it is not this leadership that decided: foreign imperialism guided Chiang Kai-shek by threats, by promises, by its direct assistance. The Communist International directed Ch'en Tu-hsiu. Two leaderships of world dimensions crossed swords here. That of the Communist International, through all the stages of the struggle, appeared as absolutely worthless and it thus facilitated to the highest degree the task for the imperialist leadership. In such conditions, the transformation of the revolutionary situation into bourgeois stabilization is not only not "impossible," but is absolutely inevitable. Even more: it is accomplished, and within certain limits it is completed.

Bukharin has announced a new period of "organic" stabilization for Europe. He gave assurances that one need not expect, in the course of the coming years in Europe, any renewal of the Vienna events and in general any revolutionary conclusions. Why? One does not know. The struggle for the conquest of power is entirely thrust aside by the struggle to be conducted against the war. On the other hand, the stabilization in China is denied, just as the Fifth Congress denied it in Germany after the defeat of the revolution of 1923. Everything passes and everything changes, except the mistakes of the leadership of the Communist International.

The defeat of the workers and the peasants in China corresponds inevitably to a political consolidation of the Chinese ruling classes; and that is precisely the point of departure for the economic stabilization. A certain establishment of order in domestic circulation and in foreign commercial relations, following upon the pacification or the abatement of the civil war regions, automatically brings with it a restoration of economic activity. The vital needs of the completely devastated and exhausted country must make a path for themselves to some degree or other. Commerce and industry must begin to reestablish themselves. The number of employed workers must increase.

It would be blindness to close one's eyes to the existence of certain political premises for the subsequent development of the productive forces of the country which, of course, take on the forms of capitalist servitude. The political premises alone do not suffice. There is still needed an economic impulsion without which the disorganization could be overcome only with relative slowness. This external shock may be furnished by the influx of foreign capital. America has already cut across the field, outstripping Japan and Europe, by consenting, for the sake of form, to conclude an "equal treaty." The domestic depression, in the face of the available resources, makes more than likely an extensive economic intervention in China by the United States, before which the Kuomintang will evidently hold the door wide "open." One cannot doubt the fact that the European countries, especially Germany, fighting against the rapidly aggravated crisis, will seek to debouch upon the Chinese market.

Given the vast area of China and the multitudinous population, even feeble success in the field of road construction, even a simple growth in transportation security, accompanied by a certain regulation of the exchange, must automatically produce a considerable increase of commercial circulation and by the same sign an enlivening of industry. At the present time, the most important capitalist countries, among them and far from occupying last place, the United States, preoccupied with an outlet for their automobiles, are interested in the establishment of all kinds of roads.

In order to stabilize the Chinese exchange and to mark out the roads, a large loan from abroad is required. The possibility of concluding it is discussed and recognized as quite real in the influential Anglo-Saxon financial press. They speak of an international banking consortium to amortize the old debts of China and to grant it new credits. The well-informed press is already calling the future affair "the most important in world history."

It is impossible to predict to what extent these grandiose projects will be put into effect without being better acquainted with all the documents, which relate in part to operations that take place behind the scenes. But there can be no doubt about the fact that for the near future the course of events will follow this direction. Right now, the press is bringing out dozens of news items indicating that the extremely relative pacification of China and its still more relative unification have already given an impetus in the most diversified fields of economic life. A good harvest in almost the whole of China is acting in the same sense. The diagrams of domestic circulation, of imports and exports, show patent signs of progress.

Manifestly, one should not repeat the mistake committed yesterday, only the other way around. One should not attribute to semicolonial capitalist stabilization I do not know what rigid, unchangeable—in a word, metaphysical—traits. It will be a very lame stabilization, exposed to all the winds of world politics as well as to the still uneliminated internal dangers. Nevertheless, this very relative bourgeois stabilization is radically distinguished from a revolutionary situation. To be sure, the fundamental material relations of the classes have remained the same. But the political relationships of their forces for the period in view have been rudely altered. This is expressed also by the fact that the Communist Party has been almost completely driven back to its starting point. It will have to regain its political influence by proceeding almost from the beginning.

What has been gained is experience. But this gain also will be positive instead of negative on the single condition that the experience is judiciously assimilated. In the meanwhile, the bourgeoisie is acting with greater assurance, with greater cohesion. It has gone over to the offensive. It is setting itself great tasks for the morrow. The proletariat is falling back; it is far from always offering resistance to blows. The peasantry, deprived of any kind of centralized leadership, boils over here and there without having any real chances of success. Now, world capital is coming to the aid of the Chinese bourgeoisie with the clear intention of pushing down still lower to the ground, through the intermediary of the latter, the Chinese toiling masses. There is the mechanism of the process of stabilization. The day after tomorrow, when Bukharin runs his head into the facts, he will proclaim that heretofore the stabilization might have been considered as "incidental," but it is now clear that it is "organic." In other words, here too he will jump over the fence, only this time with his right foot forward.

The process of economic recovery will, in turn, correspond to the mobilization of new tens and hundreds of thousands of Chinese workers, to the tightening up of their ranks, to the increase of their specific gravity in the social life of the country and by that an increase in their revolutionary self-confidence. It is superfluous to explain that the reanimation of Chinese commerce and industry will soon give point to the problem of imperialism. However, were the Communist Party of China, influenced by the scholasticism of Bukharin and Lominadze, to turn its back to the process really taking place in the country, it would lose an economic point of support for the recovery of the workers' movement.

At the beginning, the augmentation of the specific gravity and the class self-confidence of the proletariat will make itself felt in a rebirth of the strike struggle, in the consolidation of the trade unions. It is needless to say that serious possibilities are thus opened up before the Chinese Communist Party. Nobody knows how long it will have to remain in a clandestine existence. In any case, it is necessary to reinforce and to perfect the illegal organizations in the course of the coming period. But this task cannot be accomplished outside of the life and the struggle of the masses. The illegal apparatus will have all the greater possibilities to develop itself if the legal and semilegal organizations of the working class surround it closely and the more profoundly it will penetrate into them. The Chinese Communist Party must not have doctrinary blinkers over its eyes, and it must keep its hands on the pulse of the economic life of the country. It must put itself at the head of strikes at the proper time, charge itself with the resurrection of the trade unions and the struggle for the eight-hour day. It is only under these conditions that its participation in the political life of the country can obtain a serious foundation.

*   *   *

"There cannot even be any question," said one of the Chinese delegates at the congress, "of a consolidation of the power of the Kuomintang" (*Pravda,* August 28, 1928). This is false. There most assuredly can be a "question" of a certain consolidation, even fairly considerable, of the power of the Kuomintang for a certain period of time, even for a fairly important period.

The Chinese bourgeoisie, with an ease which it never expected, has won decisive victories, for the period in view, against the workers and the peasants. The reawakening of its class consciousness that followed made itself clearly felt at the economic conference which met at the end of June in Shanghai and which represented, so to speak, the economic preparliament of the Chinese bourgeoisie. It showed that it wanted to reap the fruits of its triumph. Across this road stand the militarists and the imperialists with whose aid it vanquished the masses. The bourgeoisie wants customs autonomy, that stumbling block to economic independence, to the completest possible unification of China; the abolition of internal customs that disorganize the market; suppression of the arbitrariness of the military authorities who confiscate the rolling stock of the railroads and infringe upon private property; finally, the reduction of armaments which today constitute a too heavy burden upon the economy of the country. It is to this, also, that belongs the creation of a single monetary value and the establishment of order in administration. The bourgeoisie has formulated all its demands in its economic preparliament. From the formal point of view, the Kuomintang has taken note of it, but being entirely divided among the regional military cliques, it constitutes at the present time an obstacle to the realization of these measures.

The foreign imperialists represent an even stronger one. The bourgeoisie considers, and not without cause, that it will exploit the contradictions between the imperialists with all the greater success, and that it will obtain an all the more favorable compromise with them, should it be successful in compelling the military cliques of the Kuomintang to submit to the centralized apparatus of the bourgeois state. It is in this sense that the aspirations of the most "progressive" elements of the bourgeoisie and of the democratic petty bourgeoisie are now being directed. It is out of this that is born the idea of the national assembly to crown the victories won, a means of bridling the militarists, the authorized state representative of the Chinese bourgeoisie for doing business with foreign capital. The economic animation that is already visible cannot but give courage to the bourgeoisie, obliging it to regard with particular hostility anything that impairs the regularity of the circulation of merchandise and disorganizes the national market. The first stage of the economic stabilization will surely increase the chances of success of Chinese parliamentarism and will consequently require that the Chinese Communist Party give evidence, in this question too, of timely political initiative.

For the Chinese bourgeoisie, having vanquished the workers and peasants, it can only be a question of an archcensored assembly, perhaps by simply giving formal representation to the commercial and industrial associations on the basis of which the economic conference of Shanghai was convoked. The petty-bourgeois democracy, which will inevitably begin to stir, seeing that the revolution declines, will formulate more "democratic" slogans. In this manner, it will seek to establish contact with the higher strata of the popular masses of town and country.

The "constitutional" development of China, at least in its next stage, is intimately bound up with the internal evolution of the Kuomintang, in whose hands the state power is at present concentrated in every respect. The last plenum of the Kuomintang in August decided, so far as can be understood, to convene for January 1, 1929, the party congress that was adjourned for so long a time out of the center's fear of losing power (as we see, the peculiarity of "China" is not very peculiar). The agenda of the congress includes the problem of the Chinese constitution. It is true that certain internal or external events may cause the collapse not only of the January congress of the Kuomintang but also of the whole constitutional era of stabilization of the Chinese bourgeoisie. This eventuality always remains a possibility. But unless new factors intervene, the question of the state regime in China, the constitutional problems, will occupy the center of public attention in the next period.

What attitude will the Communist Party take? What will it set up against the Kuomintang's draft of a constitution? Can the Communist Party say that since it is preparing, as soon as a new rise takes place, to create soviets in the future, it makes no difference to it *up to then* whether there exists or does not exist in China a national assembly, that it matters little if it is censored or embraces the whole people? Such an attitude would be superficial, empty, and passive.

The Communist Party can and should formulate the slogan of the constituent assembly with full powers, elected by universal, equal, direct, and secret suffrage. In the process of agitation for this slogan, it will obviously be necessary to explain to the masses that it is doubtful if such an assembly will be convened, and even if it were, it would be powerless so long as the material power remains in the hands of the Kuomintang generals. From this flows the possibility of broaching in a new manner the slogan of the arming of the workers and the peasants. The revival of political activity, connected with that of economy, will once more shift to the foreground the agrarian problem. But for a certain period, it may find itself posed on the parliamentary field, that is, on the field of the attempts by the bourgeoisie and primarily by the petty-bourgeois democracy to "solve" it by legislative means. Obviously, the Communist Party cannot adapt itself to bourgeois legality, that is, to capitulate before bourgeois property. It can and should have its own finished and rounded-out project for the solution of the agrarian problem on the basis of the confiscation of landed property exceeding a certain area, varying in accordance with the different provinces. The communist project of the agrarian law must be in essence the formula of the future agrarian revolution. But the Communist Party can and should introduce its own formula into the struggle for the national assembly and into the assembly itself, should it ever be convened.

The slogan of the national (or constituent) assembly is thus intimately linked up with those of the eight-hour day, the confiscation of the land, and the complete national independence of China. It is precisely in these slogans that the democratic stage of the development of the Chinese revolution will express itself. In the field of international policy, the Communist Party will demand an alliance with the USSR. By judiciously combining these slogans, by advancing each of them at the proper time, the Communist Party will be able to tear itself out of its clandestine existence, make a bloc with the masses, win their confidence, and thus speed the coming of the period of the creation of soviets and of the direct struggle for power.

Well-defined historical tasks are deduced from the democratic stage of the revolution. But by itself the democratic character of these tasks does not at all determine as yet what classes, and in which combination, will solve these problems. At bottom, all the great bourgeois revolutions solved problems of the same type, but they did it through a different class mechanism. By fighting for democratic tasks in China in the interrevolutionary period, the Communist Party will reassemble its forces, will check up on itself, upon its slogans and its methods of action. If it should succeed, in this connection, in passing over a period of parliamentarism (which is possible, even probable, but far from inevitable), this will permit the proletarian vanguard to scrutinize its enemies and adversaries by examining them through the prism of parliament. In the course of the preparliamentary and parliamentary period, this vanguard will have to conduct an intransigent struggle to win influence over the peasants, to guide the peasantry directly from the political point of view. Even if the national assembly should be realized in an archdemocratic manner, the fundamental problems would nevertheless have to be solved by force. Through the parliamentary period, the Chinese Communist Party would arrive at a direct and immediate struggle for power, but by possessing a maturer historical basis, that is, surer premises for victory.

We have said that the existence of the parliamentary stage was probable, but not inevitable. A new disintegration of the country, as well as external causes, may prevent its realization; at all events, in the first case, a movement in favor of parliaments for various regions might come forward. But all this does not remove the importance of the struggle for a democratically convoked national assembly which would by itself be an entering wedge between the groupings of the possessing classes and would broaden the framework of the proletariat's spirit of activity.

We know in advance that all the "leaders" who preached the bloc of four classes, the arbitration commissions instead of strikes, who gave telegraphic orders that the agrarian movement should not be extended, who counseled that the bourgeoisie should not be terrorized, who prohibited the creation of soviets, who subordinated the Communist Party to the Kuomintang, who acclaimed Wang Ching-wei as the leader of the agrarian revolution—that all these opportunists, guilty of the defeat of the revolution, will now attempt to outbid the left wing and to charge our way of putting the question with containing "constitutional illusions" and a "Social Democratic deviation." We deem it necessary to warn the communists and the advanced Chinese workers in time against the hollow, false radicalism of yesterday's favorites of Chiang Kai-shek. One cannot rid himself of a historical process by faked quotations, by confusion, by mile-long resolutions, in general, by every sort of apparatus and literary trick, which seeks to escape facts and classes. Events will come and furnish the test. Those who have not enough of the tests of the past, have only to wait for the future. Only, let them not forget that this verification nevertheless is effected on the bones of the proletarian vanguard.

3. The Soviets and the Constituent Assembly

We hope that it is not necessary to raise here the general question of formal, that is, of bourgeois democracy. Our attitude toward it has nothing in common with the sterile anarchist negation. The slogan and the norms of democracy, from the formal point of view, are deduced in a different way for the various countries of a well-defined stage in the evolution of bourgeois society. The democratic slogans contain for a certain period not only illusions, not only deception, but also an animating historical force.

> Of course, we shall have to utilise it. And until the time comes for the struggle of the working class for full power it is incumbent on us to make use of the forms of bourgeois democracy. [Lenin, "Report at the Second All-Russian Trade Union Congress," January 20, 1919, *Collected Works,* vol. 28, p. 414.]

From the *political* point of view, the question of formal democracy is for us not only that of the attitude to be observed toward the petty-bourgeois masses, but also toward the worker masses, to the extent that the latter have not yet acquired a revolutionary class consciousness. Under the conditions of the progress of the revolution, during the offensive of the proletariat, the eruption of the lower strata of the petty bourgeoisie in political life* was manifested in China by agrarian revolts, by conflicts with the governmental troops, by strikes of all kinds, by the extermination of lower administrators. At the present moment, all the movements of this type are obviously diminishing. The triumphant soldiery of the Kuomintang dominates society. Every day of stabilization will lead more and more to collisions between this militarism and the bureaucracy on the one hand, and on the other, not only the advanced workers but also the petty-bourgeois masses who predominate in the population of the country and town, and even, within certain limits, the big bourgeoisie. Before these collisions develop to the point of becoming an open revolutionary struggle, they will pass, from all the available facts, through a "constitutional" stage.

The conflicts between the bourgeoisie and its own military cliques will inevitably draw in the upper layer of the petty-bourgeois masses, through the medium of the "Third Party"[99] or by other means. From the standpoint of economics and of culture, the latter are extraordinarily feeble. Their political strength lies in their numbers. Therefore, the slogans of formal democracy win over, or are capable of winning over, not only the petty-bourgeois masses but also the broad working masses, precisely because they reveal to them the possibility, which is essentially illusory, to oppose their will to that of the generals, the country squires, and the capitalists. The proletarian vanguard educates the masses by using this experience, and leads them forward.

The experience of Russia shows that during the progress of the revolution, the proletariat organized in soviets can, by a correct policy, directed toward the conquest of power, draw behind it the peasantry, fling it against the front of formal democracy embodied in the constituent assembly, and switch it onto the rails of soviet democracy. In any case, these results were not attained by simply opposing the soviets to the constituent assembly, but by drawing the masses toward the soviets while maintaining the slogans of formal democracy up to the very moment of the conquest of power and even after it.

It is an absolutely incontestable and fully established historical fact that, in September–November 1917, the urban working class and the soldiers and peasants of Russia were, because of a number of special conditions, exceptionally well prepared to accept the Soviet system and to disband the most democratic of bourgeois parliaments. Nevertheless, the Bolsheviks did *not* boycott the Constituent Assembly, but took part in the elections both before *and after* the proletariat conquered political power. . . .

The conclusion which follows from this is absolutely incontrovertible: it has been proved that, far from causing harm to the revolutionary proletariat, participation in a bourgeois-democratic parliament, even a few weeks before the victory of a Soviet republic and even *after* such a victory, actually helps that proletariat to *prove* to the backward masses why such parliaments deserve to be done away with; it *facilitates* their successful dissolution, and *helps* to make bourgeois parliamentarianism "politically obsolete." [Lenin, "'Left-Wing' Communism—An Infantile Disorder," April-May 1920, *Collected Works,* vol. 31, pp. 59-60.]

When we adopted direct practical measures to disperse the Constituent Assembly, I recall that Lenin insisted particularly on having sent to Petrograd one or two regiments of Latvian light infantry, composed largely of agricultural workers. "The Petrograd garrison is almost entirely peasant; may it not hesitate in face of the Constituent?" That is how Lenin formulated his preoccupations. It was not at all a question of political "traditions"; indeed, the Russian peasantry could have no serious traditions of parliamentary democracy. The essence of the question lies in the fact that the peasant mass, aroused to historical life, is not at all inclined to place confidence in advance in a leadership coming from the cities, even if it is proletarian, especially during a nonrevolutionary period; this mass seeks a simple political formula that would express *directly* its own political strength, that is, the predominance of numbers. The political expression of the domination of the majority is formal democracy.

Naturally, to affirm that the popular masses can and should never and under no conditions "leap" over the "constitutional" step, would be to manifest a ridiculous pedantry in the spirit of Stalin. In certain countries, the epoch of parliamentarism lasts long decades and even centuries. In Russia, it was only prolonged for the few years of the pseudoconstitutional regime and one day of existence of the Constituent. From the historical point of view, one can perfectly well conceive of situations where even these few years and this one day would not exist.

Also, if the revolutionary policy had been correct, if the

Communist Party had been completely independent of the Kuomintang, if the soviets had been established in 1925-27, the revolutionary development could already have led China today to the dictatorship of the proletariat by passing beyond the democratic phase. But even in that case, it is not impossible that the formula of the constituent assembly, not tried by the peasantry at the most critical moment, not tested, and consequently still containing illusions, could, at the first serious difference between the peasantry and the proletariat, on the very morrow of the victory, become the slogan of the peasants and the petty bourgeoisie of the cities against the proletariat. Important conflicts between the proletariat and the peasantry, even in face of favorable conditions for the alliance, are quite inevitable, as is witnessed by the experience of the October revolution. Our greatest advantage lay in the fact that the majority of the Constituent Assembly, which had grown in the struggle of the dominant parties for the continuation of the war and against the confiscation of the land by the peasants, had profoundly compromised itself, even in the eyes of the peasantry, already at the moment of the convocation of the Constituent Assembly.

*   *   *

How does the resolution of the congress, adopted after a reading of Bukharin's report, characterize the present period of the development of China and the tasks to be deduced from this period? Paragraph 54 of this resolution says:

> At the present time, the principal task of the party, in the period between two waves of revolutionary progress, is to fight to win the masses, that is, mass work among the workers and the peasants, the reestablishment of their organizations, the utilization of all discontent against the landed proprietors, the bourgeoisie, the generals, the foreign imperialists. . . .

There is really a classic example of double meaning in the manner of the most renowned oracles of antiquity. The present period is characterized as being "between two waves of revolutionary progress." We know this formula. The Fifth Congress applied it to Germany. A revolutionary situation does not develop uniformly, but by following waves of ebb and flow. This formula has been chosen with premeditation, so as to be able to interpret it as recognizing the existence of a revolutionary situation, in which there takes place simply a "calm" before the tempest. At all events, they will also be able to explain it by pretending to acknowledge a whole period between two revolutions. In both cases, they will be able to begin the new resolution with the words: "as we foresaw" or "as we predicted."

Every historical prognosis inevitably contains a conditional element. The shorter the period over which this prognosis extends, the greater is this element. In general, it is impossible to establish a prognosis with which the leaders of the proletariat would, in the future, no longer have need of analyzing the situation. A prognosis has not an importance of command but rather of orientation. One can and one must make reservations on the point up to which it is conditional. In certain situations, one can furnish a number of variants of the future, delimiting them with reflection. One can, finally, in a turbulent atmosphere, completely abandon prognosis for the time being and confine oneself to giving the advice: Wait and see! But all this must be done clearly, openly, honestly. However, in the course of the last five years, the prognoses of the Communist International have constituted not directives but rather traps for the leaderships of the parties of the various countries. The principal aim of these "prognoses" is: to inspire veneration toward the wisdom of the leadership, and in case of defeat, to save its "prestige," that supreme fetish of weak people. It is a method of oracular announcement and not of Marxist investigation. It presupposes the existence on the scene of action of "scapegoats." It is a demoralizing system. The ultraleftist mistake committed by the German leadership in 1925 flowed precisely from this same perfidious, double meaning manner of formulating the question on the subject of the "two waves of revolutionary progress." The resolution of the Sixth Congress can cause just as many misfortunes.[100]

We have known the wave before Shanghai, and then that of Wuhan. There have been many more partial and localized waves. They all rose in the general revolutionary progress of 1925-27. But this historical ascension is exhausted. This must be understood and said clearly. Important strategic consequences are to be deduced from it.

The resolution speaks of the necessity of utilizing "all discontent against the landed proprietors, the bourgeoisie, the generals, the foreign imperialists." This is incontestable, but it is too indefinite. Utilize it how? If we find ourselves between two waves of continuous revolutionary progress, then every manifestation of discontent, no matter how small its importance, can be considered as the famous (according to Zinoviev-Bukharin) "beginning of the second wave." Then the propaganda slogan of the armed insurrection will have to be transformed immediately into a slogan of action. From this can grow a "second wave" of putschism. The party will utilize quite differently the discontent of the masses, if it considers it by reckoning with a correct historical perspective. But the Sixth Congress does not dispose of this "bagatelle": a correct historical perspective, in any question. The Fifth Congress was a failure because of this deficiency. It is on this score that the whole Communist International can also break its neck.

After having once more condemned the putschistic tendencies for which it itself prepares the ground, the resolution of the congress continues: "On the other hand, certain comrades have fallen into an opportunist error: they put forward the slogan of the national assembly."

The resolution does not explain what the opportunism of this slogan consists of. Once burned, twice shy.

Only the Chinese delegate, Strakhov,[101] in his closing speech on the lessons of the Chinese revolution, tried to furnish an explanation. Here is what he says:

> From the experience of the Chinese revolution, we see that when the revolution in the colonies [?] draws close to the decisive moment, the question is clearly posed: either the dictatorship of the landed proprietors and the bourgeoisie, or of the proletariat and the peasantry.

Naturally, when the revolution (and certainly not only in the colonies) "draws close to the decisive moment," then every mode of action in the Kuomintang style, that is to say, all collaborationism, is a crime involving fatal consequences; one can then conceive only of a dictatorship of the possessors or a dictatorship of the workers. But as we have already seen, even in such moments, in order to triumph over parliamentarism as revolutionists, one must have nothing in common with the sterile negation of it. Strakhov, however, goes even further:

> There [in the colonies], bourgeois democracy cannot exist; only the

bourgeois dictatorship, operating openly, is possible. . . . It cannot have there . . . any constitutional path.

This is a doubly inexact extension of a correct thought. If, during "decisive moments" of the revolution, bourgeois democracy is inevitably torpedoed (and that not only in the colonies), this in no way signifies that it is impossible during interrevolutionary periods. But it is Strakhov and the whole congress who do not want to recognize that the "decisive moment," during which it was precisely the communists who occupied themselves with the worst democratic fictions within the Kuomintang, has already passed. Now, before a new "decisive moment," a long period must be passed through, during which the *old* questions will have to be approached in a *new* manner.

To assert that in the colonies there can be no constitutional or parliamentáry periods of evolution is to renounce the utilization of methods of struggle that are essential to the highest degree, and is, above all, to make hard for oneself a correct political orientation by driving the party into a blind alley.

To say that for China, as, moreover, for all the other states of the world, there is no way out toward a free, in other words, a socialist development, by following the parliamentary path, is one thing, is right. But to claim that in the evolution of China, or of the colonies, there can be no constitutional period or stage, that is another thing, that is wrong. There was a parliament in Egypt, which is at the present time dissolved. It may come to life again. There is a parliament in Ireland, in spite of the semicolonial existence of the country. The same holds true for all the states of South America, not to speak of the dominions of Great Britain. There exist semblances of "parliaments" in India. They can also develop later on: in such matters, the British bourgeoisie is pretty flexible. What reason is there for asserting that after the crushing of the revolution that has just taken place, China will not pass through a parliamentary or pseudoparliamentary phase, or that it will go through a serious political struggle to gain this stage of evolution? Such an assertion has no foundation at all.

The same Strakhov says that it is precisely the Chinese opportunists who aspire to substitute the slogan of the national assembly for that of soviets. This is possible, probable, even inevitable. It was proved by all the experience of the world labor movement, of the Russian movement in particular, that the opportunists are the first to cling to parliamentary methods, in general to everything that resembles parliamentarism, or even approaches it. The Mensheviks clung to activity in the Duma *as against* revolutionary activity. The utilization of parliamentary methods inevitably brings up all the dangers connected with parliamentarism: constitutional illusions, legalism, a penchant for compromises, etc. These dangers and maladies can only be combatted by a revolutionary course in all policies. But the fact that the opportunists put forward the slogan of the struggle for the national assembly in no way constitutes an argument in favor of a formal, negative attitude on our part toward parliamentarism. After the coup d'etat of June 3, 1907, in Russia, the majority of the leading elements of the Bolshevik party were favorable to the boycott of the mutilated and tricked Duma. This did not prevent Lenin from coming forward resolutely in favor of the utilization of even the "parliamentarism" of June 3 at the party conference which at that time still united the two factions.[102]

Lenin was the only Bolshevik who voted with the Mensheviks in favor of participation in the elections. Obviously, Lenin's "participation" had nothing in common with that of the Mensheviks, as was shown by the whole subsequent march of events; it was not opposed to the revolutionary tasks, but served them for the epoch between two revolutions. While utilizing the counterrevolutionary pseudoparliament of June 3, our party, in spite of its great experience of the soviets of 1905, continued to conduct the struggle for the constituent assembly, that is, for the most democratic form of parliamentary representation. The right to renounce parliamentarism must be won by uniting the masses around the party and by leading them to struggle openly for the conquest of power. It is naive to think that one can simply substitute for this work the mere renunciation of the revolutionary utilization of the contradictory and oppressive methods and forms of parliamentarism. This is the crudest error of the resolution of the congress, which makes here a flippant ultraleftist leap.

Just see how everything is turned topsy-turvy. According to the logic of the present leadership, and in conformity with the sense of the resolutions of the Sixth Congress of the Communist International, China is not approaching its 1917, but rather its 1905. *That is why,* the leaders conclude mentally: Down with the slogan of formal democracy! There really does not remain a single joint that the epigones have not taken care to dislocate.

How can the slogan of democracy, and especially the most radical one, the democratic representation of the people, be rejected in the condition of a nonrevolutionary period, if the revolution has not accomplished its most immediate tasks from the point of view of the unity of China and its purging of all its feudal and military-bureaucratic rubbish?

So far as I know, the Chinese party has not had a program of its own. The Bolshevik party arrived at the October revolution and accomplished it while armed with its old program, in the political part of which the slogans of democracy occupied an important place. In his time, Bukharin attempted to suppress this minimum program, just as he came forward later on against transitional demands in the program of the Communist International. But this attitude of Bukharin remained recorded in the history of the party only as an anecdote. As is known, it was the dictatorship of the proletariat that accomplished the democratic revolution in Russia. The present leadership of the Communist International absolutely does not want to understand this either. But our party led the proletariat to the dictatorship only because it defended with the greatest energy, doggedness, and devotion all the slogans and demands of democracy, including popular representation based upon universal suffrage, responsibility of the government to the representatives of the people, etc. Only such an agitation permits the party to preserve the proletariat from the influence of petty-bourgeois democracy, to undermine its influence among the peasantry, to prepare the alliance of the workers and the peasants, and to draw into its ranks the most resolute revolutionary elements. Was all this nothing but opportunism? "Sing, my sweet, don't be shy!"[103]

*   *   *

Strakhov says that we have the slogan of soviets and that only opportunists can substitute for it the slogan of the national assembly. This argument unmasks in most exemplary manner the erroneous character of the congress resolution. In the discussion, nobody confuted Strakhov. On the contrary, his position was approved; it was ratified in the principal tactical resolution. It is only now that one sees clearly how numerous are those in the present leadership who went through the experience of one, two, or even three revolutions, letting themselves be drawn in by the course of events and the leadership of Lenin, but without themselves reflecting upon the meaning of what was happening and without assimilating the greatest lessons of history. One is therefore obliged to repeat again certain elementary truths.

In my criticism of the program of the Communist International, I have showed how the epigones have monstrously disfigured and mutilated the thought of Lenin, which affirms that the soviets are organs of insurrection and organs of power. From it was drawn the conclusion that soviets can be created only on the "eve" of the insurrection. This grotesque idea found its most consummate expression in the same resolution, recently revealed by us, of the November plenum of the Chinese Central Committee held last year. It says there:

> Soviets can and should be created as organs of revolutionary power only in case we are in the midst of an important, incontestable progress of the revolutionary movement of the masses and when the *solid* victory of the uprising is *assured*.

The first condition, "important progress," is incontestable. The second condition, "guarantee of victory," and what is more of a "solid" one, is simply pedantic stupidity. In the rest of the text of the resolution this stupidity, however, is developed at length:

> The creation of soviets cannot obviously be approached when the victory is not yet absolutely guaranteed, for it might then happen that all attention is concentrated solely upon elections to the soviets and not upon the military struggle, as a consequence of which petty-bourgeois democratism might install itself, which would weaken the revolutionary dictatorship and would create a danger for the leadership of the party.

The spirit of Stalin, refracted through the prism of the infant prodigy, Lominadze, hovers over these immortal lines. However, all this is simply absurd. During the Hong Kong strike, during the Shanghai strikes, during all the subsequent violent progress of the workers and the peasants, soviets should and could have been created as organs of an open revolutionary mass struggle which, *sooner or later* and not at all at one blow, would lead to the insurrection and the conquest of power. If, in the phase under consideration, the struggle did not rise to the point of insurrection, obviously the soviets too would be reduced to nothing. They cannot become "normal" institutions of the bourgeois state. But in that case, too, that is, if the soviets are liquidated before the insurrection, the working masses make an enormous acquisition, familiarizing themselves with the soviets in practice, identifying themselves with their mechanism. During the following stage of the revolution, the more successful and more extensive creation of soviets will thus be guaranteed: although, even in the phase that follows it may be that they do not lead directly to victory, or even to the insurrection.

Let us recall this very distinctly: the slogan of soviets can and must be put forward from the first stages of the revolutionary progress of the masses. But it must be a real progress. The working masses must flock to the revolution, rally under its standard. The soviets furnish an expression, from the organizational point of view, to the centripetal force of revolutionary progress. But in this way, it holds true at the same time that during the period of revolutionary ebb tide and of the development of centrifugal tendencies in the masses, the slogan of soviets will be doctrinaire, lifeless, or what is just as bad, it will be the slogan of adventurists. The Canton experience showed it better than anything else in a striking and tragic manner.

At the present time, the slogan of soviets in China has an importance only from the point of view of perspective, and in this sense it has a propaganda value. One would not be conforming to anything at all by opposing the soviets, the slogan of the third Chinese revolution, to the national assembly, that is, to the slogan that flows from the debacle of the second Chinese revolution. Abstentionism, in an interrevolutionary period, especially after a cruel defeat, would be a suicidal policy.

One might say (for there are many sophists in the world) that the resolution of the Sixth Congress does not at all mean abstentionism: there is no national assembly, nobody is as yet convoking it or promising to convoke it, consequently there is nothing to boycott. Such reasoning, however, would be too pitiable, purely formal, infantile, Bukharinistic. If the Kuomintang were compelled to proclaim the convocation of a national assembly, would we boycott it in the given situation? No. We would pitilessly unmask the lie and duplicity of the Kuomintang's parliamentarism, the constitutional illusions of the petty bourgeoisie; we would demand the complete extension of electoral rights; at the same time we would throw ourselves into the political arena to oppose, in the struggle for the parliament, in the course of the elections and in the parliament itself, the workers and the poor peasants to the possessing class and their parties. Nobody would presume to foretell how great would be the results thus obtained for the present party, debilitated and reduced to a clandestine existence. If the policy were correct, the advantages could be very considerable. But in this case, is it not clear that the party can and must not only participate in the elections if the Kuomintang promulgates them, but also demand that they be held by mobilizing the masses around this slogan?

From the political point of view the question is already posed, every new day will confirm it. In our criticism of the program, we spoke of the probability of a certain economic stabilization in China. The newspapers have since then carried dozens of indications of the economic revival that is beginning (see the *Bulletin of the Chinese University*). Now it is no longer a supposition, but a fact, in spite of the fact that it is only in its very first phase. But it is just in the course of the first phase that the tendencies must be perceived, otherwise it will not be a revolutionary policy that is pursued, but a dragging at the tail of events.

The same holds true for the political struggle around the questions of the constitution. It is now no longer a theoretical forecast, that is, a simple possibility, but something more concrete. It is not for nothing that the Chinese delegate frequently returns to the theme of the national assembly; it is not by chance that the congress thought it necessary to adopt a special (and a particularly false) resolution on the subject of this question. It is not the Opposition that has posed this question, but rather the evolution of Chinese political life. Here too one must know how to perceive a tendency at the very outset. The more audaciously and resolutely the Communist Party comes forward with the slogan of the democratic constituent assembly, the less place it will leave all sorts of intermediary parties, the more solid will be its own success.

If the Chinese proletariat is obliged to live a few more years (even if it were only another year) under the regime of the Kuomintang, could the Chinese Communist Party abandon the struggle for the extension of legal possibilities of all sorts, for the freedom of press, of assembly, of organization, to strike, etc.? Were it to abandon this struggle, it would transform itself into a lifeless sect. But that is a struggle on the democratic plane. The soviet power signifies the monopoly of the press, of assembly, etc., in the hands of the proletariat. Perhaps the Chinese

Communist Party will put forward these slogans precisely at this time? In the situation under consideration, it would be an admixture of childishness and madness. The Communist Party is fighting at present not for power, but to maintain, to consolidate, and to develop its contact with the masses for the sake of the struggle for power in the future. The struggle to win the masses is inevitably bound up with the struggle conducted against the violence that the Kuomintang bureaucracy practices toward the mass organizations, their meetings, their press, etc. During the period that is to follow immediately, will the Communist Party fight for freedom of press or will it leave this to be done by the "Third Party"? Will the Communist Party confine itself to presenting democratic, isolated, partial demands (freedom of press, of assembly, etc.), which would amount to liberal reformism, or will it put forward the most consistent slogans of democracy? In the political sphere, this signifies popular representation based upon universal suffrage.

*   *   *

One might ask if the democratic constituent assembly is "realizable" after a defeated revolution in a semicolonial China encircled by the imperialists. This question can only be answered by conjectures. But the simple criterion of the possibility of realizing some demand, in the face of conditions existing in bourgeois society or in a given state of this society, is not decisive for us. It is very probable, for example, that the monarchical power and the House of Lords will not be swept away before the establishment of the revolutionary dictatorship of the proletariat. Nevertheless, the British Communist Party must formulate among its partial demands this one as well.

It is not by devoting oneself to empirical conjectures as to the possibility of realizing some transitional demand or not that the question relating to it is settled. It is its social and historical character that decides: Is it progressive from the point of view of the subsequent development of society? Does it correspond to the historical interests of the proletariat? Does it strengthen the consciousness of the latter? Does it bring it closer to its dictatorship? Thus, for example, the demand for the prohibition of trusts is petty bourgeois and reactionary and, as the experiences of America have shown, it is completely utopian. Under certain conditions, on the contrary, it is entirely progressive and correct to demand workers' control over the trusts, even though it is more than doubtful that this will ever be realized within the framework of the bourgeois state. The fact that this demand is not satisfied so long as the bourgeoisie rules, must push the workers to the revolutionary overthrow of the latter. Thus, the impossibility of realizing a slogan from the political point of view can be no less fruitful than the relative possibility of putting it into practice.

Will China come for a certain period to democratic parliamentarism? What will be the degree of its democratism? What strength and what duration will it have? All this is a matter of conjecture. But it would be radically wrong to base oneself on the supposition that parliamentarism is unrealizable in China in order to conclude that we cannot haul the cliques of the Kuomintang before the tribunal of the Chinese people. The idea of the representation of the entire people, as has been shown by the experience of all the bourgeois revolutions and especially those which liberated nationalities, is the most elementary, the most simple, and the one most apt to embrace really vast popular strata. The more the ruling bourgeoisie resists this demand of the "entire people," and the more the proletarian vanguard rallies around our banner, the riper the political conditions will become to win the real victory against the bourgeois state, whether it be the military state of the Kuomintang or the parliamentary.

It may be said: A real constituent assembly will not be convoked except through the soviets, that is, through the insurrection. Would it not be simpler to begin with soviets and to confine oneself to them? No, it would not be simpler. It would be just like putting the cart before the horse. It is very likely that it will not be possible to convoke the constituent assembly except through the soviets and that in this way the assembly might become superfluous even before its birth. This may happen, just as it may not happen. If the soviets, through whose medium a "real" constituent assembly might be called together, were already here, we would see if it is still necessary to proceed with its convocation. But there are no soviets at the present time. One cannot start to establish them except at the beginning of a new advance of the masses, which may take place in two or three years, in five years, or more. There are no soviet traditions at all in China. The Communist International conducted an agitation in this country against the soviets and not in favor of them. In the meantime, however, the constitutional questions are beginning to emerge from every cranny.

Can the Chinese revolution, in the course of its new stage, leap over formal democracy? It follows from what has been said above that, from the historical point of view, such a possibility is not excluded. But it is entirely inadmissible to approach the question by being guided by this eventuality which is the most distant and the least likely. It is to manifest light-mindedness in the political domain. The congress adopts its decisions for more than one month, and even, as we know, for more than a year. How then can the Chinese communists be left bound hand and foot, by designating as opportunism the form of political struggle that, from the next stage onward, may acquire the greatest importance?

*   *   *

It is incontestable that by entering the path of struggle for the constituent assembly, the Menshevik tendencies in the Chinese Communist Party may be revived and strengthened. It is no less important to fight against opportunism when the policy is directed toward parliamentarism or toward the struggle for it, than when one is confronted with a direct revolutionary offensive. But, as has already been said, it does not follow from this that the democratic slogans should be called opportunistic, but that guarantees and Bolshevik methods of struggle for these slogans must be worked out. In broad outline, these methods and guarantees are the following:

1. The party must have in mind and must explain that in comparison to its principal aim, to the conquest of power with arms in hand, the democratic slogans have only an auxiliary, a provisional, an episodic character. Their fundamental importance consists of the fact that they permit us to embark on the revolutionary road.

2. In the process of the struggle for the slogans of democracy, the party must shatter the constitutional and democratic illusions of the petty bourgeoisie and of the reformists who express their opinions, by explaining that power in the state is not obtained by the democratic forms of the vote, but by property and by the monopoly of information and armaments.

3. While making full use of the differences of views existing within the petty and the big bourgeoisie on the subject of constitutional questions; while opening up every possible road toward an openly exercised field of activity; while fighting for the legal existence of the trade unions, the workers' clubs, the labor

press; while creating, whenever and wherever possible, legal political organizations of the proletariat under the direct influence of the party; while trying as soon as possible to legalize more or less the various fields of activity of the party; the latter must above all assure the existence of its illegal, centralized, well-built apparatus, directing all the branches of the party's activity, legal as well as illegal.

4. The party must develop a systematic revolutionary work among the troops of the bourgeoisie.

5. The leadership of the party must implacably unmask all the opportunist hesitations seeking a reformist solution of the problems confronting the proletariat of China and must cut off all the elements who consciously pull toward the subordination of the party to bourgeois legalism.

It is only by taking these conditions into account that the party will preserve the necessary proportions in the various branches of its activity, will not let pass a new turn in the situation that leads toward a revolutionary advance, so that its first steps proceed along the road of the creation of soviets, of mobilizing the masses around them, and of opposing them to the bourgeois state, with all its parliamentary and democratic camouflage, should it happen to be realized.

4. Once More on the Slogan of the Democratic Dictatorship

The slogan of the constituent assembly is just as little opposed to the formula of the democratic dictatorship as it is to that of the dictatorship of the proletariat. Theoretical analysis and the history of our three revolutions indicate that.

In Russia, the formula of the democratic dictatorship of the proletariat and the peasantry was the algebraic expression, in other words, the most general, the most extensive expression of the collaboration of the proletariat and the lower strata of the peasantry in the democratic revolution. The logic of this formula was conditioned by the fact that its fundamental magnitude had not been verified in action. In particular, it was not possible to predict quite categorically if, in the conditions of the new epoch, the peasantry would be capable of becoming a more or less *independent* political power, to what extent it would be such, and what would be the reciprocal political relations of the allies in the dictatorship that would result from it.

The year 1905 did not bring the question to the point of a decisive verification. The year 1917 showed that when the peasantry bears on its back a party (the Social Revolutionaries) independent of the vanguard of the proletariat, this party proves to be in complete dependence upon the imperialist bourgeoisie. In the course of the period from 1905 to 1917, the growing imperialist transformation of the petty-bourgeois democracy as well as of the international Social Democracy, made gigantic progress. It is because of this that in 1917 the slogan of the democratic dictatorship of the proletariat and the peasantry was actually realized in the dictatorship of the proletariat, drawing with it the peasant masses. By this very token, the "transformation by growth" of the revolution, passing from the democratic phase to the socialist stage, already took place under the dictatorship of the proletariat.

In China, the slogan of the democratic dictatorship of the proletariat and the peasantry might still have had a certain political logic, much more limited and episodic than in Russia, if it had been formulated at the right time in 1925-26, in order to test out the animating forces of the revolution, so as to be replaced, also at the right time, by the dictatorship of the proletariat drawing behind it the poor peasants. All that is necessary has been said about this in "The Criticism of the Draft Program." Here, there still remains to ask: Does not the present interrevolutionary period, bound up with a new regrouping of class forces, allow one to discern possibilities of the rebirth of the slogan of the democratic dictatorship? To this we reply: No, it makes this possibility disappear completely.

The period of interrevolutionary stabilization corresponds to the development of the productive forces, to the growth of the national bourgeoisie, to the growth and the increase of the cohesion of the proletariat, to the accentuation of the differentiation in the villages, and to the continuation of the capitalist degeneration of democracy à la Wang Ching-wei or any other petty-bourgeois democrat, with their "Third Party," etc. In other words, China will pass through processes analogous in their broad outlines to those through which Russia passed under the regime of June 3. We were certain in our time that this regime would not be eternal, nor of long duration, and that it would terminate by a revolution. That is what happened (with a little bit of aid from the war). But the Russia that came out of the regime of Stolypin was no longer what it had been when it entered it.

The social changes that the interrevolutionary regime will introduce in China depend especially upon the duration of this regime. But the general tendency of these modifications is henceforth indisputable: it is the sharpening of the class contradictions and the complete elimination of the petty-bourgeois democracy as an independent political power. But this signifies precisely that in the third Chinese revolution, a "democratic" coalition of the political parties would acquire a still more reactionary and more antiproletarian content than that of the Kuomintang in 1925-27. There is therefore nothing left to do but to make a coalition of classes under the direct leadership of the proletarian vanguard. That is the road of October. It involves many difficulties, but there exists no other.

5. APPENDIX

A Remarkable Document on the Policy and the Regime of the Communist International

We referred above several times to the remarkable resolution of the plenum of the Central Committee of the Chinese Communist Party (November 1927), precisely the one that the Ninth Plenum of the Executive Committee of the Communist International charged with "Trotskyism," and about which Lominadze justified himself in such a variegated manner while Stalin very monotonously slunk off in silence. In reality, this resolution is a combination of opportunism and adventurism, reflecting with perfect precision the policy of the Executive Committee of the Communist International before and after July 1927. In condemning this resolution *after the defeat of the Canton insurrection*, the leaders of the Communist International not only did not publish it but did not even quote from it. It was too embarrassing for them to show themselves in the Chinese mirror. This resolution was published in a special issue of *Documentation* accessible to very few, printed by the Chinese Sun Yat-sen University (no. 10).

No. 14 of the same publication, which reached our hands when our work (*The Chinese Question After the Sixth Congress*) was already completed, contains a no less remarkable document, even though of a different, that is, of a critical character: it is a resolution adopted by the Kiangsu Provincial Committee of the Chinese Communist Party on May 7, 1928, in connection with the decisions of the Ninth Plenum of the Executive Committee of the Comintern.[104] Remember that Shanghai and Canton are part of the province of Kiangsu.[105]

This resolution, as has already been said, constitutes a truly remarkable document, in spite of the errors in principle and the political misunderstandings it contains. The essence of the resolution amounts to a deadly condemnation not only of the decisions of the Ninth Plenum of the Executive Committee of the Communist International, but in general, of the whole leadership of the Comintern in the questions of the Chinese revolution. Naturally, in conformity with the whole regime existing in the Comintern, the criticism directed against the Executive Committee of the CI bears a camouflaged and conventionally diplomatic character. The immediate point of the resolution is directed against the Central Committee itself as against a responsible ministry under an irresponsible monarch who, as is known, "can do no wrong." There are even polite eulogies for certain parts of the resolution of the ECCI. This whole way of approaching the question by "maneuvering" is in itself a harsh criticism of the regime of the Communist International; hypocrisy is inseparable from bureaucratism. But what the resolution says in essence about the political leadership and its methods has a much more damning character.

"After the August 7 (1927) conference," the Kiangsu Committee relates, "the Central Committee formulated a judgment on the situation which was tantamount to saying that even though the revolution had suffered a triple defeat, it is nevertheless going through a rising phase." This appreciation is entirely in conformity with the caricature that Bukharin makes of the theory of the permanent revolution, a caricature that he applied first to Russia, then to Europe, and finally to Asia. The actual events of the struggle, that is, the three defeats, are one thing and the permanent "rise" is another.

The Central Committee of the Chinese party draws the following conclusion from the resolution adopted by the Eighth Plenum of the Executive Committee of the Communist International (in May [1927]):

"Wherever this is objectively possible, we must *immediately* prepare and organize armed insurrections."

What are the political premises for this? The Kiangsu Committee declares that in August 1927 the political report of the Central Committee pointed out that the *workers* of Hunan, after the cruel *defeat, are abandoning the leadership of the party,* that we are not confronted with an objectively revolutionary situation . . . but in spite of this . . . the Central Committee says plainly that the general situation, from the economic, political, and social [precisely!—L.T.] point of view is favorable to the insurrection. Since *it is already no longer possible to launch revolts in the cities,* the armed struggle must be transferred to the villages. That is where the centers of the uprising must be, while the town must be an auxiliary force. [Ibid., p. 4.]

Let us recall that immediately after the May plenum of the Executive Committee of the Communist International, which entrusted the leadership of the agrarian revolution to the left Kuomintang, the latter began to exterminate the workers and peasants. The position of the ECCI became completely untenable. At all costs, there had to be, and that without delay, "left" actions in China to refute the "calumny" of the Opposition, that is, its irreproachable prognosis. That is why the Chinese Central Committee, which found itself between the hammer and the anvil, was obliged, in August 1927, to turn the proletarian policy topsy-turvy all over again. Even though there was no revolutionary situation and the working masses were abandoning the party, this committee declared that the economic and social situation was, in its opinion, "favorable to the insurrection." In any case, a triumphant uprising would have been very "favorable" to the prestige of the Executive Committee of the Comintern. Given the fact that the workers were abandoning the revolution, it was therefore necessary to turn one's back to the towns and endeavor to launch isolated uprisings in the villages.

Already at the May plenum (1927) of the ECCI, we pointed out that the adventurist uprisings of Ho Lung and Yeh T'ing were inevitably doomed to defeat because of insufficient political preparation and because they were bound up with no movement of the masses. That is just what happened. The resolution of the Kiangsu Committee says on this subject:

In spite of the defeat of the armies of Ho Lung and Yeh T'ing in Kwangtung, even after the November plenum the Central Committee persists in clinging to the tactic of immediate uprisings and takes as its point of departure an estimation leading to the direct ascent of the revolution.

For understandable reasons, the Kiangsu Committee passes in

silence over the fact that this appreciation was also that of the Executive Committee of the Comintern itself, which treated as "liquidators" those who correctly estimated the situation, and the fact that the Chinese Central Committee was forced, in November 1927, on pain of being immediately overthrown and expelled from the party, to present the decline of the revolution as its rise.

The Canton insurrection sprang up by basing itself upon this tip-tilted manner of approaching the question; manifestly, this uprising was not regarded as a rearguard battle (only raging madmen could have urged passing over to the insurrection and to the conquest of power through a "rearguard battle"); no, this uprising was conceived as part of a general coup d'etat. The Kiangsu resolution says on this point:

> During the Canton insurrection of December, the Central Committee decided once more to launch an immediate uprising in Hunan, Hupeh, and Kiangsu in order to defend Kwangtung, in order to extend the framework of the movement all over China (this can be verified from the information letters of the Central Committee, nos. 16 and 22). These measures flowed from a subjective estimation of the situation and did not correspond to the objective circumstances. Obviously, under such conditions defeats will be inevitable. [Ibid., p. 5.]

The Canton experience frightened the leaders not only of China but also of Moscow. A warning was issued against putschism, but in essence the political line did not change. The orientation remained the same: toward the insurrection. The Central Committee of the Chinese Communist Party transmitted this ambiguous instruction to the lower bodies; it also warned against the tactic of skirmishes, while setting down in its circulars academic definitions of adventurism.

"But being given the fact that the Central Committee based itself in its estimation of the revolutionary movement upon an uninterrupted advance," as the Kiangsu resolution says correctly and pointedly,

> no modifications were brought into this question at bottom. The forces of the enemy are far too greatly underrated and at the same time, no attention is paid to the fact that our organizations have lost contact with the masses. . . . Therefore, in spite of the fact that the Central Committee had sent its information letter no. 28 (on

putschism) everywhere, it did not at the same time correct its mistakes. [Ibid.]

Once more, it is not a question of the Central Committee of the Chinese party. The February plenum of the Executive Committee of the Communist International introduced no modifications into its policy either. While warning against the tactics of skirmishes in general (in order to assure itself against all eventualities), the resolution of this plenum pounced furiously upon the Opposition which spoke of the necessity of a resolute change in the whole orientation. In February 1928, the course continued as before to lead toward the insurrection. The Central Committee of the Chinese Communist Party only served as a mechanism to transmit this instruction. The Kiangsu Committee says:

> The Central Committee circular no. 38, of March 6 [take careful note: March 6, 1928!—L.T.] shows very clearly that the Central Committee still finds itself under the influence of illusions about a favorable situation for the general insurrection in Hunan, Hupeh, and Kiangsu, and the possibility of conquering power throughout the province of Kwangtung. The radical quarrel over the choice of Changsha or Hankow as the center of insurrection still continued between the Political Bureau of the Central Committee and the instructor of the Central Committee in Hunan and Hupeh. [Ibid.]

Such was the disastrous significance of the resolution of the February plenum, not only false in principle, but deliberately ambiguous from the practical point of view. The thought concealed behind this resolution was always the same: if, contrary to expectations, the uprising extends itself, we shall refer to that part which speaks against the liquidators; if the insurrection goes no further than partisan frays, we will point a finger at that part of the resolution which warns against putschism.

Even though the Kiangsu resolution nowhere dares to criticize the Executive Committee of the Communist International (everybody knows what this costs), nevertheless, in none of its documents has the Opposition dealt such deadly blows to the leadership of the Comintern as does the Kiangsu Committee in its arraignment, aimed formally at the Central Committee of the Chinese Communist Party. After listing chronologically the policies of adventurism month after month, the resolution turns to the general causes for the disastrous course.

How is one to explain [asks the resolution] this erroneous estimation of the situation established by the Central Committee which influenced the practical struggle and contained serious errors? It is to be explained as follows:

1. The revolutionary movement was estimated as an uninterrupted ascent [the "permanent revolution" à la Bukharin-Lominadze!—L.T.].

2. No attention was paid to the loss of contact between our party and the masses, nor to the decomposition of the mass organizations at the turning point of the revolution.

3. No account was taken of the new regrouping of class forces inside the enemy camp during this turn.

4. No consideration was given to leading the movement in the cities.

5. No attention was paid to the importance of the anti-imperialist movement in a semicolonial country.

6. During the insurrection, no account was taken of the objective conditions, nor of the necessity of applying different methods of struggle in conformity with them.

7. A peasant deviation manifested itself.

8. The Central Committee, in its estimation of the situation, was guided by a subjective point of view.

It is doubtful whether the Kiangsu Committee has read what the Opposition wrote and said on all these questions. One can even say with certainty that it did not read it. As a matter of fact, if it had, it would have feared to formulate with such precision its considerations, coinciding entirely in this part with ours. The Kiangsu Committee repeated our words without suspecting it.

The eight points enumerated above, characterizing the false line of the Central Committee (that is, of the Executive Committee of the Communist International) are equally important. If we wish to say a few words on the fifth point, it is simply because we have here a particularly striking confirmation "by facts" of the justice of our criticism in its most essential features. The Kiangsu resolution charges the policy of the Central Committee with neglecting the problems of the anti-imperialist movement in a semicolonial country. How could this happen? By the force of the dialectic of the false political line; mistakes have their dialectic like everything else in the world.

The point of departure of official opportunism was that the Chinese revolution is essentially an anti-imperialist revolution, and that the yoke of imperialism welds together all the classes or at the very least "all the living forces of the country." We objected that a successful struggle against imperialism is only possible by means of an audacious extension of the class struggle, and consequently, of the agrarian revolution. We rose up intransigently against the attempt to subordinate the class struggle to the abstract criterion of the struggle against imperialism (substitution of arbitration commissions for the strike movement, telegraphic advice not to stir up the agrarian revolution, prohibiting the formation of soviets, etc.). This was the first stage of the question. After Chiang Kai-shek's coup, and especially after the "treason" of the "friend" Wang Ching-wei, there was a turnabout of 180 degrees. Now, it turns out to be that the question of customs' independence, that is, of the economic "(and consequently, the political)" sovereignty of China is a secondary "bureaucratic" problem (Stalin).

The essence of the Chinese revolution was supposed to consist of the agrarian upheaval. The concentration of power in the hands of the bourgeoisie, the abandonment of the revolution by the workers, the schism between the party and the masses, were appraised as secondary phenomena in comparison with the peasant revolts. Instead of a genuine hegemony of the proletariat, in the anti-imperialist as well as in the agrarian struggle, that is, in the democratic revolution as a whole, there took place a wretched capitulation before the primitive peasant forces with "secondary" adventures in the cities. However, such a capitulation is the fundamental premise of putschism. The whole history of the revolutionary movement in Russia, as well as in other countries, is witness to that. The events in China of the past year have confirmed it.

In its estimation and its warnings, the Opposition took as its point of departure general theoretical considerations, basing itself upon official information, very incomplete and sometimes deliberately distorted. The Kiangsu Committee has as its point of departure facts that it observed directly at the center of the revolutionary movement; from the theoretical point of view this committee still writhes in the toils of Bukharinist scholasticism. The fact that its empirical conclusions coincide completely with our own has, in politics, the same significance as, for example, the discovery in laboratories of a new element—whose existence was predicted in advance on the basis of theoretical deductions— has in chemistry. Unfortunately, the triumph from the theoretical point of view of our Marxist analysis, in the case before us, has as its political foundation mortal defeats for the revolution.

The abrupt and essentially adventurist turn in the policy of the Executive Committee of the Communist International in the middle of 1927 could not but provoke painful shocks in the Chinese Communist Party, which was taken off guard by it. Here we pass from the political line of the Executive Committee of the Communist International to the regime of the Comintern and to the organizational methods of the leadership. Here is what the Kiangsu Committee resolution says on this point:

> After the conference of August 7 (1927), the Central Committee should have assumed the responsibility for the putschist tendencies, for it demanded rigorously of the local committees that the *new political line* be applied; if anybody was not in agreement with *the new line,* without further ceremony he was not permitted to renew his party card and even comrades who had already carried out this operation were expelled. . . . At this time, the putschist mood was making headway throughout the party; if anybody expressed doubts about the policy of uprisings, he was immediately called an opportunist and pitilessly attacked. This circumstance provoked great friction within the party organizations. [p. 6.]

All this took place with the accompaniment of pious academic warnings against the dangers of putschism "in general."

The policy of the sudden, hastily improvised armed insurrection demanded a speedy overhauling and a regrouping of the entire party. The Central Committee tolerated in the party only those who silently acknowledged the course of armed insurrection in the face of an obvious decline of the revolution. It would be well to publish the instructions furnished by the Executive Committee of the Communist International during this period. They could be reduced to one: an instruction for the organization of defeat. The Kiangsu resolution sets forth that

> The Central Committee continues not to take notice of the defeats and the depressed mood of the workers; it does not see that this situation is the result of the mistakes of its leadership. [Ibid.]

But that is not all:

> The Central Committee accuses someone or other [Just so!—L.T.] for the fact that:
> (a) the local committees have not sufficiently well checked up on the reorganization;
> (b) the worker and peasant elements are not *pushed ahead;*

(c) the local organizations are not purged of opportunist elements, etc.

All this happens abruptly, by telegraph: somehow or other, the mouth of the Opposition must be closed. But nevertheless since matters are in a bad way, the Central Committee asserts that "'the disposition of the masses would be entirely different if the signal for revolt had been given at least in one single province.' Does not this last indication bespeak a one hundred percent putschism of the Central Committee itself?" asks the Kiangsu Committee with full justice, passing over in prudent silence that the Central Committee only executed the instructions of the Executive Committee of the Communist International.

For five years the party was led and educated in an opportunist spirit. At the present moment, it is demanded of it that it be ultraradical and "that it immediately put" forward worker-leaders. How? . . . Very simply: by fixing a certain percentage of them. The Kiangsu Committee complains:

1. No account is taken of the fact that the ones who are to supplement the leading cadres should be advanced in the course of the struggle. Whereas the Central Committee confines itself to a formal establishment of a percentage fixed in advance of workers and peasants in the leading organs of the various organizations.

2. In spite of the numerous failures, they do not examine the point to which our party is already restored, but they simply say formally that it is necessary to reorganize. . . .

3. The Central Committee simply says dictatorially that the local organizations do not put forward new elements, that they do not rid themselves of opportunism; at the same time, the Central Committee makes baseless attacks upon the militant cadres and replaces them light-mindedly.

4. Without paying attention to the mistakes of its own leadership, the Central Committee nevertheless demands the most severe party discipline from the rank-and-file militants.

Does it not seem as though all these paragraphs are copied from the *Platform of the Opposition?*[106] No, they are copied from life. But since the *Platform* is also copied from life, there is a coincidence. Where then is the "peculiarity" of Chinese conditions? Bureaucratism levels down every and all peculiarities. The policy as well as the regime is determined by the Executive Committee of the Communist International, more exactly by the Central Committee of the Communist Party of the Soviet Union.

The Central Committee of the Chinese Communist Party drives both of them down into the lower organs. Here is how this takes place according to the Kiangsu resolution:

> The following declaration made by a comrade of a district committee is very characteristic: "At present it is very difficult to work; but the Central Committee shows that it has a very subjective manner of regarding the problem. It pounces down with accusations and says that the Provincial Committee is no good; the latter in its turn accuses the rank-and-file organizations and asserts that the district committee is bad. The latter also begins to accuse and asserts that it is the comrades working on the spot who are no good. And the comrades declare that the masses are not revolutionary." [p. 8.]

There you really have a striking picture. Only, there is nothing peculiarly Chinese about it.

Every resolution of the Executive Committee of the Communist International, in registering new defeats, declares that on the one hand all had been foreseen and that on the other it is the "executors" who are the cause of the defeats because they did not understand the line that had been pointed out to them from above. There remains unexplained how the perspicacious leadership was able to foresee everything save that the executors do not measure up to its instructions. The essential thing in the leadership does not consist of presenting an abstract line, of writing a letter without an address, but of selecting and educating the executors. The correctness of the leadership is tested precisely in execution. The reliability and perspicacity of the leadership are confirmed only when words and deeds harmonize. But if chronically, from one stage to the other, in the course of many years, the leadership is obliged post factum to complain at every turn that it has not been understood, that its ideas have been deformed, that the executors have ruined its plan, that is a sure sign that the fault devolves entirely upon the leadership. This "self-criticism" is all the more murderous by the fact that it is involuntary and unconscious.

According to the Sixth Congress, the leadership of the Opposition must be held responsible for every group of turncoats; but per contra the leadership of the Communist International should in no way have to answer for the Central Committee of all the national parties in the most decisive historical moments. But a leadership that is answerable for nothing is an irresponsible leadership. In that is to be found the root of all the evils.

In protecting itself against the criticism of the ranks, the Central Committee of the Chinese Communist Party bases itself on the Executive Committee of the Communist International, that is, it draws a chalk line on the floor that cannot be stepped over. Nor does the Kiangsu Committee overstep it. But within the confines of this chalk line, it tells some bitter truths to its Central Committee that automatically extend to the Executive Committee of the Communist International. We are once more forced to quote an extract from the remarkable document of Kiangsu:

> The Central Committee says that the whole past leadership was exercised in accordance with the instructions of the Communist International. As if all these hesitations and errors depended only upon the rank-and-file militants. If one adopts such a manner of regarding the question, the Central Committee will itself be unable either to repair the mistakes or to educate the comrades to study this experience. It will not be able to strengthen its ties with the lower party apparatus. The Central Committee always says that its leadership was right; it charges the rank-and-file comrades with all the mistakes, always especially underscoring the hesitations of the rank-and-file party committees.

A little further on:

> If the leadership only attacks light-mindedly the local leading comrades or organs by pointing out their errors, but without actually analyzing the source of these mistakes, this only produces friction within the party; such an attitude is disloyal ["rude and disloyal."— L.T.[107]] and can do no good to the revolution and to the party. If the leadership itself covers up its errors and throws the blame on others, such conduct will do no good to the party or to the revolution. [p. 10.]

A simple but classic characterization of bureaucratic centrism's work of decaying and devastating the consciousness.

The Kiangsu resolution shows in an entirely exemplary manner how and by what methods the Chinese revolution was led to numerous defeats, and the Chinese party to the brink of catastrophe. For the imaginary hundred thousand members who figure on paper in the Chinese Communist Party only represent a gross self-deception. They would then constitute one-sixth of the total membership of the Communist parties of all the capitalist countries. The payments that Chinese communism must make for the crime of the leadership are still far from completed.

Further decline is ahead. There will be great difficulty in rising again. Every false step will fling the party into a deeper ditch. The resolution of the Sixth Congress dooms the Chinese Communist Party to errors and false steps. With the present course of the Communist International, under its present regime, victory is impossible. The course must be changed. This is what the resolution of the Kiangsu Provincial Committee says once more.

From *Problems of the Chinese Revolution.*

CHINA AND THE
CONSTITUENT ASSEMBLY

December 1928

Certain comrades, while completely agreeing with my point of view in estimating the forces behind the Chinese revolution and in assessing the perspectives of this revolution, raise objections to the democratic slogan of the constituent assembly. Naturally, this difference of opinion does not have the same importance from the standpoint of principles as the problem of evaluating the main tendencies and forces of the revolution. Nevertheless, at a certain point this question can acquire an enormous importance, as was the case with the Bolsheviks in regard to the attitude to be taken toward the Third Duma. To my great surprise, one comrade, in criticizing the slogan for a constituent assembly, seriously claimed to see in this a maneuver that I was supposedly carrying out with the aim of "deceiving" the Chinese bourgeoisie. It was for this reason that he cited against me a quotation drawn from my "Criticism of the Draft Program of the Communist International" that began with the following words: "Classes cannot be deceived . . . ," etc.

There is an obvious misunderstanding here of the greatest importance. Everything of political significance on the slogan of the constituent assembly for China has been said in my essay, "The Chinese Question After the Sixth Congress." I will not repeat it here. If one looks in the "Criticism of the Draft Program" for the general theoretical basis given to the argumentation on this slogan, it will be found in the chapter on "The Fundamental Peculiarities Inherent in the Strategy of the Revolutionary Epoch," which says:

Without an extensive and generalized dialectical comprehension of the present epoch as an epoch of abrupt turns, a real education of the young parties, a correct strategical leadership of the class struggle, a correct combination of tactics, and, above all, a sharp and bold and decisive re-arming at each successive breaking point of the situation is impossible. [*The Third International After Lenin* (New York: Pathfinder Press, 1970), p. 86.]

One of my critics declares: "It is the slogan of the abolition of the *tuchüns* and the unification of China under the power of the soviets that remains correct." As for the call for the constituent assembly, that would be "unacceptable." I ask why? If one regards as correct the resolution of the February plenum (1928) of the Executive Committee of the Communist International in declaring that "it is correct to continue to orient toward the insurrection," then, clearly, one must also grant the correctness of the slogan of soviets. This is only logical. But I considered, and I still consider, that proclaiming an insurrectional course in February 1928 was the most criminal stupidity that can be imagined.

Well before February the counterrevolution in China overwhelmed the working class and the party. In "The Chinese Question After the Sixth Congress" I clearly established the main chronological milestones of the changes in the situation in China, basing my presentation on indisputable facts and documents. This country is at present going through not a revolution but rather a counterrevolution. In the course of such a period the slogan of soviets makes no sense *except for a limited number of cadres,* in preparing them for the third Chinese revolution, in the future.

This preparation clearly has an enormous importance. To accomplish it, the slogan of soviets must be accompanied by the slogan of the struggle of the proletariat for its dictatorship at the head of all the impoverished masses of the population, and, above all, of the poor peasants. But side by side with theoretical and propagandistic preparation of the revolutionary cadres for the future revolution there still remains the question of *mobilizing the broadest possible layers of the workers to participate actively in the political life of the period we are in.*

The country is now being administered by a military dictatorship serving the top sectors of the bourgeoisie and the foreign imperialists. This dictatorship, which was recently installed after the revolutionary struggle (which we shamefully and criminally lost), cannot yet be stable. It seeks only to become stable by establishing a "transitional regime" on the road to the creation of the Five Chambers of Sun Yat-sen.[108] This absurd and reactionary invention (which one hears praised among ourselves without much critical sense, even at a time when these ideas above all retard the revolutionary development of China), this philistine fantasy now becomes an instrument serving as "national," "constitutional" camouflage for the fascist regime, that is to say, for the military domination by a centralized party, the Kuomintang, representing the interests of capital in their most concentrated form.[109]

By the same token, questions of the political regime and of the state are on the agenda in China. These problems are inevitably of interest to large working class circles. In a situation that is not revolutionary it is impossible to give any other reply to these questions than the slogans and formulas of political democracy.

When the mass movement progresses, under the conditions of a general revolutionary crisis, the soviets, arising through this movement, serve its current needs, become a natural form of the unity of the masses, comprehensible, close to the "national" point of view, and aid the party to bring the masses to the insurrection. But what does the slogan of soviets signify now, under the present circumstances in China? Don't forget that there is no soviet tradition there. Such a tradition would have remained even in the event of a defeat, but it didn't exist. The cause of that is the reactionary leadership of Stalin-Bukharin.

The slogan of soviets, which is not sustained by a mass movement and which is not even supported by the experience of the past, is only an empty phrase: *do as they did in Russia,* that is to say, it is the slogan of the socialist revolution in its purest, most abstract, and most absolute form.

Soviets have to be created to win power by the proletariat and the poor peasants through an insurrection. But *today* it is necessary to oppose to the fascist machine of the Kuomintang the slogans of democracy, that is, those which, under the domination of the bourgeoisie, open the widest avenue for popular political activity.

The stage of democracy has a great importance in the evolution of the masses. Under definite conditions, the revolution can allow the proletariat to pass beyond this stage. But it is precisely to facilitate this future development, which is not at all easy and not at all guaranteed to be successful in advance, that it is necessary to utilize to the fullest the interrevolutionary period to exhaust the democratic resources of the bourgeoisie. This can be done by developing democratic slogans before the broad masses and by compelling the bourgeoisie to place itself in contradiction to them at each step.

The anarchists have never understood this Marxist policy. The opportunists conducting the Sixth Congress, mortally frightened by the fruits of their labor, do not understand it either. But we, thank heavens, are neither anarchists, nor opportunists covered with shame, but Bolshevik-Leninists, that is, revolutionary dialecticians who have understood the meaning of the imperialist epoch and the dynamic of its abrupt turns.

Published in English for the first time. From *Contre le Courant* (Paris), nos. 27-28, April 12, 1929. Translated from the French for this volume by Les Evans.

THE POLITICAL SITUATION IN CHINA AND THE TASKS OF THE BOLSHEVIK-LENINIST OPPOSITION[110]

June 1929

At the February [1928] plenum of the ECCI and the Sixth Congress of the Comintern a basically false evaluation of the situation in China was made. So as to cover up for the terrible defeats, it was declared that the revolutionary situation is maintained ("between two waves"), and that as before the course is toward armed uprising and soviets.

In fact, the second Chinese revolution of 1925-27 ended in a series of crushing defeats, without having completed its tasks. Now we have an interrevolutionary period, under the complete sway of bourgeois counterrevolution and with a strengthening of the position of foreign imperialism.

It is impossible to predict how long the interrevolutionary period will last, since it depends on many factors, internal and international. But the rise of a third revolution is inevitable; it is absolutely and completely grounded in the conditions of the defeat of the second revolution.

The tasks of the Chinese Communist Opposition, i.e., the Bolshevik-Leninists, are to understand the causes of the defeats clearly, to evaluate correctly the present situation, to regroup the staunchest, bravest, and most tested elements of the proletarian vanguard, to seek again the paths to the masses on the basis of transitional demands, and in all fields of social life to prepare the working class for the third Chinese revolution.

The second Chinese revolution was defeated in three stages in the course of 1927: in Shanghai, Wuhan, and Canton. All three defeats were the direct and immediate consequence of the basically false policy of the Communist International and the Central Committee of the Chinese Communist Party.

The completely opportunist line of the Comintern found its expression in the four questions which determined the fate of the Chinese revolution:

1. *The question of the party.* The Chinese Communist Party entered a bourgeois party, the Kuomintang, while the bourgeois character of this party was disguised by a charlatan philosophy about a "workers' and peasants' party" and even about a party of "four classes" (Stalin-Martynov). The proletariat was thus deprived of its own party at a most critical period. Worse yet: the pseudo-Communist Party was converted into an additional tool of the bourgeoisie in deceiving the workers. There is nothing to equal this crime in the whole history of the world revolutionary movement. The responsibility falls entirely on the ECCI and Stalin, its inspirers.

Since even now in India, Korea, and other countries "workers' and peasants'" parties, i.e., new Kuomintangs, are still being instituted, the Chinese Communist Opposition considers it necessary, on the basis of the experience of the second Chinese revolution, to declare:

Never and under no circumstances may the party of the proletariat enter into a party of another class or merge with it organizationally. An absolutely independent party of the proletariat is a first and decisive condition for communist politics.

2. *The question of imperialism.* The false course of the Comintern was based on the statement that the yoke of international imperialism is compelling all "progressive" classes to go together. In other words, according to the Comintern's Stalinist theory, the yoke of imperialism would somehow change the laws of the class struggle. In fact, the economic, political, and military penetration of imperialism into China's life brought the internal class struggle to extreme sharpness.

While at the bottom, in the agrarian bases of the Chinese economy, the bourgeoisie is organically and unbreakably linked with feudal forms of exploitation, at the top it is just as organically and unbreakably linked with world finance capital. The Chinese bourgeoisie cannot on its own break free either from agrarian feudalism or from foreign imperialism.

Its conflicts with the most reactionary feudal militarists and its collisions with the international imperialists always take second place at the decisive moment to its irreconcilable antagonism to the poor workers and peasants.

Having always behind it the help of the world imperialists against the Chinese workers and peasants, the so-called national bourgeoisie raises the class struggle to civil war more rapidly and more mercilessly than any other bourgeoisie in the world, and drowns the workers and peasants in blood.

It is a gigantic and historical crime that the leadership of the Comintern helped the Chinese national bourgeoisie to mount the backs of the workers and peasants, while shielding it from the criticism and protests of revolutionary Bolsheviks. Never in the history of all revolutions has the bourgeoisie had such a cover-up and such a disguise as the Stalinist leadership created for the Chinese bourgeoisie.

The Opposition reminds the Chinese workers and the workers of the whole world that as little as a few days before the Shanghai coup of Chiang Kai-shek, Stalin not only suddenly called for trust and support for Chiang Kai-shek, but also subjected to fierce repressions the Bolshevik-Leninists ("Trotsky-ists") who had given warning in time of the defeat in store for the revolution.

The Chinese Opposition declares that all who support or spread or defend in relation to the past the legend that the "national" bourgeoisie is able to lead the masses to a revolutionary struggle are traitors. The tasks of the Chinese revolution can really be solved only on condition that the Chinese proletariat, at the head of the oppressed masses, throws off bourgeois political leadership and seizes power. There is no other way.

3. *The question of the petty bourgeoisie and the peasantry.* In this question too, which has decisive importance for China, just as for all countries of the East, the policy of the Comintern constitutes a Menshevik falsification of Marxism. When we, the Opposition, spoke of the necessity for a revolutionary alliance of the proletariat and the petty bourgeoisie, we had in mind the oppressed masses, the tens and hundreds of millions of poor of town and countryside. The Comintern leadership understood and understands by the petty bourgeoisie those petty-bourgeois summits, overwhelmingly intellectuals, who, under the form of democratic parties and organizations, exploit the rural and urban poor, selling them out at the decisive moment to the big bourgeoisie. For us, it is not a matter of an alliance with Wang Ching-wei against Chiang Kai-shek, but of an alliance with the toiling masses against Wang Ching-wei and Chiang Kai-shek.

4. *The question of soviets.* The Bolshevik theory of soviets was

replaced by an opportunist falsification, subsequently supplemented by adventurist practice.

For the countries of the East, just as for the countries of the West, soviets are the form of organization which can and must be created *from the very first stage of a broad revolutionary upsurge.* Soviets usually arise as revolutionary strike organizations, and then extend their functions and increase their authority in the eyes of the masses. At the next stage they become the organizations of a revolutionary uprising. *Finally,* after the victory of the uprising they are transformed into the organs of revolutionary power.

In hindering the Chinese workers and peasants from creating soviets, the Stalinist leadership of the Comintern artificially disarmed and weakened the toiling masses before the bourgeoisie and gave it the opportunity to crush the revolution. The subsequent attempt in December 1927 to set up a soviet in Canton in twenty-four hours was nothing but a criminal adventure, and it prepared only for the final defeat of the heroic workers of Canton by the unrestrained military.

These are the basic crimes of the Stalinist Comintern leadership in China. Taken together they indicate a substitution of Menshevism, perfected and taken to its limits, for Bolshevism. The crushing of the second Chinese revolution is above all a defeat for the strategy of Menshevism, which this time appeared under a Bolshevik mask. It is not by chance that in this the whole of the international Social Democracy was in solidarity with Stalin and Bukharin.

Without understanding the great lessons for which the Chinese working class has paid so dearly there can be no movement forward. The Chinese Left Opposition bases itself on these lessons, wholly and completely. The Chinese bourgeoisie, after the defeat of the popular masses, was compelled to endure the dictatorship of the military. This is for the given period the only possible form of state power, flowing from the irreconcilable antagonisms of the bourgeoisie toward the popular masses on the one hand and the dependence of the bourgeoisie on foreign imperialism on the other. Individual layers and provincial groups of the bourgeoisie are not content with the rule of the sword, but the big bourgeoisie as a whole cannot keep itself in power otherwise than with the sword.

The inability of the "national" bourgeoisie to stand at the head of a revolutionary nation makes democratic parliamentarism unacceptable to it. Under the name of a temporary regime of "guardianship of the people," the "national" bourgeoisie is establishing the rule of military cliques.

These last, which reflect the special and local interests of various groups of the bourgeoisie, come one after the other into conflicts and open wars, which are the reward for a crushed revolution.

It would be pitiful and contemptible now to try to determine which of the generals is "progressive," so as to again bind up the fate of the revolutionary struggle to his sword.

The task of the Opposition is to counterpose the workers and the poor to the whole social mechanism of the counterrevolutionary bourgeoisie. It is not the Stalinist policy of collaboration and alliances with leaders, but the irreconcilable class policy of Bolshevism that will be the Opposition's line.

From the end of 1927 the Chinese revolution gave way to counterrevolution which is still continuing to deepen. The clearest expression of this process is the fate of the Chinese party. At the Sixth Congress the number of members of the Chinese Communist Party was boastfully given as one hundred thousand. The Opposition said then that after 1927 the party would hardly be able to keep even ten thousand members. In fact, the party today musters not more than three to four thousand, and its decline is still going on. The false political orientation, which at every step comes into irreconcilable contradiction with the facts, is destroying the Chinese Communist Party and will inevitably lead it to its doom, if the Communist Opposition does not secure a basic change in its whole policy and in the whole party regime.

In continuing to cover up for its errors, the present leadership of the Comintern is clearing the way in the Chinese workers' movement for two enemies: *Social Democracy* and *anarchism*. The revolutionary movement can only be defended from these complementary dangers by the Communist Opposition, which wages an irreconcilable struggle against both the opportunism and the adventurism which inevitably flow from the Stalinist leadership of the Comintern.

There is at present no mass revolutionary movement in China. All that can be done is to prepare for it. The preparation must consist in attracting ever wider circles of workers into the political life of the country, on the basis that exists now in an epoch of triumphant counterrevolution.

The slogan of soviets, as a slogan for the present, is now adventurism or empty talk.

The struggle against the military dictatorship must inevitably assume the form of *transitional revolutionary democratic demands,* leading to the demand for a Chinese constituent assembly on the basis of universal direct, equal, and secret voting, for the solution of the most important problems facing the country: the introduction of the eight-hour day, the confiscation of the land, and the securing of national independence for China.

Having rejected transitional revolutionary democratic slogans, the Sixth Congress left the Chinese Communist Party without any slogans and thereby denied it the possibility of approaching the task of mobilizing the masses under conditions of counterrevolution.

The Chinese Opposition condemns the lifeless irrelevance of such a policy. The Chinese Opposition predicts that as soon as the workers start to emerge from their paralysis they will inevitably put forward democratic slogans. If the communists stand back, the revival of political struggle will go to the benefit of petty-bourgeois democracy, and it is possible to predict in advance that the present Chinese Stalinists will follow in its wake, giving the democratic slogans not a revolutionary, but a conciliatory interpretation.

The Opposition therefore considers it necessary to make clear in advance that the real road to a solution of the problems of national independence and the raising of the standard of living of the mass of the people is a basic change in the whole social structure by means of a third Chinese revolution.

At present, it is still difficult to predict when and in what ways the revolutionary revival in the country will start. There are, however, symptoms which allow the conclusion to be drawn that political revival will be preceded by a certain *economic revival,* with a greater or lesser participation of foreign capital.

An economic upsurge, even a weak one of short duration, will again assemble the workers in the factories, raise their feeling of class self-confidence, and thereby create the conditions for the setting up of trade union organizations and for a new extension of the influence of the Communist Party. An industrial upsurge would in no case liquidate the revolution. On the contrary, in the last analysis it would revive and sharpen all the unsolved problems and all the now repressed class and subclass antagonisms (between the military, the bourgeoisie, and "democracy," between the "national" bourgeoisie and imperialism, and, finally, between the proletariat and the bourgeoisie as a whole). The upsurge would lead the Chinese popular masses out of oppression and passivity. The inevitable new crisis after this could serve as a new revolutionary impulse.

Of course, factors of an international character could hinder or possibly accelerate these processes.

The Opposition therefore does not bind itself to any ready-made scheme. Its duty is to follow the actual development of the internal life of the country and the whole world situation. All the tactical turns of our policy must be timed to the real situation of each new stage. And our general strategic line must lead to the conquest of power.

The dictatorship of the Chinese proletariat must include the Chinese revolution in the international socialist revolution. The victory of socialism in China, just as in the USSR, is thinkable only in the conditions of a victorious international revolution. The Opposition categorically rejects the reactionary Stalinist theory of socialism in one country.

The immediate tasks of the Opposition are:

(a) to publish the most important documents of the Bolshevik-Leninists (Opposition);

(b) to commence as soon as possible publication of a weekly political and theoretical organ of the Opposition;

(c) to select, on the basis of a clear conception, the best, most reliable elements of communism, capable of withstanding the pressure of counterrevolution, creating a centralized faction of Bolshevik-Leninists (Opposition), and preparing themselves and others for a new upsurge;

(d) to maintain constant active contact with the Left Opposition in all other countries, so as to attain in the shortest possible time the construction of a strong, ideologically united international faction of Bolshevik-Leninists (Opposition).

Only such a faction, openly and boldly coming out under its own banner, both inside the Communist parties and outside them, is capable of saving the Communist International from decay and degeneration and returning it to the path of Marx and Lenin.

From *Writings of Leon Trotsky (1929)*. Text from *Biulleten Oppozitsii* (Paris), nos. 1-2, July 1929. Translated by Iain Fraser.

THE CAPITULATION OF RADEK, PREOBRAZHENSKY, AND SMILGA[111]

July 27, 1929

As befits all self-respecting bankrupts, the trio certainly could not fail to cover themselves from *the permanent revolution* side. Of this powder, there is an inexhaustible supply in Yaroslavsky's snuffbox.[112] What is most tragic in all the new historical experience of the defeats of opportunism—the Chinese revolution—the three capitulators dismiss with a cheap oath in which they declare they have nothing in common with the theory of permanent revolution. It would be more correct to say that these gentlemen have nothing in common with Marxism on the fundamental questions of world revolution.

Radek and Smilga stubbornly supported the subordination of the Chinese Communist Party to the bourgeois Kuomintang, and this not only before Chiang Kai-shek's coup d'etat but also after. Preobrazhensky mumbled something vague, as he usually does on political questions. A remarkable fact: *all those in the Opposition who had supported the subordination of the Communist Party* to the Kuomintang have become capitulators. Not one of the Oppositionists who remained faithful to their banner carries this mark, a mark of notorious shame. Three-quarters of a century after the *Communist Manifesto* came into the world, a quarter of a century after the foundation of the Bolshevik party, these unfortunate "Marxists" thought it possible to defend the communists being in the Kuomintang cage! In reply to my accusation, Radek, as he now does in his letter of surrender, raised the fear of "the isolation" of the proletariat from the peasantry should the Communist Party leave the bourgeois Kuomintang. Shortly before that, Radek described the Canton government as a *workers' and peasants'* government, helping

410   *Leon Trotsky on China*

Stalin to camouflage enslavement of the proletariat to the bourgeoisie. How cover oneself from these shameful acts, consequences of this blindness and stupidity, this betrayal of Marxism? *How? With an indictment of the permanent revolution!* Yaroslavsky's snuffbox is at your service.

As early as 1928, having begun to look for arguments in order to capitulate, Radek associated himself immediately with *the resolution of the February 1928 plenum* of the ECCI on the Chinese question. This resolution described the Trotskyists as liquidators because they called a defeat a defeat and did not agree to describe the victorious Chinese counterrevolution as the highest stage of the Chinese revolution. In this February resolution the course toward armed insurrection and soviets was proclaimed. For anyone with the slightest political sense helped by revolutionary experience, this resolution offered itself as a sample of disgusting, irresponsible adventurism. Radek associated himself with it. Smilga was thoughtfully silent because what was the Chinese revolution to him when he had already begun to smell the "concrete" odor of the figures of the five-year plan?[113] Preobrazhensky involved himself in the matter in a no less subtle manner than Radek, but from the opposite end. The Chinese revolution is defeated, he wrote, and will be for a long time. A new revolution won't come soon. In that case, is it worthwhile quarreling with the centrists over China? Preobrazhensky sent lengthy messages on the subject. Reading them at Alma-Ata, I had a feeling of shame. What had these people learned in the school of Lenin? I asked myself several times. Preobrazhensky's premises were completely the opposite of Radek's, yet their conclusions were identical: both would have liked very much for Yaroslavsky to embrace them fraternally, through the mediation of Menzhinsky. Oh, to be sure, it's for the good of the revolution. They aren't careerists; no, they aren't careerists—they are simply people without hope, exhausted of ideas.

To the adventurist resolution of the plenum of the ECCI of February 1928, I had already counterposed at the time the course of mobilizing the Chinese masses around democratic slogans, including the slogan of *a Chinese constituent assembly*. But here the unfortunate trio rushed into ultraleftism; that was cheap and committed them to nothing. Democratic slogans? Never. "It is a gross mistake by Trotsky." Only Chinese soviets, and not a penny less. It is difficult to invent anything more stupid than this apology for a position. To use the slogan of soviets in a period of bourgeois reaction is to trifle, i.e., to make a mockery of soviets. Even at the time of the revolution, i.e., in the period of directly building soviets, we didn't withdraw democratic slogans. We withdrew them only when *the real soviets,* which had already captured power, clashed, before the eyes of the masses, with *the real institutions of democracy.* In the language of Lenin (and not in the mishmash of Stalin and his parrots) that meant: *not jumping over the democratic stage in the development of the country.*

Without a program for democracy—the constituent assembly, the eight-hour day, national independence for China, confiscation of the land, the right of nationalities to self-determination, etc.— without this program for democracy, the Chinese Communist Party would find itself bound hand and foot and would be obliged passively to clear the ground for the Chinese Social Democracy which, helped by Stalin, Radek, and Company, might supplant it.

So: when he followed in the wake of the Opposition, Radek missed what was most important in the Chinese revolution, for he defended the subordination of the Communist Party to the bourgeois Kuomintang. Radek missed the Chinese counterrevolution, supporting the course to armed insurrection which followed the Canton adventure. Now, Radek jumps over the period of the counterrevolution and the struggle for democracy, keeping himself apart from the tasks of the transition period by the abstract idea of soviets outside of time and place. But in compensation, Radek swears he has nothing in common with permanent revolution. That is gratifying. That is comforting. It is true that Radek does not understand the motive forces of revolution; he does not understand its changing periods; he does not understand the role and meaning of the proletarian party; he does not understand the relation between democratic slogans and the struggle for power; but in compensation—oh, supreme compensation!—he takes no strong drink and if he comforts himself on difficult days, it is not with the alcohol of permanent revolution but with innocent pinches from Yaroslavsky's snuff-box.

But, no, these "pinches" are not so innocent. On the contrary, they are very dangerous. They bear in themselves a very great threat for the coming Chinese revolution. The anti-Marxist theory of Stalin-Radek bears in itself a repetition, changed but not improved, of the Kuomintang experiment, for China, for India, and for all the other countries of the East.

On the basis of all the experiences of the Russian and Chinese revolutions, on the basis of the teachings of Marx and Lenin, having thought the matter out in the light of these experiences, the Opposition affirms:

A new Chinese revolution can overthrow the existing regime and hand power over to the mass of the people *only in the form of the dictatorship of the proletariat.*

"The democratic dictatorship of the proletariat and the peasantry"—substituting for *the dictatorship of the proletariat leading the peasantry and carrying out the democratic program*—is a fiction, a self-deception, or, worse still, Kerenskyism or Kuomintangism.

Between the regime of Kerensky or Chiang Kai-shek on the one hand and the dictatorship of the proletariat on the other, *there is not nor can there be any intermediate revolutionary regime,* and whoever puts forward such a naked formula shamefully deceives the workers of the East and prepares fresh catastrophes.

The Opposition says to the workers of the East: The machinations of the capitulators gnawing within the party help Stalin to sow the seeds of centrism, to throw sand in your eyes, to stop up your ears, to befog your minds. On the one hand, you are weakened in the face of the regime of an oppressive bourgeois dictatorship because you are forbidden to develop the struggle for democracy. On the other hand, there is drawn for you a perspective of some kind of dictatorship, cheap and nonproletarian, thus facilitating the future reshaping of the Kuomintang, i.e., the future defeat of the revolution of the workers and peasants.

Such forecasters utter treacheries. Workers of the East, learn to distrust them, learn to despise them, learn to drive them out of your ranks!

Excerpted from "A Wretched Document," in *Writings of Leon Trotsky (1929).* Text from *Biulleten Oppozitsii* (Paris), nos. 3-4, September 1929. Translated by Fred Buchman.

THE SINO-SOVIET CONFLICT
AND THE OPPOSITION[114]

August 4, 1929

On July 22 I gave the following statement in answer to an American news agency questionnaire:

I can give my view on Sino-Soviet relations, of course, only as an individual. I have no information except what is in the newspapers. In cases of this kind, information in the newspapers is always insufficient.

There can be no doubt that aggressiveness has been manifested not by the Soviet, but by the Chinese government. The managing apparatus of the Chinese Eastern Railroad has existed for a number of years. The workers' organizations that the Chinese regime has attacked have also existed for some time. The existing administrative arrangement for the Chinese Eastern Railroad was carefully worked out this last time by a special commission under my chairmanship. The commission's decisions were approved in April 1926 and completely protect Chinese interests.

The conduct of the present Chinese government is explained by the fact that it was made stronger by the crushing defeat of the workers and peasants. I will not discuss here the reasons for the defeat of the revolutionary movement of the Chinese people because I have dealt sufficiently with this theme in my previously published works. The government, having risen out of a completely routed revolution, as always in such cases, feels weak in relation to those forces against which the revolution was directed, i.e., above all against British and Japanese imperialism. Therefore, it is compelled to try to enhance its power and influence by making adventuristic gestures toward its revolutionary neighbor.

Must this provocation that developed out of the defeat of the Chinese revolution lead to war? I don't think so. Why? Because the *Soviet government does not want war,* and the Chinese government *is not capable of waging it.*

The army of Chiang Kai-shek was victorious in 1925-27 [against the warlords] thanks to the revolutionary upsurge of the masses. In turning against them, the army has forfeited its chief source of strength. As a purely military organization, Chiang Kai-shek's army is extremely weak. Chiang Kai-shek cannot help but realize that the Soviet government is well aware of the weakness of his army. It is unthinkable that Chiang Kai-shek could wage a war against the Red Army *without the aid of other powers*. It is more accurate to say that Chiang Kai-shek would wage war only if his army were merely the auxiliary detachment to the forces of another power. I do not believe that at this time such a combination is very likely, especially in light of the Soviet government's sincere desire, as indicated above, to settle problems by peaceful means. . . .

It goes without saying that in the event that war is imposed on the Soviet people, the Opposition will devote itself fully to the cause of defending the October revolution.

I thought that in this statement I had expressed the viewpoint of the Communist Left Opposition as a whole. I regret to say that this is not entirely true. Individuals and groups have come forward in the Opposition that, on the occasion of their first serious political test, have taken either an equivocal or a basically wrong position, a position outside their own revolutionary Opposition camp or one which brought them very close to the camp of the Social Democracy.[115]

In *Die Fahne des Kommunismus,* no. 26, there was an article written by one H. P. According to this article, the conflict was caused by an encroachment on China's right of self-determination by the Soviet republic. In other words, it was in essence a defense of Chiang Kai-shek. I shall not deal with this article, since H. P. received a correct reply from Comrade Kurt Landau, who dealt with this question as behooves a Marxist.

The editor of *Fahne des Kommunismus* printed the article as a discussion article, with a note that he is not in solidarity with the author. It is incomprehensible that a discussion could be opened on a question that is so elementary for every revolutionary, particularly at a time political action is called for. The thing became even worse when the editor of the paper also published Landau's contribution as a "discussion article." H. P.'s article expresses the prejudices of vulgar democracy combined with those of anarchism. Landau's article formulates the Marxist position. And what about the position of the editor?

Something incomparably worse occurred in one of the numerous groups of the French Opposition. Number 35 of *Contre le*

Courant (July 28, 1929) had an editorial on the Sino-Soviet conflict which is a sorry mess of errors from beginning to end, partly of a Social Democratic and partly of an ultraleft character. The editorial begins with the statement that the adventuristic policy of the Soviet bureaucracy is responsible for the conflict; in other words, the paper assumes the role of Chiang Kai-shek's attorney. The editorial puts the policy of the Soviet government toward the Chinese Eastern Railroad in the category of a capitalist, imperialist policy, which resorts to the support of the imperialist powers.

"The Communist Opposition," the editorial states, "cannot support Stalin's war, which is not a defensive war of the proletariat but a semicolonial war." Elsewhere it says: "The Opposition must have the courage *to tell the working class that it is not falling into line with the Stalinist bureaucrats, that it is not for their adventuristic war.*" This sentence is emphasized in the original, and not by accident. It expresses the whole point of the editorial and thereby puts the author into implacable opposition to the Communist Left.

In what sense is the Stalinist bureaucracy responsible for the present conflict? In this sense and no other: that it helped Chiang Kai-shek by its previous policy to destroy the revolution of the Chinese workers and peasants. I wrote about this in an article directed against Radek and Company: "Chiang Kai-shek's provocation is the settlement of expenses incurred by Stalin in the defeat of the Chinese revolution. We gave warning hundreds of times: after Stalin has helped Chiang Kai-shek to settle in the saddle, Chiang Kai-shek would, at the first opportunity, draw his whip on him. That is what has happened."

Chiang Kai-shek's provocation was preceded by his crushing of the Chinese revolution. What we have now is an adventure of the Bonapartist military power headed by Chiang Kai-shek. This provocation is at the root of the Sino-Soviet conflict.

According to the editorial, the principal cause of the conflict is the imperialist "claim" of the Soviet republic on the Chinese Eastern Railroad. Hands off China! shout the involuntary defenders of Chiang Kai-shek, repeating not only the slogans but also the basic arguments of the Social Democrats. Up until now we believed that only the capitalist bourgeoisie as a class could be the representatives of an imperialist policy. Is there anything to indicate the contrary? Or has such a class taken power in the USSR? Since when? We are fighting against the centrism of the

Stalinist bureaucracy (remember: centrism is a tendency within the working class itself) because centrist policies *may help* the bourgeoisie to gain power, first the petty and middle bourgeoisie and, eventually, finance capital. This is the historical danger; but this is a process that is by no means at the point of completion.

In the same issue of *Contre le Courant,* there is a so-called draft of a platform. In it we read among other things: "We cannot say that Thermidor has already taken hold." This shows that continual repetition of the general formulas of the Opposition is far from equivalent to a political understanding of those formulas. If we cannot say that Thermidor is an accomplished fact, then we cannot say that Soviet policy has become a capitalist, or imperialist, policy. Centrism zigzags between the proletariat and the petty bourgeoisie. To identify centrism with big capital is to understand nothing, and thereby to support finance capital not only against the proletariat, but also against the petty bourgeoisie.[116]

The theoretical wisdom of the ultralefts in Berlin and Paris boils down to a few democratic abstractions, which have a geographical, not a socialist basis. The Chinese Eastern Railroad runs through Manchuria, which belongs to China. China has a right to self-determination; therefore, the claim of Soviet Russia to this railroad is imperialism. It should be turned over. To whom? To Chiang Kai-shek? Or to the son of Chang Tso-lin?

During the Brest-Litovsk peace negotiations, von Kuhlmann introduced the demand for an independent Latvia and Estonia, referring to the fact that the Landtags established there with the aid of Germany had instructed him to demand separation. We refused to sanction this, and we were denounced by the entire official German press as imperialists.[117]

Let us assume that in the Caucasus there is an outbreak of counterrevolution which, with the help of, say, England, achieves victory. Let us also assume that the workers of Baku, with the help of the Soviet Union, succeed in keeping the whole area of Baku in their hands. It goes without saying that the Transcaucasian counterrevolution would lay claim to this district of Baku. It is perfectly clear that the Soviet republic would not consent to this. Is it not also clear that in such a case the enemy would accuse the Soviet government of imperialism?

Had the revolution of the Chinese workers and peasants been victorious, there wouldn't be any difficulty whatsoever about the Chinese Eastern Railroad. The lines would have been turned over to the victorious Chinese people. But the fact of the matter is that the Chinese people were defeated by the ruling Chinese bourgeoisie, with the aid of foreign imperialism. To turn over the railroad to Chiang Kai-shek under such conditions would mean to give aid and comfort to the Chinese Bonapartist counterrevolution against the Chinese people. This itself is decisive. But there is another consideration of equal weight. Chiang Kai-shek never could get those lines by virtue of his own financial-political means—let alone keep them. It is hardly an accident that he tolerates the actual independence of Manchuria existing under a Japanese protectorate. The railroad lines transferred to Chiang Kai-shek would only become security for the foreign loans he received. They would pass into the hands of the real imperialists and would become their most important economic and strategic outpost in the Far East—against a potential Chinese revolution and against the Soviet republic. We are well aware that the imperialists understand perfectly how to utilize the slogan of self-determination for their own dirty deals. But I don't believe that Marxists are under obligation to help them put it over.

The point of departure for the ultralefts is the fact that it was the greedy and thievish imperialism of the tsar that took the Chinese Eastern Railroad from the Chinese people. This is a fact that cannot be disputed. Yet they forget to point out this was the same imperialism that dominated the Russian people. Yes, this railroad was constructed for the purpose of robbing the Chinese workers and peasants. But it was constructed by the exploitation and the robbery of the Russian workers and peasants. Then the October revolution took place. Did this alter the mutual relations of the Chinese and the Russians? On the foundation of the revolution, after a period of reaction, the state structure was rebuilt. Did Russia now return to the starting point? Can we now imagine, from a historical viewpoint—regardless of Stalin and Molotov, regardless of the exile of the Opposition, etc., etc.—can we imagine an ownership of the Chinese Eastern Railroad that would be more beneficial from the point of view of the international proletariat and the Chinese revolution than that of the Soviet Union? This is how we ought to put the question.

All the White Guard emigrés look upon this question from a class viewpoint, not from a nationalist or a geographical one. In spite of internal dissension, the leading groups of the Russian emigrés agree that the internationalization of the Chinese Eastern Railroad, that is, its transference to the control of world imperialism, would be more advantageous to the "coming," that is, bourgeois, Russia than leaving it in the possession of the Soviet state. By the same token, we can say that its remaining under the control of the Soviet government would be more advantageous to an independent China than turning it over to any of the present claimants.

Does this mean that the managing apparatus of the line is perfect? No! Indeed not. Tsarist imperialism has left its traces. All the zigzags of Soviet internal policy are undoubtedly also reflected in the apparatus of the lines. The tasks of the Opposition extend to these questions as well.

I would like to refer to my personal experience in this matter. I had to fight more than once for an improvement in the administration of the Chinese railroad. The last time I worked on this question was in March 1926 on a special commission of which I was chairman. The members of the commission were Voroshilov, Dzerzhinsky, and Chicherin. In full agreement with the Chinese revolutionaries, not only the communists but also the representatives of the then functioning Kuomintang, the commission considered absolutely necessary: "strictly keeping the actual apparatus of the CER in the hands of the Soviet government—which in the next period is the only way to protect the railroad from imperialist seizure. . . . "

With regard to the administration in the interim, the resolution adopted on the question had this to say:

> It is necessary to immediately adopt broad measures of a cultural-political nature aimed at *Sinification* of the railroad.
> (a) The administration should be bilingual; station signs and instructions posted in the stations and in the cars, etc., should be bilingual. (b) Chinese schools for railroad workers should be established combining technical and political training. (c) At appropriate points along the railroad, cultural-educational institutions should be established for the Chinese workers and the Chinese settlements adjacent to the railroad. ["Problems of Our Policy with Respect to China and Japan" (March 25, 1926).]

With regard to the policy of the Russian representatives toward China, the resolution said:

> There is absolutely no doubt that in the actions of the various departmental representatives there were inadmissible great-power mannerisms compromising the Soviet administration and creating an impression of Soviet imperialism.

It is necessary to impress upon the corresponding agencies and persons the vital importance for us of such a policy and of even such an *external form* of the policy in relation to China so that any trace of suspicion of great-power intentions will be eliminated. This policy— based on the closest attention to China's rights, on emphasizing its sovereignty, etc.—must be carried out on every level. In every individual instance of a violation of this policy, no matter how slight, the culprits should be punished and this fact brought to the attention of Chinese public opinion.

In addition to this I must point out that the Chinese owners of the railroad, including Chiang Kai-shek, put against the management of the railroad not a Chinese but mainly a White-Guardist apparatus on the payroll of the imperialists of the world. The White Guards employed in the police and military squads of the Chinese lines have frequently committed acts of violence against the railroad workers. Regarding this, the resolution passed by the commission said the following:

> it is necessary right now to carefully compile (and subsequently examine) all cases of tyranny and violence on the part of Chinese militarists, police, and Russian White Guard elements against Russian workers and employees of the CER, and also all cases of conflict between Russians and Chinese on national-social grounds. It is also necessary to devise the course and means for defending the personal and national dignity of Russian workers so that conflicts on this basis rather than kindling chauvinist sentiments on both sides, on the contrary, will have a political and educational significance. It is necessary to set up special conciliation commissions or courts of honor attached to the trade unions, with both sides participating on an equal basis, under the actual guidance of serious communists who understand the full importance and acuteness of the national question.

I believe that this is a far cry from imperialism. I believe that the ultralefts have a good chance to learn something from this. I am also ready to admit that not all of our resolutions have been carried out. There were probably more unlawful acts on the railroad than in Moscow. That is precisely why the Opposition wages an implacable struggle. Yet it is a poor politician who throws out the baby with the bath water.

I have already shown the sense in which the Stalinist faction is responsible for Chiang Kai-shek's provocations. But even if we assume that Stalin's bureaucrats have acted foolishly again, and have thereby helped the enemy to strike a blow against the Soviet republic, what conclusions should we draw? The conclusion that we must not defend the Soviet republic? Or the conclusion that we must free the Soviet republic from the Stalinist leadership? The *Contre le Courant* editorial has outrageously come to the first conclusion. It states that we must not support Stalin's bureaucracy and its adventuristic war, as though in the event of war the Stalinist bureaucracy would be at stake and not the October revolution and its potentialities. In order to display more of its wisdom, the editorial continues: "It is not up to the Opposition to find some special remedy in the present crisis." We cannot imagine a worse position. This is not the view of a revolutionary, but of a disinterested spectator. What shall the Russian revolutionary do? What shall the fighters of the Opposition do in case of war? Shall they perhaps take a neutral position? The author of the editorial does not seem to think of this. And that is because he is not guided by the viewpoint of a revolutionary who will unconditionally enlist in the war, but proceeds like a notary who records the actions of both parties without intervening.

The Stalinists have accused us more than once of being defeatists or conditional defensists. I spoke on this subject at a joint plenary session of the Central Committee and the Central Control Commission on August 1, 1927. I said: "The lie of conditional defensism . . . we fling back into the faces of the calumniators."

In this way I repudiated the idea of neutrality and of conditional defense, called it a slander, and hurled the slander back into the teeth of the Stalinists. Did the author of the editorial fail to notice this? And if he didn't—why did he not attack me? The speech to which I refer was printed in my recent book, published in French under the title *La Révolution défigurée*.[118]

When I spoke, I did not deal with a specific war, but with any war that might be waged against the Soviet republic. Only an ignoramus could fail to see from the combination of the preceding events a basic antagonism between the imperialist powers and Soviet Russia. Yes, concerning my visa the imperialists are in cheerful accord with Stalin.[119] But when it comes to the question of the Soviet republic, they all remain its mortal enemies, *irrespective of Stalin*. Every war would expose this antagonism and inevitably result in endangering the very existence of the Soviet Union. That is why I said in that speech:

Do we, the Opposition, cast any doubts on the defense of the socialist fatherland? Not in the slightest degree. It is our hope not only to participate in the defense, but to be able to teach others a few things. Do we cast doubts on Stalin's ability to sketch a correct line for the defense of the socialist fatherland? We do so and, indeed, to the highest possible degree. . . .

The Opposition is *for* the victory of the USSR; it has proved and will continue to prove this in action, in a manner inferior to none. But Stalin is not concerned with that. Stalin has essentially a different question in mind, which he dares not express, namely, "Does the Opposition really think that the leadership of Stalin is incapable of assuring victory to the USSR?" Yes, we think so.

Zinoviev: Correct!

. . . Not a single Oppositionist will renounce his right and his duty, on the eve of war, or during the war, to fight for the correction of the party's course—as has always been the case in our party—because therein lies the most important condition for victory. To sum up. For the socialist fatherland? Yes! For the Stalinist course? No!

I believe that this position retains its full force at the present moment as well.

From *Writings of Leon Trotsky (1929)*. Text from the *Militant* (New York), September 15, 1929.

WHAT IS HAPPENING IN CHINA?

A Question Every Communist Must Ask Himself

November 9, 1929

Among the dispatches in *Pravda* there has been communicated several times during October, in the smallest type, that an armed communist detachment under the command of Comrade Chu Te is advancing successfully toward Chaochow (Kwangtung), that this detachment has grown from 5,000 to 20,000, etc. Thus we learn, as if incidentally, from the laconic dispatches of *Pravda* that the Chinese communists are conducting an armed struggle against Chiang Kai-shek. What is the meaning of this struggle? Its origins? Its perspectives? Not a word is breathed to us about it. If the new revolution in China has matured to the point that the communists have taken to arms, then it would seem necessary to mobilize the whole International in the face of events of such gigantic historical importance. Why then do we hear nothing of the sort? And if the situation in China is not such as puts on the order of the day the armed struggle of the communists for power, then how and why has a communist detachment begun an armed struggle against Chiang Kai-shek, that is, against the bourgeois-military dictatorship?[120]

Yes, why have the Chinese communists risen in rebellion? Perhaps because the Chinese proletariat has already found the time to heal its wounds? Because the demoralized and debilitated Communist Party has found the time to rise on the revolutionary wave? Have the city workers assured their contact with the revolutionary masses of the country? Have strikes spread throughout the country? Has the general strike pushed the proletariat to the insurrection? If such is the case, then everything is clear and in order. But then why does *Pravda* communicate these events in a few lines and in small print?

Or perhaps the Chinese communists have risen in rebellion because they have received the latest comments of Molotov on the resolution on the "third period"?[121] It is no accident that Zinoviev who, in contrast to the other capitulators, still pretends to be alive, has come out in *Pravda* with an article which shows that the domination of Chiang Kai-shek is entirely similar to the temporary domination of Kolchak, that is, is only a simple episode in the process of the revolutionary rise. This analogy is of course bracing to the spirit. Unfortunately, it is not only false, but simply stupid. Kolchak organized an insurrection in one province against the dictatorship of the proletariat already established in the greater part of the country. In China, bourgeois counterrevolution rules in the country and it is the communists who have stirred up an insurrection of a few thousand people in one of the provinces. We think, therefore, we have the right to pose this question: Does this insurrection spring from the situation in China or rather from the instructions concerning the "third period"? We ask further, what is the political role of the Chinese Communist Party in all this? What are the slogans with which it mobilized the masses? What is the degree of its influence upon the workers? We hear nothing about all this. The rebellion of Chu Te appears to be a reproduction of the adventurist campaigns of Ho Lung and Yeh T'ing in 1927 and the Canton uprising timed for the moment of the expulsion of the Opposition from the Russian Communist Party.

Perhaps the rebellion broke out spontaneously? Well and good. But then what is the meaning of the communist banner unfurled above it? What is the attitude of the official Chinese Communist Party toward the insurrection? What is the position of the Comintern in this question? And why, finally, in communicating this fact to us, does the Moscow *Pravda* abstain from any comment?

But there is still another explanation possible, which is perhaps the most alarming one: Have the Chinese communists risen in rebellion because of Chiang Kai-shek's seizure of the Chinese Eastern Railroad? Has this insurrection, wholly partisan in character, as its aim to cause Chiang Kai-shek uneasiness at his rear? If that is what it is, we ask who has given such counsel to the Chinese communists? Who bears the political responsibility for their passing over to guerrilla warfare?

It is not long ago that we decisively condemned the ramblings on the necessity of handing over so important an instrument as the Chinese Eastern from the hands of the Russian revolution to those of the Chinese counterrevolution. We called to mind the elementary duty of the international proletariat in this conflict to defend the republic of the Soviets against the Chinese bourgeoisie and all its possible instigators and allies. But on the other hand, it is quite clear that the proletariat of the USSR, which has the power and the army in its hands, cannot demand that the vanguard of the Chinese proletariat begin a war at once against Chiang Kai-shek, that is, that it apply the means which the Soviet government itself does not find it possible, and correctly so, to apply.

Had a war begun between the USSR and China, or rather between the USSR and the imperialist patrons of China, the duty of the Chinese communist would be to transform this war in the shortest time into a civil war. But even in that case the launching of the civil war would have to be subordinated to general revolutionary policy; and even then the Chinese communists would be unable to pass over arbitrarily, and at any moment at all, to the road of open insurrection, but only after having assured themselves of the necessary support of the worker and peasant masses. The rebellion at Chiang Kai-shek's rear, in this situation, would be the extension of the front of the Soviet workers and peasants; the fate of the insurgent Chinese workers would be intimately bound up with the fate of the Soviet republic; the tasks, the aims, the perspectives would be quite clear.

But what is the perspective opened up by this uprising of the today isolated Chinese communists in the absence of war or revolution? The perspective of a terrific debacle and of an adventurist degeneration of the remnants of the Communist Party.

In the meantime, it must be said openly: Calculations based upon guerrilla adventure correspond entirely to the general nature of Stalinist policy. Two years ago, Stalin expected gigantic gains for the security of the Soviet state from the alliance with the imperialists of the General Council of the British trade unions. Today, he is quite capable of calculating that a rebellion of the Chinese communists, even without any hope, would bring "a little profit" in a precarious situation. In the first case, the calculation was grossly opportunist; in the second, openly adventurist; but in both cases, the calculation is made independent of the general tasks of the world labor movement, against these tasks, and to the detriment of the correctly understood interests of the Soviet republic.

We have not at our disposal all the necessary data for a definite conclusion. That is why we ask:

What is happening in China? Let it be explained to us! The communist who does not pose the question to himself and to the leadership of his party will be unworthy of the name of communist. The leadership that would like to remain discreetly on the sidelines in order, in case of a defeat of the Chinese partisans, to wash its hands and transfer responsibility to the Central Committee of the Chinese Communist Party—such a leadership would dishonor itself—not for the first time, it is true—by the most abominable crime against the interests of the international revolution.

We ask: What is happening in China? We will continue to pose this question until we have forced a reply.

From *Problems of the Chinese Revolution.*

A REPLY TO THE
CHINESE OPPOSITIONISTS[122]

December 22, 1929

Dear Comrades:

On December 20 I received your letter of November 15; it took thirty-five days from Shanghai to Constantinople. For my reply to reach you, at least as many days must be allowed. Nothing can be done about it. Neither airmail nor radio are as yet at the service of the Opposition.

The most important thing in your letter is the announcement that you have published a *platform* of the Chinese Opposition. You should immediately translate it into at least one European language. The whole international Opposition must have the possibility of knowing this highly important document. I await your platform with the greatest impatience.

In your letter you pose two questions connected with the platform: the constituent assembly and the United States of Asia. The second question is entirely new; I must put off my reply until I can devote a special article to it. On the question of the constituent assembly I will reply briefly:

The political task of the Chinese Communist Party, weakened and driven into illegality, is to mobilize not only the workers but also the broad social layers of the city and the countryside against the bourgeois-military dictatorship. It is this end that the simplest and most natural slogan under present conditions, the constituent assembly, must serve. Tireless agitation must be carried on under this slogan in correlation with other slogans of the democratic revolution: the transfer of the land to the poor peasants, the eight-hour day, the independence of China, the right of self-determination for the people who constitute it.

Agitation must be supplemented by propaganda that will make

426

at least the most advanced sections of the proletariat understand that the road leading to the constituent assembly can only pass through the insurrection against the military usurpers and the seizure of power by the popular masses.

The government that will emerge from the victorious revolution of the workers and peasants can only be a government of the *dictatorship of the proletariat,* leading the majority of the exploited and oppressed people. But the difference must be clearly understood between the general *revolutionary perspective* which we must tirelessly develop in articles and in theoretical and propaganda speeches and the *current political slogan* under which we can, beginning today, mobilize the masses by actually organizing them in opposition to the regime of the military dictatorship. Such a *central political slogan* is the slogan of the *constituent assembly.*

This slogan is dealt with briefly in the draft of the platform of the Chinese Opposition, drawn up in Constantinople by some Chinese and foreign comrades. My young friend, N.,[123] I know, has transmitted this draft to you. With all the greater impatience do I await your platform so as to be able to judge, documents in hand, if there are differences between you and Comrade N. and if the separate existence of two groups is justified. Until I can become acquainted with the facts and the documents, I am obliged to refrain from formulating any judgment on this important question.

You report that Chinese Stalinists fired at an Oppositionist in the streets of Canton. Outrageous as this act may be, I do not consider it impossible. In his "Testament," Lenin accused Stalin personally of a tendency to abuse power, that is, of violence. Since then this trait has developed monstrously in the apparatus of the Communist Party of the Soviet Union and has been extended to the Communist International. Naturally, the dictatorship of the proletariat is inconceivable without the use of force, even against certain sectors of the proletariat itself. The workers' state, however, also requires that workers' democracy exercise the most vigilant control in order to know why, how, and in whose name violence is employed. This question presents itself in an entirely different manner in the bourgeois countries, where the revolutionary party constitutes only a small minority of the working class and where it has to struggle in order to win the majority. Under such conditions, the use of violence against ideological opponents—not strikebreakers, or provocateurs, or fascists attacking treacherously, but ideological opponents, honest Social Democratic workers included—is an enormous crime and madness that must inevitably turn upon the revolutionary party itself. In the bitter struggle that the Bolsheviks conducted against the Narodniks and the Mensheviks during the fifteen years that preceded the October revolution, there was never a question of employing methods of physical violence. As for individual terror, we Marxists rejected it even with regard to the tsarist satraps. Nevertheless, in recent times the Communist parties, or rather their apparatus people, have resorted more and more frequently to the disruption of meetings and to other methods for the mechanical suppression of adversaries, notably the Left Opposition. Many bureaucrats are sincerely convinced that this is what real Bolshevism consists of. They avenge themselves on other proletarian groups for their impotence against the capitalist state, and thereby transform the bourgeois police into an arbiter between us.

It is difficult to imagine the depravity engendered by this combination of impotence and violence. The youth become more and more accustomed to thinking that the fist is a surer weapon than argument. In other words, political cynicism is cultivated, which more than anything else prepares individuals for passing over into the fascist camp. An implacable struggle must be waged against the brutal and disloyal methods of Stalinism, by denouncing them in the press and in meetings, by cultivating among the workers a hatred and contempt for all these pseudorevolutionists who, instead of appealing to the brain, take a crack at the skull.

Concerning the Ch'en Tu-hsiu group, I am pretty well acquainted with the policy it followed in the years of the revolution: it was the Stalin-Bukharin-Martynov policy, that is, a policy in essence of right-wing Menshevism. Comrade N. wrote me, however, that Ch'en Tu-hsiu, basing himself on the experience of the revolution, has come considerably closer to our position. It goes without saying that this can only be welcomed. In your letter, however, you categorically dispute Comrade N.'s information. You even contend that Ch'en Tu-hsiu has not broken from Stalin's policy, which presents a mixture of opportunism and adventurism. But up to now I have read only one declaration of program by Ch'en Tu-hsiu and therefore am in no position to express myself on this question.

In other respects, I conceive a solidarity in principle on the

Chinese question only on the basis of clear replies to the following questions:

As far as the first period of the revolution is concerned:

1. Did the anti-imperialist character of the Chinese revolution give the "national" Chinese bourgeoisie the leading role in the revolution (Stalin-Bukharin)?

2. Was the slogan of the "bloc of four classes"—the big bourgeoisie, the petty bourgeoisie, the peasantry, and the proletariat (Stalin-Bukharin)—correct, even for an instant?

3. Were the entry of the Chinese Communist Party into the Kuomintang and the admission of the latter into the Comintern (resolution of the Politburo of the Soviet Communist Party) permissible?

4. Was it permissible, in the interests of the Northern Expedition, to curb the agrarian revolution (telegraphic directives in the name of the Politburo of the Soviet Communist Party)?

5. Was it permissible to renounce the slogan of soviets at the time the broad movement of workers and peasants developed, that is, in 1925-27 (Stalin-Bukharin)?

6. Was the Stalinist slogan of a "workers' and peasants'" party, that is, the old slogan of the Russian Narodniks, acceptable for China, even for an instant?

As far as the second period is concerned:

7. Was the resolution of the Communist International which said that the crushing of the workers' and peasants' movement by the Kuomintang of the right and the left signified a "transition of the revolution to a higher stage" (Stalin-Bukharin) correct?

8. Under these conditions, was the slogan of insurrection, issued by the Communist International, correct?

9. Was the tactic of guerrilla warfare, reinstituted by Ho Lung and Yeh T'ing and approved by the Comintern at the moment of the political ebb tide of the workers and peasants, correct?

10. Was the organization of the Canton uprising by the agents of the Comintern correct?

As far as the past in general is concerned:

11. Was the 1924-27 struggle in the Communist International against the Opposition on the Chinese question a struggle of Leninism against Trotskyism or, on the contrary, a struggle of Menshevism against Bolshevism?

12. Was the 1927-28 struggle in the Communist International against the Opposition a struggle of Bolshevism against

"liquidationism" or, on the contrary, a struggle of adventurism against Bolshevism?

As far as the future is concerned:

13. Under the present conditions of victorious counterrevolution, is the mobilization of the Chinese masses under democratic slogans, particularly that of the constituent assembly, necessary, as the Opposition believes, or is there any ground for limitation to the abstract propaganda of the slogan of soviets, as the Comintern has decided?

14. Has the slogan of the "workers' and peasants' democratic dictatorship" still a revolutionary content, as the Comintern thinks, or is it necessary, on the contrary, to sweep away this masked formula of the Kuomintang and to explain that the victory of the alliance of the workers and peasants in China can lead only to the dictatorship of the proletariat?

15. Is the theory of socialism in one country applicable to China or, on the contrary, can the Chinese revolution triumph and accomplish its task to the very end only as a link in the chain of the world revolution?

These are, in my opinion, the principal questions that the platform of the Chinese Opposition must necessarily answer. These questions have great importance for the whole International. The epoch of reaction that China is now passing through must become, as has always happened in history, an epoch of theoretical preoccupation. What characterizes the young Chinese revolutionists at the present time is the passion to understand, to study, to embrace the question in its entirety. The bureaucracy, lacking an ideological basis, stifles Marxist thinking. But I do not doubt that in the struggle with the bureaucracy the Chinese vanguard of the proletariat will produce from its ranks a nucleus of notable Marxists who will render service to the whole International.

With Opposition greetings,
L.D. Trotsky

From *Writings of Leon Trotsky (1929)*. Text from the *Militant* (New York), February 1, 1930.

SOME RESULTS
OF THE SINO-SOVIET CONFLICT

January 3, 1930

1. In its last stage the conflict revealed, as is known, the complete military impotence of the present Chinese government. This in itself clearly demonstrates that there has not been a victorious bourgeois revolution in China, as Louzon, Urbahns, and others think,[124] for a victorious revolution would have consolidated the army and the state. In China there was a victorious counterrevolution, directed against the overwhelming majority of the nation and therefore incapable of creating an army.

2. At the same time it strikingly demonstrates the inconsistency of the Menshevik policy of Stalin-Martynov, based since the beginning of 1924 on the assumption that the "national" Chinese bourgeoisie is capable of leading the revolution. In reality the bourgeoisie, with political support from the Comintern and material aid from the imperialists, was capable only of smashing the revolution and thereby reducing the Chinese state to complete impotence.

3. The Sino-Soviet conflict, in its military stage, revealed the enormous superiority of the [Russian] proletarian revolution, although weakened by the erroneous policy of the leadership in the last years, over the [Chinese] bourgeois counterrevolution, which had at its disposal substantial diplomatic and material support from imperialism.

4. The victory of the October revolution over the April counterrevolution (the coup by Chiang Kai-shek in April 1927) can in no sense be considered a victory for Stalin's policy. On the contrary, that policy has suffered a series of heavy defeats. The seizure of the railroad was Chiang Kai-shek's payment for the

services rendered by Stalin. Stalin's subsequent wager on Feng Yü-hsiang was equally inconsistent. The Opposition warned against the adventurist anti–Chiang Kai-shek bloc with Feng Yü-hsiang after April 1927 as energetically as it had protested against Stalin's bloc with Chiang Kai-shek.

5. The unprincipled wager on the Kellogg Pact also resulted in a heavy loss.[125] The Soviet government's adherence to the pact of American imperialism was a capitulation of the Soviet government as shameful as it was useless. By signing the pact, the so-called instrument of peace, Stalin openly assisted the American government in deceiving the working masses of America and Europe. What was the purpose of adherence to the pact? Obviously to gain the goodwill of the United States and thereby hasten diplomatic recognition. As should have been expected, this end was not achieved, for the American government had no reason to pay for what it got for nothing. New York, basing itself on the Kellogg Pact, took the first opportunity to play the role of China's protector against the Soviet republic. Moscow was obliged to reply with a sharp rebuke. That was correct and inevitable. But this necessary demonstration against the American government's attempt to intervene disclosed Stalin's criminal light-mindedness in joining the Kellogg Pact.

6. There still remains the question of the revolutionary communist detachment under the leadership of Chu Te. *Pravda* wrote about this on the eve of the transition of the conflict into a military stage. After that, we heard no more about these Chinese workers and peasants whom someone sent into armed battle under the banner of communism. What were the aims of the struggle? What was the role of the party in it? What was the fate of this detachment? And, finally, in whose back room are all these questions decided?

On this last point, no less important than all the rest, a final balance sheet cannot yet be drawn. But everything points to the fact that bureaucratic adventurism in this instance as in the others bears the responsibility for the weakening and exhaustion of the reserves of the Chinese revolution.

From *Writings of Leon Trotsky (1930)*. Text from the *Militant* (New York), February 8, 1930.

THE SLOGAN OF
A NATIONAL ASSEMBLY IN CHINA[126]

April 2, 1930

It seems to me that our Chinese friends deal with the question of political slogans of democracy too metaphysically, even scholastically.

The "intricacies" begin with the name: constituent assembly or national assembly. In Russia until the revolution we used the slogan of a constituent assembly because it most clearly emphasized a break with the past. But you write that it is difficult to formulate this slogan in Chinese. If so, the slogan of a national assembly can be adopted. In the consciousness of the masses, the slogan's content will depend, firstly, on the implication revolutionary agitation gives it and, secondly, on events. You ask, "Is it possible to carry on agitation for a constituent assembly while denying that it can be achieved?" But why should we decide in advance that it cannot be? Of course the masses will support the slogan only if they consider it feasible. Who will institute a constituent assembly and how will it function? Only suppositions are possible. In case of a further weakening of the military-Kuomintang regime and increasing discontent among the masses, particularly in the cities, it is possible that an attempt will be made by a part of the Kuomintang together with the "Third Party" to convene something on the style of a national assembly. They will, of course, cut into the rights of the more oppressed classes and layers as much as they can.

Would we communists enter such a restricted and manipulated national assembly? If we are not strong enough to replace it, that is, to take power, we certainly would enter it. Such a stage would not at all weaken us. On the contrary, it would help us to gather

434   *Leon Trotsky on China*

together and develop the forces of the proletarian vanguard. Inside this spurious assembly, and particularly outside of it, we would carry on agitation for a new and more democratic assembly. If there were a revolutionary mass movement, we would simultaneously build soviets. It is very possible that in such a case the petty-bourgeois parties would convene a relatively more democratic national assembly, as a dam against the soviets. Would we participate in this kind of assembly? Of course we would participate; again, only if we were not strong enough to replace the assembly with a higher form of government, that is, soviets. Such a possibility, however, reveals itself only at the apex of revolutionary ascent. But at the present time we are far from there.

Even if there were soviets in China—which is not the case—this in itself would not be a reason to abandon the slogan of a national assembly. The majority in the soviets might be—and in the beginning would certainly be—in the hands of the conciliatory and centrist parties and organizations. We would be interested in exposing them in the open forum of the national assembly. In this way, the majority would be won over to our side more quickly and more certainly. When we succeeded in winning a majority, we would counterpose the program of the soviets to the program of the national assembly, we would rally the majority of the country around the banner of the soviets, and this would enable us, in deed and not on paper, to replace the national assembly, this parliamentary-democratic institution, with soviets, the organ of the revolutionary class dictatorship.

In Russia the Constituent Assembly lasted only one day. Why? Because it made its appearance too late; the Soviet power was already in existence and came into conflict with it. In this conflict, the Constituent Assembly represented the revolution's yesterday. But let us suppose that the bourgeois Provisional Government had been sufficiently decisive to convene the Constituent Assembly in March or April [1917]. Was that possible? Of course it was. The Cadets used every legal trick to drag out the convening of the Constituent Assembly in the hope that the revolutionary wave would subside. The Mensheviks and the Social Revolutionaries took their cue from the Cadets. If the Mensheviks and the Social Revolutionaries had had a little more revolutionary drive, they could have convened the Constituent Assembly in a few weeks. Would we Bolsheviks have participated in the elections and in the assembly itself? Undoubtedly, for it was *we who demanded all this time the speediest convening of the Constituent Assembly.* Would the course of the revolution have changed to the disadvantage of the proletariat by an early convening of the assembly? Not at all. Perhaps you remember that the representatives of the Russian propertied classes and, imitating them, also the conciliators, were for postponing all the important questions of the revolution "until the constituent assembly," meanwhile delaying its convening. This gave the landowners and capitalists a chance to mask to a certain degree their property interests in the agrarian question, industrial question, etc.

If the Constituent Assembly had been convened let us say in April 1917, then all the social questions would have confronted it. The propertied classes would have been compelled to show their cards; the treacherous role of the conciliators would have become apparent. The Bolshevik faction in the Constituent Assembly would have won the greatest popularity and this would have helped to elect a Bolshevik majority in the soviets. Under these circumstances the Constituent Assembly would have lasted not one day but possibly several months. This would have enriched the political experience of the working masses and, rather than retard the proletarian revolution, would have accelerated it. This in itself would have been of the greatest significance. If the second revolution had occurred in July or August instead of October, the army at the front would have been less exhausted and weakened and the peace with the Hohenzollerns might have been more favorable to us. Even if we assume that the proletarian revolution would not have come a single day sooner because of the Constituent Assembly, the school of revolutionary parliamentarism would have left its mark on the political level of the masses, making our tasks the day after the October revolution much easier.

Is this type of variant possible in China? It is not excluded. To imagine and expect that the Chinese Communist Party can jump from the present conditions of the rule of the unbridled bourgeois-military cliques, the oppression and dismemberment of the working class, and the extraordinarily low ebb of the peasant movement to the seizure of power is to believe in miracles. In practice this leads to adventurist guerrilla activity, which the Comintern is now covertly supporting. We must condemn this policy and guard the revolutionary workers from it.

The political mobilization of the proletariat in leadership of the peasant masses is the first task that must be solved under the present circumstances—the circumstances of the military-bourgeois counterrevolution. The power of the suppressed masses is in their numbers. When they awaken they will strive to express their strength of numbers politically by means of universal suffrage. The handful of communists already knows that universal suffrage is an instrument of bourgeois rule and that this rule can be liquidated only by means of the proletarian dictatorship. You can educate the proletarian vanguard in this spirit beforehand. But the millions of the toiling masses can be drawn to the dictatorship of the proletariat only on the basis of their own political experience, and the national assembly would be a progressive step on this road. This is why we raise this slogan in conjunction with four other slogans of the democratic revolution: the transfer of the land to the peasant poor, the eight-hour working day, the independence of China, and the right of self-determination of the nationalities included in the territory of China.

It is understood that we cannot rule out the perspective—it is theoretically admissible—that the Chinese proletariat, leading the peasant masses and basing itself on soviets, will come to power before the achievement of a national assembly in one or another form. But for the immediate period at any rate this is improbable, because it *presupposes the existence of a powerful and centralized revolutionary party of the proletariat.* In its absence, what other force will unite the revolutionary masses of your gigantic country? Meanwhile it is our misfortune that there is no strong centralized Communist Party in China; it has yet to be formed. The struggle for democracy is precisely the necessary condition for that. The slogan of the national assembly would bring together the scattered regional movements and uprisings, give them political unity, and create the basis for forging the Communist Party as the leader of the proletariat and all the toiling masses on a national scale.

That is why the slogan of the national assembly—on the basis of universal, direct, equal, secret ballot—must be raised as energetically as possible and a courageous, resolute struggle developed around it. Sooner or later the sterility of the purely negative position of the Comintern and the official leadership of the Chinese Communist Party will be mercilessly exposed. The more decisively the Communist Left Opposition initiates and develops its campaign for democratic slogans, the sooner this will happen. The inevitable collapse of the Comintern policy will greatly strengthen the Left Opposition and help it to become the decisive force in the Chinese proletariat.

From *Writings of Leon Trotsky (1930)*. Text from the *Militant* (New York), June 14, 1930.

TWO LETTERS TO CHINA

August 22 and September 1, 1930

August 22, 1930

Dear Comrade "N.,"[127]

2.[128] Today I finally received a copy of Comrade Ch'en Tu-hsiu's letter of December 10, 1929.[129] I feel that this letter is an extremely good document. Totally clear and correct attitudes are taken in answer to all the important questions; especially on the question of a democratic dictatorship, Comrade Tu-hsiu takes a completely correct stand. At the time you wrote to me explaining why you could not unite with Ch'en Tu-hsiu, your reason was that he still seemed to support the "democratic dictatorship" viewpoint. I feel this question to be a decisive one, because if you do not have a proletarian dictatorship leading the poor peasants, then it is the same as a democratic dictatorship, which in reality is only another name for a new Kuomintang policy, that's all! There can be no compromise on this question! But it is clear from the letter of December 10 that Comrade Ch'en's position is correct. Because of this, how can I explain and defend your position? What other differing opinions have you? None, I think, unless there are some unexpected difficulties. How can we get together on the question of a national assembly? What kind of role would the parliamentary system play in China? On fundamental questions we are in complete accord. As for the unexpected or more complicated questions, some are merely academic, while others are tactical questions. These questions will be decided as events unfold. Here, I must honestly tell you that your opinions on the national assembly and the parliamentary system cannot stand, in my view. It is true that *Wo-men-ti-hua* says that this is Kautskyism, but there is no basis for this.[130]

When we have such an outstanding revolutionary as Ch'en Tu-hsiu, who formally breaks with the party, is then thrown out of the party, and finally announces that his stand is 100 percent in accord with the International Opposition, how can we ignore him? Is it possible that you have many Communist Party members who are as experienced as Ch'en Tu-hsiu? He made many mistakes in the past, but he is already aware of them. To become aware of one's past mistakes is very valuable to revolutionists and leaders. We have many young people in the Opposition who can and should learn from Comrade Ch'en Tu-hsiu!

3. You attack the Wo-men-ti-hua group for incorrectly assessing the general political situation in China and denying the utility of slogans about striving for democracy. I have received a long letter from them, and it appears that the differences of principle about which you speak have all been eliminated. You wrote that they have revised the agenda of the conference. If this is so, they have revised it for the better and, moreover, are even closer to us. You attack them for their underhanded methods (such as bringing up old disputes and revising the agenda). Naturally, this problem carries its own meaning, but if they feel there are some mistakes, and everyone agrees to revise the agenda, that isn't such a terrible crime. Isn't it a fact that they are still doing all this revising in a Marxist spirit? The three other points that you raised (the most important being whether to work inside or outside the party) are really not questions of principle, for there has not been one Opposition section that has taken as its mission the creation of a second party. We must continue to look upon ourselves as factions within the party. Naturally, we must recruit new members into the Communist Party ranks, that is, into the Opposition. The correct mixture of work both inside and outside the party can only be attained through practical work. No matter what, our work outside the party must be of the following nature: comrades inside the party must look upon us as friends, not enemies. Let's look at the European experience. In that case, the Opposition in France and Germany has recently grown closer to the party, and yet there has been absolutely no lessening in the struggle between the party and the Opposition. This strategy has already obtained the very best results in France and is fast doing so in Germany.

4. *Biulleten Oppozitsii,* in its current issue, is giving great space to the China question.[131] It's too bad that, up to now, you

have not sent any materials regarding China's peasant (soviet) movement, in order that we might adopt a correct stand. It is very important that we collect all information and carefully research all facts; otherwise we just might kill our opportunity to affect the whole situation.

Isn't there still a chance that the peasant war will converge with the workers' movement? This is an extremely important question. Theoretically, it doesn't discard the possibility of making gains while underground. That is, under the influence of the peasant insurrection, the revolution in the cities can intensify and quickly move forward. If this comes about, then the peasant insurrection takes on a different objective meaning. Naturally, our fundamental mission is to improve upon the ordinary peasant insurrection and, at the same time, to fuse with it. In addition, we must explain to the workers the true nature of peasant insurrections and what might be obtained through them in the future. Furthermore, we must devise a means to raise the workers' spirits through these insurrections. At the same time, we must visibly support the insurrectionists in their demands and programs, while opposing the landlords, officials, and bourgeoisie in their rumors, slanders, and repression. It is upon this foundation, and only this foundation, that we can expose the tricks of the Comintern organizations. They say that "soviet regimes" have been established in China—without a proletarian dictatorship! It has even reached the point where the workers refuse to actively participate in the movement. I expect that the "International" [International Left Opposition] will soon issue a manifesto on this question to inform China's Communist Party members.

5. It seems to be a fine time for me to send you a copy of *The Permanent Revolution*.[132] You should receive it soon.

6. I am afraid that the address I have for Ch'en Tu-hsiu is no good. Please send him my regards, and tell him that I was very happy to read his letter of last December 10. I firmly hope we can work together in the future.

A warm handshake,
Trotsky

September 1, 1930

Dear Comrades,

I have already received your letter of July 27 (from the Shih-yueh she). I will only answer very simply, because the International Left Opposition is at this time planning to discuss the problems of China's present situation in a special manifesto. So I will merely repeat what has been written to the other groups.

1. It is the policy of the International Opposition not to side with any particular group of the Chinese Left Opposition against any other group. The reason being: nothing in any of our materials suggests the existence of serious differences requiring continued disunity.

2. In light of this, no single group of the Chinese Left Opposition can consider itself the sole representative of the International Left Opposition and attack any other group.

3. The same goes for Comrade Ch'en Tu-hsiu's group. Not long ago I received an English translation of Comrade Ch'en's open letter of December 10, 1929. Comrade Ch'en expressed views on fundamental issues which were in total agreement with our general stand. Realizing this, I fail to understand why some of our Chinese comrades still call Comrade Ch'en's group "rightist." At the same time, none of the other groups have furnished us with any documentary proof of this charge.

4. Because of this, we feel it is necessary that these four groups publicly unite in a sincere fashion, basing themselves on commonly held principles. Recently, the International Opposition has advised these groups on the basic points that should be incorporated in the party platform to be drafted by the platform committee, and on the methods of organizing for unification.

5. As for the question of the national assembly, I have already discussed that in previous articles. It seems that some of our Chinese comrades seek to "split hairs" with us over this question. If we struggle amongst ourselves over this question and its concomitant problems (personally, I don't think this will happen), then this dispute will certainly manifest itself throughout the drafting of a party platform. Only after we have received alternate analyses can the International Opposition gauge the depth of this dispute. However, we sincerely hope that the analyses we do receive are not written in a contentious way; rather, they should be written in such a way as to enable the Chinese Left Opposition to unify on a firm foundation of commonly held principles.

> Communist greetings,
> Trotsky

P.S: I am sending you two copies of this letter; forward one to Comrade Ch'en Tu-hsiu, as I do not know his address.

From *Writings of Leon Trotsky (1930)*. Text from *Wu-ch'an-che,* no. 4, October 30, 1930. Translated from the Chinese by Joseph T. Miller.

STALIN AND THE
CHINESE REVOLUTION

Facts and Documents

August 26, 1930

The Chinese revolution of 1925-27 remains the greatest event of modern history after the 1917 revolution in Russia. Over the problems of the Chinese revolution the basic currents of communism come to clash. The present official leader of the Comintern, Stalin, has revealed his true stature in the events of the Chinese revolution. The basic documents pertaining to the Chinese revolution are dispersed, scattered, forgotten. Some are carefully concealed.

On these pages we want to reproduce the basic stages of the Chinese revolution in the light of articles and speechs by Stalin and his closest assistants, as well as decisions of the Comintern dictated by Stalin. For this purpose we use genuine texts from our archives. We especially present excerpts from the speech of Chitarov, a young Stalinist, at the Fifteenth Congress of the Communist Party of the Soviet Union, which were concealed from the party by Stalin. The readers will convince themselves of the tremendous significance of the testimony of Chitarov, a young Stalinist functionary-careerist, a participant in the Chinese events, and at the present time one of the leaders of the Communist Youth International.

In order to make the facts and citations more comprehensible, we think it useful to remind the readers of the sequence of the most important events in the Chinese revolution.

March 20, 1926—Chiang Kai-shek's first overturn in Canton.

Autumn of 1926—the Seventh Plenum of the ECCI with the

participation of a Chiang Kai-shek delegate from the Kuomintang.

April 12, 1927—coup d'etat by Chiang Kai-shek in Shanghai.

The end of May 1927—the counterrevolutionary overturn of the "left" Kuomintang in Wuhan.[133]

The end of May 1927—the Eighth Plenum of the ECCI proclaims it the duty of communists to remain within the "left" Kuomintang.

August 1927—the Chinese Communist Party proclaims a course toward an uprising.

December 1927—the Canton insurrection.

February 1928—the Ninth Plenum of the ECCI proclaims for China the course toward armed insurrection and soviets.

July 1928—the Sixth Congress of the Comintern renounces the slogan of armed insurrection as a practical slogan.

1. The Bloc of Four Classes

Stalin's Chinese policy was based on a bloc of four classes. Here is how the Berlin organ of the Mensheviks appraised this policy:

> On April 10 [1927], Martynov, in *Pravda,* most effectively and . . . in a quite "Menshevik manner," showed . . . the correctness of the *official* position which insists on the necessity of retaining the "bloc of four classes," on not hastening to overthrow the coalition government in which the workers sit side by side with the big bourgeoisie, not to impose "socialist tasks" upon it prematurely. [*Sotsialistichesky Vestnik,* no. 8, April 23, 1927, p. 4.]

What did the policy of coalition with the bourgeoisie look like? Let us quote an excerpt from the official organ of the Executive Committee of the Comintern:

> On January 5, 1927, the Canton government made public a new strike law in which the workers are prohibited from carrying weapons at demonstrations, from arresting merchants and industrialists, from confiscating their goods, and which establishes compulsory arbitration for a series of conflicts. This law contains a number of paragraphs protecting the interests of the workers. . . . But along with these paragraphs there are others, which limit the freedom to strike more than is required by the interests of defense during a revolutionary war. [*Die Kommunistische Internationale,* March 1, 1927, no. 9, p. 408.]

In the rope placed around the workers by the bourgeoisie the threads ("paragraphs") favorable to the workers are traced. The shortcoming of the noose is that it is tightened more than is required "by the interests of defense" (of the Chinese bourgeoisie). This is written in the central organ of the Comintern. Who does the writing? Martynov. When does he write? On February 25, six weeks before the Shanghai bloodbath.

2. The Perspectives of the Revolution According to Stalin

How did Stalin evaluate the perspectives of the revolution led by his ally, Chiang Kai-shek? Here are the least scandalous parts of Stalin's declaration (the most scandalous parts of it were never made public):

> The revolutionary armies in China [that is, the armies of Chiang Kai-shek] are the most important factor in the struggle of the Chinese workers and peasants for their liberation. For the advancement of the Cantonese means a blow at imperialism, a blow at its agents in China, and freedom of assembly, freedom of press, freedom of organization for all the revolutionary elements in China in general and for the workers in particular. [*On the Perspectives of the Chinese Revolution*, p. 46.]

The army of Chiang Kai-shek is the army of workers and peasants. It bears freedom for the whole population, "for the workers in particular."

What is needed for the success of the revolution? Very little:

> The student youth (revolutionary youth), the working youth, the peasant youth—all these are a force that can advance the revolution with seven-league boots, if it is subordinated to the ideological and political influence of the Kuomintang. [Ibid., p. 55.]

In this manner, the task of the Comintern consisted not of liberating the workers and peasants from the influence of the bourgeoisie, but on the contrary, of subordinating them to its influence. This was written in the days when Chiang Kai-shek, armed by Stalin, marched at the head of the workers and peasants subordinated to him, "with seven-league boots," toward . . . the Shanghai coup.

3. Stalin and Chiang Kai-shek

After the Canton coup, engineered by Chiang Kai-shek in March 1926, and which our press passed over in silence, when the communists were reduced to miserable appendages of the Kuomintang and even signed an obligation not to criticize Sun Yat-senism, Chiang Kai-shek—a remarkable detail indeed!—came forward to insist on the acceptance of the Kuomintang into the Comintern: in preparing himself for the role of an executioner, he wanted to have the cover of world communism and—he got it. The Kuomintang, led by Chiang Kai-shek and Hu Han-min, was accepted into the Comintern (as a "sympathizing" party). While engaged in the preparation of a decisive counterrevolutionary action in April 1927, Chiang Kai-shek at the same time took care to exchange portraits with Stalin. This strengthening of the ties of friendship was prepared by the journey of Bubnov, a member of the Central Committee and one of Stalin's agents, to Chiang Kai-shek. Another "detail": Bubnov's journey to Canton coincided with Chiang Kai-shek's March coup. What about Bubnov? He made the Chinese communists submit and keep quiet.

After the Shanghai overturn, the bureaus of the Comintern, upon Stalin's order, attempted to deny that the executioner Chiang Kai-shek still remained a member of the Comintern. They had forgotten the vote at the Political Bureau, when everybody against the vote of one (Trotsky), sanctioned the admission of the Kuomintang into the Comintern with a consultative voice. They had forgotten that at the Seventh Plenum of the ECCI, which condemned the Left Opposition, "Comrade Shao Li-tzu," a delegate from the Kuomintang, participated. Among other things he said:

Comrade Chiang Kai-shek in his speech to the members of the Kuomintang, declared that the Chinese revolution would be inconceivable if it could not correctly solve the agrarian, that is, the peasant question. What the Kuomintang strives for is that there should not be created a bourgeois domination after the nationalist revolution in China, as happened in the West, as we see it now in all the countries, except the USSR. . . . We are all convinced, that under the leadership of the Communist Party and the Comintern, the Kuomintang will fulfill its historic task. [*Minutes of the Enlarged Executive of the Communist International* (German edition), November 30, 1926, pp. 303-04.]

This is how matters stood at the Seventh Plenum in the autumn of 1926. After the member of the Comintern, "Comrade Chiang Kai-shek," who had promised to solve all the tasks under the leadership of the Comintern, solved only one: precisely the task of a bloody crushing of the revolution, the Eighth Plenum in May 1927 declared in the resolution on the Chinese question:

"The ECCI states that the events fully justified the prognosis of the Seventh Plenum."

Justified, and right to the very end! If this is humor, it is at any rate not arbitrary However, let us not forget that this humor is thickly colored with Shanghai blood.

4. The Strategy of Lenin and the Strategy of Stalin

What tasks did Lenin set before the Comintern with regard to the backward countries?

the need for a determined struggle against attempts to give a communist colouring to bourgeois-democratic liberation trends in the backward countries. . . . ["Draft Theses on the National and Colonial Questions," June 5, 1920, *Collected Works*, vol. 31, p. 149.]

In carrying this out, the Kuomintang, which had promised to establish in China "not a bourgeois regime," was admitted into the Comintern.

Lenin, it is understood, recognized the necessity of a temporary alliance with the bourgeois-democratic movement, but he understood by this, of course, not an alliance with the bourgeois parties, duping and betraying the petty-bourgeois revolutionary democracy (the peasants and the small city folk), but an alliance with the organizations and groupings of the masses themselves— against the national bourgeoisie. In what form, then, did Lenin visualize the alliance with the bourgeois democracy of the colonies? To these, too, he gives an answer in his thesis written for the Second Congress:

The Communist International must enter into a temporary alliance with bourgeois democracy in the colonial and backward countries, but should not merge with it, and should under all circumstances uphold the independence of the proletarian movement even if it is in its most embryonic form. [Ibid., p. 150.]

It seems that in executing the decision of the Second Congress, the Communist Party was made to join the Kuomintang and the Kuomintang was admitted into the Comintern. All this summed up is called Leninism.

5. The Government of Chiang Kai-shek as a Living Refutation of the State

How the leaders of the Communist Party of the Soviet Union appraised the government of Chiang Kai-shek one year after the first Canton coup (March 20, 1926) may be seen clearly from the public speeches of the members of the party Political Bureau.

Here is how Kalinin spoke in March 1927, at the Moscow factory Gosznak:

> All the classes of China, beginning with the proletariat and ending with the bourgeoisie, hate the militarists as the puppets of foreign capital; all the classes of China look upon the Canton government as the national government of the whole of China in the same way. [*Izvestia*, March 6, 1927.]

Another member of the Political Bureau, Rudzutak, spoke a few days later at a gathering of the streetcar workers. The *Pravda* report states:

> Pausing further on the situation in China, Comrade Rudzutak pointed out that the revolutionary government has behind it all the classes of China. [*Pravda*, March 9, 1927.]

Voroshilov spoke in the same spirit more than once.

Truly in vain did Lenin clear the Marxist theory of the state of petty-bourgeois garbage. The epigones succeeded in a short time in covering it with twice as much refuse.

As late as April 5, Stalin spoke in the Hall of the Columns in defense of the communists' remaining inside the party of Chiang Kai-shek, and what is more, he denied the danger of a betrayal by his ally: "Borodin is on guard!" The overturn occurred exactly one week later.

6. How the Shanghai Overturn Took Place

In this connection we have the exceptionally valuable testimony of a witness and participant, the Stalinist Chitarov, who arrived from China on the eve of the Fifteenth Congress and appeared there with his information. The most important points of his narrative have been deleted by Stalin from the minutes with the consent of Chitarov himself; the truth cannot be made public if it so crushingly proves all the accusations the Opposition directed against Stalin. Let us give the floor to Chitarov (Sixteenth Session of the Fifteenth Congress of the AUCP, December 11, 1927):

> The first bloody wound was inflicted upon the Chinese revolution in Shanghai by the execution of the Shanghai workers on April 11-12.
> I would like to speak in greater detail about this overturn because I know that in our party little is known about it. In Shanghai there existed for a period of twenty-one days the so-called People's Government in which the communists had a majority. We can therefore say that for twenty-one days Shanghai had a communist government. This communist government, however, revealed a complete inactivity in spite of the fact that the overturn by Chiang Kai-shek was expected any day.
> The communist government, in the first place, did not begin to work for a long time under the excuse that, on the one hand, the bourgeois part of the government did not want to get to work, sabotaging it, and, on the other hand, because the Wuhan government did not approve of the composition of the Shanghai government. Of the activity of this government three decrees are known, and one of them, by the way, speaks of the preparation of a triumphal reception to Chiang Kai-shek who was expected to arrive in Shanghai.
> In Shanghai, at this time, the relations between the army and the workers became acute. It is known, for instance, that the army [that is, Chiang Kai-shek's officers—L.T.] deliberately drove the workers into slaughter. The army for a period of several days stood at the gates of Shanghai and did not want to enter the city because they knew that the workers were battling against the Shantungese, and they wanted the workers to bleed in this struggle. They expected to enter later. Afterward the army did enter Shanghai. But among these troops there was one division that sympathized with the workers—the First Division of the Canton army. The commander, Hsueh Yueh, was in disfavor with Chiang Kai-shek, who knew about his sympathies for the mass movement, because this Hsueh Yueh himself came from the ranks. He was at first the commander of a company and later commanded a division.
> Hsueh Yueh came to the comrades in Shanghai and told them that there was a military overthrow in preparation, that Chiang Kai-shek had summoned him to headquarters, had given him an unusually cold reception and that he, Hsueh Yueh, would not go there any

longer because he fears a trap. Chiang Kai-shek proposed to Hsueh
Yueh to get out of the city with his division and to go to the front; and
he, Hsueh Yueh, proposed to the Central Committee of the Communist Party to agree that he should not submit to Chiang Kai-shek's
order. He was ready to remain in Shanghai and fight together with
the Shanghai workers against the military overthrow that was in
preparation. To all this, our responsible leaders of the Chinese
Communist Party, Ch'en Tu-hsiu included, declared that they know
about the overturn being prepared, but that they do not want a
premature conflict with Chiang Kai-shek. The First Division was let
out of Shanghai, the city was occupied by the Second Division of Pai
Ch'ung-hsi and, two days later, the Shanghai workers were massacred.

Why was this truly stirring narrative left out of the minutes (p.
32)? Because it was not at all a question of the Chinese
Communist Party but of the Political Bureau of the Communist
Party of the Soviet Union.

On May 24, 1927, Stalin spoke at the plenum of the ECCI:

> The Opposition is dissatisfied because the Shanghai workers did
> not enter into a decisive battle against the imperialists and their
> myrmidons. But it does not understand that the revolution in China
> cannot develop at a fast tempo. It does not understand that one
> cannot take up a decisive struggle under unfavorable conditions. The
> Opposition does not understand that not to avoid a decisive struggle
> under unfavorable conditions (when it can be avoided), means to
> make easier the work of the enemies of the revolution. . . .

This section of Stalin's speech is entitled: "The Mistakes of the
Opposition." In the Shanghai tragedy Stalin found mistakes . . .
of the Opposition. In reality the Opposition at that time did not
yet know the concrete circumstances of the situation in Shanghai, that is, it did not know how much more favorable the
situation still was for the workers in March and the beginning of
April in spite of all the mistakes and crimes of the leadership of
the Comintern. Even from the deliberately concealed story of
Chitarov it is clear that the situation could have been saved even
at that time. The workers in Shanghai are in power. They are
partly armed. There is all the possibility of arming them far more
extensively. Chiang Kai-shek's army is unreliable. There are
sections of it where even the commanding staff is on the side of
the workers. But everything and everyone is paralyzed at the top.
We must not prepare for the decisive struggle against Chiang
Kai-shek, but for a triumphal reception to him. Because Stalin

gave his categorical instructions from Moscow: not only do not resist the ally, Chiang Kai-shek, but on the contrary, show your loyalty to him. How? Lie down on your back and play dead.

At the May plenum of the ECCI, Stalin still defended on technical, tactical grounds this terrible surrender of positions without a struggle, which led to the crushing of the proletariat in the revolution. Half a year later, at the Fifteenth Congress of the AUCP, Stalin was already silent. The delegates at the congress extended Chitarov's time so as to give him a chance to end his narrative which gripped even them. But Stalin found a very simple way out of it by deleting Chitarov's narrative from the minutes. We publish this truly historic document here for the first time.

Let us note in addition one interesting circumstance: While smearing up the course of events as much as possible and concealing the really guilty one, Chitarov singles out for responsibility Ch'en Tu-hsiu whom the Stalinists had until then defended in every way against the Opposition, because he had merely carried out their instructions. But at that time it was already becoming clear that Comrade Ch'en Tu-hsiu would not agree to play the role of a silent scapegoat, that he wanted openly to analyze the reasons for this catastrophe. All the hounds of the Comintern were let loose upon him, not for mistakes fatal to the revolution, but because he would not agree to deceive the workers and to be a cover for Stalin.

7. The Organizers of the "Infusion of Workers' and Peasants' Blood"

The leading organ of the Comintern wrote on March 18, 1927, about three weeks prior to the Shanghai overturn:

> The leadership of the Kuomintang is at present ill with a lack of revolutionary workers' and peasants' blood. The Chinese Communist Party must aid in the infusion of this blood, and then the situation will radically change.

What an ominous play on words! The Kuomintang is in need of "workers' and peasants' blood." The "aid" was rendered in the fullest measure: in April-May, Chiang Kai-shek and Wang Ching-wei received a sufficient "infusion" of workers' and peasants' blood.

With regard to the Chiang Kai-shek chapter of Stalin's policy, the Eighth Plenum (May 1927) declared:

> The ECCI assumes that the tactic of the bloc with the national bourgeoisie in the already declining period of the revolution was absolutely correct. The Northern Expedition alone [!] serves as historic justification for this tactic. . . .

And how it serves!

Here is Stalin all the way through. The Northern Expedition, which incidentally proved to be an expedition against the proletariat, serves as a justification of his friendship with Chiang Kai-shek. The ECCI has done everything it could to make it impossible to draw the lessons of the bloodbath of the Chinese workers.

8. Stalin Repeats His Experiment with the "Left" Kuomintang

Further on, the following remarkable point is left out of Chitarov's speech:

> After the Shanghai coup, it has become clear to everyone that a new epoch is beginning in the Chinese revolution; that the bourgeoisie is retreating from the revolution. This was recognized and immediately so stated. But one thing was left out of sight in connection with this—that while the bourgeoisie was retreating from the revolution, the Wuhan government did not even think of leaving the bourgeoisie. Unfortunately, among the majority of our comrades, this was not understood; they had illusions with regard to the Wuhan government. They considered the Wuhan government almost an image, a prototype of the democratic dictatorship of the proletariat and peasantry. [The omission is on page 33.]
>
> After the Wuhan overturn, it became clear that the bourgeoisie is retreating. . . .

This would be ridiculous if it were not so tragic. After Chiang Kai-shek slew the revolution, confronting the workers disarmed by Stalin, the penetrating strategists finally "understood" that the bourgeoisie was "retreating." But having recognized that his friend Chiang Kai-shek was retreating, Stalin ordered the Chinese communists to subordinate themselves to that same Wuhan government which, according to Chitarov's information at the Fifteenth Congress, "did not even think of leaving the bourgeoisie." Unfortunately "our comrades did not understand this." What comrades? Borodin, who clung to Stalin's telegraph wires? Chitarov does not mention any names. The Chinese revolution is dear to him, but his hide—is still dearer.

However, let us listen to Stalin:

> Chiang Kai-shek's coup means that there will now be two camps, two governments, two armies, two centers in the South: a revolutionary center in Wuhan and a counterrevolutionary center in Nanking.

Is it clear where the center of the revolution is located? In Wuhan!

> This means that the revolutionary Kuomintang in Wuhan, leading a decisive struggle against militarism and imperialism, will in reality be transformed into an organ of the revolutionary democratic dictatorship of the proletariat and peasantry. . . .

Now we finally know what the democratic dictatorship of the proletariat and peasantry looks like!

> From this it follows further [Stalin continues] that the policy of close collaboration of the lefts and the communists inside the Kuomintang acquires a particular force and a particular significance at the present stage . . . that without such a collaboration the victory of the revolution is impossible. [*Questions of the Chinese Revolution,* pp. 125-27.]

Without the collaboration of the counterrevolutionary bandits of the "left" Kuomintang, "the victory of the revolution is impossible"! That is how Stalin, step after step—in Canton, in Shanghai, in Hankow—assured the victory of the revolution.

9. Against the Opposition—For the Kuomintang!

How did the Comintern regard the "left" Kuomintang? The Eighth Plenum of the ECCI gave a clear answer to this question in its struggle against the Opposition.

> The ECCI rejects most determinedly the demand to leave the Kuomintang. . . . The Kuomintang in China is precisely that specific form of organization where the proletariat collaborates directly with the petty bourgeoisie and the peasantry.

In this manner the ECCI quite correctly saw in the Kuomintang the realization of the Stalinist idea of the "two-class workers' and peasants' party."

The not unknown Rafes, who was at first a minister under Petlyura and afterward carried out Stalin's instructions in China, wrote in May 1927 in the theoretical organ of the Central Committee of the AUCP:

> Our Russian Opposition, as is known, also considers it necessary for the communists to leave the Kuomintang. A consistent defense of this viewpoint would lead the adherents of the policy to leave the Kuomintang to the famous formula proclaimed by Comrade Trotsky in 1917: "No tsar, but a workers' government!,"[134] which, for China, might have been changed in form: "Without the militarists, but a workers' government!" We have no reason to listen to such consistent defenders of leaving the Kuomintang. [*Proletarskaya Revolutsya*, p. 54.]

The slogan of Stalin-Rafes was: "Without the workers, but with Chiang Kai-shek!" "Without the peasants, but with Wang Ching-wei!" "Against the Opposition, but for the Kuomintang!"

10. Stalin Again Disarms the Chinese Workers and Peasants

What was the policy of the leadership during the Wuhan period of the revolution? Let us listen to the Stalinist Chitarov on this question. Here is what we read in the minutes of the Fifteenth Congress:

> What was the policy of the CC of the Communist Party at this time, during this whole [Wuhan] period? The policy of the CC of the Communist Party was carried on under the slogan of *retreat*. . . .
> Under the slogan of retreat—in the revolutionary period, at the moment of the highest tension of the revolutionary struggles—the Communist Party carries on its work and under this slogan surrenders one position after another without a battle. To this surrender of positions belongs: the agreement to subordinate all the trade unions, all the peasant unions, and other revolutionary organizations to the Kuomintang; the rejection of independent action without the permission of the Central Committee of the Kuomintang; the decision on the voluntary disarming of the workers' pickets in Hankow; the dissolution of the pioneer organizations in Wuhan; the actual crushing of all the peasant unions in the territory of the national government, etc.

Here is pictured quite frankly the policy of the Chinese Communist Party, the leadership of which actually helps the "national" bourgeoisie to crush the people's uprising and to annihilate the best fighters of the proletariat and the peasantry.

But the frankness here is treacherous: the above citation is printed in the minutes after the omission cited above by the elipse. Here is what the section concealed by Stalin says:

> At the same time, some responsible comrades, Chinese and *non-Chinese,* invented the so-called theory of retreat. They declared: The reaction is advancing upon us from all sides. We must therefore immediately retreat in order to save the possibility of legal work, and if we retreat, we will save this possibility, but if we defend ourselves or attempt to advance, we will lose everything.

Precisely in those days (end of May 1927), when the Wuhan counterrevolution began to crush the workers and peasants, in the face of the left Kuomintang, Stalin declares at the plenum of the ECCI (May 24, 1927):

> The agrarian revolution is the basis and content of the bourgeois-democratic revolution in China. *The Kuomintang in Hankow and the Hankow government are the center of the bourgeois-democratic revolutionary movement.* [*Minutes* (German edition), p. 71, emphasis added.]

To a written question of a worker as to why no soviets are being formed in Wuhan, Stalin replied:

> It is clear that whoever calls at present for the immediate creation of soviets of workers' deputies in this [Wuhan] district is attempting to jump [!] over the *Kuomintang phase of the Chinese revolution,* and he risks putting the Chinese revolution in a most difficult position. [Emphasis added.]

Precisely: In a "most difficult" position! On May 13, 1927, in a conversation with students, Stalin declared:

> Should soviets of workers' and peasants' deputies, in general, be created in China? Yes, they should, absolutely they should. They will have to be created *after the strengthening of the Wuhan revolutionary government,* after the unfolding of the agrarian revolution, in the transformation of the agrarian revolution, of the bourgeois-democratic revolution into the revolution of the proletariat. [Emphasis added.]

In this manner, Stalin did not consider it permissible to strengthen the position of the workers and peasants through soviets, so long as the positions of the Wuhan government, of the counterrevolutionary bourgeoisie, were not strengthened.

Referring to the famous theses of Stalin which justified his Wuhan policy, the organ of the Russian Mensheviks wrote at that time:

> Very little can be said against the essence of the "line" traced there [in Stalin's theses]. As much as possible to remain in the Kuomintang, and to cling to its left wing and to the Wuhan government to the last possible moment; "to avoid a decisive struggle under unfavorable conditions"; not to issue the slogan "All power to the soviets" so as not "to give new weapons into the hands of the enemies of the Chinese people for the struggle against the revolution, for creating new legends that it is not a national revolution that is taking place in China, but an artificial transplanting of Moscow sovietization"—what can actually be more sensible. . . ? [*Sotsialisti-chesky Vestnik,* no. 9 (151), p. 1.]

On its part, the Eighth Plenum of the ECCI which was in session at the end of May 1927, that is, at a time when the crushing of the workers' and peasants' organizations in Wuhan had already begun, adopted the following decision:

> The ECCI insistently calls the attention of the Chinese Communist Party to the necessity of taking all possible measures for the strengthening and development of all mass organizations of workers and peasants . . . within all these organizations it is necessary to carry on an agitation *to enter the Kuomintang,* transforming the latter into a mighty mass organization of the revolutionary petty-bourgeois democracy and the working class.

"To enter the Kuomintang" meant to bring one's head voluntarily to the slaughter. The bloody lesson of Shanghai passed without leaving a trace. The communists, as before, were being transformed into cattle herders for the party of the bourgeois executioners (the Kuomintang)—into suppliers of "workers' and peasants' blood" for Wang Ching-wei and Company.

11. The Stalinist Experiment with Ministerialism

In spite of the experience of the Russian Kerenskiad and the protest of the Left Opposition, Stalin wound up his Kuomintang policy with an experiment in ministerialism: two communists entered the bourgeois government in the capacity of ministers of labor and agriculture—the classic posts of hostages!—under the direct instructions of the Comintern to paralyze the class struggle with the aim of retaining the united front. Such directives were constantly given from Moscow by telegraph until August 1927.

Let us hear how Chitarov depicted communist "ministerialism" in practice before the audience of delegates at the Fifteenth Congress of the AUCP: "You know that there were two communist ministers in the government," says Chitarov. The rest of this passage is deleted from the minutes:

> Afterwards, they [the communist ministers] stopped coming around to the ministries altogether, failed to appear themselves, and put in their places a hundred functionaries. During the activity of these ministers not a single law was promulgated which would ease the position of the workers and peasants. This reprehensible activity was wound up with a still more reprehensible, shameful end. The ministers declared that one of them was ill and the other wished to go abroad, etc., and therefore asked to be released. They did not resign with a political declaration in which they would have declared: You are counterrevolutionists, you are traitors, you are betrayers—we will no longer go along with you. No. They declared that one was allegedly ill. In addition, *T'an P'ing-shan* wrote that *he could not cope with the magnitude of the peasant movement,* therefore he asked that his release be granted. Can a greater disgrace be imagined? A communist minister declares that he cannot cope with the peasant movement. Then who can? It is clear, the military, and nobody else. This was an open legalization of the rigorous suppression of the peasant movement, undertaken by the Wuhan government.

This is what the participation of the communists in the "democratic dictatorship" of the workers and peasants looked like. In December 1927, when Stalin's speeches and articles were still fresh in the minds of all, Chitarov's narrative could not be printed, even though the latter—young but precocious!—in looking after his own welfare, did not say a word about the Moscow leaders of Chinese ministerialism and even referred to Borodin only as "a certain non-Chinese comrade."

T'an P'ing-shan complained—Chitarov raged hypocritically—that he could not cope with the peasant movement. But Chitarov could not help knowing that this was just the task that Stalin set before T'an P'ing-shan. T'an P'ing-shan came to Moscow at the end of 1926 for instructions and reported to the plenum of the

ECCI how well he coped with the "Trotskyists," that is, with those communists who wanted to leave the Kuomintang in order to organize the workers and peasants. Stalin was sending T'an P'ing-shan telegraphic instructions to curb the peasant movement in order not to antagonize Chiang Kai-shek and the bourgeois military staff. At the same time, Stalin accused the Opposition of . . . underestimating the peasantry.

The Eighth Plenum even adopted a special "Resolution on the Speeches of Comrades Trotsky and Vujovic at the Plenary Session of the ECCI." It read:

> Comrade Trotsky . . . demanded at the plenary session the immediate establishment of dual power in the form of soviets and the immediate adoption of a course toward the overthrow of the left Kuomintang government. This apparently [!] ultraleft [!!] but in reality opportunist [!!!] demand is nothing but the repetition of the old Trotskyist position of jumping over the petty-bourgeois, peasant stage of the revolution.

We see here in all its nakedness the essence of the struggle against Trotskyism: the defense of the bourgeoisie against the revolution of the workers and peasants.

12. Leaders and Masses

All the organizations of the working class were utilized by the "leaders" in order to restrain, to curb, to paralyze the struggle of the revolutionary masses. Here is what Chitarov related:

> The congress of the trade unions [in Wuhan] was postponed from day to day and when it was finally convened no attempt whatsoever was made to utilize it for the organization of resistance. On the contrary, on the last day of the congress, it was decided to stage a demonstration before the building of the national government with the object of expressing their sentiment of loyalty to the government.
>
> (*Lozovsky:* I scared them there with my speech.)

Lozovsky was not ashamed at that moment to put himself forward. "Scaring" the same Chinese trade unionists whom he had thrown into confusion, with bold phrases, Lozovsky succeeded on the spot, in China, in not seeing anything, not understanding anything, and not foreseeing anything. Returning from China, this "leader" wrote: "The proletariat has become the dominant force in the struggle for the national emancipation of China" (*Workers' China*, p. 6).

This was said about a proletariat whose head was being squeezed in the iron manacles of Chiang Kai-shek. This is how the general secretary of the Red International of Labor Unions deceived the workers of the whole world. And after the crushing of the Chinese workers (with the aid of all sorts of "general secretaries"), Lozovsky derides the Chinese trade unionists: Those "cowards" got scared, you see, by the intrepid speeches of the most intrepid Lozovsky. In this little episode lies the art of the present "leaders," their whole mechanism, the whole of their morals!

The might of the revolutionary movement of the masses of the people was truly incomparable. We have seen that in spite of three years of mistakes the situation could still have been saved in Shanghai by receiving Chiang Kai-shek not as a liberator but as a mortal foe. Moreover, even after the Shanghai coup the communists could still have strengthened themselves in the provinces. But they were ordered to submit themselves to the "left" Kuomintang. Chitarov gives a description of one of the most illuminating episodes of the second counterrevolution carried out by the left Kuomintang:

> The overturn in Wuhan occurred on May 21-22. . . . The overturn took place under simply unbelievable circumstances. In Changsha the army consisted of 1,700 soldiers, and the peasants made up a majority of the armed detachments gathered around Changsha to the number of 20,000. In spite of this, the military command succeeded in seizing power, in shooting all the active peasants, in dispersing all revolutionary organizations, and in establishing its dictatorship only because of the cowardly, irresolute, conciliatory policy of the leaders in Changsha and Wuhan. When the peasants learned of the overturn in Changsha they began to prepare themselves, to gather around Changsha in order to undertake a march on it. The march was set for May 21. The peasants started to draw up their detachments in increasing numbers toward Changsha. It was clear that they would seize the city without great effort. But at this point *a letter arrived from the Central Committee of the Chinese Communist Party in which Ch'en Tu-hsiu wrote that they should presumably avoid an open conflict and transfer the question to Wuhan.* On the basis of this letter, the District Committee dispatched to the peasant detachments an order to retreat, not to advance any further; but this order failed to reach two detachments. Two peasant detachments advanced on Wuhan and were there annihilated by the soldiers. [*Minutes,* p. 34, emphasis added.]

This is approximately how matters proceeded in the rest of the

provinces. Under Borodin's guidance—"Borodin is on guard!"—
the Chinese communists carried out very punctiliously the
instructions of Stalin not to break with the left Kuomintang, the
chosen leaders of the democratic revolution. The capitulation at
Changsha took place on May 31, that is, a few days after the
decisions of the Eighth Plenum of the ECCI and in full
conformity with these decisions.

The leaders indeed did everything in order to destroy the cause
of the masses!

In that same speech of his, Chitarov declares:

> I consider it my duty to declare that in spite of the fact that the
> Chinese Communist Party has for a long time committed unheard-of
> opportunist errors . . . we do not, however, need to blame the party
> masses for them. . . . In my deep conviction (I have seen many
> sections of the Comintern), there isn't another such section so devoted
> to the cause of communism, so courageous in its fight for our cause as
> are the Chinese communists. There are no other communists as
> courageous as the Chinese comrades. [*Minutes,* p. 36.]

Undoubtedly, the revolutionary Chinese workers and peasants
revealed exceptional self-sacrifice in the struggle. Together with
the revolution, they were crushed by the opportunist leadership.
Not the one that had its seat in Canton, Shanghai, and Wuhan
but the one that was commanding from Moscow. Such will be the
verdict of history!

13. The Canton Uprising

On August 7, 1927, the special conference of the Chinese
Communist Party condemned, according to previous instructions
from Moscow, the opportunist policy of its leadership, that is, its
whole past, and decided to prepare for an armed insurrection.
Stalin's special emissaries had the task of preparing an
insurrection in Canton timed for the Fifteenth Congress of the
Communist Party of the Soviet Union, in order to cover up the
physical extermination of the Russian Opposition with the
political triumph of the Stalinist tactic in China.

On the declining wave, while the depression still prevailed
among the urban masses, the Canton "Soviet" uprising was
hurriedly organized, heroic in the conduct of the workers,
criminal in the adventurism of the leadership. The news of the
new crushing of the Canton proletariat arrived exactly at the
moment of the Fifteenth Congress. In this manner, Stalin was

smashing the Bolshevik-Leninists exactly at the moment when his ally of yesterday, Chiang Kai-shek, was crushing the Chinese communists.

It was necessary to draw up new balance sheets, that is, once more to shift the responsibility on to the executors. On February 7, 1928, *Pravda* wrote: "The provincial armies fought undividedly against Red Canton and this proved to be the greatest and *oldest shortcoming of the Chinese Communist Party, precisely insufficient political work for the decomposition of the reactionary armies*" (emphasis added).

"The oldest shortcoming"! Does this mean that it was the task of the Chinese Communist Party to decompose the armies of the Kuomintang? Since when?

On February 25, 1927, a month and a half prior to the crushing of Shanghai, the central organ of the Comintern wrote:

> The Chinese Communist Party and the conscious Chinese workers must not *under any circumstances* pursue a tactic that would disorganize the revolutionary armies just because the influence of the bourgeoisie is to a certain degree strong there . . . [*Die Kommunistische Internationale,* February 25, 1927, p. 19.]

And here is what Stalin said—and repeated on every occasion—at the plenum of the ECCI on May 24, 1927:

> Not unarmed people stand against the armies of the old regime in China, but an armed people in the form of the Revolutionary Army. In China, an armed revolution is fighting against armed counterrevolution.

In the summer and autumn of 1927, the armies of the Kuomintang were depicted as an armed people. But when these armies crushed the Canton insurrection, *Pravda* declared the "oldest [!] shortcoming" of the Chinese communists to be their inability to decompose the "reactionary armies," the very ones that were proclaimed "the revolutionary people" only on the eve of Canton.

Shameless mountebanks! Was anything like it ever seen among real revolutionists?

14. The Period of Putschism

The Ninth Plenum of the ECCI met in February 1928, less than two months after the Canton insurrection. How did it estimate the situation? Here are the exact words of its resolution:

> The ECCI makes it the duty of all its sections to fight against the slanders of the Social Democrats and the Trotskyists who assert that the Chinese revolution has been liquidated.

What a treacherous and at the same time miserable subterfuge! The Social Democracy considers in reality that the victory of Chiang Kai-shek is the *victory* of the national revolution (the confused Urbahns went astray on this very same position). The Left Opposition considers that the victory of Chiang Kai-shek is the *defeat* of the national revolution.

The Opposition never said and never could have said that the Chinese revolution *in general* is liquidated. What was liquidated, confused, deceived, and crushed was "only" the *second* Chinese revolution (1925-27). That alone would be enough of an accomplishment for the gentlemen of the leadership!

We maintained, beginning with the autumn of 1927, that a period of ebb is ahead in China, the retreat of the proletariat, the triumph of the counterrevolution. What was Stalin's position? On February 7, 1928, *Pravda* wrote:

> The Chinese Communist Party is heading toward an armed insurrection. The whole situation in China speaks for the fact that this is the correct course. . . . Experience proves that the Chinese Communist Party must concentrate all its efforts on the task of the day-to-day and widespread careful preparation of the armed insurrection.

The Ninth Plenum of the ECCI, with ambiguous bureaucratic reservations on putschism, approved this adventurist line. The object of these reservations is known: to create holes for the "leader" to crawl into in the event of a new retreat.

The criminally light-minded resolution of the Ninth Plenum meant for China: new adventures, new skirmishes, breaking away from the masses, the loss of positions, the consuming of the best revolutionary elements in the fire of adventurism, the demoralization of the remnants of the party. The whole period between the conference of the Chinese party on August 7, 1927, and the Sixth Congress of the Comintern on July 8, 1928, is permeated through and through with the theory and practice of putschism. This is how the Stalinist leadership was dealing the final blows to the Chinese revolution and the Communist Party.

Only at the Sixth Congress did the leadership of the Comintern recognize that:

"The Canton uprising was objectively already a 'rearguard battle' of the receding revolution" (*Pravda,* July 27, 1928).

"Objectively"! And subjectively? That is, in the consciousness of its initiators, the leaders? Such is the masked recognition of the adventurist character of the Canton insurrection. However that may be, one year after the Opposition, and what is more important, after a series of cruel defeats, the Comintern recognized that the second Chinese revolution had terminated together with the Wuhan period, and that it cannot be revived through adventurism. At the Sixth Congress, the Chinese delegate, Chan Fu Yun reported:[135]

> The defeat of the Canton insurrection has delivered a still heavier blow to the Chinese proletariat. The first stage of the revolution was in this manner ended with a series of defeats. In the industrial centers, a depression is being felt in the labor movement. [*Pravda,* July 17, 1928.]

Facts—are stubborn things! This had to be recognized also by the Sixth Congress. The slogan of armed insurrection was eliminated. The only thing that remained was the name "second Chinese revolution" (1925-27), "the first stage" of which is separated from the future second stage by an undefined period. This was a terminological attempt to save at least a part of the prestige.

15. After the Sixth Congress

The delegate of the Chinese Communist Party, Siu, declared at the Sixteenth Congress of the AUCP[136]

> Only Trotskyist renegades and Chinese Ch'en Tu-hsiuists say that the Chinese national bourgeoisie has a perspective of independent [?] development [?] and stabilization [?].

Let us leave aside the abuse. These unfortunate people would never be in the Lux boarding house if they did not address their abuse to the Opposition.[137] This is their only resource. T'an P'ing-shan thundered in exactly the same manner against the "Trotskyists" at the Seventh Plenum of the ECCI before he went over to the enemy.[138] What is curious in its naked shamelessness is the attempt to father us, Left Oppositionists, with the idealization of the Chinese "national bourgeoisie" and its "independent development." Stalin's agents, as well as their leaders, fulminate because the period after the Sixth Congress once more revealed their complete incapacity to understand the change in circumstances and the direction of its further development.

After the Canton defeat, at a time when the ECCI, in February 1928, was steering the course toward an armed insurrection, we declared in opposition to this:

The situation will now change in the exactly opposite direction; the working masses will temporarily retreat from politics; the party will grow weak which does not exclude the continuation of peasant uprisings. The weakening of the war of the generals as well as the weakening of the strikes and uprisings of the proletariat will inevitably lead in the meantime to some sort of an establishment of elementary processes of economic life in the country and consequently to somewhat of a commercial and industrial rise, even though very weak. The latter will revive the strike struggles of the workers and permit the Communist Party, under the condition of correct tactics, once more to establish its contact and its influence in order that later, on a higher plane, the insurrection of the workers may be interlocked with the peasant war. That is what our so-called liquidationism consisted of.

But aside from abuse, what did Siu say about China in the last two years? First of all, he stated after the fact:

"In Chinese industry and commerce a certain revival was to be marked in 1928."

And further:

In 1928, 400,000 workers went on strike, in 1929, the number of strikers had already reached 750,000. In the first half of 1930, the labor movement was still further fortified in the tempo of development.

It is understood that we must be very cautious with the figures of the Comintern, including Siu's. But regardless of the possible exaggeration of the figures, Siu's exposition bears out entirely our prognosis at the end of 1927 and the beginning of 1928.

Unfortunately, the leadership of the ECCI and the Chinese Communist Party took their point of departure from the directly opposite prognosis. The slogan of armed insurrection was dropped only at the Sixth Congress, that is, in the middle of 1928. But aside from this purely negative decision the party did not receive any new orientation. The possibility of economic revival was not taken into consideration by it. The strike movement went on to a considerable extent apart from it. Can one doubt for an instant that if the leadership of the Comintern had not occupied itself with stupid accusations of liquidationism against the Opposition and had understood the situation in time, as we did, the Chinese Communist Party would have been considerably stronger, especially in the trade union movement? Let us recall that during the highest ascent of the second revolution, in the first half of 1927, there were 2.8 million workers organized in trade unions under the influence of the Communist Party. At the present time, there are, according to Siu, around 60,000. This in the whole of China!

And these miserable "leaders," who have worked their way into a hopeless corner, who have done terrific damage, speak about the "Trotskyist renegades" and think that by this slander they can make good the damage. Such is the school of Stalin! Such are its fruits!

16. Soviets and the Class Character
of the Revolution

What, according to Stalin, is the role of soviets in the Chinese revolution? What place has been assigned to them in the alternation of its stages? With the rule of what class are they bound up?

During the Northern Expedition, as well as in the Wuhan period, we heard from Stalin that soviets can be created only *after* the completion of the bourgeois-democratic revolution, only on the *threshold* of the proletarian revolution. Precisely because of this the Political Bureau, following right behind Stalin, stubbornly rejected the slogan of soviets advanced by the Opposition:

"The slogan of soviets means nothing but an immediate skipping over the stage of the bourgeois-democratic revolution and the organization of the power of the proletariat" (from the written "Reply of the Political Bureau" to the Opposition theses, April 1927).

On May 24, after the Shanghai coup d'etat and during the

Wuhan overturn, Stalin proved the incompatibility of soviets with bourgeois-democratic revolution in this manner:

> But the workers will not stop at this if they have soviets of workers' deputies. They will say to the communists—and they will be right: If we are the soviets, and the soviets are the organs of power, then can we not squeeze the bourgeoisie a little, and expropriate "a little"? The communists will be empty windbags if they do not take the road of expropriation of the bourgeoisie with the existence of soviets of workers' and peasants' deputies. Is it possible to and should we take this road at present, at the present phase of the revolution? No, we should not.

And what will become of the Kuomintang after passing over to the proletarian revolution? Stalin had it all figured out. In his discourse to the students on May 13, 1927, which we previously quoted, Stalin replied:

> I think that in the period of the creation of soviets of workers' and peasants' deputies and the preparation for the Chinese October, the Chinese Communist Party will have to substitute for the present bloc inside the Kuomintang the bloc outside the Kuomintang.

Our great strategists foresaw everything—decidedly they foresaw everything, except the class struggle. Even in the matter of going over to the proletarian revolution Stalin solicitously supplied the Chinese Communist Party with an ally, with the same Kuomintang. In order to carry out the socialist revolution, the communists were only permitted to get out of the ranks of the Kuomintang, but by no means to break the bloc with it. As is known, the alliance with the bourgeoisie was the best condition for the preparation of the "Chinese October." And all this was called Leninism. . . .

Be that as it may, in 1925-27 Stalin posed the question of soviets very categorically, connecting the formation of soviets with the immediate socialist expropriation of the bourgeoisie. It is true he needed this "radicalism" at that time not in defense of the expropriation of the bourgeoisie but on the contrary in defense of the bourgeoisie from expropriation. But the principled posing of the question was at any rate clear: *the soviets can be only and exclusively organs of the socialist revolution.* Such was the position of the Political Bureau of the AUCP, such was the position of the ECCI.

But at the end of 1927 an insurrection was carried out in Canton to which a soviet character was given. The communists had the power. They decreed measures of a purely socialist character (nationalization of the land, banks, dwellings, industrial enterprises, etc.). It would seem we were confronted with a proletarian revolution. But no. At the end of February 1928, the Ninth Plenum of the ECCI drew up the balance of the Canton insurrection. And what was the result?

> The current year in the Chinese revolution is a period of bourgeois-democratic revolution, which has not been completed. . . . The tendency toward jumping over the bourgeois-democratic stage of the revolution with the simultaneous appraisal of the revolution as a "permanent" revolution is a mistake similar to the one made by Trotsky in 1905.

But ten months before that (April 1927) the Political Bureau declared that the very slogan of soviets (not Trotskyism, but the slogan of soviets!) means the inadmissible skipping of the bourgeois-democratic stage. But now, after a complete exhaustion of all the variations of the Kuomintang, when it was necessary to sanction the slogan of soviets, we were told that only Trotskyists can connect this slogan with the proletarian dictatorship. This is how it was revealed that Stalin, during 1925-27, was a . . . "Trotskyist," even though the other way around.

It is true that the program of the Comintern also made a decisive turn in this question. Among the most important tasks of the colonial countries, the program mentioned: "The establishment of a democratic dictatorship of the proletariat and peasantry based on the soviets." Truly miraculous! What was yesterday incompatible with the democratic revolution was today proclaimed to be its foundation base. One would seek in vain for any explanation of this complete somersault. Everything was done in a strictly administrative manner.

In what instance was Stalin wrong? When he declared the soviets incompatible with the democratic revolution or when he declared the soviets to be the basis of the democratic revolution? In both instances. Because Stalin does not understand the meaning of the democratic dictatorship, the meaning of the proletarian dictatorship, their mutual relationship, and what role the soviets play in connection with them.

He once more revealed it best, even though in a few words, at the Sixteenth Congress of the AUCP.

17. The Chinese Question at the Sixteenth Congress of the AUCP

In his ten-hour report Stalin, however anxious he was to do so, could not completely ignore the question of the Chinese revolution. He devoted to it exactly five sentences. And what sentences! Indeed, "a lot in a little," as the Romans said (*multum in parvo*). Desiring to avoid all sharp corners, to refrain from risking generalizations and still more from concrete prognoses, Stalin in five sentences succeeded in making all the mistakes still left for him to make.

> It would be ridiculous to think [Stalin said] that this misconduct of the imperialists will pass for them unpunished. The Chinese workers and peasants have already replied to this by the creation of soviets and a Red army. It is said that a soviet government has already been created there. I think that if this is true then there is nothing surprising in it. There is no doubt that only soviets can save China from complete dismemberment and impoverishment. [*Pravda*, June 29, 1930.]

"It would be ridiculous to think." Here is the basis for all the further conclusions. If the misconduct of the imperialists will inevitably provoke a reply in the form of soviets and Red army, then how is it that imperialism still exists in the world?

"It is said that a soviet government has already been created there." What does it mean: "It is said"? Who says so? And what's most important, what does the Chinese Communist Party say about it? It is part of the Comintern and its representative spoke at the congress. Does it mean that the "soviet government" was created in China without the Communist Party and without its knowledge? Then who is leading this government? Who are its members? What party has the power? Not only does Stalin fail to give a reply, but he does not even pose the question.[139]

"I think that if [!] this is true then [!] there is nothing surprising in it." There is nothing surprising in the fact that in China a soviet government was created about which the Chinese Communist Party knows nothing and about whose political physiognomy the highest leader of the Chinese revolution can give us no information. Then what is there left in the world to be surprised at?

"There is no doubt that only soviets can save China from dismemberment and impoverishment." Which soviets? Up to now, we have seen all sorts of soviets: Tseretelli's soviets, Otto Bauer's and Scheidemann's, on the one hand, Bolshevik soviets on the other. Tseretelli's soviets could not save Russia from dismemberment and impoverishment. On the contrary, their whole policy went in the direction of transforming Russia into a colony of the Entente. Only the Bolsheviks transformed the soviets into a weapon for the liberation of the toiling masses. What kind of soviets are the Chinese? If the Chinese Communist Party can say nothing about them, then it means that it is not leading them. Then who is? Apart from the communists, only accidental, intermediate elements, people of a "Third Party," in a word, fragments of the Kuomintang of the second and third rank, can come to the head of the soviets and create a "soviet government."

Only yesterday Stalin thought that "it would be ridiculous to think" of the creation of soviets in China prior to the completion of the democratic revolution. Now he seems to think—if his five sentences have any meaning at all—that in the democratic revolution the soviets can save the country even without the leadership of the communists.

To speak of a soviet government without speaking of the dictatorship of the proletariat means to deceive the workers and to help the bourgeoisie deceive the peasants. But to speak of the dictatorship of the proletariat without speaking of the leading role of the Communist Party means once more to convert the dictatorship of the proletariat into a trap for the proletariat. The Chinese Communist Party, however, is now extremely weak. The number of its worker members is limited to a few thousand.[140] There are about fifty thousand workers in the Red trade unions. Under these conditions, to speak of the dictatorship of the proletariat as an *immediate* task is obviously unthinkable.

On the other hand, in South China a broad peasant movement is unfolding itself in which partisan bands participate. The influence of the October revolution, in spite of the year of epigone leadership, is still so great in China that the peasants call their movement "soviet" and their partisan bands—"Red armies." This shows once more the depths of Stalin's philistinism in the period when, coming out against soviets, he said that we must not scare off the masses of the Chinese people by "artificial sovietization." Only Chiang Kai-shek could have been scared off by it, but not the workers, not the peasants, to whom, after 1917, the soviets had become symbols of emancipation. The Chinese peasants, it is understood, inject no few illusions into the slogan of soviets. It is pardonable in them. But is it pardonable in the leading tailendists who confine themselves to a cowardly and ambiguous generalization of the illusions of the Chinese peasantry, without explaining to the proletariat the real meaning of events?

"There is nothing surprising in it," says Stalin, if the Chinese peasants, without the participation of the industrial centers and without the leadership of the Communist Party, created a soviet government. But we say that the appearance of a soviet government under these circumstances is absolutely impossible. Not only the Bolsheviks but even the Tseretelli government or half-government of the soviets could make its appearance only on the basis of the cities. To think that the peasantry is capable of creating its soviet government *independently* means to believe in miracles. It would be the same miracle to create a peasant Red army. The peasant partisans played a great revolutionary role in the Russian revolution, but under the existence of centers of proletarian dictatorship and a centralized proletarian Red army.

With the weakness of the Chinese labor movement at the present moment, and with the still greater weakness of the Communist Party, it is difficult to speak of a dictatorship of the proletariat as the *task of the day* in China. This is why Stalin, swimming in the wake of the peasant uprising, is compelled, in spite of all his earlier declarations, to link the peasant soviets and the peasant Red army with the bourgeois-democratic dictatorship. The leadership of this dictatorship, which is too heavy a task for the Communist Party, is delivered to some other political party, to some sort of a revolutionary *x*. Since Stalin hindered the Chinese workers and peasants from conducting their struggle for the dictatorship of the proletariat, then somebody must now help Stalin by taking charge of the soviet government as the organ of the bourgeois-democratic dictatorship. As a motivation for this new perspective we are presented with five arguments in five sentences. Here they are: (1) "It would be ridiculous to think"; (2) "it is said"; (3) "if it is true"; (4) "there is nothing surprising in it"; (5) "there is no doubt." Here it is, administrative argumentation in all its power and splendor!

We warn: the Chinese proletariat will again have to pay for this whole shameful concoction.

18. The Character of Stalin's "Mistakes"

There are mistakes and mistakes. In the various spheres of human thought, there can be very considerable mistakes that flow from an insufficient examination of the object, from insufficient factual data, from a too great complexity of the factors to be considered, etc. Among these we may consider, let us say, the mistakes of meteorologists in foretelling the weather, which are typical of a whole series of mistakes in the sphere of politics. However, the mistakes of a learned, quick-witted meteorologist are often more useful to science than the conjecture of an empiric, even though it is accidentally substantiated by facts. But what should we say of a learned geographer, of a leader of a polar expedition who would take as his point of departure that the earth rests on three whales? Yet the mistakes of Stalin are almost completely of this last category. Never rising to Marxism as a method, making use of one or another "Marxist-like" formula in a ritualist manner, Stalin in his practical actions takes as his point of departure the crassest empirical prejudices. But such is the dialectic of the process. These prejudices became Stalin's main strength in the period of revolutionary decline. They were the ones that permitted him to play the role which subjectively he did not want.

The cumbersome bureaucracy, separating itself from the revolutionary class that conquered power, seized upon Stalin's empiricism for his mercenariness, for his complete cynicism in the sphere of principles, in order to make him its leader and in order to create the legend of Stalin which is the holiday legend of the bureaucracy itself. This is the explanation of how and why the strong but absolutely mediocre person who occupied third and fourth-ranking roles in the years of the rise of the revolution proved called upon to play the leading role in the years of its ebb, in the years of the stabilization of the world bourgeoisie, the regeneration of the Social Democracy, the weakening of the Comintern, and the conservative degeneration of the broadest circles of the Soviet bureaucracy.

The French say about a man: His defects are his virtues. Of Stalin it can be said: His defects proved to be to his advantage. The gear teeth of the class struggle meshed into his theoretical limitedness, his political adaptability, his moral indiscriminateness, in a word, into his defects as a proletarian revolutionist, in order to make him a statesman of the period of the petty-bourgeois emancipation from October, from Marxism, from Bolshevism

The Chinese revolution was an examination of the new role of Stalin—by the inverse method. Having conquered power in the USSR with the aid of the strata who have been breaking away from the international revolution and with the indirect but very real aid of the hostile classes, Stalin automatically became the leader of the Comintern and by that alone the leader of the Chinese revolution. The passive hero of the behind-the-scenes apparatus mechanism had to show his method and quality in the events of the great revolutionary flow. Within this lies the tragic paradox of Stalin's role in China.

Having subordinated the Chinese workers to the bourgeoisie, put the brakes on the agrarian movement, supported the reactionary generals, disarmed the workers, prevented the appearance of soviets and liquidated those that did appear, Stalin carried out to the end that historic role which Tseretelli only attempted to carry out in Russia. The difference is that Tseretelli acted on the open arena, having arrayed against him the Bolsheviks—and he immediately and on the spot had to bear the responsibility for his attempt to betray to the bourgeoisie a fettered and duped working class. Stalin, however, acted in China primarily behind the scenes, defended by a powerful apparatus and draped in the banner of Bolshevism. Tseretelli supported himself on the repressions of the power of the Bolsheviks by the bourgeoisie. Stalin, however, himself applied these repressions against the Bolshevik-Leninists (Opposition). The repressions of the bourgeoisie were shattered by the rising wave. Stalin's repressions were fostered by the ebbing wave. This is why it was possible for Stalin to carry out the experiment with the purely Menshevik policy in the Chinese revolution to the end, that is, to the most tragic catastrophe.

But what about the present left paroxysm of the Stalinist policy? To see in this episode—and the left zigzag with all its significance will nevertheless go down in history as an episode—a contradiction to what has been said, can be done only by very nearsighted people who are foreign to an understanding of the dialectic of human consciousness in connection with the dialectic of the historic process. The decline of the revolution as well as its rise does not move along a straight line. The empirical leader of the down sliding of the revolution—"You think that you are moving but you are being moved" (Goethe)—could not help at a certain moment but take fright at that abyss of social betrayal to the very edge of which he was pushed in 1925-27 by his own qualities, utilized by forces half-hostile and hostile to the proletariat. And since the degeneration of the apparatus is not an even process, since the revolutionary tendencies within the masses are strong, then for the turn to the left from the edge of the Thermidorian abyss there were sufficient points of support and reserve forces already at hand. The turn assumed a character of panicky jumps, precisely because this empiric foresaw nothing until he had reached the very brink of the precipice. The ideology of the jump to the left was prepared by the Left Opposition—it only remained to utilize its work in bits and fragments, as befits an empiric. But the acute paroxysm of leftism does not change the basic processes of the evolution of the bureaucracy, nor the nature of Stalin himself.

The absence in Stalin of theoretical preparation, of a broad outlook, and creative imagination—those features without which there can be no independent work on a large scale—fully explains why Lenin, who valued Stalin as a practical assistant, nevertheless recommended that the party remove him from the post of general secretary when it became clear that this post might assume independent significance. Lenin never saw in Stalin a political leader.

Left to himself, Stalin always and invariably took up an opportunistic position on all big questions. If Stalin had no important theoretical or political conflicts with Lenin, like Bukharin, Kamenev, Zinoviev, and even Rykov, it is because Stalin never held on to his principled views and in all cases of serious disagreement simply kept quiet, retreated to the sidelines and waited. But for all that, Lenin very often had practical organizational-moral conflicts with Stalin, frequently very sharp ones, precisely for those Stalinist defects which Lenin, so carefully in form but so mercilessly in essence, characterized in his "Testament."

To all that has been said we must add the fact that Lenin worked hand in hand with a group of collaborators, each of whom brought into the work knowledge, personal initiative, distinct talent. Stalin is surrounded, particularly after the liquidation of the right-wing group,[141] by accomplished mediocrities, devoid of any international outlook, and incapable of producing an independent opinion on a single question of the world labor movement.

In the meantime, the significance of the apparatus has grown immeasurably since Lenin's time. Stalin's leadership in the Chinese revolution is just the fruit of the combination of theoretical, political, and national limitedness with huge apparatus power. Stalin has proved himself incapable of learning. His five sentences on China at the Sixteenth Congress are penetrated through and through with that same organic opportunism that governed Stalin's policy at all the earlier stages of the struggle of the Chinese people. The gravedigger of the second Chinese revolution is preparing before our very eyes to strangle the third Chinese revolution at its inception.

From *Problems of the Chinese Revolution.*

A HISTORY OF THE
SECOND CHINESE REVOLUTION
IS NEEDED

Published September 1930

A study of the Chinese revolution is a most important and urgent matter for every communist and for every advanced worker. It is not possible to talk seriously in any country about the struggle of the proletariat for power without a study by the proletarian vanguard of the fundamental events, motive forces, and strategic methods of the Chinese revolution. It is not possible to understand what day is without knowing what night is; it is not possible to understand what summer is without having experienced winter. In the same way, it is not possible to understand the meaning of the methods of the October uprising without a study of the methods of the Chinese catastrophe. In the meantime, the history of the Chinese revolution has been a forbidden topic for the Comintern. There is not a single book which has summed up what the lessons are of the great experiences of the battles and defeats of 1925-27. This book has not been written, and it will not and cannot be written by the Comintern leadership for the same reason that the Roman conclave will not write a scientific history of the Holy Inquisition: it is not possible to demand or expect that any institution should write the history of its own crimes.

The working up of the history of the second Chinese revolution (1925-27) can be done only by the Communist Left Opposition: First place here belongs, clearly, to our Chinese comrades. We think that this question must be included on the agenda of the international conference of the Left Opposition (Bolshevik-Leninists).

From *Writings of Leon Trotsky (1930-31)*. Text from *Biulleten Oppozitsii* (Paris), nos. 15-16, September-October 1930. Translated by Jim Burnett.

MANIFESTO ON CHINA OF THE
INTERNATIONAL LEFT OPPOSITION[142]

September 1930

During the last few months a peasant movement of consider-able scope has again appeared in certain provinces of southern China. Not only the world press of the proletariat, but the press of its enemies as well, is filled with the echoes of this struggle. The Chinese revolution, betrayed, defeated, exhausted, shows that it is still alive. Let us hope that the time when it will again lift its proletarian head is not far off. And in order to be prepared for this, we must put the problems of the Chinese revolution on the agenda of the working class of the world.

We, the International Communist Left Opposition (Bolshevik-Leninists), consider it our duty to raise our voices now in order to attract the attention of all communists, all advanced revolution-ary workers, to the task of liberating this great country of East Asia and at the same time to warn them against the false policy of the dominant faction of the Communist International, which obviously threatens to undermine the coming Chinese revolution as it ruined the 1925-27 revolution.

The signs of the rebirth of the Chinese revolution in the countryside indicate its inner forces and immense potentialities. But the task is to transform these potentialities into reality. The first condition for success is to understand what is happening, that is, to make a Marxist analysis of the motive forces and to estimate correctly the current stage of the struggle. On both counts, the ruling circle of the Comintern is wrong.

The Stalinist press is filled with communications about a "soviet government" established in vast provinces of China under the protection of a Red army. Workers in many countries are greeting this news with excitement. Of course! The establish-

476

ment of a soviet government in a substantial part of China and the creation of a Chinese Red army would be a gigantic success for the international revolution. But we must state openly and clearly: *this is not yet true.*

Despite the scanty information which reaches us from the vast areas of China, our Marxist understanding of the developing process enables us to reject with certainty the Stalinist view of the current events. It is false and extremely dangerous for the further development of the revolution.

For centuries the history of China has been one of formidable uprisings of a destitute and hungry peasantry. Not less than five times in the last two thousand years the Chinese peasants succeeded in effecting a complete redivision of landed property. Each time the process of concentration began anew and continued until the growth of the population again produced a partial or general explosion. This vicious cycle was an expression of economic and social stagnation.

Only the inclusion of China in the world economy opened up new possibilities. Capitalism invaded China from abroad. The backward Chinese bourgeoisie became the intermediary between foreign capital and the mercilessly exploited masses of their own country. The foreign imperialists and the Chinese bourgeoisie combine the methods of capitalist exploitation with the methods of feudal oppression and enslavement through usury.

The fundamental idea of the Stalinists was to transform the Chinese bourgeoisie into a leader of the national revolution against feudalism and imperialism. The results of this political strategy ruined the revolution. The Chinese proletariat paid a heavy price for knowledge of the truth that their bourgeoisie cannot, does not want to, and never will fight either against so-called feudalism, which constitutes the most important part of its own system of exploitation, or against imperialism, whose agent it is and under whose military protection it operates.

As soon as it was clear that the Chinese proletariat, in spite of all the obstacles put in its path by the Comintern, was ready to proceed on its own independent revolutionary road, the bourgeoisie, with the help of the foreign imperialists, beginning in Shanghai, crushed the workers' movement. As soon as it was clear that friendship with Moscow could not paralyze the uprising of the peasants, the bourgeoisie shattered the peasants' movement. The spring and summer of 1927 were the months of the greatest crimes of the Chinese bourgeoisie.

Frightened by the consequences of its mistakes, at the end of 1927 the Stalinist faction abruptly tried to compensate for its blunders of the past years. The Canton insurrection was organized. The Stalinist leaders assumed that the revolution was still on the rise; actually, it was already on the decline. The heroism of the vanguard workers could not prevent the disaster caused by the adventure of these leaders. The Canton insurrection was drowned in blood. The second Chinese revolution was completely destroyed.

From the beginning, we, the representatives of the International Left Opposition, the Bolshevik-Leninists, were against entering the Kuomintang and for an independent proletarian policy. From the very beginning of the revolutionary upsurge, we urged that the organization of workers', soldiers', and peasants' soviets be initiated; we urged that the workers take their place at the head of the peasant insurrection and carry through the agrarian revolution to its conclusion. Our course was rejected. Our supporters were persecuted and expelled from the Comintern; those in the USSR were arrested and exiled. In the name of what? In the name of a bloc with Chiang Kai-shek.

After the counterrevolutionary coup d'etat in Shanghai and Wuhan we, the Communist Left Oppositionists, warned insistently that the second Chinese revolution was finished, that a temporary triumph of the counterrevolution had supervened, and that an attempt at insurrection by the advanced workers in the face of the general demoralization and fatigue of the masses would inevitably bring additional criminal blows against the revolutionary forces. We demanded a shift to the defensive, a strengthening of the underground organization of the party, the participation in the economic struggles of the proletariat, and the mobilization of the masses under democratic slogans: the independence of China, the right of self-determination for the different nationalities in the population, a constituent assembly, the confiscation of the land, the eight-hour workday. Such a policy would have allowed the communist vanguard to emerge gradually from its defeat, to reestablish connections with the trade unions and with the unorganized urban and rural masses, and to prepare to meet the new revolutionary upsurge fully armed.

The Stalinist faction denounced our policy as "liquidationist," while it, not for the first time, went from opportunism to adventurism. In February 1928, when the Chinese revolution was at its lowest point, the Ninth Plenum of the Executive Committee of the Communist International announced a policy of armed insurrection in China. The results of this madness were the further defeat of the workers, the murder of the best revolutionaries, a split in the party, demoralization in the ranks of the workers.

The decline of the revolution and a temporary lessening of the struggle between the militarists permitted a limited economic revival in the country. Strikes occurred again. But these were conducted independently of the party, which, not understanding the situation, was absolutely unable to present a new perspective to the masses and to unite them under the democratic slogans of the transitional period. As a result of new errors, opportunism, and adventurism, the Communist Party now counts in its ranks only a few thousand workers. In the Red trade unions, according to the figures given by the party itself, there are about sixty thousand workers. In the months of the revolutionary upsurge there were about three million.

The counterrevolution left its mark more directly and much more ruthlessly on the workers than on the peasants. The workers in China are few in number and are concentrated in the industrial centers. The peasants are protected to a certain extent by their numbers and their diffusion over vast areas. The revolutionary years trained quite a few rural local leaders, and the counterrevolution did not succeed in eliminating them all. A considerable number of revolutionary workers hid from the militarists in the countryside. In the last decade a large amount of arms was widely dispersed. In conflicts with local administrators or military units, these arms were obtained by the peasants and Red guerrilla bands were organized. Agitation flared up in the armies of the bourgeois counterrevolution, at times leading to open revolts. Soldiers, with their guns, deserted to the side of the peasants, sometimes in groups, sometimes in whole companies.

It is quite natural, therefore, that even after the defeat of the revolution, waves of the peasant movement continued to roll through the various provinces of the country and have now forcefully rushed ahead. Armed peasant bands drive out and exterminate local landlords, as many as can be found in their regions, and especially the so-called gentry and *tuchüns,* the local representatives of the ruling class—the bureaucrat-proprietors, the usurers, the rich peasants.

When the Stalinists talk about a soviet government established by the peasants in a substantial part of China, they not only reveal their credulity and superficiality; they obscure and misrepresent the fundamental problem of the Chinese revolution. The peasantry, even the most revolutionary, cannot create an independent government; it can only support the government of another class, the dominant urban class. The peasantry at all decisive moments follows either the bourgeoisie or the proletariat. So-called peasant parties may disguise this fact, but they cannot annul it. Soviets are the organs of power of a revolutionary class in opposition to the bourgeoisie. This means that the peasantry is unable to organize a soviet system on its own. The same holds true for an army. More than once in China, and in Russia and other countries too, the peasantry has organized guerrilla armies which fought with incomparable courage and stubbornness. But they remained guerrilla armies, connected to a local province and incapable of centralized strategic operations on a large scale. *Only the predominance of the proletariat in the decisive industrial and political centers of the country* creates the necessary basis for the organization of a Red army and for the extension of a soviet system into the coutryside. To those unable to grasp this, the revolution remains a book closed with seven seals.

The Chinese proletariat is just beginning to recover from the paralysis of the counterrevolution. The peasant movement at the present time is advancing, to a large degree, independently of the workers' movement, according to its own laws and at its own tempo. But the heart of the problem of the Chinese revolution consists in the political coordination and organizational combination of the proletarian and peasant uprisings. Those who talk about the victory of the soviet revolution in China, although confined to separate provinces in the South and confronted with passivity in the industrial North, ignore the dual problem of the Chinese revolution: the problem of an alliance between the workers and peasants and the problem of the leading role of the workers in this alliance.

The vast flood of peasant revolts can unquestionably provide the impulse for the revival of political struggle in the industrial centers. We firmly count on it. But this does not mean in any case that the revolutionary awakening of the proletariat would lead immediately to the conquest of power or even to the struggle for power. The resurgence of the proletariat might at first assume the character of partial economic and political defensive and offensive struggles. How much time would the proletariat, and particularly the communist vanguard, require to rise to its role as leader of a revolutionary nation? At any rate, more than weeks or months. Bureaucratic command is no substitute for the independent growth of the class and its party.

At this juncture the Chinese communists need a long-range policy. They must not scatter their forces among the isolated flames of the peasant revolt. Weak and small in number, the party will not be able to take hold of this movement. The communists must concentrate their forces in the factories and the shops and in the workers' districts in order to explain to the workers the meaning of what is happening in the provinces, to lift the spirits of the tired and discouraged, to organize groups of workers for a struggle to defend their economic interests, and to raise the slogans of the democratic-agrarian revolution. Only through the process of activating and uniting the workers will the Communist Party be able to assume leadership of the peasant insurrection, that is, of the national revolution as a whole.

To support the illusions of adventurism and to conceal the weakness of the proletarian vanguard, the Stalinists say that a democratic dictatorship, not a proletarian, is the issue. On this central point their adventurism relies entirely on the premises of opportunism. Not satisfied with their Kuomintang experiment, the Stalinists are devising a new formula for the coming revolution with which to put to sleep and chain the working class, the "democratic dictatorship."

When the vanguard workers in China advanced the slogan of *soviets,* they were saying: we want to do what the Russian workers did. Only yesterday the Stalinists replied to this: no, you must not, you have the Kuomintang, and it will do what is necessary. Today the same leaders respond more cautiously: you will have to organize soviets, not for a proletarian but for a democratic dictatorship. They thereby tell the proletariat that the dictatorship will not be in their hands, that there is some other as-yet-undiscovered force which can introduce the revolutionary dictatorship in China. In this way the formula of the democratic dictatorship opens the gates to a new deception of the workers and peasants by the bourgeoisie.

To justify the slogan of the "democratic dictatorship," the Stalinists describe the Chinese counterrevolution as "feudal-militarist and imperialist." Thus they exclude the bourgeoisie from the counterrevolution, that is, they again as before idealize the bourgeoisie. In reality the militarists express the interests of the Chinese bourgeoisie, which are inseparable from feudal interests and relations. The Chinese bourgeoisie is too hostile to the people, too closely tied up with the foreign imperialists, and too afraid of the revolution to be eager to rule in its own name by parliamentary methods. The militarist-fascist regime of China is an expression of the antinational, antirevolutionary character of the Chinese bourgeoisie. The Chinese counterrevolution is not a counterrevolution of feudal barons and slaveowners against bourgeois society. It is a counterrevolution of all property holders—and first of all bourgeois—against the workers and peasants.

The proletarian insurrection in China can and will develop only as a direct and immediate revolution against the bourgeoisie. The peasants' revolt in China, much more than it was in Russia, is a revolt against the bourgeoisie. A class of landlords as a separate class does not exist in China. The landowners and the bourgeoisie are one and the same. The gentry and *tuchüns,* against whom the peasant movement is immediately directed, represent the lowest link to the bourgeoisie and to the imperialist exploiters as well. In Russia the October revolution, in its first stage, counterposed all the peasants as a class against all the landlords as a class, and only after several months began to introduce the civil war within the peasantry. In China every peasant uprising is, from the start, a civil war of the poor against the rich peasants, that is, against the village bourgeoisie.

The middle peasantry in China is insignificant. Almost 80 percent of the peasants are poor. They and they alone play a revolutionary role. The problem is not to unite the workers with the peasants as a whole, but with the village poor. They have a common enemy: the bourgeoisie. No one but the workers can lead the poor peasants to victory. Their mutual victory can lead to no other regime but the dictatorship of the proletariat. Only such a regime can establish a soviet system and organize a Red army, which will be the military expression of the dictatorship of the proletariat supported by the poor peasants.

The Stalinists say that the democratic dictatorship, as the next stage of the revolution, will grow into a proletarian dictatorship at a later stage. This is the current doctrine of the Comintern, not only for China but for all the Eastern countries. It is a complete departure from the teachings of Marx on the state and the conclusions of Lenin on the function of the state in a revolution. The democratic dictatorship differs from the proletarian in that it is a *bourgeois*-democratic dictatorship. The transition from a bourgeois to a proletarian dictatorship cannot occur as a peaceful process of "growing over" from one to the other. A dictatorship of the proletariat can replace a democratic, or a fascist, dictatorship of the bourgeoisie only through armed insurrection.

The peaceful "growing over" of a democratic revolution into a socialist revolution is possible only under the dictatorship of one class—the proletariat. The transition from democratic measures to socialist measures took place in the Soviet Union under the regime of the proletarian dictatorship. This transition will be accomplished much faster in China because its most elementary democratic problems have much more of an anticapitalist and antibourgeois character than they had in Russia. The Stalinists apparently need one more defeat, paid for by the workers' blood, before they can bring themselves to say: "The revolution has reached the highest stage, whose slogan is the dictatorship of the proletariat."

At this moment nobody can tell the extent to which the present peasant insurrection combines the reflection of the second revolution with the summer lightning of the third. Nobody can foretell now whether the hearths of the peasant revolt can keep a fire burning through the whole long period of time which the proletarian vanguard will need to gather its own strength, bring the working class into the fight, and coordinate its struggle for power with the general offensive of the peasants against their most immediate enemies.

What distinguishes this movement in the countryside today is the desire of the peasants to give it the form of soviets, at least in name, and to fashion their own guerrilla armies as much as possible after the Red Army. This shows how intensely the peasants are seeking a political form that would enable them to overcome their dispersion and impotence. From this point of departure, the communists can proceed successfully.

But it must be understood in advance that in the consciousness of the Chinese peasant the general slogan of soviets does not by any means signify the dictatorship of the proletariat. The peasants cannot speak for the proletarian dictatorship a priori. They can be led to it only through the experience of a struggle that will prove to them in life that their *democratic* problems cannot be solved in any way except through the *dictatorship of the proletariat.* This is the fundamental reason why *the Communist Party cannot lead the proletariat to a struggle for power except under democratic slogans.*

The peasant movement, although adorned with the name of soviets, remains scattered, local, provincial. It can be elevated to a national movement only by connecting the struggle for land and against oppressive taxes and burdens of militarism with the ideals of the independence of China and the sovereignty of the people. A democratic expression of this connection is the sovereign constituent assembly. Under such a slogan the communist vanguard will be able to unite around itself the vast masses of workers, the oppressed small townspeople, and the hundreds of millions of poor peasants for an insurrection against foreign and native oppressors.

The organization of workers' soviets can be attempted only on a rising tide of revolution in the cities. In the meantime we can prepare for it. To prepare means to gather strength. At present we can do it only under consistent and courageous revolutionary democratic slogans.

And we must explain to the vanguard elements of the working class that a constituent assembly is only a step on the revolutionary road. We are setting our course toward the dictatorship of the proletariat in the form of a soviet regime.

We do not shut our eyes to the fact that such a dictatorship will place the most difficult economic and international problems before the Chinese people. The proletariat in China constitutes a smaller part of the population than the proletariat in Russia did on the eve of the October revolution. Chinese capitalism is more backward than was Russia's. But difficulties are conquered not by illusions, not by an adventurist policy, not by hopes in a Chiang Kai-shek or in a "democratic dictatorship." Difficulties are conquered by clear thinking and revolutionary will.

The Chinese proletariat will take power not in order to resurrect the Chinese Wall and under its protection construct national socialism. By winning power the Chinese proletariat will win one of the most important strategic positions for the international revolution. The fate of China, like that of the USSR, is bound up with the fate of the revolutionary movement of the world proletariat. This is the source of greatest hope and the justification of highest revolutionary courage.

The cause of the international revolution is the cause of the Chinese revolution. The cause of the Chinese revolution is the cause of the international revolution.

From *Writings of Leon Trotsky (1930-31)*. Text from the *Militant* (New York), October 1, 1930.

A RETREAT IN FULL DISORDER

Manuilsky on the "Democratic Dictatorship"

November 1930

In the anniversary number of *Pravda* (November 7, 1930), Manuilsky once more shows the value of the present leadership of the Comintern. We will analyze briefly that part of his anniversary reflections devoted to China, and which amounts in essence to a cowardly, deliberately confused, and therefore all the more dangerous, semicapitulation to the theory of the permanent revolution.

1. "A revolutionary democratic dictatorship of the peasantry and proletariat in China," writes Manuilsky, "will differ essentially from the democratic dictatorship outlined [!] by the Bolsheviks in the 1905-06 revolution."

The democratic dictatorship was "outlined" by the Bolsheviks not only in 1905, but also in 1917, and in all the years between the two revolutions. But only *outlined*. Events served as a test. Manuilsky, like his teacher Stalin, does not reflect upon the points of resemblance and the points of difference of the Chinese revolution with the three Russian revolutions—no, with such comparison they would be unable to preserve the fiction of the democratic dictatorship, and along with it, the fiction of their theoretical reputations. Therefore these gentlemen do not compare the Chinese revolution with the real Russian revolution, but with the one that was "outlined." It is much easier in this way to cónfuse and to throw dust in the eyes.

2. In what respect then does the revolution taking place in

China differ from the one "outlined" in Russia? In the fact, we are taught by Manuilsky, that the Chinese revolution is directed against the "whole system of world imperialism"! It is true that this was the basis upon which Manuilsky yesterday depended for the revolutionary role of the Chinese bourgeoisie as against the Bolshevik position "outlined in 1905." Today, however, Manuilsky's conclusions are different: "The difficulties of the Chinese revolution are tremendous; and this is precisely why the victorious movement of the Chinese Red Army upon the industrial centers of China had to halt at Changsha." It would have been much more simple and honest to say that the partisan peasant detachments, *in the absence of revolutionary uprisings in the cities,* found themselves powerless to take possession of the industrial and political centers of the country. Wasn't this clear to Marxists beforehand?

But Manuilsky has to save Stalin's speech at the Sixteenth Congress. Here is how he fulfills this task:

> The Chinese revolution has at its disposal a Red army, it is in possession of a considerable territory, at this very moment it is creating on this territory a soviet system of workers' and peasants' power in whose government the communists are in the majority. And this condition permits the proletariat to realize not only an ideological but also *a state hegemony over the peasantry.* [Our emphasis.]

The fact that the communists, as the revolutionary and most self-sacrificing elements, appear at the head of the peasant movement and the armed peasant detachments, is quite natural in itself and is also exceptionally important in the symptomatic sense. But this does not change the fact that the Chinese workers find themselves throughout their vast country under the heel of the Chinese bourgoisie and foreign imperialism. In what way can the proletariat realize "state hegemony" over the peasantry, when the state power is not in its hands? It is absolutely impossible to understand this. The leading role of the isolated communists and the isolated communist groups in the peasant war does not decide the question of power. Classes decide and not parties. The peasant war may support the dictatorship of the proletariat, if they coincide in point of· time, but under no circumstances can it be substituted for the dictatorship of the proletariat. Is it possible that the "leaders" of the Comintern have not learned even this from the experiences of the three Russian revolutions?

3. Let us listen further to Manuilsky: "All these [?] conditions lead to the fact that a revolutionary democratic dictatorship in China will be confronted with the necessity of a *consistent confiscation of the enterprises belonging to foreign and Chinese capital*" (our emphasis).

"All these conditions" is a commonplace whose purpose is to cover up the gap created in the old position. But the center of gravity in the phrase quoted above is not in "all these conditions" but in one single "condition": Manuilsky has been instructed to maneuver away from the democratic dictatorship and to cover up the traces. This is why Manuilsky so diligently, but not very skillfully, wags his tail.

The democratic dictatorship can be contrasted only to the proletarian socialist dictatorship. The one differs from the other by the character of the class holding power and by the social content of its historical work. If the democratic dictatorship is to occupy itself not with clearing the road for capitalist development, as stated in the Bolshevik schema "outlined in 1905," but on the contrary, with a "consistent confiscation of the enterprises belonging to foreign and Chinese capital," as "outlined" by Manuilsky, then we ask: Wherein does this *democratic* dictatorship differ from the *socialist?* In no way. Then does it mean that Manuilsky, for the second time after a lapse of twelve years, has bitten into the apple of the "permanent" theory?[143] He bit without really taking a bite: this will yet be seen.

4. We read one phrase after another. "The presence of socialist elements will be the specific [!] peculiarity of the revolutionary democratic dictatorship of the proletariat and peasantry in China." Not a bad "specific" peculiarity!

The democratic dictatorship was always thought of by the Bolsheviks as a *bourgeois*-democratic dictatorship, and not as a supraclass one, and was contrasted to the *socialist* dictatorship only in this—the only possible—sense. Now it appears that in China there will be a "democratic dictatorship with socialist elements." Between the bourgeois and socialist regimes, the class abyss thus disappears, everything is dissolved into pure democracy, and this pure democracy is supplemented gradually and planfully by "socialist elements."

Who did these people learn from? From Victor Chernov. It is precisely he who, in 1905-06, outlined such a Russian revolution as would be neither bourgeois nor socialist, but democratic, and would gradually be supplemented by socialist elements. No, Manuilsky did not make much use of the apple of wisdom!

5. Further: the Chinese revolution in its transition from capitalism to socialism will have more intermediate stages than our October revolution; but the periods of its *growing over* into a socialist revolution will be considerably shorter than the periods outlined (!) by the Bolsheviks for the democratic dictatorship in 1905.

Our astrologer has drawn the balance to everything in advance: to the stages, the periods, and the length of the periods. He only forgot the ABCs of communism. It appears that under democracy, capitalism will *grow over* into socialism in a series of stages. And the power—will it remain the same in this process or will it change? What class will hold power under the democratic dictatorship and what class under the socialist? If different classes will hold power then they can supplant each other only by a new revolution, and not through the "growing over" of the power of one class into the power of another. On the other hand, if it is assumed that in both periods one and the same class will dominate, that is, the proletariat, then what is the meaning of the democratic dictatorship as against the proletarian? To this there can be no answer. And there will not be. Manuilsky is ordered not to clear up the question but to cover up the traces.

In the October revolution, the democratic *tasks* grew over into socialist—under the unaltered domination of the proletariat. One can therefore draw a distinction (it is understood, only relatively) between the democratic period of the October revolution and the socialist period; but one cannot distinguish between the democratic and the socialist dictatorships because the democratic was—nonexistent.

In addition, we have heard from Manuilsky that in China the democratic dictatorship, from the very beginning, will be confronted with a consistent confiscation of the enterprises, which means the expropriation of the bourgeoisie. This means that there will not even be a democratic stage of the proletarian dictatorship. Under these conditions, where will the democratic dictatorship come from?

Manuilsky's injudicious construction would be entirely impossible were he to compare the Chinese revolution with the Russian as it actually developed, and not with the one that was "outlined," and at that, to confuse and distort the outline. And all this to what end? In order to retreat without retreating, in order to give up the reactionary formula of the democratic dictatorship, or, as they say in China, to save face. But on the face of Stalin-Manuilsky there is already written, first, Chiang Kai-shek and then Wang Ching-wei. Enough! The face is already sufficiently descriptive. They cannot save it any more. Manuilsky's theoretical confusion is directed against the basic interests of the Chinese revolution. The Chinese Bolshevik-Leninists will reveal this.

From *Problems of the Chinese Revolution.*

A LETTER TO MAX SHACHTMAN[144]

December 10, 1930

You are quite right when you point out that the Russian Opposition, as late as the first half of 1927, did not demand openly the withdrawal from the Kuomintang. I believe, however, that I have already commented on this fact publicly somewhere. I personally was from the very beginning, that is, from 1923, resolutely opposed to the Communist Party joining the Kuomintang, as well as against the acceptance of the Kuomintang into the "Kuomintern." Radek was always with Zinoviev against me. The younger members of the Opposition of 1923 were with me almost to a man. Rakovsky was in Paris and not sufficiently informed. Up to 1926, I always voted independently in the Political Bureau on this question, against all the others.

In 1925, simultaneously with the theses on the Chinese Eastern Railroad which I have quoted in the Opposition press, I once more presented the formal proposal that the Communist Party leave the Kuomintang instantly.[145] This was unanimously rejected and contributed a great deal to the baiting later on. In 1926 and 1927, I had uninterrupted conflicts with the Zinovievists on this question. Two or three times, the matter stood at the breaking point. Our center consisted of approximately equal numbers from both of the allied tendencies, for it was after all only a bloc. At the voting, the position of the 1923 Opposition was betrayed by Radek, out of principle, and by Pyatakov, out of unprincipledness. Our faction (1923) was furious about it, demanded that Radek and Pyatakov be recalled from the center. But since it was a question of splitting with the Zinovievists, it was the general decision that I must submit publicly in this question and acquaint the Opposition in writing with my

490

standpoint. And that is how it happened that the demand was put up by us so late, in spite of the fact that the Political Bureau and the plenum of the Central Committee always contrasted my view with the official view of the Opposition.

Now I can say with certainty that I made a mistake by submitting formally in this question. In any case, this mistake became quite clear only by the further evolution of the Zinoviev-ists. At that time, the split with them appeared to the overwhelming majority of our faction as absolutely fatal. Thus, the manifesto in no way contradicts the facts when it contends that the Russian Opposition, the real one, was against the Communist Party joining the Kuomintang.[146] Out of the thousands of imprisoned, exiled, etc., hardly a single one was with Radek in this question. This fact too I have referred to in many letters, namely, that the great majority of the capitulators were not sure and firm in the Chinese and the Anglo-Russian questions. That is very characteristic! . . .

From *Problems of the Chinese Revolution.*

TO THE CHINESE LEFT OPPOSITION

January 8, 1931

Dear Comrades:

During the last few months I have received from you a great number of documents and letters in English, French, and Russian, as well as a large number of Opposition publications in Chinese. Pressing work, followed by illness prevented me from answering you sooner. During the last days I have carefully studied all the documents received—except, alas, the Chinese—in order to be able to answer the questions you have raised.

To begin with, I will say that in studying the new documents I finally became convinced that there is no difference in principle at all among the various groups that have entered on the road to unification. There are nuances in tactics, which in the future, depending on the course of events, *could* develop into differences. However, there are no grounds for assuming that these differences of opinion will necessarily coincide with the lines of the former groupings. Further on, I will attempt to analyze the controversial and semicontroversial questions as I see them from here.

1. The entrance of the Communist Party into the Kuomintang was a mistake from the very beginning. I believe that this must be stated openly—in one or another document—especially since in this instance the Russian Opposition to a large extent shares the guilt. Our group (the 1923 Opposition) was from the first, with the exception of Radek and a few of his closest friends, *against* the entry of the Communist Party into the Kuomintang and against the admission of the Kuomintang into the Comintern. The Zinovievists held the opposite position. With his vote, Radek put them in a majority in the Opposition center. Preobrazhensky and Pyatakov thought that we should not break our bloc with the

Zinovievists because of this question. As a result, the United Opposition took an equivocal position on this question, which was reflected in a whole series of documents, even in the Opposition platform.[147] It is worthy of note that all the Russian Oppositionists who adopted the Zinovievist or a conciliatory position on this question subsequently capitulated. On the other hand, all the comrades who are today in jails or in exile were from the very beginning opponents of the entry of the Communist Party into the Kuomintang. This shows the power of a principled position!

2. The slogan *dictatorship of the proletariat and the poor* does not contradict the slogan *dictatorship of the proletariat* but only supplements the latter, and makes it more understandable to the people. In China the proletariat is only a small minority. It can only become a force by uniting around it the majority, i.e., the city and village poor. This idea is in fact expressed by the slogan *dictatorship of the proletariat and the poor*. Naturally, we must point out in the platform and in programmatic articles clearly and distinctly that the role of leadership is concentrated in the hands of the proletariat, which acts as the guide, teacher, and defender of the poor. However, in agitation it is completely correct to employ the term *dictatorship of the proletariat and the poor* as a short slogan. In this form, it has nothing in common with "democratic dictatorship of the proletariat and the peasantry."

In a long document (December 15, 1929) signed by Ch'en Tu-hsiu and others, the problem is formulated in the following manner:

> The tasks of the bourgeois-democratic revolution in China (national independence, state unity, and agrarian revolution) can be solved only on condition that the Chinese proletariat, in alliance with the city and village poor and *as their leader* seizes political power. In other words, the conclusion and the victory of the bourgeois-democratic revolution in China can only be attained in the Russian way, i.e., by way of a Chinese October.[148]

I believe that this formulation is completely correct and excludes the possibility of any misunderstandings whatever.

3. On the question of the character of the Chinese revolution the Comintern leadership has reached an impasse. The experience of the events and the critiques of the Left Opposition have completely destroyed the conception of a "democratic dictatorship." However, if this formula is given up, then no other recourse

is left except to turn to the theory of the permanent revolution. The pathetic "theoreticians" of the Comintern stand between these two theories in the unenviable position of Buridan's ass.[149] The anniversary article (*Pravda,* November 7, 1930) of Manuilsky is the very latest revelation on this subject. A baser mixture of ignorance, cretinism, and villainy cannot be imagined. The Buridanish theory of the Stalinist bureaucrats has been analyzed in the last number of the *Biulleten Oppozitsii* (nos. 17-18).[150] On this fundamental question at any rate we do not have the least difference with you, as all your documents demonstrate.

4. In some letters, complaints have been made about some groups or individual comrades taking a wrong position with regard to the Chinese "Red Army" by likening its detachments to bandits. If that is true, then a stop must be put to it. Of course, lumpenproletarian elements and professional bandits are joining the revolutionary peasant detachments. Yet the movement as a whole arises from wellsprings deep in the conditions of the Chinese village, and these are the same sources from which the dictatorship of the proletariat will have to nourish itself later on. The policy of the Stalinists toward these detachments is a policy of criminal bureaucratic adventurism. This policy must be mercilessly exposed. We do not share or encourage the illusions of the leaders and the participants of the partisan detachments. We must explain to them that without a proletarian revolution and the seizure of power by the workers the partisan detachments of the peasantry cannot lead the way to victory. However, we must conduct this work of clarification as real friends, not detached onlookers and—especially—not as enemies. Without abandoning our own methods and tasks, we must persistently and courageously defend these detachments against the Kuomintang repression and bourgeois slander and persecution. We must explain the enormous *symptomatic* significance of these detachments. Naturally, we cannot throw our own forces into the partisan struggle—at present we have another field of endeavor and other tasks. Nevertheless, it is very desirable to have our people, Oppositionists, at least in the larger divisions of the "Red Army," to share the fate of these detachments, to observe attentively the relations between these detachments and the peasantry, and to keep the Left Opposition informed.

In case of a postponement of the revolution, of a new economic revival in China, and of a development of parliamentary tendencies (all these are interconnected), the detachments will inevitably degenerate, antagonizing the poor peasantry. Therefore it is all the more necessary for us to keep an eye on these detachments, in order to be able to adjust our position as necessary.

5. In several letters, the question of a national assembly is brought up anew. The problem of our political tasks is lost beneath guesses as to whether a national assembly will be set up, in what form, the relationship that might develop between the national assembly and the soviets, etc. Running through such speculation is a strong thread of political scholasticism. Thus, for instance, one of the communications reads:

> We believe that the national assembly will most likely not be realized. Even if it should be realized, it could not be transformed into a "provisional government," since all the material forces are in the hands of the Kuomintang militarists. Regarding the government that will be organized after the insurrection, that will undoubtedly be the government of the proletarian dictatorship, and in that case it will not convoke a national assembly.

This supposition is extremely incomplete and one-sided, and therefore, leaves considerable room for misunderstandings and mistakes.

(a) First of all, we must not exclude the possibility that the bourgeois classes themselves may be forced to convoke *something like* a national assembly. If the reports of the European papers are correct, Chiang Kai-shek is nursing the idea of substituting control over some kind of sham parliament for his control over the Kuomintang, which is now restricting him. Certain circles of the big and the middle bourgeoisie which have come into conflict with what they find to be an exasperating party dictatorship may look with favor upon such a project. At the same time, a "parliament" would serve better as a cover for the military dictatorship in face of American public opinion. As the papers report, Chiang Kai-shek has adopted Americanized Christianity in the not unfounded hope that this will facilitate his credit rating with the Jewish bankers in Wall Street; Americanized Christianity, American Jewish moneylenders, and a Chinese pseudoparliament—all these harmonize splendidly with one another.

In case of a parliamentary variant, the urban petty bourgeoisie, the intellectuals, the students, the "Third Party"—all will be set into motion. The questions of a constitution, suffrage, and parliamentarism will come onto the agenda. It would be nonsense to contend that the masses of the Chinese people have already left all this behind them. Up to the present, they have only gone through the Stalin–Chiang Kai-shek school, i.e., the basest of all schools. The problems of democracy will inevitably, for a certain period, absorb the attention not only of the peasantry, but of the workers also. This must take place *under our leadership.*

Will Chiang Kai-shek convoke his own parliament? It is quite possible. But it is possible that the constitutional-democratic movement will go beyond the bounds planned by Chiang Kai-shek, and this will force him to go further than he wants to at present. It is possible even that the movement will sweep away Chiang Kai-shek together with all his plans. No matter what the constitutional-parliamentary variants, we will not remain on the sidelines. We shall participate in the struggle under our slogans; above all, under the slogans of revolutionary and consistent ("100 percent") democracy. If the revolutionary wave does not immediately sweep away Chiang Kai-shek and his parliament, we will be forced to participate in this parliament, exposing the lies of comprador parliamentarism, and advancing our own tasks.

(b) Can we assume that the revolutionary democratic movement may take on such dimensions that Chiang Kai-shek will no longer be able to keep the military apparatus under control, while the communists are not yet in a position to seize power? Such a transitional period is very likely. It could advance some sort of Chinese variety of *dual power,* a new provisional government, a bloc of the Kuomintang with the Third Party, etc., etc. Such a regime would be very unstable. It could only be a step toward the dictatorship of the proletariat. But such a step is possible.

(c) "After the victorious insurrection," says the document which we have quoted, "a proletarian dictatorship might be instituted and in that case a national assembly would not be convoked." Here, too, the question is oversimplified. At what moment will the insurrection take place and under what slogans? If the proletariat has assembled the poor peasantry under the slogans of democracy (land, national assembly, etc.) and in a united onslaught overthrows the military dictatorship of the bourgeoisie, then, when it comes into power, the proletariat will have to convoke a national assembly in order not to arouse the mistrust of the peasantry and in order not to provide an opening for bourgeois demagogy. Even after the October insurrection the Bolsheviks had to convoke the Constituent Assembly. Why should we conclude that this variant is impossible for China? The peasantry does not develop at the same rate as the proletariat. The proletariat can anticipate many things, but the peasantry will only learn from the facts. It may be that the Chinese peasantry will need to go through the living experience of a national assembly.

Since the bourgeoisie in Russia delayed convoking the Constituent Assembly for a long time, and the Bolsheviks exposed this, they were compelled, after they had come into power, to convoke the Constituent Assembly rapidly, on the basis of the old election results, which put them in a minority. The Constituent Assembly came into conflict with the soviets before the eyes of all the people and it was dissolved.

In China we can conceive of another variant. After it comes to power, the proletariat may, under certain conditions, postpone convoking a national assembly for several months, develop a broad agitation in the countryside, and assure a communist majority in the national assembly. The advantage would be that the soviet system would be formally sanctioned by the national assembly, immediately depriving the bourgeoisie of a popular slogan in the civil war.

6. Of course, the variations we have considered above are only *historical hypotheses*. There is no way of predicting what the actual course of developments will be. The general course, toward the dictatorship of the proletariat, is clear in advance. We should not engage in speculation over possible variations, stages, and combinations, but instead intervene as the revolutionary factor in what is happening and develop powerful agitation around democratic slogans. If we take the initiative in this field, the Stalinist bureaucracy will be brushed aside and the Bolshevik-Leninists will become within a short time a powerful political force.

7. The question of determining what possibilities may open up in the near future for Chinese capitalism is not a matter of principle but of fact. To decide in advance that capitalist development in China can no longer take a step forward would be the purest doctrinairism. A significant inflow of foreign capital into China is not at all excluded. Because of the world crisis, idle capital is accumulating that needs a field of investment. It is true that at present even American capital, the most powerful of all, is paralyzed, perplexed, apprehensive, and deprived of initiative, since only recently it fell from the peaks of prosperity into the

depths of the depression. But it has already begun to look for an international bridgehead as the springboard from which it could touch off a new economic upsurge. It is beyond doubt that under these conditions China offers serious possibilities. To what degree will these be realized? This is not easy to predict either. Here we must not guess a priori, but watch the actual economic and political processes. All the same, it is not at all excluded that while the bulk of the capitalist world is still struggling in the grip of the crisis, the inflow of foreign capital will create an economic revival in China. We must be prepared for this variant, too, by focusing our attention in good time on organizing and strengthening the trade unions and assuring them a correct leadership.

Naturally, an economic upsurge in China would postpone immediate revolutionary perspectives for some time, but this revival will in turn open up new possibilities, new forces, and new sources of strength for victory. In any case, the future belongs to us.

8. Some of the letters from Shanghai pose the question: Should we carry out a complete unification in the individual localities, fuse the press of all the groups, and convoke a conference on the basis of the unification that has already been achieved, or should we permit separate groups to continue within the united Opposition until all the tactical problems have been solved? In such organizational matters, it is difficult to offer advice from afar. It is even possible that the advice would arrive too late. Still, I cannot refrain from saying this to you: *Dear friends, fuse your organizations and your press definitively this very day!* We must not drag out the preparations for the unification a long time, because in that way, without wanting to, we can create artificial differences.

By this I do not mean to say that all the questions have already been settled and that you (or more correctly, *we*) are assured that no differences will arise in the future. No, there is no doubt that the day after tomorrow and the day after that, new tasks will arise, and with them new differences. Without this the development of a revolutionary party is impossible. But the new differences will create new groupings in the framework of the united organization. We must not tarry too long over the past. We must not mark time. We must go onward toward the future.

9. That new differences are inevitable is proved by the experiences of all the sections of the Left Opposition. The French League, for example, was formed from various groups. Thanks to

its weekly journal, the League has accomplished very serious and very valuable work, not only from the national, but from the international point of view as well. It has demonstrated that the unification of the different groups was a progressive step. But in recent months some very serious differences have arisen in the League, particularly on the trade union question. A right wing has formed and taken a position that is false to the core. This question is so important and so profound that it can even lead to a new split. Naturally, absolutely everything will have to be done to avoid this. But if that does not succeed, it will not at all prove that the unification of yesterday was a mistake. We do not make a fetish of unity, nor of splits. It all depends upon the conditions of the moment, on the depth of the differences, on the character of the problems.

10. In Spain, conditions are apparently different from those in all the other countries. Spain is at present going through a period of clear and definite revolutionary upsurge. The heated political atmosphere should greatly facilitate the work of the Bolshevik-Leninists as the boldest and most consistent revolutionary wing. The Comintern has smashed the ranks of Spanish communism, it has weakened and rendered lifeless the official party. As in all other important cases, the Comintern leadership has let a revolutionary situation slip by. The Spanish workers have been left to their own devices at a most crucial moment. Left almost without leadership, they are developing a struggle through revolutionary strikes of notable scope. Under these conditions, the Spanish Bolshevik-Leninists are issuing the slogan of *soviets*. According to the theory of the Stalinists and the practice of the Canton insurrection, it appears that soviets must be created only on the eve of the insurrection. Disastrous theory and disastrous practice! Soviets must be created when the real and living movement of the masses manifests the need for that type of organization. Soviets are formed at first as broad strike committees. This is precisely the case in Spain. There is no doubt that under these conditions the initiative of the Bolshevik-Leninists (Opposition) will receive a sympathetic response from the proletarian vanguard. A broad perspective can open up in the near future for the Spanish Opposition. Let us wish our Spanish friends complete success.

11. In conclusion, I come once more to the question of unity, in order to point out the extremely pitiful experiences of Austria in this domain.

For a year and a half, three Austrian groups occupied themselves with "unification" and each thought up in turn such conditions as to make the unification impossible. This criminal game only reflected the generally sorry state of the Austrian Opposition which has been overcome by the decay of the official Communist Party. This year each of the Austrian groups has succeeded in more than amply demonstrating that it is ready to give up the ideas and principles of the International Opposition but in no case its own sectarian pretensions. The more barren the ideological base of these groups, the more venomous the nature of their internal struggles. They delight in dragging the banner of the International Opposition into the mud and demand that the International Opposition use its authority to cover up their unworthy work.

Obviously the International Opposition is not going to do this. To bring unprincipled groups into the International Opposition would mean poisoning one's own organism. In this respect, strict selection is demanded. I hope that at its conference the International Opposition will adopt the "twenty-one conditions" for the admission of organizations into its ranks and that these conditions will be sufficiently severe.[151]

In contrast to the Austrian Opposition, the Chinese Opposition did not develop on the basis of petty backroom intrigues, but from the experiences of a great revolution that was lost by an opportunist leadership. Its great historic mission places exceptional responsibilities on the Chinese Opposition. All of us here hope that the Chinese Opposition will rid itself of the spirit of clannishness, and, rising to its full height, prove equal to the tasks it faces.

Yours,
L. Trotsky

From *Writings of Leon Trotsky (1930-31)*. Text from *Biulleten Oppozitsii* (Paris), no. 19, March 1931. The translation is by *Intercontinental Press*.

THE STRANGLED REVOLUTION

February 9, 1931

The book by André Malraux, *Les Conquérants,*[152] has been sent to me from various parts and I think in four copies, but to my regret I read it after a delay of a year and a half or two. The book is devoted to the Chinese revolution, that is, to the greatest subject of the last five years. A fine and well-knit style, the discriminating eye of an artist, original and daring observation— all confer upon the novel an exceptional importance. If we write about it here it is not because the book is a work of talent, although this is not a negligible fact, but because it offers a source of political lessons of the highest value. Do they come from Malraux? No, they flow from the recital itself, unknown to the author, and they go against him. This does honor to the author as an observer and an artist, but not as a revolutionist. However, we have the right to evaluate Malraux from this point of view, too; in his own name and above all in the name of Garine, his other self, the author does not hesitate with his judgments on the revolution.

This book is called a novel. As a matter of fact, we have before us a romanticized chronicle of the Chinese revolution, from its first period to the period of Canton. The chronicle is not complete. Social vigor is sometimes lacking from the picture. But for that there pass before the reader not only luminous episodes of the revolution but also clear-cut silhouettes which are graven in the memory like social symbols.

By little colored touches, following the method of *pointillisme,* Malraux gives an unforgettable picture of the general strike, not, to be sure, as it is below, not as it is carried out, but as it is observed from above: the Europeans do not get their breakfast, they swelter in the heat, the Chinese have ceased to work in the kitchens and to operate the ventilators. This is not a reproach to the author. The foreign artist could undoubtedly not have dealt with his theme otherwise. But there is a reproach to be made, and not a small one: the book is lacking in a congenital affinity between the writer, in spite of all he knows, understands, and can do, and his heroine—the revolution.

The active sympathies of the author for insurgent China are unmistakable. But chance bursts upon these sympathies. They are corroded by the excesses of individualism and by aesthetic caprice. In reading the book with sustained attention one sometimes experiences a feeling of vexation when in the tone of the persuasive recital one perceives a note of protective irony toward the barbarians capable of enthusiasm. That China is backward, that many of its political manifestations bear a primitive character—nobody asks that this be passed over in silence. But a correct perspective is needed which puts every object in its place. The Chinese events, on the basis of which Malraux's "novel" unfolds itself, are incomparably more important for the future destiny of human culture than the vain and pitiful clamor of European parliaments and the mountain of literary products of stagnant civilization. Malraux seems to feel a certain fear to take this into account.

In the novel, there are pages, splendid in their intensity, which show how revolutionary hatred is born of the yoke, of ignorance, of slavery, and is tempered like steel. These pages might have entered into the anthology of the revolution if Malraux had approached the masses with greater freedom and intrepidity, if he had not introduced into his observations a small note of blasé superiority, seeming to excuse himself for his transient contact with the insurrection of the Chinese people, as much perhaps before himself as before the academic mandarins in France and the traffickers in spiritual opium.

*   *   *

Borodin represents the Comintern in the post of "high counsellor" in the Canton government. Garine, the favorite of the author, is in charge of propaganda. All the work is done within the framework of the Kuomintang. Borodin, Garine, the Russian "General" Galen, the Frenchman Gérard, the German Klein, and others, constitute a first bureaucracy of the revolution raising itself above the insurgent people and conducting its own "revolutionary" policy instead of the policy of the revolution.

The local organizations of the Kuomintang are defined as follows: "groups of fanatics—brave . . . of a few plutocrats out for notoriety or for security—and crowds of students and coolies" (p. 24). Not only do bourgeois enter into every organization but they completely lead the party. The communists are subordinate to the Kuomintang. The workers and the peasants are persuaded to take no action that might rebuff the devoted friends of the bourgeoisie. "Such are the societies that we control (more or less, do not fool yourself on this score)." An edifying avowal! The bureaucracy of the Comintern tried to "control" the class struggle in China, like the international bankocracy controls the economic life of the backward countries. But a revolution cannot be controlled. One can only give a political expression to its internal forces. One must know to which of these forces to link his destiny.

"Today coolies are beginning to discover that they exist, simply that they exist" (p. 26). That's well aimed. But to feel that they exist, the coolies, the industrial workers, and the peasants must overthrow those who prevent them from existing. Foreign domination is indissolubly bound up with the domestic yoke. The coolies must not only drive out Baldwin or MacDonald but also overthrow the ruling classes. One cannot be accomplished without the other. Thus, the awakening of the human personality in the masses of China, who exceed ten times the population of France, is immediately transformed into the lava of the social revolution. A magnificent spectacle!

But here Borodin appears on the scene and declares: "In the revolution the workers must do the coolie work for the bourgeoisie," as Ch'en Tu-hsiu wrote in an open letter to the Chinese communists.[153] The social enslavement from which they want to liberate themselves, the workers find transposed into the sphere of politics. To whom do they owe this perfidious operation? To the bureaucracy of the Comintern. In trying to "control" the Kuomintang, it actually aids the bourgeoisie which seeks "notoriety and security" in enslaving the coolies who want to exist.

Borodin, who remains in the background all the time, is characterized in the novel as a "man of action," as a "professional revolutionist," as a living incarnation of Bolshevism on the soil of China. Nothing is further from the truth! Here is the political biography of Borodin: in 1903, at the age of nineteen, he emigrated to America; in 1918, he returned to Moscow where, thanks to his knowledge of English, he "insured contact with the foreign parties"; he was arrested in Glasgow in 1922; then he was delegated to China as representative of the Comintern. Having quit Russia *before* the first revolution and having returned *after* the third, Borodin appeared as the consummate representative of that state and party bureaucracy that recognized the revolution only after its victory. When it is a question of young people, it is sometimes nothing more than a matter of chronology. With people of forty or fifty, it is already a political characterization. If Borodin rallied successfully to the victorious revolution in Russia, it does not in the least signify that he was called upon to assure the victory of the revolution in China. People of this type assimilate without difficulty the gestures and intonations of "professional revolutionists." Many of them, by their protective coloration, not only deceive others but also themselves. The audacious inflexibility of the Bolshevik is most usually metamorphosed with them into that cynicism of the functionary ready for anything. Ah! to have a mandate from the Central Committee! This sacrosanct safeguard Borodin always had in his pocket.

Garine is not a functionary, he is more original than Borodin and perhaps even closer to the revolutionary type. But he is devoid of the indispensable education; dilettante and theatrical, he gets hopelessly entangled in the great events and he reveals it at every step. With regard to the slogans of the Chinese revolution, he expresses himself thus: ". . . democratic chatter— 'the rights of the proletariat,' etc." (p. 32). This has a radical ring but it is a false radicalism. The slogans of democracy are execrable chatter in the mouth of Poincaré, Herriot, Léon Blum, sleight-of-hand artists of France and jailors of Indochina, Algeria, and Morocco. But when the Chinese rebel in the name of the "rights of the proletariat," this has as little to do with chatter as the slogans of the French revolution in the eighteenth century. At Hong Kong, the British birds of prey threatened, during the strike, to reestablish corporal punishment. "The rights of man and of the citizen" meant at Hong Kong the right of the Chinese not to be flogged by the British whip. To unmask the democratic rottenness of the imperialists is to serve the revolution. To call the slogans of the insurrection of the oppressed "chatter" is to aid involuntarily the imperialist.

A good inoculation of Marxism would have preserved the author from fatal contempt of this sort. But Garine in general considers that revolutionary doctrine is "doctrinary rubbish" (*le fatras doctrinal*). He is, you see, one of those to whom the revolution is only a definite "state of affairs." Isn't this astonishing? But it is just because the revolution is a "state of affairs," that is, a stage in the development of society conditioned by objective causes and subjected to definite laws, that a scientific mind can foresee the general direction of processes. Only the study of the anatomy of society and of its physiology permits one to react to the course of events by basing oneself upon scientific foresight and not upon a dilettante's conjectures. The revolutionist who "despises" revolutionary doctrine is not a bit better than the healer who despises medical doctrine which he does not know, or than the engineer who rejects technology. People who without the aid of science try to rectify the "state of affairs" that is called a disease are called quacks or charlatans and are prosecuted by law. Had there existed a tribunal to judge the quacks of the revolution, it is probable that Borodin, like his Muscovite inspirers, would have been severely condemned. I am afraid Garine himself would not have come out of it unscathed.

Two figures are contrasted to each other in the novel, like the two poles of the national revolution; old Chen-Dai, the spiritual authority of the right wing of the Kuomintang, the prophet and saint of the bourgeoisie, and Hong, the young leader of the terrorists. Both are depicted with great force. Chen-Dai embodies the old Chinese culture translated into the language of European breeding; with this exquisite garment, he "ennobles" the interests of all the ruling classes of China. To be sure, Chen-Dai wants national liberation, but he dreads the masses more than the imperialists; he hates the revolution more than the yoke placed upon the nation. If he marches toward it, it is only to pacify it, to subdue it, to exhaust it. He conducts a policy of passive resistance on two fronts, against imperialism and against the revolution, the policy of Gandhi in India, the policy which, in definite periods and in one form or another, the bourgeoisie has conducted at every longitude and latitude. Passive resistance flows from the tendency of the bourgeoisie to canalize the movement of the masses and to make off with it.

When Garine says that Chen-Dai's influence rises above politics, one can only shrug one's shoulders. The masked policy of the "upright man" in China as in India expresses in the most sublime and abstractly moralizing form the conservative interests of the possessors. The personal disinterestedness of Chen-Dai is in no sense in opposition to his political function: the exploiters need "upright men" like the corrupted ecclesiastical hierarchy needs saints.

Who gravitates around Chen-Dai? The novel replies with meritorious precision: a world of "aged mandarins, smugglers of opium and of obscene photographs, of scholars turned bicycle dealers, of Parisian barristers, of intellectuals of every kind" (p. 124). Behind them stands a more solid bourgeoisie bound up with England, which arms General Tang against the revolution. In the expectation of victory, Tang prepares to make Chen-Dai the head of the government. Both of them, Chen-Dai and Tang, nevertheless continue to be members of the Kuomintang which Borodin and Garine serve.

When Tang has a village attacked by his armies, and when he prepares to butcher the revolutionists, beginning with Borodin and Garine, his party comrades, the latter with the aid of Hong, mobilize and arm the unemployed. But after the victory won over Tang, the leaders do not seek to change a thing that existed before. They cannot break the ambiguous bloc with Chen-Dai because they have no confidence in the workers, the coolies, the revolutionary masses; they are themselves contaminated with the prejudices of Chen-Dai whose qualified arm they are.

In order "not to rebuff" the bourgeoisie they are forced to enter into struggle with Hong. Who is he and where does he come from? "The lowest dregs" (p. 36). He is one of those who are making the revolution and not those who rally to it when it is victorious. Having come to the idea of killing the English governor of Hong Kong, Hong is concerned with only one thing: "When I have been sentenced to capital punishment, you must tell the young to follow my example" (p. 36). To Hong a clear program must be given: to arouse the workers, to assemble them, to arm them, and to oppose them to Chen-Dai as to an enemy. But the bureaucracy of the Comintern seeks Chen-Dai's friendship, repulses Hong and exasperates him. Hong exterminates bankers and merchants one after another, the very ones who "support" the Kuomintang, Hong kills missionaries: "those who teach people to support misery must be punished, Christian priests or others. . ." (p. 274). If Hong does not find the right road, it is the fault of Borodin and Garine, who have placed the revolution in the hands of the bankers and the merchants. Hong reflects the mass which is already rising but which has not yet rubbed its eyes or softened its hands. He tries by the revolver and the knife to act *for* the masses whom the agents of the Comintern are paralyzing. Such is the unvarnished truth about the Chinese revolution.

*   *   *

Meanwhile, the Canton government is "oscillating, in its attempt to stay straight, between Garine and Borodin, who control the police and the trade unions, on the one hand, and Chen-Dai, who controls nothing, but who exists all the same, on the other" (p. 68). We have an almost perfect picture of the duality of power. The representatives of the Comintern have in their hands the trade unions of Canton, the police, the cadet school of Whampoa, the sympathy of the masses, the aid of the Soviet Union. Chen-Dai has a "moral authority," that is, the prestige of the mortally distracted possessors. The friends of Chen-Dai sit in a powerless government willingly supported by the conciliators. But isn't this the regime of the February revolution, the Kerenskyist system, with the sole difference that the role of the Mensheviks is played by the pseudo-Bolsheviks? Borodin has no doubt of it even though he is made up as a Bolshevik and takes his makeup seriously.

The central idea of Garine and Borodin is to prohibit Chinese and foreign boats, cruising toward the port of Canton, from putting in at Hong Kong. By the commercial boycott these people, who consider themselves revolutionary realists, hope to shatter British domination in South China. They never deem it necessary first of all to overthrow the government of the Canton bourgeoisie which only waits for the moment to surrender the revolution to England. No, Borodin and Garine knock every day at the door of the "government," and hat in hand, beg that the saving decree be promulgated. One of them reminds Garine that at bottom the government is a phantom. Garine is not disconcerted. Phantom or not, he replies, let it go ahead while we need it. That is the way the priest needs relics that he himself fabricates with wax and cotton. What is concealed behind this policy which weakens and debases the revolution? The respect of a petty-bourgeois revolutionist for a solid conservative bourgeois. It is thus that the reddest of the French Radicals is always ready to fall on his knees before Poincaré.

But perhaps the masses of Canton are not yet mature enough to overthrow the power of the bourgeoisie? From this whole atmosphere, the conviction arises that without the opposition of the Comintern the phantom government would long before have been overthrown under the pressure of the masses. But let us suppose that the Cantonese workers were still too weak to establish their own power. What, generally speaking, is the weak spot of the masses? Their inclination to follow the exploiters. In this case, the first duty of revolutionists is to help the workers liberate themselves from servile confidence. Nevertheless, the work done by the bureaucracy of the Comintern was diametrically opposed to this. It inculcated in the masses the notion of the necessity to submit to the bourgeoisie and it declared that the enemies of the bourgeoisie were their own enemies.

Do not rebuff Chen-Dai! But if Chen-Dai withdraws in spite of this, which is inevitable, it would not mean that Garine and Borodin will be delivered of their voluntary vassaldom toward the bourgeoisie. They will only choose as the new focus of their activity Chiang Kai-shek, son of the same class and younger brother of Chen-Dai. Head of the Whampoa Military Academy, founded by the Bolsheviks, Chiang Kai-shek does not confine himself to passive resistance; he is ready to resort to bloody force, not in the plebeian form, the form of the masses, but in the military form and only within limits that will permit the bourgeoisie to retain an unlimited power over the army. Borodin and Garine, by arming their enemies, disarm and repulse their friends. This is the way they prepare the catastrophe.

But are we not overestimating the influence of the revolutionary bureaucracy upon the events? No, it showed itself stronger than it might have thought, if not for good then at least for evil. The coolies who are only beginning to exist politically require a courageous leadership. Hong requires a bold program. The revolution requires the energies of millions of rising men. But Borodin and his bureaucrats require Chen-Dai and Chiang Kaishek. They strangle Hong and prevent the worker from raising his head. In a few months, they will stifle the agrarian insurrection of the peasantry so as not to repulse the bourgeois army command. Their strength is that they represent the Russian October, Bolshevism, the Communist International. Having usurped authority, the banner, and the material resources of the greatest of revolutions, the bureaucracy bars the road to another revolution which also had all chances of being great.

The dialogue between Borodin and Hong (pp. 182-84) is the most terrific indictment of Borodin and his Moscow inspirers. Hong, as always, is after decisive action. He demands the punishment of the most prominent bourgeois. Borodin finds this sole objection: Those who are "paying" must not be touched. "Revolution is not so simple," says Garine for his part. "Revolution involves paying an army," adds Borodin. These aphorisms contain all the elements of the noose in which the Chinese revolution was strangled. Borodin protected the bourgeoisie which, in recompense, made contributions to the "revolution," the money going to the army of Chiang Kai-shek. The army of Chiang Kai-shek exterminated the proletariat and liquidated the revolution. Was it really impossible to foresee this? And wasn't it really foreseen? The bourgeoisie pays willingly only for the army which serves it against the people. The army of the revolution does not wait for donations: it makes them pay. This is called the revolutionary dictatorship.

Hong comes forward successfully at workers' meetings and thunders against the "Russians," the bearers of ruin for the revolution. The way of Hong himself does not lead to the goal but he is right as against Borodin. "Had the T'aip'ing leaders Russian advisers? Had the Boxers?" (p. 190).[154] Had the Chinese revolution of 1924-27 been left to itself it would perhaps not have come to victory immediately but it would not have resorted to the methods of hara-kiri, it would not have known shameful capitulations, and it would have trained revolutionary cadres. Between the dual power of Canton and that of Petrograd there is the tragic difference that in China there was no Bolshevism in evidence; under the name of Trotskyism, it was declared a counterrevolutionary doctrine and was persecuted by every method of calumny and repression. Where Kerensky did not succeed during the July days,[155] Stalin succeeded ten years later in China.

Borodin and "all the Bolsheviks of his generation," Garine assures us, were distinguished by their struggle against the anarchists. This remark was needed by the author so as to prepare the reader for the struggle of Borodin against Hong's group. Historically it is false. Anarchism was unable to raise its head in Russia not because the Bolsheviks fought successfully against it but because they had first dug up the ground under its feet. Anarchism, if it does not live within the four walls of intellectuals' cafes and editorial offices, but has penetrated more deeply, translates the psychology of despair in the masses and signifies the political punishment for the deceptions of democracy and the treachery of opportunism. The boldness of Bolshevism in posing the revolutionary problems and in teaching their solution left no room for the development of anarchism. But if Malraux's historical investigation is not exact, his recital shows admirably how the opportunist policy of Stalin-Borodin prepared the ground for anarchist terrorism in China.

Driven by the logic of this policy, Borodin consents to adopt a decree against the terrorists. The firm revolutionists, driven onto the road of adventurism by the crimes of the Moscow leaders, are declared outlaws by the bourgeoisie of Canton—with the benediction of the Comintern. They reply with acts of terrorism against the pseudorevolutionary bureaucrats who protect the monied bourgeoisie. Borodin and Garine seize the terrorists and destroy them, no longer defending the bourgeoisie alone but also their own heads. It is thus that the policy of conciliation inexorably slips down to the lowest degree of treachery.

The book is called *Les Conquérants*. With this title, which has a double meaning when the revolution confuses its aims with those of imperialism, the author refers to the Russian Bolsheviks, or more exactly, to a certain part of them. The conquerors? The Chinese masses rose for a revolutionary insurrection, with the influence of the October upheaval as their example and with Bolshevism as their banner. But the "conquerors" conquered nothing. On the contrary, they surrendered everything to the enemy. If the Russian revolution called forth the Chinese revolution, the Russian epigones strangled it. Malraux does not make these deductions. He does not even suspect their existence. All the more clearly do they emerge upon the background of his remarkable book.

From *Problems of the Chinese Revolution.*

WHAT IS HAPPENING IN THE CHINESE COMMUNIST PARTY?

Published March 1931

Pravda of December 25, 1930, tells us:

> In the fall of 1930, the Chinese Communist Party numbered 200,000 members. The party has uprooted the remnants of the ideas of Ch'en Tu-hsiu and has destroyed Trotskyism ideologically. [!]
>
> However, the complicated circumstances of struggle have recently given rise to certain reservations of a "leftist" semi-Trotskyist character inside the party. A whole number of leading comrades, who believe that a revolutionary situation has matured on an international scale, have posed the question of beginning an immediate struggle for power on a full national plane, ignoring the necessity of consolidating the soviet power in the regions already occupied by the Red Army. Proceeding from such an estimate, they consider it possible to cease the economic struggle of the proletariat and to liquidate the revolutionary unions.

This quotation gives one an idea of the chaos that reigns in the minds of the leading functionaries of the Chinese party. They have destroyed Trotskyism "ideologically"—that goes without saying—but immediately following this destruction, reservations of a "semi-Trotskyist character" rise anew. Such things have happened time and again. These reservations have arisen even among a "number of leading comrades." That also has happened before.[156]

What are these new semi-Trotskyist reservations? They manifest themselves, first of all, in the demand to begin an "immediate struggle for power on a full national plane." But the Left Opposition since the fall of 1927 has advanced the exact opposite demand: to withdraw the slogan of armed insurrection as an immediate slogan. Even today our Chinese comrades put on the agenda not the armed uprising, but the mobilization of the masses around the social demands of the proletariat and the peasantry and the slogans of revolutionary democracy; not adventurist experiments in the countryside, but the building up of the trade unions and the party! If *Pravda* is not indulging in slander (which is very likely), if the new opposition really voices demands "to cease the economic struggle of the proletariat and to liquidate the unions," then this is directly contrary to the proposals of the Left Opposition (Bolshevik-Leninists).

We read further on that the new opposition ignores "the necessity of consolidating the soviet power in the regions already occupied by the Red Army." Instead of such consolidation, it is as though the opposition were calling for a general national uprising. This too has nothing in common with the position of Bolshevik-Leninists. If the Chinese "Red Army" is regarded as the weapon of a proletarian uprising, then the Chinese communists must be guided by the laws of every revolutionary uprising. They must take the offensive, extend their territory, conquer the strategic centers of the country. Without this, every revolutionary uprising is hopeless. To delay, to remain on the defensive instead of taking the offensive, spells defeat for the uprising. In this sense, the new opposition, if its point of view has been correctly stated, is far more consistent than the Stalinists, who believe that "soviet power" in the countryside can be maintained for years or that soviet power can be transported from one end of the country to another in the baggage car of the partisan detachments labeled the "Red Army." But neither position resembles our own; both flow from a wrong point of departure. They renounce the class theory of soviet power. They dissolve the revolution into provincial peasant revolts, linking up the entire fate of the Chinese Communist Party with them in an adventurist manner.

What does the Communist Party represent? Quite unexpectedly we learn from this article that the Communist Party in the fall of 1930 numbered about "200,000 members." The figure is given without explanation. Last year, however, the Chinese party numbered only about six to seven thousand members. If this tremendous growth of the party during the last year is a fact, then this should be a symptom of a radical change in the situation in favor of the revolution. Two hundred thousand members! If in reality the party were to number fifty, forty, or even twenty thousand workers, after it had experienced the second Chinese revolution and had absorbed its lessons, we would say that this is a powerful force, and invincible; with such cadres, we can transform all of China. But we would also have to ask: Are these twenty thousand workers members of the unions? What kind of work are they carrying on within them? Is their influence growing? Are they linking up their organizations with the masses of the unorganized and of the rural periphery? And under what slogans?

The fact is that the leadership of the Comintern is concealing something from the proletarian vanguard. We can be certain that the lion's share of these 200,000—let us say from 90 to 95 percent—come from regions where the detachments of the "Red Army" are active. One has only to imagine the political psychology of the peasant detachments and the conditions under which they carry on their activity to get a clear political picture: the partisans, most probably, are almost all enrolled in the party, and after them the peasants in the occupied regions. The Chinese party, as well as the "Red Army" and the "soviet power," has abandoned the proletarian rails and is heading toward the rural districts and the countryside.

In seeking a way out of the impasse, the new Chinese opposition advances, as we have read, the slogan of a proletarian uprising on a national plane. Obviously this would be the best outcome, if the prerequisites for it were to exist. But they do not exist today. What, then, can be done? We must develop slogans for the interval between revolutions, the length of which no one can tell in advance. These are the slogans of the democratic revolution: land to the peasants, the eight-hour workday, national independence, the right of national self-determination for all people, and, finally, the constituent assembly. Under these slogans the provincial peasant uprisings of the partisan detachments will break out of their provincial isolation and fuse with the general national movement, linking their own fate with it. The Communist Party will emerge, not as the technical guide of the Chinese peasantry, but as the political leader of the working class of the entire country. There is no other road!

Excerpted from "Notes of a Journalist" in *Writings of Leon Trotsky (1930-31)*. Text from the *Militant* (New York), April 15, 1931.

A STRANGLED REVOLUTION
AND ITS STRANGLERS

June 13, 1931

Urgent work prevented me from reading sooner the article by Malraux in which he defends, against my criticism, the Communist International, Borodin, Garine, and himself. As a political publicist, Malraux is at a still greater distance from the proletariat and from the revolution than as an artist. By itself, this fact would not justify these lines, for it is nowhere said that a talented writer must necessarily be a proletarian revolutionist. If I nevertheless return to the same question again, it is for the sake of the subject, and not of Malraux.

The best figures of the novel, I said, attained the stature of social symbols. I must add: Borodin, Garine, and all their "collaborators" represent the symbol of the quasi-revolutionary bureaucracy, of that new "social type" which was born thanks to the existence of the Soviet state on the one hand, and on the other to a definite regime in the Comintern.

I declined to classify Borodin among the "professional revolutionists," as he is characterized in the novel. Malraux endeavors to show me that Garine has enough mandarin's buttons to give him the right to this title. Here, Malraux finds it in place to add that Trotsky has a greater quantity of buttons. Isn't it ridiculous? The type of the professional revolutionist is not at all some sort of an ideal type. But in all events, it is a *definite* type, with a definite political biography and with salient traits. Only Russia created this type during the last decades; in Russia, the most perfect of this type was created by the Bolshevik party.

The professional revolutionists of the generation to which Borodin belonged began to take shape on the eve of the first revolution, they were put to the test in 1905, they tempered and educated (or decomposed) themselves during the years of the counterrevolution; they stood the supreme test in 1917. From 1903 up to 1918, that is, during the whole period when, in Russia, this type of professional revolutionist was being formed, Borodin, and hundreds, thousands of Borodins, remained outside of the struggle. In 1918, after the victory, Borodin arrived to offer his services. This does him honor: it is worthier to serve the proletarian state than the bourgeois state. Borodin charged himself with perilous missions. But the agents of bourgeois states in foreign countries, especially in colonial countries, also, and that quite frequently, accomplish perilous tasks. Yet they do not become revolutionists because of that. The type of the functionary-adventurer and the type of the professional revolutionist, at certain moments and by certain qualities, can find points of similarity. But by their psychological formation as much as by their historical function, they are two opposite types.

The revolution pursues its course together with its class. If the proletariat is weak, if it is backward, the revolution confines itself to the modest, patient and persevering work of the creation of propaganda circles, of the preparation of cadres; supporting itself upon the first cadres, it passes over to mass agitation, legal or illegal, according to the circumstances. It always distinguishes its class from the enemy class, and conducts only such a policy as corresponds to the strength of its class and consolidates this strength. The French, the Russian, or the Chinese proletarian revolutionist, will look upon the Chinese workers as his own army, of today or of tomorrow. The functionary-adventurer raises himself above all the classes of the Chinese nation. He considers himself predestined to dominate, to give orders, to command, independently of the internal relationship of forces in China

Since the Chinese proletariat is weak today and cannot assure the commanding positions, the functionary conciliates and joins together the different classes. He acts as the inspector of the nation, as the viceroy for the affairs of the colonial revolution. He arranges combinations between the conservative bourgeois and the anarchist, he improvises a program *ad hoc,* he erects policies upon ambiguities, he creates a bloc of four classes, he swallows swords and scoffs at principles. With what result? The bourgeoisie is richer, more influential, more experienced. The functionary-adventurer does not succeed in deceiving it. But for that, he deceives the workers, filled with the spirit of abnegation, but not experienced, by turning them over to the hands of the bourgeoisie. Such was the role of the bureaucracy of the Comintern in the Chinese revolution.

Considering as natural the right of the "revolutionary" bureaucracy to command independently of the forces of the proletariat, Malraux informs us that one could not participate in the Chinese revolution without participating in the war, and one could not participate in the war without participating in the Kuomintang, etc. . . . To this, he adds: the break with the Kuomintang would have meant, for the Communist Party, the necessity of passing into illegality. When one thinks that these arguments sum up the philosophy of the representatives of the Comintern in China, he cannot refrain from saying: Indeed, the dialectic of the historical process sometimes plays bad jokes upon organizations, upon men, and upon ideas! How easy it is to solve the problem—in order to participate successfully in the events directed by the enemy class, one must submit to this class; in order to avoid repressions on the part of the Kuomintang, one must paint himself up in its colors! There you have the secret of Borodin-Garine.

Malraux's political estimate of the situation, of the possibilities and the tasks in China in 1925, is entirely false; it hardly reaches the borderline where the real problems of the revolution begin. I have said elsewhere all that had to be said on this subject, and Malraux's article gives no ground for a reexamination of what has been said. But even by standing on the ground of the false estimate Malraux gives of the situation, one can in no case justify the policy of Stalin-Borodin-Garine. In order to protest in 1925 against this policy, certain things had to be foreseen. In order to defend in it 1931, one must be incurably blind.

Did the strategy of the functionaries of the Comintern bring the Chinese proletariat anything but humiliations, the extermination of its cadres, and above all, a terrific confusion of mind? Did the shameful capitulation before the Kuomintang avert repression for the party? On the contrary, it only accumulated and concentrated the repressions. Was not the Communist Party compelled to pass into illegality? And when? In the period of the crushing of the revolution! If the communists had begun by illegal work, at the beginning of the revolutionary tide, they would have emerged upon the open arena at the head of the masses. By effacing and demoralizing the party with the aid of the Borodins and Garines, Chiang Kai-shek compelled it later, with all the greater success, to take refuge in illegality during the years of the counterrevolution. The policy of Borodin-Garine entirely served the Chinese bourgeoisie. The Chinese Communist Party must begin all over again at the beginning, and that on an arena encumbered with debris, with prejudices, with uncomprehended mistakes, and with the distrust of the advanced workers. Those are the results.

The criminal character of this whole policy reveals itself with particular acuteness in isolated questions. Malraux presents as a merit of Borodin and Company the fact that in turning over the terrorists to the hand of the bourgeoisie, he deliberately pushed under the knife of the terror the leader of the bourgeoisie, Chen-Dai. This machination is worthy of a bureaucratic Borgia or of the "revolutionary" Polish *szlachta* [gentry and nobility] who always preferred to fire with the hands of others behind the backs of the people. No, the task was not to kill Chen-Dai in ambush, but to prepare the overthrow of the bourgeoisie. When the party of the revolution is obliged to kill, it does it on its own responsibility, in the name of tasks and immediate aims understood by the masses.

Revolutionary morals are not abstract Kantian norms, but rules of conduct that place the revolutionist under the control of the tasks and aims of his class. Borodin and Garine were not bound up with the masses, they did not absorb the spirit of responsibility before the class. They are bureaucratic supermen who consider that "everything is permitted" . . . within the limits of the mandate received from above. The activity of such men, effective as it may be at certain moments, can only be directed, in the last instance, against the interests of the revolution.

After having killed Chen-Dai with the hands of Hong, Borodin and Garine then turn over Hong and his group to the hands of the executioners. This stamps their whole policy with the brand of Cain. Here too Malraux poses as a defender. What is his argument? Lenin and Trotsky also punished the anarchists. It is hard to believe that this is said by a man who came near the revolution, even if but for a moment. Malraux forgets or does not understand that the revolution takes place in the name of the domination of one class over another, that it is only from this task that revolutionists draw their right to violence.

The bourgeoisie exterminates the revolutionists, sometimes also the anarchists (more and more infrequently, because they become ever more obedient) in the name of safeguarding the regime of exploitation and baseness. Under the domination of the bourgeoisie, the Bolsheviks always defend the anarchists against the Chiappes.[157] After having conquered power, the Bolsheviks did everything to draw the anarchists over to the side of the dictatorship of the proletariat. They succeeded in actuality in drawing the majority of the anarchists behind them. Yes, the Bolsheviks severely punished those anarchists who undermined the dictatorship of the proletariat. Were we right or weren't we? That depends upon the manner in which one evaluates our revolution and the regime instituted by it. But can one imagine for a single instant that the Bolsheviks—under Prince Lvov or under Kerensky, under the bourgeois regime—would act as its agents in the extermination of anarchists? It is enough to formulate the question clearly, to turn aside in disgust. Just as Bridoison interests himself only in the form and ignores the essence, so the quasi-revolutionary bureaucracy and its literary attorney interest themselves only in the mechanics of the revolution, ignoring the question of what class and what regime they should serve. Here lies the abyss between the revolutionist and the functionary of the revolution.

What Malraux says about Marxism is a joke. The Marxist policy was not applicable in China because, you see, the proletariat was not class conscious. It would seem then that from this flows the task of awakening this class consciousness. But Malraux deduces a justification of the policy directed against the interests of the proletariat.

The other argument is no more convincing and still less amusing: Trotsky speaks of the need of Marxism for revolutionary politics; but isn't Borodin a Marxist? And Stalin, isn't he a Marxist? Then it is not a question of Marxism. I defend, against Garine, the revolutionary doctrine, just as I would defend, against a sorcerer, the medical sciences. The sorcerer will say to me in his defense that diplomaed doctors also very often kill their patients. It is an argument unworthy of a moderately educated burgher, and not only of a revolutionist. The fact that medicine is not omnipotent, that the doctors do not always effect cures, that one finds among them ignoramuses, blockheads and even poisoners—can this fact serve as an argument for giving the right to practice medicine to sorcerers, who have never studied medicine and who deny its significance?

I must make one correction, after having read Malraux's article. In my article I expressed the idea that an inoculation of Marxism would do Garine good. I don't think so any more.

From *Problems of the Chinese Revolution.*

THE SOVIET UNION AND
JAPAN'S MANCHURIAN ADVENTURE[158]

November 26, 1931

5. The tsarist adventure in Manchuria led to the Russo-Japanese War; the war—to the 1905 revolution. The present Japanese adventure in Manchuria can lead to revolution in *Japan*.

At the beginning of the century, the feudal-military regime of that country could still successfully serve the interests of the young Japanese capitalism. But in the last quarter of a century, capitalist development has brought extraordinary decomposition in the old social and political forms. Since that time, Japan has more than once been on the brink of revolution. But she lacked a strong revolutionary class to accomplish the tasks imposed on it by the developments. The Manchurian adventure may accelerate the revolutionary catastrophe for the Japanese regime.

Present-day China, no matter how enfeebled it may be by the dictatorship of the Kuomintang clique, differs greatly from the China which Japan, following the European powers, despoiled in the past. China has not the strength to drive out the Japanese expeditionary forces immediately, but the national consciousness and activity of the Chinese people have grown enormously; hundreds of thousands, millions of Chinese have gone through military training. The Chinese will rig up newer and yet newer armies. The Japanese will feel themselves besieged. The railroads will be of far greater service for war than for economic purposes. More and more new troops will have to be sent out. The Manchurian expedition spreading out will begin to exhaust Japan's economic organism, increase the discontent inside the country, sharpen the contradictions, and thereby accelerate the revolutionary crisis.

6. In *China*, the necessity for a determined defense against the

imperialist invasion will also provoke serious internal political consequences. The Kuomintang regime arose out of the national revolutionary mass movement which was exploited and strangled by the bourgeois militarists (with the aid of the Stalinist bureaucracy). Precisely for this reason, the present regime, shaky and full of contradictions, is incapable of initiating a revolutionary war. The necessity for a defense against the Japanese tyrants will turn more and more against the Kuomintang regime, nourishing the revolutionary sentiments of the masses. With a correct policy, the proletarian vanguard can, under these conditions, make up for all that was so tragically lost in the course of the years 1924-27.

7. The present events in *Manchuria* prove particularly how naive those gentlemen were who demanded of the Soviet Union the simple return of the Chinese Eastern Railroad to China. That would have meant surrendering it voluntarily to Japan, in whose hands the railroad would have become a weapon against China as well as against the USSR. If anything at all had hitherto prevented the Japanese military cliques from intervention in Manchuria, and if anything may still hold them within the bounds of caution today, it is the fact that the Chinese Eastern Railroad is the property of the Soviets.

8. Cannot the Manchurian adventure of the Japanese nevertheless lead to war with the USSR? It goes without saying that this is not excluded even with the wisest and most cautious policy on the part of the Soviet government. The internal contradictions of feudal-capitalistic Japan have obviously unbalanced her government. There is no lack of instigators (France). And from the historical experiences of tsarism in the Far East, we know what an unbalanced military-bureaucratic monarchy is capable of.

The struggle unfolding in the Far East is, of course, carried on not for the sake of the railroads, but over the fate of all of China. In this gigantic historical struggle, the Soviet government cannot be neutral, cannot take the same position with regard to China and Japan. It is duty bound to stand completely and fully on the side of the Chinese people. Only the unflinching loyalty of the Soviet government to the struggle for the liberation of the oppressed peoples can really protect the Soviet Union on the eastern frontier against Japan, Britain, France, the United States.

The ways in which the Soviet government will support the struggle of the Chinese people in the coming period depend upon the concrete historical circumstances. If it would have been absurd to surrender the Chinese Eastern Railroad voluntarily to Japan earlier, then it would be just as absurd to subordinate the entire policy in the Far East to the question of the Chinese Eastern Railroad. There is much to suggest that the behavior of the Japanese military clique on this question has a consciously provocatory character. The direct instigators of this provocation are the French rulers. The aim of the provocation is to tie the Soviet Union down in the East. All the more firmness and farsightedness is required on the part of the Soviet government.

The fundamental conditions of the East—its immense expanse, its countless human masses, its economic backwardness—give all processes a slow, drawn out, and crawling character. In any case, there is no immediate or acute threat to the existence of the Soviet Union from the Far East. During the coming period, the main events will unfold in Europe. Here great opportunities may arise, but from the same source also, great dangers threaten. For the present, only Japan has tied its hands in the Far East. The Soviet Union must, for the present, keep its hands free.

Excerpted from "Germany, the Key to the International Situation" in *The Struggle Against Fascism in Germany* (New York: Pathfinder Press, 1971). Translated by Sam Gordon and Morris Lewitt.

PEASANT WAR IN CHINA AND THE PROLETARIAT

September 22, 1932

Dear Comrades:

After a long delay, we received your letter of June 15. Needless to say we were overjoyed by the revival and the renascence of the Chinese Left Opposition, despite the most ferocious police persecutions it had endured.[159] So far as one may judge from here, handicapped as we are by extreme lack of information, the position expressed in your letter coincides with ours.

Our irreconcilable attitude toward the vulgar democratic Stalinist position on the peasant movement has, of course, nothing in common with a careless or passive attitude toward the peasant movement itself. The manifesto of the International Left Opposition that was issued two years ago and that evaluated the peasant movement in the southern provinces of China declared: "The Chinese revolution, betrayed, defeated, exhausted, shows that it is still alive. Let us hope that the time when it will again lift its proletarian head is not far off." Further on it says: "The vast flood of peasant revolts can unquestionably provide the impulse for the revival of political struggle in the industrial centers. We firmly count on it."

Your letter testifies that under the influence of the crisis and the Japanese intervention, against the background of the peasant war, the struggle of the city workers is burgeoning once again. In the manifesto we wrote about this possibility with necessary caution: "Nobody can foretell now whether the hearths of the peasant revolt can keep a fire burning through the whole long period of time which the proletarian vanguard will need to gather its own strength, bring the working class into the fight, and coordinate its struggle for power with the general offensive of the peasants against their most immediate enemies."

At the present time it is evident that there are substantial grounds for expressing the hope that, through a correct policy, it will be possible to unite the workers' movement, and the urban movement in general, with the peasant war; and this would constitute the beginning of the third Chinese revolution. But in the meantime this still remains only a hope, not a certainty. The most important work lies ahead.

In this letter I want to pose only one question which seems to me, at least from afar, to be the most important and acute. Once again I must remind you that the information at my disposal is altogether insufficient, accidental, and disjointed. I would indeed welcome any amplification and correction.

The peasant movement has created its own armies, has seized great territories, and has installed its own institutions. In the event of further successes—and all of us, of course, passionately desire such successes—the movement will become linked up with the urban and industrial centers and, through that very fact, it will come face to face with the working class. What will be the nature of this encounter? Is it certain that its character will be peaceful and friendly?

At first glance the question might appear to be superfluous. The peasant movement is headed by communists or sympathizers. Isn't it self-evident that in the event of their coming together the workers and the peasants must unanimously unite under the communist banner?

Unfortunately the question is not at all so simple. Let me refer to the experience of Russia. During the years of the civil war the peasantry in various parts of the country created its own guerrilla detachments, which sometimes grew into full-fledged armies. Some of these detachments considered themselves Bolshevik, and were often led by workers. Others remained nonparty and most often were led by former noncommissioned officers from among the peasantry. There was also an "anarchist" army under the command of Makhno.

So long as the guerrilla armies operated in the rear of the White Guards, they served the cause of the revolution. Some of them were distinguished by exceptional heroism and fortitude. But within the cities these armies often came into conflict with the workers and with the local party organizations. Conflicts also arose during encounters of the partisans with the regular Red Army, and in some instances they took an extremely painful and sharp character.

The grim experience of the civil war demonstrated to us the necessity of disarming peasant detachments immediately after the Red Army occupied provinces which had been cleared of the White Guards. In these cases the best, the most class-conscious and disciplined elements were absorbed into the ranks of the Red Army. But a considerable portion of the partisans strived to maintain an independent existence and often came into direct armed conflict with the Soviet power. Such was the case with the anarchist army of Makhno, entirely kulak in spirit. But that was not the sole instance; many peasant detachments, which fought splendidly enough against the restoration of the landlords, became transformed after victory into instruments of counterrevolution.

Regardless of their origin in each isolated instance—whether caused by conscious provocation of the White Guards, or by tactlessness of the communists, or by an unfavorable combination of circumstances—the conflicts between armed peasants and workers were rooted in one and the same social soil: the difference between the class position and training of the workers and of the peasants. The worker approaches questions from the socialist standpoint; the peasant's viewpoint is petty bourgeois. The worker strives to socialize the property that is taken away from the exploiters; the peasant seeks to divide it up. The worker desires to put palaces and parks to common use; the peasant, insofar as he cannot divide them, inclines to burning the palaces and cutting down the parks. The worker strives to solve problems on a national scale and in accordance with a plan; the peasant, on the other hand, approaches all problems on a local scale and takes a hostile attitude to centralized planning, etc.

It is understood that a peasant also is capable of raising himself to the socialist viewpoint. Under a proletarian regime more and more masses of peasants become reeducated in the socialist spirit. But this requires time, years, even decades. It should be borne in mind that in the initial stages of revolution, contradictions between proletarian socialism and peasant individualism often take on an extremely acute character.

But after all aren't there communists at the head of the Chinese Red armies? Doesn't this by itself exclude the possibility of conflicts between the peasant detachments and the workers' organizations? No, that does not exclude it. The fact that individual communists are in the leadership of the present armies does not at all transform the social character of these armies, even if their communist leaders bear a definite proletarian stamp. And how do matters stand in China?

Among the communist leaders of Red detachments there indubitably are many declassed intellectuals and semi-intellectuals who have not gone through the school of proletarian struggle. For two or three years they live the lives of partisan commanders and commissars; they wage battles, seize territories, etc. They absorb the spirit of their environment. Meanwhile the majority of the rank-and-file communists in the Red detachments unquestionably consists of peasants, who assume the name communist in all honesty and sincerity but who in actuality remain revolutionary paupers or revolutionary petty proprietors. In politics he who judges by denominations and labels and not by social facts is lost. All the more so when the politics concerned is carried out arms in hand.

The true Communist Party is the organization of the proletarian vanguard. But we must not forget that the working class of China has been kept in an oppressed and amorphous condition during the last four years, and only recently has it evinced signs of revival. It is one thing when a Communist Party, firmly resting on the flower of the urban proletariat, strives through the workers to lead a peasant war. It is an altogether different thing when a few thousand or even tens of thousands of revolutionists, who are truly communists or only take the name, assume the leadership of a peasant war without having serious support from the proletariat. This is precisely the situation in China. This acts to augment to an extreme the danger of conflicts between the workers and the armed peasants. In any event, one may rest assured there will be no dearth of bourgeois provocateurs.

In Russia, in the period of civil war, the proletariat was already in power in the greater part of the country, the leadership of the struggle was in the hands of a strong and tempered party, the entire commanding apparatus of the centralized Red Army was in the hands of the workers. Notwithstanding all this, the peasant detachments, incomparably weaker than the Red Army, often came into conflict with it after it victoriously moved into peasant guerrilla sectors.

In China the situation is radically different, and moreover completely to the disadvantage of the workers. In the most important regions of China the power is in the hands of bourgeois militarists; in other regions, in the hands of leaders of armed peasants. Nowhere is there any proletarian power as yet. The trade unions are weak. The influence of the party among the workers is insignificant. The peasant detachments, flushed with victories they have achieved, stand under the wing of the Comintern. They call themselves "the Red Army," i.e., they identify themselves with the armed forces of the Soviets. What results consequently is that the revolutionary peasantry of China, in the person of its ruling stratum, seems to have appropriated to itself beforehand the political and moral capital which should by the nature of things belong to the Chinese workers. Isn't it possible that things may turn out so that all this capital will be directed at a certain moment *against* the workers?

Naturally the peasant poor, and in China they constitute the overwhelming majority, to the extent they think politically, and these comprise a small minority, sincerely and passionately desire alliance and friendship with the workers. But the peasantry, even when armed, is incapable of conducting an independent policy.

Occupying in daily life an intermediate, indeterminate, and vacillating position, the peasantry at decisive moments can follow either the proletariat or the bourgeoisie. The peasantry does not find the road to the proletariat easily but only after a series of mistakes and defeats. The bridge between the peasantry and the bourgeoisie is provided by the urban petty bourgeoisie, chiefly by the intellectuals, who commonly come forward under the banner of socialism and even communism.

The commanding stratum of the Chinese "Red Army" has no doubt succeeded in inculcating itself with the habit of issuing commands. The absence of a strong revolutionary party and of mass organizations of the proletariat renders control over the commanding stratum virtually impossible. The commanders and commissars appear in the guise of absolute masters of the situation and upon occupying cities will be rather apt to look down from above upon the workers. The demands of the workers might often appear to them either inopportune or ill-advised.

Nor should one forget such "trifles" as the fact that within cities the staffs and offices of the victorious armies are established not in the proletarian huts but in the finest city buildings, in the houses and apartments of the bourgeoisie; and all this facilitates the inclination of the upper stratum of the peasant armies to feel itself part of the "cultured" and "educated" classes, in no way part of the proletariat.

Thus, in China the causes and grounds for conflicts between

the army, which is peasant in composition and petty bourgeois in leadership, and the workers not only are not eliminated but, on the contrary, all the circumstances are such as to greatly increase the possibility and even the inevitability of such conflicts; and in addition the chances of the proletariat are far less favorable to begin with than was the case in Russia.

From the theoretical and political side the danger is increased many times because the Stalinist bureaucracy covers up the contradictory situation by its slogan of "democratic dictatorship" of workers and peasants. Is it possible to conceive of a snare more attractive in appearance and more perfidious in essence? The epigones do their thinking not by means of social concepts, but by means of stereotyped phrases; formalism is the basic trait of bureaucracy.

The Russian Narodniks used to accuse the Russian Marxists of "ignoring" the peasantry, of not carrying on work in the villages, etc. To this the Marxists replied: "We will arouse and organize the advanced workers and through the workers we shall arouse the peasants." Such in general is the only conceivable road for the proletarian party.

The Chinese Stalinists have acted otherwise. During the revolution of 1925-27 they subordinated directly and immediately the interests of the workers and the peasants to the interests of the national bourgeoisie. In the years of the counterrevolution they passed over from the proletariat to the peasantry, i.e., they undertook that role which was fulfilled in our country by the SRs when they were still a revolutionary party. Had the Chinese Communist Party concentrated its efforts for the last few years in the cities, in industry, on the railroads; had it sustained the trade unions, the educational clubs and circles; had it, without breaking off from the workers, taught them to understand what was occurring in the villages—the share of the proletariat in the general correlation of forces would have been incomparably more favorable today.

The party actually tore itself away from its class. Thereby in the last analysis it can cause injury to the peasantry as well. For should the proletariat continue to remain on the sidelines, without organization, without leadership, then the peasant war even if fully victorious will inevitably arrive in a blind alley.

In old China every victorious peasant revolution was concluded by the creation of a new dynasty, and subsequently also by a new group of large proprietors; the movement was caught in a vicious circle. Under present conditions the peasant war by itself, without the direct leadership of the proletarian vanguard, can only pass on the power to a new bourgeois clique, some "left" Kuomintang or other, the "Third Party," etc., etc., which in practice will differ very little from the Kuomintang of Chiang Kai-shek. And this would signify in turn a new massacre of the workers with the weapons of "democratic dictatorship."

What then are the conclusions that follow from all this? The first conclusion is that one must boldly and openly face the facts as they are. The peasant movement is a mighty revolutionary factor insofar as it is directed against the large landowners, militarists, feudalists, and usurers. But in the peasant movement itself are very powerful proprietary and reactionary tendencies, and at a certain stage it can become hostile to the workers and sustain that hostility already equipped with arms. He who forgets about the dual nature of the peasantry is not a Marxist. The advanced workers must be taught to distinguish from among "communist" labels and banners the actual social processes.

The activities of the "Red armies" must be attentively followed, and the workers must be given a detailed explanation of the course, significance, and perspectives of the peasant war; and the immediate demands and the tasks of the proletariat must be tied up with the slogans for the liberation of the peasantry.

On the bases of our own observations, reports, and other documents we must painstakingly study the life processes of the peasant armies and the regime established in the regions occupied by them; we must discover in living facts the contradictory class tendencies and clearly point out to the workers the tendencies we support and those we oppose.

We must follow the interrelations between the Red armies and the local workers with special care, without overlooking even the minor misunderstandings between them. Within the framework of isolated cities and regions, conflicts, even if acute, might appear to be insignificant local episodes. But with the development of events, class conflicts may take on a national scope and lead the revolution to a catastrophe, i.e., to a new massacre of the workers by the peasants, hoodwinked by the bourgeoisie. The history of revolutions is full of such examples.

The more clearly the advanced workers understand the living dialectic of the class interrelations of the proletariat, the peasantry, and the bourgeoisie, the more confidently will they seek unity with the peasant strata closest to them, and the more successfully will they counteract the counterrevolutionary provocateurs within the peasant armies themselves as well as within the cities.

The trade union and the party units must be built up, the advanced workers must be educated, the proletarian vanguard must be brought together and drawn into the battle.

We must turn to all the members of the official Communist Party with words of explanation and challenge. It is quite probable that the rank-and-file communists who have been led astray by the Stalinist faction will not understand us at once. The bureaucrats will set up a howl about our "underestimation" of the peasantry, perhaps even about our "hostility" to the peasantry. (Chernov always accused Lenin of being hostile to the peasantry.) Naturally such howling will not confuse the Bolshevik-Leninists. When prior to April 1927 we warned against the inevitable coup d'etat of Chiang Kai-shek, the Stalinists accused us of hostility to the Chinese national revolution. Events have demonstrated who was right. Events will provide a confirmation this time as well.

The Left Opposition may turn out to be too weak to direct events in the interests of the proletariat at the present stage. But we are sufficiently strong right now to point out to the workers the correct road and, in the development of the class struggle, to demonstrate to the workers our correctness and political insight. Only in this way can a revolutionary party gain the confidence of the workers, only in this way will it grow, become strong, and take its place at the head of the popular masses.

Postscript, September 26, 1932

In order to express my ideas as clearly as possible, let me sketch the following variant, which is theoretically quite possible.

Let us assume that the Chinese Left Opposition carries on in the near future widespread and successful work among the industrial proletariat and attains the preponderant influence over it. The official party, in the meantime, continues to concentrate all its forces on the "Red armies" and in the peasant regions. The moment arrives when the peasant troops occupy the industrial centers and are brought face to face with the workers. In such a situation, in what manner will the Chinese Stalinists act?

It is. not difficult to foresee that they will counterpose the peasant army to the "counterrevolutionary Trotskyists" in a hostile manner. In other words, they will incite the armed peasants against the advanced workers. This is what the Russian SRs and the Mensheviks did in 1917; having lost the workers, they fought might and main for support among the soldiers, inciting the barracks against the factory, the armed peasant against the worker Bolshevik. Kerensky, Tseretelli, and Dan, if they did not label the Bolsheviks outright as counterrevolutionists, called them either "unconscious aides" or "involuntary agents" of counterrevolution. The Stalinists are less choice in their application of political terminology. But the tendency is the same: malicious incitement of the peasant, and generally petty-bourgeois, elements against the vanguard of the working class.

Bureaucratic centrism, as centrism, cannot have an independent class support. But in its struggle against the Bolshevik-Leninists it is compelled to seek support from the right, i.e., from the peasantry and the petty bourgeoisie, counterposing them to the proletariat. The struggle between the two communist factions, the Stalinist and the Bolshevik-Leninists, thus bears in itself an inner *tendency* toward transformation into a class struggle. The revolutionary development of events in China may draw this tendency to its conclusion, i.e., to a civil war between the peasant army led by the Stalinists and the proletarian vanguard led by the Leninists.

Were such a tragic conflict to arise, due entirely to the Chinese Stalinists, it would signify that the Left Opposition and the Stalinists ceased to be communist factions and had become hostile political parties, each having a different class base.

However, is such a perspective inevitable? No, I don't think so at all. Within the Stalinist faction (the official Chinese Communist Party) there are not only peasant, i.e., petty-bourgeois tendencies but also proletarian tendencies. It is extremely important for the Left Opposition to seek to establish connections with the proletarian wing of the Stalinists by presenting to them the Marxist evaluation of "Red armies" and the interrelations between the proletariat and the peasantry in general.

While maintaining its political independence, the proletarian vanguard must be ready always to assure united action with revolutionary democracy. While we refuse to identify the armed peasant detachment with the Red Army as the armed power of the proletariat and have no inclination to shut our eyes to the fact that the communist banner hides the petty-bourgeois content of the peasant movement, we, on the other hand, take an absolutely clear view of the tremendous revolutionary democratic significance of the peasant war. We teach the workers to appreciate its significance and we are ready to do all in our power in order to achieve the necessary military alliance with the peasant organizations.

Consequently our task consists not only in preventing the political-military command over the proletariat by the petty-bourgeois democracy that leans upon the armed peasant, but in preparing and ensuring the proletarian leadership of the peasant movement, its "Red armies" in particular.

The more clearly the Chinese Bolshevik-Leninists comprehend the political events and the tasks that spring from them, the more successfully will they extend their base within the proletariat. The more persistently they carry out the policy of the united front in relation to the official party and the peasant movement led by it, the more surely will they succeed not only in shielding the revolution from a terribly dangerous conflict between the proletariat and the peasantry and in ensuring the necessary united action between the two revolutionary classes, but also in transforming their united front into the historical step toward the dictatorship of the proletariat.

From *Writings of Leon Trotsky (1932)*. Text from the *Militant* (New York), October 15, 1932.

FOR A STRATEGY OF ACTION,
NOT SPECULATION

A Letter to Friends in Peking

October 3, 1932

What are at present the chief elements of the political situation in China?

The two most important revolutionary problems, the national problem and the agrarian problem, have again become aggravated. The pace of the peasant war, slow and crawling but generally victorious, is evidence that the Kuomintang dictatorship has proved incapable of satisfying the countryside or of intimidating it further. The Japanese intervention in Shanghai and their effective annexation of Manchuria have placed in relief the military bankruptcy of the Kuomintang dictatorship. The crisis of power, which at bottom has not stopped for a single moment during these last years, had to grow fatally worse. The struggle between the militarist cliques is destroying what remains of the unity of the country.

If the peasant war has radicalized the intellectuals who have connections with the countryside, the Japanese intervention, on the other hand, has politically stimulated the petty bourgeoisie of the cities. This again has only aggravated the crisis of power. There is not a single section of the bourgeoisie called "nationalist" which does not tend to arrive at the conclusion that the Kuomintang regime devours much and gives little. To demand an end to the period of "tutelage" by the Kuomintang is to demand that the military dictatorship give way to parliamentarism.

The Left Opposition press has sometimes labeled the regime of Chiang Kai-shek as fascist. This definition was derived from the fact that in China, as in Italy, the military-police power is concentrated in the hands of a single bourgeois party to the exclusion of all other parties and, notably, of the workers' organizations. But after the experience of the last years, an experience complicated by the confusion the Stalinists brought to the question of fascism, it would not be correct to identify the dictatorship of the Kuomintang with fascism. Hitler, like Mussolini before him, supports himself above all on the counter-revolutionary petty bourgeoisie: this is the essence of fascism. The Kuomintang does not have this point of support. In Germany the peasants march behind Hitler and by this fact indirectly support von Papen; in China the peasants carry on a raging struggle against Chiang Kai-shek.

The regime of the Kuomintang contains more of Bonapartist traits than of fascist; not possessing a social base, not even the smallest, the Kuomintang stands between the pressure of the imperialists and compradors on the one hand and of the revolutionary movement on the other. But Bonapartism can make a pretense of stability only when the land hunger of the peasants is satisfied. This is not true in the case of China. Hence the impotence of the military dictatorship which can only maintain itself thanks to the dispersion of its enemies. But under their growing attack even this begins to fall apart.

In the revolution of 1925-27, it was the proletariat that morally and physically suffered the most. That is why the workers are now in the rear of the other classes, not only of the petty bourgeoisie, starting with the students, but also in a certain sense of the peasants. It is precisely this which proves that the third Chinese revolution cannot win, cannot even develop, as long as the working class has not again entered into the struggle.

The slogans of revolutionary democracy correspond best to the prerevolutionary political situation in China today.

It is elementary for a Marxist that the peasants, whatever their banner, fight for the aims of agrarian petty-bourgeois democracy. The slogan of the independence of China, raised anew to a white heat by the Japanese intervention, is a slogan of national democracy. The impotence of the military dictatorship and the division of the country among the militarist cliques put on the agenda the slogan of political democracy.

The students cry: "Down with the Kuomintang government!" Groups of the workers' vanguard support this slogan. The "national" bourgeoisie demands a constitutional regime. The peasants revolt against the dearth of land, the yoke of the militarists, government officials, usurious loans. Under these circumstances, the party of the proletariat must support as the central political slogan the call for a constituent assembly.

Does this mean—it will be asked—that we demand the government convoke the constituent assembly or that we attempt to organize it ourselves? This way of posing the question, at least at this stage, is too formalistic. For a number of years the Russian revolution coordinated two slogans: "Down with absolutism" and "Long live the constituent assembly." To the question who would convoke the constituent assembly we answered: the future will tell, that is, the relation of forces, as they establish themselves in the process of the revolution itself. This approach to the question is equally correct for China. If the Kuomintang government at the moment of its collapse tries to convoke some kind of a representative assembly, what shall our attitude be toward it, that is, how shall we best utilize it in the interests of the revolution, by boycotting the elections or participating in them? Will the revolutionary masses succeed in forming an independent governmental body that takes on itself the convocation of a constituent assembly? Will the proletariat succeed, in the course of the struggle for democratic demands, in creating soviets? Will the existence of soviets make the convocation of a constituent assembly superfluous? These questions cannot be answered in advance. But our task consists not in making predictions on a calendar but in mobilizing the workers around the slogans that flow from the political situation. Our strategy is a strategy of revolutionary action, not abstract speculation.

Today, by the force of events, revolutionary agitation is directed above all against the Kuomintang government. We explain to the masses that the dictatorship of Chiang Kai-shek is the main obstacle that stands in the way of the constituent assembly and that we can rid China of the militarist cliques only by means of an armed insurrection. Agitation, spoken and written, strikes, meetings, demonstrations, boycotts, whatever concrete goals they aim at, must have as a corollary the slogans: "Down with the Kuomintang!" "Long live the constituent assembly!"

In order to achieve real national liberation it is necessary to overthrow the Kuomintang. But this does not mean we postpone the struggle until such time as the Kuomintang is overthrown. The more the struggle against foreign oppression spreads, the more difficulties the Kuomintang will have. The more we mobilize the masses against the Kuomintang, the more the struggle against imperialism will develop.

At the critical moment of Japanese intervention the workers and the students called for arms. From whom? From the Kuomintang. It would be a sectarian absurdity to abandon this demand on the plea that we want to overthrow the Kuomintang. We want to overthrow it, but we haven't yet reached that point. The more energetically we demand the arming of the workers, the sooner we shall reach it.

The official Communist Party, despite its ultraleftism, favors "the resumption of Russian-Chinese diplomatic relations." This is a slogan that is directed against the Kuomintang. To advance it does not at all mean that one has "confidence" in the Kuomintang. On the contrary, the effect of this slogan is to make the government's situation more difficult before the masses. Certain Kuomintang leaders already have had to take up the slogan for the reestablishment of relations with the USSR. We know that with these gentlemen there is a big gap between words and deeds, but here, as in all other questions, mass pressure will decide.

If under the whip of the revolution the Kuomintang government begins to make petty concessions on the agrarian question, tries to call a semblance of a constituent assembly, is forced to give arms to the workers or to reestablish relations with the USSR, it goes without saying that we will at once take advantage of these concessions. We will firmly cling to them at the same time that we correctly show their insufficiency and in this way use these concessions by the Kuomintang as a weapon to overthrow it. Such in general is the reciprocal relation of reforms and revolution in Marxist politics.

But doesn't the scope the peasant war is reaching mean that there is no longer time or place for the slogans and problems of parliamentary democracy in China? Let us go back to this question.

If today the revolutionary Chinese peasants call their fighting organizations "soviets," we have no reason to give up that name. We must simply not get intoxicated with words. To believe that soviet power in essentially rural regions can be an important stable revolutionary power is proof of great frivolity. It is impossible to be ignorant of the experience offered by the only country where soviet power has been effectively established. Although in Petrograd, Moscow, and other industrial centers and regions of Russia soviet power has been firm and constant since November 1917, in all the immense peripheral areas (Ukraine, Northern Caucasus, Transcaucasia, Urals, Siberia, Central Asia, Archangel, Murmansk) this power has appeared and disappeared several times, not only because of foreign intervention but also thanks to internal revolts. The Chinese soviet power has an essentially rural, peripheral character, and to this day entirely lacks a point of support in the industrial proletariat. The less stable and sure this power is, the less it can be described as soviet power.

Ko Lin's article, which appeared in the German paper *Der Rote Aufbau,* claims that in the Red armies the workers represent 36 percent, the peasants 57 percent, and the intellectuals 7 percent. I confess that these figures arouse serious doubts. If the figures apply to all the insurrectionary armed forces, which according to the author number 350,000, the army includes about 125,000 workers. If the 36 percent applies only to the Red armies, of 150,000 soldiers there are more than 50,000 workers. Is this really so? Did they previously belong to the unions, to the party? Did they take part in the revolutionary struggle? But even that does not settle the question. Because of the absence of strong, independent proletarian organizations in the industrial centers, the revolutionary workers, inexperienced or too little experienced, become totally lost in the peasant, petty-bourgeois environment.

Wang Ming's article, which appeared at the beginning of the year in the Comintern press, singularly exaggerates, as far as I can judge, the scope of the movement in the cities, the degree of independence of the workers in the movement, and the importance of the influence of the Communist Party. The trouble with the present official press is that it mercilessly distorts facts for its factional interests. Thus it is not hard to realize, even by Wang Ming's article, that the leading place in the movement that began in the autumn of last year belonged to the students and to the school youth in general. The university strikes had an appreciable importance, greater than the factory strikes.

To arouse the workers, to organize them, to give them the possibility of relating to the national and agrarian movements in order to take the leadership of both: such is the task that falls to us. The immediate demands of the proletariat as such (length of the workday, wages, right to organize, etc.) must form the basis of our agitation. But that alone is not enough. Only these three slogans can raise the proletariat to the role of the head of the nation: the independence of China, land to the poor peasants, the constituent assembly.

The Stalinists imagine that the minute the insurgent peasants call their organizations soviets, the stage of revolutionary parliamentarism is already over. This is a serious mistake. The rebel peasants can serve as a point of support to soviets only if the proletariat shows in practice its ability to lead. Without the leadership of the proletariat, the peasant movement can only serve to advance one bourgeois clique against another, finally to break up into provincial factions. The constituent assembly, thanks to its importance as a centralizing force, would mark a serious stage in the development of the agrarian revolution. The existence of rural "soviets" and "Red armies" would help the peasants to elect revolutionary representatives. At the present stage this is the only way to link up the peasant movement politically with the national and proletarian movements.

The official Chinese Communist Party declares that its current "principal slogan" is that of the national-revolutionary war against Japanese imperialism (see Wang Ming's article in the *Communist International,* no. 1 in 1932). This is a one-sided and even adventurist way to pose the question. It is true that the struggle against imperialism, which is the essential task of the Chinese proletariat, cannot be carried through to the end except by insurrection and revolutionary war. But it does not follow in the least that the struggle against Japanese imperialism constitutes the central slogan at the *present* moment. The question must be solved in an international context.

At the beginning of the year, they thought in Comintern circles that Japan had launched its military action against China in order to immediately push things to a war against the Soviet Union. I wrote then that the Tokyo government would have to be completely out of its mind to run the risk of a war with the Soviet Union before it had at least to some extent consolidated the military base that Manchuria represents for it. In reply to this evaluation of the situation, the American Stalinists, the most vulgar and stupid of all, declared that I was working in the interests of the Japanese general staff. Yet what have the events of these last months shown? The fear of the consequences of a military adventure in Japan's leading circles was so great that the military clique had to liquidate a certain number of Japanese statesmen in order to arouse the mikado's government to complete the annexation of Manchuria.[160] There is no doubt that even today a war against the Soviet Union remains a very real perspective, but in politics *time* is very important.

If the Soviet government considered war with Japan right now inevitable, it would have neither the right nor the possibility of carrying out a peace policy, that is, an ostrich policy. In fact, in the course of the year, the Soviet government has concluded an agreement with Japan to furnish Soviet naphtha to the Japanese war fleet. If war is inevitable right now, furnishing naphtha to Japan is equivalent to committing treason toward the proletarian revolution. We won't discuss here the question of knowing to what extent this or that declaration or step of the Soviet government is correct. One thing is clear: contrary to the American Stalinists, whose zeal is beyond measure, the Moscow Stalinists have been oriented toward peace with Japan, not war.

Pravda of September 24 writes: "With vast impatience the world bourgeoisie was expecting a Japanese-Soviet war. But the fact that the USSR has rigorously abstained from intervening in the Sino-Japanese conflict and the firm peace policy she is following has forestalled war. . . ." An admission that if the attitude of the American and other windbags had any political meaning at all, it was this: to push the Soviet power on the same road the world bourgeoisie was pushing it. We don't mean that they were consciously serving the Japanese general staff. Suffice it to say they are incapable of consciously serving the proletarian revolution.

The Chinese proletariat inscribes on its banner not only the resumption of diplomatic relations with the Soviet Union but also the conclusion of a close offensive and defensive alliance with it. This indicates that the policy of the Chinese proletariat must be in conformity with the whole of the international situation and above all with the policy of the Soviet Union. If Japan were to thrust war upon the Soviet Union today, drawing China into that war would be a life-and-death question for the Chinese proletariat and its party. The war would open up boundless horizons for the Chinese revolution. But to the extent that the international situation and internal conditions oblige the Soviet Union to make serious concessions in the Far East in order to avoid war, or to defer it as long as possible, to the extent that Japan does not feel itself strong enough to begin hostilities, the war against Japanese imperialism cannot constitute, at least at the present time, the central fighting slogan of the Chinese Communist Party.

Wang Ming quotes the following slogans of the Left Opposition in China: "Reconstitution of the mass movement," "Convocation of the constituent assembly," and "Resumption of diplomatic relations between China and the Soviet Union." Simply because these slogans seem to be poorly motivated in an article appearing in the legal organ of the Opposition, Wang Ming calls the Left Opposition in China a "counterrevolutionary Trotskyist–Ch'en Tu-hsiu group."

Even if we were to admit that the revolutionary slogans were poorly motivated, this does not make the slogans or the organization that formulated them counterrevolutionary. But Wang Ming and his like have to speak about the counterrevolutionary spirit of the "Trotskyists" if they want to keep their jobs and their pay.

While they express themselves so sharply against the Bolshevik-Leninists, who have been proved right in the course of events in China from 1924 to 1932, the Stalinists are extremely indulgent toward themselves, toward their uninterrupted chain of errors.

When Japan attacked Shanghai, the Kuomintang proposed "the united front of the workers, peasants, soldiers, merchants, and students to combat imperialism." But this is the famous "bloc of four classes" of Stalin-Martynov! Since the second revolution, foreign oppression has not weakened, but on the contrary has grown. The antagonism between the needs of the country's development on the one side and the regime and imperialism on the other has also sharpened. The rationale of the old Stalinist arguments in favor of the bloc of four classes has acquired double strength. But now the Stalinists have interpreted the Kuomintang's proposal as a new attempt to deceive the masses. Very well! But they have forgotten to explain why the Comintern leadership helped the Chinese bourgeoisie's fatal deception, and why the philosophy which consisted in being at the beck and call of the Kuomintang found expression in the program of the Comintern.

It is clear that we can and must support the slogan of democratic self-government: of the election of representatives by the people, etc. The democratic program represents a great step forward in relation to the regime of military dictatorship. We must tie in the isolated, partial democratic slogans with the principal slogans and connect them to the problems of the revolutionary organization and arming of the workers.

The question of "patriotism" and "nationalism," like some other questions contained in your letter, is of a terminological rather than fundamental character. The Bolsheviks, in favor of the national liberation of oppressed people by revolutionary means, support the movement of the masses of the people for national liberation by any means, not only against the foreign imperialists, but also against the bourgeois exploiters of the Kuomintang type inside the national movement.

Must we introduce the term "patriotism," which has been thoroughly discredited and corrupted? I doubt it. Isn't this a tendency to adapt to petty-bourgeois ideology and terminology? If such a tendency were really to appear in our ranks, we would have to fight it mercilessly.

Many questions of a tactical and strategic character will appear insoluble if approached formalistically. But they will fall into place if we pose them dialectically, that is, in the context of the living struggle of classes and parties. The revolutionary dialectic is best assimilated in action. I have no doubt that our Chinese friends and comrades in ideas, the Bolshevik-Leninists, not only passionately discuss the complex problems of the Chinese revolution, but also no less passionately participate in the developing struggle. We are for a strategy of action, not speculation.

From *Writings of Leon Trotsky (1932)*. Text from *Class Struggle* (New York), June 1933.

DISCUSSIONS WITH
HAROLD R. ISAACS[161]

August 1935

August 8, 1935

. . . On the problem of the united front with the bourgeoisie: Trotsky did not believe Liu Jen-ching's conclusion that Ch'en Tu-hsiu has become an opportunist. He thinks that Liu's argument was undialectical and that it tended to throw around ambiguous terminology. For instance, Trotsky thinks there should be a distinction between "united fronts" and "common action" . . . and he was rather amused by Liu's arrogant attitude of being a self-appointed representative of the Bolshevik tendency in the Chinese revolutionary movement.

August 9, 1935

To resume yesterday's discussion, Trotsky read my draft and pointed out a few weaknesses on the first page. He felt that my analysis of the different layers of the bourgeoisie and their subjective and objective viewpoints was insufficient and undialectical. He said that if we used such a pat formula, we would tend to be dogmatic and opportunist. He emphasized:

"Common action, especially a short-term common action, is one thing, but capitulation to the bourgeoisie in the form of a permanent 'united front' such as the French Popular Front is another. They are entirely different. It is good to keep our organization completely independent; but the heart of the matter is how to use this independence. We should continually carry out 'common action' with the students' and peasants' organizations."

I said that the question is not one of our relationship to the petty bourgeoisie and the peasantry. On this point, Ch'en Tu-hsiu had adopted an emptier and more abstract formula than Liu Jen-ching. At any rate, I had to send Sneevliet a telegram to ask him to send me Liu's document, "Five Years of the Chinese Left Opposition." (I had not brought it with me because I had thought Trotsky already had this document. We will discuss it more fully later on.)

August 9 (afternoon)

My oral report on the Chinese Red Army took up almost the whole meeting. In this report I also touched on the general political situation in China. Dr. F. and N. Sedova were also present. I drew a map and talked for an hour and a half. I talked about the origins, initial development, internal evolution, and eventual fate of the Chinese Red Army. I dealt with it as completely as possible so that at the conclusion there were almost no questions to be answered.

Trotsky only said that its general development verified the Opposition's prediction that without the leadership of the working class movement, the fate of the Red Army would either depend on the upper strata (merchants and middle and rich peasants) within its jurisdiction, or it would be suppressed by the superior military forces of the Kuomintang and the imperialists. Our viewpoint was that at present the Red Army wanted to go to Sinkiang province because only there could they answer the Soviet Union's diplomatic needs by establishing a buffer zone between the Soviet Union and the Japanese forces from Mongolia.[162] Trotsky considered this viewpoint correct, logical, and most likely. Near the end of the meeting, I raised the problem of the political perspective in China. I described Liu's ideological evolution on the problem of economic reconstruction, and also mentioned his search for a new solution and his attention to the Red Army and the possibility of its expansion into Szechwan province. At the end, I mentioned that the political perspective had to be clarified because this will be the foundation of the program of the Chinese Bolshevik-Leninist faction. This problem will be discussed in the later meetings.

August 13 (morning)

We discussed Liu's document. I could only cite major arguments and read the important quotations to him, and let him read it. We only had time to discuss the introduction and the chapters on the national assembly and the bourgeoisie. When I read the part (page 14) where Liu said the masses considered the national assembly and the dictatorship of the proletariat to be "the same thing" (i.e., the national assembly is the popular formula for the dictatorship of the proletariat), Trotsky interrupted me and said: "It would be more exact to say that Liu considers what is in his mind and what is in the minds of the masses to be 'the same thing.'" He continued:

"One might say, looking at the historical development of countries such as England and France, that a long period of democracy is required before reaching socialism, and that this period could last several centuries. But in Russia, semidemocracy of the parliamentary period lasted only several years. Democracy during the February revolution lasted only eight months. In China, this period may not even last eight months. At any rate, the masses always want democracy in the beginning. Only when they follow this road will they be able to accept the soviet system and to seize power. For this matter we cannot form a detailed plan in advance; we have to rely on the thinking and actions of the masses to determine our action. In China the period of democracy may be very short, or even nonexistent. But this does not mean that the masses will think of the national assembly, or any democratic concept, and the dictatorship of the proletariat as 'the same thing.'"

I continued to read. He shook his head and said: "It is ridiculous to hinder our first steps with worrying about future problems. The first step should be to conduct propaganda and agitation for the national assembly. When the Kuomintang capitulates to the Japanese imperialists, the people should do something themselves. How? Call a national assembly! As simple as that! We should spread this idea among all strata of the people. The students, as before, could play a very big role in the initial stage. We have two tasks: (1) to arouse and to participate in the democratic mass movement; (2) to draw the proletariat into this movement so as to prepare them for the proletarian revolution. If we can recruit ten or a hundred cadres, they will be the future leaders of the proletariat.

"The problems of the future perspective are part of cadre education, but these problems should not be allowed to paralyze and interfere with our propaganda work for a national assembly. The most important task at the moment is to do everything possible to promote the idea of a national assembly. Then we will watch the result of this agitation closely. For instance, if Chiang Kai-shek attempts to call his own national assembly—which will eventually cause a split among the bourgeoisie—the right wing will oppose this idea and the left wing will try to utilize the movement. Then we will attack it and expose it. If the radical wing of the bourgeoisie attempted to carry out the national assembly, we should on the one hand push them to act, for instance to overthrow Chiang Kai-shek and form their own government; and on the other hand we have to expose their deception to the masses. We should start now to agitate for the national assembly. We will discuss the second step later."

"But," I interrupted, "you said we should participate in this democratic mass movement. This is a problem, because at the moment we do not have such a movement. Our task is to create one in order to resurrect mass activity." I then briefly described the present situation of pessimism, discontent, and lack of organization of the workers and of the petty-bourgeois intellectuals. Trotsky said:

"It frequently happens that we cannot push the masses forward. We cannot create a miracle. The defeat of the revolution was deeply felt by the masses. It is a fact that we recognized the defeat in 1928. On the one hand, there was a certain impulse imparted by this defeat (the Red Army, etc.), and on the other hand there were the deepening psychological effects among the masses. If simultaneously the economic crisis deepens, the number of workers declines, production shrinks, and the peasant movement is suppressed, this will mean that the counterrevolution has deepened. But its basis is still undetermined. We will then have to carry out the task of education through our cadres. We will use all means to spread the idea of a national assembly, and we will watch the effect of our propaganda. If there is not yet a response, we will try again, again, and again, until we get a response.

"In the past, we made a theoretical assumption that if the Red Army were to occupy large cities, it would awaken the workers' movement. We also said that this was probable but not inevitable, and that if an economic boom should coincide with advances by the Red Army, it could accelerate the rise of the mass movement. But these lucky coincidences did not occur. Therefore we have to start over again, go back to 1922-23. But if and when the movement rises for the second time, its tempo will be much quicker. The entire contents of the second revolution will be run through again as a brief overture to the third revolution. We will start with our democratic slogan. The slogan of the national assembly can play a big role among the masses. We will talk to the workers through literature and conversations. We should get some response from the workers. This is the only way to advance our work."

Trotsky then described the circumstances of the revival of mass political activity in Russia in 1893, after ten years of reaction following the suppression of the "People's Will." Plekhanov and his group published a document that year evaluating the progress of the Marxist movement in which they expressed their disappointment at the small results. But it was to be in that very year that Marxism was to grow into a big movement that swept the whole country.[163]

"But I have to explain that the revival was the result of ten years of growth and development of Russian capitalism, which had completely changed the face of the nation. If the deepening of the counterrevolution in China is paralleled by an economic crisis, then our agitation will have no results. Then we will have to prepare our cadres and wage our propaganda. Although our results seem small, we are preparing our future leaders and we do not expect any miracles. What then can bring about the revival of the revolutionary mass movement? Various factors can have this effect: war or revolution in other countries—a new war will bring a new revolution—such was the effect of the Russo-Japanese War in 1905. Don't forget that without our 1905 revolution, there would have been no Persian revolution, and there would have been no 1911 revolution in China.[164] Our 1905 made a big impact on the Far East.

"As for who will convoke the national assembly, at the moment that is still a hypothetical question. Our agitation should concentrate on the need for a national assembly. First the masses must become convinced of the need for a national assembly. As our agitation progresses, we will proceed further on the basis of the results of the last step. In all events, we must start to agitate around the demand for a national assembly to oppose Kuomintang rule. Comrades participating in this struggle must have an adequate slogan, a slogan that covers various possible circumstances.

"I do not yet thoroughly understand these controversies [between Ch'en and Liu] so I cannot express my opinion. I shall study them more carefully. But I can say one thing: even if Ch'en Tu-hsiu holds some opportunist ideas, he is, after all, older and has a lifetime of experience. It is possible that he can contribute many good ideas. I have the impression—with some reservations—that Liu Jen-ching has exaggerated this disagreement. Maybe Ch'en posed his opinion as a tactical formula, and Liu considered it a strategic one. If this is Ch'en's strategic line, then many of Liu's criticisms may be right. But I think these differences have been greatly exaggerated. I think it is impermissible to conduct a split with Ch'en Tu-hsiu.[165] We need his cooperation in the Fourth International. The unfortunate thing is not that a serious dispute has arisen over a small difference, but that this small difference has blocked our action."

Published in English for the first time. Translated from the Chinese edition of *Problems of the Chinese Revolution* (Shanghai: New Banner, 1947).

JAPAN AND CHINA[166]

July 30, 1937

Japan at present represents the weakest link in the capitalist chain. Its military-financial superstructure rests on a foundation of semifeudal agrarian barbarism. The periodic explosions of the Japanese army simply reflect the unbearable tension of social relations in that country. The entire regime maintains itself only through the dynamic of military seizures. The decapitation of the Red Army and the demoralizing influence upon it of a series of staged trials has freed the hands of Japanese militarism for new adventures.[167]

The probable military successes of Japan against China will be of significance only as historical episodes. China's resistance, closely linked with the rebirth of that nation, will grow stronger from year to year. Japan's growing difficulties will end in military catastrophe and social revolution.

With the introduction of serious social reforms, the Chinese government could arouse enormous enthusiasm among the popular masses and mobilize them for the struggle against Japanese intervention. Past experience does not permit us to foster illusions regarding the social program of Marshal Chiang Kai-shek. But if there exists in the world a *just war,* it is the war of the Chinese people against its oppressors. All workers' organizations, all progressive forces in China, without abandoning their programs or their political independence, will carry out to the end their duty in the war of liberation, regardless of their attitude toward the government of Chiang Kai-shek.

The current military skirmish, as has happened more than once in the past, can be followed by a rotten compromise. But it will not be long lasting. Japan is too deeply enmeshed on the

547

continent to retreat. The national awakening of China will not endure protracted capitulations. For its part, the USSR cannot long remain a passive spectator of this great historical struggle. The interests of self-preservation of the Soviet state will come to the fore over the interests of self-preservation of the present ruling clique. The USSR will extend its hand to China, and will aid in the construction and armament of the Chinese army. All of progressive world opinion will be on China's side. The defeat of Japanese militarism is inevitable, and it is a matter of the not-too-distant future.

From *Writings of Leon Trotsky (1937-38)*. Text from *Biulleten Oppozitsii* (Paris), nos. 58-59, September-October 1937. The translation is by George Saunders.

A DISCUSSION ON CHINA[168]

August 11, 1937

Li Fu-jen: The question I wish to raise first is that outlined in the short thesis by one of our Chinese comrades, namely, the question as to whether our organization should, when opportunity occurs, take the initiative in forming anti-Japanese organizations in localities where such do not already exist. The CC of our Chinese organization is divided on this question. One section contends that such organizations can be no different from comparable organizations set up by the Stalinists on an international scale, e.g., the League Against Imperialism, League Against War and Fascism, etc. Opponents of this view declare that at this time, when the labor movement is largely passive and when the political life of the masses is expressed principally in anti-Japanese activity, the revolutionists must form such organizations in order to lead the masses in struggle and prevent them from falling under the influence of bourgeois and petty-bourgeois political organizations.

Trotsky: Can you give us approximate estimates of the strength of the CP, the trade unions, the Third Party, if it exists, and how strong are the Salvation organizations?

Li Fu-jen: The CP, outside of the "soviet" districts (which, by the way, are no longer called soviet), has practically ceased to exist as a party. In Shanghai, formerly the main center of party activity, there is an apparatus but no party organization. The illegal party organ long since ceased publication. Representatives of the party have taken part in the recent strike movement, but only in order to sabotage it. For example, at a large silk mill where a strike was in progress a Stalinist representative

549

addressed a meeting at which he declared that the foremost task of the Chinese proletariat was to "save the country" from Japanese imperialism. A worker replied: "It seems to me that our first task is to save ourselves—we are starving." The Stalinists have raised the slogan: "Don't strike in Chinese-owned factories." This is completing the process of their isolation from the workers which began after the defeat of the revolution in 1927.

It is very difficult to ascertain the real situation in the "soviet" districts, because of the news censorship exercised by the Kuomintang government. But there is reason for believing that there is very little distinction between the CP and the "soviet" government apparatus. The main force of the "Red Army" (recently renamed the People's Anti-Japanese Army) is now located in the northeastern part of Shensi province, in China's Northwest. If one strikes a fair average of several estimates made, this force numbers 80,000 men, not all of whom are equipped with modern weapons. Beyond this, there are several smaller armies and peasant partisan bands operating in such provinces as Fukien and Honan. Over these smaller forces the "soviet" government, according to its chairman, Mao Tse-tung, is not able to exercise any direct control, with the result that land expropriation and other measures of the agrarian revolution are still being carried out in contradiction to the new class-collaborationist line of the CP. The party has completely capitulated to the Kuomintang, humbly asking in return that the Kuomintang government conduct a "sincere" struggle against Japanese imperialism, that it cease conducting civil war against "its own" people, that it inaugurate a "democratic" regime, and that it release the political prisoners. It is impossible to say whether any formal agreement has been arrived at between the CP and the Kuomintang. When the CCP made its first overtures to the Kuomintang, the latter flatly demanded unconditional surrender, declaring that nothing short of the liquidation of the "soviet" government, disbandment of the "Red Army," and complete abandonment by the CP of its class-struggle policy would be acceptable. That some sort of "agreement" has been reached is indicated in reports that the Nanking government has been sending money and supplies—motor trucks, munitions, and food—into the "soviet" areas in northeastern Shensi.

There has been nothing to indicate that the "Red Army" ranks have shown any opposition to the new capitulationist course of the leadership. But then it must be remembered that the force itself is greatly different from the one that held the "soviet" area in Kiangsi against successive Nanking attacks between 1930 and 1935, until compelled to evacuate it in the summer of 1935. During the Long March from Kiangsi to Shensi, many of the seasoned fighters dropped from the ranks or were killed and their places were filled by youthful recruits from among the poor peasants in the localities through which the army retreated, who saw in the "Red Army" a means of filling their rice bowls. This diluted force has proved more pliable in the hands of the CCP than the army which left Kiangsi with a great fighting tradition.

Genuine trade unions, in the sense of voluntary organizations of the workers, scarcely exist, although in some industries, in recent times, there have been attempts to create such organizations. In 1929, the Kuomintang government passed a Trade Union Law which, as in Italy and Germany, provides for governmental supervision and control of the industrial organizations of the workers. In accordance with this law, "trade unions" have been formed but they exist merely as government agencies in the ranks of the workers. Offices are maintained, manned by functionaries, but union meetings are rare. Calls to strike are seldom an official union act, and when a strike does break out the union apparatus acts only to bring about a settlement. The workers thus have no real organizations of their own.

The Third Party is a political grouping of very small proportions which centers its attention on an agrarian program. It was formed in Europe by remnants of the "left" Kuomintang, left high and dry by the collapse of the Wuhan government in 1927. Among its early adherents was T'an P'ing-shan, right-wing CCP leader who participated in the Wuhan government as minister of agriculture. The party emerged on the China arena early in 1930 under the leadership of Teng Yen-ta, who had then just returned from Moscow, where Stalin is reported to have offered him the leadership of the Chinese Communist Party in succession to Ch'en Tu-hsiu. Teng was executed by Chiang Kai-shek late in 1931. The Third Party, expounding a reformist land program and plans for the development of "national capital" through struggle against imperialism, never succeeded in growing. Obliged to live an outlaw existence under the Kuomintang dictatorship, it maintained its headquarters and centered most of its activity in the British colony of Hong Kong. In the field of agrarian policy it was unable to compete with the CCP for leadership of the peasants, since the CCP was conducting a policy of land expropriation. But it has gained a new lease on life now that the CCP, in line with the decisions of the Seventh Congress of the Comintern, has thrown overboard its program of agrarian revolution. The Third Party now criticizes the CCP from the "left," charging it with traitorous abandonment of the cause of the peasantry.

The fascist organization referred to in the resolution is not really a fascist organization. The term "fascist" derives in this case from the name of the organization, which is known as the Blue Shirts. The Blue Shirts are not a party, but a personal organization of Chiang Kai-shek created for the purpose of buttressing his power both inside and outside the Kuomintang and the government. One of their tasks has been the assassination of Chiang's opponents. Chiang rules by a military dictatorship and there is neither need nor basis for a fascist movement after the Italian or German models. The petty bourgeoisie, above all the peasants, are opposed to Chiang's dictatorship and cannot (now at any rate) become a social basis for fascism. The Stalinists, to the extent that they still wield any influence over the peasantry and over the petty bourgeoisie of the cities, are helping by their class-collaborationist policy to drive these classes back under Chiang's influence. But the Blue Shirts at the present time, as an organ of Chiang's power, have their membership exclusively in the Kuomintang government apparatus, although they have succeeded in influencing the upper layers of the numerous student bodies, especially in Shanghai.

The National Salvation Association is a federal patriotic organization with headquarters in Shanghai. It embraces local patriotic societies formed of students, teachers, small businessmen, and in some cases workers, although the latter are very few. The leadership consists exclusively of upper petty-bourgeois elements close to the big bourgeoisie. The NSA is the present organizational manifestation of the patriotic movement which arose with Japan's seizure of Manchuria in 1931-32. At that time, a student movement of great proportions got under way. Thousands of students deserted their classes, took possession of trains, and proceeded to Nanking to protest against the government's policy of nonresistance to the Japanese invasion. The vastness of the demonstrations that ensued frightened the government, but when the students failed to find a basis and support in the workers and other sections of the exploited the government took courage and ended the movement by a show of force.

During the ensuing years, up to 1936, the student movement was practically dead despite continued Japanese aggression. In 1936, however, Japan began pressing its demands in North China and Sung Che-yuan, head of Nanking's administration in the area, made numerous economic concessions to Japanese imperialism. This led to a revival of the student movement and Sung became the target of considerable student demonstrations. But the Stalinists, fairly influential at that time in the North, sabotaged the movement, declaring that the students were disrupting "national unity" by demonstrating against Sung Che-yuan. They told the students that Sung was obliged to make concessions to Japan because the people did not give him sufficient support. This killed the movement. Students were heard to declare: "If the communists will not lead us, who will?"

Meanwhile, in Shanghai and other parts of the country, "Salvation Associations" arose, composed mainly of students, intellectuals, and petty-bourgeois elements generally, and including even some representatives of the big bourgeoisie. Some workers, few in number, also adhered to these patriotic organizations from which the National Salvation Association finally emerged.

Within the association, two policies made their appearance. The reactionary elements, who predominated, steered the organization along the course of support for the Kuomintang government, on the ground that it was necessary to help the government fight Japan. Their opponents declared that the government was selling out the country to Japan and should be criticized and attacked in order to prevent fresh betrayals. Chang Nai-ch'i, the principal leader of the organization, interviewed Chiang Kai-shek in Nanking and was believed to have pledged full support to the government. This action precipitated a split, the anti-Nanking elements withdrawing from all activity. Strangely enough, Chiang Kai-shek proceeded to arrest all the leaders, including Chang Nai-ch'i, but recently they were released.[169]

Trotsky: Was it on the order of Tokyo?

Li Fu-jen: That was the common belief, since Tokyo had made repeated protests against "organized anti-Japanese activity," but for Chiang it was also a precautionary measure. When the leaders were arrested, the National Salvation Association virtually collapsed as the arrested men had control of the finances, records, etc. The leaders were visited in prison by other members of the association and asked to hand over control, but they refused to do so, taking the attitude that the association was their own private property. The association was never formally proscribed, but the arrested leaders were charged with "endangering the existence of the republic" and having maintained relations with the CCP (with which Nanking was negotiating at that time). In the home of one of the arrested men, Tsou T'ao-fen, was found a copy of our paper, *Struggle,* and this was to have been used to prove the charge of endangering the republic—the same charge, incidentally, upon which Ch'en Tu-hsiu was condemned to prison for eleven years.

There is not much to be told concerning the provincial affiliates of the NSA. Shanghai was the main center of the movement and the federated bodies were for the most part used as money-collecting agencies. Stalinist influence within the NSA was considerable and was used to direct the organization into Kuomintang channels.

Trotsky: I don't see clearly the material content of the discussion. If the leaders of the Salvation organizations were arrested, it's clear that an anti-Japanese organization built up by our comrades can't have a legal existence—then it must be illegal.

Li Fu-jen: The proponents of the idea think we could get others to cooperate with us in order to give such anti-Japanese associations a legal basis. We could then have fractions within them.

Trotsky: Yes, we can have an illegal fraction. But then I don't see clearly the point of difference. The difference resides merely in the point of taking the initiative of organizing such organizations, where they don't exist. I don't understand very clearly why that question is put in the forefront, and not the question of our participation in the strike movement which must have in China a very great importance. If it would be a question of legal mass organizations, I could understand the viewpoint but, as it is, I would propose to the proponents: try to do it and show me; it's a question of possibility and result. What practical experience in that respect did the proponents have? What concrete incident brought forth the discussion?

Li Fu-jen: The question arose when we were drafting the political resolution, a document intended to furnish political directives to our comrades. It was said that our comrades should take part in the work of the patriotic organizations in order to win the best elements to our banner. Others then contended that if it was correct to participate in the existing organizations, it would also be correct to form such organizations with the aim of capturing them.

Trotsky: We can penetrate religious organizations in order to do antireligious work but that does not mean that we have to form religious organizations.

Li Fu-jen: My view of the proposal is that it reveals the impatience of our comrades. Our work is now very difficult and unspectacular. The comrades are tired of being a small group, isolated, issuing a small paper. They would like to jump over this period. Their proposal to form anti-Japanese organizations is a product of their search for easier contacts with the masses.

Trotsky: Such an attitude has its pitfalls: it can become dangerous. In the thesis I find little about trade union work: the necessity to organize them in order to spread trade union propaganda and in order to be ready to give leadership when a strike breaks out. That I believe is a thousand times more important than to create or discuss the creation of Salvation organizations.

Naturally in case the present acute situation leads directly to a great war between Japan and China, the war question will become the focus of attention of the activity of the whole people and thereby of the working class. In that event, it would not be necessary for us to take the initiative to create patriotic organizations. They will arise from the soil from all sides. Our duty would be to separate the workers inside and outside from the bourgeoisie, take care of the arming of the workers and also of the material interests of the workers and soldiers: not to give up the right to strike even during the war when war industries will flourish and cede tremendous profits to the bourgeois patriots.

The question of economic revival is not sufficiently treated in the political thesis—it's glossed over. I believe it was in 1931-32 that I wrote in a letter to the Chinese comrades that if there will not set in for some years a rise of the workers' movement the Red Army will degenerate. Only when an economic revival begins, the workers' movement can gain new life and support the Red Army. The prognosis that an economic revival is not possible—which was the idea of Niel Shih—was wrong. He said that the military regime makes a revival absolutely impossible. I wrote then of the necessity and importance of the question and about the full possibility—inevitability—of an economic revival, especially in China; now it is a fact.

In the last months there was some very interesting correspondence concerning investments of foreign capital in China. It is
true that China is not a sure arena but where is there a sure
arena? Relatively, China is now an attractive field for foreign
capital. In spite of the very bad situation in France, France sent
400 million francs to Nanking in order to reinforce the currency.
Czechoslovakia invested money in China through the government. It is a result of the fact that in the last years Nanking
showed a certain stability. It is a fact, it has some authority, it is
sustained by the British government. The fact is that Great
Britain economically and politically is a very important factor in
the country through the Nanking government. France not only
gave 400 million francs but is investing capital in railroad
construction. Though the official French correspondent, sent by
Comité des Forges, writes that "we must be very cautious; the
stability is not absolute; in a moment we will meet a catastrophe," it is a fact that capital looks toward China where there is
a relative "prosperity."

It is possible that we will have an influx of foreign capital to
China and China can now make important progress—capitalist
progress, naturally, by transformation of the country into a more
colonial country. But there is this important difference from
India, that in India it is Great Britain that is ruling and deciding,
whereas in China we have different imperialisms, thus giving
more possibility to the government and to the revolutionary
elements for maneuvering. It creates elbowroom. If we were at the
top, we would maneuver between British and Japanese imperialisms. These symptoms, if true, signify that we now have an
important revival of the Chinese economy: that gives a perspective of a revival of the workers' movement. The worker who
answered, "First we must save ourselves" was correct. We should
not begin by building anti-Japanese organizations—(naturally
we are for the independence of China); but we must realize that
the most important task is in the trade union movement. The
revival of industry, of economic life, revives the trade unions. All
our energies must be concentrated in the strike movement. Here
the resolution merely mentions the revival, with some embarrass-
ment, as if the reality would be against our prognosis. We must
underline the fact that there is a revival, that the capitalists,
bankers, compradors make very good business in China whilst
the workers still starve. In order to save China, it's necessary to
save the workers.

In the thesis there is the slogan, "For an immediate war

against Japanese imperialism"—I don't believe we can issue such a slogan. There was preparation for war in February; there is now. We spoke then and we speak now of "immediate war." The question of war does not depend upon us but is decided by circumstances. The most important preparation for war is to create trade union committees and a party organization: a systematic propaganda for the liberation from all imperialisms, in the first place from Japanese imperialism, not by diplomatic maneuvers, capitulations, but by a revolutionary military struggle, by a war of the Chinese people against the imperialists. What is important is to create a point of support which in time can become the basis for the mobilization of the people, rather than put forward the slogan of immediate war. That latter slogan can seem adventuristic.

Li Fu-jen: The slogan is intended to contrast with Chiang Kai-shek's position. He keeps on saying he is *preparing* for war. Hence our slogan for *immediate* war with Japan.

Trotsky: The danger is that you reinforce the attitude of Chiang Kai-shek by such a slogan. The question of preparation gives us the possibility of agitation, of denunciation of the politics of Chiang Kai-shek. I can say, for example, in concrete circumstances, that on February 3 we must begin the war, but as a slogan, "immediate war," in unknown circumstances, is unrealistic. Why is the question of Japan a question of immediate armed struggle—and what about the question of different imperialisms? It is necessary to say that all imperialists are brigands; they differ merely in their proceedings. We don't deny the right to oppose one imperialism against the other and to utilize the antagonisms between them. But only a revolutionary people's government is capable of doing it without becoming an instrument of one imperialism against the other. The present government can't oppose Japanese imperialism without becoming a servile tool of British imperialism. They will answer: the Bolsheviks also used one imperialism against the other and why do you criticize us for our bloc with Great Britain? A bloc depends on the relationship of forces; if I am the stronger I can use it for my purposes; if I am the weaker, I become a tool. Only a revolutionary government could be the stronger.

In the thesis, the term "patriotic" is applied to the Stalinists and Salvation organizations. At the same time the thesis recognizes the necessity of fighting for the independence of the country. That's patriotic. It is a question of terminology. We deny the working class the right to be patriotic to its imperialists, its imperialist state; we do not deny the workers the right to be patriotic to a workers' state; or of a colonial people against its imperialists. There is a great difference in using the term "patriotic." Japanese workers' organizations have no right to be patriotic but Chinese have a right. Stalinists will make use of this wrong terminology. If we don't use it correctly, this word can become a very important question in our fight with the Stalinists. In China I would say: I will never use that word in an insulting, derisive sense and I can say to Chiang: you wish to be patriotic but you are antipatriotic because the bourgeoisie, the comprador can only betray the country. I would say: Chiang Kai-shek cannot save the fatherland, the workers can, by their own movement, by mobilizing the workers around the vanguard, the revolutionary party. We say: we are the genuine patriots. But it is necessary to embody that with the content of revolutionary struggle, of class struggle, etc.

The question of the United States is given little space in the thesis. The question of the relations of Japanese imperialism and British duplicity is very well elaborated—all its movements against Japan in order to conclude an agreement with that same Japan—that is excellently done. But the question of the United States is very important, especially now when there is a change in the policy of the U.S. and a concentration of the fleet in the Pacific, the fortification of the islands, the question concerning fishing, Alaska, and the question of the Philippines: these questions can become extremely acute when the Roosevelt "prosperity" will break up. The humanitarian pacifist Wilson pushed the U.S. into war; the same is possible with Roosevelt: he promised the country a new deal, a new fate—his transfusion of blood has some influence. He has three years more. If during these three years there is a sharp change of conjuncture—big business has a good scent: they know a year ahead. All this great movement would be a tremendous movement. The question of China will become the first important arena. Why, Great Britain doesn't wish now to make agreements with the U.S. against the aggression of Japan because it would signify the victory of the predominating force.

It would be good to introduce into the thesis a word on the U.S. which can become a decisive factor in China against Japan—one of the possible factors of the world war. I was a bit astonished that the U.S. didn't have a great influence in the anti-Japanese struggle. That was because it was in a state of somnolence—American imperialism during the period of crisis. But it's changing its policy, its expectative, cowardly policy.

Li Fu-jen: America's abstention is the result of a conscious policy. Washington proceeds first by consolidating its positions in South America (Pan-American Union) and by building up its armaments. Then it will be able to try conclusions with Japan. If we accept this view of America's position, American intervention in the Far East struggle cannot be expected for a long time.

Trotsky: That is no contradiction to what I say. But Washington does not have all factors in its hands; a sharp crisis would force a change. You say long-term perspective: what is a long term? There are armaments programs of three to four years, then a new American world program would be more or less apparent. It is possible that it will be done in two to three years to show Great Britain that they are technically more powerful.

W: China is now on a gold basis. In the whole naval program and the speeding up of that program and in the aviation program the U.S. has been sharply opposing Japan.

Li Fu-jen: The preponderance of British and Japanese influence in China has prevented the U.S. from getting a real foothold. It was Britain, for example, which arranged China's departure from the silver standard and reform of China's currency system. Britain is also leading in capital investments. The enormous Boxer indemnity which China pays annually to Britain is now being refunded and applied to the construction of railroads and other enterprises, all the material for which is purchased from British manufacturers. American intervention in China in the recent period has taken the form largely of diplomatic demarches and these have not been very sharp. As evidence of the present weakness of America's position may be cited the fact that Japan succeeded in preventing Pan-American Airways from establishing its trans-Pacific terminal in China and the company was forced to go to the Portuguese colony of Macao. Japan also compelled Nanking to abandon a contract with the Mackay Radio Corporation of America. The role of the U.S. in China in recent times has thus been very weak and there is no present indication that it will become stronger.

Trotsky: One great country that used the period of crisis for an aggressive policy was Japan, then Italy in Abyssinia.[170] Germany used it only for armaments. All the other countries, for example, Great Britain, had the possibility of influence in China because it had an old basis but Britain was internationally totally paralyzed. Baldwin in his famous stupid speech said, "I cannot say all the truth about my bankruptcy." And on the question of Spain: France and Great Britain were helpless. The position of the U.S. in China was analogous to the position of Great Britain in Spain, expectative, cowardly. But for Japan success is also the greatest burden. Great Britain has trouble with India though it is a possession of hundreds of years. But China is a country of 400 million. And now the five northern provinces. For a little poor country like Japan to have the domination of China with the proximity of the Soviet Union, with the competition of Great Britain, with the great menace of the U.S.— all that will arouse the Chinese people, and the period of economic revival has made it more powerful than in 1924-27. It is the new juncture which is for China a kind of industrial revolution. It is a promise for a new patriotic upheaval. For Japan even Korea can become a trap. Even in a war with the Soviet Union Japan has to approach in the direction of Irkutsk. In Manchuria live 30 million Chinese people absolutely hostile to Japan. I believe that the military situation of Japan in a world war is absolutely falsely appraised by the bourgeois strategists because they don't estimate the possibility of revolutionary national movements, and most of them are full of reminiscences of the Russo-Japanese War. There is a great difference: Manchuria then was a little people of 5 million—now it is 30 million genuine Chinese peasants. In any case we can expect China to give a greater resistance. Now we face a very important period in the history of China.

Li Fu-jen: An interesting feature of foreign investments in China is that they are very largely, if not principally, placed in communications, first of all railroads. But railroads in China facilitate the marketing of foreign manufactured products. Thus these investments, far from helping develop Chinese economy, assist the sale of foreign commodities.

Trotsky: The influence is of a dialectical character. In Russia too they began with the construction of railroads. The year 1905 was a revolution of railroads. We had also a big industry but the most important industrial development began after 1905, it was the period 1909-14. The foreigners created railroads, gave to the country a more centralized character, a government power. The government, in turn, became more independent of foreign capital—the customs duty fight of Witte. The Nanking government is now politically sustained by Great Britain but precisely the railroads will give a real basis to the Nanking government and it will become more independent of Great Britain. The general strike in Russia in 1905 was in the first place a strike of railroads—the paralysis of the railroads is a tremendous fact.

R: Isn't it also true that the United States' seeming passive attitude toward Japan in China is due to the fact that it is looking for a base from which to fight Japan and hence her relationship with Russia?

Trotsky: Yes, it is the last period of the U.S. policy of "splendid isolation." The first premise for a turn was created by the recognition of the USSR by Roosevelt. There was a cooling off of relationships but now there is again a rapprochement and the visit of the squadron of the American navy to Vladivostok has a great symbolic importance. Naturally, the question of the generals' trial has been for the U.S. an obstacle because they are doubtful whether the Soviet Union is a worthy ally.[171] But this is an episode. They are beginning to abandon the policy of "splendid isolation" and there is a rapprochement with the USSR, very cautious but clear, and it is directed not only against Japan but also against Great Britain.

Then there is the question of the national policy of the Chinese bourgeoisie itself. The categoric statement in this thesis that Chiang will never fight against Japan is not correct. The general political considerations are absolutely correct and excellently formulated; the class line in the fight against Japan. But we said the same in the fight against tsarism: our liberals and bourgeoisie are absolutely incapable of fighting, and, in essence, that was correct. But the bourgeoisie in the position where they had to choose between death and the monarchy, abandoned the palace of the tsars to its fate. The Duma became oppositionist, they participated in the revolution: they killed Rasputin, it was the beginning of the separation of the tsarist family. The Chinese bourgeoisie can't fight freely against imperialism because it must mobilize the working masses and that's very dangerous. But foreign capital and the Chinese masses can create a situation for the bourgeoisie in which it will not have much choice. By the same reason that now the Chinese bourgeoisie is obliged to support Japanese imperialism, it may break in the last moment with Japanese imperialism to save itself and by that help us. So in Russia they tried in February 1917 to sacrifice the monarchy to save themselves; Rodzianko then became the head of the "revolution," the Russian "Mirabeau."[172] The Chinese bourgeoisie, to save themselves, can sacrifice Japanese garrisons, banks, interests, but save their own interests; they are very close friends but they are not the same and should not be put in the same bag.

And there is one word to be said concerning terminology: the phrase "petty bourgeoisie" is employed in the thesis only in the sense of urban petty bourgeoisie. But the peasantry is also a part of the petty bourgeoisie—a very different part but of the same class. Here the peasantry is opposed to the petty bourgeoisie, and it's not made clear that it is opposed to the *urban* petty bourgeoisie.

For China, what means the slogan: "Down with the preparation for a new world war"? We must be *ready* for the new world war. We must demand a revolutionary peoples' army, armed workers and peasants in China. The policy of Chiang is the policy of submission to Great Britain. Chiang Kai-shek will be the tool of Great Britain in the world war. Our slogan should be: Down with the policy of Chiang which will transform China into an abject tool of Great Britain. Our task is to prepare for a workers' and peasants' government.

The slogan: "For unity with the Soviet Union, with the proletariat of the whole world" should rather be: "Unity with the proletariat of the whole world and for an alliance with the Soviet Union on the basis of a concrete program in the interests of the liberation of China." The Soviet Union is now the bureaucracy—no blind confidence in the Soviet Union!

Li Fu-jen: If the Nanking government should enter into an alliance with the Soviet Union, and the alliance should be of such a nature as to harm China and benefit only the Soviet Union, what should our attitude be toward it?

Trotsky: A military alliance against Japan would be in any case preferable for China even with the bureaucracy as it is. But then we must say that we demand that the Soviet Union deliver munitions, arms for the workers and peasants; special committees must be created in Shanghai, in workers' centers; the treaty must be elaborated with the participation not only with the Kuomintang but also with the workers' and peasants' organizations. We ask for an open proclamation from the Soviet bureaucracy that at the end of the war no point of China would be occupied without the consent of the Chinese people, etc.

Li Fu-jen: Do you then think that the Soviet Union could be capable of conducting an imperialistic policy?

Trotsky: If it is capable of organizing frame-ups, killing the revolutionaries, it is capable of all possible crimes.

Now as to the question of the international character of the revolution. We will be asked: can you, a backward country, begin the revolution when there are defeats in other countries? Can you have a dictatorship of the proletariat when in other countries the counterrevolution is victorious? We must say: Yes, because our revolution, even only partially victorious, will arouse movements in Japan and other countries and emphasize not so much the influence that other revolutions can have upon China, but the influence the Chinese revolution will have on other countries.

And we must warn our comrades to be as conspiratorial as possible. Now with the agreement of Stalin with Chiang, they will all be exterminated overnight—they must be very conspiratorial. No movement in the world has ever been so persecuted as ours. If the agreement is concluded, they will kill Ch'en Tu-hsiu; a movement must be started for him, you can take the initiative in that.[173]

Is it not possible to create in New York a commission on the Chinese question and the colonial question in general in order to elaborate resolutions for the next congress of the Fourth International? The IS [International Secretariat] has decided to convoke an international conference in October but personally I find this date too near. We must have for the conference an independent party in the U.S.[174] It will be necessary to defer the international conference till January-February.

AFTERWORD
by Trotsky

September 3, 1937

[Stenographer's note: The *Afterword* was dictated as a reply to a question of Comrade Li Fu-jen (asked after the discussion took place): Isn't it true that the present military operations in China would so disorganize the Chinese economy as to wipe out the gains of the economic revival and even throw the economy farther back than before? If the economic revival is destroyed for a long time by the devastating war, is there any other basis upon which a revival of the workers' movement can take place?]

1. The discussion about the Chinese question was held in English and, as my command of that language is very bad, the stenogram could not clearly express my thoughts. Unfortunately, I have not the time to correct or add to the English text. Also, the situation since the time of the conversation has changed considerably. On August 11, when the discussion took place, it was not yet clear how sharp the conflict between Japan and China would become. At the present time, the conflict turned into an open war, although it is now still hard to tell, at least from here, whether the military operations will end in some sort of compromise or whether, on the contrary, they will develop into a great war.

2. In any case, the question about independent "anti-Japanese" organizations assumes a more immediate meaning than it did a few weeks ago. However, now, too, it seems to me that our adherents cannot take upon themselves the initiative of forming "anti-Japanese" organizations without a more exact definition of their aims. It appears to me that it would be much more correct to try to create "war" organizations on a class basis, for the carrying out of the work which, in a corresponding situation, the trade unions would carry out. For example, if in a given plant, several workers went off to war, it would then be necessary to organize a group for keeping connections with them and for rendering them and their families material and moral aid. Similar work one has to carry out in the villages, trying to organize a special workers' center for that purpose in the city. Such workers' and peasants' unions for help to those who leave for the front can and must insist before bourgeois political organizations and before government organs on their rendering help to the families of the revolutionary soldiers, etc.

3. It would be incorrect to think that war would *at once* paralyze the economic revival in the country. On the contrary, there are all grounds to think that the war will produce a feverish revival of industry. Also, one has to add that the tremendous space of China, especially to the south and west, will remain not only not in the field of military operations but, to a considerable extent, not under direct influence of the factors of war. One can, in that way, expect that the industrial revival will continue, especially if the war will be financed by Great Britain, the U.S.,

or the Soviet Union. The dependence of the army and the government on internal production will immeasurably raise the role and importance of the Chinese industrial workers. All branches of industry, especially those which immediately work for defense, will make big profits. This circumstance opens wide opportunities for economic struggle of the workers. The government will have to be more careful in its repressions in order not to break down the tempo of war industry. Of course, the scoundrels of the Kuomintang and the no lesser scoundrels of the Stalinist party will cry that an economic struggle in time of war is "anti-patriotic." However, the working masses will hardly sympathize with this advice, especially if the real revolutionaries will be able to expose the tremendous profits of the capitalists and the rapaciousness of the bureaucrats.

All the work will not only not cause injury to the war, but, on the contrary, will serve toward its support. A war against Japan can assume a genuine national character only in the event that the bourgeoisie is unsuccessful in throwing the whole burden on the working masses. That is why demands for workers' control over industry, especially over war industry, have such a tremendous significance—not only to "control" profits but to make it hard for the capitalists to furnish the army with bad products of poor quality. Daily life during the time of war will furnish hundreds and thousands of means for the organization of different kinds of unions and committees, in which the workers will participate side by side with the students and the petty bourgeoisie in general. It is necessary that such organizations have before them, though, a narrow but fully concrete program, tied to the interests of the army and the workers. There is no reason to repeat that the worker-revolutionists, actively participating in the war and the services connected with the war, cannot and should not take upon themselves the slightest political responsibility for the bourgeois government. The vanguard of the proletariat remains during the time of war in irreconcilable opposition to the bourgeoisie. The task of the vanguard consists in that, basing itself on the experience of the war, it is to weld the workers around the revolutionary vanguard, to rally the peasants around the workers, and by that prepare for the genuine worker-peasant government, i.e., the dictatorship of the proletariat, leading behind it millions of peasants.

From the point of view of the noted aim, the preservation of a close tie with the revolutionary workers in the army (correspondence, sending of products), every kind of fraternization between the workers, the peasants, and the soldiers, etc., etc., has a tremendous significance.

Such are the short additional remarks which I can add to our discussion of August 11.

From *Internal Bulletin,* Organizing Committee for the Socialist Party Convention (New York), no. 3, December 1937.

ON THE SINO-JAPANESE WAR[175]

September 23, 1937

Dear Comrade Diego Rivera:

During the past few days I have been reading some of the lucubrations of the Oehlerites and the Eiffelites[176] (yes, there is a tendency of that sort!) on the civil war in Spain and on the Sino-Japanese War. Lenin called the ideas of these people "infantile disorders." A sick child arouses sympathy. But twenty years have passed since then. The children have become bearded and even bald. But they have not ceased their childish babblings. On the contrary, they have increased all their faults and all their foolishness tenfold and have added ignominies to them. They follow us step by step. They borrow some of the elements of our analysis. They distort these elements without limit and counterpose them to the rest. They correct us. When we draw a human figure, they add a deformity. When it is a woman, they decorate her with a heavy moustache. When we draw a rooster, they put an egg under it. And they call all this burlesque Marxism and Leninism.

I want to stop to discuss in this letter only the Sino-Japanese War. In my declaration to the bourgeois press, I said that the duty of all the workers' organizations of China was to participate actively and in the front lines of the present war against Japan, without abandoning, for a single moment, their own program and independent activity. But that is "social patriotism!" the Eiffelites cry. It is capitulation to Chiang Kai-shek! It is the abandonment of the principle of the class struggle! Bolshevism preached revolutionary defeatism in the imperialist war. Now, the war in Spain and the Sino-Japanese War are both imperialist wars. "Our position on the war in China is the same. The only

567

salvation of the workers and peasants of China is to struggle independently against the two armies, against the Chinese army in the same manner as against the Japanese army." These four lines, taken from an Eiffelite document of September 10, 1937, suffice entirely for us to say: we are concerned here with either real traitors or complete imbeciles. But imbecility, raised to this degree, is equal to treason.

We do not and never have put all wars on the same plane. Marx and Engels supported the revolutionary struggle of the Irish against Great Britain, of the Poles against the tsar, even though in these two nationalist wars the leaders were, for the most part, members of the bourgeoisie and even at times of the feudal aristocracy . . . at all events, Catholic reactionaries. When Abd-el-Krim rose up against France, the democrats and Social Democrats spoke with hate of the struggle of a "savage tyrant" against the "democracy." The party of Léon Blum supported this point of view. But we, Marxists and Bolsheviks, considered the struggle of the Riffians against imperialist domination as a progressive war.[177] Lenin wrote hundreds of pages demonstrating the primary necessity of distinguishing between imperialist nations and the colonial and semicolonial nations which comprise the great majority of humanity. To speak of "revolutionary defeatism" in general, without distinguishing between exploiter and exploited countries, is to make a miserable caricature of Bolshevism and to put that caricature at the service of the imperialists.

In the Far East we have a classic example. China is a semicolonial country which Japan is transforming, under our very eyes, into a colonial country. Japan's struggle is imperialist and reactionary. China's struggle is emancipatory and progressive.

But Chiang Kai-shek? We need have no illusions about Chiang Kai-shek, his party, or the whole ruling class of China, just as Marx and Engels had no illusions about the ruling classes of Ireland and Poland. Chiang Kai-shek is the executioner of the Chinese workers and peasants. But today he is forced, despite himself, to struggle against Japan for the remainder of the independence of China. Tomorrow he may again betray. It is possible. It is probable. It is even inevitable. But today he is struggling. Only cowards, scoundrels, or complete imbeciles can refuse to participate in that struggle.

Let us use the example of a strike to clarify the question. We do not support all strikes. If, for example, a strike is called for the exclusion of Negro, Chinese, or Japanese workers from a factory, we are opposed to that strike. But if a strike aims at bettering—insofar as it can—the conditions of the workers, we are the first to participate in it, whatever the leadership. In the vast majority of strikes, the leaders are reformists, traitors by profession, agents of capital. They oppose every strike. But from time to time the pressure of the masses or of the objective situation forces them into the path of struggle.

Let us imagine, for an instant, a worker saying to himself: "I do not want to participate in the strike because the leaders are agents of capital." This doctrine of this ultraleft imbecile would serve to brand him by his real name: *a strikebreaker.* The case of the Sino-Japanese War, is from this point of view, entirely analogous. If Japan is an imperialist country and if China is the victim of imperialism, we favor China. Japanese patriotism is the hideous mask of worldwide robbery. Chinese patriotism is legitimate and progressive. To place the two on the same plane and to speak of "social patriotism" can be done only by those who have read nothing of Lenin, who have understood nothing of the attitude of the Bolsheviks during the imperialist war, and who can but compromise and prostitute the teachings of Marxism. The Eiffelites have heard that the social patriots accuse the internationalists of being the agents of the enemy and they tell us: "You are doing the same thing." In a war between two *imperialist* countries, it is a question neither of democracy nor of national independence, but of the oppression of backward nonimperialist peoples. In such a war the two countries find themselves on the same historical plane. The revolutionaries in both armies are defeatists. But Japan and China are not on the same historical plane. The victory of Japan will signify the enslavement of China, the end of her economic and social development, and the terrible strengthening of Japanese imperialism. The victory of China will signify, on the contrary, the social revolution in Japan and the free development, that is to say unhindered by external oppression, of the class struggle in China.

But can Chiang Kai-shek assure the victory? I do not believe so. It is he, however, who began the war and who today directs it. To be able to replace him it is necessary to gain decisive influence among the proletariat and in the army, and to do this it is necessary not to remain suspended in the air but to place oneself in the midst of the struggle. We must win influence and prestige in the *military* struggle against the foreign invasion and in the *political* struggle against the weaknesses, the deficiencies, and the internal betrayal. At a certain point, which we cannot fix in advance, this political opposition can and must be transformed into armed conflict, since the civil war, like war generally, is nothing more than the continuation of the political struggle. It is necessary, however, to know when and how to transform political opposition into armed insurrection.

During the Chinese revolution of 1925-27 we attacked the policies of the Comintern. Why? It is necessary to understand well the reasons. The Eiffelites claim that we have changed our attitude on the Chinese question. That is because the poor fellows have understood nothing of our attitude in 1925-27. We never denied that it was the duty of the Communist Party to participate in the war of the bourgeoisie and petty bourgeoisie of the South against the generals of the North, agents of foreign imperialism. We never denied the necessity of a military bloc between the CP and the Kuomintang. On the contrary, we were the first to propose it. We demanded, however, that the CP maintain its entire political and organizational independence, that is, that during the civil war against the internal agents of imperialism, as in the national war against foreign imperialism, the working class, while remaining in the front lines of the *military* struggle, prepare the *political* overthrow of the bourgeoisie. We hold the same policies in the present war. We have not changed our attitude one iota. The Oehlerites and the Eiffelites, on the other hand, have not understood a single bit of our policies, neither those of 1925-27, nor those of today.

In my declaration to the bourgeois press at the beginning of the recent conflict between Tokyo and Nanking, I stressed above all the necessity of the active participation of revolutionary workers in the war against the imperialist oppressors. Why did I do it? Because first of all it is correct from the Marxist point of view; because, secondly, it was necessary from the point of view of the welfare of our friends in China. Tomorrow the GPU, which is in alliance with the Kuomintang (as with Negrín in Spain), will represent our Chinese friends as being "defeatists" and agents of Japan. The best of them, with Ch'en Tu-hsiu at the head, can be nationally and internationally compromised and killed. It was necessary to stress, energetically, that the Fourth International was on the side of China as against Japan. And I added at the same time: *without abandoning either their program or their independence.*

The Eiffelite imbeciles try to jest about this "reservation." "The Trotskyists," they say, "want to serve Chiang Kai-shek in action and the proletariat in words." To participate actively and consciously in the war does not mean "to serve Chiang Kai-shek" but to serve the independence of a colonial country *in spite of* Chiang Kai-shek. And the words directed against the Kuomintang are the means of educating the masses for the overthrow of Chiang Kai-shek. In participating in the *military* struggle under the orders of Chiang Kai-shek, since unfortunately it is he who has the command in the war for independence—to prepare *politically* the overthrow of Chiang Kai-shek . . . that is the only revolutionary policy. The Eiffelites counterpose the policy of "class struggle" to this "nationalist and social patriotic" policy. Lenin fought this abstract and sterile opposition all his life. To him, the interests of the world proletariat dictated the duty of aiding oppressed peoples in their national and patriotic struggle against imperialism. Those who have not yet understood that, almost a quarter of a century after the World War and twenty years after the October revolution, must be pitilessly rejected as the worst enemies on the inside by the revolutionary vanguard. This is exactly the case with Eiffel and his kind!

L. Trotsky

From *Writings of Leon Trotsky (1937-38)*. Text from *Internal Bulletin,* Organizing Committee for the Socialist Party Convention (New York), no. 1, October 1937.

PACIFISM AND CHINA[178]

September 25, 1937

The so-called peace organizations, including the working class organizations, do not in the least constitute an obstacle to the war. The numerous peace conferences, organized mainly by the Comintern, are purely theatrical enterprises without the least effectiveness; in time of war all these peace leaders, all these pious and humanitarian ladies and gentlemen, will return to their governments to support them in the war as they did in 1914-18.

The only political factor which today hinders the outbreak of war is the fear, on the part of the governments, of the social revolution. Hitler himself has said it many times. We must draw the logical conclusions from this: the more revolutionary the working class, the more it opposes the ruling imperialist class, the more are these latter prevented from carrying out their designs to make a new division of the world by armed force.

At the same time we must carefully distinguish between the imperialist countries and the backward countries, colonial and semicolonial. The attitude of the working class organizations in and toward these two groupings cannot be the same. The present war between China and Japan is a classic example. It is absolutely indisputable that, on the part of Japan, it is a war of rapine and that, on the part of China, it is a war of national defense. Only conscious or unconscious agents of Japanese imperialism can put the two countries on the same plane.

That is why we can only feel pity or hatred for those who in the face of the Sino-Japanese War declare that they are opposed to all wars, to wars altogether. The war is already a fact. The working class movement cannot remain neutral in a struggle between those who wish to enslave and those who are enslaved. The working class movement in China, Japan, and in the entire world must oppose with all its strength the Japanese imperialist bandits and support the people of China and their army.

This does not at all suppose a blind confidence in the Chinese government and in Chiang Kai-shek. In the past, above all in 1925-27, the general was already dependent upon working class organizations in his military struggle against the Chinese generals of the North, agents of foreign imperialism. In the end, he crushed the working class organizations by armed force in 1927-28. We must learn the lessons from this experience which resulted from the fatal policies of the Comintern. In participating in the legitimate and progressive national war against Japanese invasion, the working class organizations must preserve their entire *political independence* of the Chiang Kai-shek government. The Communist Party of China again, as in 1924-25, is making violent efforts to turn over the Chinese working class movement politically to Chiang Kai-shek and the Kuomintang. It is a crime all the more horrible because it is being committed for the second time.[179]

At the same time, the remedy does not lie in the working class organizations declaring themselves "against all wars" and folding their arms in an attitude of passive treason, but rather in participating in the war, aiding the Chinese people materially and morally, and simultaneously educating the masses of peasants and workers in a spirit of total independence of the Kuomintang and its government. We do not attack Chiang Kai-shek for conducting the war. Oh, no. We attack him for doing it badly, without sufficient energy, without confidence in the people and especially in the workers.

A pacifist who has the same attitude toward China as toward Japan in this terrible conflict is like one who would identify a lockout with a strike. The working class movement is against a lockout by the exploiters and for a strike of the exploited. At the same time, strikes are often led by misleaders who are capable of betraying the working class movement during the strike. This is no reason for workers to refuse to participate in the strike but it is reason for mobilizing the working masses against the defections and the treason of the leadership. It often happens that during or after a strike the organized masses change their leadership. This can very well happen in China. But this change can be favorable for the people only if the Chinese and international working class organizations support China against Japan.

From *Writings of Leon Trotsky (1937-38).* Text from *Socialist Appeal* (New York), October 16, 1937.

CONCERNING THE RESOLUTION
ON THE WAR

October 27, 1937

International Secretariat

Dear Comrades:

After a great delay I shall write you briefly about your resolution on Japan and China. The delay was determined by my supposition that my previous letters on the matter were sufficient. I see now that this is not so. Some comrades, guided by ultraleftist considerations, who wished to remain more or less "neutral" between Chiang Kai-shek and the mikado, now try to retreat to a second line trench presented, according to their belief, by your resolution.

I cannot object to any part of your document and even to any sentence of it. Every assertion in itself is correct, but the proportion between different parts seems to me not sufficiently realistic. We have a war. The first question is, should our Chinese comrades and with them all the others accept this war as *their* war or reject is as a war imposed upon them by the ruling class? The ultraleftists try to avoid the answering of this fundamental question. They begin by denouncing Chiang Kai-shek with his former and future crimes. This is a totally doctrinaire approach which is possible in New York (Oehlerites) or in Brussels, but not in China and especially not in Shanghai. We know Chiang Kai-shek well enough as the hangman of workers. But this same Chiang Kai-shek is now obliged to lead a war which is *our* war. In this war our comrades should be the best fighters. Politically they should criticize Chiang Kai-shek not for making war but for making it in an ineffective manner, without high taxation of the bourgeois class, without sufficient arming of workers and peasants, etc.

Our comrades in different countries scarcely know that the most important slogan of our Chinese section in the previous period was: "Prepare the war against Japan." And this was correct. Now our Chinese comrades have the great advantage of having been the strongest protagonists for anti-Japanese war and military preparedness. They must continue their political activity on the same plane. I believe that we cannot make in this respect any concessions to the ultraleftists who are . . . yes, yes,—potential social patriots. They remain passive internationalists insofar as they are ready to reject "any war" in order to preserve their virginal "neutrality." But when events force these comrades to distinguish between war and war, they can easily slip into social patriotism.

The Chinese-Japanese war is a classic example given to us for preparing our cadres for the coming world war, as the Spanish revolution is a precious example for preparing our cadres for the international revolution. Here the imperialist robbers are engaged in an isolated fight with a semicolonial country in order to transform it into a completely colonial country. The Japanese worker must say: "My exploiters imposed this dishonest war upon me." The Chinese worker must say: "The Japanese robbers imposed this war of defense upon my people. It is my war. But unfortunately the leadership of the war is in bad hands. We must survey its direction severely, and we must prepare to replace it." This is the only real plan for agitation and propaganda.

I have heard the following argument: "The Chinese army is a bourgeois army, but we can support only a proletarian Red army." This argument is a "militarized" expression of the lack of understanding of the difference between a bourgeois (semibourgeois-semifeudal) colonial country and a country of imperialistic slaveholders. As a bourgeois army the Chinese army can of course suppress workers' strikes and peasant rebellions in the interest of the owners. In all these cases we oppose it by all possible means. But in the war against Japan the same army defends—not sufficiently, not conscientiously, etc.—the progressive national interest of the Chinese people. So far we support it. To identify the Chinese army with the Japanese signifies simply identifying the oppressors and the oppressed, the robbers and their victims.

I have also heard arguments such as this: "By supporting this war under the leadership of Chiang Kai-shek against Japanese imperialism, we render service to British and American imperialism and can become their tools." Ultraradicalism again becomes a handicap upon revolutionary action.

An example: In a plant, company guards attack the workers, wound, and kill several of them. The workers are so indignant that even the trade union fakers are obliged to call a strike. Our ultraleftist appears on the scene with a warning finger raised over his head. "We should not strike," he says, "not only because the trade union leaders are fakers, incapable of assuring us our full liberation, but also because by our strike we render a service to the competitive plant and become in this way simple tools of another exploiter."

In the case of a strike such arguments can only be received with indignation by the workers. But projected on the grandiose scale of war, the same attitude is incomparably more infuriating and criminal. Chiang Kai-shek cannot assure the *liberation* of China, it is clear; but he tries to stop the further enslavement of China and it is a small step to further liberation. With all our energy we take part in this small step.

In the last analysis it is not correct that we "help" Great Britain. A people that is capable of defending itself with arms in hand against one robber will be capable tomorrow of repulsing the other. A revolutionary party that understands this and that consciously and courageously takes its place at the head of a people who defend the remains of their independence—only such a party is capable of mobilizing the workers during the war and after the war to conquer power from the national bourgeoisie.

The situation in the Far East, I repeat, is so classically clear, that one must ask himself again and again how and why our leading Belgian comrades, at a critical moment when a real war was beginning, could find it possible to place a question mark over my very simple statement to the press: We are totally on the side of China without abandoning our program. All our previous work on the war question beginning with 1914 had as its aim the preparation of at least our leading comrades to meet every new war situation with open eyes. Yet we see unfortunately that at the outbreak of the most clear and unquestionable conflict some of our Belgian comrades have no other instrument of propaganda than a question mark.

In one of my previous letters I explained that the character of my above-mentioned statement to the press (July 30, 1937), emphasizing the duty of the Chinese workers to participate actively in the war, was dictated also by consideration of the specific situation facing our Chinese comrades. It was clear that the Stalinist hangmen connected with Chiang Kai-shek would try to slander the Chinese Bolsheviks as "agents of Japan." Now this has occurred. The GPU agents in China have sent to the New York organ of the GPU (*Daily Worker*) a cable announcing a new frame-up, this time on Chinese territory. Genuine internationalism does not consist in repeating stereotyped phrases on every occasion but in thinking over the specific conditions and problems of each one of our sections in order to facilitate its task. In view of the terribly difficult situation facing the Chinese Bolsheviks, the incomprehensible question marks of our Belgian paper are a very grave error.

That is why we cannot make the slightest concession on this question to the ultraleft, centrists, doubters, and quibblers. The fight on this question should be fought out to the end.

> With best greetings,
> L. Trotsky

From *Writings of Leon Trotsky (1937-38)*. Text from *Internal Bulletin*, Organizing Committee for the Socialist Party Convention (New York), no. 1, October 1937.

REVOLUTION AND WAR IN CHINA[180]

January 5, 1938

First of all, the mere fact that the author of this book belongs to the school of historical materialism would be entirely insufficient in our eyes to win approval for his work. In present-day conditions the Marxist label would predispose us to mistrust rather than to acceptance. In close connection with the degeneration of the Soviet state, Marxism has in the past fifteen years passed through an unprecedented period of decline and debasement. From an instrument of analysis and criticism, it has been turned into an instrument of cheap apologetics. Instead of analyzing facts, it occupies itself with selecting sophisms in the interests of exalted clients.

In the Chinese revolution of 1925-27 the Communist International played a very great role, depicted in this book quite comprehensively. We would, however, seek in vain in the library of the Communist International for a single book which attempts in any way to give a rounded picture of the Chinese revolution. Instead, we find scores of "conjunctural" works which docilely reflect each zigzag in the politics of the Communist International, or, more correctly, of Soviet diplomacy in China, and subordinate to each zigzag facts as well as general treatment. In contrast to this literature, which cannot arouse anything but mental revulsion, Isaacs' book represents a scientific work from beginning to end. It is based on a conscientious study of a vast number of original sources and supplementary material. Isaacs spent more than three years on this work. It should be added that he had previously passed about five years in China as a journalist and observer of Chinese life.

The author of this book approaches the revolution as a

revolutionist, and he sees no reason for concealing it. In the eyes of a philistine, a revolutionary point of view is virtually equivalent to an absence of scientific objectivity. We think just the opposite: only a revolutionist—provided, of course, that he is equipped with the scientific method—is capable of laying bare the objective dynamics of the revolution. Apprehending thought in general is not contemplative, but active. The element of will is indispensable for penetrating the secrets of nature and society. Just as a surgeon, on whose scalpel a human life depends, distinguishes with extreme care between the various tissues of an organism, so a revolutionist, if he has a serious attitude toward his task, is obliged with strict conscientiousness to analyse the structure of society, its functions and reflexes.

To understand the present war between Japan and China one must take the second Chinese revolution as a point of departure. In both cases we meet not only identical social forces, but frequently the same personalities. Suffice it to say that the person of Chiang Kai-shek occupies the central place in this book. As these lines are being written it is still difficult to forecast when and in what manner the Sino-Japanese War will end. But the outcome of the present conflict in the Far East will in any case have a provisional character. The world war which is approaching with irresistible force will review the Chinese problem together with all other problems of colonial domination. For it is in this that the real task of the second world war will consist: to divide the planet anew in accord with the new relationship of imperialist forces. The principal arena of struggle will, of course, not be that lilliputian bathtub, the Mediterranean, nor even the Atlantic Ocean, but the basin of the Pacific. The most important object of struggle will be China, embracing about one-fourth of the human race. The fate of the Soviet Union—the other big stake in the coming war—will also to a certain degree be decided in the Far East. Preparing for this clash of titans, Tokyo is attempting today to assure itself of the broadest possible drill ground on the continent of Asia. Great Britain and the United States are likewise losing no time. It can, however, be predicted with certainty—and this is in essence acknowledged by the present makers of destiny—that the world war will not produce the final decision: it will be followed by a new series of revolutions which will review not only the decisions of the war but all those property conditions which give rise to war.

This prospect, it must be confessed, is very far from being an idyll, but Clio, the muse of history, was never a member of a ladies' peace society. The older generation which passed through the war of 1914-18 did not discharge a single one of its tasks. It leaves to the new generation as heritage the burden of wars and revolutions. These most important and tragic events in human history have often marched side by side. They will definitely form the background of the coming decades. It remains only to hope that the new generation, which cannot arbitrarily cut loose from the conditions it has inherited, has learned at least to understand better the laws of its epoch. For acquainting itself with the Chinese revolution of 1925-27 it will not find today a better guide than this book.

Despite the unquestionable greatness of the Anglo-Saxon genius, it is impossible not to see that the laws of revolutions are least understood precisely in the Anglo-Saxon countries. The explanation for this lies, on the one hand, in the fact that the very appearance of revolution in these countries relates to a long-distant past, and evokes in official "sociologists" a condescending smile, as would childish pranks. On the other hand, pragmatism, so characteristic of Anglo-Saxon thinking, is least of all useful for understanding revolutionary crises.

The English revolution of the seventeenth century, like the French revolution of the eighteenth, had the task of "rationalizing" the structure of society, i.e., cleansing it of feudal stalactites and stalagmites, and subjecting it to the laws of free competition, which in that epoch seemed to be the laws of "common sense." In doing this, the Puritan revolution draped itself in biblical dress, thereby revealing a purely infantile incapacity to understand its own significance. The French revolution, which had considerable influence on progressive thought in the United States, was guided by formulas of pure rationalism. Common sense, which is still afraid of itself and resorts to the mask of biblical prophets, or secularized common sense, which looks upon society as the product of a rational "contract," remain to this day the fundamental forms of Anglo-Saxon thinking in the domains of philosophy and sociology.

Yet the real society of history has not been constructed, following Rousseau, upon a rational "contract," nor, as according to Bentham, upon the principle of the "greatest good," but has unfolded "irrationally," on the basis of contradictions and antagonisms. For revolution to become inevitable, class contradictions have to be strained to the breaking point. It is precisely this historically inescapable necessity for conflict, which depends neither on good nor ill will but on the objective interrelationship of classes, that makes revolution, together with war, the most dramatic expression of the "irrational" foundation of the historic process.

"Irrational" does not, however, mean arbitrary. On the contrary, in the molecular preparation of revolution, in its explosion, in its ascent and decline, there is lodged a profound inner lawfulness which can be apprehended and, in the main, foreseen. Revolutions, as has been said more than once, have a logic of their own. But this is not the logic of Aristotle, and even less the pragmatic demilogic of "common sense." It is the higher function of thought: the logic of development and its contradictions, i.e., the dialectic.

The obstinacy of Anglo-Saxon pragmatism and its hostility to dialectical thinking thus have their material causes. Just as a poet cannot attain to the dialectic through books without his own personal experiences, so a well-to-do society, unused to convulsions and habituated to uninterrupted "progress," is incapable of understanding the dialectic of its own development. However, it is only too obvious that this privilege of the Anglo-Saxon world has receded into the past. History is preparing to give Great Britain as well as the United States serious lessons in the dialectic.

The author of this book tries to deduce the character of the Chinese revolution not from a priori definitions and not from historical analogies, but from the living structure of Chinese society and from the dynamics of its inner forces. In this lies the chief methodological value of the book. The reader will carry away not only a better-knit picture of the march of events but—what is more important—will learn to understand their social mainsprings. Only on this basis is it possible correctly to appraise political programs and the slogans of struggling parties—which, even if neither independent nor in the final analysis the decisive factors in the process, are nevertheless its most manifest signs.

In its immediate aims the incompleted Chinese revolution is "bourgeois." This term, however, which is used as a mere echo of the bourgeois revolutions of the past, actually helps us very little. Lest the historical analogy turn into a trap for the mind, it is necessary to check it in the light of a concrete sociological analysis. What are the classes which are struggling in China?

What are the interrelationships of these classes? How, and in what direction, are these relations being transformed? What are the objective tasks of the Chinese revolution, i.e., those tasks dictated by the course of development? On the shoulders of which classes rests the solution to these tasks? With what methods can they be solved? Issacs' book gives the answers to precisely these questions.

Colonial and semicolonial—and therefore backward—countries, which embrace by far the greater part of mankind, differ extraordinarily from one another in their degree of backwardness, representing an historical ladder reaching from nomadry, and even cannibalism, up to the most modern industrial culture. The combination of extremes in one degree or another characterizes all of the backward countries. However, the hierarchy of backwardness, if one may employ such an expression, is determined by the specific weight of the elements of barbarism and culture in the life of each colonial country. Equatorial Africa lags far behind Algeria, Paraguay behind Mexico, Abyssinia behind India or China. With their common economic dependence upon the imperialist metropolises, their political dependence bears in some instances the character of open colonial slavery (India, Equatorial Africa), while in others it is concealed by the fiction of state independence (China, Latin America).

In agrarian relations backwardness finds its most organic and cruel expression. Not one of these countries has carried its democratic revolution through to any real extent. Halfway agrarian reforms are absorbed by semiserf relations, and these are inescapably reproduced in the soil of poverty and oppression. Agrarian barbarism always goes hand in hand with the absence of roads, with the isolation of provinces, with "medieval" particularism, and absence of national consciousness. The purging of social relations of the remnants of ancient and the encrustations of modern feudalism is the most important task in all these countries.

The achievement of the agrarian revolution is unthinkable, however, with the preservation of dependence upon foreign imperialism, which with one hand implants capitalist relations while supporting and re-creating with the other all the forms of slavery and serfdom. The struggle for the democratization of social relations and the creation of a national state thus uninterruptedly passes into an open uprising against foreign domination.

Historical backwardness does not imply a simple reproduction of the development of advanced countries, England or France, with a delay of one, two, or three centuries. It engenders an entirely new "combined" social formation in which the latest conquests of capitalist technique and structure root themselves into relations of feudal or prefeudal barbarism, transforming and subjecting them and creating peculiar relations of classes.

Not a single one of the tasks of the "bourgeois" revolution can be solved in these backward countries under the leadership of the "national" bourgeoisie, because the latter emerges at once with foreign support as a class alien or hostile to the people. Every stage in its development binds it only the more closely to the foreign finance capital of which it is essentially the agency. The petty bourgeoisie of the colonies, that of handicrafts and trade, is the first to fall victim in the unequal struggle with foreign capital, declining into economic insignificance, becoming de-classed and pauperized. It cannot even conceive of playing an independent political role. The peasantry, the largest numerically and the most atomized, backward, and oppressed class, is capable of local uprisings and partisan warfare, but requires the leadership of a more advanced and centralized class in order for this struggle to be elevated to an all-national level. The task of such leadership falls in the nature of things upon the colonial proletariat, which, from its very first steps, stands opposed not only to the foreign but also to its own national bourgeoisie.

Out of the conglomeration of provinces and tribes, bound together by geographical proximity and the bureaucratic apparatus, capitalist development has transformed China into the semblance of an economic entity. The revolutionary movement of the masses translated this growing unity for the first time into the language of national consciousness. In the strikes, agrarian uprisings, and military expeditions of 1925-27 a new China was born. While the generals, tied to their own and the foreign bourgeoisie, could only tear the country to pieces, the Chinese workers became the standard-bearers of an irresistible urge to national unity. This movement provides an incontestable analogy with the struggle of the French third estate against particularism,[181] or with the later struggle of the Germans and Italians for national unification. But in contrast to the first-born countries of capitalism, where the problem of achieving national unity fell to the petty bourgeoisie, in part under the leadership of the bourgeoisie and even of the landlords (Prussia!), in China it was the proletariat that emerged as the primary motive force and potential leader of this movement. But precisely thereby, the proletariat confronted the bourgeoisie with the danger that the leadership of the unified fatherland would not remain in the latter's hands. Patriotism has been throughout all history inseparably bound up with power and property. In the face of danger the ruling classes have never stopped short of dismembering their own country so long as they were able in this way to preserve power over one part of it. It is not at all surprising, therefore, if the Chinese bourgeoisie, represented by Chiang Kai-shek, turned its weapons in 1927 against the proletariat, the standard-bearer of national unity. The exposition and explanation of this turn, which occupies the central place in Isaacs' book, provides the key to the understanding of the fundamental problems of the Chinese revolution as well as of the present Sino-Japanese War.

The so-called "national" bourgeoisie tolerates all forms of national degradation so long as it can hope to maintain its own privileged existence. But at the moment when foreign capital sets out to assume undivided domination of the entire wealth of the country, the colonial bourgeoisie is forced to remind itself of its "national" obligations. Under pressure of the masses it may even find itself plunged into a war. But this will be a war waged against one of the imperialist powers, the one least amenable to negotiations, with the hope of passing into the service of some other, more magnanimous power. Chiang Kai-shek struggles against the Japanese violators only within the limits indicated to him by his British or American patrons. Only that class which has nothing to lose but its chains can conduct to the very end the war against imperialism for national emancipation.

The above developed views regarding the special character of the "bourgeois" revolutions in historically belated countries are by no means the product of theoretical analysis alone. Before the second Chinese revolution (1925-27) they had already been submitted to a grandiose historical test. The experience of the three Russian revolutions (1905, February and October 1917) bears no less significance for the twentieth century than the French revolution bore for the nineteenth. To understand the destinies of modern China the reader must have before his eyes the struggle of conceptions in the Russian revolutionary movement, because these conceptions exerted, and still exert, a direct and, moreover, powerful influence upon the politics of the

Chinese proletariat and an indirect influence upon the politics of the Chinese bourgeoisie.

It was precisely because of its historical backwardness that tsarist Russia turned out to be the only European country where Marxism as a doctrine and the Social Democracy as a party attained powerful development before the bourgeois revolution. It was in Russia, quite naturally, that the problem of the correlation between the struggle for democracy and the struggle for socialism, or between the bourgeois revolution and the socialist, was submitted to theoretical analysis. The first to pose this problem in the early eighties of the last century was the founder of the Russian Social Democracy, Plekhanov. In the struggle against so-called Populism (Narodnikism), a variety of socialist utopianism, Plekhanov established that Russia had no reason whatever to expect a privileged path of development; that like the "profane" nations, it would have to pass through the stage of capitalism and that along this path it would acquire the regime of bourgeois democracy indispensable for the further struggle of the proletariat for socialism. Plekhanov not only separated the bourgeois revolution as a task distinct from the socialist revolution—which he postponed to the indefinite future—but he depicted entirely different combinations of forces. The bourgeois revolution was to be achieved by the proletariat in alliance with the liberal bourgeoisie, and thus clear the path for capitalist progress; after a number of decades and on a higher level of capitalist development, the proletariat would carry out the socialist revolution in direct struggle against the bourgeoisie.

Lenin—not immediately, to be sure—reviewed this doctrine. At the beginning of the present century, with much greater force and consistency than Plekhanov, he posed the agrarian problem as the central problem of the bourgeois revolution in Russia. With this he came to the conclusion that the liberal bourgeoisie was hostile to the expropriation of the landlords' estates, and precisely for this reason would seek a compromise with the monarchy on the basis of a constitution on the Prussian pattern. To Plekhanov's idea of an alliance between the proletariat and the liberal bourgeoisie, Lenin opposed the idea of an alliance between the proletariat and the peasantry. The aim of the revolutionary collaboration of these two classes he proclaimed to be the establishment of the "bourgeois-democratic dictatorship of the proletariat and peasantry" as the only means of cleansing the tsarist empire of its feudal-police refuse, of creating a free farmers' system, and of clearing the road for the development of capitalism along American lines. Lenin's formula represented a gigantic step forward in that, in contrast to Plekhanov's, it correctly indicated the central task of the revolution, namely, the democratic overturn of agrarian relations, and equally correctly sketched out the only realistic combination of class forces capable of solving this task. But up to 1917 the thought of Lenin himself remained bound to the traditional concept of the "bourgeois" revolution. Like Plekhanov, Lenin proceeded from the premise that only after the "completion of the bourgeois-democratic revolution" would the tasks of the socialist revolution come on the order of the day. Lenin, however, contrary to the legend later manufactured by the epigones, considered that after the completion of the democratic overturn, the peasantry, as peasantry, could not remain the ally of the proletariat. Lenin based his socialist hopes on the agricultural laborers and the semiproletarianized peasants who sell their labor-power.

The weak point of Lenin's conception was the internally contradictory idea of the "bourgeois-democratic dictatorship of the proletariat and the peasantry." A political bloc of two classes whose interests only partially coincide excludes a dictatorship. Lenin himself emphasized the fundamental limitation of the "dictatorship of the proletariat and the peasantry" when he openly called it *bourgeois*. By this he meant to say that for the sake of maintaining the alliance with the peasantry the proletariat would, in the coming revolution, have to forego the direct posing of the socialist tasks. But this would signify, to be precise, that the proletariat would have to give up the dictatorship. In that event, in whose hands would the revolutionary power be concentrated? In the hands of the peasantry? But it is least capable of such a role.

Lenin left these questions unanswered up to his famous Theses of April 4, 1917. Only here did he break for the first time with the traditional understanding of the "bourgeois" revolution and with the formula of the "bourgeois-democratic dictatorship of the proletariat and the peasantry." He declared the struggle for the dictatorship of the proletariat to be the sole means of carrying out the agrarian revolution to the end and of securing the freedom of the oppressed nationalities. The regime of the proletarian dictatorship, by its very nature, however, could not limit itself to the framework of bourgeois property. The rule of the proletariat automatically placed on the agenda the socialist revolution, which in this case was not separated from the democratic revolution by any historical period, but was uninterruptedly connected with it, or, to put it more accurately, was an organic outgrowth of it. At what tempo the socialist transformation of society would occur and what limits it would attain in the nearest future would depend not only upon internal but upon external conditions as well. The Russian revolution was only a link in the international revolution. Such was, in broad outline, the essence of the conception of the permanent (uninterrupted) revolution. It was precisely this conception that guaranteed the victory of the proletariat in October.

But such is the bitter irony of history: the experience of the Russian revolution not only did not help the Chinese proletariat but, on the contrary, it became in its reactionary, distorted form, one of the chief obstacles in its path. The Comintern of the epigones began by canonizing for all countries of the Orient the formula of the "democratic dictatorship of the proletariat and peasantry" which Lenin, influenced by historical experience, had acknowledged to be without value. As always in history, a formula that had outlived itself served to cover a political content which was the direct opposite of that which the formula had served in its day. The mass plebeian, revolutionary alliance of the workers and peasants, sealed through the freely elected soviets as the direct organs of action, the Comintern replaced by the bureaucratic bloc of party centers. The right to represent the peasantry in this bloc was unexpectedly given to the Kuomintang, i.e., a thoroughly bourgeois party vitally interested in the preservation of capitalist property, not only in the means of production but in land. The alliance of the proletariat and the peasantry was broadened into a "bloc of four classes": workers, peasants, urban petty bourgeoisie, and the so-called "national" bourgeoisie. In other words, the Comintern picked up a formula discarded by Lenin only in order to open the road to the politics of Plekhanov and, moreover, in a masked and therefore more harmful form.

To justify the political subordination of the proletariat to the bourgeoisie, the theoreticians of the Comintern (Stalin, Bukharin) adduced the fact of imperialist oppression which supposedly impelled "all the progressive forces in the country" to an alliance. But this was precisely in its day the argument of the Russian Mensheviks, with the difference that in their case the place of imperialism was occupied by tsarism. In reality, the subjection of the Chinese Communist Party to the Kuomintang signified its break with the mass movement and a direct betrayal of its historical interests. In this way the catastrophe of the second Chinese revolution was prepared under the direct leadership of Moscow.

To many political philistines who in politics are inclined to substitute "common sense" guesses for scientific analysis, the controversy among the Russian Marxists over the nature of the revolution and the dynamics of its class forces seemed to be sheer scholasticism. Historical experience revealed, however, the profoundly vital significance of the "doctrinaire formulas" of Russian Marxism. Those who have not understood this up to today can learn a great deal from Isaacs' book. The politics of the Communist International in China showed convincingly what the Russian revolution would have been converted into if the Mensheviks and the Social Revolutionaries had not been thrust aside in time by the Bolsheviks. In China the conception of the permanent revolution was confirmed once more, this time not in the form of a victory, but of a catastrophe.

It would, of course, be impermissible to identify Russia and China. With all their important common traits, the differences are all too obvious. But it is not hard to convince oneself that these differences do not weaken but, on the contrary, strengthen the fundamental conclusions of Bolshevism. In one sense tsarist Russia was also a colonial country, and this found its expression in the predominant role of foreign capital. But the Russian bourgeoisie enjoyed the benefits of an immeasurably greater independence from foreign imperialism than the Chinese bourgeoisie. Russia itself was an imperialist country. With all its meagerness, Russian liberalism had far more serious traditions and more of a basis of support than the Chinese. To the left of the liberals stood powerful petty-bourgeois parties, revolutionary or semirevolutionary in relation to tsarism. The party of the Social Revolutionaries managed to find considerable support among the peasantry, chiefly from its upper layers. The Social Democratic (Menshevik) Party led behind it broad circles of the urban petty bourgeoisie and labor aristocracy. It was precisely these three parties—the Liberals, the Social Revolutionaries, and the Mensheviks—who for a long time prepared, and in 1917 definitely formed, a coalition which was not yet then called the People's Front but which had all of its traits. In contrast to this the Bolsheviks, from the eve of the revolution in 1905, took up an irreconcilable position in relation to the liberal bourgeoisie. Only this policy, which achieved its highest expression in the "defeatism" of 1914-17, enabled the Bolshevik party to conquer power.

The differences between China and Russia—the incomparably greater dependence of the Chinese bourgeoisie on foreign capital, the absence of independent revolutionary traditions among the petty bourgeoisie, the mass gravitation of the workers and peasants to the banner of the Comintern—demanded a still more irreconcilable policy—if such were possible—than that pursued in Russia. Yet the Chinese section of the Comintern, at Moscow's command, renounced Marxism, accepted the reactionary scholastic "principles of Sun Yat-sen," and entered the ranks of the Kuomintang, submitting to its discipline. In other words, it went much further along the road of submission to the bourgeoisie than the Russian Mensheviks or Social Revolutionaries ever did. The same fatal policy is now being repeated in the conditions of the war with Japan.

How could the bureaucracy emerging from the Bolshevik revolution apply in China, as throughout the world, methods fundamentally opposed to those of Bolshevism? It would be far too superficial to answer this question with a reference to the incapacity or ignorance of this or that individual. The gist of the matter lies in this: together with the new conditions of existence the bureaucracy acquired new methods of thinking. The Bolshevik party led the masses. The bureaucracy began to order them about. The Bolsheviks won the possibility of leadership by correctly expressing the interests of the masses. The bureaucracy was compelled to resort to command in order to secure its own interests against those of the masses. The method of command was naturally extended to the Communist International as well. The Moscow leaders began quite seriously to imagine that they could compel the Chinese bourgeoisie to move to the left of its interests and the Chinese workers and peasants to the right of theirs, along the diagonals drawn in the Kremlin. Yet it is the very essence of revolution that the exploited as well as the exploiters invest their interests with the most extreme expression. If hostile classes would move along diagonals, there would be no need for a civil war. Armed by the authority of the October revolution and the Communist International, not to mention inexhaustible financial resources, the bureaucracy transformed the young Chinese Communist Party from a motive force into a brake at the most important moment of the revolution. In contrast to Germany and Austria, where the bureaucracy could shift part of the responsibility for defeat to the Social Democracy, there was no Social Democracy in China. The Comintern had the monopoly in ruining the Chinese revolution.

The present domination of the Kuomintang over a considerable section of Chinese territory would have been impossible without the powerful national-revolutionary movement of the masses in 1925-27. The massacre of this movement on the one hand concentrated power in the hands of Chiang Kai-shek, and on the other doomed Chiang Kai-shek to half-measures in the struggle against imperialism. The understanding of the course of the Chinese revolution has in this way the most direct significance for an understanding of the course of the Sino-Japanese War. This historical work acquires thereby the most *actuel* political significance.

War and revolution will be interlaced in the nearest future history of China. Japan's aim, to enslave forever, or at least for a long time to come, a gigantic country by dominating its strategic centers, is characterized not only by greediness but by wooden-headedness. Japan has arrived much too late. Torn by internal contradictions, the empire of the mikado cannot reproduce the history of Britain's ascent. On the other hand, China has advanced far beyond the India of the seventeenth and eighteenth centuries. Old colonial countries are nowadays waging with ever greater success a struggle for their national independence. In these historic conditions, even if the present war in the Far East were to end with Japan's victory, and even if the victor himself could escape an internal catastrophe during the next few years— and neither the former nor the latter is in the least assured— Japan's domination over China would be measured by a very brief period, perhaps only the few years required to give a new impulse to the economic life of China and to mobilize its laboring masses once more.

The big Japanese trusts and concerns are already following in the wake of the army to divide the still unsecured booty. The Tokyo government is seeking to regulate the appetites of the financial cliques that would tear North China to pieces. If Japan were to succeed in maintaining its conquered positions for an interval of some ten years, this would mean, above all, the intensive industrialization of North China in the military interests of Japanese imperialism. New railways, mines, power stations, mining and metallurgical enterprises, and cotton plantations would rapidly spring up. The polarization of the Chinese nation would receive a feverish impulse. New hundreds of thousands and millions of Chinese proletarians would be mobilized in the briefest possible space of time. On the other hand, the Chinese bourgeosie would fall into an ever greater dependence on Japanese capital. Even less than in the past would it be capable of standing at the head of a national war, no less a national revolution. Face to face with the foreign violator would stand the numerically larger, socially strengthened, politically matured Chinese proletariat, called to lead the Chinese village. Hatred of the foreign enslaver is a mighty revolutionary cement. The new national revolution will, one must think, be placed on the agenda still in the lifetime of the present generation. To solve the tasks imposed upon it, the vanguard of the Chinese proletariat must thoroughly assimilate the lessons of the Chinese revolution. Isaacs' book can serve it in this sense as an irreplaceable aid. It remains to be hoped that the book will be translated into Chinese as well as other foreign languages.

From *The Tragedy of the Chinese Revolution* by Harold R. Isaacs (London: Secker & Warburg, 1938).

THE GREAT LESSON OF CHINA[182]

May 1940

The tragic experience of China is a great lesson for the oppressed peoples. The Chinese revolution of 1925-27 had every chance for victory. A unified and transformed China would constitute at this time a powerful fortress of freedom in the Far East. The entire fate of Asia and to a degree the whole world might have been different. But the Kremlin, lacking confidence in the Chinese masses and seeking the friendship of the generals, utilized its whole weight to subordinate the Chinese proletariat to the bourgeoisie and so helped Chiang Kai-shek to crush the Chinese revolution. Disillusioned, disunited, and weakened, China was laid open to Japanese invasion.

Like every doomed regime, the Stalinist oligarchy is already incapable of learning from the lessons of history. At the beginning of the Sino-Japanese War, the Kremlin again placed the Communist Party in bondage to Chiang Kai-shek, crushing in the bud the revolutionary initiative of the Chinese proletariat. This war, now nearing its third anniversary, might long since have been finished by a real catastrophe for Japan, if China had conducted it as a genuine people's war based on an agrarian revolution and setting the Japanese soldiery aflame with its blaze. But the Chinese bourgeoisie fears its own armed masses more than it does the Japanese ravishers. If Chiang Kai-shek, the sinister hangman of the Chinese revolution, is compelled by circumstances to wage a war, his program is still based, as before, on the oppression of his own workers and compromise with the imperialists.

The war in eastern Asia will become more and more interlocked with the imperialist world war. The Chinese people will be able to reach independence only under the leadership of the youthful and self-sacrificing proletariat, in whom the indispensable self-confidence will be rekindled by the rebirth of the world revolution. They will indicate a firm line of march. The course of events places on the order of the day the development of our Chinese section into a powerful revolutionary party.

Excerpted from "Manifesto of the Fourth International on the Imperialist War and the Proletarian World Revolution," in *Writings of Leon Trotsky (1939-40)*. Text from *Socialist Appeal* (New York), June 29, 1940.

CHINA AND THE
RUSSIAN REVOLUTION[183]

July 1940

The day I learned that my *History of the Russian Revolution* was to be published in the Chinese language was a holiday for me. Now I have received word that the work of the translation has been speeded up and that the first volume will be issued next year.

Let me express the firm hope that the book will prove profitable to Chinese readers. Whatever may be the shortcomings of my work, one thing I can say with assurance: Facts are there presented with complete conscientiousness, that is, on the basis of verification with original sources; and in any case, not a single fact is altered or distorted in the interests of this or that preconceived theory or, what is worse yet, in the interests of this or that personal reputation.

The misfortune of the present young generation in all countries, among them China, consists in this: that there has been created under the label of Marxism a gigantic factory of historical, theoretical, and all other kinds of falsifications. This factory bears the name "Communist International." The totalitarian regime, i.e., the regime of bureaucratic command in all spheres of life, inescapably seeks to extend its rule also over the past. History becomes transformed into raw material for whatever constructions are required by the ruling totalitarian clique. This fate was suffered by the October revolution and by the history of the Bolshevik party. The latest and to date most finished document of falsification and frame-up is the *History of the Communist Party of the Soviet Union,* issued some time ago under the personal direction of Stalin. In the entire library of mankind I do not know, and hardly anyone else knows, of a book in which facts, documents—and furthermore facts known to everyone—are so dishonestly altered, mangled, or simply deleted from the march of events in the interests of glorifying a single human being, namely Stalin.

Thanks to the unlimited material resources at the disposal of the falsifiers, the rude and untalented falsification has been translated into all the languages of civilized mankind and circulated by compulsion in millions and tens of millions of copies.

We have at our disposal neither such financial resources nor such a colossal apparatus. But we do dispose of something greater: concern for historical truth and a correct scientific method. A falsification, even one compiled by a mighty state apparatus, cannot withstand the test of time and in the long run is blown up because of its internal contradictions. On the contrary, historical truth, established through a scientific method, has its own internal persuasiveness and in the long run gains mastery over minds. The very necessity of reviewing, i.e., recasting and altering—still more precisely, falsifying—the history of the revolution, arose from this: that the bureaucracy found itself compelled to sever the umbilical cord binding it to the Bolshevik party. To recast, i.e., to falsify the history of the revolution, became an urgent necessity for the bureaucracy which usurped the revolution and found itself compelled to cut short the tradition of Bolshevism.

The essence of Bolshevism was the class policy of the proletariat, which alone would bring about the conquest of power in October. In the course of its entire history, Bolshevism came out irreconcilably against the policy of collaboration with the bourgeoisie. Precisely in this consisted the fundamental contradiction between Bolshevism and Menshevism. Still more, the struggle within the labor movement, which preceded the rise of Bolshevism and Menshevism, always in the last analysis revolved around the central question, the central alternative: either collaboration with the bourgeoisie or irreconcilable class struggle. The policy of "People's Fronts" does not include an iota of novelty, if we discount the solemn and essentially charlatan name. The matter at issue in all cases concerns the political subordination of the proletariat to the left wing of the exploiters, regardless of whether this practice bears the name of coalition or Left Bloc (as in France) or "People's Front" in the language of the Comintern.

The policy of the "People's Front" bore especially malignant fruit because it was applied in the epoch of the imperialist decay of the bourgeoisie. Stalin succeeded in conducting to the end, in the Chinese revolution, the policy which the Mensheviks tried to realize in the revolution of 1917. The same thing was repeated in Spain. Two grandiose revolutions suffered catastrophe owing to this: that the methods of the leadership were the methods of Stalinism, i.e., the most malignant form of Menshevism.

In the course of five years, the policy of the "People's Front," by subjecting the proletariat to the bourgeoisie, made impossible the class struggle against war. If the defeat of the Chinese revolution, conditioned by the leadership of the Comintern, prepared the conditions for Japanese occupation, then the defeat of the Spanish revolution and the ignominious capitulation of the "People's Front" in France prepared the conditions for the aggression and unprecedented military successes of Hitler.

The victories of Japan, like the victories of Hitler, are not the last word of history. War this time, too, will turn out to be the mother of revolution. Revolution will once again pose and review all the questions of the history of mankind in advanced as well as in backward countries, and make a beginning for overcoming the very distinction between advanced and backward countries.

Reformists, opportunists, routinists will be flung aside by the course of events. Only revolutionists, tempered revolutionists enriched by the experience of the past, will be able to rise to the level of great events. The Chinese people are destined to occupy the first place in the future destinies of mankind. I shall be happy if the advanced Chinese revolutionists will assimilate from this history certain fundamental rules of class politics which will help them to avoid fatal mistakes in the future, mistakes that led to the shipwreck of the revolution of 1925-27.

From *Writings of Leon Trotsky (1930-40)*. Text from *Fourth International* (New York), March 1941.

APPENDIX

Appeal to All the Comrades
of the Chinese Communist Party[184]

December 10, 1929

Dear Comrades:

Since 1920 (the ninth year of the republic) I have worked with the comrades, in founding the party, in sincerely carrying out the opportunist policy of the International's leaders, Stalin, Zinoviev, Bukharin, and others, bringing the Chinese revolution to a shameful and sad defeat. Though I have worked night and day, yet my demerits exceed my merits.

Of course, I should not imitate the hypocritical confessions of some of the ancient Chinese emperors: "I, one person, am responsible for all the sins of the people"; take upon my own shoulders all the mistakes that caused the failure. Nevertheless I feel ashamed to adopt the attitude of some responsible comrades at times—only criticizing the past mistakes of opportunism and excluding oneself. Whenever my comrades have pointed out my past opportunist errors, I earnestly acknowledged them. I am absolutely unwilling to ignore the experiences of the Chinese revolution obtained at the highest price paid by proletarians in the past. (From the August 7 Conference [1927] to the present time, I not only did not reject proper criticism against me, but I even kept silent about the exaggerated accusations against me.)

Not only am I willing to acknowledge my past errors, but now or in the future, if I should make any opportunist errors in thought or action, I likewise expect comrades to criticize me mercilessly with theoretical argument and fact. I humbly accept or shall accept all criticism, but not rumors and false accusations. I cannot have such self-confidence as Ch'ü Ch'iu-pai and Li Li-san. I clearly recognize that it is never an easy thing for anybody or any party to avoid the errors of opportunism. Even such veteran Marxists as Kautsky and Plekhanov were guilty of unpardonable opportunism when they were old; those who followed Lenin for a long time like Stalin and Bukharin are now also acting like shameful opportunists. How can superficial Marxists like us be self-satisfied? Whenever a man is self-satisfied, he prevents himself from making progress.

Even the banner of the Opposition is not the incantation of the "Heavenly Teacher" Chang [the Taoist pope]. If those who have not fundamentally cleared out the ideology of the petty bourgeoisie, and have not plainly understood the system of past opportunism, and decisively participated in struggles, merely stand under the banner of the Opposition to revile the opportunism of Stalin and Li Li-san, and then think that the opportunist devils will never approach, they are suffering from an illusion. The only way of avoiding the errors of opportunism is continually and humbly to learn from the teachings of Marx and Lenin in the struggles of the proletarian masses and in the mutual criticism of comrades.

I decisively recognize that the objective conditions were second in importance as the cause of the failure of the last Chinese revolution. The main cause was the error of opportunism, the error of our policy in dealing with the bourgeois Kuomintang.* All the responsible comrades of the Central Committee at that time, especially myself, should openly and courageously recog-

---

 * Stalin said: "Was the policy of the Bolsheviks in the 1905 Revolution a correct one? Yes, it was. Why, then, did the 1905 Revolution suffer defeat, despite the existence of Soviets, despite the correct policy of the Bolsheviks? Because the feudal survivals and the autocracy proved at that time to be stronger than the revolutionary movement of the workers. . . . Can it be affirmed that communist policy in China has not enhanced the fighting capacity of the proletariat, has not multiplied its ties with the broad masses, and has not increased its prestige among these masses? Clearly, it cannot" [Stalin, *On the Opposition* (Peking: Foreign Languages Press, 1974), pp. 747-48]. The correct policy, of course, is not the only guarantee of success but an erroneous policy is the chief guarantee of failure. If we think that the power of the enemy is stronger though there is a correct policy, and yet the revolution cannot succeed, then the failure of the Russian revolution in 1905 and the failure of the Chinese revolution in 1927 and all other failures of the workers' revolutionary movement are predestined. I do not want to have Stalin defend the Chinese party like this, and am even more unwilling to defend myself with Stalin's words.

nize that this policy was undoubtedly wrong. But it is not enough merely to recognize the error. We must sincerely and thoroughly acknowledge that the past error was the internal content of the policy of opportunism, examine the causes and results of that policy, and reveal them clearly. Then we can hope to stop repeating the errors of the past, and the repetition of former opportunism in the next revolution. When our party was first founded, though it was quite young, yet, under the guidance of the Leninist International, we did not commit any great mistakes. For instance, we decisively led the struggle of the workers and recognized the class nature of the Kuomintang. In 1921, our party induced the delegates of the Kuomintang and other social organizations to participate in the conference of the Toilers of the Far East, which was called by the Comintern. The conference resolved that in the colonial countries of the East the struggle for the democratic revolution must be carried out, and that in this revolution peasant soviets should be organized.

In 1922, at the Second Congress of the Chinese party, the policy of the united front in the democratic revolution was adopted, and based upon this we expressed our attitude toward the political situation. At the same time, the representative of the Communist Youth International, Dalin, came to China and suggested to the Kuomintang the policy of a united front of the revolutionary groups. The head of the Kuomintang, Sun Yat-sen, stubbornly rejected this, agreeing only to allow the members of the Chinese Communist Party and the Youth League to join the Kuomintang as individuals and obey it, denying any unity outside of the party.

Soon after the adjournment of our party congress the Communist International sent its delegate Maring to China. He invited all the members of the Central Committee of the Chinese Communist Party to hold a meeting at the West Lake in Hangchow, in Chekiang province, at which he suggested to the Chinese party that it join the Kuomintang organization. He strongly contended that the Kuomintang was not a party of the bourgeoisie but the joint party of various classes and that the proletarian party should join it in order to improve this party and advance the revolution.

At that time, the five members of the Central Committee of the CCP—Li Shou-ch'ang, Chang T'e-li, Ts'ai Ho-sen, Kao Chün-yü, and I—unanimously opposed the proposal.[185] The chief reason was: To join the Kuomintang was to confuse the class organizations and curb our independent policy. Finally, the delegate of the Third International asked if the Chinese party would obey the decision of the International.

Thereupon, for the sake of respecting international discipline the Central Committee of the CCP could not but accept the proposal of the Communist International and agree to join the Kuomintang. After this, the international delegate and the representatives of the Chinese party spent nearly a year in carrying out the reorganization of the Kuomintang.[186] But from the very outset the Kuomintang entirely neglected and resisted it. Many times Sun Yat-sen said to the delegates of the International: "Since the Chinese CP has joined the Kuomintang, it should obey the discipline of the KMT and should not openly criticize it. If the communists do not obey the Kuomintang I shall expel them from it; if Soviet Russia stands on the side of the CCP I shall immediately oppose Soviet Russia." As a result, a dejected Maring returned to Moscow. Borodin, who took over Maring's post in China, brought with him a large sum of material aid for the Kuomintang. It was then, in 1924, that the KMT began the policy of reorganization and alliance with Soviet Russia.

At this time the Chinese communists were not very much tainted with opportunism. We were able to lead the railroad workers' strike on February 7, 1923, and the May Thirtieth Movement of 1925, since we were not restrained by the KMT and at times severely criticized its compromising policy. But as soon as the proletariat raised its head in the May Thirtieth Movement, the bourgeoisie was immediately aroused. In response, Tai Chi-t'ao's anticommunist pamphlet appeared in July.[187]

At the enlarged plenum of the Central Committee of the CCP held in Peking in October of 1925, I submitted the following proposal to the Political Resolution Committee:

Tai Chi-t'ao's pamphlet was not accidental but the indication that the bourgeoisie was attempting to strengthen its own power for the purpose of checking the proletariat and going over to the counterrevolution. We should be ready immediately to withdraw from the Kuomintang. We should maintain our [public] political face, lead the masses, and not be held in check by the policy of the Kuomintang.

At that time both the delegate of the Comintern and the responsible comrades of the Central Committee unanimously opposed my suggestion, saying that it was to propose to the comrades and the masses to take the path of opposing the Kuomintang. I, who had no decisiveness of character, could not insistently maintain my proposal. I respected international discipline and the opinion of the majority of the Central Committee.

Chiang Kai-shek's coup d'etat on March 20, 1926, was made to carry out Tai Chi-t'ao's principles. Having arrested the communists in large numbers, disarmed the Canton-Hong Kong Strike Committee's guards for the visiting Soviet group (most of whom were members of the Central Committee of the AUCP) and for the Soviet advisers, the Central Committee of the Kuomintang decided that all communist elements should be removed from the supreme party headquarters of the KMT, that criticism of Sun Yat-senism by communists be prohibited, and that a list of the names of the members of the Communist Party and of the [Youth] League who had joined the KMT should be handed over to the latter. All these conditions were accepted.

At the same time we resolved to prepare our independent military forces in order to be equal to the forces of Chiang Kai-shek. Comrade P'eng Shu-chih was sent to Canton as representative of the Central Committee of the Chinese party to consult the international delegate about our plan. But the latter did not agree with us, and tried his best to continually strengthen Chiang Kai-shek. He insistently advocated that we use all our strength to support the military dictatorship of Chiang Kai-shek, to build up the Canton government, and to carry on the Northern Expedition. We demanded that he take 5,000 rifles out of those given to Chiang Kai-shek and Li Chi-shen, so that we might arm the peasants of Kwangtung province. He refused, saying:

"The armed peasants cannot fight against the forces of Ch'en Chiung-ming nor take part in the Northern Expedition, but they can incur the suspicion of the Kuomintang and make the peasants oppose it."

This was the most critical period. Concretely speaking it was the period when the bourgeois KMT openly compelled the proletariat to follow its guidance and direction, when we formally called on the proletariat to surrender to the bourgeoisie, to follow it, and be willing to be subordinates of the bourgeoisie. (The international delegates said openly: "The present period is a period in which the communists should do the coolie service for the Kuomintang.") By this time the party was already not the party of the proletariat, having become completely the extreme left wing of the bourgeoisie, and beginning to fall into the deep pit of opportunism.

After the coup of March 20, I stated in a report to the

Comintern my personal opinion that cooperation with the Kuomintang by means of joint work within it should be changed to cooperation outside the KMT. Otherwise, we would be unable to carry out our own independent policy or win the confidence of the masses. After having read my report, the International published an article by Bukharin in *Pravda* severely criticizing the Chinese party on [the question of] withdrawing from the Kuomintang, saying:

"There have been two mistakes: the advocacy of withdrawal from the yellow trade unions and from the Anglo-Russian Trade Union Unity Committee; now the third mistake has been produced: the Chinese party advocates withdrawal from the Kuomintang." At the same time, the head of the Far Eastern Bureau, Voitinsky, was sent to China to correct our tendency to withdraw from the KMT. At that time, I again failed to maintain my proposal strongly, for the sake of honoring the discipline of the International and the opinion of the majority of the members of the Central Committee.

Later on, the Northern Expedition army set out. We were very much persecuted by the KMT because in *Hsiang-tao* we criticized the curbing of the labor movement in the rear, and the compulsory collection of the military fund from the peasants for the use of the Northern Expedition. In the meantime the workers in Shanghai were about to rise up to oust the Chihli-Shantung troops. If the uprisings were successful, the problem of the ruling power would be posed. At that time, in the minutes of the [discussion of the] political resolution of the enlarged plenum of the Central Committee I suggested:

The Chinese revolution has two roads: One is that it be led by the proletariat, then we can reach the goal of the revolution; the other is that it be led by the bourgeoisie, and in that case the latter must betray in the course of the revolution. And though we may cooperate with the bourgeoisie at the present, we must nevertheless seize the leading power. However, all the members of the Far Eastern Bureau of the Comintern residing in Shanghai unanimously opposed my opinion, saying that such an opinion would influence our comrades to oppose the bourgeoisie too early. Further, they declared, if the Shanghai uprising succeeds, the ruling power should belong to the bourgeoisie and that it was unnecessary to have any participation by workers' delegates. At that time, I again could not maintain my opinion because of their criticism.

About the time the Northern Expedition army took Shanghai in 1927, [Ch'ü] Ch'iu-pai paid great attention to the selection of the Shanghai municipal government and how to unite the petty bourgeoisie (the middle and small traders) in opposition to the big bourgeoisie. P'eng Shu-chih and Lo I-nung were in agreement with my opinion, that the immediate problem was not the municipal elections. The central problem was that if the proletariat was not strong enough to win a victory over Chiang Kai-shek's military forces the petty bourgeoisie would not support us. Chiang Kai-shek, at the instigation of the imperialists, would be certain to carry out a massacre of the masses. Then not only would the municipal elections be reduced to empty talk, but we would face the beginning of a defeat throughout China. When Chiang Kai-shek openly betrayed the revolution it could not be just an individual action but would be the signal for the bourgeoisie in the whole country to go over to the reactionary camp.

At that time [P'eng] Shu-chih went to Hankow to state our opinion before the international delegate and the majority of the members of the Central Committee of the Chinese Communist Party and to consult with them on how to attack Chiang Kai-shek's forces. But they did not care very much about the impending coup in Shanghai. They telegraphed to me several times urging me to go to Wuhan. They thought that since the Nationalist government was then at Wuhan, all important problems should be solved there. At the same time, the International telegraphed to us instructing us to hide or bury all the workers' weapons to avoid a military conflict between the workers and Chiang Kai-shek, in order not to disturb the occupation of Shanghai by the armed forces. Having read this telegram, [Lo] I-nung became very angry, and threw it on the floor. At that time I again obeyed the order of the International and could not maintain my own opinion. Based upon the policy of the International toward the Kuomintang and the imperialists, I issued a shameful manifesto with Wang Ching-wei.

At the beginning of April I went to Wuhan. When I first met Wang Ching-wei, I heard some reactionary things from him, far different from what he had said while in Shanghai. I told this to Borodin; he said that my observations were right and that as soon as Wang Ching-wei reached Wuhan he was surrounded by Hsü Ch'ien, Ku Meng-yü, Ch'en Kung-po, T'an Yen-k'ai, and others, and became gradually colder.[188] After Chiang Kai-shek

and Li Chi-shen began their massacre of the workers and
peasants, the [Wuhan] Kuomintang came to hate the power of the
proletariat more every day, and the reactionary attitude of Wang
Ching-wei and of the Central Committee of the Kuomintang
rapidly hardened. At the meeting of our Political Bureau, I made
a report on the status of the joint meeting of our party and of the
Kuomintang:

"The danger involved in cooperation between our party and the
Kuomintang is more and more serious. What they tried to seize on
seemed to be this or that small problem; what they really wanted
was the whole of the central power. Now there are only two roads
before us: either to give up the authority of leadership or to break
with them."

Those attending the meeting answered my report with silence.

After the coup [May 21 at Changsha] in Hunan province, I
twice suggested withdrawal from the Kuomintang. Finally, I
said: "The Wuhan Kuomintang has followed in the footsteps of
Chiang Kai-shek! If we do not change our policy, we too will end
up on the same road."

At that time only Jen Pi-shih said, "That is so!" Chou En-lai
said, "After we withdraw from the Kuomintang the labor and
peasant movement will be freer but the military movement will
suffer too much." All the rest still answered my suggestion with
silence. At the same time I discussed this with [Ch'ü] Ch'iu-pai.
He said: "We should let the Kuomintang expel us; we cannot
withdraw by ourselves." I consulted Borodin. He said: "I quite
agree with your idea but I know that Moscow will never permit
it."

At that time I once more observed the discipline of the
International and the opinion of the majority of the Central
Committee and was unable to maintain my own opinion. From
the beginning I could not persistently maintain my opinion; but
this time I could no longer bear it. I then tendered my resignation
to the Central Committee. My chief reason for this was:

"The International wishes us to carry out our own policy, on
the one hand, and does not allow us to withdraw from the
Kuomintang on the other. There is really no way out and I cannot
continue with my work."

From the beginning to the end, the International recognized the
Kuomintang as the main body of the Chinese national democrat-
ic revolution. In Stalin's mouth, the words "leadership of the
Kuomintang" were shouted very loudly (see "The Errors of the

Opposition" in "Questions of the Chinese Revolution"). So it wished us throughout to surrender in the organization of the Kuomintang and to lead the masses under the name and the banner of the Kuomintang. This was continued up to the time when the whole Kuomintang of Feng Yü-hsiang, Wang Ching-wei, T'ang Sheng-chih, Ho Chien, etc., became openly reactionary and abolished the so-called three-point policy: to unite with the Soviet Union, to allow the CP to join the Kuomintang, and to help the labor and peasant movement. The International instructed us by telegram: "Only withdraw from the Kuomintang government, not from the Kuomintang."

So, after the August 7 Conference, from the Nanchang uprising to the capture of Swatow, the Communist Party still hid behind the blue-white banner of the left clique of the Kuomintang. To the masses it seemed that there was trouble within the Kuomintang, but nothing more. The young Chinese Communist Party, produced by the young Chinese proletariat, had not had a proper period of training in Marxism and class struggles. Shortly after the founding of the party, it was confronted by a great revolutionary struggle. The only hope of avoiding a very grave error was correct guidance by the proletarian policy of the International. But under the guidance of such a consistently opportunist policy how could the Chinese proletariat and the Communist Party clearly see their own future? And how could they have their own independent policy? They only surrendered to the bourgeoisie step by step and subordinated themselves to the bourgeoisie. So when the latter suddenly massacred us we did not know what to do about it. After the coup in Changsha, the policy given to us by the International was:

1. Confiscate the land of the landowners from the lower strata, but not in the name of the Nationalist government, and do not touch the land of military officers. (There was not a single one of the bourgeoisie, landlords, tuchüns, and gentry of Hunan and Hupeh provinces who was not the kinsman, relative, or old friend of the officers of that time. All the landowners were directly or indirectly protected by the officers. To confiscate the land is only empty words if it is conditioned by "do not touch the land of the military officers.")

2. Restrain the peasants' "over-zealous" actions with the power of the party headquarters. (We did execute this shameful policy of checking the peasants' over-zealous actions; afterward the International criticized the Chinese party for having "often

become an obstacle to the masses" and considered it as one of the greatest opportunist errors.)

3. Destroy the present unreliable generals, arm twenty thousand communists, and select fifty thousand worker and peasant elements from Hunan and Hupeh provinces for organizing a new army. (If we could get so many rifles, why should we not directly arm the workers and peasants and why should we still recruit new troops for the Kuomintang? Why couldn't we establish soviets of workers, peasants, and soldiers? If there were neither armed workers and peasants nor soviets, how and with whom could we destroy the said unreliable generals? I suppose that we could have continued to pitifully beg the Central Committee of the Kuomintang to discharge them. When the Comintern representative Roy showed Wang Ching-wei these instructions from the International it was, of course, for this purpose.[189])

4. Put new worker elements into the Central Committee of the Kuomintang to take the place of old members. (If we had the power to deal freely with the old committee and reorganize the Kuomintang, why could we not organize soviets? Why must we send our worker and peasant leaders to the bourgeois Kuomintang, which has already been massacring the workers and peasants? And why should we decorate such a Kuomintang with our leaders?)

5. Organize a revolutionary court with a well-known member of the Kuomintang (one who is not a member of the CCP) as its chairman, in order to judge the reactionary officers. (How can an already reactionary leader of the Kuomintang judge the reactionary officers in the revolutionary court?)

Those who attempted to implement such a policy within the Kuomintang were still opportunists, of a left stripe. There was no change at all in the fundamental policy; it was like taking a bath in a urinal vessel! At that time, if we wanted to carry out a genuinely left, that is, a revolutionary, policy, the fundamental line had to be changed. The Communist Party had to withdraw from the Kuomintang and be really independent. It had to arm the workers and peasants, as many as possible, establish soviets of workers, peasants, and soldiers, and seize the leading power from the Kuomintang. Otherwise, no matter what kind of left policy was adopted, there was no way to realize it.

At that time the Central Political Bureau wired to the Communist International in answer to its instructions: We accept the instructions and will work according to their directions, but they cannot be realized immediately.

All the members of the Central Committee recognized that the International's instructions were impractical. Even Fan K'e, a participant in the Central Committee meeting (it was said that he was Stalin's private deputy),[190] also thought that there was no possibility of carrying them out. He agreed with the telegraphic answer of the Central Committee, saying: "This is the best reply we can give."

After the August 7 Conference, the Central Committee tried to propagate the idea that the Chinese revolution had failed because the opportunists did not accept the Communist International's instructions to immediately change tactics. (Of course, the instructions were the above mentioned ones; besides these, there were no instructions!) We did not know: How could the policy be changed from inside the Kuomintang? And who were the so-called opportunists?

Once the party had committed such a fundamental error, a continual series of other smaller or larger subordinate errors were naturally inevitable. I, whose perception was not clear, whose opinion was not decisive, became immersed in the atmosphere of opportunism and sincerely carried out the opportunist policy of the Third International. I unconsciously became the tool of the narrow faction of Stalin. I could not save the party and the revolution. All this, both I and other comrades should be held responsible for. The present Central Committee says: "You attempt to place the failure of the Chinese revolution on the shoulders of the Comintern in order that you might throw off your own responsibility!" This statement is ridiculous. One does not permanently lose his right to criticize the opportunism of the party leadership, or to return to Marxism and Leninism because he has himself committed opportunist errors.

At the same time, nobody can take the liberty of avoiding his responsibility for executing an opportunist policy because the opportunism originated in high places. The source of the opportunist policy is the Comintern; but why did not the leaders of the Chinese party protest against the Comintern, and instead loyally carry out its policies? Who can absolve us of this responsibility? We should very frankly and objectively recognize that all the past and present opportunist policies originated in the Communist International. The International should bear the responsibility. The young Chinese party has not yet the ability of itself to invent any theories and settle any policy; but the leading organ of the Chinese party ought to bear the responsibility for blindly implementing the opportunist policy of the Comintern without a little bit of judgment and protest.

If we mutually excuse each other and all of us think that we have committed no mistakes, was it then the error of the masses? This is not only too ridiculous but also does not assume any responsibility toward the revolution! I strongly believe that if I, or other responsible comrades, could at that time have clearly recognized the falsity of the opportunist policy and made a strong argument against it, even to the point of mobilizing the entire party for a passionate discussion and debate, as Comrade Trotsky has been doing, the result would inevitably have been a great help to the revolution. It would not have made the revolution such a shameful failure, though I might have been expelled from the Communist International and a split in the party might have taken place. I, whose perception was not clear and whose opinion was not resolute, did not do so after all! If the party were to base itself on such past mistakes of mine or on the fact that I strongly maintained the former erroneous line, as grounds for giving me some severe punishment, I would earnestly accept it without uttering a word.

But these are the reasons given by the present Central Committee for expelling me from the party:

1. They said: "Fundamentally, he is not sincere in recognizing his own error of opportunist leadership in the period of the great revolution, and has not decided to recognize where his real past error lies, so it is inevitable that he will continue his past erroneous line." In reality, I was expelled because I sincerely recognized where the error of the former opportunist leadership lay, and decided to oppose the present and future continuation of wrong lines.

2. They said: "He is not satisfied with the decisions of the Communist International. He is obdurately unwilling to go to Moscow to be trained by the International."[191] I have been trained enough by the Communist International. Formerly, I made many mistakes because I accepted the opinions of the Third International. Now I have been expelled because I am not satisfied with those opinions.

3. Last August 5, I wrote a letter to the Central Committee in which there were the following sentences: "Besides, what is the continuing fundamental contradiction of 'economic class interests' between these two classes [the bourgeoisie and the landlords]?!" "Before and after the Canton uprising. . . . I wrote

several letters to the Central Committee pointing out that the ruling power of the Kuomintang would not collapse as quickly as you estimated." "At present, though there are some mass struggles it is not enough to take them as the symptoms of the coming revolutionary wave." "The wholly legal movement, of course, is an abandonment of the attempt at revolution. But under certain circumstances, when it is necessary to build up our strength, as Lenin said, 'except in eruptions of a white-hot intensity, we should also make use of all possible legal measures in this (transitional) period.'"

The Central Committee changed these sentences to read ambiguously:

"There is no contradiction between the bourgeoisie and the feudal forces." "The present ruling class is not going to be overthrown and the revolutionary struggle is not beginning to revive but is declining more and more." He advocates "the adoption of legal forms."

Furthermore, they put quotation marks around each sentence so as to make them seem like my original statements. This is another reason for my expulsion.

4. I wrote another letter to the Central Committee on October 10 saying: "The present period is not a period of the revolutionary wave, but a period of counterrevolution. We should elaborate democratic slogans as our general demands. For instance, besides the eight-hour-day demand and the confiscation of land, we should issue the slogans 'Nullify the unequal treaties,' 'Against the military dictatorship of the Kuomintang,' 'Convoke the national assembly,' etc., etc. It is necessary to bring the broad masses into activity under these democratic slogans; then we can shake the counterrevolutionary regime, go forward to the revolutionary wave, and make our fundamental slogans—'Down with the Kuomintang government,' 'Establish the soviet regime,' etc.—the slogans of action in the mass movement."

On October 26, Comrade P'eng Shu-chih and I wrote a letter to the CC saying: "This is not the transitional period to direct revolution, and we must have general political slogans adapted to this period; then we can win the masses. The workers' and peasants' soviets is merely a propaganda slogan at present. If we take the struggle to organize soviets as a slogan of action, we will certainly get no response from the proletariat." But the CC claimed that in place of the slogans "Down with the Kuomintang government" and "Establish the soviet regime" we wish to substitute as the present general political slogan the demand "Convoke the national assembly." This is also one of the reasons for my expulsion.

5. I said in a letter that we should point out "the policy of treason or spoliation of the country by the Kuomintang in the handling of the Chinese Eastern Railroad," making the "broad masses still imbued with nationalist spirit able to sympathize with us and oppose the maneuver of the imperialists to attack the Soviet Union by utilizing the Kuomintang and making the Chinese Eastern Railroad problem an excuse." This was to help the slogan of defense of the USSR penetrate the masses. But the CC said I wanted to issue the slogan of opposing the spoliation of the country by the Kuomintang in place of the slogan of supporting the USSR. This is another reason why I was expelled.

6. I wrote the CC several letters dealing with the serious political problems within the party. The CC kept them from the party for a long time. Further, the delegates of the Comintern and the CC told me plainly that the principle is that different political opinions cannot be expressed in the party. Because there is no hope of correcting the mistakes of the Central Committee by means of a legal comradely discussion, I hold that I should not be bound by the routine discipline of the organization, and still less should comrades be prevented from passing my letters to others to be read. This is also one of the reasons why I am expelled.

7. Since the August 7 Conference, the CC has not allowed me to participate in any meetings, nor has it given me any work to do. Then, on October 6 (only forty days before my expulsion), they suddenly wrote me a letter saying: "The CC has decided to ask you to undertake the work of editing in the CC under the political line of the party, and to write an article, 'Against the Opposition,' within a week." As I had criticized the Central Committee more than once for continuing the line of opportunism and putschism, they tried to create some excuse for my expulsion. Now I have recognized fundamentally that Comrade Trotsky's views are identical with Marxism and Leninism. How would I be able to write false words, contrary to my opinions?

8. We know that Comrade Trotsky has decisively opposed the opportunist policy of Stalin and Bukharin. We cannot listen to the rumors of the Stalin clique and believe that Comrade Trotsky, who led the October revolution hand in hand with Lenin, really is a counterrevolutionist. (It may be "proved" by rumors created about us by the Chinese Stalinist clique, Li Li-san, etc.) Because

we spoke of Trotsky as a comrade, the Central Committee accused us of "having already left the revolution, left the proletariat, and gone over to the counterrevolution," and expelled us from the party.

Comrades! The Central Committee has now invented these false reasons in order to expel me from the party and brand me as a "counterrevolutionist" without any proof. I believe that most of the comrades are not clear about this case. Even the CC itself has said: "There may be some who do not understand it!" But they expelled me and said I went over to the counterrevolution even though some comrades do not understand it. Nevertheless, I understand quite well why they falsely accuse us as "counterrevolutionists." This is a weapon created by up-to-date Chinese for attacking those who differ from them. For instance, the Kuomintang accuses the communists of being "counterrevolutionists" in order to cover its own sins. Chiang Kai-shek tries to deceive the masses with the signboard of revolution, portraying himself as the personification of revolution. Those who oppose him are "counterrevolutionists" and "reactionary elements."

Many comrades know that the false reasons I have cited, given by the CC for expelling me, are only the formal and official excuse. In reality, they have become tired of hearing my opinions expressed in the party and of my criticism of their continued opportunism and putschism and their execution of a bankrupt policy.

In any number of the bourgeois countries of the world, there are feudal survivals and methods of semifeudal exploitation (Blacks, and slaves of the South Sea archipelago, are like those of the prefeudal slave system), and there exist remnants of feudal forces. China is even more like this. In the revolution, of course, we cannot neglect this; but the Comintern and the CC unanimously hold that in China the feudal remnants still occupy the dominant position in the economy and politics and are the ruling power. As a result, they consider these survivals as the object of the revolution and disregard the enemy, the suppressor of the revolution—the forces of the bourgeoisie. They pass off all reactionary actions of the bourgeoisie as those of the feudal forces.

They say that the Chinese bourgeoisie is still revolutionary, that it can never be reactionary, and that all those who are reactionary cannot be the bourgeoisie. Thus, they do not recognize that the Kuomintang represents the interests of the bourgeoisie or that the Nationalist government is the regime representing the interests of the bourgeoisie. The conclusion must be that besides the Kuomintang, or the Nanking section of it, there is or will be, now or in the future, a nonreactionary, revolutionary bourgeois party. Therefore, in tactics and in practical actions they now simply follow the Reorganizationists and do the military work of overthrowing Chiang Kai-shek.[192] In the platform they say that the character of the third revolution in the future must still be that of a bourgeois-democratic revolution, opposing anything that would antagonize the economic forces of the bourgeoisie and opposing issuing the slogan for the dictatorship of the proletariat.* Such illusions in the bourgeoisie and such continual attraction to it are calculated not only to perpetuate the opportunism of the past but to deepen it. It must lead to a more shameful and miserable failure in the future revolution.

If we consider the slogan "Establish the soviet regime" as a slogan of action, we can issue it only when the objective conditions have ripened into a revolutionary wave. It cannot be issued at any time at will.** In the past, during the revolutionary wave, we did not adopt the slogans "Organize soviets" and "Establish the soviet regime." Naturally, this was a grave error. In the future, when the revolution takes place, we shall immediately have to organize the workers', peasants', and

---

* At the present time, the Chinese revolution is in a stage of retreat. It may be that the present defensive democratic movement might lead toward revolution, but this movement is not the revolution. Regarding the anti-Chiang Reorganizationist movement, this is merely an internal conflict within the reactionary Kuomintang. There is no way that this movement might be considered a democratic movement. Only when the mass movement is so highly developed that it overthrows the whole bourgeois Kuomintang regime can we speak of this as revolution. When the Sixth Congress states that "the present stage of the revolution in China is a revolutionary stage," it should, in actuality, refer to the third revolution of the future. Because they consider the present stage to be a revolutionary one, they have come up with the confusing "Political Program for the Present Stage of the Chinese Revolution," that is, the so-called Ten Great Demands of the Chinese Revolution. This program is simply a hybrid of opportunism and putschism.

** When, in April 1917, some Bolsheviks led by [the Petrograd party committee] brought forth the slogan "All Power to the Soviets," Lenin scolded them for their prematurity in advocating this slogan, saying that this was adventurism.

soldiers' soviets. Then we shall mobilize the masses to struggle for the slogan "Establish the soviet regime." Furthermore, it would be the soviet of the dictatorship of the proletariat, and not the soviet of the workers' and peasants' democratic dictatorship.

In the present period when the counterrevolutionary forces are entirely victorious and when there is no wave of mass revolutionary action, the objective conditions for "armed uprising" and the establishment of soviets have not matured. At the present time, "Organize soviets" is only a propaganda and educational slogan. If we use it as a slogan of action, and mobilize the working class at once to struggle in practice to "Organize soviets" we will be completely unable to generate a response from the masses.

In the present situation, we should adopt the democratic slogan, "Struggle for the convocation of the national assembly." The objective conditions for this movement have matured and at present only this slogan can take large masses through the legal political struggle and toward the revolutionary rise and the struggle for the "armed uprising" and the "Establishment of the soviet regime."

The present CC, continuing its putschism, does not do this. They consider that the rebirth of the revolution has matured,* and reproach us for regarding the slogan of the "Establishment of workers' and peasants' soviets" as only a propaganda slogan; thus, they logically consider it a slogan of action. In consequence, they are continually ordering party members into the streets for demonstrations in workers' quarters, and ordering employed comrades to strike. Every small daily struggle is artificially blown up into a big political battle, leading to more and more

---

* Recently the Comintern has sent instructions claiming that the revival of the conditions for the Chinese revolution have reached full maturity. At first, when these instructions were received, the CC of the Chinese Communist Party thought that there must be some error in translation regarding the word "maturity." After the original text was checked by the propaganda department it was ascertained that there was no mistake. During the Kiangsu representative conference mentioned above, a majority of the delegates were also suspicious about the term "maturity," and there was much argument. Later, the stubborn insistence of the CCP CC members who attended the conference revealed that the revival of the Chinese revolution to full maturity had taken place in their heads! (Probably they regarded the Reorganizationists' anti-Chiang movement as the revolutionary revival.)

defections from the party by the working masses and employed comrades.

More than that, at the Kiangsu representative conference recently, it was resolved "to organize the great strike movement," and "local uprisings." Since last summer there have been signs of small struggles among the Shanghai workers, but as they appear they have been defeated through the party's putschist policy. Henceforth, of course, they will all be crushed; if the resolutions of the Kiangsu representative conference are carried out, these workers' struggles will be destroyed. Our party is no longer the guide, helping the coming wave of workers' revolutionary struggles; it is becoming the executioner destroying the workers' struggles at their roots.

The present Central Committee, sincerely basing itself upon the bankrupt line of the Sixth Congress, and under the direct guidance of the Comintern,* is executing the above bankrupt policy and capping the opportunism and putschism of the past by liquidating the party and the revolution. No matter whether it was the Comintern or the Chinese Communist Party that committed the opportunist errors in the past and made the revolution fail, it was a crime. Now these errors have been pointed out plainly by the comrades of the Opposition, but they

---

* The bankrupt line adopted by the Sixth Congress was put down in black and white in resolutions that included passages such as these: "The existing stage of the Chinese revolution is that of the bourgeois-democratic revolution"; "carry out the democratic dictatorship of the workers and the peasantry"; "the rich peasants have not yet lost their revolutionary nature . . . struggles should not be mounted against them"; "regarding the present status of the revolutionary movement and the general line of the Chinese Communist Party, signs of the new revolution are already quite apparent. . . . There are great possibilities for a rising revolutionary wave in one or several provinces and the establishment of a soviet regime"; "a new revolutionary wave will soon arrive"; and so forth. It is exactly this bankrupt line that is being faithfully carried out by the Central Committee. Hsiang Ying, Li Fu-ch'un, Ho Meng-hsiung, and other compromisers feel that the resolutions of the Sixth Congress are correct and it is only that the Central Committee has not carried them out correctly. This clearly illustrates that the compromisers not only misunderstand the political line of the Opposition, but they also misunderstand the political line laid down at the Sixth Congress under the direct guidance of the Comintern. They themselves have no line whatsoever.

still do not acknowledge their past mistakes and consciously continue their past erroneous line. Moreover, for the sake of covering up the errors of a few individuals, they deliberately violate the organizational norms of Bolshevism, abuse the authority of the supreme party organs, and prevent self-criticism within the party, expelling numerous comrades from the party for expressing different political opinions and deliberately splitting the party. This is the crime of crimes, the most stupid and the most shameful.

No Bolshevik should be afraid of open self-criticism before the masses. The only way for the party to win the masses is to carry out self-criticism courageously, never losing the masses for fear of self-criticism. To cover up one's own mistakes, like the present Central Committee, is certainly to lose the masses.

The majority of comrades have felt these mistakes and the party crisis to varying degrees. As long we do not simply expect to make our living through the party, as long as we have some feeling of responsibility for the party and the revolution, any comrade should stand up and resolutely make a self-criticism of the party in order to rescue it from this crisis. To silently watch, arms folded, while our party comes close to destruction would surely be criminal!

Comrades! We all know that whoever opens his mouth to express some criticism of the errors of the party is himself expelled, while the mistake remains uncorrected. But we should draw a balance. Which is more important: to save the party from danger or save ourselves from having our names dropped from the party list?

Since the August 7 Conference, which adopted the "general line of armed uprising," and the uprisings that followed in several places, I have written many letters to the Central Committee, pointing out that the revolutionary sentiment of the masses was not then at a high point, that the Kuomintang regime could not be quickly exploded, that uprisings that lacked objective conditions only weaken the power of the party and isolate it further from the masses. I proposed that we change from the policy of uprisings to a policy of winning and uniting the masses in their daily struggles. The Central Committee thought that widespread uprisings were an absolutely valid new line for correcting opportunism, and that to take account of the objective conditions for the uprisings and to consider how to insure the success of the uprisings, is opportunism. Of course, they never took my opinion into consideration and regarded my words as a joke. They propagated them everywhere, saying that it was proof that I had not corrected my opportunist mistakes. At that time, I was bound by the discipline of the party organization, and took a negative attitude, being unable to go over the head of the organization to wage a determined struggle against the policy of the Central Committee which was destroying the party.

I accept responsibility for this. After the Sixth Congress, I still had a false comprehension and still entertained the illusion that the new Central Committee had received so many lessons from events that they themselves would awaken to the fact that it was not necessary after all to follow blindly the erroneous line of the Comintern. I still continued my negative attitude and did not hold any different theories that would have involved a dispute within the party, though I was fundamentally dissatisfied with the line of the Sixth Congress. After the war between Chiang Kai-shek and the Kwangsi cliques, and the "May 30 anniversary movement," I felt deeply that the Central Committee would obstinately continue its opportunism and putschism, and manifestly could not change by itself: that except through an open discussion and criticism by the party members, from the lowest to the highest ranks, the seriously false line of the leading organ could not be corrected. But all the party members are under the domination and restriction of party discipline, in a state of "daring to be angry but not daring to speak."

At that time, I could not bear to see the party (created by the warm blood of innumerable comrades) destroyed and ruined by the enduring and essentially false line. Thus I could not do otherwise than to begin to express my opinion, from August onward, in order to fulfill my responsibility. Some comrades sought to dissuade me, saying that the people in the Central Committee regard the interests of a few leaders as more important than the interests of the party and the revolution, that they have attempted everywhere to cover up their mistakes and could never accept the criticism of comrades, and that since I was criticizing them so frankly, they would use it as an excuse for expelling me from the party. But my regard for the party compelled me to resolutely follow the path of not caring for my own interests.

The Communist International and the Central Committee have for a long time opposed any review of the record of failure of the Chinese revolution. And now, because I have continued to criticize them, they have suddenly invented the following declaration: "He [i.e., I] is not sincere in recognizing his own error of opportunist leadership in the period of the great revolution and has not decided to recognize where his real past error lies, so it is inevitable that he will continue his past erroneous line."

These words are an accurate description of their authors. In reality, if I were to stultify my mind and care nothing about the interests of the proletariat, if I had not decided to recognize my real past errors and had been willing to do their dirty work and let them continue with their past false line, they would, as before, rely on the old opportunist's pen and mouth and use me to attack so-called Trotskyism in order to cover up their errors. How could they expel me from the party?

Am I, who have struggled against evil social forces for the greater part of my life, willing to do such a base work—to confuse right and wrong? Li Li-san said: "The Chinese opportunists* are unwilling to absorb accurately the lessons of the failure of the past great revolution, but try to hide behind the banner of Trotskyism in order to cover up their own mistakes." In reality

---

* As far as attitudes toward opportunism, Li Li-san and those like him are not willing to help the party as a whole understand the mistakes of the completely opportunist line. They hope to use the party propaganda organs and their authority to concentrate the attention of all the party comrades on some individuals who serve as symbols of opportunism in order to produce a kind of mass psychology that would allow them to escape charges of opportunism themselves. Their propaganda regarding putschism is just the same, causing comrades to pay attention to the putschist symbols represented by Ch'ü Ch'iu-pai, thus taking the spotlight away from their own putschism. In the Hankow period [April-July 1927], Ch'ü Ch'iu-pai in reports on the peasants' department scolded peasants' "excesses" and referred to their movement as the activities of vagabonds. He ordered party headquarters at all levels to follow the general policies of the Nationalist government. Following the May 21 coup at Changsha, Comintern representative M. N. Roy said: "The Central Committee of the Kuomintang is already counterrevolutionary!" Immediately a red-faced Li Li-san raised his voice in protest: "When Comrade Roy speaks in this manner, he is sending a coffin to the Chinese Communist Party!" Ts'ai Ho-sen tried to disarm the Hankow Main Inspectors' Corps so that conflicts with Kuomintang troops could be avoided. I would like to ask, what kind of consciousness, what kind of theory, does all of this reflect? Yang Yin and Lo I-yüan have personally told me: "When Li Li-san was responsible for the Kwangtung Provincial Committee, he was more putschist than any other comrade in the party."

the documents of Comrade Trotsky censure me much more severely than do those of Stalin and Bukharin; and I could not but recognize that the lessons of the past revolution pointed out by him are one hundred percent correct, and I could never reject his words because he criticizes me. I am willing to accept the severest criticism of my comrades, but unwilling to bury the lessons and experiences of the revolution. I would rather be expelled now by Li Li-san and a few others than to see the party crisis without attempting to save the party, and be blamed in the future by the masses of the party members.

I would much rather have peace of mind while suffering oppression by evil forces in my struggle for the interests of the proletariat. I am unwilling to merely follow along with any cruel and corrupt bureaucratic elements!

Comrades! I know that my expulsion from the party by the Central Committee is the act of a few men for the purpose of covering up their errors. They not only want to save themselves the "trouble" of hearing my opinions expressed within the party and hearing me advocate an open discussion on political problems, but also to demonstrate by my expulsion that all the comrades must keep their mouths closed. I know that the masses of the party members never entertained the idea of expelling me. Though I have been expelled by a few leaders at the top of the party, yet there has never been any hostility or bad feeling between the masses in the ranks and myself. I shall continue to serve the proletariat hand in hand with all those comrades both in the International and in China who are not following the opportunist policy of Stalin's clique.

Comrades! The present errors of the party are not partial or accidental problems: As in the past, they are the manifestation of the whole opportunist policy conducted by Stalin in China. The responsible heads of the Central Committee of the Chinese Communist Party, who are willing to be the phonograph of Stalin, have never shown any political consciousness and are growing worse and worse: they can never be saved. At the Tenth Congress of the Russian party [1921], Lenin said: "Only when there exist within the party fundamentally different political opinions and there is no other way to resolve them, then factional groupings are proper." Based on this theory he led the Bolshevik movement at that time.

Now, in our party, there is no other way permitted (legal or open discussion in the party) to overcome the party crisis. Every party member has the obligation of saving the party. We must return to the spirit and political line of Bolshevism, unite together solidly, and stand straightforward on the side of the International Opposition led by Comrade Trotsky, that is, under the banner of real Marxism and Leninism. We must decisively, persistently, and thoroughly fight against the opportunism of the Comintern and the Central Committee of the Chinese party. We are opposed not only to the opportunism of Stalin and his like, but also to the compromising attitude of Zinoviev and others. We are not afraid of the so-called "jumping out of the ranks of the party" and do not hesitate to sacrifice everything in order to save the party and the Chinese revolution!

> With proletarian greetings,
> Ch'en Tu-hsiu

From the *Militant* (New York), November 15 and December 1, 1930; January 1 and 15, and February 1, 1931.

NOTES

1. This article was written for the Soviet press in response to the May Thirtieth Incident in 1925 which marked the beginning of the second Chinese revolution. Twelve students were killed by British troops while protesting the murder of a Chinese worker at a Japanese-owned factory in Shanghai. This touched off a general strike that soon spread throughout the country. At this time the Left Opposition, formed by Trotsky in October 1923 to fight for inner-party democracy through the program he and Lenin worked out jointly in 1922, had suffered a serious defeat. Stalin's control of the apparatus had succeeded in grossly inflating the votes of the Zinoviev-Kamenev-Stalin bloc at the Thirteenth Party Conference in January 1924. In the year that followed, punitive demotions and organized hooliganism sharply cut the strength of the Opposition and reduced it to near-silence. In January 1925 Trotsky was forced to resign as president of the Revolutionary Military Council, the head of the Soviet Red Army. He retained his seat on the Politburo and the ECCI and had some access to the press, although he was not permitted to reply to the venomous campaign against "Trotskyism" that had been raging since 1923. In May 1925, after four months without an assignment, Trotsky was appointed to the Supreme Council of the National Economy under Dzerzhinsky. At the time of this article a rift had already appeared in the Politburo between Stalin and the other two "triumvirs," Zinoviev and Kamenev, but it would be another ten months before they would seek common cause with Trotsky against Stalin and Bukharin.

2. This document is the report of a special Politburo commission charged with preparing recommendations for Soviet foreign policy in the Far East. Trotsky chaired the commission, whose other members were Chicherin, Dzerzhinsky, and Voroshilov, all supporters of the Stalin-Bukharin Politburo majority. The report was approved by the Politburo. It is of interest not only as a statement of Soviet diplomatic objectives in the Far East but because it has been cited by several historians to show that Trotsky had no serious differences with Stalin on the China question

as late as March 1926. Also, that Trotsky was pessimistic about the prospects of defeating the Northern warlords, headed by Chang Tso-lin, and saw no great revolutionary possibilities in China. As the reader can see, the commission took up only Soviet governmental diplomacy, which from the time of the October revolution was based on dealing with existing governments even when the parallel Comintern policy strove for their overthrow. The commission does not take up at all the question that was in dispute: the course to be followed by the CCP in the areas under KMT rule. Nor is Trotsky's appointment to the commission a mystery. The split between Stalin and Zinoviev had reached a showdown at the Fourteenth Party Congress in December 1925. The new Politburo was dominated by Bukharin's supporters. (Out of nine members, three were Bukharinists, two were Stalinists, two wavered between Stalin and Bukharin, plus Zinoviev and Trotsky.) The unusual weakness of Stalin's personal faction made him anxious to prevent an open bloc between Trotsky and Zinoviev. The commission appointment was a gesture aimed at neutralizing Trotsky by offering him the hope of future collaboration. A few weeks later, in April, the Politburo discussed CCP policy in China and Trotsky raised the demand for withdrawal from the KMT. The same month the United Opposition was formed. This put an end to Stalin's overtures. While the commission's report did not take up the KMT's Northern Expedition, it should be noted that in the discussion in the Politburo Stalin proposed an amendment strongly opposing the action. Chiang rejected Stalin's advice and began the Northern Expedition in July 1926.

3. The Locarno Pact was a series of five treaties and arbitration conventions signed in December 1925 by Germany, Belgium, France, Italy, Great Britain, Czechoslovakia, and Poland, "guaranteeing" the continuation of peace and existing territorial boundaries.

4. Under the Treaty of Portsmouth which codified the Japanese victory in the Russo-Japanese War of 1905, Japan took over the tsarist territorial concessions in southern Manchuria. Russia retained the Pacific port of Vladivostok as well as the Chinese Eastern Railroad (CER), the section of the Trans-Siberian Railroad that went through Manchuria to the coast. Japan, however, acquired the South Manchurian Railroad, the spur line beginning at the junction with the CER at Harbin and running south through Mukden (now Shenyang) to Lushunkou (Port Arthur) at the tip of the Kwantung peninsula. After the overthrow of the Ch'ing dynasty in 1911 Manchuria became a virtual Japanese protectorate under the Chinese warlord Chang Tso-lin.

5. Mukden (Shenyang) was Chang Tso-lin's Manchurian capital. Harbin, on the route of the Chinese Eastern Railroad, was the principal Russian settlement in Manchuria.

6. At the time this report was drafted, Wu P'ei-fu, the warlord leader of the Honan-Hupeh-Hunan area of Central China, was engaged in a successful offensive against the armies of the "Christian General" Feng

Yü-hsiang, who was allied to the Kuomintang. The term "people's armies" here refers to the pro-Kuomintang troops.

7. Rakovsky was Soviet ambassador to France at this time.

8. Leonid Serebryakov, deputy people's commissar for communications and a member of the Left Opposition, met with Chang Tso-lin in April 1926 to discuss the railroad situation, then proceeded to Tokyo where he met with Japanese Minister of Railroads Mitsugu Sengoku on May 14. "Dobuchi" has not been identified. The name has been transliterated from the Russian script and may not be spelled according to standard usage.

9. This evidently refers to the article "The Russian Opposition: Questions and Answers," a statement of the basic positions of the United Opposition in question-and-answer format that was circulated in hand-copied editions in the USSR from the late fall of 1926. Radek, who was a member of the center established by the United Opposition, appears to have been assigned to write the document, but in the end Trotsky himself wrote it in September 1926. The text will be included in the second volume of *The Challenge of the Left Opposition* to be published by Pathfinder Press.

10. Soviet and British union representatives formed the Anglo-Russian Trade Union Unity Committee in May 1925. Its British members, officials of the General Council of the Trades Union Congress, used the authority gained by their alliance with Soviet Russia to isolate the left wing in the British unions. On May 1, 1926, the British coal miners began a bitterly contested strike that brought the British labor movement to the brink of revolution. On May 3 the Trades Union Congress called a general strike in solidarity with the coal miners, but after nine days the General Council of the TUC called off the strike and left the coal miners to fight on alone until November. The Soviet government, over Trotsky's objections, remained a party to the Anglo-Russian Committee while the general strike was being sabotaged, and continued to support the body until its British members, no longer needing it, walked out in September 1927. For Trotsky's discussion of these events see *Leon Trotsky on Britain* (New York: Monad Press, 1973).

11. This is evidently a letter to the leaders of the United Opposition calling on them to prepare for a discussion in the Politburo of communist policy in China in light of the successes of the Northern Expedition.

12. The workers of Shanghai, under Communist Party leadership, took control of the city from its warlord masters the day this letter was written. On orders from Moscow they invited the occupation of the city by Chiang's Northern Expedition troops. Chiang's coup came on April 12.

13. This is the only place in all of Trotsky's writings that he proposed a coalition government with the Kuomintang. This should be distinguished from Trotsky's position of support to the KMT against the Northern warlords (and later against the Japanese imperialist invasion of China), which remained a consistent part of his program. Trotsky advanced this

proposal as a means of setting in motion the dynamic of CCP withdrawal and its independent contest for the allegiance of the masses. It should be read in conjunction with his prediction from the fall of 1926 that CCP withdrawal would precipitate a split in the Kuomintang between the bourgeois wing and the radical petty bourgeoisie (see "The Chinese Communist Party and the Kuomintang" of September 27, 1926). He made an important reevaluation of the capacities of the KMT left wing in the week after this letter was written. The next document—the "Letter to Alsky"—shows that he rejected the revolutionary pretensions of all wings of the KMT and proposed the realization of the worker-peasant alliance in China through the formation of soviets.

14. The Hungarian Soviet Republic was proclaimed on March 21, 1919, and lasted 133 days. On the day the republic was formed, the Communist and Social Democratic parties merged into the Hungarian Socialist Party. Within this amalgam the communists found themselves working at cross purposes with the former Social Democratic functionaries, who were hostile to the revolutionary aims of the Comintern. The resulting administrative and political confusion contributed to the fall of the regime.

15. The theory of the possibility of building a complete socialist society within the borders of a single country, even an industrially backward one like Russia, was first enunciated by Stalin in the fall of 1924. It became the ideological cover for promoting the national interests of the Soviet state and its bureaucratic rulers at the expense of the working class of other countries. Trotsky defended against this theory the traditional Marxist position that socialism required an advanced industrial basis and an international division of labor. The particular argument Trotsky advances here may seem strange to readers familiar with both his and Stalin's later views. Later it would be Trotsky who would insist on the possibility of socialist revolution in even the most backward country, and Stalin who would seek to keep all revolutionary movements within the bounds of capitalist property relations. The real point of difference here, however, is entirely consistent with the later views of both men. Stalin and Bukharin, in defending the "two-stage" revolution, had put forward the demagogic argument that continued CCP subordination to the Kuomintang would result in strong communist influence in the National-ist government at the end of the Northern Expedition, when the country had been unified and the warlords defeated. This, they promised, would make possible a dramatic shift to the left of the KMT regime and a direct transition to "socialism." Their immediate policy, however, was contin-ued support to the KMT. Trotsky advocated that the workers and peasants break from the KMT, take power, and form their own government. He rejected, however, the Stalinist notion that a self-contained socialist society could be built in a single country, particularly one as backward as China. In September 1927 he would add the important idea that a workers' government in a colonial country could abolish capitalist property relations and hence take a "noncapitalist"

road. (See "New Opportunities for the Chinese Revolution, New Tasks, and New Mistakes" later in this volume.) This would be only a first step toward the world socialist society required by the expansion of industry and trade as described by Marx and Lenin.

16. The Hong Kong-Canton Strike Committee was organized in June 1925 following the May Thirtieth Incident in Shanghai. At the height of the general strike, directed at British shipping in Hong Kong, some 250,000 workers participated. The strike committee was organized on the basis of one elected delegate for every fifty workers. The delegates formed a Strikers' Delegates Conference, which in turn selected a thirteen-member executive committee. The strike committee operated its own hospitals, schools, and courts, and auctioned confiscated British goods to raise revenues. It was this strike that brought the Kuomintang to power in Canton.

17. This article was submitted for publication to the Soviet press. It was prohibited on Stalin's order.

18. Nanking was occupied by Kuomintang troops on March 24, 1927. British and American gunboats anchored in the Yangtze river shelled the city in retaliation, killing twelve and wounding nineteen Chinese civilians.

19. Hankow is part of the present city of Wuhan on the Yangtze river in Hupeh province. Wuhan is a triple city, formed by the fusion of the three cities of Hankow, Hanyang, and Wuchang. Wuhan fell to the Northern Expedition forces in October 1926. In December the KMT government was moved there from Canton over Chiang Kai-shek's objections. After Chiang's April 1927 coup in Shanghai, he established a rival regime in Nanking, while the Wuhan KMT leaders maintained themselves as the "left Kuomintang," under the leadership of Wang Ching-wei. This government is referred to as both the Wuhan and Hankow regime.

20. The term "Bonapartism" as used by Marxists denotes a dictatorship or regime with certain features of a dictatorship that arises in a period of social crisis; it is based on the military, police, and the state bureaucracy, rather than on parliamentary parties and has the appearance of extraordinary power owing to the fact that it balances between contending social classes, appearing to rise above them. Such governments are usually headed by a single dictator.

21. In a revolutionary situation, dual power appears when organs of workers' power, such as soviets, begin to assume governmental authority while the old bourgeois government remains more or less intact. By their nature such periods are transitory and are resolved by the victory of one class or the other. For a discussion of this concept in the Russian revolution of 1917 see Trotsky's *History of the Russian Revolution,* vol. 1, ch. XI.

22. Shortly before the Shanghai massacre, Chiang Kai-shek, as a leader of a "sympathizing party" of the Comintern, sent copies of his photograph to Stalin, Rykov, Voroshilov, and Trotsky, through the intermediary of Andrei S. Bubnov, who visited China occasionally as a

representative of the Soviet government. It is known that Stalin accepted the portrait of Chiang and sent his own picture in return.

23. Trotsky's "A Protest to the Central Control Commission" (May 17, 1927) describes his efforts to have this article and "The Sure Road" (May 12, 1927) published in the Soviet press. The main text of "The Chinese Revolution and the Theses of Comrade Stalin" was completed on May 7, 1927. After it was rejected for publication, Trotsky added the postscript of May 17 and submitted it to the Secretariat of the Central Committee for the discussion bulletins of the party. It is not known if it was printed.

24. Aleksandr Guchkov (1862-1936) was a Moscow industrialist; he served as minister of war in the first Provisional Government after the February revolution of 1917. Aleksandr Nikolaievich Potressov (1869-1934) was a founder of the Russian Social Democracy and in 1917 was a right-wing Menshevik. K. A. Gvozdyov was a Menshevik and minister of labor in the Provisional Government. Nikolai Semenovich Chkeidze (1864-1926) was a Georgian Menshevik, first chairman of the Petrograd Soviet in 1917, and a supporter of coalition with the Russian bourgeoisie.

25. The Paris Commune, the first workers' government in world history, was proclaimed on March 28, 1871, in the aftermath of the French defeat in the Franco-Prussian war. The Commune lasted for seventy-two days and was finally crushed by the bourgeois government at Versailles. After the military defeat of the Paris workers, some 30,000 persons were executed by the Versaillese in reprisal for the rebellion.

26. Louis-Eugène Cavaignac (1802-1857) was a French general and a leader of the moderate bourgeois republicans in 1848. As war minister in the French cabinet he ordered the execution of 3,000 Paris workers after the June 1848 uprising. Alexandre Auguste Ledru-Rollin (1808-1874) was a leader of the liberal republicans in the 1848 revolution; he supported the crushing of the workers' movement. Louis Blanc (1811-1882) was a utopian socialist and pacifist, and a member of the Provisional Government established by the February 1848 revolution in France. He sought to reconcile capital and labor.

27. Trotsky refers here to the Central Committee of the Wuhan section of the KMT, not that section still controlled by Chiang Kai-shek at Nanking, Canton, and Shanghai.

28. This letter, signed by N. Nassonov, N. Fokine, and A. Albrecht, and dated March 17, 1927, was published in English as an appendix to *Problems of the Chinese Revolution* under the title "The Letter from Shanghai." The authors were anti-Trotskyists.

29. This refers to the General Council of the British Trades Union Congress, which participated in the Anglo-Russian Trade Union Unity Committee.

30. At the April 1927 meeting of the Anglo-Russian Trade Union Unity Committee in Berlin, which took place almost a year after the betrayal of the British general strike by the British section of the committee, Tomsky and the other representatives of the Soviet trade unions, in the resolution adopted, called the General Council of the Trades Union Congress the

"only representative" of the British workers and pledged themselves to "noninterference" in the affairs of the British trade union movement.

31. The document referred to here is "The Letter from Shanghai" (see note 28) which cites an alleged statement by Chiang Kai-shek to the commander of the KMT's Sixth Army Corps: "I am not at all opposed to the Russian Communists, I am only against the Right wing of the C.P.S.U. at whose head stands Stalin, but I know that a Left wing also exists in the C.P.S.U., led by Trotsky and Zinoviev. I am ready to work together with them because the Left is for the complete support of the national revolution in China and for the withdrawal of the Communists from the Kuo Min Tang, while the Right wing, represented by Borodin, Galen and others, though also for supporting the national revolution, are, however, against the withdrawal of the Communists from the Kuo Min Tang. If they would send Radek or Karakhan here, I would be able to work with them." The authors of the letter comment on this statement: "While Chiang Kai-shek disguises himself as a 'Russian Left Communist' . . . he has conducted a rabid hunt against the Communists, and finally came forward on February 21 with a veritable pogrom speech against the Communist Party of China." The letter was never made public by the Soviet government or the Comintern.

32. In Germany in 1923 the French occupation of the Ruhr sparked a mass protest movement against the Versailles Treaty. The Communist Party (KPD) planned an uprising for October, to begin in Saxony, where the KPD was in a bloc with the Social Democrats who controlled the state government. At the last minute the KPD leadership canceled the rising, although an isolated insurrection took place in Hamburg. Trotsky considered this to have signaled the loss of a unique revolutionary opportunity and he blamed not only the German party leadership but principally the Comintern, led at that time by Stalin and Zinoviev. The German defeat was an important factor in the decision to form the Russian Left Opposition at the end of 1923.

33. The Fifth Congress of the CCP was held in Hankow April 27–May 6, 1927 (according to some accounts, May 9). Ch'en Tu-hsiu was reelected general secretary, although he was forced to make a confession of past errors.

34. From the internal evidence this document appears to have been written for circulation to the Left Oppositionists or perhaps to the United Opposition as a whole (including the supporters of Zinoviev and Kamenev). The main text was written May 10, with a postscript of June 8-9. Trotsky refers to Radek's letter of March 3, 1927, which was in reply to his letter of August 30, 1926, and which Trotsky answered in his "Second Letter to Radek" (see above in this volume). The list of enclosures at the end of this document, including the Radek letter, Trotsky's reply, the unaddressed "Brief Note" of March 22, and the letter to Alsky of March 29, are all part of the internal discussion within the Opposition and would not have been appended to a document addressed to the Politburo and hence to the Stalin faction.

35. The Amsterdam International was the popular name for the International Federation of Trade Unions, headquartered at Amsterdam and dominated by the reformist socialists of the Second International. It had collapsed during World War I but was revived in 1919.

36. The Third Plenum of the Central Executive Committee of the Kuomintang was held at Hankow, March 10-17, 1927. The plenum took place on the eve of the split of the KMT into two separate governments as well as on the eve of Chiang's Shanghai massacre. It sought to offset the growing power of Chiang by increasing the authority of the various KMT committees and by recalling Wang Ching-wei from Europe, where he had been in exile since a clash with Chiang in 1926. Wang did not actually attend the plenum, arriving back in China only on April 1. His views were made known to the organizers of the meeting, and he immediately assumed the leadership of the Wuhan government on his return. On April 18 Chiang proclaimed his own government at Nanking. The March plenum—in which Chiang also did not participate—prohibited the Communist Party from publishing anything that would violate the "principle of cooperation with the Kuomintang" (*People's Tribune,* March 15, 1927).

37. Two CCP members accepted ministerial posts in the Wuhan Kuomintang government at the time of the March 1927 Hankow plenum of the KMT CEC. These were T'an P'ing-shan, who became minister of agriculture, and Su Chao-cheng, minister of labor.

38. On May 9, 1927, Zinoviev addressed a mass meeting in Moscow celebrating the fifteenth anniversary of *Pravda.* He criticized *Pravda* for boycotting the views of the Opposition. His speech was condemned by the Central Committee and the question turned over to the Control Commission for disciplinary action.

39. Ch'en Tu-hsiu's speech of April 29, 1927, to the Fifth Congress of the CCP was discussed by Trotsky in the appendix to "The Chinese Revolution and the Theses of Comrade Stalin" earlier in this volume.

40. After the AUCP Politburo's rejection of the Opposition's request for a closed plenum to discuss the Chinese question, Trotsky invoked his statutory right to appeal to the Executive Committee of the Communist International, whose Eighth Plenum opened in Moscow on May 18, 1927. In this letter to the AUCP Secretariat Trotsky announces that he is forwarding his documents to the ECCI. *Pravda,* before the opening of the plenum, denounced Trotsky's appeal as a violation of discipline and an act of disloyalty. The ECCI, however, was compelled by its statutes to hear the appeal and Trotsky was given speaking time.

41. The Eighth Plenum of the ECCI was held in Moscow, May 18-30, 1927. It marked a point of disastrous setbacks for the Stalin-Bukharin foreign policy. The Berlin conference of the Anglo-Russian Trade Union Unity Committee had refused to endorse the CP-backed proposal for a "Hands Off China" campaign. More serious, on May 12 British police had raided the Soviet trade corporation in London, Arcos Ltd., and opened a

witch-hunt against the Soviet Union. In China, Chiang Kai-shek had completed his coup in Shanghai, and on May 21, while the plenum was in session, left Kuomintang General Hsü K'e-hsiang began a massacre of communists and trade unionists in Changsha, the capital of Hunan province. This was the first step in the rupture with the left KMT government at Wuhan, which was allied with Hsü and which was to follow his example in July. The plenum was held in the strictest secrecy so as not to provide a public platform for the Opposition. For the first time, the delegates from the secondary leadership of the AUCP were excluded from the sessions. The proceedings, except for the formal resolutions, were never published—a break with the practice of all previous Comintern gatherings. Zinoviev, although he was a former president of the Comintern, was barred from attending. The Opposition was represented only by Trotsky and Voja Vujovic, a Yugoslav delegate from the Communist Youth International. The plenum approved the line of the Stalin-Bukharin faction, stating that "the tactic of a bloc with the national bourgeoisie in the period of the revolution already passed was fully correct" and projecting a "great revolutionary role" for the left Kuomintang government at Wuhan. The plenum also adopted a resolution directed at the Opposition, empowering the Presidium of the ECCI and the International Control Commission "to effect the formal expulsion of Comrade Trotsky and Vujovic from the ECCI in the event of the [internal factional] struggle continuing" (*International Press Correspondence,* English edition, vol. 7, no. 35, June 16, 1927). The statement published here was drafted by Trotsky in the course of the plenum in rebuttal to the Stalinist resolution on the Opposition and submitted in the name of Trotsky and Vujovic.

42. While the Eighth Plenum was in session, British Foreign Secretary Austen Chamberlain announced a break in diplomatic relations with the USSR. These actions of the Conservative government went effectively unopposed by the TUC officials and the Labour Party. This development posed the possibility of war with Britain and was used by the Stalinists to try to proscribe discussion and silence the Opposition.

43. During the ECCI plenum, eighty-three leading members of the AUCP submitted a declaration to the Politburo in support of the United Opposition. The "Declaration of the Eighty-three" was later circulated among the ranks, where despite virtually certain expulsion and, by the end of the year, imprisonment, for signing, some 3,000 party members added their names.

44. One of the principal Stalinist slanders against the Left Opposition focused not on its political program but on Trotsky's "non-Bolshevik" past. By this time the Stalin faction had recruited large numbers of former Mensheviks, such as Martynov, and others even further to the right, who had opposed the Russian revolution that Trotsky helped to lead.

45. The document known as Lenin's Testament was dictated by him between December 23 and 31, 1922. It called for "removing Stalin" from

the post of party general secretary in order to prevent a split with Trotsky. This document was suppressed by Stalin during his lifetime, although it was published by Trotsky in the West after his expulsion from the Soviet Union in 1929. It was first published in the USSR in 1956 under Khrushchev and can be found in the fourth edition of the English-language *Collected Works* of Lenin (Moscow: Progress Publishers, 1960-70 , vol. 37, pp. 593-611) under the title "Letter to the Congress."

46. The already long-delayed Sixth Congress of the Comintern was scheduled at this time to be held in 1927. It was again postponed and finally met in Moscow in the summer of 1928. As a result of the postponement the Fifteenth Party Congress of the AUCP came first, opening on December 2. Trotsky and the Opposition were expelled from both the ECCI and from the AUCP before the congress began.

46. The Presidium of the Eighth Plenum of the ECCI gave Trotsky forty-five minutes to present the Opposition's position on China, with time for a summary after the discussion. The exact date of the first speech is not established, but internal evidence suggests that it was on May 23.

48. Zinoviev's "Theses on the Chinese Revolution" of April 14, 1927, were published as an appendix to *Problems of the Chinese Revolution.*

49. Radek's correspondence of July and September 1926 with the Politburo on China was quoted by Vujovic in his speech to the Eighth ECCI Plenum. This speech was published as an appendix to *Problems of the Chinese Revolution.*

50. This is "The Letter from Shanghai" of March 17, 1927, by Nassonov, Fokine, and Albrecht.

51. Trotsky is speaking here as a representative of the United Opposition, which refused as a faction to approve his position for immediate CCP withdrawal from the Kuomintang. Several times in public he states the United Opposition's formal stand of approving continued entry provided the CCP also carry on independent activities in its own name. See his "Why Have We Not Called for Withdrawal from the Kuomintang Until Now?" (June 23, 1927), which is directed to the Zinoviev wing of the joint faction.

52. See section 40 of "The Chinese Revolution and the Theses of Comrade Stalin," which appears earlier in this volume.

53. The Politburo of the AUCP discussed the question of the Chinese Eastern Railroad on March 25, 1926, at the same time that it received the report of the special commission on Far Eastern policy published earlier in this volume ("Problems of Our Policy with Respect to China and Japan"). Trotsky proposed that the Soviet government repeat its pledge contained in the Sino-Soviet Treaty of May 1924, to return the CER to China as soon as a unified and democratic Chinese government existed that could guarantee that it would not fall into the hands of foreign imperialists, particularly Japan. The Politburo postponed action on this pledge. At the May 1927 ECCI plenum Bukharin accused Trotsky of having proposed to turn over the CER to Chang Tso-lin in March 1926.

This charge was picked up and repeated by the Stalinist press. No stenographic record was taken at the Politburo meeting. A reading of the commission's report shows that the charge is false. In 1935, however, Stalin turned the railroad over to the Japanese puppet government of "Manchukuo." The CER was returned to the USSR at Yalta in 1945. In contrast to Stalin's readiness to turn over Chinese territory to imperialist Japan, he refused to relinquish it to Mao Tse-tung when the CCP came to power in 1949. It was returned to China only in 1952 after extensive negotiations.

54. Part of the text appears to be missing here ("I have already observed. . ."). The great party discussion Trotsky refers to, however, is clearly the debate over the terms of the peace treaty with Germany in the spring of 1918 in which the new Soviet government withdrew from participation in World War I. Negotiations were begun with the Germans at the town of Brest-Litovsk in the Ukraine, with Trotsky, then commissar of foreign affairs, in charge. The Bolshevik leadership was divided on what policy to pursue. The largest group, led by Bukharin, advocated a "revolutionary war" of self-defense. Trotsky advocated a delaying tactic in hopes of securing better terms or at the least showing the world that the Soviet government had signed under duress. Lenin, in a small minority, advocated immediate signing of whatever terms the Germans proposed. Faced with an imminent German offensive, Trotsky in the end voted with Lenin, giving him a majority against Bukharin. Bukharin's claim in 1927 that debate was out of order when war threatened the Soviet state stood in sharp contrast to the party's actual practice in a real war under the regime of Lenin.

55. This is Trotsky's summary speech at the Eighth Plenum of the ECCI in Moscow. Stalin had conspicuously absented himself from Trotsky's initial presentation. Then, during the discussion, he took the floor and accused the Opposition of being objectively in league with British imperialism for wishing to prolong discussion at a time when the Conservative government of Britain threatened war with the USSR. "Some threaten the party with war and intervention," Stalin said, "others with a split. There comes into being something like a united front from Chamberlain to Trotsky." This accusation had been made anonymously in *Pravda* earlier, but this was the first time it had been said publicly by a leader of the Stalin-Bukharin faction. Trotsky's speech was probably given on May 24.

56. At the Seventh Plenum of the ECCI in November-December 1926, Stalin "recalled" that Kamenev, shortly after the February revolution in 1917, had added his name to a telegram congratulating Prince Mikhail Romanov for having been named by the abdicating Tsar Nicholas II as his successor. This story would have been sensational if true, but it was first circulated in 1917 by opponents of the Bolsheviks, investigated by the party, and rejected, including a public denial by Lenin.

57. This document was directed to the Eighth Plenum of the ECCI,

which was in session until May 30. It presents a counterresolution to the one submitted by Bukharin on China.

58. General Feng Yü-hsiang, whose troops held Shensi province and the northern part of Honan province, had joined the Kuomintang in September 1926. In the spring of 1927 he wavered between the Wuhan regime of Wang Ching-wei and the Nanking government of Chiang Kai-shek. As Trotsky predicts here, Feng joined forces with Chiang Kai-shek, following a conference with Chiang at Soochow, June 19-21, 1927.

59. This letter to the United Opposition indicates the different positions held within the bloc by Trotsky and by the Zinoviev-Kamenev group, which opposed the call for complete withdrawal from the KMT. Trotsky's fullest discussion of these differences appears in his letter to Max Shachtman (December 10, 1930), which appears later in this volume.

60. The "Declaration of the Eighty-three" (see note 43) opened with the statement: "The big mistakes committed or tolerated in the leadership of the Chinese revolution have contributed to a heavy defeat. We can only extricate ourselves from this situation by following the road marked out by Lenin. Great tensions are created in the party by the abnormal conditions in which we examine the questions raised by the Chinese revolution. The unilateral 'discussion' carried on in *Pravda* and *Bolshevik* is a systematic distortion of the position of the Opposition (for example, attributing to the Opposition the demand for withdrawal from the Kuomintang). This shows the desire of the leading group in the Central Committee to hide its failings behind the attack on the Opposition. All of this focuses the attention of the party in a wrong direction."

61. This letter was undated, but it refers to the suppression of the Communist Party in Wuhan, which began July 15, 1927. The manuscript contains a handwritten note by Trotsky: "Probably comes from Zinoviev."

62. In June 1927, Smilga, one of the most popular leaders of the Zinoviev group, was ordered to leave Moscow to take a post in Khabarovsk on the border with Manchuria. Several thousand Oppositionists gathered to see him off at Moscow's Yaroslavl station; both Trotsky and Zinoviev spoke. Stalin then ordered the two central leaders of the United Opposition brought before the Central Committee and the Central Control Commission, sitting together as the party's highest tribunal. Stalin called for their removal from the Central Committee on the grounds of their participation in the meeting at Yaroslavl station and their appeal to the ECCI on the China question. Although the tribunal was packed with Stalin's and Bukharin's supporters, the charges were so contrary to party rules and traditions that Stalin could not secure a conviction. Trotsky appeared before the Presidium of the Central Control Commission first on July 24. The Presidium adjourned without reaching a verdict. From July 29 to August 9 the full plenum of the Central Committee and the Control Commission met and Trotsky defended the Opposition before it. Again Stalin was unable to have his charges against

Trotsky sustained. These are excerpts from Trotsky's opening speech.

63. Ho Lung and Yeh T'ing were hailed by Bukharin for leading the KMT units they commanded in the Nanchang uprising of August 1, 1927, which took the capital of Kiangsi province for the CCP. The rebellion, carried out in the name of the KMT, was defeated in five days. Ho and Yeh retreated southward, capturing Swatow briefly at the end of September, after which their units were dispersed. Remnants of these forces participated in the creation of various "soviet" areas in Southeast China in 1928.

64. *Pravda* on July 25, 1927, said: "The communists must immediately begin to propagate the idea of soviets, in order to be able, in case the struggle to win the Kuomintang fails, to call on the masses to create soviets. . . ."

65. The Red Spears were a rural secret society, based in North China. A July 1926 CCP Central Committee plenum had called for alliances with the Red Spears.

66. At the meeting of the British Trades Union Congress at Edinburgh in September 1927 the General Council passed a formal motion to sever relations with the Anglo-Russian Trade Union Unity Committee.

67. Three prominent leaders of the left Kuomintang regime in Wuhan broke with Wang Ching-wei in July 1927, opposing the suppression of the CCP: Soong Ch'ing-ling, Sun Yat-sen's widow; Teng Yen-ta, director of the political department of the KMT army during the Northern Expedition and one of Sun Yat-sen's young military associates in Sun's last years; and Eugene Ch'en, foreign minister of the Wuhan government. All three briefly sought refuge in Moscow after the Wuhan debacle, where they were played up by the official press as the nucleus of a projected "Revolutionary Committee" of the Kuomintang that would continue collaboration with the CCP. Ch'en was later reconciled to the Chiang Kai-shek KMT, where he functioned as a loyal opposition; Teng founded the splinter "Third Party" that opposed both the Kuomintang and the Communist Party; Soong became a fellow traveler of the CCP and was rewarded with a post in the CCP government after it came to power in 1949.

68. On September 27, 1927, Trotsky and Vujovic were expelled from the Executive Committee of the Communist International. These are excerpts from Trotsky's speech to the Presidium of the ECCI in defense of the Opposition. Published here are the first nine points of Trotsky's outline. The rest of the speech included "The Fight Against War" (point 10), "Questions of Discipline and Organizational Rules" (points 11-21), and "Where Is the Solution?" (points 22-25). The full text will be included in the second volume of *The Challenge of the Left Opposition* to be published by Pathfinder Press.

69. On November 15, 1927, Trotsky and Zinoviev were expelled from the AUCP. The expulsions were ordered on the eve of the Fifteenth Party Congress, which met in Moscow December 2-19, thus depriving the

Opposition of a voice at the congress. On December 11, while the congress was in session, the Comintern representatives in China led an uprising in Canton, to provide a successful action in China that would bolster the Stalin-Bukharin line. The "Canton Commune" was defeated on December 14. The Fifteenth Party Congress expelled all members of the United Opposition. This brief excerpt from Trotsky's article "On the New Stage," written in late December 1927, shows his immediate reaction to the news of the Canton uprising. His views of this event are more fully developed in his letters to Preobrazhensky of March and April 1928 and in his "Summary and Perspectives of the Chinese Revolution" which appear later in this volume.

70. On October 15, 1927, the Central Executive Committee of the USSR issued a manifesto in celebration of the tenth anniversary of the October revolution. The manifesto promised extravagant improvements in the living standards of the workers and peasants in the near future, a move designed to win popularity for the Stalin-Bukharin faction in the last stage of the inner-party fight with the United Opposition. The manifesto pledged the institution of the seven-hour day and the five-day week, old-age pensions for peasants, and abolition of the death penalty for all but the most serious crimes against the state. The seven-hour day has yet to be attained in the USSR, the workweek was reduced to five days only in 1967, and peasants received their pensions only in 1969 (collective farmers in 1965). The death penalty was soon brought into use against any form of dissent in the great purges of the 1930s.

71. Following the defeat of the German revolution of 1923 through the inaction of the German CP, a putschist insurrection was ordered in Estonia. On December 1, 1924, some 200 armed communists assaulted government buildings and strategic points. Lacking serious preparation among the masses, the insurrection was crushed in four hours. (See note 32 above for the German events of 1923.)

72. In January 1928 there were mass deportations of the expelled Oppositionists to remote areas of Soviet Asia. This precipitated the breakup of the United Opposition. Zinoviev and Kamenev capitulated to Stalin, publicly denouncing Trotsky. Trotsky was deported on January 16 to Alma-Ata in Soviet Turkestan on the Chinese border. Published here are brief excerpts on the question of China from the "Appeal of the Deportees" issued by Trotsky, Rakovsky, Radek, Smilga, Ivan Smirnov, Valentinov, Serebryakov, Preobrazhensky, and a number of other Old Bolsheviks on going into exile. The full text will appear in volume three of *The Challenge of the Left Opposition* to be published by Pathfinder Press.

73. At the time of first publication in 1936 the editors of the *New International* were able to verify only the date of Trotsky's first letter. A copy of Preobrazhensky's reply in the Trotsky Archive at Harvard bears the date of March 27, 1928. From the internal evidence this would date Trotsky's second and third letters as late April. Preobrazhensky's letter was published with the Trotsky correspondence in the April 1936 *New International*.

74. Zinoviev, Kamenev, and Rykov were opposed to the insurrection in the October revolution. Their opposition was based not only on purely technical grounds but also on the long-held expectation of the Bolshevik party that the Russian revolution would be bourgeois-democratic and not socialist in character.

75. 'The Ninth Plenum of the ECCI was held in Moscow, February 9-25, 1928.

76. Zinoviev and Kamenev wrote a public letter on January 17, 1928, denouncing Trotsky.

77. Hong Kong is a British crown colony. It consists of Hong Kong island, ninety miles southeast of Canton, and the Kowloon peninsula which has a direct rail link to Canton. The British supported the crushing of the Canton uprising.

78. The last convention of the CCP had been the August 7, 1927, "Emergency Conference" where a rump body removed Ch'en Tu-hsiu from the leadership and replaced him with Ch'ü Ch'iu-pai. The new special Comintern representative who ran this conference was Vissarion Lominadze who is presumably the "Comrade N" referred to here. The other principal Comintern representative to China at this time was Heinz Neumann, who was the main organizer of the Canton uprising. While there is some dispute, the standard histories say that Neumann arrived in China only in October and did not attend the August 7 conference.

79. The German revolution of November 1918 began with a naval mutiny under the impact of Germany's defeat in World War I. A Bavarian Socialist Republic was proclaimed on November 8, in Munich, while in Berlin, workers' and soldiers' soviets were formed. The German empire collapsed and Kaiser Wilhelm II fled to Holland. The Social Democratic leader Ebert became head of a provisional government in Berlin which acted as a caretaker regime for German capitalism.

80. The chapter in *Problems of the Chinese Revolution* entitled "The Canton Insurrection" (erroneously dated July) was an excerpt (subheads 2 through 5 inclusive) from the essay which appears here in full. "Summary and Perspectives of the Chinese Revolution" is the portion devoted to China of Trotsky's book-length "The Draft Program of the Communist International—A Criticism of Fundamentals," published in English under the title *The Third International After Lenin* (Pathfinder Press). It was written at Alma-Ata in the spring and early summer of 1928 for submission to the Sixth World Congress of the Comintern, to which Trotsky was appealing his expulsion. Until 1933 the Left Opposition considered itself an expelled faction of the Comintern and sought to reform its program and leadership and to win over its ranks. Before 1928 the Comintern had never officially adopted a formal program. It had considered drafts at its Fourth Congress in 1922 and Fifth Congress in 1924. These were withdrawn and a new draft was submitted in the names of Stalin and Bukharin to the Sixth Congress which met in Moscow July 17–September 1, 1928. Trotsky's criticism was distributed by the apparatus to the Program Commission but it was not

given to the delegates. It reached the West through James P. Cannon, a central leader of the American Communist Party and a member of the Program Commission. Cannon became convinced of the correctness of Trotsky's views on reading the document, smuggled a copy of it out of the Soviet Union, and became a founding leader of the American Trotskyist Opposition.

81. Sun's basic views on relations with foreign imperialism are outlined in his *Wu-chih chien-she* (1919) published in English in 1920 as *The International Development of China*. He proposed the rapid industrialization of China through the investment of astronomical amounts of foreign capital on terms mutually profitable to the imperialists and China's people. His plan aroused little interest in financial circles in the West.

82. The Chinese tariff was limited to 5 percent *ad valorem* by the Treaty of Nanking of 1842 imposed on China after its defeat in the first Anglo-Chinese War. Chinese demands for an upward revision at the Versailles Conference were ignored. Formal tariff autonomy was not granted until January 1931 as a concession to Chiang Kai-shek to help stabilize his government. Imperialist pressure kept this concession more formal than real.

83. This is a reference to the fact that after the February 1917 Russian revolution the Social Revolutionaries and the Mensheviks headed workers' soviets.

84. There were approximately 12,000 American, British, French, Japanese, and Italian troops stationed in the foreign "concessions" of China's port cities in 1927, not counting police and warships.

85. Nestor Makhno (1889-1934) was a Ukrainian anarchist leader. He formed a guerrilla band in 1918 and fought against the German occupiers of the Ukraine and various White Guard forces. He refused to integrate his troops into the Red Army and eventually came into armed clashes with the Soviet power, whereupon his forces were dispersed and he went into exile. The term "Makhnoism" came to be used to designate isolated, adventuristic, rural partisan warfare.

86. *Problems of Leninism*, published in Moscow in 1926 and republished in English in 1928 by International Publishers under the title *Leninism*, is a collection of Stalin's writings beginning with his January 1926 pamphlet of the same title as the Russian edition. The words quoted by Trotsky are from Stalin's speech of May 18, 1925, "Political Tasks of the University of the Peoples of the East," first published in *Pravda*, no. 115, May 22, 1925, and appearing on p. 278 of the International Publishers' edition. In Stalin's *Works* this paragraph appears on p. 149, vol. 7, English language edition. In Stalin's *Works*, however, although the speech is still purportedly taken from *Pravda* of 1925, the mention of the Kuomintang has disappeared.

87. John Pepper was the pseudonym of the Hungarian communist Jozsef Pogany (1886-1937). He was a member of Bela Kun's short-lived Hungarian Soviet Republic in 1919, which declared the outright

nationalization of the land, alienating the peasantry and hastening the government's downfall. Pepper then migrated to the U.S. where he established himself as Comintern representative to the American CP. In 1923 Pepper masterminded the ill-fated CP takeover of the Federated Farmer-Labor Party which precipitated the walkout of most of the non-CP trade unionists from the body. To recover its lost strength, Pepper proposed that the Federated Farmer-Labor Party endorse the third-party candidacy of Wisconsin's Progressive Republican Senator Robert M. La Follette (1855-1925) in the 1924 presidential elections. Opposition within the CP, principally from William Z. Foster and James P. Cannon, won referral of this decision to the Comintern where it was set aside as class collaborationist.

88. Early in the German revolution of 1918-19, Rudolf Hilferding, one of the leaders of the German Social Democracy, proposed a constitutional structure for the new republic that would combine workers' councils with a parliament, the latter to exercise all decisive legislative and executive powers. This "combined" form led to the dissolution of the workers' councils.

89. "Krestintern" is an acronym for the Peasants' International, an auxiliary organization of the Comintern founded in October 1923. Its purpose was "to coordinate peasant organizations and the efforts of the peasants to achieve workers' and peasants' governments." It held one further conference in November 1927 and was officially dissolved in 1939.

90. The Kuomintang's admission to the Comintern as a sympathizing party was voted in March 1926 over Trotsky's opposition. Chiang Kai-shek was at that time made an honorary member of the Presidium of the ECCI.

91. "Profintern" is the acronym for the Red International of Labor Unions, formed in July 1921 as a rival to the reformist Amsterdam trade union international. It ceased activity in 1937.

92. Article 58 of the Soviet penal code provided for punishment of those engaged in counterrevolutionary activity against the Soviet state. Under Stalin it was used to victimize his political opponents within the Communist Party.

93. This letter was sent to members of the Left Opposition by Trotsky along with the document that follows, "The Chinese Question After the Sixth Congress." The manuscript is undated.

94. An analogy with the year after the defeat of the revolutions of 1848.

95. The *Otzovists* (recallers) were a faction that arose in the Bolshevik party in 1908 under the leadership of A. A. Bogdanov. They opposed Bolshevik participation in the Third Duma and demanded immediate recall of the party's deputies. The Ultimatists, called "bashful Otzovists" by Lenin, proposed an ultimatum to the Bolshevik deputies to either adopt a more uncompromising stance in the Duma or resign. Lenin opposed both factions.

96. In Greek mythology the Danaides stabbed their husbands on their

wedding night. As punishment in Hades they were compelled to fill with water a large cask with holes in the bottom.

97. The August 7, 1927, CCP Emergency Conference which deposed Ch'en Tu-hsiu also ordered the Autumn Harvest Uprisings in Hupeh, Kiangsi, and Hunan provinces. Mao Tse-tung, elected in absentia as an alternate member of the Politburo, was assigned to lead the Hunan section of the uprisings. After their collapse Mao was criticized by the party leadership in November 1927 for "military adventurism" and stripped of his membership in the CCP's Hunan Committee and his place on the Politburo. The Sixth Comintern Congress also condemned the uprisings, which had been ordered by the representatives of the ECCI.

98. On July 15, 1927, a mass spontaneous workers' demonstration erupted in Vienna when it became known that two members of an Austrian fascist group on trial for the murder of left-wing workers had been acquitted. Mounted police and troops attacked the Viennese workers, leaving 150 dead and 1,500 injured. Out of weakness of the CP and irresoluteness of the Social Democrats, the government regained the initiative and opened a period of repression.

99. The so-called Third Party was founded by Teng Yen-ta. Teng had taken refuge in Moscow in August 1927, after the anticommunist purge in Wuhan. Stalin at first hoped to win Teng to continued collaboration with the CCP, but on November 1, 1927, Teng issued a manifesto calling for the formation of a Third Party opposed to both Chiang Kai-shek and the CCP. This was formally launched in September 1930 under the official name of the Provisional Action Committee of the Kuomintang. Teng was executed by the KMT in 1931. In 1947 the Third Party was renamed the China Peasants and Workers Democratic Party. It participated in the coalition government set up by Mao and Chou En-lai in 1949.

100. The Fifth Congress of the Comintern in 1924, refusing to recognize the defeat in Germany the previous year and the period of capitalist stabilization that had opened, approved over Trotsky's objections an ultraleft line proposed by Zinoviev, predicated on an imminent new rise of the revolutionary wave. During this period Brandler and Thalheimer, the leaders at the time of the defeat in October 1923, were made scapegoats for the Comintern's failure in 1923 to call for an insurrection. Throughout 1925 the German CP continued to act, on the basis of the analysis provided by the Comintern, as if revolution were imminent. At the Sixth Enlarged Plenum of the ECCI in February-March 1926 acknowledgment of the stabilization of German capitalism was belatedly made through the device of castigating the current German CP leaders for their ultraleft "errors."

101. Strakhov was the pseudonym of Ch'ü Ch'iu-pai (Ch'ü and Strakhov both mean "fear" in their respective languages).

102. On June 3, 1907, tsarist Prime Minister Stolypin dissolved the Second Duma, calling new elections under a revised electoral law designed to return a more conservative body. The majority of the

Bolsheviks were for boycotting the elections. The Mensheviks, however, favored participation in the elections, and the two factions, along with the Bund, had reunited in a single party at the Stockholm Congress of April-May 1906. At the August 1907 party conference, Lenin came out against the boycott tactic. Finding himself in a minority of one among the Bolshevik delegates, he voted with the Mensheviks and the Bund on this question.

103. From a popular Russian song.

104. The important Kiangsu Provincial Committee had its headquarters in Shanghai, as did the CCP Central Committee in 1928. The secretary of the committee at this time and the author of the resolution was Wang Jo-fei, a member of the CCP from 1922 who had been secretary for the Central Committee under Ch'en Tu-hsiu and Peng Shu-tse. Wang attended the Sixth Congress of the CCP in Moscow June 18-July 11, 1928, where he was under a political cloud because of his criticisms. He expressed sympathy for Trotsky's views to Oppositionists he met in Moscow. Wang was kept on in Moscow for three years. In his absence the Kiangsu Provincial Committee was reorganized and placed under the control of the apparatus, which after the Sixth Congress was in the hands of Li Li-san. Wang returned to China in 1931, was arrested, and spent almost six years in prison. On his release he became a prominent CCP official until his death in a plane crash in 1946.

105. Trotsky is in error here. Shanghai is in Kiangsu province, although it became an autonomous municipality in 1927. Canton is located in Kwangtung province on the South China coast, some 800 miles to the southwest.

106. The *Platform of the Opposition* was submitted to the Central Committee of the AUCP in early September 1927. It was signed by thirteen members of the Central Committee including Trotsky, Zinoviev, Kamenev, Smilga, Evdokimov, Rakovsky, and Pyatakov. This was two months before the expulsion of Trotsky and Zinoviev from the party. It will be included in volume two of *The Challenge of the Left Opposition,* to be published by Pathfinder Press.

107. The reference is to Lenin's Testament, where he characterized Stalin as "too rude" and called for his replacement as general secretary of the party by someone "more loyal, more polite and more considerate to the comrades, less capricious, etc." (*Collected Works,* vol. 36, p. 596).

108. Sun Yat-sen envisaged the development of a modern bourgeois China in three stages. First would be a military dictatorship of the Kuomintang that would eliminate the old autocracy; second would be a period of political "tutelage" of the masses in which the military rulers would create local institutions of government; finally there would be the establishment of a constitutional republic. In the final constitutional phase, Sun had proposed a division of powers on the American model between five equal bodies (called *yüan*): legislative, executive, judicial, civil service examinations, and censorship. A prototype of this five-yüan

setup was established at Nanking by Chiang Kai-shek in October 1928.

109. This is one of the few places where Trotsky refers to the Kuomintang regime as fascist. He later reconsidered this position and in his letter to the Chinese Trotskyists of October 3, 1932 ("For a Strategy of Action, Not Speculation"), he gave his reasons for considering this definition to be incorrect.

110. In February 1929, Trotsky and Natalia Sedova were deported from the Soviet Union to Constantinople, Turkey. There, Trotsky organized the publication of the Russian-language *Biulleten Oppozitsii,* which was printed in Paris. The manifesto printed here appeared in the first issue. The following editorial statement in the *Biulleten* explained the authorship and the circumstances in which this manifesto was drafted: "The document printed below is the platform of the Chinese Bolshevik-Leninists (Opposition). The working out of this document was preceded by numerous discussions among the Chinese Oppositionists. The initial draft was then submitted for the approval of comrades from the Russian, French, and Austrian Oppositions. Thus the present program of the Chinese Communist Left Opposition is at the same time an international document, not only in its political significance but in its origin. After a private discussion between representatives of the four national groups of Oppositionists named above (Chinese, Russian, French, and Austrian), the necessity was recognized of proceeding immediately to the setting up of an international faction of Bolshevik-Leninists, with the programmatic documents of the Russian Opposition as its basis. The first step on this road must be the setting up of a leading theoretical and political journal of the international Opposition."

111. After the capitulation of the Zinovievites at the end of 1927, the remaining, Trotskyist, wing of the Opposition came under severe repression with jailings and deportations to Siberia. In February 1928 a wave of defections to Stalin took place, headed by Pyatakov, Antonov-Ovseenko, and Krestinsky. This coincided with a turn to ultraleftism by Stalin. In July 1929, on the eve of the opening of the Tenth Plenum of the ECCI, Radek, Preobrazhensky, and Smilga led the capitulation of four hundred former Left Oppositionists to Stalin. Trotsky's article "A Wretched Document," of which these are excerpts, answered their statement of capitulation of July 10.

112. Earlier in this article Trotsky had pointed out that all the arguments used against him by the capitulators had been taken directly from the writings of Stalin's literary henchman Yemelyan M. Yaroslavsky (1878-1943), who had authored the charges in 1927 that expelled the capitulators as well as Trotsky from the AUCP: "As is known, capitulators in general do not invent gunpowder. They borrow snuff from Yaroslavsky's snuffbox and pass it off as gunpowder."

113. One of the long-standing demands of the Left Opposition had been the institution of a five-year plan for industrial growth, for which Trotsky had been denounced as a "superindustrializer." The Sixteenth Party Conference in April 1929 approved the First Five-Year Plan in a

resolution predating the plan's beginning to October 1928. Many of the capitulators rationalized their action by the argument that Stalin was adopting the Opposition's program.

114. In May 1929 Manchurian warlord Chang Hsueh-liang (son of Chang Tso-lin, who had been assassinated the previous year by the Japanese) ordered a police raid on the Soviet consulate at Harbin. (Chang had affiliated to the KMT government of Chiang Kai-shek in December 1928, so his action was taken to represent the policy of Nanking.) On July 10, Chang's troops seized the Chinese Eastern Railroad, ousting the Soviet administrators. The Soviet government demanded restoration and war was threatened. Armed clashes between Soviet and Chinese troops took place in Manchuria on August 15, shortly after Trotsky's article was written. In mid-November Soviet troops seized the CER. Nanking at this point proposed that Chang Hsueh-liang not contest the return of the railroad and this was codified in the Khabarovsk Protocol of December 22, 1929.

115. The German Leninbund and some French and Belgian Oppositionists took the position that Soviet claims to the CER were a continuation of tsarist expansion into Chinese territory and that efforts by the Soviet Union to retake the railroad were signs of Soviet imperialism. These events also became an issue in China in the fight between the Left Opposition of Ch'en Tu-hsiu and Peng Shu-tse and the Stalin-imposed leadership of Li Li-san. The Chinese Oppositionists accepted Trotsky's policy of defending the Soviet Union in the clash with Chang Hsueh-liang but differed with the ultraleft CCP line on how this could best be done. Li Li-san issued the slogan "Defend the Soviet Union." Ch'en proposed instead the slogan "Oppose the Kuomintang's Mistaken Policy," on the grounds that this would be better understood by the Chinese masses, while adequately fulfilling the task of supporting the Soviet government if war should break out. This dispute was the immediate pretext for Ch'en and Peng's expulsion from the CCP in November 1929.

116. Trotsky's use of the terms Thermidor and centrism in relation to the rising Stalinist bureaucracy went through an evolution as the bureaucracy took on more definite shape in the early 1930s. He ultimately concluded that the bureaucracy could no longer be described as centrist because it had become a hardened conservative caste. At the same time he modified the analogy with the overthrow of the radical Jacobin wing of the French revolution on 9 Thermidor (July 27), 1794, concluding that the Soviet Thermidor did not necessarily mean the restoration of capitalism but simply a sharp shift to the right, politically dispossessing the Soviet working class but leaving intact "the social foundation of the revolution" which defined the class character of the Soviet state. His mature views on these questions are best stated in his article "The Workers' State, Thermidor and Bonapartism" (February 1, 1935) in *Writings of Leon Trotsky (1934-35)*.

117. The German merchant and feudal aristocracy that had ruled the

Baltic states from the thirteenth century continued in power even after the integration of these countries into the Russian empire at the end of the eighteenth century. During World War I the German occupation forces used the remnants of these social layers to set up "independent" governments sympathetic to Germany. Richard von Kuhlmann (1873-1948) headed the German delegation at Brest-Litovsk in the negotiations with Trotsky.

118. The speech Trotsky refers to is "The War Danger—The Defense Policy and the Opposition," brief excerpts of which appeared earlier in this volume under the title "What About China?" *La Révolution défigurée* was published in August 1929 in French. A somewhat revised English edition was brought out by Pioneer Publishers in 1937 under the title *The Stalin School of Falsification*.

119. After Trotsky's exile to Turkey he applied to all the major governments of Europe and America for the right to reside as a political exile. Without exception his requests were refused, even by such bastions of "democracy" as Britain and the United States. He describes this experience in the final chapter of his autobiography, *My Life* (Pathfinder Press, 1970), which was entitled "The Planet without a Visa." Although he was later permitted to live briefly in France and in Norway he was finally forced to leave both these countries and only Mexico would grant him an entry permit.

120. After the failure of the Autumn Harvest Uprising, Mao Tse-tung with the remnants of his forces established a base camp in the Chingkang mountains on the Hunan-Kiangsi border. He was joined there by Chu Te and Lin Piao in April 1928. After withstanding two attacks by KMT forces in May and July 1928, the situation became untenable and the Fourth Red Army under Chu's command, and with Mao as political commissar, broke out of the encirclement in January 1929. It was the exploits of these forces that were reported in the Comintern press. Throughout 1929 the Chu-Mao units were on the move in the area where the provinces of Kiangsi, Fukien, and Kwangtung meet. At the beginning of 1930 there were approximately fifteen separate small "soviet" areas in Southeast China, of which the largest was the so-called Kiangsi Soviet of Chu Te and Mao, headquartered at Juichin, which underwent considerable growth in the early 1930s. At this time Chiang Kai-shek was tied down in military clashes with warlord generals who had nominally adhered to the KMT. In 1931 he concentrated his forces on the rural CP "soviets" and by the end of 1934 had eliminated them from South China.

121. The "third period" theory was first formally adopted by a Comintern gathering at the Tenth Plenum of the ECCI in July 1929, although it was claimed in the resolution, with some justice, that the theory could be found in the program adopted by the Sixth Congress the previous year. The Sixth Congress had signaled Stalin's break with Bukharin and it was there that Molotov emerged as Stalin's principal theoretician. According to the Stalinists the post-World War I epoch could

be divided into three periods: the first period, of revolutionary upheaval, had run from 1917 to 1923; the second, of capitalist stabilization, had lasted from 1924 to 1928. The "third period," which was to see the final collapse of capitalism, was said to have opened in 1928. The tactics favored by the Stalinists at this time and which they maintained until 1934 included the rejection of the united front, refusal to work in existing trade unions, and promotion of rural guerrilla warfare in China and Southeast Asia.

122. Trotsky is replying here to a letter from "Peter," a leader of the Wo-men-ti-hua (Our Words) group in Shanghai. ("Peter's" letter, signed "P.," was published in the New York *Militant,* January 25, 1930.) There were at this time four Trotskyist groups in China. The largest was the Wu-ch'an-che she (Proletarian Society), led by Ch'en Tu-hsiu and Peng Shu-tse. (This group was organized within the CCP before Ch'en and Peng's expulsion in December 1929, under the name Tso-p'ai fan-tui-p'ai [Left Opposition], which remained the group's formal name until 1931, though from 1930 it was better known by the name of its magazine, *Wu-ch'an-che.*) In addition there were three smaller groups, composed mainly of Chinese students who had been won to the Left Opposition while in Moscow, and who at this time were generally critical of Ch'en and Peng. These groups were: the Shih-yueh she (October Society), led by Liu Jen-ching; the Chan-tou she (Combat Society); and the Wo-men-ti-hua group. In May 1931 the four groups united to form the Communist League of China, a name that was retained until 1948 when it was changed to the Revolutionary Communist Party.

123. The document Trotsky refers to is "The Political Situation in China and the Tasks of the Bolshevik-Leninist Opposition" (June 1929), which appears earlier in this volume. "N." was Liu Jen-ching, who visited Trotsky at Prinkipo in 1929. Liu wrote for the world Trotskyist press under the name Niel Shih from Shanghai in the early 1930s.

124. Trotsky's major polemic against the ultraleftists among the Left Oppositionists on the Sino-Soviet conflict appears in his pamphlet "Defense of the Soviet Republic and the Opposition" (September 7, 1929), in *Writings of Leon Trotsky (1929).* He discusses in particular the views of the French syndicalist Robert Louzon and the German Hugo Urbahns.

125. The Kellogg Pact (after Frank B. Kellogg, U.S. secretary of state [1925-29]) was an agreement signed by fifteen nations in 1928 calling for the renunciation of war as an instrument of national policy. It was later ratified by a total of sixty-three countries, including the Soviet Union.

126. This article, which is described as a reply to questions raised by Chinese Oppositionists, was first published in *Biulleten Oppozitsii,* no.11, May 1930. The text here is taken from the *Militant* and has been slightly revised after comparison with the Russian. Neither source indicated which group of Chinese Oppositionists Trotsky was writing to. The only regular liaison with Trotsky and with the world Trotskyist press at this time was through Liu Jen-ching of the Shih-yueh she.

127. "N." here as before is Liu Jen-ching. The newspaper, *Wu-ch'an-che*, in which this correspondence appeared was that of Ch'en Tu-hsiu and Peng Shu-tse.

128. Point 1 of Trotsky's letter, which was summarized by the editors of *Wu-ch'an-che*, was Trotsky's correction of the geographical error in his "The Chinese Question After the Sixth Congress" (see note 105 above).

129. This document appears as an appendix to this volume.

130. See note 122 above.

131. The September-October 1930 issue of *Biulleten Oppozitsii* (nos. 15-16), which was in preparation at the time of this letter, contained Trotsky's "Stalin and the Chinese Revolution," the September 1930 "Manifesto on China of the International Left Opposition," and excerpts from Ch'en Tu-hsiu's "Letter to the Comrades," all of which appear later in this volume.

132. *The Permanent Revolution*, written in October 1928, while Trotsky was at Alma-Ata, was first published in a Russian edition in Berlin early in 1930. The English edition appeared in 1931.

133. It is usual to date the break between the Wuhan government and the CCP from the expulsion of the CCP from the Kuomintang in Wuhan on July 15, 1927. However, the May 21-22 massacre in Changsha, the capital of neighboring Hunan, one of the bloodiest episode of the counterrevolution, was engineered by Wuhan supporters, not the allies of Chiang Kai-shek. It was the Wuhan government of Wang Ching-wei, not Chiang's Nanking regime, that appointed General T'ang Sheng-chih to "investigate" his subordinate in Changsha, General Hsü K'e-hsiang. As can be seen from Trotsky's citation of the Stalinist Chitarov's report from the Minutes of the Fifteenth Congress of the AUCP on page 459 of this volume, the Stalinists after the fact also regarded the anticommunist turn by the Wuhan regime to date from May and not July. The Changsha coup took place while the Eighth Plenum of the ECCI was in session.

134. The slogan "No tsar, but a workers' government!" was falsely attributed to Trotsky at the time of the 1905 revolution and cited repeatedly later by the Stalinists as "proof" that Trotsky had ignored the peasantry in 1905 and sought to "leap over" the stage of the bourgeois-democratic revolution. The slogan was actually used on a leaflet issued in Europe not by Trotsky but by Parvus (Alexander Helphand) in the summer of 1905. At this time Trotsky was working underground in St. Petersburg. The embellishment by Rafes, who attributed this slogan to Trotsky in 1917, was even more ill-chosen, as Rafes was then an anti-Bolshevik member of the Bund who served in the anticommunist Ukrainian Central Rada headed by Simon V. Petlyura. Trotsky discusses the circumstances surrounding this Stalinist campaign in *The Permanent Revolution*, pp. 221-24.

135. This report appears in the English-language *International Press Correspondence*, vol. 8, no. 40, July 26, 1928. There is no indication who "Chan Fu Yun" is. Between the pseudonyms used by delegates and the

haphazard transliteration of Chinese names the editors have been unable to identify the author of the report.

136. The Sixteenth Congress of the AUCP was held in Moscow, June 26–July 13, 1930. "Siu's" comments are reported in the English-language *International Press Correspondence*, vol. 10, no. 36, August 7, 1930, pp. 735-36. He is identified only as a representative of the CCP.

137. The Hotel Lux in Moscow was used to house Comintern visitors and officials.

138. T'an P'ing-shan, the communist minister of agriculture in the Wuhan government, after participating in the Nanchang uprising and the Ho Lung–Yeh T'ing campaign, quit the CCP in October 1927 and joined the Third Party of Teng Yen-ta. He rejoined the KMT in 1937.

139. A local "soviet government" had in fact been proclaimed in China, in Kiangsi province in February 1930. Led by Chu Te and Mao, it did not include the then central leaders of the CCP, in particular Li Li-san and Chou En-lai, who were functioning underground in Shanghai. A National Congress of Delegates from Soviet Areas was held on the outskirts of Shanghai beginning May 31, which issued a manifesto calling for the formation of a Chinese Soviet Republic at a congress to be held on November 7, 1930. This was to unite the various scattered rural areas held by the CCP. As part of the preparation for this event the CCP, under the direction of Li Li-san, ordered attacks on major cities. The most important of these, which took Changsha for a few days in late July and early August 1930, ended in defeat and the congress was postponed for a year.

140. *Hung-ch'i* (Red flag), the CCP's theoretical journal, reported in its issue of March 20, 1930, that whereas workers had comprised 66 percent of the party membership in 1926, in 1930 they were only 8 percent.

141. The right-wing Bukharinists were maneuvered from power slowly, beginning at the Sixth Congress of the Comintern in July 1928 and ending with Bukharin's removal from the Politburo of the AUCP in November 1929 amidst a campaign against the "right danger."

142. This manifesto written by Trotsky was signed by Alfred Rosmer, Kurt Landau, and Markin (Leon Sedov) for the Provisional International Secretariat of the International Left Opposition, and by the following representatives of its sections: L. Trotsky for the Russian Opposition; A. Rosmer, Communist League of France; K. Landau, United Left Opposition of the German Communist Party; J. Andrade and J. Gorkin, Spanish Opposition; A. Hennaut, Belgian Opposition; M. Shachtman, Communist League of America; D. Karl and C. Mayer, Communist Left of Austria; J. Frey, Communist Party of Austria (Opposition); Frank, "Internal Group" of the Austrian CP; W. Krieger, Czechoslovak Opposition; Candiani, Italian Left Faction; Santini and Blasco [Pietro Tresso], new Italian Opposition; R. Negrete, Mexican Opposition. The International Left Opposition was formed in April 1930 as an outgrowth of the Russian Left Opposition. Its members were called "Trotskyists" or "Trotskyites" by the Stalinists and others—Trotsky avoided the use of this term.

143. In 1918 Manuilsky wrote the following: "Russian Bolshevism, born in the nationally confined revolution of 1905-06, had to go through the purification ritual of liberation from all the typical features of national peculiarity in order to receive full citizenship rights as an international ideology. Theoretically, this purging of Bolshevism of the national varnish that clung to it was carried through by Trotsky in 1905, who endeavored to connect the Russian revolution with the whole international movement of the proletariat in the idea of the permanent revolution." This was quoted by the Opposition at the November 1926 ECCI plenum, to Manuilsky's discomfort.

144. These excerpts from Trotsky's letter are quoted by Shachtman in his August 7, 1931, introduction to *Problems of the Chinese Revolution.* No copy of the full text is presently available, although it may exist in the closed section of the Trotsky archive at Harvard.

145. Trotsky's recollection of the date here is wrong. The theses on the Chinese Eastern Railroad were drafted on March 25, 1926 (they appear earlier in this collection under the title "Problems of our Policy with Respect to China and Japan").

146. "From the beginning, we, the representatives of the International Left Opposition, the Bolshevik-Leninists, were against entering the Kuomintang and for an independent proletarian policy."—"Manifesto on China of the International Left Opposition" (September 1930). The manifesto appears earlier in this volume.

147. This refers to the "Platform of the Opposition" (1927).

148. "A Statement of Our Political Views" *(Wo-men-ti cheng chih i-chien-shu)* (Shanghai 1929). This was signed by eighty Oppositionists besides Ch'en Tu-hsiu.

149. Buridan's ass: after the fourteenth century French scholastic philosopher who is traditionally credited with posing the paradox of a donkey placed before two identical bunches of hay who starves to death for inability to choose between them.

150. This is the article "A Retreat in Full Disorder" (November 1930) printed earlier in this volume.

151. "Twenty-one conditions" were adopted by the Second World Congress of the Comintern (July-August 1920) to prevent the affiliation of centrist parties that had not fully broken from reformism. The conditions were drafted by Lenin (see his *Collected Works,* vol. 31). The ILO's first conference was held in February 1933 in Paris, where eleven points were adopted governing future admissions to the ILO (see *Writings of Leon Trotsky [1932-33]).*

152. This was published in English translation as *The Conquerors* (New York: Harcourt, Brace, and Company, 1929). *The Conquerors* (1928) was the first of Malraux's two novels based on the Chinese revolution of 1925-27. The second and more famous was *Man's Fate* (1933). Trotsky's review of *Les Conquérants* was published in the April 1931 issue of *Nouvelle Revue Francais* (Paris) along with a rebuttal by Malraux.

Trotsky replied to Malraux's article in "A Strangled Revolution and Its Stranglers" (June 13, 1931), which appears later in this volume.

153. See the appendix to this volume.

154. The T'aip'ing (great peace) rebellion (1851-64) was a revolt against the Ch'ing dynasty led by Hung Hsiu-ch'üan, a Christian mystic. This great peasant revolt was finally defeated by the intervention of British military forces. The so-called Boxer rebellion (this name is not used in China) was an antiforeign uprising led by the I-ho Ch'üan (Righteous and Harmonious Fists) secret society in 1899-1900. It was crushed after the sacking of Peking in August 1900 by an eight-power expeditionary force including troops from the U.S., France, Britain, Germany, Austria, Italy, Russia, and Japan. The Ch'ing government was compelled to pay reparations to the imperialist governments after the uprising was suppressed.

155. The July days of 1917 began with mass spontaneous demonstrations by Russian workers in Petrograd against the bourgeois Provisional Government of Aleksandr Kerensky. Kerensky retaliated against the Bolsheviks with severe repression, arresting Trotsky and forcing Lenin into hiding.

156. After the failure of P'eng Te-huai's troops to hold Changsha in August 1930, the Comintern decided to make Li Li-san the scapegoat for the failure of its line of using the rural-based CCP armies to take industrial centers. Li Li-san was removed from the Politburo on November 25 and sent to Moscow in December, immediately before the *Pravda* article Trotsky quotes. Li and his supporters were denounced for putschism and "Trotskyism." Li was replaced by Pavel Mif's young protégés, headed by Ch'en Shao-yü (Wang Ming).

157. Jean Chiappe (1878-1940) was prefect of police in Paris (1928-34) and was noted for his violent procedure against revolutionists.

158. Japan invaded Manchuria on September 18, 1931, securing its conquest almost immediately. In February 1932 Tokyo established the puppet state of Manchukuo in the occupied territory, and launched a brief punitive expedition against Shanghai. The occupation of Manchuria was followed by six years of uneasy truce, until the Japanese invasion of central China in the summer of 1937 which opened the Sino-Japanese War.

159. The Chinese Left Opposition suffered severe repression shortly after its founding conference in May 1931. Many of its leading members were arrested. After the Japanese invasion of Shanghai in January 1932 the organization underwent considerable growth as a result of the inability of the KMT government to mount serious resistance, and of sectarian abstentionism by the CCP. By the early fall of 1932 a majority of the industrial cells of the CCP in Shanghai had gone over to the Left Opposition. Shortly after Trotsky's letter, however, on October 15, 1932, eight of the central leaders of the Chinese Opposition, includeng Ch'en Tu-hsiu and Peng Shu-tse, were arrested. Their trial, before a military

court in Nanking, lasted for two years. Ch'en and Peng were sentenced to thirteen years in prison; they served five and were released when the prison was destroyed by Japanese bombers at the outbreak of the Sino-Japanese War in 1937.

160. The Japanese attack on Manchuria in September 1931 was executed by the Kwantung Army, Japan's standing army in Manchuria, without official permission from the civilian cabinet. The same was true of the naval invasion of Shanghai in January 1932. This precipitated a struggle between the party politicians who controlled the cabinet and the military leadership. On February 9, 1932, former Finance Minister Junnosuke Inoue was murdered, followed on March 5 by the assassination of Baron Takuma Dan of the house of Mitsui. On May 15, 1932, Prime Minister Ki Tsuyoshi Inukai was assassinated, ending the control of the cabinet by party representatives and initiating an era of military governments.

161. Trotsky had left Turkey for France in July 1933, and was in turn expelled from that country under Stalinist and right-wing pressure in 1935. He and his family arrived in Norway in June 1935. In 1933, with the collapse of the German CP's opposition to Hitler without a struggle, Trotsky called for an end of the International Left Opposition's status as a faction of the Comintern and for the replacement of the bankrupt Comintern with a new, Fourth International. From 1933 on, the Fourth Internationalists throughout the world sought to construct independent parties in competition with the Stalinists for the allegiance of the working class. Shortly after Trotsky's arrival in Norway he was visited by Harold R. Isaacs, a member of the Chinese section and later of the American section of the International Communist League. The ICL was the predecessor of the Fourth International, which was to be founded in 1938. (Isaacs broke from the Socialist Workers Party in the United States during World War II and moved to the right.) In August 1935, Isaacs was writing his *Tragedy of the Chinese Revolution*, based on several years of research he had carried out in China. He reported to Trotsky on the Communist League of China and on the general developments in Chinese politics. This account is taken from Isaacs' travel diary. A copy was sent to the Chinese Trotskyists who translated it into Chinese and later included it in the 1947 Chinese edition of Trotsky's *Problems of the Chinese Revolution*. Isaacs has informed the editors that he is unable to locate his original diary notes, so the version published here has had to be retranslated from the Chinese.

162. These discussions took place during the Long March. Under massive military assault by Chiang Kai-shek, the CCP territories were reduced to five or six counties in south-central Kiangsi by the summer of 1934. In October the main elements of the First Front Army, numbering about 90,000 persons, broke through the KMT cordon and set out on a year-long trek on foot that took them 6,600 miles into Northwest China. While Trotsky and Isaacs were meeting, the main forces of the Long

March were camped at Maoerhkai in northwest Szechwan province near the border of Tsinghai. There, a debate was taking place between Mao Tse-tung, who advocated breaking through to the Northeast, and Chang Kuo-t'ao, who advocated roughly the route Isaacs expected them to take into Sinkiang on the Soviet border. Mao carried the majority and the First Front Army, reduced to less than 6,000, arrived at Wuch'ichen, Shensi, on October 20, 1935.

163. The first political party of the revolutionary Russian intelligentsia was the Zemlya i Volya (Land and Freedom). This organization split in October 1879 into a terrorist wing, the Narodnaya Volya (People's Will) and the Cherny Peredel (General Redivision), the latter led by George Plekhanov. The Narodnaya Volya was crushed after it succeeded in assassinating Tsar Alexander II in March 1881. Plekhanov, forced into exile in 1880, was won to Marxism and founded Russia's first Marxist organization, the Emancipation of Labor Group, in 1883. The first decade of Russian Marxism was one of extreme political reaction which by 1893 saw the organization hardly larger that it had been at its founding and still confined to a handful of emigrés with few contacts inside Russia. But 1893 proved to be a year of deep radicalization in which Marxist ideas became widely popular among Russian radicals and marked the beginning of the period of "legal Marxism" (1893-99) in which many Marxist and semi-Marxist works were published in Russia and became the center of heated debate.

164. The Persian revolution (1906-09) began with protests against the shah by merchants and the Islamic clergy (*ulema*). Soon demands for a republic and a constitution became dominant. Under mass pressure the shah granted the creation of a *Majlis* (assembly), but sought to restrict its authority. The most radical center of the revolution was Tabriz, where a plebeian opposition to the monarchy took power in 1907, resisting the shah's armies for eleven months. It was finally crushed only with the intervention of tsarist Russian troops in 1909. (The country's name was offically changed to Iran in 1935.) The Chinese revolution of 1911 ended Manchu rule and created a republic for the first time in Chinese history. Beginning with a military uprising at Wuhan on October 10, 1911, the rebellion was victorious in fifteen of China's eighteen provinces by the end of November. Although Sun Yat-sen was briefly proclaimed president of China, the power went to local military commanders who soon dismembered the country into provincial warlord states.

165. Ch'en, who was in prison at this time, had in fact begun to develop serious differences with Trotsky. The Central Committee of the Communist League of China, led by a few very young members, voted to expel him from the organization, but this decision was rescinded. After his release from prison in 1937, Ch'en objected to public criticism of the Kuomintang on the grounds of the need for a common front against the Japanese invasion of China in the summer of that year. He later rejected Trotsky's position of defending the Soviet Union against imperialist

attack. Ch'en broke with Trotskyism after his positions were defeated at the Communist League's August 1941 convention. In ill health, he died the following year. Liu Jen-ching broke from Trotsky before Ch'en, capitulating to the KMT in 1937.

166. The Sino-Japanese War began with a clash between Chinese and Japanese soldiers at the Marco Polo Bridge near Peking on July 7, 1937. Trotsky was at this time in Mexico, where he had arrived from Norway in January 1937. This document was a statement for the bourgeois press.

167. During the great purges of the 1930s Stalin struck against the general staff of the Soviet Red Army. The acting commander in chief, Marshal Tukhachevsky, was arrested in May 1937 and executed in early June along with most of the experienced generals. This was followed by the imprisonment or execution of 25,000 lower ranking officers, one-third of the total.

168. This is a transcript, uncorrected by the participants, of a discussion held at Trotsky's home at Coyoacan, Mexico, between Trotsky and several Fourth Internationalists. The person identified in the text as "W" was Jack Weber, a leading American Trotskyist. "R" was Raya Dunayevskaya, one of Trotsky's secretaries in Mexico. She took the stenogram of the China discussion. The session opened with a report by Li Fu-jen on the political situation in China.

169. Chiang's arrest of seven leaders of the National Salvation Association in November 1936 provoked a great outcry in China in defense of the civil liberties of the "Seven Gentlemen" and led to massive recruitment by the NSA which made it briefly the third largest political organization in China after the KMT and the CCP.

170. Italy invaded Ethiopia (Abyssinia) in October 1935.

171. The Soviet government announced that a secret trial of the Red Army generals had been held in early June 1937, prior to their execution. There are conflicting accounts as to whether the trial actually took place or if the officers were simply shot.

172. Mikhail Rodzianko (1859-1924) played in the Russian revolution of February 1917 a part analogous to that of Honoré Mirabeau (1749-1791) in the French revolution of 1789. A constitutional monarchist who desired nothing more than a parliamentary reform, he found himself thrust momentarily to the head of a revolution that destroyed the monarchy altogether.

173. Ch'en Tu-hsiu was released from prison on August 19, 1937, after serving five years.

174. The American Trotskyists had joined the Socialist Party in the spring of 1936 as a way of establishing contact with newly radicalizing militants who were then attracted to the SP. The SP right wing began expelling the left in August 1937. The expelled left-wing branches met in convention December 31, 1937–January 3, 1938, in Chicago where they founded the Socialist Workers Party. The SWP affiliated to the Fourth International at the International's founding conference later in 1938.

175. This is a letter to the Mexican artist Diego Rivera (1886-1957). Rivera had been a member of the Central Committee of the Mexican Communist Party from 1922. He opposed the expulsion of the Left Opposition in 1927, and later became a supporter of Trotsky. He was instrumental in gaining Trotsky's entry into Mexico. In 1939 Trotsky broke with him when Rivera supported the candidacy of the right-wing general Almazar in the 1940 presidential election. Rivera later returned to the Communist Party.

176. The Oehlerites were followers of Hugo Oehler, who led a sectarian faction within the Workers Party of the United States opposing fusion with the Socialist Party. He was expelled in October 1935 for violations of discipline and organized the Revolutionary Workers League. The Eiffelites were followers of Paul Eiffel, leader of a tiny split-off from Oehler's RWL in 1936. He opposed military support to Loyalist Spain against Franco or to Chiang Kai-shek against the Japanese invasion.

177. The Berber tribes of the Rif region of Morocco revolted against Spanish colonial rule in 1921 under the leadership of Abd-el-Krim. Defeating the Spanish forces in 1924, the Riffians attacked the French sector the following year but were defeated in 1926 by a combined Spanish and French army.

178. This article was in answer to questions by a journalist, Roger Devlin.

179. The rapprochement between the CCP and Chiang began with the Sian Incident of December 1936, where the CCP intervened to secure Chiang's release after his arrest by Manchurian KMT troops angry at his foot-dragging in the war with Japan, which occupied their homeland. In a telegram to Chiang on February 10, 1937, the CCP agreed to halt land reform, cease all efforts to overthrow the KMT, reorganize its territories around Yenan as a subdivision of Chiang's government, place their troops under the command of the KMT, and accept fully the political leadership of Chiang Kai-shek for the duration of the war. The KMT accepted these concessions in the fall of 1937 when the war had begun in earnest. In 1938 Chou En-lai demonstratively rejoined the KMT and was appointed vice-minister of the political training board of the Military Council.

180. This essay appeared as the introduction to the first edition of Harold R. Isaacs' book *The Tragedy of the Chinese Revolution* (London: Secker & Warburg, 1938). Isaacs later broke with Marxism and deleted Trotsky's introduction in two subsequent editions (1951 and 1961) which were politically revised to give the book an anticommunist slant. The first edition of Isaacs' book was completed in collaboration with Trotsky who discussed its thesis with the author as well as providing the introduction. The later editions, although they no longer have the same content Trotsky describes here, remain the fullest and best-documented account of the Chinese revolution of 1925-27.

181. The French third estate, the representatives of the cities or

commons, in 1789 succeeded in prevailing over the first two estates (nobles and clergy) to force the creation of a national assembly, marking the beginning of the French revolution.

182. The "Manifesto of the Fourth International on the Imperialist War and the Proletarian World Revolution," from which these excerpts are taken, was adopted by the Emergency Conference of the Fourth International held May 19-26, 1940, in New York. This was the first world gathering of the Fourth International after the outbreak of World War II in September 1939.

183. This article was intended to be the introduction to the Chinese edition of Trotsky's *History of the Russian Revolution*. It was begun in July 1940 and remained unfinished when Trotsky was assassinated by Stalin's agent on August 20, 1940.

184. On November 15, 1929, the Politburo of the CCP, then headed by Li Li-san, adopted a motion calling for the expulsion of Ch'en Tu-hsiu and Peng Shu-tse. This document is Ch'en's open letter to the party ranks answering the charges brought against him. The motion was approved by the Central Committee on June 11, 1930. Ch'en's letter first appeared in English in the *Militant* in serial form between November 1930 and February 1931, under the title "How Stalin-Bukharin Destroyed the Chinese Revolution." The version that appears here is based on the *Militant*'s translation, revised after comparison with the Chinese original by Joseph T. Miller. Only the first of Ch'en's footnotes appeared in the *Militant;* they have been restored in the text that appears here.

185. Ch'en uses the courtesy names *(tzu),* customarily adopted by Chinese at the age of twenty, for two of the CC members listed here. Li Shou-ch'ang is known in the West as Li Ta-chao and Chang T'e-li is better known as Chang Kuo-t'ao.

186. Maring (Henricus Sneevliet) had met with the CCP leadership in Hangchow in August 1922. On September 4, 1922, Sun Yat-sen announced plans for a reorganization of the KMT and set up a committee to carry this out, of which Ch'en Tu-hsiu was a member. The committee's plans, outlining a structure based on that of the RCP(B), were reported in January 1923, but not implemented until the KMT's First National Congress in January 1924. In October 1923 Mikhail Borodin came to China as representative of the Soviet government. He immediately took over the de facto responsibilities as chief Comintern representative as well.

187. This pamphlet was entitled *The Nationalist Revolution and the Chinese Nationalist Party.*

188. Hsü Ch'ien (1871-1940) became minister of justice in the KMT government in the summer of 1926. He was among the first of the left wing KMT leaders at Wuhan to instigate the break with the CCP, helping in June 1927 to persuade Feng Yü-hsiang to side with Chiang Kai-shek over the issue of suppression of the CCP. Ku Meng-yü (1889-   ), a professor of economics at Peking University, replaced Mao Tse-tung as

head of the KMT's propaganda department in May 1926. He was prominent in the Wuhan government. Since the early 1950s he has been a professor at the University of California at Berkeley. Ch'en Kung-po (1892?-1946) joined the Communist Party in Canton in 1920, went over to the Kuomintang in 1922, where he sided with Wang Ching-wei. He served in Wang's collaborationist regime under the Japanese in Nanking during World War II. T'an Yen-k'ai (1879-1930) was governor of Hunan province in the 1912-20 period. T'an was one of the chief negotiators for the Wuhan side in the fall of 1927 in the discussions leading to reunification with Chiang Kai-shek's wing of the KMT. In October 1928 T'an became president of the Executive Yüan at Nanking, a post equivalent to premier.

189. Ch'en is referring to M. N. Roy. Roy's indiscretion with the Comintern directive was the immediate precipitator of the suppression of the CCP in Wuhan in July 1927.

190. The editors have been unable to identify "Fan K'e" except to verify that he was a Russian.

191. Stalin had already begun the practice of detaining foreign communists in Moscow for long periods to isolate them from their own parties. The Comintern's invitation to Ch'en to come to the Soviet Union was reiterated in February 1930, ostensibly to discuss the motion for his expulsion from the CCP. Ch'en, already outside the CCP by this time, refused to go.

192. The Reorganizationist faction of the KMT was formed in October 1928 by Wang Ching-wei around a demand to purge the party of "reactionaries" in the pattern of the 1924 reorganization. In the winter of 1929-30 the Reorganizationists backed a military revolt against Chiang Kai-shek by T'ang Sheng-chih. When that failed, Wang Ching-wei joined with Feng Yü-hsiang and Yen Hsi-shan in establishing yet another rival bourgeois government at Peking. The revolt was crushed in October 1930.

GLOSSARY

Alsky, M.—Old Bolshevik, hero of Soviet civil war, Left Oppositionist, signer of Declaration of the Forty-six (1923). Deported to Siberia (1928).

AUCP(B)—All-Union Communist Party (Bolsheviks)—Name adopted by Russian Communist Party (Bolsheviks) in 1925. Party was founded as Russian Social Democratic Labor Party (RSDLP) in 1898. Split into Bolshevik (majority) and Menshevik (minority) wings in 1903. RSDLP(Bolsheviks) renamed Russian Communist Party (Bolsheviks) (RCP[B]) in 1918. Name changed from AUCP(B) to Communist Party of Soviet Union (CPSU) in 1952.

Baldwin, Stanley (1867-1947)—British Conservative Party prime minister (1923, 1924-29, 1935-37).

Biulleten Oppozitsii (Bulletin of the Opposition)—Russian-language magazine founded by Trotsky in exile in Turkey in 1929. Trotsky was its editor until his death in 1940; his son Leon Sedov was managing editor until his death in 1938. Printed in Paris (1929-31), Berlin (1931-32), Paris (1933-34), Zurich (1934-35), Paris (1935-39), and New York (1939-41).

Black Hundreds—Common name for Union of the Russian People, ultrareactionary monarchist group known for instigation of anti-Semitic and antisocialist pogroms under tsarist regime.

Blanquism—After Louis Auguste Blanqui (1805-1881), French utopian communist revolutionary, known for his theory of socialist revolution through insurrection by small conspiratorial group. His followers were prominent in Paris Commune (1871).

Blücher, Vassily Konstantínovich (1889-1938)—Main Soviet military adviser to Canton KMT government (1924-27) under pseudonym Galen. Arrested on Stalin's orders (1937) and executed.

Blum, Léon (1872-1950)—Principal leader of French Socialist Party in 1930s and premier of first Popular Front government (1936-37).

Bolsheviks—Majority faction formed in Russian Social Democratic Labor Party at Second Congress (1903). Led by Lenin. Became separate party in 1912. Organized October revolution in 1917 that established first workers' state. Changed name to Russian Communist Party (Bolsheviks) in 1918.

Borodin, Mikhail Markovich (1884-1951)—Stalin's chief representative in China (September 1923–July 1927). Later served as editor of Moscow *Daily News*. Arrested in 1949. Died in concentration camp.

Bukharin, Nikolai Ivanovich (1887-1938)—Joined Bolsheviks in 1906. In 1918 was spokesman of "left communists" but after Lenin's death became chief theoretician of right wing of AUCP. President of Comintern (1926-29). Formed Right Opposition to Stalin in 1928. Capitulated in 1929. Defendant in March 1938 Moscow trial, he "confessed" and was shot.

The Bund (General Jewish Workers Union of Russia and Poland)— Formed in 1897 at Vilna. Affiliated to Russian Social Democratic Labor Party in 1898, claiming special autonomous rights to represent Jewish workers. Broke from RSDLP in 1903; rejoined in 1906, allied with Mensheviks. Supported bourgeois Provisional Government after February 1917. Split in 1920, majority joining RCP(B), minority forming a Social Democratic Bund which was active in exile until World War II.

Cadets—Members of the Constitutional Democratic Party of Russia, founded in 1905 and led by Pavel N. Milyukov. A liberal bourgeois party, committed to constitutional monarchy. Briefly dominated Provisional Government after February 1917 Russian revolution.

Chamberlain, Joseph Austen (1863-1937)—Conservative British foreign secretary (1924-29).

Chang Fa-k'uei (1896-   )—Commander of KMT's Fourth Army during Northern Expedition. Supported Wuhan KMT in split with Chiang Kai-shek. Led KMT troops in crushing of communist-led Nanchang uprising; August 1927. Retired to Hong Kong in 1949.

Chang Hsueh-liang (1898-   )—Known as the Young Marshal. Son of Chang Tso-lin, from whom he inherited control of Manchuria in 1928. Joined KMT in December 1928. Best known for arresting Chiang Kai-shek at Sian in 1936. After CCP's intervention secured Chiang's release, Chang was imprisoned by Chiang, first in China and later in Taiwan. Given nominal amnesty in 1961 but still restricted to Taiwan.

Chang Kuo-t'ao (1897-   )—Attended founding conference of CCP (1921). Labor leader during 1920s. Leader of Oyüwan "soviet" area after 1931. Headed section of Long March (1935), but clashed with Mao Tse-tung and took his troops into Southwest China, not north to Shensi. Left CCP in 1938 and joined KMT. Ceased political activity after 1949.

Chang Tso-lin (1873-1928)—Manchurian militarist, gained control of Manchuria in 1919. Captured Peking (1924). Opposed KMT regime. He was assassinated by Japanese officers and succeeded in power by his son, Chang Hsueh-liang.

Ch'en Chiung-ming (1878-1933)—Anti-Manchu revolutionary and Cantonese military leader. Helped Sun Yat-sen take power in Canton in

1920, but broke with Sun in 1922 and seized power himself. Defeated in Canton early in 1923, he retained a military base in eastern Kwangtung until 1925.

Ch'en, Eugene (1878-1944)—Lawyer, born in Trinidad. Went to China in 1912, where he became Sun Yat-sen's legal adviser. Elected to Central Executive Committee of KMT in January 1926; appointed foreign minister in June. Supported Wang Ching-wei in April 1927 split with Chiang Kai-shek. Critical of Wuhan's break with the CCP, he fled to USSR in July 1927. Reconciled with KMT in February 1928.

Ch'en Shao-yü (1904-1974)—Known under pseudonym Wang Ming. Leader of the Russian returned-student group (Chinese students from Moscow's Sun Yat-sen University) used by Comintern representative Pavel Mif to replace Li Li-san as head of CCP in 1930-31 power struggle. CCP representative to Comintern (1931-37). His group was defeated by Mao Tse-tung during Long March (1935). Held nominal posts in CCP regime after 1949 but from mid-1950s lived in Moscow.

Ch'en Tu-hsiu (1879-1942)—Took part in bourgeois revolution of 1911. Principal literary and political leader of May Fourth Movement (1919). Founder and first general secretary of CCP. Central leader of CCP in revolution of 1925-27. Deposed at Stalin's order at August 1927 CCP CC rump Emergency Conference. Supported Trotskyist Left Opposition. Expelled from CCP in November 1929. With Peng Shu-tse a founding leader of Chinese Left Opposition. Imprisoned by KMT (1932-37). Developed differences with Trotsky in late 1930s and broke with Communist League of China in 1941.

Chernov, Viktor Mikhaylovich (1876-1952)—Founder and leader of Russian Social Revolutionary Party. Minister of agriculture in bourgeois Provisional Government (May-September 1917). Opposed Bolshevik revolution.

Chiang Kai-shek (1887-1975)—Joined Sun Yat-sen's personal following in Japan in 1913. Became operations officer of Ch'en Chiung-ming's Kwangtung Army in 1918. Supported Sun against Ch'en Chiung-ming in 1922. Became chief of staff in Sun's Canton headquarters in 1923. Assigned by First National KMT Congress (January 1924) to head Whampoa Military Academy. Principal military leader of KMT after death of Sun in March 1925. Blocked with Wang Ching-wei and Borodin at January 1926 KMT congress to defeat right-wing Western Hills faction. On March 20, 1926, staged coup in Canton, ousting Wang Ching-wei and imposing strict conditions on CCP to remain in KMT. During Northern Expedition, led bloody coup against Shanghai workers' government on April 12, 1927. Organized rival KMT government on April 18, in opposition to official KMT regime at Wuhan. Headed reunified KMT after March 1928 and the Nationalist government established in October 1928. Fled to Taiwan in December 1949 following CCP victory on mainland.

Chicherin, Georgi Vasilyevich (1872-1936)—Prominent Soviet diplomat. Member of tsarist diplomatic corps until 1904. Joined Social

Democrats in 1905 and went into exile. Returned to USSR in 1918. Commissar of foreign affairs (1918-30).

Chinese Communist Party (CCP)—Dates from formation of communist groupings in Peking, led by Li Ta-chao, and in Shanghai, led by Ch'en Tu-hsiu, in spring of 1920, following discussions with Comintern representative Grigori Voitinsky. This led to founding of Socialist Youth Corps in Shanghai (August 1920). First Congress of CCP held in Shanghai, July 1921.

Chitarov, F.—Stalinist secretary of Communist Youth International in 1920s.

Chou En-lai (1898-1976)—Joined CCP in France in 1922. Served as KMT political commissar at Whampoa Military Academy under Chiang Kai-shek (1924-26). Arrested during Chiang Kai-shek's March 20, 1926, Canton coup. Participated in Shanghai workers' uprising in March 1927 and barely escaped during Chiang Kai-shek's April 12 bloodbath. Chief lieutenant of Li Li-san until January 1931. Then supported Wang Ming, and finally Mao Tse-tung after 1935. Intervened at Sian in December 1936 to save Chiang Kai-shek's life. Chief CCP negotiator with Chiang's government until 1949. Premier of People's Republic of China from 1949 until his death.

Ch'ü Ch'iu-pai (1899-1935)—Chosen by Lominadze to replace Ch'en Tu-hsiu as acting head of CCP at August 7, 1927, Emergency Conference. Was made scapegoat for failures of ultraleft putschist course and deposed at CCP Sixth Congress held in Moscow (June-July 1928). During early 1930s worked underground in Shanghai as leader of Stalinist-inspired League of Left-Wing Writers. Spent 1934 at Juichin. Left behind because of ill health when Long March began, was imprisoned and executed by KMT.

Chu Te (1886-   )—Republican soldier from 1911. Joined CCP in 1922. Participated in Nanchang uprising of August 1, 1927. Combined forces with Mao at Chingkangshan in spring 1928. Commander of Fourth Red Army. Principal military leader of Kiangsi "Soviet Republic." CCP's chief military figure in Long March, Sino-Japanese War, and civil war with Chiang. One of few old CCP leaders to survive purges of 1960s and 1970s.

Citrine, Walter (1887-   )—General secretary of British Trades Union Congress (1926-46).

Comité des Forges—French association of iron, steel, and coal interests.

Communist International (Comintern)—Founded in 1919 in Moscow to unite world Communist parties and coordinate revolutionary struggles. Transformed in 1920s into instrument of Soviet diplomacy under Stalin. Dissolved in 1943 as goodwill gesture to Stalin's democratic imperialist allies in World War II.

Communist League of China—Chinese section of International Left Opposition and, after 1938, of Fourth International. Formed in May 1931 at Shanghai through unification of four Chinese Trotskyist organizations. In 1948 name was changed to Revolutionary Communist Party.

Contre le Courant (Against the Stream)—French Left Opposition journal published in Paris between November 1927 and October 1929. Ceased publication after a number of Opposition groups succeeded in unifying around a new weekly, *La Verité*.

Dalin, Sergei A.—A leader of Russian Young Communists after October 1917 revolution. Sent on a mission to China in April 1922 by Communist Youth International. Met with both CCP and Sun Yat-sen to urge collaboration with KMT.

Dan, Fyodor Ilyich (1871-1947)—Leader of Russian Mensheviks. Member of Presidium of Petrograd Soviet after February 1917 revolution. Arrested in 1921; deported in 1922. Edited Menshevik journals in exile.

Dashnaks—Members of Dashnaktsutiun, or Armenian Revolutionary Federation, established 1890, with populist program. Set up government in Armenia in 1918 opposed to Soviet Union. Defeated in 1920.

Dzerzhinsky, Feliks Edmundovich (1877-1926)—A founder of Social Democratic Party of Poland and Lithuania. Elected to CC of RSDLP in 1906. After October revolution became chairman of All-Russian Extraordinary Commission for Combatting Counterrevolution and Sabotage (Cheka). Supporter of Stalin.

ECCI—Executive Committee of the Communist International.

Die Fahne des Kommunismus (The Banner of Communism)—Journal launched at beginning of 1927 by expelled leaders of left wing of German CP, Ruth Fischer, Arkadi Maslow, and Hugo Urbahns. Became organ of Leninbund when it was founded in March 1928. Leninbund moved close to Left Opposition in 1928 but in 1930 Urbahns expelled supporters of Trotsky.

Feng Yü-hsiang (1882-1948)—North Chinese warlord known as the Christian General. Headed personal army, the Kuominchün. Persuaded by Borodin to join KMT in spring 1926, Feng spent three months in Moscow in summer. In June 1927 allied with Chiang Kai-shek against Wuhan regime and against CCP. War broke out between Feng and Chiang in October 1929 in western Honan province. Feng was defeated in October 1930.

Fourth International—The World Party of Socialist Revolution, founded in 1938.

Galen—Pseudonym of Vassily K. Blücher.

Galliffet, Gaston, Marquis de (1830-1909)—French general infamous for his savage suppression of Paris Commune of 1871.

GPU—Initials of Soviet secret police in 1930s. Known earlier as Cheka and later as NKVD, MVD, and KGB.

Guchkov, Aleksandr Ivanovich (1862-1936)—Wealthy Russian politician. Founder of Octobrists. President of Central War Industries Committee during World War I. First minister of war and navy in Provisional Government after February revolution. Went into exile after October revolution.

Hicks, George—Secretary of National Federation of Building Operatives in Britain. Member of General Council of Trades Union Congress during betrayal of 1926 general strike.

Ho Chien (1887-1956)—Military leader of Wuhan KMT's July 1927 suppression of CCP. Later governor of Hunan (1929-37).

Ho Lung (1896-   )—A local commander in a provincial Hunan army, Ho joined KMT in 1925. A key leader of August 1, 1927, Nanchang uprising, though he had not yet joined CCP. Prominent CCP military figure on Long March and in Sino-Japanese War. Elevated to Politburo (1956), he was purged in Cultural Revolution of 1960s.

Hsiang-tao chou-pao (The Guide Weekly)—The main public newspaper of CCP in 1920s. The party did not publish a daily.

Hsü K'e-hsiang—Commander of Thirty-third Regiment of National Revolutionary Army at Changsha. Led KMT troops in May 21, 1927, assault on Changsha General Labor Union.

Hu Han-min (1879-1936)—Top leader of KMT right wing. Elected to KMT CEC at First National Congress (January 1924). Represented KMT in Moscow (October 1925-April 1926). Became chairman of Chiang Kai-shek's anticommunist Nanking government (April 1927). President of Legislative Yüan from formation of national KMT government (October 1928). His arrest by Chiang Kai-shek in February 1931 precipitated formation of rival KMT regime at Canton. Restored to nominal KMT posts before his death.

International Press Correspondence (Inprecor)—Unofficial organ of Comintern published in several languages.

Izvestia (News)—Daily newspaper begun in March 1917 as organ of Petrograd Soviet. After October 1917, official newspaper of Soviet government.

Jaurès, Jean Auguste (1859-1914)—Most prominent leader of pre-World War I French socialists. Founder of newspaper *l'Humanité*. Advocate of socialist participation in bourgeois governments. Assassinated by French officers for his pacifist views on eve of war.

Jen Pi-shih (1904-1950)—Joined CCP in Moscow (1922). Elected to CCP CC at Fifth Congress (Wuhan, April-May 1927). Leader of Youth League in revolution of 1925-27. A political officer of Red Army (1933-38).

Joffe, Adolf Abramovich (1883-1927)—Joined Russian socialist movement in 1890s. Supporter of Trotsky in innerparty controversies before 1917. Joined Bolsheviks with Trotsky and was elected to CC. Member of Petrograd Revolutionary Military Committee during October revolution. Later Soviet diplomat, participating in Brest-Litovsk negotiations with Germans (1918). First Soviet ambassador to China (1922-23). Negotiated agreement with Sun Yat-sen for CCP entry into KMT. Supported Left Opposition. Committed suicide when refused foreign visa to obtain medical treatment.

Kalinin, Mikhail Ivanovich (1875-1946)—Old Bolshevik and later Stalinist. Elected to Politburo (1926). Chairman of Supreme Soviet of USSR (1938-46).

Kamenev, Lev Borisovich (1883-1936)—Joined RSDLP in 1901. Headed Bolshevik fraction in Duma before World War I. With Zinoviev opposed October 1917 insurrection. After Lenin's death a member with Zinoviev and Stalin of ruling triumvirate. With Zinoviev formed United Opposition with Trotsky (1926-27). Expelled from party in December 1927. Recanted and was readmitted. Defendant in first Moscow trial (1936). "Confessed" and was executed.

Karakhan, Lev Mikhailovich (1889-1937)—Joined RSDLP in 1904. Member of Trotsky's Mezhraiontsy group (1913-17). Deputy commissar for foreign affairs (1918). Soviet ambassador to Peking warlord government (1923-26). Executed in purges.

Kautsky, Karl (1854-1938)—Leader of German Social Democracy and a founder of Second International (1889). Best known Marxist theoretician before 1914. Took pacifist position during World War I. Opposed Bolshevik revolution in 1917.

Kerensky, Aleksandr Fyodorovich (1882-1970)—Joined Socialist Revolutionary Party in 1905. In 1912 represented the allied Trudovik grouping in state Duma. Prime minister of Provisional Government established by February 1917 Russian revolution. Overthrown by Bolsheviks in October 1917.

Kornilov, General Lavr Georgievich (1870-1920)—Siberian Cossack. Appointed commander in chief of Russian army by Provisional Government (July 1917). Led counterrevolutionary putsch in September 1917. Escaped after arrest. Killed in action leading White Guard forces in Soviet civil war.

kulak—Literally "fist." Popular name for Russian well-to-do peasantry.

Kun, Bela (1886-1939)—Joined Hungarian Social Democratic Party before World War I. Founder of Hungarian CP (1918). Headed short-lived Hungarian Soviet Republic (March-July 1919). Later served as Comintern functionary. Arrested in 1937. Died in purges.

Kuomintang (KMT—Nationalist Party)—Bourgeois nationalist party founded by Sun Yat-sen in August 1912 as an outgrowth of earlier T'ung-meng-hui (Alliance Society), an underground anti-Manchu organization created by Sun in exile in Japan in 1905. After being forced out of Republican government at Peking by Yuan Shih-k'ai in 1913, Sun's KMT sought military base in South China. Captured Canton (1917). At first

Sun hoped to reform Peking regime. Later KMT became involved in struggles with local militarists. After Sun's death, KMT established strong government in Canton (July 1925) and began campaign to defeat warlords of North China. Under Chiang Kai-shek, who captured control of party after April 1927, KMT became ruling bourgeois party in China, establishing Nationalist government over whole territory in October 1928. Defeated in civil war with CCP (1946-49), KMT remains ruling party in Taiwan.

Kuusinen, Ottomar Vilgelmovich (1884-1964)—Leader of Finnish Socialist Party before World War I. Fled to Moscow after collapse of Finnish revolution (April 1918). Stalinist spokesman and a secretary of Comintern (1922-31).

Landau, Kurt (d. 1937)—Austrian Left Oppositionist. Headed German United Left Opposition when it was formed in 1930. Split from Left Opposition in 1931. Assassinated by Stalinists in Spain during civil war.

Lassalle, Ferdinand (1825-1864)—German socialist. Founder of General Union of German Workers (1863), which after his death fused with Marx's followers to form Social Democratic Party.

Left Opposition (Bolshevik-Leninists)—Faction formed by Trotsky within Russian Communist Party in 1923 to defend his and Lenin's views against Zinoviev-Kamenev-Stalin triumvirate. Organized on a world scale in 1930 under name International Left Opposition. Following Hitler's rise to power in 1933, decided to end status as expelled faction of Comintern and seek to build new revolutionary Marxist parties, changing its name to International Communist League, predecessor organization of Fourth International, founded in 1938.

Li Chi-shen (1886-1959)—Governor of Kwangtung during Northern Expedition. Ordered suppression of Ho Lung-Yeh T'ing occupation of Swatow and Chaochow (September 1927). Headed short-lived Fukien rebellion against Chiang Kai-shek (November 1933–January 1934). Expelled from KMT (1947). Organized splinter bourgeois party, the Kuomintang Revolutionary Committee. Given governmental posts in People's Republic after 1949.

Li Fu-jen—While working as a journalist in Shanghai in 1930s wrote extensively on Chinese developments for world Trotskyist press.

Li Li-san (1889-   ?)—Joined Chinese Communist student group in France (1920). Labor organizer in Hunan during early 1920s. Elected to Politburo of CCP at Fifth Congress (Wuhan, April-May 1927). Participated in Nanchang uprising (August 1, 1927). Attended Sixth CCP Congress (Moscow, June-July 1928), where Ch'ü Ch'iu-pai was removed as party general secretary, the post going to Hsiang Chung-fa, a colorless figurehead whom Li Li-san soon replaced as de facto head of CCP. Came under attack by Comintern in fall 1930 as scapegoat for failure of Stalin's line of seizing major cities. Called to Moscow (December 1930). Formally deposed at Fourth Party Plenum (Shanghai—1931). Remained in exile in

Moscow until 1945. Given minor posts under Maoist regime. Made public self-criticism at CCP's Eighth Congress (1956). Attacked in Cultural Revolution and reportedly committed suicide.

Li Ta-chao (1888-1927)—With Ch'en Tu-hsiu one of two principal founders of CCP. Directed CCP work in North China. Arrested during Chang Tso-lin's April 6, 1927, raid on Soviet embassy in Peking. Executed three weeks later.

Liberationists—Liberals of the Union of Liberation, prominent in early phase of 1905 Russian revolution.

Liu Jen-ching (1899-   )—joined Marxist study group in Peking led by Li Ta-chao in 1920. Attended founding meeting of CCP (July 1921). Spent mid-1920s in Moscow, where he joined Left Opposition. Met Trotsky in Prinkipo, Turkey, in 1929. Organized Shih-yueh she (October Society) after his return. Participated in unification conference of Chinese Oppositionists (May 1931). Wrote for world Trotskyist press under name Niel Shih. Split from Trotskyist movement in 1937. Joined KMT and became anticommunist propagandist. Remained in China after 1949, recanted his past, and was given minor posts in CCP regime.

Lloyd George, David (1863-1945)—Liberal Party prime minister of Britain (1916-22). Engineered British intervention against Bolsheviks in Soviet civil war.

Lo I-nung (1901-1928)—Joined Socialist Youth League at its inception (August 1920). Student in USSR (1921-25). Returned to China to work as labor organizer in Canton. Leader of Shanghai general strike (March 21, 1927). Participated in Autumn Harvest uprising in south Hupeh. Arrested in International Settlement in Shanghai (April 1928), was turned over to KMT and executed.

Lominadze, Vissarion (1898-1934)—Joined Bolshevik party in March 1917. Leader of various Comintern-sponsored youth organizations. Stalin's delegate to China (July-December 1927). Dominated August 7 Emergency Conference of CCP, where rump body deposed Ch'en Tu-hsiu. With Heinz Neumann, directed Canton insurrection (December 1927). Opposed Stalin's policy of forced collectivization. Stripped of all posts (1930). Expelled from AUCP(B) in fall of 1934. Committed suicide after Kirov assassination (December 1934).

Louzon, Robert (1882-   )—French revolutionary syndicalist. Briefly a member of French CP in 1920s. A founder of Révolution prolétarienne group.

Lozovsky, Solomom Abramovich (1878-1952)—Joined RSDLP in 1901. Active as trade unionist. Expelled from Bolshevik party in 1918; rejoined next year. Secretary of Profintern (1921-37). Supported Stalin in purges of 1930s. Arrested in 1949 during Stalin's anti-Semitic campaign, he was later shot.

MacDonald, James Ramsey (1866-1937)—Britain's first Labour Party prime minister (1924). Returned to office (1929-31), he broke with Labour Party to form coalition cabinet with Tories (1931-35).

Malraux, André (1901-   )—French novelist; author of two novels about Chinese revolution of 1925-27: *The Conquerors* (1929) and *Man's Fate* (1933). Collaborated with Stalinists in Popular Front period. After World War II became a Gaullist government official.

Manuilsky, Dmitri Zakharovich (1883-1959)—Joined Bolsheviks in 1903. Member of Stalin faction. Elevated to Secretariat of Comintern Presidium in 1926, a post he held until Comintern's dissolution in 1943. A principal Stalinist spokesman for Comintern after 1930. Soviet diplomat after 1944.

Mao Tse-tung (1893-   )—Attended founding conference of CCP (July 1921). Elected to CCP CC in 1923. Elected as alternate member of KMT CEC in 1924. Worked under Hu Han-min in Shanghai KMT apparatus. Head of KMT Propaganda Department (November 1925-May 1926). Appointed head of Wuhan KMT Central Land Commission (March 1927), which acted to restrain peasant "excesses." Elected as alternate member of CCP Politburo at August 7, 1927, rump Emergency Conference, which deposed Ch'en Tu-hsiu. Assigned to lead section of Autumn Harvest uprisings in Hunan. After failure, was removed from Politburo (November 1927). Founded military base in Chingkang mountains that led to formation of Kiangsi "soviet." Became party chairman during Long March (1935). Initiated collaboration with Chiang Kai-shek government (1936-46). Political head of CCP in civil war (1946-49). Has headed People's Republic of China since 1949.

Maring—Pseudonym of Henricus Sneevliet.

Martynov, Aleksandr Samoylovich (1865-1935)—Joined RSDLP in 1899. Extreme right-wing Menshevik after 1905. Principal Menshevik theorist of "two-stage" revolution. Opposed Bolshevik revolution. Joined Martov's Menshevik-Internationalists in 1917. Joined Russian CP in 1923 and was assigned to Comintern. Authored class-collaborationist theory of "bloc of four classes" in China.

Maslow, Arkadi (1891-1941)—Pioneer German communist. Part of ultraleftist leadership that replaced Brandler group after failure of 1923 German revolution. Expelled from German CP in 1926 along with Ruth Fischer in move directed at Zinoviev faction. Supported United Opposition, capitulating with Zinoviev at beginning of 1928. Refused readmission to German CP. Formed Leninbund with Fischer and Hugo Urbahns in March 1928. Joined movement for Fourth International along with Ruth Fischer in mid-1930s but left before founding of Fourth International in 1938.

Mensheviks—Minority faction in RSDLP formed at Second Congress (1903). Became separate party after 1912. Supported bourgeois Provisional Government created by February 1917 Russian revolution and opposed Bolshevik seizure of power in October. Remained part of Second International.

Menzhinsky, Vyacheslav Rudolfovich (1874-1934)—Joined RSDLP in 1902. Cheka official after 1919. Headed GPU (1926-34). Reportedly executed in purges.

Mif, Pavel (1899- ?   )—Joined Bolsheviks after October revolution. Visited China for Comintern in 1926. Replaced Karl Radek as head of Moscow's Sun Yat-sen University (1928). Returned to China in 1930 with twenty-eight of his students to depose Li Li-san leadership, succeeding at January 1931 CC plenum. Arrested in 1937 and disappeared in purges.

The Militant—Newspaper of American Left Oppositionists, first published in November 1928.

Milyukov, Pavel Nikolaevich (1859-1943)—Russian bourgeois liberal politician and historian. Founder and principal leader of Cadet Party (1905). Minister of foreign affairs in Provisional Government (March-July 1917). Emigrated to Paris (1919).

Milyutin, Vladimir Pavlovich (1884-1938)—Joined Bolsheviks in 1910. CC member from 1917. People's commissar for agriculture in first Soviet government. Killed in purges.

Molotov, Vyacheslav Mikhailovich (1890-   )—Joined RSDLP in 1906. Elected to RCP(B) CC in 1920. Stalin's chief spokesman in Comintern (1928-29). Chairman of Council of People's Commissars (1930-41). Became foreign minister in 1938. Opposed "de-Stalinization" in 1956. Expelled from CPSU in 1962.

Muralov, Nikolai Ivanovich (1877-1937)—Joined Bolsheviks in 1903. Organizer of Bolshevik insurrection in Moscow in 1917. Held important military posts in civil war. Supported Left Opposition and was expelled from party in 1927, deported to Siberia in 1928. Victim of second Moscow trial (1937).

Narodniks (Populists)—Tendency in Russian bourgeois-democratic revolutionary movement from 1860s. Stressed peasantry as leading force in coming revolution and utopian socialism or democratic reform as its aim. Represented in 1880s by Narodnaya Volya (People's Will) party. Populist tradition was continued in twentieth century by Social Revolutionary Party (SRs), who were close to Mensheviks in political outlook.

Negrin López, Juan (1889-1956)—Spanish Republican premier. Replaced Largo Caballero as head of Popular Front government in May 1937. Resigned in exile in France at end of civil war (March 1939).

Nepmen—Disparaging term for petty traders, merchants, and swindlers who took advantage of profitmaking opportunities under relaxed restrictions on business activity of New Economic Policy (NEP) proclaimed by Soviet government in March 1921.

Neumann, Heinz (1902-1937?)—Joined German CP in 1921. Assigned to Comintern staff (1925). Supported Stalin in suppression of Left Opposition. Stalin's representative in China during winter 1927-28. Chief organizer of abortive Canton Commune (December 1927). Prominent in leadership of German CP until 1932. Arrested in Moscow in 1937 and disappeared in purges.

New International—Theoretical magazine of American Trotskyists

(1934-40). Later published under names *Fourth International* (1940-56) and *International Socialist Review* (from 1956).

Northern Expedition—First publicly projected by Sun Yat-sen in spring 1921, when his Canton regime disavowed legitimacy of military government in Peking. Postponed because of local revolt by Kwangtung warlord Ch'en Chiung-ming. Finally begun in summer 1926. Petty warlord states rapidly collapsed as National Revolutionary Army moved north, sparking wave of peasant and worker uprisings. Northern Expedition was completed after KMT's counterrevolutionary purges of April-July 1927. Nationalist government formed at Nanking in October 1928 marked defeat or capitulation of all major warlord forces, although periodic local rebellions and putsches continued into 1930s.

Octobrists—Members of Russian League of October Seventeenth, bourgeois monarchist party formed in 1905 in support of tsar's Manifesto of October 17, 1905, establishing State Duma.

Papen, Franz von (1879-1969)—Rightist dictatorial chancellor of Germany (May-November 1932); vice-chancellor under Hitler (1933-34); acquitted of war crimes in 1946.

P'eng Shu-chih—Alternate spelling of Peng Shu-tse.

Peng Shu-tse (1896-   )—Joined Socialist Youth League in 1920. Attended Communist University for Toilers of the East in Moscow (1921-23). Elected to CCP CC and to Politburo Central Standing Committee by Fourth Congress (January 1925). Chief editor of *Hsiang-tao chou-pao* (Guide Weekly) and *Hsin Ch'ing-nien* (New Youth). Expelled from CCP with Ch'en Tu-hsiu in November 1929 for supporting Left Opposition. Founding leader of Chinese Trotskyist movement. Imprisoned by KMT (1932-37). Forced into exile by Stalinist victory in 1949. A leader of the Fourth International.

Pilsudski, Jozef (1867-1935)—Began political career as Polish nationalist. Sentenced to Siberian exile for conspiring to assassinate Tsar Alexander III. Founder of Polish Socialist Party (1892). Headed Polish Republic after 1918. Invaded Ukraine in 1920; defeated by Trotsky's Red Army. Dictator of Poland from 1926 to his death.

Plekhanov, George Valentinovich (1856-1918)—Broke with Narodniks to found Emancipation of Labor group (1883), Russia's first Marxist organization. Outstanding Marxist theorist. Main leader of RSDLP until 1903. Supported Mensheviks in split with Lenin. Became social-patriot during World War I. Opposed October 1917 revolution.

Poincaré, Raymond (1860-1934)—French bourgeois statesman and writer. Headed Republican Party. President of France (1913-20); prime minister (1922-24, 1926-29).

Pravda (Truth)—Newspaper of CC of CPSU. First published in April 1912, became a daily in March 1917.

Preobrazhensky, Evgeny Alekseyevich (1886-1937)—Joined Bolsheviks in 1903. Fought in civil war. Leading Bolshevik economist and author of *The New Economics* (1926). Expelled from AUCP in 1927 as Left Oppositionist. Capitulated in 1929, readmitted. Expelled again in 1931 and again readmitted. Refused to confess during purges and was shot without trial.

Proudhonists—Followers of Pierre-Joseph Proudhon (1809-1865), French utopian socialist whose theory of a society based on direct exchange between individual producers without state intervention laid basis for anarchist movement.

Purcell, Albert A. (1872-1935)—British left Labourite and MP. Founding member of British CP (1920), which he left two years later. Leader of Trades Union Congress General Council during general strike of 1926.

Pyatakov, Yuri Leonidovich (1890-1937)—Joined Bolsheviks in 1910. In his Testament, Lenin called him one of "two ablest young men in the party." Joined Left Opposition in 1923. Expelled from party in 1927; capitulated and was reinstated (1928). Headed State Bank during First Five-Year Plan. Defendant in second Moscow trial; executed.

Radek, Karl Berngardovich (1885-1939)—Active in German and Polish Social Democratic parties from 1910. Came to Russia with Lenin in April 1917. Member of Presidium of Comintern. Supporter of Left Opposition. Capitulated to Stalin (1929). Worked as Stalinist propagandist in 1930s. Defendant in second Moscow trial (1937); sentenced to ten years, died in prison.

Rafes, Moisei Grigorievich (1883-1942)—Joined Bund in 1903. Member of Bund CC (1912-1919). Participated in anticommunist Ukrainian government of Simon V. Petlyura (1917-18). Joined RCP(B) in 1919. Assigned by Stalinists to Comintern section directing Chinese CP in late 1920s. Arrested in Stalin's purges.

Rakovsky, Khristian Georgievich (1873-1941)—Of Bulgarian and Romanian ancestry, was prominent in leadership of revolutionary socialist movement of both countries before World War I. Joined Bolsheviks in Russia in 1917. President of Ukrainian Soviet government (1919-23) and later ambassador to France. One of Trotsky's closest collaborators in leadership of Left Opposition. Expelled from AUCP in 1927 and exiled at Barnaul in Siberia. Remained in opposition until 1934 when he recanted. Sentenced to twenty years' imprisonment in third Moscow trial (1938). Died in prison.

Raskolnikov, Fyodor Fyodorovich (1892-1939)—Joined Bolsheviks in 1910. Appointed deputy people's commissar of navy (1918). Ambassador to Afghanistan (1921-22). Directed Far East Bureau of Comintern briefly in 1920s. Supported Stalin in struggle with Left Opposition. Soviet diplomat in 1930s. Denounced in April 1938 as "enemy of the people" over his memoirs of October revolution. Fled to France; drafted open letter to Stalin along lines similar to Left Opposition. Died under mysterious circumstances.

Rasputin, Grigori Efimovich (1871?-1916)—Illiterate Siberian monk and mystic who gained great influence over tsar and tsarina after 1907. Assassinated by Russian aristrocrats.

RCP(B)—Russian Communist Party (Bolsheviks). Name adopted by Bolsheviks in 1918. Changed to All-Union Communist Party (Bolsheviks) in 1925. See **AUCP(B)** and **RSDLP.**

Remmele, Hermann (1880-1937)—A leader of German CP before Hitler's rise to power. A Stalinist, he fled to USSR in 1933. Arrested and executed by GPU in 1937.

Renaudel, Pierre (1871-1935)—Right-wing French socialist leader. Took patriotic stance during World War I. Expelled from French SP in 1933.

Rennenkampf, Pavel Karlovich (1854-1918)—Tsarist general of cavalry. Scored initial success against Germans in World War I but suffered disastrous defeat at Masurian Lakes in East Prussia (August 1914). Later commander in chief of northern front (1916). Shot by Bolsheviks (1918).

Der Rote Aufbau (Red Reconstruction)—Newspaper published in Berlin by the Stalinist Willi Münzenberg.

Roy, M. N. (1887-1954)—Active in Indian nationalist movement in his home state of Bengal until 1915. Recruited to communism by Mikhail Borodin in Mexico (1919). With Lenin, led discussion on colonial question at Second Comintern Congress (1920). Elected to ECCI (1921). Went to China in May 1927 to replace Borodin as CI representative. Criticized for "rightist deviation" at Sixth Comintern Congress (1928) and expelled from Comintern in November 1929. Imprisoned in India in early 1930s, he joined Congress Party in 1936 and edited a publication entitled *The Radical Humanist.*

RSDLP (Russian Social Democratic Labor Party)—Forerunner of CPSU. First Congress held at Minsk (1898), broken up by police. Split at Second Congress (London, 1903), into Bolshevik and Menshevik wings. The two factions reunited at Fourth Congress (Stockholm, 1906), only to split definitively in 1912. The Seventh Congress (1918) voted to change name to Russian Communist Party (Bolshevik). See **RCP(B)** and **AUCP(B).**

Rudzutak, Yan Ernestovich (1887-1938)—Joined RSDLP in 1905. Active in October revolution. From 1920 a member of RCP(B) CC. A leader of Stalin faction. People's commissar for communications (1924-30). Arrested in 1938 and disappeared.

Rykov, Aleksei Ivanovich (1881-1938)—Joined RSDLP in 1899. Succeeded Lenin as head of state. With Bukharin, led Right Opposition (1928-29). Recanted. Sentenced to death in third Moscow trial (1938).

Safarov, Georgi (1891-1942)—Joined Bolsheviks in 1908. Headed Comintern section for Middle and Far East (1921-24). Prominent member of Zinoviev group. Expelled from party in December 1927. Recanted and was readmitted. Arrested in 1934 and deported to forced labor camps.

Sedova, Natalia (1882-1962)—Trotsky's companion and political collaborator from 1903 until his death in 1940. Active in Russian Marxist movement from late 1890s. Member of Paris section of *Iskra* group led by Lenin. Assigned to Commissariat of Public Education after October revolution. Accompanied Trotsky in his years of exile from USSR. Developed political differences with Fourth International after Trotsky's death and severed her political ties in 1951.

Serebryakov, Leonid Petrovich (1888-1937)—Joined Bolsheviks in 1905. Secretary of party CC (1919-20) and deputy people's commissar for communications in mid-1920s. Visited China and Japan (1926) to negotiate railroad agreements. Supporter of Left Opposition. Expelled from RCP(B) in October 1927. Recanted (1929); readmitted (1930). Defendant in second Moscow trial (1937); shot.

Shih, Niel—Pseudonym of Liu Jen-ching.

Smeral, Bohumir (1880-1941)—A leader of Czech Social Democratic Party before World War I, where he stood in right wing. Became head of Czechoslovak CP when it was founded (1921). Elected to ECCI and its Presidium (1922). Supported Stalin in fight with Left Opposition.

Smilga, Ivan Tenisovich (1892-1938)—Joined Bolsheviks in 1907. Elected to party CC in April 1917. Deputy chairman of Supreme Economic Council after civil war. A leader of Left Opposition, he was deported (1928); capitulated (1929). Disappeared during purges.

Smirnov, Ivan Nikitich (1881-1936)—Joined RSDLP in 1899. Bolshevik from 1903. Leader of Red Army on Siberian front during civil war. Member of CC from 1920. Left Oppositionist. Expelled (1927); capitulated (1929); arrested (1933). Sentenced to death in first Moscow trial.

Sneevliet, Henricus (1883-1942)—Joined Dutch Social Democratic Party in 1902. Emigrated to Java where he founded Social Democratic Union (1914), predecessor of Indonesian Communist Party. Became a communist after Russian revolution. Elected to ECCI (1920) under name Maring. Comintern representative to China (1921-23). Proposed CCP entry into KMT (August 1922). Returned to Holland (1924), where as a leader of Dutch CP he came out for Left Opposition. Broke with CP (1927) and formed Revolutionary Socialist Party (1929), which joined the International Communist League in 1933. In 1935 RSP fused with another revolutionary group in Holland to form Revolutionary Socialist Workers Party. Broke with international Trotskyist movement and did not participate in founding of Fourth International in 1938. During German occupation, was arrested by Nazis and executed.

Social Revolutionary Party (SRs)—Russian populist party founded in 1900. At first congress, held in Finland (1905), adopted program drafted by Viktor Chernov projecting struggle for a bourgeois-democratic republic through mobilization of peasantry. Majority of SRs supported Kerensky government in 1917 and opposed October revolution. Left SRs participated in coalition government with Bolsheviks; led anti-Bolshevik insurrection in July 1918 which was suppressed.

Soong Ch'ing-ling (1892-   )—Member of wealthy, Americanized Soong family. Married Sun Yat-sen in 1914 and was his constant companion and political collaborator until his death in 1925. Member of State Council of KMT government at Wuhan (1926-27). Opposed suppression of CCP in July 1927; took refuge in Moscow, where she remained for two years. During this period her sister Soong Mei-ling married Chaing Kai-shek. Soong Ch'ing-ling became honorary chairwoman of Li Chi-shen's splinter bourgeois party, the Kuomintang Revolutionary Committee, when it was organized in 1947. Remained in China after CCP victory and has held various honorary posts in government of People's Republic.

Sotsialistichesky Vestnik (Socialist Herald)—Journal published in Berlin prior to 1933 by foreign bureau of Russian Menshevik party.

Stolypin, Pyotr Arkadyevich (1862-1911)—Tsarist politician. Minister of interior (police) from April 1906 and prime minister from July. Headed regime of police terror in suppression of 1905 revolution. Proposed agrarian reforms in 1910-11 aimed at winning peasant support for tsarism. Assassinated by a police agent.

Su Chao-cheng (1885-1929)—Cantonese seaman and labor organizer; major figure in 1925-26 Canton–Hong Kong strike. Joined CCP in 1925. Chairman, All-China Federation of Labor (1926). Communist minister of labor in Wuhan KMT government (1927). Participated in Canton uprising (December 1927).

Sukhanov, Nikolai Nikolaievich (1882-193?)—Joined SRs in 1903. Became a Menshevik in 1909. Member of Executive Committee of Petrograd Soviet after February 1917 revolution. Well-known intellectual and historian of Russian revolution. Worked in Soviet economic apparatus. Sentenced to ten years in "Menshevik trial" of 1931. Released after hunger strikes, reportedly rearrested in 1937 and shot.

Sun Yat-sen (1866-1925)—Bourgeois nationalist leader of Chinese revolution of 1911. Founder of KMT. Joined anti-Manchu underground in 1893. Organized Hsing-chung hui (Revive China Society) in Honolulu (1894). Lived in exile in Japan after failure of revolt in Canton (1895). Founded T'ung-meng-hui (1905). Same year formulated ideology of "Three People's Principles": nationalism, democracy, and the people's livelihood. Served briefly (January 1912) as provisional president of China's first republic after October 1911 revolution against Manchus. Forced to abdicate to General Yuan Shih-k'ai. Formed Kuomintang (Nationalist Party) in Peking (August 1912). Forced into exile in Japan (1913-16). Established military government at Canton (1917); forced to resign by local militarists (1919). Regained power in 1920; declared his Canton regime sole legal government of China (April 1921). Lost power to Ch'en Chiung-ming in 1922. Sought alliance with Soviet Union and CCP. Returned to Canton (February 1923). Died in Peking, March 1925, during fruitless negotiations with Northern warlords.

Tai Chi-t'ao (1891-1949)—Journalist and personal secretary to Sun Yat-sen. After Sun's death in 1925 became leading anticommunist theorist of KMT right wing. President of Examination Yüan (1928-48).

Committed suicide on eve of CCP victory.

T'an P'ing-shan (1887-1956)—Joined T'ung-meng-hui in 1906. Joined Li Ta-chao's communist study group in Peking (1920). Elected to CEC of KMT at First National Congress (January 1924). Headed KMT organization department (1924-May 1926). Communist minister of agriculture in Wuhan KMT government (March-June 1927), acting to suppress peasant land seizures. Headed brief CCP government at Nanchang (August 1927). Made a scapegoat for failures at August 7 Emergency Conference; expelled from CP in November. Joined so-called Third Party of Teng Yen-ta. Rejoined KMT in 1937. Participated with Li Chi-shen in formation of Kuomintang Revolutionary Committee (1947). Given nominal posts in People's Republic after 1949.

T'ang Sheng-chih (1890-   )—Hunanese militarist. Affiliated to KMT in June 1926, participating in Northern Expedition in command of six divisions in Hunan. Helped take Wuhan for KMT (August-October 1926). Became military chief of "left" KMT government at Wuhan after split with Chiang Kai-shek in April 1927. Whitewashed Changsha anticommunist massacre of May 21. Led military suppression of CCP in Wuhan (July 1927). Later led several abortive military revolts against Chiang Kai-shek. Remained in China after CCP victory and held various minor posts in new government.

TASS—Acronym for Telegraphic Agency of the Soviet Union, official Soviet news service.

Thälmann, Ernst (1886-1944)—Joined German Social Democracy in 1903. Supported left wing and joined CP in 1920. Originally associated with party ultraleft—Maslow, Fischer, and Urbahns—but his shift to Stalinism saved him from expulsion and brought him party chairmanship in 1925. Carried out Stalin's ultraleft policy leading to Hitler's victory in 1933. Arrested in March 1933; after eleven years in prison, executed at Buchenwald.

Thermidor—Eleventh month of calendar adopted in France after revolution of 1789. On 9 Thermidor (July 27), 1794, Robespierre and the Jacobin left wing were overthrown, marking a sharp shift to right in policies of revolutionary government. By analogy in debates in communist movement of 1920s, Stalin faction was described as Thermidorian to indicate its direction.

Thomas, James H. (1874-1949)—British trade union leader. Colonial secretary in 1924 Labour Party government. Union negotiator with Baldwin government during 1926 general strike. Deserted Labour Party along with MacDonald to form coalition government with Tories (1931) and was expelled from National Union of Railwaymen.

Tomsky, Mikhail Pavlovich (1880-1936)—Joined RSDLP in 1904. Chairman of CC of Soviet trade unions (1922-29). Member of RCP(B) Politburo from 1922. Allied with Bukharin in right-wing tendency in party. Removed from posts in purge of Right Opposition (1928-29). Recanted. Committed suicide during first Moscow trial.

Treint, Albert (1889-1971)—Joined French Socialist Party in 1912. A founder of French CP (1920). Elected to ECCI at Fifth Comintern Congress (1924). Supported United Opposition and was expelled from PCF in January 1928. Belonged to French Left Opposition for a few years, then founded a small syndicalist group.

Trud (Work)—Newspaper of Soviet Trade Union Council.

Trudoviks (Toilers group)—Second largest grouping in first Duma (1907). Best known member was Aleksandr Kerensky, who headed bourgeois Provisional Government after February 1917 revolution. Vacillated between Cadets and Social Democrats. Generally considered a faction of Social Revolutionary Party.

Tseretelli, Irakly Georgievich (1882-1960)—Georgian Menshevik leader. Supported Russian participation in World War I. Elected to Executive Committee of Soviets after February 1917 revolution. Held ministerial posts in Provisional Government (May-August 1917). Participated in Menshevik government of Georgia after October revolution. Emigrated abroad in 1919.

tuchün—Local military governor or petty warlord.

United Opposition—Bloc between Trotsky's Left Opposition (Bolshevik-Leninists), which had been formed in 1923, and Leningrad Opposition led by Zinoviev and Kamenev, which came into open collision with rightwing (Bukharin) and center (Stalin) factions in AUCP in fall of 1925. The United Oppositon, in formation from April 1926, was proclaimed at CC meeting in July. It broke up shortly after Trotsky and Zinoviev's expulsion from party (November 1927), when Zinovievists capitulated to Stalin. Sometimes translated as Joint Opposition.

Urbahns, Hugo (1890-1947)—Joined German Social Democrats before World War I, and German CP in 1920. Closely associated with ultraleft leadership of Ruth Fischer and Arkadi Maslow. Criticized by ECCI in September 1925; expelled from German CP (1926). Helped to found Leninbund in March 1928, which supported Left Opposition until 1930, when Urbahns took control of group and expelled Trotsky's supporters. Emigrated to Sweden after 1933, where he died in exile.

Ustryalov, N. V. (1890- ?)—Member of Cadet Party. Took part in civil war on anticommunist side, in Kolchak's Siberian White Guard army. After Kolchak's collapse, collaborated with Soviet government at Harbin, Manchuria, supporting Stalin against Trotsky in hopes Stalin would restore capitalism. Returned to Soviet Union (1935) to assume university post; arrested (1937), convicted of anti-Soviet activity, disappeared.

Vandervelde, Émile (1866-1938)—Leader of Belgian Socialist Party and president of Second International (1900-18). Accepted minsterial post in bourgeois government during World War I.

Voitinsky, Grigori (1893-1953)—Joined RCP(B) in 1918. Assigned to Comintern Far East bureau in 1920. Helped recruit first Chinese communists in spring 1920, meeting with Ch'en Tu-hsiu and Li Ta-chao. Headed Comintern Far Eastern Secretariat (1921-24). Returned to China

(1924-25 and 1927) as a Comintern representative. Active in scientific research and education from early 1930s.

Voroshilov, Kliment Efremovich (1881-1969)—Delegate to 1906 and 1907 congresses of RSDLP. Distinguished military record in civil war. Supported Stalin against Trotsky. Member of Politburo from 1926. Presided over Stalin's purge of Red Army (1936-38). Soviet head of state (1953-60).

Vujovic, Voja (1895- ?)—Born in Serbia (later part of Yugoslavia). Joined left wing of French SP while a student in Paris before World War I. A founding member and leader of Communist Youth International (1919), and its secretary-general after 1922. Elected to ECCI as youth representative (1924). Supporter of Zinoviev and participant in United Opposition. Expelled from Comintern (September 1927); exiled to Siberia (January 1928). Capitulated to Stalin in 1929 and was assigned to Balkan Secretariat of Comintern. Arrested after Kirov assassination in December 1934, exiled to Verkhneuralsk and disappeared.

Wang Ching-wei (1883-1944)—Became an associate of Sun Yat-sen in 1905 while a student in Tokyo. Imprisoned in Peking (1910) for attempt to assassinate Manchu prince regent; released during 1911 revolution. Elected second-ranking member of KMT executive, following Hu Han-min, at First Congress (January 1924). Elected chairman of Nationalist government formed at Canton, July 1925. Became leader of left wing of KMT, favoring alliance with CCP and USSR. Forced to resign after Chiang Kai-shek's March 20, 1926, anticommunist coup in Canton; went into exile in Europe. After Nationalist government moved to Wuhan at beginning of 1927, Wang was invited to return to offset growing power of Chiang Kai-shek at Nanking. Arrived in China in April, taking charge of Wuhan regime on eve of Chiang's Shanghai coup and declaration of secessionist KMT regime at Nanking. Wang followed Chiang's example in purging CCP and trade unions in Wuhan in July 1927. After reunification of two wings of KMT in fall 1927 Wang headed Reorganizationist faction (1928-31) which clashed with Chiang Kai-shek, including backing military revolt at Peking (1930). Headed KMT Executive Yüan (1932-35). Went over to Japanese imperialists and headed collaborationist regime at Nanking, then under Japanese occupation (1940-44). Died in Japan while undergoing medical treatment.

Wang Ming—Pseudonym of Ch'en Shao-yü.

Warski-Warszawski, Adolf (1868-1937)—Founding leader of Polish Social Democracy; also held membership in RSDLP and was elected to its CC (1906). Helped found Polish CP (1918). Active in work of ECCI (1921-24). Supported Stalin faction, but was removed from posts in 1924. Sought refuge in USSR in 1929. Arrested and executed in August 1936.

Whampoa Military Academy—KMT military training center at Whampoa, Kwangtung province, ten miles down Pearl river from Canton. First projected in discussions between Soviet ambassador Adolf Joffe and KMT in 1923. Plans approved at KMT First National Congress (January

1924). Sun Yat-sen designated Chiang Kai-shek commandant when school opened (May 1924). Largely Soviet funded. Top KMT leaders served as instructors, including Liao Chung-k'ai, Hu Han-min, Wang Ching-wei, and Tai Chi-t'ao. On CCP side, staff included Chou En-lai (head of Political Department of academy, late 1925–March 1926), as well as Yeh Chien-ying, and Nieh Jung-chen.

Wilson, Joseph Havelock (1859-1929)—Headed British National Union of Seamen until his death. Kept his union out of general strike (1926) and backed breakaway scab miners' union, for which he was expelled from Trades Union Congress (1927).

Witte, Count Sergei Yulievich (1849-1915)—Tsarist minister of finance (1892-1903). Premier (1905-06).

Yeh T'ing (1897-1946)—Served in Ch'en Chiung-ming's Kwangtung Army in early 1920s. Joined KMT in 1922. Studied military technique in Moscow (1924-25); joined CCP branch in Moscow (1925). A leader of August 1, 1927, CCP putsch at Nanchang and commander with Ho Lung of CCP forces that retreated south after defeat at Nanchang, taking Swatow in September. Commanded CCP troops in Canton Commune (December 1927). Made a scapegoat for failures of putschist policy, Yeh withdrew from activity for five years, living in Europe. Appointed commander of CCP-led New Fourth Army in South China (1937), during Sino-Japanese War. Arrested after Chiang Kai-shek's ambush of New Fourth Army (1941) and imprisoned by KMT (1941-46). Killed in plane crash when returning to Yenan after his release.

yüan—A public institution or department. Used to designate five branches of government under KMT after October 1928 (Executive Yüan, Legislative Yüan, Judicial Yüan, Examination Yüan, and Control [censorship] Yüan).

Zetkin, Clara (1857-1933)—Active in German socialist movement from 1878. A founder of Second International (1889) and a leader of pre-World War I German Social Democracy. Joined German CP (1919). Editor of *Gleichheit* (Equality), a women's rights newspaper. Member of ECCI and of Comintern's International Women's Secretariat. Supported Stalinists against Left Opposition.

Zinoviev, Grigori Yevseyevich (1883-1936)—Joined RSDLP in 1901. Lenin's closest associate during World War I. With Kamenev opposed decision for October 1917 Bolshevik insurrection. After Lenin's death main public figure of secret anti-Trotsky faction, with Kamenev and Stalin. Broke with Stalin in 1925 and formed United Opposition with Trotsky (1926-27). Expelled in November 1927 and exiled to Siberia. Capitulated almost immediately and was readmitted (1928). Expelled again (1932) and again recanted. Arrested in 1935, following assassination of Kirov; sentenced to ten years on trumped-up charges. A principal defendant in first Moscow trial (1936). "Confessed" and was executed.

INDEX

BOOKS AND PAMPHLETS BY LEON TROTSKY*

Against Individual Terrorism
The Age of Permanent Revolution
Between Red and White
The Bolsheviki and World Peace
(War and the International)
The Case of Leon Trotsky
The Challenge of the Left Opposition (1923-25) (incl. The New Course, Lessons of October, Problems of Civil War, and Toward Socialism or Capitalism?)
Europe and America: Two Speeches on Imperialism
Fascism: What It Is and How to Fight It
The First Five Years of the Communist International (2 vols.)
The History of the Russian Revolution (3 vols.)
In Defense of Marxism
Lenin: Notes for a Biographer
Lenin's Fight Against Stalinism (with V.I. Lenin; incl. On the Suppressed Testament of Lenin)
Leon Trotsky Speaks
Literature and Revolution
Marxism in Our Time
Military Writings
My Life
1905
On Black Nationalism and Self-Determination
On Britain (incl. Where Is Britain Going?)
On China (incl. Problems of the Chinese Revolution)
On the Jewish Question
On Literature and Art
On the Paris Commune

On the Trade Unions
Our Revolution
The Permanent Revolution and Results and Prospects
Problems of Everyday Life and Other Writings on Culture and Science
The Revolution Betrayed
The Spanish Revolution (1931-39)
Stalin
The Stalin School of Falsification
The Struggle Against Fascism in Germany
Terrorism and Communism
Their Morals and Ours (with essays by John Dewey and George Novack)
The Third International After Lenin
The Transitional Program for Socialist Revolution (incl. The Death Agony of Capitalism and the Tasks of the Fourth International and On the Labor Party in the U.S.)
Trotsky's Diary in Exile, 1935
Women and the Family
Writings of Leon Trotsky (1929-40) (12 vols., to be completed in 1977)
The Young Lenin

In preparation:
The Challenge of the Left Opposition (1926-29) (incl. The Platform of the Opposition)
On France (incl. Whither France?)
Political Portraits
The War Correspondence of Leon Trotsky

---

*This list includes only books and pamphlets by Leon Trotsky published in the United States and in print as of 1976.